THE · URBAN · WORLD

SECOND EDITION

THE · URBAN · WORLD

J. JOHN PALEN

Virginia Commonwealth University

McGraw-Hill Book Company

New York   St. Louis   San Francisco   Auckland   Bogotá   Hamburg
Johannesburg   London   Madrid   Mexico   Montreal   New Delhi
Panama   Paris   São Paulo   Singapore   Sydney   Tokyo   Toronto

Library of Congress Cataloging in Publication Data

Palen, J   John.
    The urban world.

    Bibliography: p.
    Includes index.
    1. Cities and towns. 2. Cities and towns—Unit-
ed States. 3. Underdeveloped areas—Urbanization.
I. Title.
HT151.P283 1981   307.7'6   80-21117
ISBN 0–07–048107–5

THE URBAN WORLD

34567890DODO8987654

The part-opening photographs are from the following sources:

Part One: © H. W. Silvester/Photo Researchers, Inc.
Part Two: Elliot Erwitt/Magnum Photos, Inc.
Part Three: Shelley Rusten
Part Four: J. A. Pavlovsky/Sygma
Part Five: J. P. Lafonte/United Nations
Part Six: Art Seitz/Black Star

The cover photograph is from Elliot Erwitt/Magnum Photos, Inc.

This book was set in Memphis Medium by Black Dot, Inc. (ECU).
The editors were Eric M. Munson and Susan Gamer;
the designer was Charles A. Carson;
the production supervisor was John Mancia.
The photo editor was Inge King.
R. R. Donnelley & Sons Company was printer and binder.

For Joseph, Beth, and Ellen,
who are growing up in an urban world

CONTENTS

List of Special Sections   xiv

Preface   xv

Part One: Focus and Development

1 **The Urban World**   2

Introduction: The Process of Urbanization   3
The Urban Explosion   5
Defining Urban Areas   6
City Size, Urbanization, and Urbanism   8
Concepts of the City   12
    The Chicago School / Rural Simplicity versus Urban Complexity /
    Urbanism in Social Theory

2 **Emergence of Cities**   17

Introduction   18
The Ecological Complex   18
First Settlements   19
Population, Technology, and Social Organization   22
Urban Revolution   24
Evolution in Social Organization   25
    Division of Labor / Kingship and Social Class

Technological Evolution and Social Revolution   27
City Size   27
Survival of the City   28
The Hellenic City   29
    Social Invention / Physical Design and Planning / Population

Rome   32
    Size and Number of Cities / Housing and Planning / Transportation /
    Life and Leisure

European Urbanization until the Industrial City   35
    The Feudal System / Medieval Revival / Characteristics of Towns /
    Plague / Cities after the Medieval Era

Industrial Cities   48
    Technological Improvements and the Industrial Revolution /
    The Second Urban Revolution

Part Two: American Urbanization

3   The Rise of Urban America   52
    Introduction   53
    Colonists as Town Builders   53
    Major Settlements   54
        New England / The Middle Colonies / The South
    Urban Influence   57
    The Growing New Republic   58
        Founding and Expansion of Cities / Marketplace Centers
    The Industrial City   62
        Technological Change / Spatial Configuration / Twentieth-Century
        Dispersion / Political Bosses: Corruption and Service / Blaming the
        Immigrants / Reform Movements
    Ambivalence toward the City   72

4   Change within and between Metropolitan Areas   76
    Metropolitan Ascendancy   77
    Urban Concentrations   78
    Decentralization within Metropolitan Areas   82
        Outmovement of Industry / Advances in Transportation and
        Communication / Movers and Stayers
    Megalopolis   87
    Nonmetropolitan Growth: The New Pattern   90
        Rural Renaissance? / A National Society
    The Rise of the Sun Belt   95
    A Note on the Functional Specialization of Cities   98
        A Seven-Category Division / A Three-Category Division

5   Ecology and Structure of the American City   101
    City Structure   102

Early Human Ecology 103
Burgess's Growth Hypothesis 105

   The Zonal Hypothesis / Invasion and Succession / The Zonal Hypothesis:
   Criticisms and Alternatives

Ecological Methodology 119

   Social-Area Analysis and Factorial Ecology / Urbanization and
   Environment

Part Three: Urban Life

6   **City Life-Styles** 126

   Introduction 127
   Theoretical Formulations 128

      Earlier Formulations / Later Formulations / The Limitations of Logical
      Constructs / The Chicago School / "Urbanism as a Way of Life" /
      Cultural Lag

   Reevaluation of Urbanism and Social Disorganization 134
   Diverse Life-Styles 139

      Cosmopolites / Singles / Ethnic Villagers / The Outcasts

   Community 153

7   **Patterns of Suburbanization** 155

   Suburban Growth 156
   Emergence of Suburbs 157

      Nineteenth Century / Electric Streetcar Era / Era of the Automobile /
      Era of Mass Suburbanization

   Causes of Suburbanization 161
   Contemporary Patterns 163

      Categories of Suburbs / Persistence of Characteristics /
      Characteristics of Suburbanites

   The Myth of Suburbia 167

      Differences—Real or Not? / Less Affluent Suburbs

   A Case Study: Levittown 172
   Exurbanites 173
   Black Suburbanization 174

      Changes / Causes

   White Flight? 176
   Maintaining Racial Diversity in Suburbs 178

      An Example: Park Forest South / Managed Integration: Oak Park

   The Suburban Poor 180
   Prognosis 181

8   **Urban Diversity: White Ethnics and Black Americans**   182

Introduction: Urban Minorities   183

White Ethnics   184

Immigration / Old Immigrants / New Immigrant Groups / "Racial
Inferiority" and Immigration / White Ethnics Today

Black Americans   191

Historical Patterns / Population Changes / Slavery in Cities / "Free
Persons of Color" / Jim Crow Laws / Movement North / End of Mass
Migration / Moving South / Urban Segregation Patterns / Diversity among
Blacks / The Future

9   **Urban Diversity: Mexican Americans, Puerto Ricans, Native
Americans, and Japanese Americans**   204

Spanish-Origin Population   205

Mexican Americans / Puerto Ricans

Native Americans   214

Chances in Life / Movement to Cities

A Note on Japanese Americans   218

The Issei and Nisei / The Internment Camps / Japanese Americans
Today

10 **Stratification and Power in Urban America**   223

Dimensions of Class   225
Measuring Social Class   226
Status Consistency   234
Mobility   236

Myths and Reality / Intergenerational Mobility / Sources of Mobility /
Intergenerational Mobility of Women / International Differences

Community Decision Making   243

Elitists / Pluralists / Variation among Communities / Middletown /
Black Powerlessness / Women and Power

Part Four: Urban Problems and Planning

11 **The Crisis of the Cities?**   254

The "Urban Crisis"   255
The City Resurrected?   256

Changing Central Business Districts / Fiscal Crisis of the Cities /
What Should Be Done?

Overview: The Future of Cities   262
Selected Current Problems   263

Redlining / Abandonment of Buildings / Burning for Profit /
Crime in the City

12 **Housing Programs and Urban Regeneration**   270

The Beginnings of Government Involvement   271
Federal Housing Administration (FHA) Subsidies   272
Urban Renewal   273

Rehabilitation / Relocation and New Housing / Critique

Public Housing   278

Pritt-Igoe: Profile of Failure / The Controversy over Title 235 / Section 8 /
Experimental Housing Allowance Program

Recent Developments   284

Conversion to Condominiums / Tax-Exempt Mortgage Bonds / Urban
Homesteading / Neighborhood Revival / Urban Growth Policies / The
Dutch Approach: An Example of Planning in Western Europe

13 **Urban Planning: Western Europe and Socialist Countries**   292

Introduction: Historical Background   293

Ancient Greece and Rome / Medieval and Later Developments

Urban Planning in Western Europe   296

Control of Land / Housing / Urban Growth Policies / The Dutch
Approach: An Example of Planning in Western Europe

Eastern European Patterns   300

The Soviet Union / Social-Class Distribution in Socialist Countries

New Towns   304

British New Towns / New Towns on the Continent and in Eastern Europe

14 **Urban Planning: The United States**   311

Eighteenth and Nineteenth Centuries   312

Washington, D.C. / Nineteenth-Century American Towns / Planned
Communities / Parks / The City Beautiful / Tenement Laws

Twentieth Century   317

The City Efficient and Zoning / Master Plans / Experiments with New
Towns / Limits to Growth / The Use of Space

Part Five: Worldwide Urbanization

15 **Less Developed Countries: Overview and Common Problems**   334

Urbanization in the Third World   335

Common or Divergent Paths? / Urban Population Explosion /
Problems of Growth

Rich Countries and Poor Countries: Some Definitions and
    Explanations   339
Characteristics of Third-World Cities   341

Employment and Industrialization / Squatter Settlements / Density and
Economic Development / Overurbanization / Primate Cities

Conclusion: The Future   350

16 **Latin American Cities**   352
   Spanish Colonial Cities   353
      Physical Structure / Policy and Traditions
   Evolving Patterns   356
      "POET" / Early Social and Economic Structure
   Recent Developments   359
      Urban Growth / Characteristics of Urban Inhabitants /
      Squatter Settlements

17 **African and Middle Eastern Urbanization**   372
   Africa   373
      Regional Variations / Early Cities / The Colonial Period /
      Contemporary Patterns
   The Middle East   392
      Physical and Social Considerations / Contemporary Urban Trends /
      Comparisons and Conclusions

18 **Urban Patterns in Asia**   400
   Introduction: Asian Cities   401
      Indigenous Cities / Colonial Cities
   India   403
      Land Use: Foreign and Indigenous Influences / Bombay / Calcutta /
      Government Intervention / India: Prognosis
   China   411
      Background / Current Urbanization Policies / Shanghai / Peking /
      Summary—China / A Note on Hong Kong
   Japan   417
      The Extent of Urbanization / Current Patterns / Tokyo / Planned Towns /
      Suburbanization
   Southeast Asia   420
      Singapore / Other Places
   Conclusion   423

Part Six: Conclusion

19 **Toward the Urban Future**   426
   Changes in the City   427
      Urban Growth / Internal Migration / Changes in Housing Trends /
      Changes in Racial Trends / Changes in the Energy Situation /
      Changes in Federal Funding

Planning for the City   432
Planning for City Dwellers / Planning Metropolitan Political Systems /
Social Planning
The "Postcity" Age   439
Superterritoriality / Nonterritoriality / The Passing of the City?

Bibliography   443

Indexes   469
Name Index
Subject Index

LIST OF SPECIAL SECTIONS

Preindustrial and Industrial Cities: A Comparison 43
A Note on Environmental Pollution 66
Defining Metropolitan Areas 80
A Land Shortage 93
Red-Light Districts and Combat Zones 110
A Note on Density 136
Categories of Local Communities 145
Leavin' the South 196
Chicago's Street Gangs 212
Skid Row 230
A Marxist View 257
Discrimination in Housing 265
Planned Capitals 295
The Approach of Jane Jacobs 319
Dependency Theory and Modernization Approaches 349
A Case Study of One Indigenous City 379

PREFACE

The first edition of *The Urban World* began by suggesting that urbanism has become the American way of life, residence in an urban area being the norm. The overwhelming majority of those reading this book have been lifelong residents of either central cities or surrounding suburbs and are now in college studying for urban professions and occupations. We can thus predict with reasonable certainty that their future lives will be spent in, and intimately bound up with, urban areas. Both intellectual and practical concerns thus demand that we know as much as possible about the nature of our cities and how urban areas have changed and can be expected to change over time.

The second edition reflects the range and depth of the changes that have taken place since the first edition was published in 1975. While the same basic organization has been kept, every chapter has been rewritten, and over half of this edition contains new or completely revised material. The purpose remains the same: to give undergraduate students up-to-date information on urbanization and the nature of urban life. The goal is to give the student having little formal exposure to urban sociology and related urban studies a coherent overview of the changing urban scene. Of course, selectivity is both inevitable and necessary. The topics included and the emphasis they receive reflect in part the state of knowledge in the social sciences, in part my own interests, and in part a conscious effort to provide for the needs of students with different backgrounds and interests.

There has also been a conscious attempt to explore the emerging developments of the 1980s. A textbook need not rehash the tired issues of a decade or two back. It should reflect contemporary debates. Thus, the material on urban renewal has been reduced, and new material discussing urban regeneration, urban homesteading, displacement, and federal programs has been added. The revision also includes thorough discussion of developments such as the unanticipated upturn in nonmetropolitan growth, the rise of sun belt cities, and new patterns of black suburbanization. For this edition, there is also an accompanying Instructor's Manual.

Finally, the revision retains its cross-cultural emphasis, looking beyond the confines of the United States. There is now material on urbanization and urban planning in socialist countries and a much-revised chapter on developments in Asia. (The chapter on Asia is heavily based on information the author gathered while in Japan, India, and southeast Asia on a grant from the Ford Foundation.)

The book consists of nineteen chapters divided into six parts. **Part One**, Focus and Development, consists of two chapters. Chapter 1, The Urban World, provides an introduction to the urban explosion and sets the scene for the chapters to follow. Chapter 2, Emergence of Cities, provides a framework for describing and analyzing the early growth and development of urban places. The emphasis is on providing a perspective for understanding the changes in our own contemporary society. The influences of technology, population growth, and environmental considerations are stressed.

Part Two, American Urbanization, is extensively revised. It contains three chapters on the development of, and contemporary changes in, American urbanization. Chapter 3, The Rise of Urban America, provides students with knowledge of the historical patterns of North American urbanization. Chapter 4, Changes within and between Metropolitan Areas, is new and contains discussions of changing patterns such as nonmetropolitan growth and the expansion of sun belt cities. Chapter 5, Ecology and Structure of the American City, concentrates on current patterns of urbanization and theories developed to account for changes in urban structure. Traditional ecological models as well as social-area analysis and factoral analysis are discussed. The chapter stresses how physical patterns reflect social organization.

Part Three, Urban Life, includes five chapters on the social, social-psychological, ethnic, and racial aspects of different urban ways of life. Chapter 6, City Life-Styles, discusses theories regarding the consequences of urban living and the varying life-styles of different urban communities. Chapter 7, Patterns of Suburbanization, examines suburban life-styles and has new material on black suburbanization and attempts by communities to manage integration. Chapter 8, Urban Diversity: White Ethnics and Black Americans, is new and contains material on the revival of white ethnicity as well as changes in black urban patterns. Chapter 9, Urban Diversity: Mexican Americans, Puerto Ricans, Native Americans, and Japanese Americans, provides separate treatment and discussion of groups that are too often either ignored or tacked onto a single chapter on race. Chapter 10, Stratification and Power in Urban America, deals with who makes the decisions—and who doesn't—in the urban area.

Part Four, Urban Problems and Planning, is a new section that takes up various urban problems and ways of planning for the future. Chapter 11—The Crisis of the Cities?—examines the scope of city problems such as the fiscal crisis, loss of jobs, disinvestment, and crime. Chapter 12, Housing Programs and Regeneration, replaces the chapter on urban renewal that appeared in the first edition. New material on urban homesteading, gentrification, and displacement is included. Chapter 13, Urban Planning: Western Europe and Socialist Countries, includes a new discussion of urban policies and housing in the Soviet Union as well as material on new towns in England, the Netherlands, and Scandinavia. Chapter 14, Urban Planning: United States, reviews this country's planning experience and evaluates American efforts at creating new towns.

Part Five, Worldwide Urbanization, consists of four chapters discussing the urban explosion in the third world and the different regional responses to resulting urban problems. In spite of the fact that developing countries will account for 90 percent of all urban growth between now and the turn of the century, most texts still tend to either ignore developing nations or lump them all together in a single chapter. The distinct ways in which developing nations differ both from American patterns and from each other are discussed in Chapter 16, Latin American Cities, Chapter 17, African and Middle Eastern Urbanization, and Chapter 18, Urban Patterns in Asia. Chapter 18 in particular is largely new material. The effects of urbanization on traditional life-styles are also discussed.

Part Six, Conclusion, consists of a single chapter: Chapter 19, Toward the Urban Future, which concentrates on expected trends in North American urbanization until the year 2000. Changes in housing trends, racial patterns, and energy costs are discussed. The conclusion also includes discussion of several plans and speculations about what the city will or should be like in the future. A plea is made for beginning with people's social needs and then planning in such a way as to fulfill them—as opposed to the more common approach of designing physical structures first and then attempting to adjust people to the new physical environment.

I would like especially to thank a number of colleagues for their careful and critical reading of the second edition—in particular, Harvey Choldin, Tom Drabek, Leo Schnore, and Ralph Thomlinson. Edgar Borgatta, Scott Greer, George Hesslink, and Ephraim Mizruchi reviewed the first edition. Special thanks go to Katherine Davis for her cheerful aid with the manuscript. I am of course solely responsible for all errors of omission and commission.

I would also like to acknowledge the invaluable assistance of Susan Gamer, editing supervisor, Inge King, photo editor, and Eric Munson, sociology editor.

J. John Palen

PART ONE

FOCUS
AND
DEVELOPMENT

CHAPTER

1

THE URBAN WORLD

All cities are mad, but the madness is gallant.
All cities are beautiful, but the beauty is grim.

INTRODUCTION: THE PROCESS OF URBANIZATION

The human species has been on this globe for well over a million years, but for the overwhelming number of these millennia humans have lived in a world without cities. Cities and urban places, in spite of our acceptance of them as an inevitable consequence of human life, are in the eyes of history a comparatively recent social invention, having existed a scant 7,000 years. Their period of social, economic, and cultural dominance is even shorter. Nonetheless, the era of cities encompasses the totality of the period we label "civilization." The saga of wars, architecture, and art—almost the whole of what we know of human triumphs and tragedies—is encompassed within that period. The story of human social and cultural development— and regression—is in major part the tale of the cities that have been built and the lives that have been lived within them.

The vital and occasionally magnificent cities of the past, however, existed as islands in an overwhelmingly rural sea. Less than 200 years ago, in the year 1800, the population of the world was still 97 percent rural. As of 1800, only 1.7 percent of the world's population resided in places of 100,000 or more, 2.4 percent in places of 20,000 or more, and 3 percent in communities of 5,000 or larger.[1] By the beginning of the twentieth century, the proportion of the world's population in cities of 100,000 or more had increased to 5.5 percent, and 13.6 percent lived in places of 5,000 or more. Thus, as recently as 1900 six-sevenths of the world's population was still rural. England was the first country to undergo the urban transformation. In the second half of the nineteenth century it was the world's only predominately urban country.[2] Not until 1920 did the United States have half its population residing in urban places.

By the latter quarter of the twentieth century this had changed radically. About a quarter of the world's population (24 percent) lived in large cities of 100,000 or more, and almost four out of ten persons (39 percent) resided in plac.es of 5,000 or larger (Figure 1-1).[3] Today we are on the threshold of living in a world that for the first time will be numerically more urban than rural. During the remaining years of this century, urbanization will accelerate dramatically, particularly in developing countries. Today, over half the world's urban population lives in developing countries.

The rapidity of the change from rural to urban life is as important as the degree of urbanization. As of 1850, not a single country—not even England—was as urban as the world is today. The highly urban United States did not even reach the present level of world urbanization until around 1900, a period still within living memory.

Because we live in an urban world where the mega-metropolis Tokyo-Yokohama already has a population of over 20 million and greater New York has over 16 million, and because almost all of us have spent at least part of our lives in

---

[1] Philip Hauser and Leo Schnore (eds.), *The Study of Urbanization*, Wiley, New York, 1965, p. 7.
[2] Adna Ferrin Weber, *The Growth of Cities in the Nineteenth Century*, Cornell University Press, Ithaca, N.Y., 1899, table 3.
[3] Kingsley Davis, *World Urbanization 1950–1970*, Volume II: *Analysis of Trends, Relationships, and Development*, University of California Press, Berkeley, 1972, p. 9.

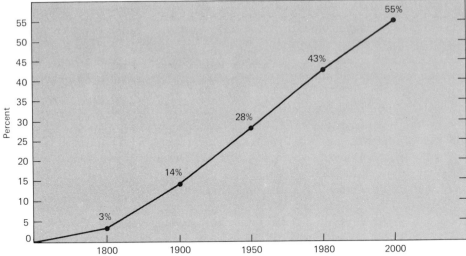

Figure 1-1. Percentage of world population living in places of 5,000 or more. (*Source:* United Nations data from *The State of World Population 1978;* and author.)

central cities or their surrounding suburbs, it is difficult for us to conceive of a world without numerous large cities. The rapidity and extent of the urban revolution can perhaps be understood if one reflects that if metropolitan Indianapolis, Indiana (1980 population, 1.2 million), had had the same population two centuries ago, it would have been the largest urban agglomeration that had ever existed in the world at any time.

According to the United Nations, as of 1972, there were 115 metropolitan areas of more than 1 million inhabitants, 27 metropolitan areas of more than 3 million, 13 areas of more than 5 million, and 4 areas of over 10 million.[4] By the year 2000, the United Nations projects a population of 31.6 million for Mexico City (over three times its present size), 26 million for São Paulo, Brazil, 19.6 million for Calcutta, and 16.3 million for greater Cairo.

Living as we do in such an urban world, it is easy for us to forget two important facts: (1) Over half the world's population is still rural-based, and (2) even in the industrialized west, massive urbanization is a recent phenomenon. Some of our difficulty in understanding or coping with urban patterns and problems can be attributed to the recency of the emergence of our contemporary urban world. As noted earlier, urbanization has accelerated until today, for the first time, we are on the threshold of living in a world that is numerically more urban than rural. Some twenty years from now the majority of the world's population will be living in urban rather than rural places. This rapid transformation from a rural to a heavily urbanized world and the development of urbanism as a way of life have been far more dramatic and spectacular than the much better known population explosion.

[4] *The State of World Population, 1978,* United Nations, New York, 1978. The best source of data for cities in earlier eras is Tertius Chandler and Gerald Fox, *3000 Years of Urban Growth,* Academic Press, New York, 1974.

THE URBAN EXPLOSION

Urban growth, which began to explode during the latter part of the eighteenth century, accelerated cumulatively during the nineteenth and twentieth centuries. By 1800 the population of London had reached almost 1 million, Paris exceeded 500,000, and Vienna and St. Petersburg had each reached 200,000. As this century began, ten cities had reached or exceeded 1 million: London, Paris, Vienna, Moscow, St. Petersburg, Calcutta, Tokyo, New York, Chicago, and Philadelphia. Today, the number of people living in cities outnumbers the entire population of

Tokyo has mushroomed as one of the world's major urban metropolises, with all the opportunities and liabilities that suggests. (Herb Levart/Photo Researchers, Inc.)

the world 150 years ago. This urban explosion, which will be discussed in greater detail in Chapter 2, Emergence of Cities, occurred for a number of reasons. Among the more important reasons were (1) a rapidly growing population, (2) scientific management of agriculture, (3) improved transportation and communication systems, (4) stable political governments, and (5) the development of the industrial revolution. While details differ from country to country, the pattern has been similar. Agriculture raised the surplus above previous subsistence levels. Then, in rather short order, this extra margin was transferred by entrepreneurs, and later by governments, into the manufacturing sector.[5] The result was urban expansion and growth fed by a demand by the burgeoning manufacturing, commercial, and service sectors for a concentrated labor force.

Whichever stereotypes we embrace, whether we are delighted by the variety and excitement of urban life or horrified by the cities' anonymity and occasional brutality, population concentration— that is, urbanization—is increasingly becoming the way of life in developing as well as developed nations. Attempts to return to a supposedly simpler rural past must be considered futile escapism. Images of a pastoral utopia where all exist in rural bliss have no chance of becoming reality. We live in an urban world; and for all our complaints about it, few would reverse the clock.

DEFINING URBAN AREAS

Before proceeding further, it is necessary to define some of the terms we will be using.

This is not altogether as simple as it might seem, since countries differ in what they mean when they call a place "urban." About thirty definitions of "urban population" are currently in use, none of them totally satisfactory.[6]

Urban settlements have been defined on the basis of an urban culture (a cultural definition), administrative functions (a political definition), the percentage of people in nonagricultural occupations (an economic definition), and the size of the population (a demographic definition). In the United States, we define places as "urban" by using population criteria along with some geographic and political elements. In terms of cultural criteria, a city is "a state of mind, a body of customs and traditions."[7] The city thus is the place, as sociologists put it, where relations are "gesellschaft" ("society" or formal role relationships) rather than "gemeinschaft" ("community" or primary relationships) and forms of social organization are organic rather than mechanical. In short, the city is large, culturally heterogeneous, and socially diverse. It is the antithesis of "folk society." The problem with the cultural definitions of an urban place is the impossibility of measurement; for example, if a city is a state of mind, who can ever say where the boundaries of the urban area lie?

[5] *Urbanization in the Second United Nations Development Decade*, United Nations, New York, 1970, p. 6.

[6] Milos Macura, "The Influence of the Definition of Urban Place on the Size of Urban Population," in Jack Gibbs (ed.), *Urban Research Methods*, Van Nostrand, New York, 1961, pp. 21–31.

[7] Robert E. Park. "The City: Suggestions for the Investigation of Human Behavior in the Urban Environment," in Robert E. Park, E. W. Burgess, and Roderick D. McKenzie (eds.), *The City*. University of Chicago Press, Chicago, 1925.

Economic standards have also been used in defining what is urban. In terms of economic criteria, a country has sometimes been described as urban if less than half its workers are engaged in agriculture. Here "urban" and "nonagricultural" are taken to be synonymous. This distinction, of course, tells us nothing about the degree of urbanization or its pattern of spatial distribution within the country. A distinction has also been made between the town as the center for processing and service functions and the countryside as the area for producing raw materials.[8] However, it is becoming increasingly difficult to distinguish among areas by means of such criteria. How far out do the producing and service functions of a New York or a Los Angeles extend?

Politically, a national government may define its urban areas as such in terms of administrative functions. The difficulty is that there is no agreement internationally on what the political or administrative criteria shall be. In many countries small administrative centers are recognized as urban regardless of their population or economic significance. Kenya, for example, has a number of "urban" administrative centers with populations well under 2,000, and the same is true of a number of other countries.

Finally, size of population is used frequently as a criterion in deciding what is urban and what is not. Demographically, a place is defined as being urban because a certain number of people live in it. Measurement and comparison of rural and urban populations within a country are relatively simple when demographic criteria are used, although the problem of making comparisons among nations still remains. Only 250 persons are necessary to qualify an area as urban in Denmark, while 10,000 are needed in Greece.

According to the definition adopted by the United States Bureau of the Census for the 1980 census, the urban population of the United States comprises all persons living in urbanized areas and all persons outside of urbanized areas who live in places of 2,500 or more. For practical purposes the urban population of the United States therefore includes anyone in a place having 2,500 or more inhabitants. By this definition, three-quarters of the United States population is urban.

The United Nations has attempted to bring some order out of the various national definitions by setting up its own classifications scheme, which it uses for publishing its international data. The definitions of the United Nations are as follows:

A *"big city"* is a locality with 500,000 or more inhabitants.
A *"city"* is a locality with 100,000 or more inhabitants.
An *"urban locality"* is a locality with 20,000 or more inhabitants.
A *"rural locality"* is a locality with less than 20,000 inhabitants.[9]

This is a reasonable classification scheme, for when data are available, they are likely to have such a basis. The major limitation of the United Nations

---

[8] Amos H. Hawley, *Human Ecology: A Theory of Community Structure.* Ronald Press, New York, 1950, p. 245.
[9] *Demographic Handbook for Africa.* United Nations Economic Commission for Africa, Addis Ababa, 1968, p. 38.

TABLE 1-1
Degree of Urbanization by World Regions

	Percent rural	Percent urban*	Percent large city†
Australia-New Zealand	15.7	84.4	61.1
North America	24.9	75.1	57.4
Europe	37.0	63.0	38.9
U.S.S.R.	37.7	62.3	31.4
Latin America	45.6	54.4	33.5
Asia	74.6	25.4	15.7
Africa	78.2	21.8	11.2

*The urban and rural percentages add up to 100.
†Percent of population living in cities of 100,000 or more.
Source: Kingsley Davis, *World Urbanization 1950-1970*, Volume II: *Analysis of Trends, Relationships, and Development.* Population Monograph Series, No. 9, University of California Press, Berkeley, 1972.

definition is not logical but practical: most of the more urbanized countries, such as the United States, simply do not use them, preferring to keep their own national definitions.[10] To make a complicated situation as simple as possible, this book will use the definitions established by the United States when presenting data for the United States and the definitions established by the United Nations when presenting international data. The reader can thus assume that outside the United States, "urban" refers to the population in places of 20,000 or more.

According to definitions established by the United Nations, the percentage of the population living in urban places varies from 2 percent in Burundi to 100 percent in the city-state of Singapore. Table 1-1 shows degrees of urbanization by world regions.

CITY SIZE, URBANIZATION, AND URBANISM

As we will see in Part Five, Urban Problems and Planning, cities in the developing world are among the largest and the fastest growing in the world. Nonetheless, it must be kept in mind that the growth of cities and a high level of urbanization are not the same thing. In the western world the two things happened at the same time, but it is quite possible to find extremely large cities in overwhelmingly rural countries. Some of the world's largest cities—for example, Shanghai, Bombay, and Cairo—exist in nations that are still overwhelmingly rural. A number of extremely large cities does not necessarily indicate an urban nation.

"Urbanization," on the other hand, refers to the changes in the proportion of the population of a nation living in urban places—that is, the process of people moving to cities or other densely settled areas. The term "urbanization" is also

[10]A team working under Kingsley Davis during the 1950s defined "metropolitan areas" for 720 of the then 1,046 areas in the world having at least 100,000 persons in their metropolitan areas and at least 50,000 in the central city (International Urban Research, *The World's Metropolitan Areas.* University of California Press, Berkeley, 1959). This system will not be used in this text, since the United Nations system is far more widely accepted and provides more current data.

used to describe the changes in social organization that occur as a consequence of population concentration. Urbanization is thus a process— the process by which rural areas become transformed into urban areas. In demographic terms, urbanization is an increase in population concentration; organizationally, it is an alteration in structure and functions. Demographically, urbanization involves two elements: the multiplication of points of concentration, and the increase in the size of individual concentrations.[11] "Organization" is more difficult to define because it includes changes in the internal spatial structure of cities, changes in economic and social structures, and other related questions that are generally treated in a special area of urban sociology known as "human ecology" (see Chapters 2 and 5). In an economically developing country, the economic and social structure changes in orientation from agriculture to industrialization.

"Urbanization," described as the percentage of a nation's total population living in urban areas, is a process that clearly has a beginning and an end. For instance, almost four-fifths of the United States population of 220 million is now urban; the maximum level of urbanizaiton is probably somewhere around 90 percent. (Places that comprise only city, such as Singapore, can be 100 percent urban.) However, even after a nation achieves a high level of urbanization, its cities and metropolitan areas can continue to grow. This is clearly the case in North American and western Europe. While there is a limit to the percentage of urbanization possible, it is not yet known what the practical limit is on the size of cities or metropolitan areas.

While "urbanization" has to do with metropolitan growth, "urbanism" refers to the conditions of life associated with living in cities. Urbanism can thus be referred to as a way of life or life-style characteristic of cities. The term "urbanism" is sometimes used in both professional and popular literature as synonomous with "urbanization," and is sometimes used to represent an entirely different concept. Thus students can be excused for sometimes confusing the two.[12] Urbanism, with its changes in the values, mores, customs, and behaviors of a population, is often seen as one of the consequences of urbanization.[13]

Under the conceptual label "urbanism" is found research concerning the social psychological aspects of urban life, urban personality patterns, and the behavioral adaptations required by city life. Urbanism as a way of life will receive detailed treatment in Chapters 6 and 7, City Life-Styles and Patterns of Suburbanization, as well as in later chapters, particularly those on developing areas.

It should be noted, though, that it is possible for an area to have a high degree of urbanization and a low level of urbanism or—less commonly—a low level of urbanization and a high level of urbanism. Examples of the former can be

[11]Hope Tisdale Eldridge, "The Process of Urbanization," in J. J. Spengler and O. D. Duncan (eds.), *Demographic Analysis*, Free Press, Glencoe, Ill., 1956, pp. 338–343.
[12]Paul Meadows and Ephraim Mizruchi (eds.), *Urbanism, Urbanization, and Change: Comparative Perspectives*, Addison-Wesley, Reading, Mass., 1969, p. 4.
[13]Leo Schnore, "Urbanization and Economic Development: The Demographic Contribution," *American Journal of Economics and Sociology*, 23:37–48, 1964.

This daily market within the city of Cairo operates in the traditional manner—i.e., with no uniform fixed prices. Note the proliferation of squatter shacks, a common feature in third world cities. (© 1979 Bernard Pierre Wolff/Photo Researchers, Inc.)

found in the large cities of the developing world, where the city is filled with immigrants who now reside in an urban place but remain basically rural in outlook. Cairo, the world's tenth-largest city, is typical of developing cities in that over one-third of its residents were born outside the city. Many of these newcomers are urban in residence but remain rural in outlook and behavior.[14] On the other hand, if the urbanization process in the United States is now one of population decentralization, the United States might in the future have a decline in urbanization while urban life-styles become even more universal.[15]

The explicit belief in most older sociological writings—and an implicit premise in much of what is written about cities today—is that cities produce a characteristic way of life known as "urbanism." Moreover, urbanism as a way of life, while often successful economically, is said to produce personal alienation,

[14]See, for example, Janet Abu-Lughod, "Migrant Adjustment to City Life: The Egyptian Case," *American Journal of Sociology*, 67:22–32, July, 1961.
[15]Brian J. L. Berry, "The Counterurbanization Process: Urban America since 1970," in *Urbanization and Counterurbanization*. Vol. II: *Urban Affairs Annual Reviews*, Sage Publications, Beverly Hills, Calif., 1976, pp. 17–39.

social disorganization, and the whole range of ills falling under the cliché "the crisis of the cities."

The classic statement of the effects of urbanization on urban behavior patterns is Louis Wirth's article "Urbanism as a Way of Life."[16] According to Wirth, "For sociological purposes a city may be defined as a relatively large, dense, permanent settlement of socially heterogeneous individuals."[17]

Wirth further suggested that these components of urbanization—size, density, and hetrogeneity—are the independent variables that create a distinct way of life called "urbanism." Urbanism, with its emphasis on competition, achievement, specialization, superficiality, anonymity, independence, and tangential relationships, is often compared—at least implicitly—with a simpler and less competitive indealized rural past (The adequacy of this approach will be addressed in detail in Chapter 6, City Life-Styles.)

Today urbanism as a way of life is virtually universal in highly urbanized nations such as the United States, with their elaborate media and communications networks. The attitudes, behaviors, and cultural patterns of rural areas in the United States are dominated by urban values and life-styles. Rural wheat farmers, cattle ranchers, and dairy farmers—with their accountants, professional lobbies, and government subsidies— are all part of a complete and highly integrated agribusiness enterprise. They are hardly innocent country bumpkins being preyed upon by city slickers. By comparison, urban consumers often appear naive.

The degree to which urbanism has permeated every aspect of American culture is documented in Vidich and Bensman's study of an upstate New York hamlet with a population of 1,700. Their book which they titled *Small Town in Mass Society*, presents a detailed and careful picture of how industrialization and bureaucratization have totally permeated the rural village.[18] Everything—from 4H clubs, and Boy Scout and Girl Scout troops, through the American Legion and national churches, to university agriculture agents, the Social Security Administration, and marketing organizations to raise the price supports for milk— influenced how the village residents thought, acted, and lived. The town was totally dependent on outside political and economic institutions for its survival.

The small-towners, though, had an entirely different conception of themselves and their hamlet. They saw themselves as rugged individualists living in a town that, in contrast to outside city life, prided itself on friendliness, neighborliness, grass roots democracy, and independence. Their town was small, self-reliant, and friendly, while the city was large, coldly impersonal, and filled with welfare loafers. In spite of the absence of a viable local culture, and the clear division of the town by socioeconomic class differences, the myth of a unique rural life-style and social equality persisted. Small-town America is totally enmeshed in an urban economic and social system despite its pride in its independence of

[16]Louis Wirth, "Urbanism as a Way of Life," *American Journal of Sociology*, **44**:1–24, July, 1938.
[17]Ibid. p. 8.
[18]Arthur J. Vidich and Joseph Bensman, *Small Town in Mass Society*, Princeton University Press, Princeton, N. J., 1958.

the city and cosmopolitan ways. The small town even relies on the mass media to help reaffirm its own fading self-image.[19]

CONCEPTS OF THE CITY

The Chicago School

The scientific study of urbanism and urbanization is a relative newcomer to the academic scene. Systematic empirical examination of cities and city life began somewhat over half a century ago, and the early work is largely associated with a remarkable group of scholars connected with the University of Chicago during the 1920s and 1930s. The "Chicago school" found sociology a loose collection of interesting facts, social work, and social reform; it converted sociology to an established academic discipline and an emerging science.

The sociologists of the Chicago school began their research during a period in which American cities were experiencing considerable transformation in terms of both industrialization and a massive influx of immigrants from the rural areas of Europe and the American south. To many observers of the time, the city, with its emphasis on efficiency, technology, and division of labor, was undermining simpler rural forms of social organization. The social consequences were disorganization, depersonalization, and the breakdown of traditional norms and values.

A typical view of urban life, given in an anonymous poem of 1916 called "While the City Sleeps," mirrors this view:

> Stand in your window and scan the sights,
> On Broadway with its bright white lights.
> Its dashing cabs and cabarets,
> Its painted women and fast cafes.
> That's when you really see New York.
> Vulgar of manner, overfed,
> Overdressed and underbred.
> Heartless and Godless, Hell's delight,
> Rude by day and lewd by night.

Rural Simplicity versus Urban Complexity

In the usual description of the transition from simple to complex forms of social organization, there is, at least implicitly, a time frame in which rural areas represent the past and traditional values, and the city represents the future with its emphasis on technology, division of labor, and emergence of new values. Such a picture of a fast-paced, alienating, stimulating, and anonymous city life along with the contrasting romanticized picture of the warm, personal, and well-

[19]Maurice R. Stein, *The Eclipse of Community*, Princeton University Press, Princeton, N. J., 1961.

As a result of rapid technological change, owning a transistor radio may be more commonplace than wearing shoes. (© Marc & Evelyne Bernheim/Woodfin Camp & Assoc.)

adjusted rural life is, of course, a stereotype. There are some indications that the actual case may even be the opposite. With the exception of the largest cities, Fischer found, for example, that on a worldwide scale there is greater evidence of rural as opposed to urban dissatisfaction, unhappiness, despair, and melancholy.[20]

Furthermore, an examination of a national probability sample of 6,672 adults suggests that those living in large cities probably have fewer mental health problems than those in smaller-sized places.[21] When the sample was divided into six categories on the basis of size of place of residence, those in the three largest-sized communities appeared to have fewer nervous breakdowns and

[20]Claude S. Fischer, "Urban Malaise," *Social Forces,* **52(2):**221, December, 1973.
[21]Leo Srole, "Urbanization and Mental Health: Some Reformulations," *American Scientist,* **60:**576–583, September-October, 1972.

psychosomatic symptoms than those in the smaller communities. Since these findings are based on a sample which was not controlled for the age—other than adult—or socioeconomic status of the respondents, the findings must be considered tentative. But at the very least, the old clichés must be reevaluated.

Urbanism in Social Theory

The cleavage between the city and the countryside is, of course, not a uniquely American idea. It is significant that the great European social theorists of the nineteenth century described the social changes that were then taking place in terms of a shift from a warm, supportive community based on kinship in which common aims are shared, to a larger, more impersonal society in which ties are based not on kinship but on interlocking economic, political, and other interests.

Ideal Types. The changes were frequently presented in terms of dichotomous logical constructs, which sociologists refer to as "ideal types." Ferdinard Tönnies had a great impact on early urban sociology with his elaborate discussion of the shift from "gemeinschaft"—a community based on ties of blood or kinship—to "gesellschaft"—a society based on common economic, political, and other interests. The great French sociologist Emile Durkheim similarly saw societies moving from a commonality of tasks and outlook to a complex division of labor. Societies based on shared sentiments and tasks were said to possess "mechanical solidarity," while those based on integrating different but complementary economic and social functions were said to possess "organic solidarity."[22] Some of the same concepts can be found in the distinction made by the German sociologist Max Weber. Weber's distinction was between "traditional society" based upon ascription, and "rational society" based on the "technical superiority" of formalized and impersonal bureaucracy.[23] This distinction between simple and complex, country and town, is also found in the works of Marx and Engels:

> The greatest division of material and mental labour is the separation of town and country. The antagonism between town and country begins with the transition from barbarism to civilization, from tribe to State, from locality to nation, and runs through the whole history of civilization to the present day. . . .
>
> Here first became the division of the population into two great classes, which is directly based on the division of labour and on the instruments of production.[24]

A twentieth-century version of the dichotomy between rural and urban places is the distinction made by the anthropologist Robert Redfield between what he characterized as "folk" and "urban" societies. Folk peasant societies were described as being:

[22]Emile Durkheim, *The Division of Labor in Society,* George Simpson (trans.), Free Press, Glencove, Ill., 1960.

[23]H. H. Gerth and C. Wright Mills (trans. and ed.), *Max Weber, Essays in Sociology,* Oxford University Press, New York, 1966.

[24]Karl Marx and Friedrich Engels, *The German Ideology,* R. Pascal (trans.), International Publishers, New York, 1947, pp. 68–69.

. . . small, isolated, non-literate, and homogeneous, with a strong sense of group solidarity. The ways of living are conventionalized into that coherent system which we call "a culture." Behavior is traditional, spontaneous, uncritical, and personal; there is no legislation, or habit of experiment and reflection for intellectual ends. Kinship, its relationships and institutions, are the type categories of experience and the familial group is the unit of action. The sacred prevails over the secular; the economy is one of status rather than market.[25]

Interestingly, Redfield never did fully define "urban life," simply saying that it was the opposite of folk society.

Assumptions. The theoretical frameworks described above contain three general assumptions: (1) The evolutionary movement is unilinear, (2) modern urban life stresses achievement over ascription, and (3) the characteristics of the city apply to urban areas as a whole. As you read through this text, note whether these assumptions are supported or rejected. These models have at least an implicit evolutionary framework: Societies follow a unilinear path of development from simple rural to complex urban. Rural areas and ways of life typify the past, while the city is the mirror to the future.

This change is assumed to be both inevitable and irreversible, and early empirical sociologists, particularly those of the Chicago school, concerned themselves with describing the effects of urbanization on immigrant and rural newcomers to the city, and the emergence of "urbanism as a way of life." Works such as *The Polish Peasant in Europe and America*, *The Ghetto*, *The Jack Roller*, and *The Gold Coast and the Slum* are minor classics describing the effects of urbanization.[26]

A subset of the belief that the city fosters secondary- rather than primary-group relationships is the unspoken but usually implicit value judgment that the old ways were better, or at least more humane. The city is presented as more efficient, but the inevitable price of efficiency is the breakdown of meaningful social relationships. The countryside exemplifies stable rules, roles, and relationships, while the city is characterized by innovation, experimentation, flexibility, and disorganization. In cultural terms the small town represents continuity, conformity, and stability, while the big city stands for heterogeneity, variety, and originality. In terms of personality, country folk are supposed to be neighborly people who help one another —they lack the sophistication of city slickers but also lack the city dwellers' guile. In short, country folk are "real," while city people are artificial and impersonal.

Fortunately, the newly emerging discipline of urban sociology did not classify or explain differences between the rural and the urban, but rather began to

[25]Robert Redfield, "The Folk Society," *American Journal of Sociology*, **52**:53–73, 1947.

[26]William I. Thomas and Florian Znaniecki, *The Polish Peasant in Europe and America*, 5 vols., University of Chicago Press, Chicago, 1918–1920; Louis Wirth, *The Ghetto*, University of Chicago Press, Chicago, 1928; Clifford R. Shaw, *The Jack Roller*, University of Chicago Press, Chicago, 1930; and Harvey W. Zorbaugh, *The Gold Coast and the Slum*, University of Chicago Press, Chicago, 1929.

examine the urban scene empirically and systematically. Eventually the original dichotomy was abandoned, and limited hypotheses began to be developed on the basis of empirical research.

Community Characteristics. As urban researchers began to define urban communities sociologically, they focused on three major sets of community characteristics or variables: (1) the city as a unique demographic structure and an ecological community, (2) the city as a characteristic form of social organization, with related social structures, and (3) the city as a set of characteristic values, attitudes, and subjective perceptions. Research from all three perspectives is presented in the following chapters; Parts One and Two place relatively greater emphasis on the relationships between physical spatial features and forms of social organization. Part Three treats the social psychological aspects of urbanism and the life-styles associated with it. Parts Four and Five then apply these perspectives to particular issues or problems and compare the American experience with that of other regions of the world.

CHAPTER

2

EMERGENCE OF CITIES

Men come together in cities for security;
they stay together for the good life.

Aristotle

INTRODUCTION

This chapter outlines the growth of urban life from the first tentative agricultural villages to the industrial cities of the nineteenth century. The goal is not to memorize a series of dates and places, but rather to develop some understanding of the process of urban development. Largely archeological and historical material is included, not because there is anything sacred about beginnings as such, but because having some understanding of the origin and function of cities helps us to better understand contemporary cities and how and why they got to be what they are today.

THE ECOLOGICAL COMPLEX

In this and the following chapters we shall be implicitly using an ecosystem framework, particularly the conceptual scheme of the ecological complex. An "ecosystem" can be defined as a natural unit in which there is an interaction of an environmental and a biotic system—that is, a community together with its habitat. At the upper extreme, the whole earth is a world ecosystem.[1]

Urban ecologists study urban growth patterns in terms of changes in the system, using a set of categories known as the "ecological complex." In basic terms, the ecological complex identifies the relationship between four concepts or classes of variables: population, organization, environment, and technology. These variables are frequently referred to by the acronym "POET." The ecological complex thus reminds one of the interrelated properties of life in urban settings, and how each class of variables is related to and has implications for the others. Each of the four variables is causally interdependent; depending on the way a problem is stated, each may serve either as an independent (or thing-explaining) or a dependent (thing-to-be-explained) variable. In sociological research, "organization" is commonly viewed as the "dependent variable" to be influenced by the other three "independent variables," but a more sophisticated view of "organization" sees it as reciprocally related to the other elements of the ecological complex. In Otis Dudley Duncan's words: "These categories: population, organization, environment, and technology (P. O. E. T.), provide a somewhat arbitrary simplified way of identifying systems of relationships in a preliminary description of ecosystem process."[2]

A major advantage of the ecological complex as a conceptual scheme is its simplicity, since economy of explanation is a basic scientific goal. The categories themselves are somewhat arbitrary, and so the boundary between them is not always precise—particularly the boundary between technology and social organization. "Population" refers to any collectivity of persons functioning as a

---

[1]See Lee R. Rice, *Man's Nature and Nature's Man: The Ecology of Human Communities,* University of Michigan Press, Ann Arbor, 1955, pp. 2–3.
[2]Otis Dudley Duncan, "From Social System to Ecosystem," *Sociological Inquiry,* **31:**145, 1961.

unit. "Organization" refers to the social structure that enables the population to sustain itself in an environment. "Environment" refers to all phenomena external to the population, including other social systems.[3] "Technology" refers to the artifacts, tools, and techniques used by the population to influence the environment.

Thus, if our interest is in social organization as the dependent variable—the thing to be explained—our focus is on how population, technology, and environment operate singly and jointly in the modification of urban social organization. For example, Otis Dudley Duncan, using the example of smog in Los Angeles, suggests that as transportation technology changed, the environment organization, and population of the city also changed.[4] In Los Angeles a favorable natural environment led to large-scale increases in population, which resulted in organizational problems (civic and governmental) and technological changes (freeways and factories). These in turn led to environmental changes (smog), which resulted in organizational changes (new pollution laws), which in turn resulted in technological changes (antipollution devices on automobiles).

This example illustrates how sociologists can use the conceptual scheme of the ecological complex to clarify significant sets of variables when studying urban growth patterns. Note, for example, the dominant importance of environmental factors in the first cities and how this in time is modified by technological and social inventions.

FIRST SETTLEMENTS

Our knowledge of the origin and development of the first human settlements and our understanding of the goals, hopes, and fears of those who lived within them must forever remain tentative. Because the first towns emerged before the invention of writing about 3,500 B.C., we must depend for our knowledge on the research of archeologists. Understandably, historians, sociologists, and other scholars sometimes differ in their interpretations of the limited archeological and historical data. Lewis Mumford has stated the problem aptly:

> Five thousand years of urban history and perhaps as many of proto-urban history are spread over a few score of only partly exposed sites. The great urban landmarks Ur, Nippur, Uruk, Thebes, Heliopolis, Assur, Nineveh, Babylon, cover a span of three thousand years whose vast emptiness we cannot hope to fill with a handful of monuments and a few hundred pages of written records.[5]

This chapter which outlines the growth of urban settlements, must necessarily be based in part on scholarly speculation as to what happened before the

[3]Brian J. Berry and John D. Kasarda, *Contemporary Urban Ecology*, Macmillan, New York, 1977, p. 14.
[4]Duncan, op. cit., pp. 140–149.
[5]Lewis Mumford, *The City in History, Its Origins, Its Transformations and Its Prospects*, Harcourt, Brace, and World, New York, 1961, p. 55.

historical era. Fortunately, though, our interest is not so much in an exact chronology of historical events as in the patterns and process of development.

It is generally believed that before the urban revolution could take place, an agricultural revolution was necessary.[6] Before the invention of the city, nomadic hunting-and-gathering bands could not accumulate, store, and transport more goods than could be carried with them. All that was to change.

Only when the agricultural system became capable of producing a surplus was it possible to withdraw labor from food production and apply it to the production of other goods.[7] The size of the urban population was thus directly related to the efficiency of agricultural workers, and agriculture remained primitive for millennia.

However, while a food surplus was essential to the emergence of cities, it was not essential that the surplus come from agriculture. Small towns and villages could manage by gathering if their ecological site was especially bountiful. Services and natural resources could also be exchanged for food. The inhabitants of ancient Jericho, for example, had sufficient civic organization and division of labor to build massive defensive walls in 8,000 B.C, a period when they had barely begun to domesticate grains.[8] Perhaps as early as 15,000 years ago, during the Mesolithic period, there were hamlets from India to the Baltic area that based their culture on the use of shellfish and fish.[9] Within these Mesolithic hamlets possibly were seen the earliest domestic animals, such as pigs, ducks, geese, and our oldest companion, the dog. Mumford suggests that the practice of reproducing food by plant cuttings—as with the date palm, the olive, the fig, and the grape—probably derives from Mesolithic culture.[10]

Eventually, some groups gained enough knowledge of the relationship between the seasons and the cycle of growth to forsake constant nomadism in favor of permanent settlement in one location. The Neolithic period is character-ized by this change from gathering food to producing it. There is fairly clear evidence that about 8,000 B.C. in the middle east there was a transformation from a specialized food-collecting culture to a culture where grains were cultivated.

Herd animals such as oxen, sheep, donkeys, and finally horses were first used during this period, allowing the available supply of food to be substantially increased and the first solid steps toward permanent settlement of a single site to be made. Animals such as the horse and the donkey could also serve, in addition

[6]Not everyone agrees with an implicit evolutionary typology such as the one used in this chapter. Bruce Trigger, for instance, strongly argues against an evolutionary approach in explaining the emergence and growth of cities, and states that "what seems to be required is a more piecemeal and institutional approach to complex societies." [Bruce Trigger, "Determinants of Urban Growth in Pre-industrial Societies," in Peter Ucko, Ruth Tringham, and G. W. Dimbleby (eds.), *Man, Settlement, and Urbanism,* Schenkman, Cambridge, Mass., 1972, p. 576.]

[7]Jane Jacobs reverses the order presented here, suggesting that intensive agriculture was the result rather than the cause of cities. This theory, however, has received little support from scholars. See Jane Jacobs, *The Economy of Cities,* Random House, New York, 1969.

[8]Dora Jane Homblin, *The First Cities,* Time-Life Books, Little, Brown, Boston, 1973, p. 15.

[9]Mumford, op. cit., p. 10.

[10]Ibid., p. 11.

to humans, as beasts of burden and a source of pulling power. In all likelihood there were decreases in the very high mortality rates, and increases in population, at this same time.

This first population explosion, by increasing a tribe to the point where hunting and gathering could no longer provide adequate food, further encouraged fixed settlements. This was most likely to occur in fertile locations where land, water, and climate favored intensive cultivation of food.

Since the plow didn't yet exist—it was not invented until sometime in the fourth century B.C.—horticulturalists of this period used a form of "slash-and burn" agriculture.[11] This meant cutting down what you could and burning off the rest before planting—an inefficient form of farming but one with a long history. It was even used by the American pioneers who first crossed the Appalachian Mountains into the new lands of Kentucky and Ohio. The first horticulturalists in ancient times soon discovered that slash-and-burn farming quickly depleted the soil, and so they were forced to migrate—thus probably spreading their knowledge by means of cultural diffusion.

The consequences of these developments were momentous; with cultivation a surplus could be accumulated, and people could plan for the future. One of the earliest permanent village farming communities so far excavated, Jarmo, in the Kurdistan area of Iraq, was inhabited between 7,000 and 6,500 B.C. It has been calculated that approximately 150 people lived in Jarmo, and archeological evidence indicates a population density of twenty-seven people per square mile (this is about the same as the population density today in that area).[12] Soil erosion, deforestation, and 10,000 years of human habitation have offset the technological advantages enjoyed by the area's present inhabitants.

The inhabitants of Jarmo had learned to domesticate dogs, goats, and possibly sheep.[13] The farmers living in Jarmo raised an early form of domesticated barley and wheat but still had to hunt and collect much of their food. Since the earliest farmers lacked plows to break the tight grassland sod, they worked the hillsides where grass was scarce and trees broke the earth. Village farming communities like Jarmo had stabilized by about 5,500 B.C., and over the next 1,500 years such settlements gradually spread from the flanks of hills into the alluvial plains of river valleys like that of the Tigris-Euphrates. A similar process took place in the great river valleys of the Nile, the Indus, and the Hwang Ho. The invention of agriculture was quite possible an independent development in China and was certainly independent in the new world.[14] The civilizations of Mesomerica were physically isolated from those of the middle east and Asia and thus had to invent independently, since they were unable to borrow.

Particularly environmentally blessed were those settlements of Mesopotamia

[11]E. Cecil Curwin and Gudmund Hart, *Plough and Pasture*, Collier Books, New York, 1961, p. 64.
[12]Robert Braidwood, "The Agricultural Revolution," *Scientific American*, September, 1960, p. 7.
[13]Ibid.
[14]Ibid., p. 3.

and the Nile River valley which could exploit the rich soil of the alluvial river beds. Egypt was among the first to adopt sedimentary agriculture. By the middle of the fourth millennium B.C. the economy of the Nile valley in Egypt had shifted once and for all from a combination of farming and food gathering to a major reliance on agriculture.[15] In the great river valley two and sometimes three crops a year were possible because the annual floods brought rich silt to replace the soil which was exhausted. To the dependable crops of wheat and barley was added the cultivation of the date palm. This was a great improvement. In Mesopotamia the palm provided more than simple food; from it were obtained wood, roofing, matting, wine, and fiber for rope.

POPULATION, TECHNOLOGY, AND SOCIAL ORGANIZATION

The immediate result of the agricultural revolution was a spurt in population size, since a larger population could be maintained on a permanent basis. Stable yields meant that larger numbers of people could be sustained in a relatively compact space. Agricultural villages could support up to twenty-five persons per square mile; this was a dramatic improvement over the maximum of three to ten persons per square mile found in hunting-and-gathering societies.[16]

The establishment of sedentary agricultural villages with growing populations increased the pressure for more intensive agriculture and more complex patterns of organization. Agriculture in the river valleys required at least small-scale irrigation systems, something not necessary in the highlands. The existence of irrigation systems also means the development of systems of control, i.e., the emergence of social stratification within the permanent settlements. Rudimentary social organization and specialization began to develop; the periodic flooding made it necessary for the village farmers to band together to create a system of irrigation canals and repair the damage done by the floods. Relatively permanent settlements in one place also allowed the structure of the family itself to change. In a hunting-and-gathering society, the only legacy parents could pass on to their progeny was their physical strength and knowledge of rudimentary skills. Agriculturalists, though, can also pass land on to their children, and all land is not equal. Over generations social stratification emerged, with some children born into prosperity and others into poverty.

Extended family forms can also more easily emerge under sedentary conditions. For example, imagine a male-dominated society where polygyny is practiced. Having more than one wife can have major economic as well as sexual advantages, since extra wives mean extra hands to tend the animals and cultivate the fields. More important, many wives mean many sons; sons to work the fields,

---

[15]Robert W. July, *A History of the African People*, Scribner, New York, 1970, p. 14.
[16]Gerhard Lenski, *Human Society*, McGraw-Hall, New York, 1970, p. 164.

Today traditional agriculture—as here, in India—may exist side by side
with modern technology. (United Nations.)

help protect what one has from the raiding of others, provide for one in old age, make offerings to the gods at one's grave, and carry one's lineage forward. The last was particularly important in many societies. For example, in the Old Testament the greatest gift God could bestow on Abraham was not wealth or fame or everlasting life, but that his descendants would number more than the grains of sand on the seashore.

Environmentally, those located on rivers had advantages not only in terms of soil fertility but also for transportation and trade. The use of rivers for transportation further encouraged the aggregation of population, for now it was relatively easy to gather food at a few centers. Thus in the valleys of the Nile, the Tigris-Euphrates, and the Indus there first developed a population surplus, which in turn permitted the rise of the first cities. By the third century B.C. Egyptian peasants from the fertile river flood plain could produce approximately three times the food they needed.[17] The result was the first cities.

URBAN REVOLUTION

V. Gordon Childe lists ten features which, he says, define the "urban revolution." They are:

1. Permanent settlement in dense aggregations
2. Nonagriculturalists engaging in specialized functions
3. Taxation and capital accumulation
4. Monumental public buildings
5. A ruling class
6. The technique of writing
7. The acquisition of predictive sciences—arithmetic, geometry, and astronomy
8. Artistic expression
9. Trade
10. The replacement of kinship by residence as the basis for membership in the community[18]

Whether all ten are necessary is debatable. For example, monumental urban places did not develop in Mesoamerica until the first century B.C., but even at that comparatively late date, these cities lacked some of the technical advances found in cities of the middle east, the Indus River area, and China at that time. Central American cities existed without the wheel, the raising of animals, the plough, the use of metals, or a writing system other than the rudimentary use of hieroglyphic symbols. They did, however, have compensatory advantages; the most significant

---

[17]July, op. cit., p. 14.
[18]V. Gordon Childe, "The Urban Revolution," *Town Planning Review*, 21:4–7, 1950.

probably was the knowledge of how to cultivate large surpluses of domesticated maize (corn). The Mayans also had made major advances in mathematics, including the invention of the concept of zero. They were accurate astronomers and had an exact calender; both of the latter were for religious purposes.

Childe's list is perhaps most useful in helping us define what we have come to accept as the general characteristics of cities. What is important for our purposes is that cities possessing these characteristics did emerge in Mesopotamia and the Nile valley.

EVOLUTION IN SOCIAL ORGANIZATION

Keep in mind that the size of an urban population was, during this period, no measure of its significance. These cities were important not because of their size but because they frequently not only tolerated but actively encouraged innovations in social organization. Even though small in number, the urban elite was the principal carrier of the all-important cultural and intellectual values of a civilization. Needless to say, the city also held economic and political sway over the more numerous country dwellers. The philosopher-sociologist Ibn Khaldun, writing in the fourteenth century, pointed out that the concentration of economic power and the proceeds of taxation in the cities led to a profound difference between the economic pattern of the city and that of the country. The concentration of governmental and educational functions in the city also stimulated new demands which affected the patterns of production and supply.

Division of Labor

The city's greater population density, along with its sedentary way of life, made possible the development of an urban culture emphasizing trade, manufacturing, and services. The earliest cities began to evolve a social organization immensely more complex than that found in the Neolithic village. The slight surplus of food permitted the emergence of a rudimentary division of labor. No longer did each person have to do everything for himself or herself. The city thus differed from a large village not only in numbers, but because it had a larger and more extensive division of labor. The consequence was the emergence of hierarchy and stratification.

Archeological records indicate that the earliest public buildings were temples, suggesting that specialized priests were the first to be released from direct subsistence functions. That the priests also assumed the role of economic administrators is indicated by ration or wage lists found in places where temples were located.[19] In Egypt the temples were also used as granaries for the

[19]Robert M. Adams, "The Origins of Cities," *Scientific American*, September, 1960, p. 7.

community surplus. This surplus could be used to carry a community through a period of famine. The technology of food storage was a major achievement of the city. The biblical story of Joseph, who was sold by his jealous brothers into slavery in Egypt, only to become advisor to the Pharaoh and predict seven good years of harvest followed by seven lean years of famine, points out the vulnerability of the nomadic Israelites to their physical environment, and the relative control of the more advanced Egyptians over their environment. Even if the nomadic Jews had received Joseph's warning, they would have been unable to profit from it. They lacked the transportation and storage technology of the more urban Egyptians. Long-term planning—whether to avoid famines, build pyramids, or construct temples—was possible only where a surplus was assured and storage was available.

Kingship and Social Class

For a long time the temples were the largest and most complex institutions that existed; kingship and dynastic political regimes developed later. Apparently, warrior-leaders were originally selected by all other males and served only during times of external threat. Eventually, those chosen as short-term leaders during periods of war came to be retained even during periods of peace. As H. G. Creel describes the process in China in the fifth century B.C.:

> Perhaps whole settlements sometimes found it was easier to set up as warriors, and let the people around them work for them, than to labor in the fields. The chiefs and their groups of warriors, no doubt, provided the farmers with "protection" whether they wanted it or not, and in return for that service they took a share of the peasant's crop.[20]

It is hardly necessary to add that the size of the warrior's share of the peasant's crop was fixed by the warrior, not the peasant. The growth of military establishments did contribute, though, to technological innovations—metallurgy for weapons, chariots for battle, and more efficient ships.

It was but a short step from a warrior class to kingship and the founding of dynasties with permanent hereditary royalty. The gradual shifting of the central focus from temple to palace was accompanied by the growth of social and economic stratification. Records of sales of land indicate that even among the agriculturists there were considerable inequalities in the ownership of productive land. As a result, social differences grew. Some few members of each new generation were born with marked hereditary social and economic advantages over the others. If they couldn't afford the luxuries of palace life, they nonetheless lived in considerable comfort. Archeologically, the emergence of social classes can be seen clearly in the increasing disparity in the richness of grave offerings.[21]

---

[20]H. G. Creel, *The Birth of China*, Reynal and Hitchcock, New York, 1937, p. 279.
[21]Adams, op. cit., p. 9.

The tombs of royalty are richly furnished with ornaments and weapons of gold and precious metals; those of others, with copper vessels; while the majority have only pottery vessels or nothing at all. The building of burial pyramids was the ultimate case of monumental graves.

TECHNOLOGICAL EVOLUTION AND SOCIAL REVOLUTION

Technology was spurred on by the existence of the palace. The military required armor, weapons, and chariots, and the court demanded ever more ornaments and other luxuries. A constant market was created for nonagricultural commodities, and the result was the establishment of a class of full-time artisans and craft workers. The near-isolation of earlier periods was now replaced with trade over long distances, which brought not only new goods but also new ideas.

The first city was far more than an enlarged village—it was a clear break with the past, a whole new social system. It was a social revolution involving the evolution of a whole new set of social institutions. Unlike the agricultural revolution that preceded it, this urban revolution was far more than a basic change in subsistence. It was "pre-eminently a social process, an expression more of change in man's interaction with his fellows than in his interaction with his environment."[22]

Once begun, the urban revolution created its own environment. Inventions that have made large settlements possible have been due to the city itself—for example, writing, accounting, bronze, the solar calendar, bureaucracy, and the beginning of science.[23] Ever since Mesopotamia, the city as a social institution has been shaping human life.

CITY SIZE

These first cities were quite small; by contemporary standards, the largest were little more than villages or small towns. However, in their own day they must have been looked upon with the same awe with which nineteenth-century immigrants viewed New York, for these first cities were ten times the size of the Neolithic villages which had previously been the largest settlements. Babylon, with its hanging gardens, one of the wonders of the ancient world, embraced a physical area of only roughly 3.2 square miles.[24] The city of Ur, located at the confluence of the Tigris and Euphrates rivers, was the largest city in Mesopotamia. With all its canals, temples, and harbors, it occupied only 220 acres.[25] Ur was estimated to

[22]H. G. Creel, op. cit., p. 279.
[23]Adams, op. cit., p. 9.
[24]Kingsley Davis, "The Origin and Growth of Urbanization in the World," *American Journal of Sociology,* **60**:430, March, 1955.
[25]V. Gordon Childe, *What Happened in History,* Penguin Books, London, 1946, p. 87.

have contained 24,000 persons; other towns ranged in population from 2,000 to 20,000 inhabitants.[26] Such cities remained urban islands in the midst of rural seas.

Hawley estimates that although these cities were large for their time, they probably represented no more than 3 or 4 percent of all the people within the various localities.[27] Even Athens at its peak had only 612 acres within its walls—an area less than 1 square mile. Ancient Antioch was roughly half this size; Carthage at its peak was 712 acres. Of all the ancient cities, only imperial Rome exceeded an area of 5 square miles. Kingsley Davis estimates that even the biggest places before the Roman period could scarcely have exceeded 200,000 inhabitants, since from fifty to ninety farmers were required to support one person in a city.[28] In an agricultural world, the size of cities was limited by how much surplus could be produced and what technology was available to transport it.

SURVIVAL OF THE CITY

It should be noted that the stable location of the city was not an unmixed blessing. It was not simply for the sake of convenience that gardens and pasturelands were found within the city walls. Cities had to be equipped to withstand a siege, since the earliest cities were vulnerable not only to conquest by other peoples but also to periodic attacks by nomadic raiders.

Mesopotamian cities were perpetually under attack by nomadic tribes.[29] The Bible, for instance, devotes considerable attention to the successes of the nomadic Israelites in taking and pillaging the cities of their more advanced enemies. The description of the fall of the Canaanite city of Jericho tells us that

> the People went out into the city, every man straight before him, and they took the city. And they utterly destroyed all that was in the city, both man and woman, young and old, and ox and sheep and ass, with the edge of the sword—and they burnt the city with fire and all that was therein (Joshua 2:20–24).

That "Joshua fit the battle of Jericho . . . and the walls came tumbling down" is known to all those who have heard the stirring spiritual, even if they have not read the Old Testament. While the walls Joshua is believed to have miraculously brought down with trumpet blasts about 1,500 B.C. have not been located, the remains of other walls dating back to 8,000 B.C. have been excavated. As with some other long-inhabited ancient sites, the walls had been breached many times—sometimes by invaders, sometimes by earthquakes.

Within the city walls there also were threats to the inhabitants, the most

---

[26]Ibid., p. 86.
[27]Amos H. Hawley, *Urban Society*, Ronald Press, New York, 1971, p. 22.
[28]Davis, loc. cit.
[29]Sturat Piggot, "The Role of the City in Ancient Civilization," in E. M. Fisher (ed.), *The Metropolis in Modern Life*, Doubleday, Garden City, New York, 1955.

dangerous being fires and epidemic diseases. City life was more exciting, but it was not necessarily more secure than the countryside.

THE HELLENIC CITY

Environmental factors played a decisive role in early cities. The history of the city can be considered the story of human attempts, through the use of technology and social organization, to lessen the impact of environmental factors. An example is Athens, widely regarded as the apex of ancient urbanism. Not only was the Greek soil thin and rocky and of marginal fertility, but the mountainous hinterland made inland transportation and communication almost impossible. Aside from the sacred ways to Delphi and Eleusis, the roads were mere paths, suitable only for pack animals or porters. It is estimated that the cost of transporting goods 10 miles from Athens was more than 40 percent of the value of the goods.[30]

But Greece was blessed with fine harbors. Consequently, Athens turned to the sea. A Greek ship could carry 7,000 pounds of grain 65 nautical miles a day, and do it at one-tenth the cost of land transportation. (Storms at sea and pirates, however, often made this an ideal rather than a reality.) There were also technological contributions to Greek prosperity: the use of the lodestone as a basic nautical compass and the development of more seaworthy ships.

Social Invention

The greatest achievement of the Greeks was not in the area of technology but in that of social organization. The social invention of the "polis," or "city-state," enabled families, phratries (groups of clans), and tribes to organize for mutual aid and protection as citizens of a common state. Because they acknowledged a common mythical ancestry among the gods, different families were able to come together in larger bodies. Gradually the principle of common worship was extended to the entire community. Citizenship within the state and the right to worship at civic shrines were two sides of the same coin.

Citizens were those who could trace their ancestry back to the god or gods responsible for the city and thus could participate in public religious worship. An Athenian citizen was one who had the right to worship at the temple of Athena, the protector of the city-state of Athens. The ancient city was a religious community, and citizenship was at its basis a religious status.[31] Socrates's questioning the existence of the gods was considered a grave offense because, by threatening established religion, he was undermining the very basis of citizenship

---

[30]Gustave Glotz, *Ancient Greece at Work,* Norton, New York, 1967, pp. 291–293.
[31]Numa Denis Fustel de Coulanges, *The Ancient City.* Doubleday, Garden City, New York, 1956 (first published 1865), p. 134.

in the city-state. As punishment for such a subversive act he was forced to take poison hemlock. Unfortunately, the Greeks never devised a system for extending citizenship to political units larger than the city-state. That was to be the great achievement of the Romans.

Being a citizen of the city was of supreme importance to the Greeks. When Aristotle wished to characterize humans as social animals, he said that "man is by nature a citizen of the city." To the Greeks, being ostracized, or forbidden to enter into the city walls, was a severe punishment. To be placed beyond the walls was to be cast out of civilized life. The terms "pagan" and "heathen" originally referred to those beyond the city walls; our adjective "urban" and our nouns "citizen" and "politics" are derived from the Latin and Greek terms for the city. The English terms "city" and "civilization" are both derived from the Latin "civis."

Physical Design and Planning

Physically, the Greek cities were of fairly similar design, a fact which is not surprising given the amount of social borrowing that took place among the various city-states and the fact that the cities were built with military defense in mind. The major city walls were built around a fortified hill called an "acropolis." Major temples were also placed upon the acropolis. The nearby "agora" served both as a meeting place, and in time, a marketplace. All major buildings were located within the city walls. Housing, except for the most privileged, was outside the walls but huddled as close to their protective shelter as was possible.

The Acropolis of Athens was the religious, civil, and military center of the city-state. (Editorial Photocolor Archives.)

In describing the Greek polis, there is a strong tendency to focus on the image of the Athenian Acropolis harmoniously crowned by the perfectly proportioned Parthenon. Separated by seas and centuries, it is perhaps natural for us to accept Pericles's own praise of his fellow Athenians as "lovers of beauty without extravagance and lovers of wisdom without unmanliness."

Yet below the inner order and harmony of the Parthenon was a sprawling jumbled town in which streets were no more than dirty winding narrow lanes and unburied refuse rotted in the sun. Housing for the masses was squalid and cramped. Today it is easy to forget that the white stone of the Parthenon was once painted garish colors. While Hippodamus designed a grid street pattern for Piraeus, the port city of Athens, Athens itself had no such ordered arrangement. Athens was the center of an empire, but little of its genius was given to urban design or municipal management.

Population

Athens had considerable population problems— partially due to the scarcity of productive land, which resulted in heavy migration from rural areas to the cities. During its peak the city achieved a population of only between 120,000 and 180,000. The major limit on population growth was the limited technological base. The city was still dependent on the surplus of agricultural activities. Much of the land within Athens itself was given over to gardening. The great sociologist Max Weber put the Greek city-states in perspective when he wrote, "The full urbanite of antiquity was a semi-peasant."[32]

Expansion of Greek cities was also limited by preference and policy. The ancient Greek preferred fairly small cities. Both Plato and Aristotle firmly believed that good government was directly related to the size of the city. Plato specified that in the ideal Republic there should be exactly 5,040 citizens, since that number had fifty-nine divisors and would "furnish numbers for war and peace, and for all contracts and dealings, including taxes and divisions of the land."[33] Why Plato chose the number 5,040 isn't known, since his totalitarian state would be governed not by citizen vote but by a small group of guardians presided over by a philosopher-king. Lewis Mumford suggests perhaps two possible reasons for the limited size: A larger population would be more difficult to control strictly; and there may have been a desire to keep the population low enough to live off the local food supply.[34] He also notes that when noncitizens such as children, slaves, and foreigners are added into the calculation, the total population of the city-state is approximately 30,000, or about the size chosen later by Leonardo da Vinci and Ebenezer for their ideal cities. (Slaves constituted perhaps a third of the population.)

---

[32]Max Weber, *The City* (trans. D. Martendale and G. Neuwirth), Free Press, New York, 1958.
[33]Plato, *The Laws*, Book V, 437 (trans. B. Jowett), 1926 ed.
[34]Lewis Mumford, op. cit., p. 180.

Aristotle informs us that the town planner Hippodamus envisioned a city of 10,000 citizens divided into three parts: one of artisans, one of farmers, and one of warriors. The land was likewise to be divided in three parts: one to support the gods, one public to support the warriors defending the state, and one private to support the farm owners.[35]

Aristotle's views on the ideal size of the city are less specific, although he recognized that increasing the number of inhabitants beyond a certain point changes the character of a city. In his view, the city-state had to be large enough to defend itself and to be economically self-sufficient, but not so large as to prevent the citizens from knowing each other's character. As he stated it:

> A state then only begins to exist when it has attained a population sufficient for a good life in the political community: it may somewhat exceed this number, but as I was saying there must be a limit. What should be the limit will be easily ascertained by experience.—If the citizens of a state are to judge and distribute offices according to merit, then they must know each other's characters: where they do not possess this knowledge, both the election to offices and the decisions of lawsuits will go wrong—Clearly then the best limit of the population of a state is the largest number which suffices for the purposes of life and can be taken at a single view.[36]

City-states were also restrained from growing overly large by the Greek policy of creating colonies. This policy reinforced the social preference for small cities. Between 479 and 431 B.C., over 10,000 families migrated from established cities to newer Greek colonial settlements. Colonization both met the needs of empire and provided a safety valve for a chronic population problem. This diffusion of population led in turn to a diffusion of Greek culture and ideas of government far beyond the Peloponnesus.

ROME

The city as a physical entity reached a high point under the Roman Caesars. Not until the nineteenth century was Europe again to see cities as large as those found within the Roman Empire. Rome itself may have contained 1 million inhabitants at its peak, although an analysis of density figures would make an estimate two-thirds that number seem more reasonable; scholarly estimates vary from a low of 250,000 to a high of 1.6 million. These wide variations are a result of different interpretations of inadequate data. The number given in the total Roman census, for example, jumped from 900,000 in 69 B.C. to over 4 million in 28 B.C. No one is quite sure what this increase indicates—perhaps an extension of citizenship, perhaps the counting of women and children, perhaps something else.[37]

---

[35]Aristotle, *Politics*, Book VII, ii, p. 8, (trans. B. Jowett), 1932 ed.
[36]Aristotle, *Politics*, Book VII, iv, 7–8.
[37]William Petersen, *Population*, Macmillan, New York, 1969, p. 369.

Readers should remind themselves that all figures on the size of cities before the nineteenth century should be taken as estimates rather than empirical census counts. At their most accurate, such figures are formed by multiplying the supposed number of dwelling units at a given period by the estimated average family size.

Size and Number of Cities

Expertise in the areas of technology and social organization enabled the Romans to organize, administer, and govern an empire containing several cities of more than 200,000 inhabitants. The population of the Roman Empire exceeded that of all but the largest twentieth-century superpowers. According to the historian Edward Gibbon, "We are informed that when the emperor Claudius [reigned A.D. 41–54] exercised the office of censor, he took account of six million nine hundred and forty-five thousand Roman citizens, who with women and children, must have amounted to about twenty million souls." He concludes that there were "about twice as many provincials as there were citizens, of either sex and of every age; and that the slaves were at least equal in number to the free inhabitants of the Roman world. The total amount of this imperfect calculation would rise to about one hundred and twenty millions."[38] The total world population at this time was roughly 250 million.

Gibbon further states that ancient Italy was said to contain 1,197 cities— however defined—and Spain, according to Pliny, had 360 cities.[39] North Africa had hundreds of cities, and north of the Alps major cities rose from Vienna to Bordeaux. Even in far-off Britain there were major cities at York, Bath, and London. What made all this possible for hundreds of years was a technology of considerable sophistication and—most important—Roman social organization. Wherever the legions conquered, they also brought Roman law and Roman concepts of government.

Housing and Planning

"Rome, Goddess of the earth and of its people, without a peer or a second" remains the wonder of the ancient world. Yet despite the emperor Augustus's proud claim that he found a city of brick and left one of marble, much of the city centuries later was still composed of buildings with wood frames and roofs on narrow crowded alleys. Fire was a constant worry, and the disastrous fires of A.D. 64 that some say Nero started left only four of the city's fourteen districts intact.

Wealthy Romans lived on the Palatine Hill where its imperial palaces overlooked the Forum with its temples and public buildings, and the Colosseum. However, as was the case in Athens, Roman municipal planning was definitely

---

[38]Edward Gibbon, *The Decline and Fall of the Roman Empire*, Dell, New York, 1879 (first published 1776), p. 53.
[39]Ibid., pp. 54–55.

limited in scope. Magnificent though it was, it did not extend beyond the center of the municipality. Once one branched off the main thoroughfare leading to the city gates, there was only a maze of narrow crooked lanes winding through the squalid tenements that housed the great bulk of the population. The masses crowded in the poor quarters were offered periodic "bread and circuses" to keep their minds off revolt. Magnificent public squares and public baths were built with public taxes for the more affluent Romans, not for the masses. As the city grew, the old city walls were torn down and rebuilt to include buildings that had been constructed on the outer fringe. In time even the Forum became crowded and congested, as the ruins still standing amply testify.

The city was supplied with fresh water through an extensive system of aqueducts. The most important of these, which brought water from the Sabine Hills, was completed in 144 B.C. Parts of aqueducts still stand—testament to the excellence of their engineering and the skill of their builders. Rome even had an elaborate sewer system—at least in the better residential areas. It is an unfortunate comment on progress to note that present-day Rome still dumps untreated sewage in the Tiber River.

In many ways provincial Roman cities such as Paris, Vienna, Cologne, Mainz, and London exhibited greater civic planning than Rome itself. These cities grew out of semipermanent military encampments and thus took the shape of the standard Roman camp. The encampments and later the cities were laid out on a rectangular grid pattern with a gate on each side. The center was reserved for the forum, the coliseum, and municipal buildings such as public baths. Markets were also generally found in the forum. The common origins of European provincial Roman cities meant that they were all remarkably similar in design.

Elsewhere in the empire, the major distinction was between preexisting cities and new provincial towns and cities. In the east there were Hellenic and other cities which the Romans simply took over and expanded under Roman jurisdiction. In the west (western Europe and Britain), on the other hand, there was no preexisting system of cities; here the Romans created a wholly new system of Roman rather than Hellenic cities. The differences between the older eastern and newer western segments of the empire were never fully resolved, with the empire eventually splitting into eastern and western sections. While eastern cities differed physically as well as politically because of their commonality of origin, the western European provincial Roman cities were all remarkably similar in design (for more detail on Hellenic and Roman planning, see Chapter 13).

Transportation

Rome was an exporter of ideas—such as Roman law, government, and engineering—which enabled it to control the hinterland. It was an importer of necessary goods and therefore depended on the hinterland not only for tribute and slaves but for its very life. The city of Rome could feed its population and also import vast quantities of goods other than food because of an unrivaled road network and peaceful routes of sea trade. (The roads were built and the galleys powered largely by slaves.) Some 52,000 miles of well-maintained roads facilitated rapid movement of goods and people. Parts of some of the original roads are still in use today, and the quality of their construction surpasses that of even the most rigorous contemporary federal standards.

With the elimination of Carthage as a rival, the Mediterranean truly became "*Mare Nostrum*" or a Roman lake. Foodstuffs for both the civilian population and the legions could be transported easily and inexpensively from the commercial farming areas of Iberia and north Africa. When the African grain-producing areas were lost to the Vandals, and the barbarians in Germany, Gaul, and England pressed the empire, disrupting vital transportation routes, the decline of Rome was inevitable. Rome lived off its hinterland.

Life and Leisure

The prosperity of the Roman Empire during its peak and the leisure it afforded the residents of the capital were imperial indeed. By the second century after Christ, between a third and a half of the population was on the dole, and even those who worked (including the third of the population who were slaves) rarely spent more than six hours at their jobs. Moreover, by that period, religious and other holidays had been multiplied by the emperors until the ratio of holidays to workdays was one to one.[40]

To amuse the populace and keep their mind off uprisings against the emperor, chariot races and gladiatorial combats were staged. The scene of the races was the colossal Circus Maximus, which seated 260,000 persons, and gladiatorial fights were staged at the Colosseum. When the emperor Titus inaugurated the Colosseum in A.D. 80 he imported 5,000 lions, elephants, deer, and other animals to be slaughtered in a single day to excite the spectators. The role Christians came to play in these amusements is well known.

EUROPEAN URBANIZATION UNTIL THE INDUSTRIAL CITY

The preceding pages discussed the development of the city through the Roman period. Here particular emphasis is placed on the reemergence of European urban places after the decline of Rome and on how such cities laid the basis for the western industrial city with which we are all so familiar.

The dissolution of the Roman Empire in the fifth century after Christ marked the effective decay of cities in western Europe for a period of 600 years. This is not the place to detail why Rome fell; it is sufficient to note that under the combined impact of the barbarian invasion and internal decay, the empire disintegrated and commerce shrank to a bare minimum. Once-proud Roman provincial centers disappeared or declined to the point of insignificance. By the end of the sixth

---

[40]Jerome Carcoping, *Daily Life in Ancient Rome*, Yale University Press, New Haven, Conn., 1940.

century, war, devastation, plague, and starvation had destroyed the glory that was Rome. From the status of megalopolis, the city was reduced to its early medieval character of a collection of separate villages whose population had taken shelter in the ruins of ancient grandeur and had dug wells to replace the aqueducts. The people were supported by the pope, rather than by the emperor, from the produce of the papal territory.[41]

Nonetheless, while the social and physical city withered and decayed into poverty and ruins, the idea and myth of Rome and a Roman Empire remained alive even in the darkest medieval periods, and led eventually in the Renaissance to a new burst of urban activity. The throttling of Mediterranean trade by the advance of Islam in the seventh century, and the pillaging raids of the Norsemen in the ninth century, did further damage to what remained of European commercial life. In the east, however, cities continued to prosper. Constantinople, created by the emperor Constantine between 324 and 330, survived as the capital of the Byzantine Empire until its conquest by the Turks in 1453.

The Feudal System

The fall of Rome meant that each locality was isolated from every other and thus had to become self-sufficient in order to survive. Local lords offered peasants in the region protection from outside raiders in return for the virtual slavery—called "serfdom"—of the peasants. Removed from outside influences, local social structures congealed into hereditary hierarchies, with the local lord at the top of the pyramid of social stratification and the serfs at the bottom.[42]

It is important to note that the economic and political base of the feudal system, unlike that of the Roman period, was *rural*, not urban. Its center was not a city but the rural manor or castle from which the local peasantry could be controlled. The economy was a subsistence agriculture based solely on what was produced in the local area; transportation of goods from one area to another was extremely difficult. Lack of communication, the virtual absence of a commonly accepted currency, and the land-tenure system that bound serfs to the soil all contributed to a narrow inward-looking localism.

However, not all former provincial cities were totally abandoned; a few managed to survive with greatly reduced populations. These were generally under the secular control of the residing bishop. The Catholic church had based its diocesan boundaries on those of the old Roman cities, and as the empire faded and then collapsed, the bishops sometimes came to exercise secular as well as religious power. By the ninth century "civitas" had come to be synonymous with these "episcopal cities."[43]

According to Henri Pirenne, the "episcopal cities" were cities in name only, for they more clearly resembled medieval fortresses than true cities. They had a maximum of 2,000 or 3,000 persons and were frequently even smaller. But they

[41]Mason Hammond, *The City in the Ancient World*, Harvard University Press, Cambridge, Mass., 1972, p. 324.
[42]Henri Pirenne, *Medieval Cities*, Princeton University Press, Princeton, N.J., 1939, particularly pp. 84–85.
[43]Max Weber, op. cit., p. 49.

were to play a crucial historical role as "stepping stones."[44] By the time of Charlemagne (ninth century) the cities—or towns—had lost most of their urban functions:

> The Carolingians used the ancient cities as places of habitation, as fortified settlements from which to dominate the surrounding countryside. The surviving physical apparatus of the old town, the walls, and buildings, served because it already existed, a convenient legacy of an earlier age.[45]

Medieval Revival

Cities began to revive, very slowly, in the eleventh century. According to Pirenne, most of these new towns were not continuations of ancient cities but new social entities. Originally they were formed as a byproduct of the merchant caravans that stopped to trade outside the walls of the medieval "episcopal cities" such as Amiens, Tours, and Cologne. Under the influence of trade the old Roman cities took on a new life and became repopulated, while new towns were also being established. Mercantile groups formed around the military burgs, along sea-coasts, on riverbanks, and at the confluences and junctions of the natural routes of trade and communication.[46]

Over time the seasonal fairs that were held outside the town gates came to take on a more or less permanent year-round character. Since at this time the merchants were not allowed inside the town walls, they settled in the outside shadow of the walls and in some cases built their own walls, which attached to those of the town. These *faubourgs,* or medieval suburbs, came to be incorporated into the town proper, and by the thirteenth century merchants had an accepted and important role in the growing medieval towns. Revitalized city life was most prominent in Italy when city-states such as Venice established extensive commerical ties with the Byzantine and even the Arab empires. Trade with Constantinople enabled the Venetians to prosper and in time create a mini-empire of their own based upon the skills of their sea captains and the size of their fleets.

Two external factors during the Middle Ages also greatly contributed to the growth of towns elsewhere in Europe: the Crusades and the overall population growth. A great impetus for the revival of trade came from the medieval religious crusades. The Crusaders returned from the urban Byzantine Empire with newly developed tastes for the consumer goods and luxuries of the east. The crusading movement provided an excellent opportunity for the town entrepreneurs to put their commercial instincts into practice.[47] Trading activities greatly accelerated despite the pillaging which traders suffered from highwaymen and the endless feudal taxes and dues the traders were forced to pay to local lords as they transported goods through their territories.

[44]Pirenne, op. cit., p. 76.
[45]Howard Saalman, *Medieval Cities*, Braziller, New York, 1968, p. 15.
[46]Fritz Rörig, *The Medieval Town*, University of California Press, Berkeley, 1967, p. 15.
[47]Ibid.

Still, the social system was definitely more stable than that of the early Middle Ages, with their marauding raiders and internal warfare. The increasing stability led to a more constant food supply, which in turn resulted in lower death rates and improvement in the rate of natural increase of the population.

Technological innovations also contributed to population growth. The moldboard plow, which had been used in Roman times, was rediscovered. This heavier plow could turn the tight soils of northern Europe, and it came to be commonly used during the tenth century. The substitution of three-field rotation for the old two-field system also brought substantial gains in agriculture. In practice it permitted three plantings a year rather than two, while at the same time raising the productivity of each planting by 16 percent. The effect was to double production and permit stable growth.

England in the time of William the Conqueror had a population of approximately 1.8 million. Three hundred years later the population had increased to roughly 2.7 million. Some of this increased population migrated to the small but growing towns. Without such increases, the growth of towns would hardly have been possible.

It should be noted that while the feudal order was basically rural, certain elements of the medieval legal system indirectly encouraged the growth of towns. Feudal lords were forbidden by custom to sell their lands, but lords badly in need of new funds could sell charters for new towns within their lands. Also, by encouraging the growth of older towns such lords could increase their annual rents. Towns were frequently able to purchase or bargain for various rights, such as the right to hold a regular market, the right to coin money and establish weights and measures, the right of citizens to be tried in their own courts, and—most important—the right to bear arms.[48] Over time cities became more or less autonomous and self-governing. City charters, in fact, bestowed the right of citizenship upon those living within the urban walls. As a result, medieval cities attracted the more skilled, the more ambitious, and probably the more intelligent of the rural population.

Characteristics of Towns

Medieval cities were quite small by contemporary standards, having hardly more inhabitants than present-day towns or villages (Table 2-1). Even during the Renaissance, cities of considerable prominence often had only 10,000 to 30,000 inhabitants.[49] Only Paris, Florence, Venice, and Milan are thought to have possibly reached populations of 100,000.[50] These figures are of course scholarly estimates of past size, rather than counts taken at the time. (For a discussion of the larger and more socially devleoped Arab cities of this period, see Chapter 17.)

Thick walls enclosed the medieval city; watchtowers and external moats added to its military defense. The internal spatial arrangement of the medieval

[48]Mumford, op. cit., p. 263.
[49]Frederick Hiorns, *Town Building in History*, Harrap, London, 1956, p. 110.
[50]Henri Pirenne, *Economic and Social History of Medieval Europe*, Harcourt, New York, 1936, p. 173.

TABLE 2-1
Estimated Populations and Areas
of Selected Medieval Cities

City	Date	Population	Land area, acres
Venice	1363	77,700	810
Paris	1192	59,200	945
Florence	1381	54,747	268
Milan	1300	52,000	415
Genoa	1500	37,788	732
Rome	1198	35,000	3,450
London	1377	34,971	720
Bologna	1371	32,000	507
Barcelona	1359	27,056	650
Naples	1278	22,000	300
Hamburg	1250	22,000	510
Brussels	1496	19,058	650
Sienna	1385	16,700	412
Antwerp	1437	13,760	880
Pisa	1228	13,000	285
Frankfort	1410	9,844	320
Liège	1470	8,000	200
Amsterdam	1470	7,476	195
Zurich	1357	7,399	175
Berlin	1450	6,000	218
Geneva	1404	4,204	75
Vienna	1391	3,836	90
Dresden	1396	3,745	140
Leipzig	1474	2,076	105

Source: J. C. Russell, *Late Ancient and Medieval Population,*
American Philosophical Society, Philadelphia, 1958, pp. 60-62.

town relected its primary function either as an "episcopal city" functioning as an administrative center for church officials or as a military, and later a commercial, center. The main thoroughfares led directly from the outer gates to the source of protection and power—the cathedral or the feudal castle.[51] Outside the medieval bourgs, land was reserved for expansion, so that when the population increased, the older fortifications could be torn down and new city walls built farther out. The magnificent ringlike boulevards of Vienna and Paris are reminders of the medieval origins of these cities. When the walls were finally demolished in the latter part of the nineteenth century, the resulting open space was used to construct the now-famous boulevards.

Within the medieval bourgs could be found a new social class of artisans, weavers, innkeepers, money changers, and metalsmiths known as the "bourgeoisie." This new class of merchants was in many ways the antithesis of the feudal nobility. They were organized into guilds, and their way of life was characterized

[51]Rose Hum Lee, *The City,* Lippincott, Chicago, 1955, p. 27.

by trade and functionally specialized production, not by the ownership of land. The rise of the medieval bourgeoisie undermined the traditional system and prepared the way for further changes, for, as a German phrase put it, *"Stadtluft macht frei"* ("City air makes one free").[52]

What eventually developed was a distinct form, a full urban community Such communities, as defined by the German sociologist Max Weber, were economically based on trading and commercial relations. They exhibited the following features: (1) a fortification, (2) a market, a court of its own, and at least partial autonomous law, (3) a related form of association, and (4) at least partial political autonomy and self-governance.[53] Weber argues convincingly that such a totally self-governing urban community could emerge only in the west, where cities had political autonomy and urban residents shared common patterns of association and social statuses.

Medieval towns sometimes became organized around a particular craft or product, but the majority of the towns developed their greatest economic strength because of their performance of trade, commercial, and financial functions. Examples of cities that grew and prospered because of trade and banking are Venice, Milan, and Marseilles in the Mediterranean area, and Bremen, Hamburg, Cologne, and later Antwerp in the north.[54] In the later Middle Ages great financial families came to dominate many of these cities both economically and politically.

By the fourteenth century it was clear that the growth of town-based commerce was turning Europe away from the earlier manorial self-sufficiency toward an urban-centered, profit-oriented economy. The more ambitious cities were starting to flex their economic muscles. The Italian port cities grew wealthy on trade and began to expand their influence over the surrounding hinterland. Economic competition among the Italian city-states was augmented by warfare. Florence eliminated the competition of Pisa and Siena by conquering them militarily. The cities to the north were equally active in carving out a hinterland under their economic domination. Rouen was the economic center for 35 villages, Metz controlled 168, and Lübeck claimed 240 dependent villages within its territory.[55]

Plague

Urban development, however, was checked in the fourteenth century by the outbreak of plague. But even the devastation of the plague could not reverse the long-term growth of cities, although it certainly wrought havoc to a degree that is difficult to exaggerate. In its first three years, from 1348 through 1350, the plague, or "black death," wiped out at least a fourth of the population of Europe. One scholar

[52]In its precise sense, the phrase refers to the medieval practice of recognizing the freedom of any serf who could manage to remain within the walls of the city for a year and a day.
[53]Weber, op. cit., p. 81.
[54]Bert Hoselitz, "The Role of Cities in the Economic Growth of Underdeveloped Countries," *Journal of Political Economy,* **61**:195–208, 1953.
[55]John H. Mundy and Peter Reisenberg, *The Medieval Town,* Van Nostrand, New York, 1958, p. 35.

The "dance of death" symbolized how the plague claimed its victims regardless of their social position. (Culver Pictures.)

of the plague simply says that "it undoubtedly was the worst disaster that has ever befallen mankind."[56] Before the year 1400, mortality due to the plague rose to more than a third of the population of Europe. Over half the population of most cities was wiped out; few cities escaped with losses of less than a third. Florence went from 90,000 to 45,000 inhabitants and Siena from 42,000 to 15,000, and Hamburg lost almost two-thirds of its inhabitants.[57]

The path of the black death, which began in India and spread to the middle east and then Europe, followed the major trade routes. Thus, the effects were most pronounced in seaports and caravan centers.[58] The greatest losses occurred at the emerging centers of development and change. While the blow to the cities was severe, the effect of the plague on the rural manorial system was fatal. The rural social structure almost totally collapsed. Those peasants who were not killed by the plague fled to the towns, thus depriving the manors of their essential labor

[56]William L. Langer, "The Black Death," in Scientific American's *Cities, Their Origin, Growth, and Human Impact*, Freeman, San Francisco, 1973, p. 106.
[57]Ibid., pp. 106–107.
[58]Andre Siegfried, *Routes of Contagion*, Harcourt, Brace and World, New York, 1965.

force. Serfs fleeing the plague often found that labor shortages had turned them into contract laborers or even town artisans.

The structure of basic social institutions such as the Catholic church was also dramatically altered by the black death. Many of the senior and most learned clergy perished; those who survived were likely to be more concerned with taking care of themselves than their flocks. New priests were hastily trained, if at all. Their desertions of their parishes when plague threatened, and their participation in the general loose living and immorality of the time, contributed to the religious upheavals that swept Europe for the next two centuries and culminated in the Protestant Reformation.

Since the plagues were considered to be a consequence of the wrath and vengeance of God, some people became fanatically religious, while the majority embraced the philosophy of "live, drink, and be merry, for tomorrow we may die." In the words of one scholar, "Charity grew cold, workers grew arrogant, revenues of Church and State dropped, people everywhere were more self-indulgent and frivolous than ever."[59] Chroniclers stress the lawlessness, depravity, and dissolute behavior of the time. In London, "In one house you might hear them roaring under the pangs of death, in the next tippling, whoring and belching out blasphemies against God."[60]

Various plagues, generally of decreasing severity, occurred in Europe until the late seventeenth century, but by the fifteenth century the cities were beginning to grow again. The plague had given the rural-based feudal system a blow from which it did not recover. From this point onward the history of western civilization was again to be the history of cities and city inhabitants.

Cities after the Medieval Era

By the sixteenth century numerous cities, and particularly the Italian city-states, had developed a wealthy patrician class which had the interest, resources, and time to devote to the development and beautification of their cities. Renaissance cities such as Florence embarked on major building programs. The revival of interest in the classical style, and in classical symmetry, perspective, and proportion, had a profound effect on the design of both public and private structures. The artistic talents even of artists such as Michelangelo and Leonardo da Vinci were used to beautify the cities; Leonardo also developed proposals for urban planning. Rather than simply building at random, the more prosperous city-states hired architects to make planned changes. The classical effect can be seen in the use of straight streets and regular squares, and particularly in the use of perspective. The early medieval city with its semirural nature had aptly symbolized that age. The sixteenth- and seventeenth-century Renaissance city symbolized the humanistic ideology of its age and proudly proclaimed its secular urban culture.

[59]George Deauz, *The Black Death*, Weybright and Talley, New York, 1969, p. 145.
[60]Langer, op. cit., p. 109.

Preindustrial and Industrial Cities: A Comparison

A comparison of the social structures of preindustrial and industrial cities helps us understand how the cities we live in differ from preindustrial cities and from the cities of the developing nations of the "third world." The industrial and preindustrial cities here described are "ideal types"—that is, they do not exist in reality but are rather abstractions or constructs obtained by carrying certain characteristics of each type of city to their logical extremes. Such "ideal types" can never exist in reality, but they are most useful in accentuating characteristics for the purposes of comparative historical research.

In his much-quoted article "Urbanism as a Way of Life," Louis Wirth gives a number of characteristics that he suggests are common to cities, and in particular to industrial cities.* For Wirth, a city is a permanent settlement possessing the following characteristics: (1) size, (2) density, (3) heterogeneity. The city is the place where large numbers of persons are crowded together in a limited space—persons who have different skills, interests, and cultural backgrounds. The result is the independence, anonymity, and cultural heterogeneity of city dwellers.

Industrial cities, he says, are characterized by (1) an extensive division of labor, (2) emphasis on innovation and achievement, (3) lack of primary ties to a localized neighborhood, (4) breakdown of primary groups, leading to social disorganization, (5) reliance on secondary forms of social control, such as the police, (6) interaction with others as players of specific roles rather than as total personalities, (7) destruction of close family life and a transfer of its functions to specialized agencies outside the home, (8) a diversity permitted in values and religious beliefs, (9) encouragement of social mobility and working one's way up, and (10) universal rules applicable to all, such as the same legal system, standardized weights and measures, and common prices. The industrial city thus is achievement-oriented and prizes a rationally oriented economic system. It is predominantly a middle-class city. (In brief, urbanism as a way of life prizes rationality, secularism, diversity, innovation, and progress. It is change-oriented. According to Wirth, "The larger, the more densely populated, the more heterogeneous the community, the more accentuated the characteristics associated with urbanism will be."† (Wirth's views will be discussed in detail in Chapter 6.)

Gideon Sjoberg paints a different picture for preindustrial cities.‡ He

---

*Louis Wirth. "Urbanism as a Way of Life," *American Journal of Sociology*, 44:1–24, July, 1938.
†Ibid., p. 9.
‡Gideon Sjoberg, *The Preindustrial City: Past and Present*, Free Press, Glencoe, Ill., 1960.

suggests that a number of factors we associate with cities are probably generic only to industrial cities. In contrast to Wirth he suggests that preindustrial cities serve primarily as governmental or religious centers and only secondarily as commercial hubs. Specialization of work is limited, and the production of goods depends on animate (human or animal) power. There is little division of labor; the artisan participates in every phase of manufacture. Home and workplace are not separate as in the industrial city; an artisan or merchant lives in back of or above the workplace. Justice is based not on what you do but on who you are. Standardization is not of major importance. Different people pay different prices for the same goods, and there is no universal system of weights and measures. In brief, the preindustrial city stresses particularism over universalism. Class and kinship systems are relatively inflexible; education is the prerogative of the rich. A small elite maintains a privileged status over the disadvantaged masses.

The continuity with rural values is obvious. Emphasis is on traditional ways of doing things; the guild system discourages innovation. Ascription rather than achievement is the norm; a worker is expected to do the job he or she was born into. A person lives and works in a particular quarter of the city and rarely moves beyond this area. Social control is the responsibility of the primary group rather than secondary groups; persons are known to one another and are subject to strict kinship control. Formal police forces are unnecessary. Family influence is strong, with the traditional extended family accepted as the ideal. Within all classes, children, and especially sons, are valued. There is great similarity in values, and little diversity in religion is tolerated. Opportunity for social mobility is severely restricted by a caste system or rigid class system. There is little or no middle class, which is the backbone of the industrial city; one is either rich or poor.

The preindustrial city lacks what the great French sociologist Emile Durkheim called "moral density" or what we today call "social integration." By contemporary standards the preindustrial city is neither socially nor economically integrated. The walled quarters of the preindustrial city are largely independent units; their physical proximity to one another does not lead to social interaction. The city as a whole may possess heterogeneity, but actual social contacts rarely extend beyond one's own group.

No real city of course conforms exactly either to the industrial model or to the preindustrial model. (Note in Chapter 2 that the preindustrial model does not appear to fit American colonial cities, although these were clearly preindustrial.) Models are best used as aids that sharpen our comparative understanding of differences; they should never be mistaken for actual places.

The sixteenth-century city gained ever greater economic and cultural domination over rural areas, but it also marked the beginning of the end of the city as a self-governing unit independent of the larger nation-state. During the medieval period, kings and city dwellers had been natural allies, since both wished to subdue the power of the local nobility. In order to cast off the last fetters of feudal restraint, the city burghers supplied the monarch with men and—most important—money to fight wars; the monarch in turn granted ever larger charter powers to the towns. Once the monarchs had subdued the rural lords, however, they turned their attention to the prosperous towns. Gradually the independent powers of the cities were reduced as they became part of nations in fact as well as in name. The structure of social organization in Europe was changing to the larger geographical unit: the nation-state. The loss of political independence, however, was compensated for by the economic advantages of being part of a nation-state rather than a collection of semi-independent feudal states and chartered cities. National government usually meant better and safer roads and therefore easier and cheaper transport of goods, and a larger potential market area. Merchants also had the advantages of reasonably unified laws, a common coinage, and standardized measures of weight and volume—all things which today we take for granted. Emergent business classes prospered from the certainty and stability provided by the king's national government.

Influences of Technology. The technological development of gunpowder and the cannon also contributed to changing the nature of the walled city. The traditional defenses of rampart, bastion, and moat were of limited utility in stopping cannon fire. Cities that hoped to resist the armies of a king or of rival cities had to shift their attention from interior architecture and urban planning to the engineering of fortifications. Only elaborate defensive outworks could stop cannon fire, and so the city unwittingly became the captive of its own horizontal defenses. While one can question Lewis Mumford's view that the decline of the city began with the end of the Middle Ages, it is certainly true that the city of the seventeenth century was changing—and probably for the worse.

Unable to grow outward, cities began to expand vertically and fill in open spaces within the city walls. The increased crowding which resulted had a bad effect on both the quality and the length of life. Filthy living conditions, combined with minimal sanitation and an absence of any knowledge of public health practices, resulted in the rapid spread of contagious diseases and consequently high death rates. As John Graut's pioneer research in the seventeenth century on the London Bills of Mortality demonstrated, London actually recorded more deaths than births. Only heavy migration from the countryside allowed the city to grow in population rather than decline as would otherwise have been the case with such a high mortality rate. As late as 1790 the city of London had three deaths for every two births.[61] A century later mortality rates in the city still exceeded those in rural

---

[61]Dorothy George, *London Life in the Eighteenth Century*, Harper Torchbooks, New York, 1964, p. 25.

In early towns the streets served as far more than arteries of transportation. (Bettmann Archive.)

districts.[62] The possibilities of jobs and excitement in the city continued to attract ruralites.

Large-scale urban growth was closely tied to the growth of the population as a whole. Until about the middle of the seventeenth century, the population of the world had been growing at a very slow rate: 0.4 percent a year. As a result, by the beginning of the eighteenth century the world population was roughly 500 million,

[62]Eric Lampara, "The Urbanizing World," in H. J. Dyds and Michael Wolfe (eds.), *The Victorian World*, Routledge & Kegan Paul, London, 1976.

or double that at the time of Christ. Then momentous changes occurred that resulted in what we call the "demographic transition" or the "demographic revolution." Population growth suddenly spurted in the latter part of the eighteenth century, not through increases in the birthrate—it was already high—but through declines in the death rate. Population increases continued in the nineteenth and twentieth centuries. The term "demographic transition" refers to this transition from a time of high birthrates matched by almost equally high death rates, through a period of declining death rates, to a period where birthrates also begin to decline, and eventually to a period where population stability is reestablished—this time through low birthrates matched by equally low death rates.

Changes in Agriculture. Much of the decline in the death rates can be attributed to technological changes in agriculture that assured both a better and a more reliable food supply. Without such increases in food supply, cities could not grow and expand.

The growth of massive cities was effectively constrained until the nineteenth century by the inability of agriculture to produce enough surplus. As late as the beginning of the nineteenth century, the produce of nine farms was still required to support one urban family. (Today each American farmer supports approximately forty-five other persons.)

At the beginning of the eighteenth century, English agriculture, for example, still practiced three-crop rotation, with the land divided into four quarters, one of which was left fallow and thus unproductive each year. Pasturelands were held in common, as were the woods which provided hunting and firewood. Water rights were also held in common. Since most animals had to be slaughtered each fall, the herds didn't increase in number. Then, within the period of half a century, English agriculture was revolutionized. Jethro Tull published the results of thirty years of research on his estates, and the new ideas were quickly adopted by much of the landed aristocracy. Tull advocated planting certain crops on fallow land to restore nutrients to the earth, thus radically increasing the usable acreage. He also recommended deep plowing and a system for foddering animals through the winter.

At the same time it was being discovered that selective breeding of animals was far superior to letting nature take its course. Striking changes can be seen by comparing the weight of animals at the Smithfield Fair in 1710 and 1795; the average weight of oxen went from 370 pounds to 800 pounds, that of calves from 50 to 150 pounds, and that of sheep from 38 to 80 pounds.

Accompanying these agricultural improvements in England were the notorious Enclosure Acts, which took the village commons from joint ownership and gave them to the lord enjoying ancient title to the land. While disastrous for the local yeoman, the larger enclosures could be worked more efficiently by the lords who were using the new agricultural knowledge. The result was an increase in both the quality and the quantity of the food supply. While it is extremely hazardous to generalize about living conditions, there apparently was an improvement over earlier centuries. Death rates began to go down, and population expanded rapidly. Some of the peasants forced from the land who migrated to the larger towns and cities provided an available labor force when factories were established and expanded.

The abandonment of traditional subsistence agriculture and the orientation to a market economy meant that rationality was replacing tradition and contract was taking the place of custom. The calculation implicit in the land-enclosure acts destroyed small peasant landholders but made it possible for London and other cities to be assured of foodstuffs and thus to grow as manufacturing and commercial centers.

INDUSTRIAL CITIES

Technological Improvements and the Industrial Revolution

The movement of agricultural surpluses was facilitated greatly by the construction of new toll roads, which were built in great numbers after 1745. The building of canals also greatly stimulated urban development. By 1800 the city of London was the second-largest in the world, with a population of 861,000.[63] (Peking was the largest at this date, with 1 million.) This was roughly 11 percent of the total British population. Without the technological breakthroughs in agriculture and transportation, this type of urban concentration would have been impossible.

Roughly at the same time that agricultural improvements were both increasing yields and releasing workers from rural bondage, inventions were being made that would allow for the growth of whole new industries. Eighteenth-century inventions in the manufacture of cloth, such as the flying shuttle and the spinning jenny, were capped in 1767 by Watt's invention of a usable steam engine. The steam engine provided a new and bountiful inanimate source of energy. The cotton industry boomed, and it was soon followed by other industries. The machines, rather than eliminating the need for workers, rapidly increased the demand for an urban work force. A factory system began to emerge based on specialization and mechanization. As a consequence, new forms of occupational structure and a more complex stratification system began to develop.

The Second Urban Revolution

Without population growth and the release of workers from the land, it is hard to see how the early industrial cities could have grown at all, for as noted earlier, unhealthful living conditions in cities meant that they were not able to maintain, much less increase, their population without in-migration from rural areas.

Thus the second urban revolution was not the emergence of cities but rather the changes that for the first time made it possible for more than 10 percent of the population to live in urban places. This new urban revolution started in Europe.

[63]Tertius Chandler and Gerald Fox, *3000 Years of Urban Growth*, Academic Press, New York, 1974, p. 323.

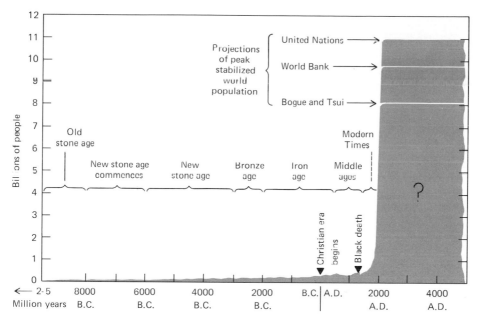

Figure 2-1. World population growth. (*Source:* Population Reference Bureau.)

Rapid expansion of population (Figure 2-1) and national economic expansion did not, however, translate into healthful living conditions in the bulging European towns that were turning into cities. Eighteenth-century London was a model of filth, crowding, and disease. The early stages of industrialism hardly did much to improve the situation. While rural mortality decreased, urban mortality was kept high by unbelievably poor sanitary conditions. The novels of Charles Dickens give an accurate portrayal of life in such cities. Cholera and other epidemics were common until the middle of the nineteenth century, and until the 1840s many of London's sewers emptied into the Thames just a few feet above the ducts that drew drinking water from the river. It was fortunate that the fascination and opportunities of the city continued to attract rural migrants, since without migration the cities would not have grown but died. Until the latter part of the nineteenth century, the old English observation "The city is the graveyard of countrymen" was all too accurate.

PART TWO

AMERICAN
URBANIZATION

CHAPTER

3

THE RISE OF URBAN AMERICA

*The din of the Market increases upon me; and that, with
frequent interruptions, has made me say some things twice over.*

Benjamin Franklin

INTRODUCTION

In this chapter we cross the ocean to the wilderness of North America and trace the coming of age of the American city. As you read through the following pages, note the major role played by environmental factors during the colonial period. (All the major early cities were seaports.) During the nineteenth century, by contrast, changing technology, particularly advances in transportation such as the railroad, came to have a far more important—if not dominant—impact. Dramatic population growth through immigration and changes in urban governance and organization also came to play a major role in the growth and development of cities. This chapter, then, takes us from Jamestown up to the dawn of the contemporary era— the 1920s when the United States formally became defined as an urban nation.

COLONISTS AS TOWN BUILDERS

We are rather new at being an urban continent. The first European colonists to arrive in North America found a land without indigenous cities. Cities as such did not exist in North America, although the Indians of the northwest coast, with their reliable food supply from the sea, had established well-built settled villages with an elaborate social structure. By and large, the North American Indian population was nomadic or lived in agricultural villages such as Taos in the southwest. Cahokia, located in the Mississippi River valley of southern Illinois, was the most populous pre-Columbian settlement north of Mexico, thriving from about A.D. 900 to A.D. 1400 as a farming and trade center. The population of North America numbered less than 1 million at the time of the Jamestown settlement (1607).

From the first, the town-building orientation of the colonists contrasted with Indian ways. The North American Indians lived in nature rather than building upon it. They viewed themselves as part of the ecology, part of the physical world. Their goal was not to master nature but to identify their niche and their relationship with the world around them. The Europeans came, on the contrary, not to adjust to the environment but to dominate and reshape it. The Puritans, for example, believed themselves to be God's chosen people. By definition the Indians were inferior.

The colonists' emphasis was on conquering nature and unfortunately for the Indians, the colonists tended to view them as a part of the environment. The Indians were treated as just another environmental problem that had to be encountered and mastered before civilization could be introduced. The implication for the future was clear. There was no niche for the Indian in the town-oriented civilization of the colonists.

What has just been said is, of course, an overgeneralization, but from our urban perspective the important point is that the concept of the city, and all the good and evil it represents, came to the new world from Europe with the first European colonist. This concept, with all the special technology, social organizations, and attitudes it entailed, was an importation from post-Renaissance Europe.

This meant, among other things, that North American cities had no feudal period.[1]

The plans of the various companies that settled the English colonies in North America called for the establishment of tight little villages and commercial centers. The first successful settlements at Jamestown and Plymouth Colony were in fact small towns. Thus, early English settlers were not primarily agriculturists but rather town dwellers coming with town expectations. In fact, the initially limited number of farmers was a problem. Jamestown nearly perished from an excess of adventurers and a dearth of skilled artisans and farmers. As John Smith wrote back to the English sponsors of the Jamestown colony,

> When you send againe I intreat you rather send but thirty Carpenters, husbandmen, gardners, fisher men, blacksmiths, masons, and diggers up of trees, roots, well provided; then a tousand of such as we haus: for except we be able both to loge them, and feed them the most will consume with what of necessaries before they can be made good for anything.[2]

The wilderness of the new world appeared strange and hostile, and the early colonists sorely missed their towns. William Bradford movingly describes the world of the Pilgrims of 1620:

> They had now no freinds to wellcome them nor inns to entertaine or refresh their weatherbeaten bodys, no houses or much less townes to repaire too, to seeke for succoure. . . . Besids, what could they see but a hidious and desolate wildernes, full of wild beasts and willd men? and what multituds ther might be of them they knew not.[3]

MAJOR SETTLEMENTS

Five communities spearheaded the urbanization of the seventeenth-century English colonies. The northernmost was Boston on New England's "stern and rockbound coast"; the southernmost was the newer and much smaller settlement of Charles Town in South Carolina.[4] Barely making an indentation in the 1,100 miles of wilderness separating these two were Newport, in the Providence Plantations of Rhode Island; New Amsterdam, which in 1664 became New York; and William Penn's Philadelphia on the Delaware River at the mouth of the Schuylkill.

Environment played a heavy role in the early development of these first five cities. All five were seaports, either on the Atlantic or—as in the case of Philadelphia—with access to the sea. Later towns such as Baltimore had similar environmental advantages. As seaports they became commercial centers funneling trade between Europe and the colonies. In terms of social structure all were

---

[1]Lewis Mumford would not agree with this statement. Mumford sees the New England villages and towns as the last flickering of the medieval order. See, for example, Lewis Mumford, *Sticks and Stones*, Liveright, New York, 1924.
[2]John Smith, *The General Historie of Virginia, New England, and the Summer Isles,* University Microfilms, Ann Arbor, Mich., 1966 (first published in London, 1624), p. 72.
[3]*Bradford's History of Plymouth Plantation* (William T. Davis, ed.), Scribner, New York, 1908, p. 96.
[4]Constance McLaughlin Green, *The Rise of Urban America,* Harper and Row, New York, 1965, p. 2.

Protestant, and against the established church, except for the ruling class of Charleston and (partially) New York. As Bridenbaugh points out, the social structure of these towns was fashioned by a background of relatively common political institutions; and the economic and cultural roots, whether English or Dutch, lay for the most part in the rising middle class of the old world.[5]

The five important urban settlements had certain similar characteristics. First, all had favorable sites. As noted above, all were seaports, or, like Philadelphia, were on a navigable river. Second, all were commercial cities emphasizing trade and commerce. Third, all had hinterlands or back country to develop, although Newport, would find its hinterland increasingly cut off by Boston in the eighteenth century. Finally, all these cities were fundamentally British. Even New York, which was more cosmopolitan than many European cities, was controlled by a British upper stratum.

New England

The story of early New England is the story of its towns, for New England from the very beginning was town-oriented. The Puritan religious dissenters who originally settled New England came heavily from the more populous centers of old England. They numbered in their midst many trades people, mechanics, and artisans. In the new world these religious dissenters sought to create tight urban communal utopias rather than spreading themselves widely over the landscape. Massachusetts Bay, according to John Winthrop, was to be "as a City upon a Hill." In that colony there existed a social system of a nature unknown outside New England. The cordial union between the clergy, the bench, the bar, and respectable society formed a tight, self-reinforcing social elite.

Boston early outstripped its rivals in both population size and economic influence and kept its lead for a century in spite of Indian wars that twice threatened its existence. Boston had barely 300 residents in the 1630s, but by 1650 there were over 2,000 residents, and a visitor could report—with some exaggeration, perhaps—that it was a sumptuous "city" and "Center Towne and Metropolis of this Wildernesse."[6]

By 1742, Boston had a population of 16,000. The barrenness of Boston's hinterland inclined Bostonians to look to the sea, and the town grew to prosperity on trade and shipbuilding. Before Boston was a generation old it had "begun to extend its control into the back country, and to develop a metropolitan form of economy that was essentially modern."[7]

Newport, the second New England city down the coast, was founded in 1639 by victims of religious bigotry in Massachusetts. Newport's growth was steady but far from spectacular; in a hundred years the population grew from 96 to 6,200. However, although Newport remained small, its growing commerce and well-

---

[5]Carl Bridenbaugh, *Cities in the Wilderness*, Capricorn Books, New York, 1964.
[6]Quoted in Kenneth T. Jackson and Stanley K. Schutty (eds.), *Cities in American History*, Knopf, New York, 1972.
[7]Carl Bridenbaugh, quoted in Charles N. Glaab and A. Theodore Brown, *A History of Urban America*, Macmillan, New York, 1967, pp. 25–26.

ordered community life gave it a significant place in emerging urban America. In Newport, as in Boston, education was encouraged; in addition, Newport had religious toleration.

The Middle Colonies

Manhattan was from the beginning the most cosmopolitan of the colonial cities, a fact reflected in the diversity of languages spoken there. Father Isaac Jogues recorded that as early as 1643 there were already "men of 18 different languages." Partially because of this mixture of national and religious backgrounds (Dutch Calvinists, Anglicans, Quakers, Baptists, Huguenots, Lutherans, Presbyterians, and after 1730 even a sprinkling of Jews), New York was by far the liveliest of towns, a position many people maintain it still holds. Interestingly enough, as of 1720 a third of New York's population was black—largely slaves and servants.[8] With the abandonment of slavery in the north—largely for economic reasons—the proportion of blacks declined substantially. New York was already an American melting pot, although the stew would still be a bit lumpy three centuries later.

New York also had decisive environmental advantages that contributed heavily to eventual emergence as "*the* American city." First, Manhattan had a magnificent deepwater natural harbor. Second, New York was blessed with a fertile soil. Third, the city had easy access to the interior hinterland by way of the Hudson River. The New England towns, by contrast, found their economic growth greatly hindered by the lack of an accessible, fertile hinterland.

Philadelphia, William Penn's "City of Brotherly Love," laid out in 1692, was the youngest of the colonial cities. This was in many ways an advantage, for by the time the city was organized, the Indians had departed and the land was already being settled. A policy of religious toleration and an extremely rich and fertile hinterland allowed rapid growth. By the time Philadelphia was six years old it had 4,000 inhabitants; by 1720 the number had risen to 10,000.[9] At the time of the first United States Census in 1790, Philadelphia had 42,000 inhabitants. It may have been, after London, the largest English-speaking city in the world. Accounts of the day noted the regularity of the town's gridiron pattern with its central square, and most frequently the substantial nature of its buildings.

> A City, and Towns were raised then,
>   Wherein we might abide,
> Planters also, and Husband-men,
>   Had Land enough beside.
> The best of Houses then was known,
>   To be of Wood and Clay,
> But now we build of Brick and Stone,
>   Which is a better way.[10]

---

[8]Green, op. cit., p. 22.
[9]Ibid., p. 27.
[10]Richard Frame, "A Short Description of Pennsylvania in 1692," in Albert Cook Myers (ed.), *Narratives of Early Pennsylvania, West New Jersey, and Delaware,* Scribner, New York, 1912; reprinted in Ruth E. Sutter, *The Next Place You Come To,* Prentice-Hall, Englewood Cliffs, N.J. 1973, p. 90.

The South

The southernmost of the colonial cities was Charles Town (Charleston), founded in 1680 on a spit of land between the mouths of the Ashley and Cooper rivers. The town grew slowly; two decades after its founding it had only 1,100 inhabitants and had "not yet produced any Commodities fit for ye markett or Europe, but a few skins—and a little cedar."[11] For decades rice, indigo, and skins formed the basis of its commerce.

Charleston's social structure was unique among the major cities. The major difference was that by the 1740s over half of Charleston's inhabitants were slaves. The middle-class artisans and shopkeepers who were the backbone of the northern cities were caught in Charleston between the aristocratic pretensions of the large landowners and the increasing skills of the trained slaves. The result was civic atrophy, the major local event being the opening of the horse-racing season. Charleston had few municipal services and could not claim even a single tax-supported school.

URBAN INFLUENCE

The relatively small populations by contemporary standards of the cities and towns of colonial America should not distract us from their seminal importance. Politically, economically, and socially these five towns dominated early colonial life. Because of their access to the sea they served as entreports, exchanging the produce of the hinterland for the finished products of Europe. In addition to their commercial function they also served as the places where new ideas and forms of social organization could be developed.

Because the colonial cities had to meet uniquely urban problems, such as paving streets, removing garbage, and caring for the poor, collective efforts developed. In the words of one historian:

> In these problems of town living which affected the entire community lay one of the vast differences between town and country society, and out of the collective efforts to solve these urban problems arose a sense of community responsibility and power that was to further differentiate the two ways of life.[12]

As a result of the town-based settlement pattern, by 1690 almost 10 percent of the colonial population was urban, a higher percentage than that found in England itself at the same time. With the subduing of the Indians and the opening up of the hinterland for cultivation, the percentage (not, of course, the actual number) of urban dwellers decreased between 1690 and 1790. The opening up of frontier hinterlands permitted greater population dispersal than had previously been possible. Not until 1830 was the urban percentage of the total population as high as it had been at the close of the seventeenth century.[13]

---

[11]Green, op. cit., p. 21.
[12]Charles N. Glaab, *The American City*, Dorsey, Homewood, Ill., 1963, p. 3.
[13]Charles N. Glaab and A. Theodore Brown, *A History of Urban America*, 2d ed., Macmillan, New York, 1976, p. 21.

Philadelphia, the nation's largest city at the end of the eighteenth century. (Culver Pictures.)

Politically, the cities were dominant. With the exception of Virginia, where the landed aristocracy did not live in cities but nonetheless followed the latest London fashions and maintained a strong commerce with Europe, the cities set the political as well as the social tone. And the merchant classes became increasingly dissatisfied with British policy. The Crown's tax measures had a bad effect on business. Boston was called "the metropolis of sedition"; and as Lord Howe, commander of the British forces at the time of the Revolution noted, "Almost all of the People of Parts and Spirit were in the Rebellion."[14] This was not surprising, since Britain's revenue policy had struck deep at urban prosperity. Business and commercial leaders were determined to resist the Crown rather than suffer financial reverses. This helps to explain the middle-class and upper-class nature of much of the support for the American Revolution.

THE GROWING NEW REPUBLIC

After the Revolutionary War the cities continued their growth, although the first United States Census, taken in 1790, revealed that only 5 percent of the new nation's 4 million people lived in places of 2,500 or more. Numerically America was overwhelmingly rural, but this demographic dominance was not reflected in

[14]Green, op. cit., p. 51.

TABLE 3-1
Great Cities of America, 1790, 1870, 1980

1790	1870	1980
New York, N.Y.	New York, N.Y.	New York, N.Y.
Philadelphia, Pa.	Philadelphia, Pa.	Chicago, Ill.
Boston, Mass.	Brooklyn, N.Y.	Los Angeles, Cal.
Charleston, S.C.	St. Louis, Mo.	Philadelphia, Pa.
Baltimore, Md.	Chicago, Ill.	Houston, Texas
Salem, Mass.	Baltimore, Md.	Detroit, Mich.
Newport, R.I.	Boston, Mass.	Dallas, Texas
Providence, R.I.	Cincinnati, Ohio	Baltimore, Md.
Gloucester, Mass.	New Orleans, La.	San Diego, Cal.
Newburyport, Mass.	San Francisco, Cal.	San Antonio, Texas

Source: U.S. Bureau of the Census and author.

the distribution of power or the composition of the leadership groups. The urban population had an influence on government, finance, and society as a whole far out of proportion to its size. The Federalist Party, which elected John Adams as the second President, was largely an urban-based party representing commercial and banking rather than agrarian interests.

Although three-quarters of the national population still lived within 50 miles of the Atlantic Ocean, there were already clear and widening differences between townspeople and rural dwellers. The farmers' orientation was toward the expanding western frontier, while the townspeople were still oriented toward Europe. Because of their status as ocean ports, the American coastal cities frequently had more in common with the old world, and certainly better communication with it, than with their own hinterlands.

The census of 1790 showed that the largest city in the young nation was Philadelphia, with 42,000 inhabitants (it was also the only city having both streetlights and sidewalks). New York was the second-largest city, with a population of 33,000 (see Table 3-1). Ten years later Philadelphia had grown to 70,000, New York to 60,000, and Boston to 25,000.

Such rapid growth of the cities after the Revolutionary War was not only the result of foreign and rural immigration; an exceptionally high rate of natural replacement also played a large part. Precise data are lacking, but the birthrate is estimated to have been at least 55 per 1,000, or near the physiological upper limit. Each married woman in 1790 bore an average of almost eight children. One result of the high birthrate and the immigration from Europe of young adults was a national median age of only sixteen years. (By comparison, the median age for the white population today is thirty years.) Between 1790 and 1860 the population would increase dramatically, doubling every twenty-three years—a rate equivalent to that in some developing countries today.

The sheer abundance of land and the almost unlimited possibilities for fee-simple tenure meant freedom from Europe's lingering feudal constraints.[15] As put by a European visitor: "It does not seem difficult to find out the reasons why

[15]Sam Bass Warner, Jr., *The Urban Wilderness,* Harper and Row, New York, 1972, p. 16.

TABLE 3-2
Percent of Population Urban, United States,
1790–1970

1790	5.1	1890	35.1
1800	6.1	1900	39.7
1810	7.3	1910	45.7
1820	7.2	1920	51.2
1830	8.8	1930	56.2
1840	10.8	1940	56.5
1850	15.3	1950 (old def.)	59.0
1860	19.8	1950 (new def.)	64.0
1870	25.7	1960	69.9
1880	28.2	1970	73.5

Source: U.S. Bureau of the Census.

people multiply faster here than in Europe. . . . There is such an amount of good land yet uncultivated that a newly married man can get a spot of ground where he may comfortably subsist with his wife and children."[16]

As Table 3-2 indicates, the percentage of the population that is urban has grown every decade except 1810–1820. The decline in that decade was chiefly due to the destruction of American commerce resulting from the Embargo Acts and the War of 1812. That war came close to destroying the costal cities; and, partially as a result of isolation from English manufactures and products, the American cities began developing manufacturing interests. Even Thomas Jefferson, an ardent opponent of cities, was forced to concede:

> He, therefore, who is now against domestic manufacture, must be for reducing us either to dependence on that foreign nation or to be clothed in skins and to live like wild beasts in dens and caverns. I am not one of them; experience has taught me that manufactures are now as necessary to our independence as to our comfort.[17]

Founding and Expansion of Cities

The period before the Civil War saw a rapid expansion of existing cities and the founding of many new ones. During the period from 1820 to 1860, cities grew at a more rapid rate than at any other time before or since in American history.[18] It is noteworthy that of the fifty largest cities in America, only seven were incorporated before 1816, thirty-nine were incorporated between 1816 and 1876, and only four have been incorporated since 1876. Cincinnati, Pittsburgh, Memphis, Louisville, Detroit, Chicago, Denver, Portland, and Seattle are all early and mid-nineteenth-century cities. In the far west, the discovery of gold and then silver did much to spur town building. Some later became ghost towns, but San Francisco prospered as *the* major city of the west.

The influence of environmental factors on the growth of nineteenth-century

---

[16]Quoted in James H. Cassedy, *Demography in Early America,* Harvard University Press, Cambridge, Mass., 1969, pp. 154–155.
[17]P. L. Ford, *The Works of Thomas Jefferson,* Putnam, New York, 1904, pp. 503–504.
[18]Glaab, op. cit., p. 65.

cities can be seen from the fact that of the nine cities which by 1860 had passed the 100,000 mark, eight were ports. The one exception really wasn't an exception; it was the then independent city of Brooklyn, which shared the benefits of the country's greatest harbor.[19]

By the eve of the Civil War the first city of the nation was clearly New York. It had both a magnificent harbor and a large hinterland to sustain growth, and relatively flat terrain westward from the Hudson River. Nonetheless, what assured New York its dominance was the willingness to speculate on the technologies of first the Erie Canal and then the railroad. Mayor DeWitt Clinton prophesied that the canal would "create the greatest inland trade ever witnessed" and allow New York to "become the granary of the world, the emporium of commerce, the seat of manufactures, the focus of moneyed operations." He was right.

The completion of the canal in 1825 greatly stimulated New York City's trade and gave it an economic supremacy which has yet to be surpassed. Thus, the original environmental advantage stimulated a technological advance—the Erie Canal—which in turn led to population growth and changes in the social organization of business and government. New York's quick acceptance of railroads as a technological breakthrough, and the possibilities thus presented, further solidified the city's dominant position. Not only was New York the most important American city, it also had become a major world metropolis by the time of the Civil War. New York grew from just over 60,000 in 1800 to over 1 million in 1860 (1,174,774, to be exact, including Brooklyn, which was then an independent municipality). Of the world's cities only London and Paris were larger. By 1860, in addition to serving as the nation's financial center, New York also handled a third of the country's exports and a full two-thirds of the imports. New York's increase in size was matched by the increasing heterogenity of its inhabitants, with their different tastes, aspirations, and needs—all of which could be best satisfied only in the large city.

Land speculation spurred the growth of cities. Fueled by a stream of immigrants and a greed for profits, cities went through periods of wild land speculation and building—only to be followed by eventually economic collapse and depression. Cincinnati, the "Queen City of the West," for example, experienced a boom during the 1820s, and during that decade its population expanded rapidly as a result of the development and use of steamboats. In other cities the technology of the railroad played a similar role in spurring growth.

Only in the deep south, where cotton was king, did the building of cities languish. In the plantation owners' view, cotton fields came before manufacturing and commerce. The dominance of agriculture can be seen in the development—or, more correctly, the lack of development—of Charleston. At the beginning of the nineteenth century Charleston was the fifth-largest American city; by 1860 it had slipped to twenty-sixth place.[20] (As a consequence of the war, a devastating earthquake, and economic stagnation, Charleston was not numbered among

[19]Blake McKelveg, *The Urbanization of America, 1860–1915,* Rutgers University Press, New Brunswick, N.J., 1963. p.4. See Howard P. Chudacoff, *The Evolution of American Urban Society,* Prentice-Hall, Englewood Cliffs, N.J., 1975, chap. 9.

[20]Nelson M. Blake, *A History of American Life and Thought,* McGraw-Hill, New York, 1963, p. 156.

even the fifty largest cities in 1900.) The post-Civil War stagnation of Charleston is reflected in the saying that Charleston was "too poor to paint and too proud to whitewash."

Marketplace Centers

Before the Civil War, American cities, while undergoing tremendous growth, retained many preindustrial characteristics. The urban economy was still in a commercial rather than an industrial stage. Businesspeople were primarily merchants who intermittently took on subsidiary functions such as manufacturing, banking, and speculating. In 1850, 85 percent of the population was still classified as rural; 64 percent was engaged in agriculture.

Physically, the city was a walking city with a radius rarely extending over 3 miles. The separation of workplace and residence so common in contemporary American cities was limited. Residences, businesses, and public buildings were intermixed with little specialization by area: "The first floor was given over to commerce, the second and third reserved for the family and clerks, and the fourth perhaps for storage. People lived and worked in the same house or at least in the same neighborhood."[21]

The separation that did occur was the obverse of the pattern of wealthy in the suburbs and poor in the city that we have come to accept as the American norm. (See Chapters 5, 6, and 7 for discussion of theories of contemporary urban growth.) In early American cities, the well-to-do tended to live not on the periphery but near the center. In an era of slow, uncomfortable, and inadequate transportation, the poor were more often relegated to the less accessible areas on the periphery.[22]

THE INDUSTRIAL CITY

The Civil War accelerated the shift from a mercantile to an industrial economy. Aided by the new protective tariffs and the inflated profits, stimulated by the war, northern industrialists began producing steel, coal, and woolen goods, most of which had previously been imported. The closing of the Mississippi was a boon to Chicago and the east-west railroads.

A century after its founding (1886), the American nation had grown to 50 million and stretched from coast to coast. The lands of the Louisiana Purchase and the Northwest Cession were already settled, while the western prairie was being peopled and plowed. However, in retrospect, this was the end, not the beginning of the age of agriculture. The census of 1880 for the first time indicated that less than half the employable population worked in agriculture. Meanwhile, foreign in-migration was swelling the cities, and urban areas held 28 percent of the

---

[21]Christopher Tunnard and Henry Hope Reed, *American Skyline: The Growth and Form of Our Cities and Towns,* New American Library, New York, 1956, p. 59.
[22]Sam Bass Warner, Jr., *The Private City: Philadelphia in Three Periods of Its Growth,* University of Pennsylvania Press, Philadelphia, 1968, p. 13.

Table 3-3
Number of Urban Places by Population Size: Selected Years, 1850–1970

Size of place	1850	1900	1950	1960	1970
Total—2,500 and over	236	1,737	4,284	5,445	6,435
1,000,000 or more	—	3	5	5	6
500,000 to 1,000,000	1	3	13	16	20
250,000 to 500,000	—	9	23	30	30
100,000 to 250,000	5	23	65	81	100
50,000 to 100,000	4	40	126	201	240
25,000 to 50,000	16	82	252	432	520
10,000 to 25,000	36	280	778	1,134	1,385
5,000 to 10,000	85	465	1,176	1,394	1,839
2,500 to 5,000	89	832	1,846	2,152	2,295

Source: U.S. Bureau of the Census, U.S. Census of Population, 1950, vol. II, and 1960, vol. 1.; and 1970, vol. 1, part A table 5.

population. By 1880 the nation already boasted four cities of over half a million inhabitants.[23]

During the last quarter of the nineteenth century, urbanism for the first time became a controlling factor in national life. This was a period of economic expansion for the nation. Industrialism was changing the nature of the economic system, rapidly changing America from a rural to an urban continent. The extent of this change can be seen in Table 3-3.

While the frontier captured the attention of writers and the imagination of the populace, the bulk of the nation's growth during the nineteenth century took place in cities. (The classic statement on the significance of the west was Frederick J. Turner's famous 1893 paper, "The Frontier in American History." A major urban response did not come until almost half a century later, with Arthur M. Schlesinger's "The City in American History."[24]) By the turn of the twentieth century, fifty cities had populations of over 100,000; the most notable of these new cities was the prairie metropolis of Chicago, which had bet heavily on the technology of the railroad. Chicago mushroomed from 4,100 at the time of its incorporation in 1833 to 1 million in 1890. Between 1850 and 1890 Chicago doubled its population every decade; in 1910 it passed 2 million. Nationally, in 100 years between 1790 and 1890 the total population grew sixteenfold, while the urban population grew 139-fold.

Technological Change

As Richard Wade aptly phrased it, "The towns were the spearhead of the frontier." This was particularly true west of the Mississippi, where the technological breakthrough of the railroad had reversed earlier patterns of settlement. Josiah Strong, writing in 1885, noted:

[23]U.S. Bureau of the Census, Historical Statistics of the United States, Colonial Times to 1957, Washington, D.C., 1960, p. 14.
[24]Arthur M. Schlesinger, "The City in American History," Mississippi Valley Historical Review, 27:43–66, June, 1940.

In the Middle States the farms were the first taken, then the town sprang up to supply its wants, and at length the railway connected it with the world, but in the West the order is reversed—first the railroad, then the towns, then the farms. Settlement is, consequently, much more rapid, and the city stamps the country, instead of the country stamping the city. It is the cities and towns which will frame state constitutions, make laws, create public opinion, establish social usages, and fix standards of morals in the West.[25]

Strong may have exaggerated his case somewhat, but the railroad was crucial in the development of the west. During the second half of the nineteenth century, the railroads expanded from 9,000 to 193,000 miles—much of it built with federal loans and land grants.[26] The railroads literally opened the west.

At the same time, changes in farming technology were converting the yeoman into an entrepreneur raising cash crops for market. Horse-drawn mechanical reapers, steel plows, and threshers heralded the shift from self-sufficient to commercial farming.

Spatial Concentration

The great cities of the east and midwest, with their hordes of immigrants, frantic pace, municipal corruption, and industrial productivity, built much of their present physical plant in the era of steam stretching from the 1880s to the depression of the 1930s. The late-nineteenth-century city was a city of concentration and centralization accentuated by industrialization. Initial industrialization encouraged centripetal rather than centrifugal forces; since steam is most cheaply generated in large quantities and must be used close to where it is produced, steam power thus fostered a compact city. Steam power encouraged the proximity of factory and power supply. It fostered the concentration of manufacturing processes in a core area that surrounded the central business district and had access to rail and often water transportation. This in turn tended to concentrate managerial and wholesale distributing activities and, above all, population near the factory.

The limited transportation technology meant that workers had to live near the factories; this in turn gave rise to row upon row of densely packed tenements. The distant separation of residence and place of work was a luxury only the very wealthy in commuting suburbs could afford. Surrounding the factories, slumlords built jaw-to-jaw tenements on every available open space. These tenements were then packed to unbelievable densities with immigrant workers—first Irish, then German, Jewish, Italian, and Polish—who could afford no other housing on the pitiful wages they made working twelve hours a day, six days a week. Slums provided the immigrant laborers with housing close to the factories, but at a horrendous price in terms of health and quality of life.

The compact trade- and commerce-oriented central business districts of northern industrial and commercial cities reflected the needs of the nineteenth century. Before the widespread use of the automobile and telephone, it was

[25]Josiah Strong, *Our Country: Its Possible Future and Its Present Crisis,* Baker and Taylor, New York, 1885, p. 206.
[26]William Petersen, *Population,* Macmillan, New York, 1961, p. 34.

Poor street urchins were a common sight in the American cities of the late nineteenth century. (Photograph by Jacob A. Riis, Jacob A. Riis Collection, Museum of the City of New York.)

necessary that business offices be close to one another so that information could be transmitted by means of messengers. High central-city land values were an inevitable result of the common business demand for a central location. Nineteenth-century inventions such as a practical steam elevator and steel-girdered buildings further enabled the core area to become even more densely inhabited. Buildings no longer had to be supported by massive outer walls, and offices and businesses could be stacked vertically upon one another as high as foundations, local ordinances, and economics would allow.

The fact that New York, Chicago, Philadelphia, and St. Louis, to name only a few, are essentially cities built before the twentieth century and before the automobile is a problem we have to cope with today. Any attempt to deal with present-day transportation or pollution problems has to take into account the fact

A Note on Environmental Pollution

It is revealing, if depressing, to recognize that the problems of pollution and environmental destruction did not begin in the twentieth century. Until late in the nineteenth century most American cities, such as Baltimore and New Orleans, still relied on open trenches for sewage. The only municipal garbage collection provided by most cities until after the Civil War was that provided by scavenging hogs and dogs and other carrion-eaters. Colonial Charleston even passed an ordinance protecting vultures because they performed a public service by cleaning the carcasses of dead animals.[*] In 1666 a Boston municipal ordinance ordered the inhabitants to bury all filth, while "all garbidge, beasts entralls &c," were to be thrown from the drawbridge into Mill Creek.[†] Colonial Boston's system of burying what you can and throwing the rest into the nearest river was used by many cities well into the modern era.

A description of Pittsburgh dating from the late nineteenth century details its air pollution in these terms:

> Pittsburgh is a smoky, dismal city, at her best. At her worst, nothing darker, dingier or more dispiriting can be imagined. The city is in the heart of the soft coal region; and the smoke from her dwellings, stores, factories, foundries, and steamboats, uniting settles in a cloud over the narrow valley in which she is built, until the very sun looks coppery through the sooty haze. According to a circular of the Pittsburgh Board of Trade, about twenty per cent, or one-fifth of all the coal used in the factories and dwellings of the city escapes into the air in the form of smoke. . . . But her inhabitants do not seem to mind it; and the doctors hold that this smoke from the carbon sulphur, and iodine contained in it, is highly favorable to the lung and cutaneous diseases, and is the sure death of malaria and its attendant fevers.[‡]

Public waterworks were luxuries found in few communities until well after the Civil War. Some medium-size cities such as Providence, Rochester, and Milwaukee relied entirely on private wells and water carriers. Sanitation fared little better. Boston, which had attained a level few communities could equal, had under 10,000 water closets for its residents.[§] Until the twentieth century, facilities were all but nonexistent in the congested tenements of the slums.

[*]Charles N. Glaab (ed.), *The American City*, Dorsey, Homewood, Ill., 1963, p. 115.
[†]Carl Bridenbaugh, *Cities In the Wilderness*, Capricorn Books, New York, 1964, p. 18.
[‡]Willard Glazier, *Peculiarities of American Cities*, Hubbard, Philadelphia, 1884, pp. 332–333.
[§]Blake McKelveg, *The Urbanization of America, 1860–1915*, Rutgers University Press, New Brunswick, N. J., 1963, p. 13.

Congestion was a serious problem in the densely packed city of the turn of the century. Pictured is downtown Chicago, ca. 1910. (Chicago Historical Society.)

that most American cities were planned and built in the nineteenth century. We still live largely in cities designed for the age of steam and the horse-drawn streetcar.

As a side note, a quick way of determining the boundaries of an early city is to note the location of cemeteries. Since cemeteries were traditionally placed on the outskirts, large cemeteries within present city boundaries effectively show earlier high-water marks of urban growth.

Twentieth-Century Dispersion

Contemporary metropolitan areas reflect dispersion rather than concentration. Three inventions contributed to this change: the telephone, the electric streetcar, and, most important, the automobile. The telephone meant that city business could be conducted other than by face-to-face contact or messenger. It enabled businesses to locate their factories separate from their offices.

Before the electric streetcar, separation of place of living from place of work was a luxury restricted to the affluent or well-to-do. Nineteenth-century suburbs developed along commuter railroad lines and were the private preserves of those who had both the time and the money to commute. The North Shore suburbs of Chicago are an example. Common people, however, walked or rode the horse streetcars to work. At the beginning of the twentieth century, the average New

Yorker lived a quarter of a mile, or roughly two blocks, from his or her place of work. Chicago at that time contained 1,690,000 inhabitants, half of them living within 3.2 miles of the city center.[27]

The electric streetcar changed all this. Perfected in 1888 in Richmond, Virginia, the streetcar moved twice as fast as the horse-drawn car and had over three times the carrying capacity. The new system of urban transportation was almost immediately adopted everywhere. By the turn of the century horsecar lines, which had accounted for two-thirds of all street railways a decade earlier, had all but vanished. Electric trolleys accounted for 97 percent of all mileage in 1902, with 2 percent still operated by cable car lines, and only 1 percent by horse cars.[28]

The result was the rapid development of outer areas of the city, and proliferation of middle-class streetcar suburbs.[29] With one's home somewhere along the streetcar line, it was possible to live as far as 12 miles from the central business district and commute relatively rapidly and inexpensively. This led to an outward expansion of the city and the establishment of residential suburbs in strips along the right-of-way of the streetcar line. Those high in the electric traction industry and corrupt politicians with influence made fortunes when streetcar lines were built to outlying areas where they just happened to own all the vacant lots.

Land lying between the "spokes" formed by the streetcar lines remained undeveloped. The cities thus came to have a rather pronounced star-shaped configuration, with the points of the star being the linear rail lines.[30] This is a shape cities would hold until the era of the automobile.

Where street rail lines intersected, natural breaks in transit took place and secondary business and commercial districts began to develop. These regional shopping areas were the equivalent of the peripheral shopping centers of today. With the coming of the automobile, the city areas between the streetcar lines filled in, and by the 1920s most of our major cities had completed the bulk of their building. The depression of the 1930s effectively stopped downtown building; thus, many central business districts remained basically unchanged until building resumed again in the early 1960s.[31]

Political Bosses: Corruption and Service

In 1853 New York was described in *Putnam's Monthly* as possessing "Filthy streets, the farce of a half-fledged and inefficient police, and the miserably bad government, generally, of an unprincipled common council, in the composition of which ignorance, selfishness, impudence and greediness seem to have an equal share." Over the following score of years the situation deteriorated. Virtually everywhere venality and urban politics became synonymous. As Arthur Schlesinger charitably put it, "This lusty urban growth created problems that taxed human

---

[27]Paul F. Cressey, "Population Succession in Chicago: 1898–1930," *American Journal of Sociology*, **44**:59, 1938.
[28]Glaab and Brown, op. cit., 2d ed., p. 144.
[29]For an excellent account of this phenomenon, see Sam Bass Warner, Jr., *Streetcar Suburbs*, Harvard and M.I.T. Presses, Cambridge, Mass., 1962.
[30]Richard Hurd, *Principles of City Land Values*, The Record and Guide, New York, 1903.
[31]For more on central business districts, see Chapter 11.

Boss William Tweed, head of the Tammany Hall political machine, as portrayed by the cartoonist Thomas Nast. Tweed plundered the New York City treasury of between $60 million and $200 million. He was convicted in 1872. (Culver Pictures.)

resourcefulness to the utmost."[32] A particularly high price was paid in the area of municipal governance. Political institutions that were adequate under simplified rural conditions but inadequate to the task of governing a complicated system of ever-expanding public services and utilities presented an acute problem. The contemporary observer Andrew White was more direct, "With very few exceptions the city governments of the United States are the worst in Christendom . . . the most expensive, the most inefficient, and the most corrupt."[33] Or as the noted British scholar James A. Bryce put it, "There is no denying that the government of cities is the one conspicuous failure of the United States."[34]

[32]Arthur M. Schlesinger, op. cit., pp. 43–66.
[33]James Bryce, *Forum*, vol. X, 1890, p. 25.
[34]James Bryce, *The American Commonwealth*, vol. 1, Macmillan, London, 1891, p. 608. Reprinted by Putnam, New York, 1959.

Boss Tweed of New York, who plundered the city of between $60 million and $200 million, was even more explicit: "The population is too helplessly split into races and factions to govern it under universal suffrage, except by bribery or patronage or corruption."[35]

On the other hand, although the political bosses emptied the public treasury, they also provided the poorer citizens with urban services, jobs, and help in solving problems. The bosses were buffers between slum dwellers and the often hostile official bureaucracy. In return for the immigrants' vote, the boss provided not abstract ideals but practical services and benefits. The boss was the one to see when you needed a job, when your child was picked up for delinquency, or when you drank a bit too much and were arrested for drunkenness. The boss would arrange something with the police at the stationhouse or even "go your bail" if the offense was serious. The boss was certain to attend every wedding and wake in the neighborhood, and often provided cash to get the newlyweds going or cover funeral expenses for a widow. The boss produced. As a Boston ward heeler, Martin Lomasney, straightforwardly expressed it, "There's got to be in every ward somebody that any bloke can come to—no matter what he's done—to get help. Help, you understand; none of your law and justice, but help."[36]

In managing the city the bosses distinguished between dishonest graft and honest graft, or "boodle." The former would include shakedowns, payoffs, and protection money for illegal gambling, liquor, and prostitution. "Boodle," on the other hand, involved using your control over contracts for municipal services and tax assessments to maximize your advantage. The boss George Washington Plunkitt in a famous passage explained how it worked.

> Just let me explain by examples. My party's in power in the city, and it's going to undertake a lot of public improvements. Well, I'm tipped off, say, that they're going to lay out a new park at a certain place. I see my opportunity and I take it. I go to that place and I buy up all the land I can in the neighborhood. Then the board of this or that makes its plan public, and there is a rush to get my land, which nobody cared particular for before. Ain't it perfectly honest to charge a good price and make a profit on my investment and foresight? of course it is. Well, that's honest graft.[37]

In an urban environment committed to the principle of free enterprise, politicians saw no reason for all the profits to go to businesspeople rather than politicians.

While the "better classes" viewed all machine bosses as rogues and thieves, the bosses were apparently far more personable and friendly than the elite captains of industry in the business community. A study of twenty city bosses described them as warm and often sentimental men who had come from poor immigrant families. All were native urbanites, and most were noted for loyalty to their families.[38] The political machine provided a route for social mobility for bright and alert young immigrants. Police departments were also an avenue of upward mobility for first- and second-generation European immigrants. Without

[35]Arthur M. Schlesinger, *Paths to the Present,* Macmillan, New York, 1949, p. 60.
[36]Quoted in Lincoln Steffens, *The Autobiography of Lincoln Steffens,* Harcourt, 1931, p. 618.
[37]Howard P. Chudacoff, op. cit, pp. 131–132.
[38]Harold Zink, *City Bosses in the United States,* Duke University Press, Durham, N. C., 1930, p. 350.

the humanitarian aid of the ward bosses, the new immigrants would have had an even rougher time than they did. For the immigrants, boss rule was clearly functional. As expressed by the sociologist Robert Merton, "The functional deficiencies of the official structure generate an alternative (unofficial) structure to fulfill existing needs somewhat more effectively.[39]

Blaming the Immigrants

The political boss was often the child of Irish immigrants. The role of immigrants will be treated in detail in Chapter 8. Suffice it to say here that the dimensions of the immigrant flood are hard to overemphasize—perhaps some 40 million persons between 1800 and 1925. From the 1840s onward, waves of immigrants landed in the major northeastern ports. The first of the mass ethnic immigrations was that of the Irish, who were driven from home in the late 1840s by the ravages of the potato blight. Later, Germans and Scandinavians poured into the middle west, particularly after the development of steamships and the opening of the railroads to Chicago.

Immigration accelerated after the Civil War, spurred on by the need for industrialization. This was a period of industrial and continental expansion. Between 1860 and 1870, twenty-five of the thirty-eight states took official action to stimulate immigration, offering not only voting rights but also sometimes land and bonuses.[40]

By 1890 New York had half as many Italians as Naples, as many Germans as Hamburg, twice as many Irish as Dublin, and two and a half times the number of Jews in Warsaw.[41] The traditions, customs, religion, and sheer numbers of these immigrants made fast assimilation impossible. Between 1901 and 1910 alone, over 9 million immigrants were counted by immigration officials. These newcomers came largely from peasant backgrounds. They were packed into teeming slums and delegated to the lowest-paying and most menial jobs. Native-born Protestant Americans suddenly became aware of the fact that 40 percent of the 1910 population was of foreign stock—that is, immigrants or the offspring of immigrants.[42] The percentage was considerably higher in the large northern industrial cities, where over half the population was invariably of foreign stock.

To WASP (white Anglo-Saxon Protestant) writers around the turn of the century, the sins of the city were frequently translated into the sins of the new immigrant groups pouring into the ghettos of the central core. Slum housing, poor health conditions, and high crime rates were all blamed on the newcomers. Those on the city's periphery and in the emerging upper-class and upper-middle-class suburbs associated political corruption with the central city. Native-born Americans tended to view city problems as being the fault of the frequently Catholic, or even Jewish, immigrants who inhabited the central-city ghettos.

---

[39]Robert K. Merton, *Social Theory and Social Structure,* Free Press, Glencoe, Ill., 1957, p. 73.
[40]Harold Zink, op. cit., p. 350. For an excellent study of the role of a twentieth-century boss, see A. Theodore Brown and Lyle W. Dorset: *K.C. A History of Kansas City, Missouri,* Pruett Publishing, Boulder, Col., 1978.
[41]Glaab and Brown, op. cit., p. 125.
[42]Donald J. Bogue, *The Population of the United States,* Free Press, Glencoe, Ill., 1969, p. 178.

Even sympathetic reformers such as Jacob Riis portrayed central-city slums as anthills teeming with illiterate immigrants. The masses in the ghettos were a threat to democracy.[43]

Reform Movements

Reformers of the period had a distinctly middle-class orientation. As today, the problems of the city were viewed as problems of and by the poor in the central core. While the bosses represented personalized politics, reform represented abstract WASP goals such as efficient administration and good accounting. The Progressive Movement at the turn of the century, at least in its urban manifestation, was an attempt by the upper middle class to reform the inner city. This, of course, meant regaining political power. Businesspeople organized in groups such as the National Municipal League. The writing of "muckrakers" like Lincoln Steffens who exposed municipal corruption, gave considerable publicity to the grosser excesses of municipal corruption, such as the deals with utility franchises. To destroy the power of the bosses and their immigrant supporters, reforms were pushed in city after city.

The National Municipal League provided model charters and moral impetus. By 1912 some 210 communities had dropped the mayor and city-council system and adopted the commission form of government. In 1913 Dayton adopted the first city-manager system, and during the following year forty-four other cities followed suit. Under the city-manager system, a nonpolitical manager is appointed to run the city in a businesslike manner. However, in the largest cities the political machines, while they lost a few battles, managed to weather the storm. The coming of World War I directed crusading energies into new channels, and the Roaring Twenties was not a decade noted for municipal reform. While there were exceptions, such as William Hoan, the socialist mayor of Milwaukee, the city after World War I was more likely to have a colorful and corrupt mayor like James ("Gentleman Jimmy") Walker in New York or Big Bill ("The Builder") Thompson in Chicago.

AMBIVALENCE TOWARD THE CITY

America has never been neutral regarding its great cities; they have been either exalted as the centers of vitality, enterprise, and excitement, or denounced as sinks of crime, pollution, and depravity. Our present ambivalence toward our cities is nothing new; even the founding fathers had great reservations about the moral worth of cities. The city was frequently equated by writers such as Thomas Jefferson with all the evils and corruption of the old world, while an idealized picture of the yeoman farmer represented the virtue of the new world. Thomas Jefferson expressed the sentiments of many of his fellow citizens when he stated in 1787 in a letter to James Madison,

> I think our governments will remain virtuous as long as they are chiefly agricultural; and this will be as long as there shall be vacant land in any part of America. When

---

[43]Jacob A. Riis, *How the Other Half Lives*, Scribner, New York, 1890.

they get piled upon one another in large cities, as in Europe, they will become corrupt as in Europe.[44]

In a famous letter to Benjamin Rush, written in 1800, Jefferson even saw some virtue in the yellow fever epidemics that periodically ravaged seaboard cities. Philadelphia, for example, lost over 4,000 persons, almost 10 percent of its population, in the epidemic of 1793. Jefferson wrote to Rush:

> When great evils happen I am in the habit of looking out for what good may arise from them as consolations to us, and Providence has in fact, so established the order of things, as that most evils are the means of producing some good. The yellow fever will discourage the growth of great cities in our nation, and I view great cities as pestilential to the morals, the health, and the liberties of man.[45]

This, however, is not the entire picture, for in spite of these sentiments Jefferson proposed a model town plan for Washington, D.C., and after the War of 1812 came to support urban manufacturing. Also, although in his writings Jefferson advised against sending Americans to Europe for education lest they be contaminated by urban customs, he himself enjoyed visiting Paris and was a social success there. Other Americans were similarly inconsistent.

Benjamin Franklin, never one to be far from the stimulation, pleasures, and excitement of the city, went so far as to say that agriculture was "the only honest way to acquire wealth . . . as a reward for innocent life and virtuous industry." Ben Franklin was many things during his long, productive life, but never a farmer; and his own way of life indicates that he never considered an innocent life or conventional virtue to be much of a reward. Writers as diverse as de Tocqueville, Emerson, Melville, Hawthorne, and Poe all had strong reservations about the city.[46] According to de Tocqueville:

> I look upon the size of certain American cities, and especially on the nature of their population, as a real danger which threatens the future security of the democratic republics of the New World; and I venture to predict they will perish from this circumstance, unless the Government succeeds in creating an armed force which while it remains under the control of the majority of the nation, will be independent of town population, and able to repress its excess.[47]

Cowley's line "God the first garden made, and the first city Cain" expresses an attitude toward cities shared by many Americans. Thoreau, sitting in rural solitude watching a sunset, is an acceptable image. Thoreau, sitting on a front stoop in Boston watching the evening rush hour, creates an entirely different image.

Americans, even while pouring into the cities, have traditionally idealized the country. The clearing of the wilderness by the pioneers, and the taming (eradication) of savages—human and animal—was considered a highly laudable enterprise. By contrast, the building of cities by the sweat and muscle of

---

[44]Quoted in Glaab, op. cit., p. 38.
[45]Andrew A. Lipscomb and Albert E. Bergh (eds.), *The Writings of Thomas Jefferson*, vol. X, The Thomas Jefferson Memorial Association, Washington, D.C., 1904, p. 173.
[46]Morton White and Lucia White, *The Intellectual versus the City*, Harvard and M.I.T. Presses, Cambridge, Mass., 1962.
[47]Alexis de Tocqueville, *Democracy in America*, Henry Reeve (trans.), New York, 1839, p. 289.

immigrants is ignored. It is as if we consider the history of the immigrants somewhat discreditable and thus best forgotten.

Vigorous attacks on the city came from writers such as Josiah Strong, who condemned it as the source of the evils of rum, Romanism, and rebellion. Strong's book *Our Country* sold a phenomenal—for that date—175,000 copies. He effectively mirrored the fears of small-town Protestant America that urban technology and the growth of foreign immigrant groups were in the process of undermining the existing social order and introducing undesirable changes such as political machines, slums, and low church attendance. Several excerpts give the general tone of his argument:

> The city has become a serious menace to our civilization. . . . It has a particular fascination for the immigrant. Our principal cities in 1880 contained 39.3 percent of our entire German population, and 45.8 percent of the Irish. Our ten larger cities at that time contained only nine percent of the entire population, but 23 percent of the foreign. . . .
>
> Because our cities are so largely foreign, Romanism finds in them its chief strength. For the same reason the saloon together with the intemperance and liquor power which it represents, is multiplied. . . .
>
> Socialism centers in the city, and the materials of its growth are multiplied with the growth of the city. Here is heaped the social dynamite; here roughs, gamblers, thieves, robbers, lawless and desperate men of all sorts congregate; men who are ready on any pretext to raise riots for the purpose of disruption and plunder; here gather the foreigners and wage-workers who are especially susceptible to socialistic arguments; here skepticism and irreligion abound; here inequality is the greatest and most obvious, and the contrast between opulence and penury the most striking; there the suffering is the sorest.[48]

An extremely influential lecture by Frederick Jackson Turner at the turn of the century, "The Winning of the West," struck a responsive chord: it glorified the pioneer and the virtues of the west. Needless to say, such homage was not paid to tenement dwellers working under oppressive conditions, who were simply trying to raise decent families. Today, television perpetuates the same myth when it gives us drama after drama concerning life in the nineteenth-century American west, but nothing about the nineteenth-century American city dweller. The cowboy, not the factory hand, is the American hero.

Criticism of the city contained some contradictory premises, although these were generally not noticed: while it was being castigated for not exhibiting rural or agrarian values, it was also being taken to task for failing to be truly urban and reach the highest ideals of an urban society. In short, the city was at the same time supposed to be both more rural and more urban.

Distrust and dislike of the city simmered during the latter part of the nineteenth century and finally crystallized around the issue of the free coinage of silver, with silver representing the agrarian west and gold the commercial and industrial east. William Jennings Bryan's campaign for the Presidency in 1896 was a major attempt by the agricultural antiurbanites to gain national political power.

---

[48]Strong, op. cit., Chap. 11.

As Bryan put it in his famous "cross of gold" speech: "Burn down your cities and leave our farms, and your cities will spring up again as if by magic; but destroy our farms, and the grass will grow in the streets of every city in the country."[49] But by the end of the nineteenth century Bryan's day had passed, and although agricultural fundamentalism still had some strength, it was no longer a commanding ideology. The city, not the farm, represented the future.

The myth of agrarian virtue nonetheless continued to outlive the reality. As Hofstadter has amusingly noted, one of President Calvin Coolidge's campaign photographs in 1924 showed him posing as a simple farmer haying in Vermont. However, the photograph said more than was intended, for the President's overalls are obviously fresh, his shoes are highly polished, and if one looks carefully, one can see his expensive Pierce Arrow, with Secret Service men waiting to rush him back to the city once the picture-taking was completed.[50] One of the lighter moments of the Watergate hearings was seeing Senator Sam Ervin, one of the sharpest constitutional lawyers in the nation, affecting country ways and referring to himself as a "simple country boy." Nor was President Carter averse to having himself pictured as a small-town "good ole boy."

Numerically, for half a century America has been a nation of urban dwellers, and with every census the percentage of urban dwellers climbs higher. Even the quarter of the population that does not live in urban places is clearly tied to an urban way of life. As noted in Chapter 1, the profits of wheat farmers, cattle ranchers, dairy farmers, and other agribusiness people are tied more to government price-support systems than to weather or other natural factors.

Today our picture of how rural life is lived and the nature of the basic rural virtues is the creation of mass media based in and directed from cities. Television shows written in New York and produced in Hollywood try to create an image of small towns, filled with friendly folk, with "down home" wisdom, rather like a Norman Rockwell painting. Urban advertising also hits hard at the same bogus theme—commercials often depend heavily on nostalgia, with old cars, fields of wheat, the old farmhouse, and the front porch swing.

What all this reflects is a deep ambivalence regarding cities and city life. As a people, we chose to glorify rural life but to live in urban areas. North America is the most urbanized of the continents (excluding Australia).

As the furor over the economic bailout of New York City indicates, our attitude toward cities is still frequently schizophrenic. Ours is an urban continent, but we treat our major cities as if we didn't fully trust them and wished they would fade away and stop causing problems.

---

[49]Glaab and Brown, op. cit., 1st ed., p. 59.
[50]Richard Hofstadter, *The Age of Reform*, Knopf, New York, 1955, p. 31.

CHAPTER

4

CHANGE WITHIN AND BETWEEN METROPOLITAN AREAS

He also built Upper-Beth-horon and Lower-Beth-horon as fortified cities with walls and barred gates, and Baalath as well as all his store-cities, and all the towns where he quartered his chariots and horses; and he carried out all his cherished plans for building in Jerusalem, in the Lebanon, and throughout his whole dominion.

Solomon's SMSA
Second Chronicles, 8:6

METROPOLITAN ASCENDANCY

The first seventy years of this century encompassed a period of dramatic metropolitan development and ascendancy, a pattern that has been modified only within the last decade. By the turn of the century, the era of the frontier was closed, and it was clear that future national growth would have an urban nexus. The ecological and demographic pattern was one of an ingathering of population into ever-larger metropolitan areas. Already rural counties were being depopulated while population in the central cities were becoming denser. The census of 1910 recognized this centripetal population movement by establishing forty-four ad hoc "metropolitan districts" whose boundaries extended beyond those of the central city. At that time, roughly one-third of the nation's population resided in metropolitan areas.

If changes in the definition of "metropolitan areas" are taken into account, *all* population growth in the contiguous United States from the turn of the century to 1970 occurred in metropolitan areas.[1] (For definitions refer back to Chapter 1.) As a result of this centripetal movement, three-quarters of the population now resides within metropolitan areas.[2] Moreover, beyond the metropolitan area there exists a commuting field that further extends metropolitan influence to virtually the entire population.[3] As far back as 1960, 95 percent of the population was within the commuting field of a metropolitan area.

Research done by Amos Hawley shows that if a "constant criterion" is used—that is, if changes in the definitions of "metropolitan area" are taken into account—metropolitan areas gained population at a rate far in excess of the rate for nonmetropolitan areas during the period from 1900 to 1970.[4] In terms of this criterion, all population growth in the United States, except for Alaska and Hawaii, occurred in metropolitan areas (see Table 4-1). A second measure of growth—the actual increase in the number of people within the area defined as "metropolitan" at the beginning of the decade (listed under the heading "Constant area" in Table 4-1)—shows a somewhat more conservative picture. According to Hawley:

> It may be seen that the amount of increase in metropolitan areas did not exceed that in nonmetropolitan areas until 1910–20; thereafter the rate of growth was more than twice as great in the former in all decades but one, the depression decade of 1930–40. In the last thirty years of the seven-decade period, metropolitan areas absorbed three quarters or more of all population increase in continental United States. The decline in the metropolitan growth rate in the 1960–70 decade was due very likely to a further enlargement of the area over which metropolitan growth is spread. Such a trend has been gathering momentum since early in the century.[5]

[1]Amos H. Hawley, *Urban Society: An Ecological Approach*, Ronald Press, New York, 1971.
[2]R. C. Forstall, "Trends in Metropolitan and Nonmetropolitan Population Growth Since 1970," U.S. Bureau of the Census, Washington, D.C., 1975.
[3]Amos H. Hawley and Vincent P. Rock (eds.), *Metropolitan America in Contemporary Perspective*, Holsted Press, New York, 1975.
[4]Hawley, op. cit., pp. 153–154.
[5]Ibid., p. 154. (Based on Amos H. Hawley, Beverly Duncan, and David Goldberg, "Some Observations of Changes in Metropolitan Population in the U.S.," *Demography*, 1:148–155, 1964.)

TABLE 4-1
Growth of Metropolitan and Nonmetropolitan Population

Decade	Conterminous United States, total	Constant criterion		Constant area	
		Metro-politan	Nonmetro-politan	Metro-politan	Nonmetro-politan
Numerical increase, millions					
1900–1910	16.0	10.6	5.4	7.5	8.5
1910–1920	13.7	11.5	2.2	8.5	5.2
1920–1930	17.1	16.0	1.1	12.4	4.7
1930–1940	8.9	5.9	3.0	5.0	3.9
1940–1950	19.0	17.6	1.4	14.4	4.6
1950–1960	27.8	27.5	.2	21.6	6.2
1960–1970	20.8	22.5	−1.7	15.1	5.7
Percentage of increase					
1900–1910	21	44	10	31	16
1910–1920	15	33	4	25	9
1920–1930	16	35	2	27	8
1930–1940	7	10	5	8	6
1940–1950	14	26	2	21	7
1950–1960	18	32	0	25	10
1960–1970	12	20	−3	13	9
Percentage distribution of increase					
1900–1910	100	66	34	47	53
1910–1920	100	84	16	62	38
1920–1930	100	94	6	72	28
1930–1940	100	66	34	56	44
1940–1950	100	92	8	76	24
1950–1960	100	99	1	78	22
1960–1970	100	108	+8	73	27

Source: Amos H. Hawley, Beverly Duncan and David Goldberg, "Some Observations of Changes in Metropolitan Population in the United States," Demography, 1:149, 1964, table 2; and Amos H. Hawley, Urban Society, Ronald Press, New York, 1971, p. 154.

The awareness that cities had become part of a larger urban complex was reflected in the pioneering works of perceptive writers such as Gras and McKenzie.[6] Half a century ago, they foresaw that the city per se had yielded its influence in the generation of change to a larger unit: the metropolitan area.

URBAN CONCENTRATIONS

Movement of population toward the largest urban concentrations (city and suburb) continued until 1970 to both depopulate rural counties and magnify urban problems.[7] The city, as opposed to most farms, not only promised excitement and liberation, it also had electricity and indoor plumbing. For a farm boy or girl of the 1920s, everything *was* up to date in Kansas City.

The magnitude of the rural out-migration is reflected in Bureau of Census

[6]N. B. S. Gras, *Introduction to Economic History*, Harper, New York, 1922; and Roderick McKenzie, *The Metropolitan Community*, McGraw-Hill, New York, 1933.
[7]Amos H. Hawley, "Urbanization as Process," in David Street (ed.), *Handbook of Contemporary Urban Life*, Jossey-Bass, San Francisco, 1978, p. 7.

figures. In 1920, 30 percent of the American population still lived on farms; by 1977 this figure had shrunk to only 3.6 percent.[8] In the half century from 1920 to 1970, the net out-migration from farms to cities was 29 million.[9] Only one person in twenty-eight lives on a farm.

For the first half of this century, while the central city increasingly found its *physical* expansion contained by surrounding suburbs, the *influence* of the central city expanded. Once independent, outlying towns, villages, and crossroad markets found themselves engulfed in an urban network. The local bank became a branch of a large city bank; local papers were replaced by metropolitan dailies; and local dairies and breweries went under, unable to compete with metropolitan-based firms. Where once such places were moderately self-sufficient, they now either declined in significance or began to perform specialized functions for the larger metropolitan area. Some previously independent communities became satellite towns, while others specialized as bedroom suburbs.[10] The consequence was the emergence of the era of the metropolitan unit.

Today about three-quarters of the urban population of the United States lives in urbanized areas, i.e., places of 50,000 or more plus their suburban areas. Nearly half (44 percent) of the American population lives within metropolitan areas of 1 million or more. One estimate is that by the turn of the century two-thirds of the population will be in areas of 1 million or more.[11] However, recent developments in nonmetropolitan growth suggest that this is unlikely to occur. In fact, the percentage—but not the number—of metropolitan residents may well decrease during the next two decades. (Nonmetropolitan growth patterns of the last decade will be examined later in this chapter.)

About half the nation's population lives in only eight of the fifty states — California, Illinois, Michigan, New Jersey, New York, Ohio, Pennsylvania, and Texas. The overall picture is as follows:

> During the decade of the 1960's the West replaced the Northeast as the most urban region, the first time in the history of the nation that the Northeast has not been the most urban region. The West's proportion of population was 82.9 percent while in the Northeast the proportion was 80.2 percent. The South, long the most rural region of the country, is now becoming urbanized at the fastest rate. In 1970, 64.4 percent of the South's people were urban, up from 58.5 percent in 1960. In the North Central region the proportion of urbanites was 71.6 percent. . . .
>
> California is the most urban state in the nation, 91 percent of its population resides in cities or towns. New Jersey with 90, Rhode Island, Massachusetts, Illinois, Florida, Utah, Nevada, and Hawaii all are more than 80 percent urban. The least urban state is Vermont with only 32 percent of its population in urban areas. West Virginia with 38 percent urban is next with South Dakota. North Dakota, and Mississippi each with 56 percent urban tied for third place.[12]

[8]U.S. Bureau of the Census, U.S. Department of Commerce and Agriculture, "Farm Population of the United States: 1977," *Current Population Reports*, series P-27, no. 51, Washington, D.C., November 1978.
[9]T. Lynn Smith and Paul E. Zopf, Jr., *Demography: Principles and Methods*, Alfred, New York, 1976.
[10]Leo F. Schnore, "Satellites and Suburbs," *Social Forces*, 36:121–127, December, 1957.
[11]U.S. Commission on Population Growth and the American Future, *Population Distribution and Policy*, Sara Mills Mazie (ed.),Washington, D.C., 1973, vol. 5.
[12]U.S. Bureau of the Census, Department of Commerce, *Small Area Data Notes*, Washington, D.C., March, 1971, vol. 6, pp. 6–7.

Defining Metropolitan Areas

The term "metropolitan area" is a popular term rather than one defined by the Bureau of the Census. It commonly refers to a large concentration of 100,000 or more inhabitants that contains as its core a legal city with 50,000 or more inhabitants and is surrounded by "suburban areas" and Standard Metropolitan Statistical Areas (SMSAs).

Urbanized Area. An urbanized area consists of a central city, or cities, of 50,000 or more and their surrounding closely settled territory, whether incorporated or unincorporated. The term thus refers to the actual urban population of an area regardless of political boundaries such as county or state lines. All those in the urbanized area are considered urban, but the population is also divided into those in the "central city" and those in the remainder of the city, or "urban fringe."

Because it is based on density (at least 1,000 persons per square mile), the urbanized area has no fixed boundaries and thus changes from census to census to reflect actual population changes. This potential strength can, however, become a weakness when one is doing longitudinal research, since the urbanized area of any city covered different land areas in the 1950, 1960, 1970, and 1980 censuses.

Standard Metropolitan Statistical Area. Standard Metropolitan Statistical Areas (SMSAs) are officially designated by the U.S. Office of Management and Budget, and are based on territory rather than population. A Standard Metropolitan Statistical Area is a county or group of counties having a central city of 50,000 or more, or twin cities with a combined population of 50,000 or more. The SMSA includes the county in which the central city is located plus any adjacent counties that are judged by the Bureau of the Census to be metropolitan in character and socially and economically integrated with the central city. In New England, where they do not have counties, SMSAs consist of townships and cities instead. Currently there are almost 300 areas designated as SMSAs. Of the fifty states, only Vermont and Wyoming contain no SMSAs.

The SMSAs have several advantages. First, since they are based on county boundaries which rarely change from decade to decade, it is easy to aggregate data about them. Second, many other data are also collected on a county basis, and thus comparisons can be made easily. Finally, the county, more than any other civil division, realistically contains the territory economically integrated with the central city.*

For use in social research, the SMSAs work best when the counties included are overwhelmingly urban in social and economic characteristics. However, some SMSAs contain considerable land outside their central cities that cannot be considered anything but rural. For example, the 1970 census indicated that there were 16 million rural people enumerated as living in SMSAs. The common practice of considering all non-central-city SMSA dwellers, wherever they live in the county, as suburbanites thus sometimes overestimates the extent of metropolitan growth.

Standard Metropolitan Consolidated Areas. In recognition of the special importance of the largest metropolitan complexes, the Bureau of the Census now defines some super-SMSAs as "Standard Metropolitan Consolidated Areas" (SMCAs). There are currently 13 SMCAs.

Megalopolis. Finally, the term "megalopolis" is sometimes used to refer to an agglomeration of closely bound metropolitan areas.† 'Megalopolis," thus, refers not to one metropolitan area but to a string of metropolitan areas. Originally, however, the term referred to the so-called "BosWash" megalopolis, stretching some 500 miles along the Atlantic coast from Boston to Washington and containing some 60 million people. An example of its extended application would be the dense urban population concentration in Tokyo-Yokohoma, totaling over 20 million people.

---

*U.S. Bureau of the Census, Census of Population: 1970, *General Social and Economic Characteristics,* Final Report PC(1)-C1, Washington, D.C., Appendix A.
†Jean Gottmann, *Megalopolis,* M.I.T. Press, Cambridge, Mass., 1961.

DECENTRALIZATION WITHIN METROPOLITAN AREAS

The twentieth century thus has witnessed a massive population implosion or ingathering of population into urban concentrations. However, within metropolitan areas the movement has been from the center toward the periphery. Throughout the twentieth century, again with annexation taken into account, the population of outer "suburban" areas has grown faster than that of central cities.[13] Almost all metropolitan growth during this period occurred in the ring beyond the central city. The redistribution of population began in the larger and older metropolitan areas and then became general for cities of all sizes except the very newest. Moreover, the highest rate of growth in nonmetropolitan counties during this period occurred in counties having metropolitan characteristics, experiencing overspill, or both. The areas of overspill commonly referred to as "exurbs," simply confirmed the patterns of metropolitan dominance.

The edges of metropolitan areas have been increasingly converted from less intensive to more intensive uses, such as housing and manufacturing. Less intensive land uses such as grain production and cattle grazing are pushed outward; near the city even agriculture is intensive—truck farms, greenhouses, chicken farms, etc. Fertility of the soil is less important than the nearness of the city: consider, for example, the intensive use of relatively poor farmland near New England cities.

Outmovement of Industry

After World War II, retail trade, service establishments, and manufacturing firms increasingly followed the population to suburban areas. For example, suburban shopping malls—virtually nonexistent 30 years ago—now number over 15,000 and account for more than half the nation's retail sales. With over three-quarters of employed suburbanites working in suburbs, old commutation patterns (residents of suburbs commuting to the central city), have also broken down. (The major role of the federal government in subsidizing suburbanization will be discussed in Chapters 7 and 13.)

In the American city of fifty years ago, industry was concentrated in an inner belt located between the central business district (CBD) and the better residential areas. Today many of the factory buildings prospered, the original space became more and more crowded. But expansion was both difficult and expensive. Internally, assembly lines or other factory operations had to be fitted into the existing building, and even moving goods from floor to floor became a serious problem. At the same time, external expansion was limited by the cost, both in land and taxes, of growing horizontally. Surrounding land was already occupied, which meant that whatever was already on the land had to be bought and torn down before the factory could expand. Transportation also became an increasing problem. Trucks had to move down busy city streets before lining up to wait to get into inadequate loading docks. Parking space for workers' cars developed into another major problem.

---

[13]Basil Zimmer, "Suburbanization and Changing Political Structures," in Barry Schwartz (ed.), *The Changing Forces of the Suburbs,* University of Chicago Press, Chicago, 1975.

The move of manufacturing and industry out of the central city was greatly accelerated by the building of interstate superhighways. The building of the interstate expressway system in the 1950s and 1960s gave industry genuine alternatives to central-city locations. Suburban land was cheap, and suburban taxes were low. Most important, the plant could be designed from the inside out. The assembly line, for example, could be laid out all on one level and then walls simply built around the work space. The size and shape of the building could be determined by the needs of the factory rather than by the size and shape of a lot or an existing plant. Suburban plants were also closer to the homes of executives who lived in the suburbs, and this was another factor encouraging the move of management to the suburbs.

Increasingly, industry has leapfrogged over intermediate city residential areas and moved directly from the inner city to suburban industrial parks. When a firm was serving only local markets, a central-city location, with its ease of access to all parts of a city, made sense. Such a location was reasonable even if the major transport between cities was done by rail. Today, however, firms with national markets usually seek a location on or near an interstate expressway, which is far more valuable than one which gives rapid access to all parts of any single city.

The location of factories in suburbs in turn encouraged workers to move to new suburban tract-type housing developments that were sprouting in the cornfields near the factories. Before long, shopping centers followed; and more and more mixed industrial-residential suburbs were born.

The ideal location for department stores is no longer in the central business district but in a suburban shopping mall near an expressway. (Everett C. Johnson/Leo DeWys, Inc.)

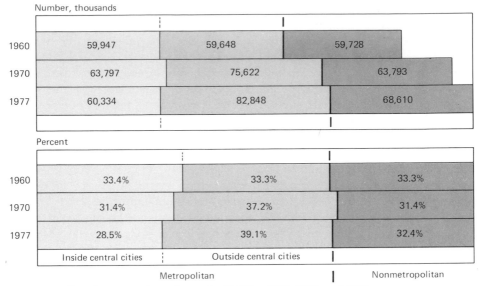

Figure 4-1   Population inside and outside SMSAs: 1960, 1970, and 1977.
(*Source:* Bureau of the Census.)

Advances in Transportation and Communication

What made the widespread outward flow of urban population (Figure 4-1) possible was technological breakthroughs in the areas of transportation and communication. The city based on steam power was transformed into one dependent on petroleum and electricity. Widespread use of automobiles, trucks, and telephones increased the movement of persons, goods, and ideas. The automobile provided mobility to the average urban dweller and allowed—and even encouraged—rapid settlement of previously inaccessible areas on the periphery of the central city. Henry Ford's Model T changed the automobile from a toy of the rich to a middle-class necessity. Automobile registration in the United States increased from 2 ½ million in 1915 to 9 million in 1920 and 26 million in 1930.

With the coming of the automobile, the maximum distance workers could live from their place of employment and commute within an hour increased from a dozen miles to perhaps 25 miles or so. (Theoretically, the automobile doubled the commuting radius, but the practicalities of poor roads and traffic congestion set lower limits.) As of 1920 a Chicago study indicated that the average distance from home to workplace was 1.5 miles.[14] By 1960 the distance had increased to 4.7 miles.[15] Just at the time when Burgess was expounding his theory of growth from

[14]Beverly Duncan, "Factors in Work-Residence Separation: Wages and Salary Workers, 1951," *American Sociological Review*, **21:**48–56, 1956.
[15]Amos H. Hawley, *Urban Society*, p. 191.

the center through intermediate zones (detailed in Chapter 5), the automobile and the truck were partially outdating his work.

What the automobile did for people, the truck did for goods. Trucks were incomparably more flexible than railroads for short hauls. Trucks were free of fixed routes and fixed schedules, needed no elaborate terminal facilities on expensive inner-city land, and could make door-to-door pick-ups and deliveries. No longer was it necessary for the factory to be on the rail line. For all but the longest hauls, the speed of motor trucks was also superior. However, during the 1920s and 1930s, the major advantage of motor transport was its lower cost per mile within the first 250 miles of the city.[16] Not only were equipment and maintenance costs far lower, but in truck cartage the cost per mile was lowest for the shortest distances. In train transport, on the other hand, the lowest cost per mile was for the longest trips. The motor truck, then, was by far the superior competitor for the short haul—an advantage that was increased considerably by the public building of new roads. The interstate expressway system, begun during the late 1950s, extended the trucks' longer-haul advantage, although this advantage is now being modified by high fuel costs.

What the motor vehicle did for transportation, the telephone did for communication. Not until 1920 did over half of all residences have telephones. By the 1920s the telephone had become a common adjunct of local business, and long-distance telephone communication was a practical—if expensive—reality. A consequence was the liberation of first residences and then factories and offices from central-city locations.

Movers and Stayers

However, decentralization has been specific rather than general as regards both industrial movement and population movement. The greatest decentralization has occurred in the larger, older cities of the northeast and middle west.[17] Decentralization of business and industry to fringe locations has also been selective. Operations which require large plants and large amounts of ground space per worker, have a high "nuisance factor" (that is, create noise, pollution, odor, and waste), and need little contact with local buyers tend to be drawn increasingly toward the periphery. Obsolete central-city plants cannot compete economically with new specifically designed single-story facilities. Automobile plants, chemical firms, steel mills, and petroleum refineries also require large areas of fringe land for their newer operations. Generally, production and distribution have decentralized; and as markets have decentralized, wholesaling has also, since it needs space as well as access to markets. The use of trucks rather than railroads for transportation also argues for the more flexible outer locations. By locating businesses outside the congested city core and near the interstate expressways,

[16]National Resources Committee, *Technological Trends and National Policy*, U.S. Government Printing Office, Washington, D.C., 1937.
[17]Brian J. L. Berry and John D. Kasarda, *Contemporary Urban Ecology*, Macmillan, New York, 1977, p. 234.

owners could reduce transportation costs. Rapid transportation provides a form of storage en route.

On the other hand, finance, management, and government have shown far less inclination to decentralize. New York City, for example, lost 42,000 manufacturing jobs between 1947 and 1955, but jobs in corporate offices, finance, insurance, and real estate increased by 28,000.[18] More recent employment data show a mixed pattern, for while central-city blue-collar jobs have been decreasing, white-collar positions have been increasing. From 1960 to 1970 there was a 12.7 percent reduction in blue-collar jobs but a concurrent 7.2 percent increase in white-collar employment. Suburbs had a much higher rate of growth in white-collar jobs, but the cities' increase occurred in spite of the decline in overall urban population. The problem of the cities is not so much a decline in employment, as a decline in jobs that could provide on-the-job training for the large pool of poor and minority-group city dwellers who lack the educational background or job experience to compete effectively for white-collar positions.[19]

While manufacturing and industry have dispersed to suburban locations, the offices that administer and control the enterprises often remain located in the central business district. Central business districts are experiencing considerable new business construction. From the mid-1960s to the early 1970s, there was over a 50 percent *increase* in office space in older cities such as New York and Chicago, while Houston doubled its office space.[20] Management, finance, government, and law still remain at the center of the city because they do not require great amounts of space per worker or need access to one another; a downtown location makes far more sense when services are oriented not to individuals but to other organizations. In the CBD, communications are easy and informal—business may be conducted over lunch, for example—and there are many services and economies available outside the firm itself. Outside specialists are readily accessible to cover areas such as advertising, legal services, accounting, tax information, and mailing. Firms located on the periphery must provide all sorts of services often not required of those in the center, such as parking lots, cafeterias, and medical services. Top management may also remain in the city so that it does not become isolated from the informal information networks about competitors, government policy, and buying patterns that are always found when a number of firms in the same sort of business are located in the same spatial area.

Retail trade has followed the population to the suburbs. Central business districts now account for less than half of all sales in personal and household items. The nation's 15,000 shopping malls have sometimes almost become cities unto themselves. San Jose has an enclosed air-conditioned center which includes

---

[18]Raymond Vernon, "Production and Distribution in the Large Metropolis," *Annals of the American Academy of Political and Social Science*, **314**:25, 1957.

[19]Anthony Downs, *Opening Up the Suburbs: An Urban Strategy for America*, Yale University Press, New Haven, 1973; and Neil N. Gold, "The Mismatch of Jobs and Low Income People in Metropolitan Areas and Its Implications for the Central-City Poor," in Sara Mills Mazie (ed.), *Population Distribution and Policy*, U.S. Commission on Population Growth and the American Future, vol. 5, U.S. Government Printing Office, Washington, D.C., 1972.

[20]Gerald Manners, "The Office in the Metropolis: An Opportunity for Shaping Metropolitan America," *Economic Geography*, **50**, 1974, pp. 93–110.

130 stores, 27 restaurants, and 9,000 parking spaces. Houston's "Galeria," which is modeled after a nineteenth-century gallery in Milan, Italy, has three levels which in addition to the usual department stores, restaurants, and shops also includes an athletic club with ten air-conditioned tennis courts and a jogging track. (Many college athletic departments would gladly exchange their facilities for those of this shopping mall.) It is connected to two high-rise office buildings and a 404-room hotel. Shopping plazas, with their fountains, film festivals, and wine-tasting contests, have come a long way from the mercantile stores of the last century. The shopping mall is replacing Main Street as the core of the community. Increasingly, the malls serve social as well as commercial functions. Columbia, Maryland, has a mall with a "crisis counseling center" and an Interfaith Center where Protestants, Catholics, and Jews share religious facilities.

However, the lineal decline of retail sales in recent decades may not be an accurate harbinger of the city to come. Downtown stores may never again have the dominance of retail trade they exercised during the centralizing era of the streetcar and subway, but so long as the downtown is a major white-collar employment center, the CBD will be a solidly profitable location for retail sales, particularly of more expensive and fashionable goods.

Retail trade outlets follow a predictable pattern of distribution. Convenience goods, such as food, and other items which have a high degree of standardization, a low price, a low margin of profit, and rapid turnover tend to be located throughout the entire metropolitan area. Shopping goods which are purchased less frequently, are less standardized (style being a factor), and have higher prices and a higher margin of profit are usually found clustered. Central shopping districts or peripheral shopping centers provide ideal locations, since they allow customers to "comparison shop." An ideal location for a furniture store is next to similar stores. Automobile dealers also find it is best to be located near their competitors. Luxury goods such as furs and works of art which are rarely purchased and have very high prices are still found downtown or near high-income areas. Since the rate of turnover of such goods is very low and emphasis is on their rarity or uniqueness rather than their standardization, a store site which has easy access from all upper-income areas is desirable. Downtown executive offices employ people who constitute a potential market for luxury goods.

MEGALOPOLIS

In the more highly industrialized sections of the world a new and larger supermetropolitan unit, called a "megalopolis," has emerged. The term "megalopolis" refers to the overlapping and interpenetration of previously separate metropolitan areas so that a continuous urbanized land area is created. Where once there was a metropolitan area made up of small towns and cities, there is now emerging a larger area where metropolitan centers are the basic units. (See Figure 4-2.)

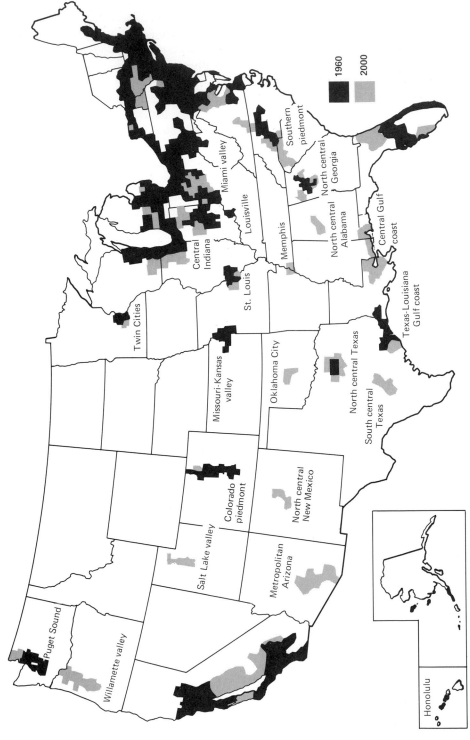

Figure 4-2 Urban regions in the United States: 1960 and 2000 (projected). (*Source*: Population Reference Bureau.)

Legend: 1960, 2000

Puget Sound
Willamette valley
Salt Lake valley
Colorado piedmont
North central New Mexico
Metropolitan Arizona
Twin Cities
Missouri-Kansas valley
Central Indiana
St. Louis
Oklahoma City
North central Texas
South central Texas
Miami valley
Louisville
Memphis
North central Alabama
Southern piedmont
North central Georgia
Central Gulf coast
Texas-Louisiana Gulf coast
Honolulu

These exploding areas are sometimes referred to as "conurbations," particularly in Britain, where Patrick Geddes coined the term; but in America the term "megalopolis" is more frequently heard. The name "Megalopolis" originally applied to a Greek colonial city that had the ambition, never realized, of becoming the largest and most powerful of the Greek city-states. Today, as a result of the writings of the geographer Jean Gottmann, "megalopolis" has come to mean the overspill of urban areas into one another, as on the northeastern coast of the United States. According to Gottmann's colorful description:

> An almost continuous system of deeply interwoven urban and suburban areas, with a total population of about 37 million people in 1960, has been erected along the Northeastern Atlantic seaboard. It straddles state boundaries, stretches across wide estuaries and bays, and encompasses many regional differences. . . . It is, *on the average,* the richest, best educated, best housed, and best serviced group of similar size (i.e., 25-to-40-million-people range) in the world. . . . It is true that many of its sections have seen pretty rural landscapes replaced by ugly industrial agglomerations or drab and monstrous residential developments; it is true that in many parts of Megalopolis the air is not clean any more, the noise is disturbing day and night, the water is not as pure as one would wish, and transportation at times becomes a nightmare.[21]

The megalopolis along the east coast of the United States, from the northern suburbs of New York in Connecticut, or even from Boston, to the suburbs of Washington, D.C., now includes a population of over 45 million. This strip city, which is sometimes called "BosWash," includes land covering ten states, the District of Columbia, and hundreds of local governments—land which is predominantly urban. It has an overall population density of more than 2,000 per mile and a median income level more than $1,000 higher than that of the rest of the country.[22] In 1970, New Jersey, much of which is within commuting distance of New York City, displaced Rhode Island as the state with the highest population density—953 people per square mile.

Is the density of this area too high? Certainly some of the commuters in the corridor think so; still, they are not leaving this crowded sector for less densely settled areas of the country. Many of those who complain the loudest would not think of leaving; what they have in mind is other people leaving. Additional megalopolises can be seen forming: from Chicago to Cleveland, or perhaps even Pittsburgh, and on the west coast from San Francisco to San Diego. As the metropolitan growth of these newer areas increases, the overwhelming dominance of BosWash has declined from over 50 percent of the nation's total metropolitan population to less than 30 percent (although its size has not declined). The remaining years of this century should see these new megalopolises take on a more definite shape and form.

---

[21]Jean Gottmann, *Megalopolis: The Urbanized Northeastern Seaboard of the United States.* ©1961 by the Twentieth Century Fund, New York. First published November, 1961. First M.I.T. Press Paperback Edition, February, 1964.
[22]Ansley J. Coale, "Population and Economic Development," in Philip M. Hauser (ed.), *The Population Dilemma,* Prentice-Hall, Englewood Cliffs, N. J., 1969, p. 73.

It is still an open question whether true supercommunities are emerging in the megalopolises or whether they are merely configurations of metropolises that share a common geographic area. On the basis of a selected analysis of thirty-one metropolises within the area Gottman described, Robert Weller concludes:

> There is but limited evidence of increasing economic interdependence among the metropolitan areas of Megalopolis. If anything their labor forces have become more homogeneous. One must therefore question the validity of concepts like Megalopolis as representing a new community form and ecological unit and consider them as clusters of large, contiguous cities until some evidence is made available to support the Megalopolis concept.[23]

The whole question of whether the megalopolis is indeed a new form remains open to further research and debate. It is, however, significant that weather reports in Washington, D.C., commonly also give the weather in the "commuter cities" which include not only New York and Boston (as expected) but with increasing frequency also Chicago. Numerous air shuttles tie all these cities together: a commuter between New York and Chicago or Los Angeles and San Francisco is able to catch a flight in either direction almost every half hour from dawn to dusk. Shuttle flights linking San Diego, Los Angeles, and San Franciso make it easier to move between these cities than around Los Angeles. It is one of the peculiarities of modern life that the air shuttles from city to city offer better, more frequent, and even faster transportation than that available between some parts of a single metropolitan area.

NONMETROPOLITAN GROWTH: THE NEW PATTERN

The classical ecological model assumed centripetal movement of population from rural hinterland to metropolitan area. This was the case for the first seventy years of this century, when the metropolitan sector—core or fringe—was growing while rural areas consistently lost population. But this pattern of increasing population concentration in metropolitan areas has come to a close.[24] The pattern of metropolitan dominance is being challenged by an emerging pattern of increased dispersion and deconcentration. In this century, for the first time, rural counties not only have stopped declining but are increasing in population. Nonmetropolitan areas added some 6 million persons (5.6 million whites and 400,000 blacks) between 1970 and 1977. During the 1960s these areas experienced a net out-migration of 3 million inhabitants. The current nonurban increases are even more significant when it is recalled that they occurred in spite of lower birthrates during the 1970s.

The nonmetropolitan turnaround is a real change. It is occurring outside of smaller as well as large "Standard Metropolitan Statistical Areas" (SMSAs) and cannot be explained simply as overspill and sprawl from metropolitan areas. The

[23]Robert H. Weller, "An Empirical Examination of Metropolitan Structure," *Demography,* **4:**743, 1967.
[24]Calvin L. Beale and Glen V. Fuguitt, "The New Pattern of Non-Metropolitan Population Change," Center for Demography and Ecology, University of Wisconsin, Madison, Center Paper 75–22, 1975.

greatest increases are occurring in counties that do not abut metropolitan areas.[25] The fastest-growing counties are those which are rural in character.

There is also a changing growth pattern within metropolitan areas. Movement from city core to suburban periphery continues, but the period of massive in-migration to metropolitan areas is no more. There now are more people moving out of than into metropolitan areas. From 1970 to 1977, there were 2.4 million more out-migrants than in-migrants.

Older central cities have been losing population for some time, but until the 1970s these losses were more than offset by suburban growth. Today metropolitan growth increasingly comes from the territorial expansion of existing SMSAs, from the designation of new SMSAs—of which thirty-four have been added since the 1970 census—or from both. Between 1950 and 1970, the Houston SMSA (an extreme case) increased by 5,071 square miles, but elsewhere outlying counties are also being rapidly absorbed into SMSAs—more than 200 between 1960 and 1970 alone.[26]

Rural Renaissance?

What is causing the nonmetropolitan turnabout? Is the recent growth of nonmetropolitan population a sign of a return to older and simpler rural ways? Is there indeed a "rural renaissance"?

No. We are experiencing a transformation in spatial settlement patterns, but this does not represent a rebirth of rural ways of life. Catchy phrases like "rural renaissance" tend to trap us in our own rhetoric. As previously noted, both the proportion and the absolute number of persons engaged in agriculture continue to decrease. Farm population declined by half, from 15.6 million persons (8.7 percent of the total population) in 1960 to 7.8 million (3.6 percent of the total population) in 1977.[27] Clearly, the rural renaissance does not mean a renaissance of the family farm or a return to agricultural pursuits.

What does it signify? The whys and wherefores of nonmetropolitan growth are not fully understood, but several factors are assumed to be significant. First, population growth signifies some growth of rural manufacturing. The transportation technology of limited-access and expressway systems that caused suburbs to boom in the 1950s and 1960s is now permitting an even more dispersed pattern of economic as well as residential development. Transportation access, coupled with lower wage rates, land costs, and taxes, has attracted some firms to localities that even a score of years ago would have been considered beyond the pale. Small communities located near major highways are particularly fortunate.[28] This

[25]Kevin F. McCarthy and Peter A. Morrison, "The Changing Demographic and Economic Structure of Non-Metropolitan Areas in the 1970s," Rand Corporation, January 1978; and Calvin L. Beale, "A Further Look at Non-Metropolitan Population Growth Since 1970," a paper presented at the annual meeting of the Rural Sociological Society, New York, 1976.

[26]Berry and Kasarda, op. cit., p. 174.

[27]U.S. Bureau of the Census, op. cit.

[28]Craig Humphrey and Ralph Sell, "The Impact of Controlled Access Highways on Population Growth in Pennsylvania and Non-Metropolitan Communities, 1940–1970," Rural Sociology, 40, Fall, 1975.

appears to represent real economic growth, not simply marginal firms locating in marginal locations.

However, the importance of new or transplanted rural manufacturing is often overstressed. While manufacturing accounted for half the nonmetropolitan growth in employment during the 1960s, it contributed only 3 percent of the growth in jobs from 1970 to 1976.[29] Of considerable importance has been the role of the military, which has concentrated its bases— and payrolls—in the less urban areas of the sun belt states.

Second, and more significant, rural growth signifies the emergence of new growth-producing activities that have a diffused spatial pattern. Foremost among these have been the specialized areas of recreation and retirement. States with much natural beauty and extensive wilderness areas, and locations attractive for recreation and leisure activities, are drawing population; and this is occurring on a year-round as well as a seasonal basis. This process in turn promotes employment, particularly in service industries, which, however, have lower pay levels than manufacturing.

Retirement patterns also increasingly involve transfer of residence. The elderly now number over a tenth of the population, and by the year 2030 there will be a minimum of 46 million elderly— double the present number. If present trends continue, those retiring will be moving in increasing numbers out of large northern metropolitan areas. Already two out of three military retirees reside in sun belt states, drawing billions of dollars in federal funds into both the metropolitan and nonmetropolitan sectors of that region. Retirement activities also create new employment opportunities—again, generally in the service sector.

Third, the growing need for energy has greatly affected selected nonmetropolitan areas. The revival of mining after the energy crisis of 1973 has created booms in rural areas from southern Appalachia to Wyoming. However, this energy-related rural revival is highly urban in character and can hardly be considered a "back to the land" movement. Much of the Rocky Mountains area is becoming one massive boomtown.

Finally, nonmetropolitan growth reflects change in American life-styles. Migration theory has long held that people move toward economic opportunity. Regardless of residential preference, most people have resided in urban areas where employment opportunities have been concentrated. Today, many families have enough money, and sufficiently flexible work schedules, to afford nonmetropolitan living. Additionally, noneconomic values such as open spaces and clean air are increasingly important factors in determining spatial location. Such considerations can be expected to increasingly influence residential patterns, even if such patterns do not reflect better employment opportunities.

There is one major factor that may radically change the pattern of urban population dispersion over an ever-widening field—the question of energy costs. Expansion of both population and manufacturing into outlying areas was based on low or at least reasonable costs for transportation and communication.

[29]McCarthy and Morrison, op. cit.

A Land Shortage?

The phrase "They aren't making land any more" is often often used to promote land investment or explain the high cost of property. The impression created is that the United States has a shortage of unbuilt land. Clearly, this is not the case. Figures compiled by the Bureau of the Census indicate that three-quarters of the population is concentrated on a mere 1 1/2 percent of the nation's land area.* Moreover, out of a total 3,536,855 square miles in the country, the amount of urban land in use totals only 54,103 square miles, or a land area roughly equal to the state of Florida. Only 2.6 percent of the nation's land area is characterized as urban or built-up.

Levels of population density very dramatically from nation to nation. The overall population density of the United States is 51 persons per square mile, compared with 970 persons per square mile in the Netherlands, which is densely settled and heavily urbanized. (The extremes range from Hong Kong with 10,066 persons per square mile to Australia and New Zealand with 5 persons.) Obviously, the United States with 10 acres per person is not suffering from an overall land shortage.

The problem is that we do not have open land in the right places—that is, in or near the cities, where it is needed. Where there is a land shortage is in the more desirable city and suburban areas. There are only a fixed limited number of lots with views, noise-free lots, smog-free lots, and low-crime lots. Because of this, land values are being forced ever higher in desirable urban areas. Open lands in Montana or Nevada are really not relevant.

However, while the amount of desirable urban land may be fixed, land use is not. England and Wales, approximately only the size of North Carolina, house nine times the population of that state while maintaining a feeling of openness.†

Comprehensive land-use policies and the prohibition of suburban sprawl can create a more livable urban environment. Chapter 13, Urban Planning: Western Europe and Socialist Countries, will discuss some of the European alternatives to American patterns of land use.

---

* *United States Department of Commerce News,* Social and Economic Statistics Administration, Washington, D.C., April 21, 1972, p. 1.
† *The Use of Land,* Rockefeller Brothers Fund, Crowell, New York, 1973, p. 103.

Inexpensive energy has made residence in the rimland possible; our currently much higher energy costs would radically alter the equation. It is still speculative whether those having freedom of residential choice will choose to bite the bullet and pay a higher price for transportation, or whether they will instead return to inner urban areas in large numbers. Either way, the remaining years of this century will exhibit a shift from the accepted conventional wisdom regarding urban ecological patterns—which until recently was all but universally accepted.

Until the extent and permanence of new patterns become clear, it is perhaps best to view nonmetropolitan growth as an extension of the metropolitan field beyond the commuting range. Over forty years ago, Louis Wirth noted that urbanism—that is, urban behavior patterns—had become the American way of life. Now, urbanization, or living in urban-defined places, has also become ubiquitous. As we continue to expand into a national metropolitan society, distinctions between metropolitan and nonmetropolitan will become even more blurred. With the number of SMSAs approaching 300 and the boundaries of existing metropolitan areas progressively expanding, it becomes increasingly difficult to distinguish between metropolitan and developing nonmetropolitan counties.

A National Society?

We are moving toward a national urban system where old differences cease to make a difference. The pattern of metropolitan dominance is being challenged by an emerging pattern of increased dispersion and deconcentration. Metropolitan areas are no longer even semi-independent. Communication and transportation advances such as WATS lines and commuter air shuttles have further reduced the friction of space. While at the turn of the century the commuter railroad line made it possible for a vanguard of businesspeople to move their residences from the city, commuter air travel now puts a premium on accessibility to an airport. In an era of air travel, the significant factor is no longer distance. Distance is increasingly measured not in miles or kilometers, but by time. Even with terrestrial travel, the question "How far is it?" commonly anticipates a temporal rather than spatial response: how long it takes to get there. Increased mobility of goods, persons, and ideas suggests that a new urban phase—a national urban unit—is in a formative stage.

The emerging pattern of a national urban society forces us to rethink traditional assumptions. In the 1950s, Otis Dudley Duncan suggested that the concept of a "rural-urban continuum," while perhaps having heuristic value, has little empirical validity.[30] Emerging nonmetropolitan growth patterns strongly suggest that the concept of a rural-urban continuum has now lost even heuristic utility. The demographic and economic growth of counties several counties removed from SMSAs increasingly suggests that any rural-urban division has lost the shards of meaning it may still have possessed even a score of years ago. New

---

[30]Otis Dudley Duncan, "Community Size and the Rural-Urban Continuum," in Paul K. Hatt and Albert J. Reiss (eds.), *Cities and Society*, Free Press, New York, 1957, pp. 35–45.

patterns also contradict the theory that the social and economic conditions of urbanization are a consequence of the distance from the point of population concentration. This change has yet to be fully reflected in policy or research.[31] As rural-urban divisions have lost all meaning, so contemporary distinctions between metropolitan and nonmetropolitan are losing utility and becoming more blurred with each passing decade. Whether we live in a metropolitan area or not, we are all part of a metropolitan society. In spite of this, we still lack a national urban policy. (See Chapter 19.)

THE RISE OF THE SUN BELT

The most dramatic urban change of the late 1970s and early 1980s—at least in terms of attention paid by the media—has been the historic shift of population and power from the old industrial heartland of the northeast to the booming metropolises of the southwest. The rise of Houston from a steamy Texas town of little interest to the booming, expanding oil capital of the world "typifies the pattern." Houston, described by the *New York Times* as "the shining buckle of the sunbelt," is now the nation's fifth-largest city and soon will be fourth behind only New York, Chicago, and Los Angeles. The sun belt, long a virtual dependent colony of the industrial northeast, has undergone an economic transformation.[32] The regional landscape has been transformed by the opening of a new urban frontier. Older northern "snow belt" cities have seen population and industry depart for the "boom" areas of the south and southwest. Businesses are attracted to such areas by a "good business climate consisting of lower wages, lower taxes, a lower rate of unionization and higher productive efficiency."

The south has attracted not only labor-intensive, low-wage industries, such as textiles and apparel, but also capital-intensive activities such as banking and insurance. Most important, while northern cities remain anchored to older industries, the south has attracted newer "leading edge" industries such as small-parts electronics and service industries such as real estate and tourism.[33]

As summed up by Kirkpatrick Sale, the writer who first focused national attention on the changing nature of the southern rim:

In broad terms there has been a shift from the traditional heavy manufacturing long associated with the industrial belt of the Northeast to the new technological industries that have grown up in the Southern Rim—areospace, defense, electronics. . . .[34]

Energy is also less costly in the south. The major sources of gas, oil, and coal

[31]The Department of Agriculture, for example, still divides nonmetropolitan counties into six types, which "describe a dimension of urban influence in which each succeeding group is affected to a lesser degree by the social and economic conditions of urban areas. This includes the influence of urban areas at a distance as well as within counties themselves." U.S. Department of Agriculture, PA-1, U.S. Government Printing Office, Washington, D.C., 1974.
[32]For details on the change and its meaning, see David D. Perry and Alfred J. Watkins (eds.), *The Rise of the Sunbelt Cities*, Sage Publications, Beverly Hills, Calif., 1977.
[33]Jeanne Biggar, "The Sunning of America: Migration to the Sunbelt," *Population Bulletin*, 34:22, March, 1979.
[34]Kirkpatrick Sale, *Power Shift: The Rise of the Southern Rim and Its Challenge to the Eastern Establishment*, Random House, New York, 1975, p. 5.

are there or nearby, and the mild climate requires less energy for heat (this is only partially offset by higher air-conditioning costs.)

Population, reversing the old trend, is now flowing southward, attracted by new jobs, the mild climate, a lower cost of living, and a life-style stressing outdoor living, year-round golf and tennis, and informal entertaining. Since 1970, urban areas in the north have generally either lost population or made only marginal gains. On the other hand, some 40 percent of the population increase of 13 million between 1970 and 1976 occurred in three sun belt states: California, Florida, and Texas. During the same period, the only northeastern states with population increases exceeding the national average of 4 percent were states better known for recreational advantages than industrial might: Maine, Vermont, and New Hampshire.

The population of the fifteen sun belt states has increased from 61 million in 1970—almost a third of the nation's total—to 85 million people, or close to 40 percent of the total. By the year 2000, the sun belt is projected to have 112 million inhabitants, or 43 percent of the nation's total population.[35]

Although the population shift to the south and southwest was long in coming, the consequences and implications for urban areas of the old industrial heartland have been recognized only recently. The northeast was long accustomed to viewing the south as an economic backwater and a cultural desert. Now expansion in the sun belt is recognized as more than crude boosterism. While cities in the north have been registering stagnancy or decline in such economic measurements as jobs, bank deposits, and construction, the corresponding figures have been bright for sun belt cities. For several years, California, Florida, and Texas have led the nation in building construction. Not only people but the tax base as well have been flowing southward. As a consequence of regional shifts, northern urban areas that have been the nation's centers of population and power for a century or more are suddenly finding themselves on the defensive.

The reaction of northern officials and officeholders to southern ascendancy has gone from initial disbelief to profound panic. Traditionally, federal funds have flowed southward. Those representing northern constituencies have been introducing congressional legislation that would rework federal distribution to favor older—i.e., northern—cities. There already have been several skirmishes in what some have dubbed the "second war between the states." What is at stake is billions of dollars in federal spending, which means jobs and economic development. In 1977, for example, northern and eastern members of Congress united against this traditional pattern, and changed housing and urban development formulas so that instead of money being allocated on the basis of population and poverty, weight is now also given to the percentage of old housing in the city and whether the city is losing population. Northern victories, however, are less certain in the future since members of Congress from the sun belt have now organized to protect their interests. As a consequence of the congressional reapportionment based on the 1980 census, the sun belt will gain at least seven new seats from snow belt states.

[35]Biggar, op. cit.

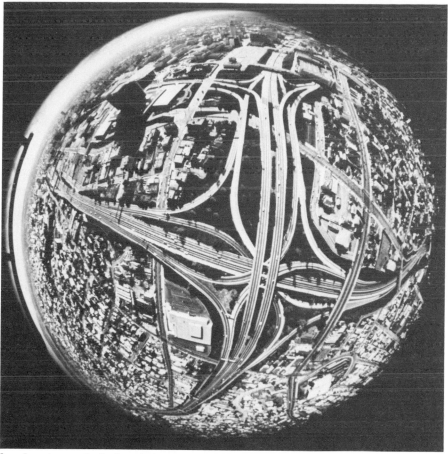

Los Angeles, a city built with the assumption of automobile ownership, is dominated by its freeways. (J. E. Eyerman/Black Star.)

However, the sun belt is not all sunshine. The rise of the sun belt has also produced problems for the expanding population. Breakneck growth has brought massive urban sprawl, overtaxed water and sewer systems, rising air pollution, environmental degradation, and traffic congestion. Sun belt cities are being pressured to expand educational opportunities, housing stock, and social services. At the same time, citizen groups are lobbying for limits on taxes like Proposition 13 in California. City officials are caught by contradictory expectations of northern-level services and southern-level taxes. There are those who even question whether all the attention given to southern ascendancy isn't largely a myth in the making.[36]

The emphasis on the growth of employment in the south should at least be balanced by the remembrance that per capita income there while at an all-time

---

[36]C. L. Jusenius and L. C. Ledebur, *A Myth in the Making: The Southern Economic Challenge and Northern Economic Decline*, Economic Development Administration, Department of Commerce, November 1976.

high, was still only 90 percent of the national average in 1976 (this is partially compensated for by lower living costs). Finally, the growing prosperity of the sun belt does not necessarily mean that this must occur at the expense of northern cities. As will be seen in Chapter 11, The Crisis of the Cities, many older cities such as Boston, Baltimore, Detroit, and even New York are showing far more vitality than was predicted by many a decade ago.

A NOTE ON THE FUNCTIONAL SPECIALIZATION OF CITIES

Even casual observation confirms the idea that the placement of cities over the landscape is anything but random. Large cities are overwhelmingly located on major bodies of water or on major navigable rivers. Historically, two other environmental considerations—suitability for defense and the fertility of the surrounding hinterland—also greatly influenced the location of cities. Only during the last century or so has it been possible for factors pertaining to technology and social organization to outweigh environmental considerations. Cities such as the Brazilian capital, Brasilia, located 600 miles inland from the coast in an area initially without roads, were impossible before modern transportation. During the initial stages of its growth, Brasilia could be reached only by air, and in recognition of the role played by technology in its founding, the city was planned to resemble the shape of an airplane.

The location of cities is related to the various economic functions they perform. Numerous activities, such as the distribution of food, are common to all cities; these are called "service activities." There are other activities which are concentrated in only some cities. The size of a particular city is related to its occupational-industrial composition. Very large cities tend to be quite diversified in terms of their economic activities.[37]

A Seven-Category Division

The most widely used classification of the economic function of cities is that developed by the geographer Chauncy Harris.[38] Several revisions have been made over the years. Basically, each of the nation's cities of over 10,000 persons is placed in one of seven categories according to its dominant function. The major categories are "manufacturing," "diversified-manufacturing," "industrial," "retailing," "diversified-retailing," "dormitory," and "specialized."[39]

Over 40 percent of the SMSAs fall into the "manufacturing" class. This includes most of the large midwestern cities, such as Chicago, Cleveland, Detroit, Milwaukee, and St. Louis. Larger cities elsewhere tend to be more diversified; over half the nation's cities with populations greater than 500,000 are listed as

---

[37]Otis D. Duncan et al., *Metropolis and Region,* Johns Hopkins Press, Baltimore, 1960.
[38]Chauncy Harris, "A Functional Classification of Cities in the United States," *Geographical Review,* **33**:86–99, January, 1943.
[39]Richard L. Forstall, "Economic Classification of Places over 10,000," *Municipal Year Book: 1967,* International City Managers Association, Chicago, 1967.

"diversified-manufacturing."[40] Boston, New York, Dallas, and Los Angeles are in this category. The pattern is for manufacturing and diversified-manufacturing cities to be most concentrated in the northeast and the midwest.

"Industrial" cities, contrary to what one might think, are found among the smaller urban places, and their number has been decreasing over the years. There are now only seventy-four places (such as Dubuque, Iowa) which are classified as "industrial." "Diversified-retailing" cities are most common in the south. There are only four such cities with over 500,000 inhabitants: New Orleans, Phoenix, San Antonio, and San Francisco. "Retailing" cities are most common in the south and the west, principally in less industrialized areas, where they serve as trading centers for agricultural hinterlands. Aberdeen, South Dakota, is an example. The "dormitory" towns are found as suburbs surrounding every great city. "Specialized-function" cities—such as university towns—provide specific services, as their name suggests. The only really large city in this category is Washington, D.C.[41]

A Three-Category Division

Another, even simpler, system divides cities into three categories: those serving as central places, those serving as transportation nodes where there is a break-in-bulk (that is, where goods must be transferred from one carrier to another, as when wheat is loaded from freight cars onto ships), and those serving specialized functions. The geographers Harris and Ullman have given this description:

1. Cities as central places performing comprehensive services for a surrounding area. Such cities tend to be evenly spaced throughout productive territory. For the moment this may be considered the "norm" subject to variation primarily in response to the ensuing factors.
2. Transport cities performing break-of-bulk and allied services along transport routes, supported by areas which may be remote and distant but close in connection because of the city's strategic location on transport channels. Such cities tend to be arranged in linear patterns along rail lines or at coasts.
3. Specialized-function cities performing one service such as mining, manufacturing, or recreation for large areas, including the general tributary areas of hosts of other cities. Since the principal localizing factor is often a particular resource such as coal, water power, or a beach, such cities may occur singly or in clusters.[42]

The first of the above categories—central-place theory—was developed largely in Europe by scholars such as von Thünen, Losch, and Christaller in order to explain the fairly regular pattern of cities in nineteenth-century Europe. The trouble is that although the model, which posits the city as providing trade and

---

[40]John C. Bollens and Henry J. Schmandt, *The Metropolis*, Harper and Row, New York, 1970, p. 74.
[41]For the question of the function of cities, see: Robert C. Atchley, "A Size-Function Typology of Cities," *Demography*, 4:721–733, 1967; Otis D. Duncan et al., *Metropolis and Region*, op. cit.; Jeffrey K. Hadden and Edgar F. Borgatta, *American Cities*, Rand McNally, New York, 1965; and Albert J. Reiss, Jr., "Functional Specialization of Cities," in Paul K. Hatt and Albert J. Reiss, Jr. (eds.), *Cities and Society*, Free Press, New York, 1957, pp. 555–575.
[42]Chauncey D. Harris and Edward L. Ullman, "The Nature of Cities," *Annals of the American Academy of Political and Social Science*, 242:8, November, 1945.

services for a tributary hinterland, roughly fits agricultural nonindustrial areas, and even parts of the American midwest, it does not really predict the location of industrial cities. And because it assumes a relatively flat terrain, it cannot deal with the often important influence of topography on urban location.

Cities in the second category—transportation centers—are likely to be located at deepwater ports or where a break-in-bulk occurs (e.g., Salt Lake City). The focusing of transportation routes alone does produce a city, but if a break in transit occurs, the point of focus becomes a natural place to process goods. The first five major American cities were all deepwater ports, and even Chicago, in the interior, has direct access to the sea and to Europe through the Great Lakes and the St. Lawrence Seaway.

Finally, cities in the third category arise because they serve as concentration points for specific purposes. The discovery of coal created Scranton and Wilkes-Barre, and the history of western mining towns such as Virginia City is well known. Las Vegas and Miami Beach specialize in tourist services; Rochester, Minnesota, with its Mayo Clinic, provides health services. The specialized function of the city frequently has a direct effect on the socioeconomic status of the population. Madison, Wisconsin, with its university, insurance, and governmental functions, has a vastly different social composition from a city such as Gary, Indiana, which is built upon the economy of the steel mills.

CHAPTER

5

ECOLOGY AND STRUCTURE OF THE AMERICAN CITY

We shape our buildings, and afterwards our buildings shape us.
Winston Churchill

CITY STRUCTURE

Much has been written of the American city: its internal structure, its forms of social organization, its peoples and life-styles, and its problems. The sociologist Louis Wirth suggested that these various topics could be viewed empirically from three interrelated perspectives: (1) as a physical structure comprising a population base, a technology, and an ecological order, (2) as a system of social organization involving a characteristic social structure, series of social institutions, and a typical pattern of social relationships, and (3) as a set of attitudes and ideas, and a constellation of personalities engaging in typical forms of collective behavior, and subject to characteristic mechanisms of social control.[1] In this chapter we shall be concerned with the first two of these perspectives: the spatial and social ecology of the city and how it affects and is affected by the city as a system of social organization. Urbanism as a system of life-styles and values will be discussed in Chapter 6, City Life-Styles.

The ecological approach is concerned with the development of the form and structure of the community. "Ecology" in its broadest sense is the study of the relationships among organisms within an environment. It is the study not of the creatures and objects themselves but rather of the relationships among them. The sum total of these many relationships among organisms in a habitat is called a "biotic community," and the community together with its physical habitat forms an "ecosystem."

The ecological school and the term "human ecology" originated with the sociologists Park and Burgess in 1921, and represented an attempt to systematically apply the basic theoretical scheme of plant and animal ecology to the study of human communities. Ecological reasoning, which traces its theoretical underpinnings to Charles Darwin's research on evolution, was first applied to the study of plants in the latter part of the nineteenth century. Animal ecology emerged in the early twentieth century, and human ecology soon followed.

Contemporary human ecology is concerned with examining the independence and interdependence of specialized roles and functions (recurrent patterns of behavior) within the society. In examining the relationship between people and their environment and people within their environment, the level of analysis focuses on the aggregate level. The issue is the properties of populations rather than the properties of the individuals who constitute them. Thus, it is based on the study of groups rather than individuals—and this focus on the group or aggregate is basic to sociology, as opposed to disciplines such as psychology in which the focus is on the individual. The focus here is on the structure of organized activity. Human ecology does not—and cannot—explain the beliefs, values, and attitudes of people while they are performing certain activities.

---

[1] Louis Wirth, "Urbanism as a Way of Life," *American Journal of Sociology,* **44:**18–19, July, 1938.

EARLY HUMAN ECOLOGY

Classical human ecology came into its own during the 1920s at the University of Chicago. Led by researchers such as Robert Park and Ernest Burgess, the so-called "Chicago school" of sociology produced a prodigious number of studies focused on the spatial-social environment of the city. The interest of the Chicago sociologists was not simply in mapping where groups and institutions were located, but rather in discovering how the sociological, psychological, and moral experiences of city life were reflected in spatial relationships. One member of the Chicago school said that human ecology "deals with the spatial aspects of symbiotic relationships of human beings and human institutions."[2]

Park was interested in how changes in the physical and spatial structure shaped social behavior. He felt that "most if not all cultural changes in society will be correlated with changes in its territorial organization, and every change in the territorial and occupational distribution of the population will effect changes in the existing culture."[3] This postulate of "an intimate congruity between the social order and physical space, between social and physical distance, and between social equality and residential proximity is the crucial hypothetical framework supporting urban ecological theories."[4]

Classical ecological theories of the human community were analogous to evolutionary theories explaining plant and animal development. A person driving from the desert into the mountains finds that different soil, water, and temperature affect the bands of growth of the plants; by analogy, in a drive from a city's business district to its outlying suburbs, there are differing zones of development. In all these theories, competition—the Darwinian struggle for existence—played a core role. In the city, as a consequence of economic competition for prime space, there emerged distinct spatial and social zones. The internal structure of the city thus evolved not as a consequence of direct planning but through competition, which changed areas through the ecological processes of invasion, succession, and segregation of new groups (e.g., immigrants) and land uses (e.g., commercial use displacing residential use).

The heavy emphasis on competition in traditional human ecology, plus the nonsocial nature of some of the variables, increasingly disturbed critics during the late 1930s and the 1940s. The human ecologists' emphasis on urban systems and how people organize themselves socially to adapt to their habitat, particularly to the habitat of cities and their environs, was felt by some not to be sufficiently sociological.

Because of its emphasis on the role of human beings in a physical environment, human ecology for years was considered by many sociologists to be only marginal to the discipline of sociology. Analogies to plant and animal life

---

[2]Roderick McKenzie, *The Metropolitan Community,* McGraw-Hill, New York and London, 1933.
[3]Robert Park, *Human Communities,* Free Press, New York, 1952, p. 14.
[4]Ralph Thomlinson, *Urban Structure,* Random House, New York, 1969, p. 9.

particularly disturbed the critics. The fact that early human ecology was heavily dependent on biology for both concepts and terminology was viewed as a damning fault by some sociologists. As one critic put it, "As the ecologists have admitted, practically all their basic hypotheses have been derived from natural science sources—and the influence of certain geographers and economists is apparent."[5] To such critics the multidisciplinary base of human ecology was a weakness rather than a source of strength. Not the ideas, but where they came from, was considered the more important factor. Fortunately such academic provincialism has few adherents today. Ecological analysis is now recognized as integral to sociology, for, as expressed by the sociologist Leo Schnore, "the central role given to organization—both as dependent or independent variable—places ecology clearly within the sphere of activities in which sociologists claim distinctive competence, i.e. analysis of social organization."[6]

Some other criticisms of traditional ecological theory had more validity. During the late 1930s a "sociocultural" school emerged which placed renewed emphasis on cultural and motivational factors in explaining urban land-use patterns. Scholars of the sociocultural school tend to feel that early human ecology overemphasized economic factors while ignoring social-psychological variables. Milla Alihan, in a broadly based critique of ecological studies, attacked bmth the theory and the application of early human ecology.[7] Another critic, Walter Firey, demonstrated in a study of land use in central Boston that many acres of valuable land in the central business district had been allowed to remain in uneconomic use, such as for example, parks and cemeteries.[8] He suggested that "sentiment" and "symbolism" play an important part in determining spatial distributions, pointing out that the 48-acre common in the heart of downtown Boston had never been developed commercially and that Beacon Hill had largely remained an upper-class residential area in spite of its proximity to the central business district. Unfortunately, mass data such as census data fail to deal with such psychological variables.

Another school of ecologists, the "neo-orthodox," see limitations in the early classical studies but also see much of value. While recognizing the importance of social-psychological variables, the members of the neo-orthodox school are more inclined toward the use of nonattitudinal data. They most frequently use mass data such as censuses, and favor interpretation on the macrosociological level. Sociologists such as Amos Hawley, Otis Dudley Duncan, and Leo Schnore are members of this school. Unlike traditional human ecology, which emphasized competition, the neoorthodox school emphasizes interdependence, as, for example, in their use of the ecological complex (POET).

[5]Warner E. Gettys, "Human Ecology and Social Theory," in George A. Theodorson (ed.), *Studies in Human Ecology*, Row, Peterson, Evanston, Ill., 1961, p. 99.
[6]Leo Schnore, "The Myth of Human Ecology," *Sociological Inquiry*, 31:139, 1961.
[7]Milla A. Alihan, *Social Ecology*, Columbia University Press, New York, 1938.
[8]Walter Firey, "Sentiment and Symbolism as Ecological Variables," *American Sociological Review*, 10:140–148, 1945.

In a reversal of the social-cultural criticisms, William Michelson has taken human ecology to task for giving too much attention to social variables and not enough to the effect of the physical environment on behavior.[9] According to Michelson, "space has been utilized as a *medium* in most human ecology rather than as a *variable* with a potential effect of its own."[10] The wheel has thus come close to full turn since the 1920s.

BURGESS'S GROWTH HYPOTHESIS

The most famous early product of the spatial-organizational concerns of the Chicago school was Burgess's concentric-zone hypothesis, first presented in 1924. This was an attempt to explain why cities grow the way they do.[11] Generations of sociology students have been exposed to the concentric-zone hypothesis—all too frequently in a form that makes it a static picture of city structure. This is unfortunate, for what Burgess was positing was the reorganization of spatial patterns that results from urban *growth,* in contrast to Gideon Sjoberg's picture of a static preindustrial city. Burgess was concerned with how industrial cities change over time from the preindustrial model, in which most of the central land is occupied by a residential elite and there is no clear segregation of city land for specific functional purposes (e.g., no central business district in sense that is characteristic of the western industrial city). His hypothesis is a model, and only a model, of how cities develop spatially as a result of competition.

Burgess noted that in industrial cities factories, homes, and retail shops were not randomly distributed within the urban area. Rather, there was a process of sorting by economic and social factors that resulted in concentration of similar populations and land uses. Competition for space meant that persons, organizations, and institutions were distributed within urban space in a nonrandom fashion. The result is the ecological pattern of American cities.

Within the urban area, competition for land means that the most valuable property—usually centrally located—goes to those functions which can use space intensively and are willing to pay the costs. Costs include not only purchase price but also taxes and nuisance (congestion, noise, pollution, etc.) from other nearby land users. Centrally located land was thus in the past taken up by those economic units, such as department stores, which could effectively use space and required heavy pedestrian traffic. Consumption-oriented commercial activities still tend to be the most centrally located; production-oriented activities are in the next ring out; and residences are the least centralized. Residential uses tend to be pushed out of areas desired for commercial purposes, since residential users

[9]William H. Michelson, *Man and His Urban Environment,* Addison-Wesley, Reading, Mass., 1970, pp. 3–32.
[10]Ibid., p. 17.
[11]Ernest W. Burgess, "The Growth of the City: An Introduction to a Research Project," *Publications of the American Sociological Society,* 18:85–97, 1924.

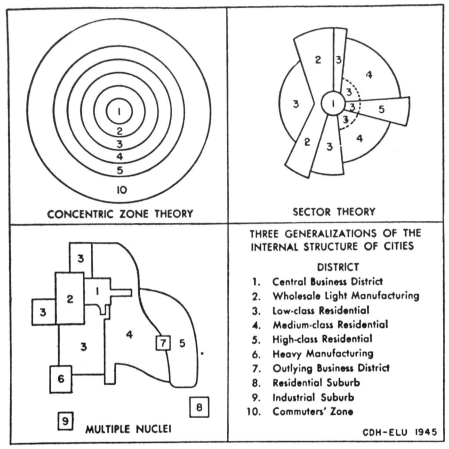

Half a century ago Burgess's zonal hypothesis provided a model of how
American cities grow.

cannot pay the high cost of central location and do not want the pollution, noise,
and congestion of trucks rumbling down the street and a factory next door.

The result is that land values are highest near the center of the city and tend
to decrease as one moves toward the periphery. This means that if housing is to be
centrally located, it must use the land intensively. As a result, the two types of
housing one finds in central areas are high-income, high-rise luxury apartments,
and tenement and slum properties. High-rise apartments escape the pollution
and noise of the city not by moving outward but by moving upward. A
fifteenth-floor apartment not only is quiet and convenient but also has a beautiful
view. Slums are likewise intensive users of space. Even when the rent per room is
low (and often it is not), the rent *per acre* is high.

Consequently, there is a tendency toward an inverse relationship between the value of land and the economic status of those who occupy it. Inner-city slum land is more expensive than land in the suburbs. In inner areas higher land costs are compensated for by density of use. Through crowding, a slumlord can get a great number of rents from a relatively small piece of land. Since land in outer areas is less valuable, less intensive use, such as single-family houses on large lots, is economically feasible. Thus, as you move out from the center of the city toward the periphery, land values and rental per acre tend to grade downward, while the rental per housing unit grades upward.

The Zonal Hypothesis

What Burgess suggested is that cities grow radially in a series of concentric zones or rings. Through a competitive struggle—expressed in ability to pay the cost of land and to tolerate nuisances such as noise and congestion—the most strategic or valuable land goes to the user who can afford to pay for it because of intensive use. Thus the ecologist would expect that the land located at the center of the transportation network, called the "central business district" (CBD), would be occupied by intensive users such as department stores, major business headquarters, and financial institutions. Near such dominant land users, one would also expect to find small establishments catering to their needs. Restaurants and coffee shops, quick printing firms, business supply houses, messenger services, and

Even in 1925, Los Angeles was an automobile city. The photograph shows a view north from Broadway and 8th Street. (United Press International.)

parking lots would be some of the related enterprises one would expect to find in the CBD. One would not expect to find used-car lots or industrial plants occupying the most costly central land.

The most familiar version of Burgess's theory divided the urban area into five zones. They are presented here essentially as they existed during the 1920s, and so they can serve as a baseline from which to examine patterns of change during the past fifty years.

Zone 1 was the central business district: the economic and (usually) the geographic center of the city. The heart of the zone was the retail shopping district, with its major department stores, theaters, hotels, banks, and central offices of economic, political, legal, and civic leaders. Consumption-oriented commercial activities tended to locate at the very core of the CBD, while the outer fringes, with lower rents, contained the wholesale business district: markets, warehouses, and storage buildings. Here also were found the wholesale markets for fresh fruits and vegetables, the markets often looking as if they had been in disrepair for a century—as they sometimes had.

Finally, at the edge of the CBD was the "red-light district," a tawdry area devoted to drink, prostitution, gambling, and such.

The "combat zone" in Boston. American cities have long had sleazy areas specializing in commercial vice, located near the downtown centers. (E. F. Bernstein/Peter Arnold, Inc.)

Red-Light Districts and Combat Zones

In Burgess's day, at one edge of the CBD was located a sleazy but highly profitable area specializing in those activities and enterprises of a disreputable nature which needed accessibility but could not for social reasons be located in the heart of the downtown area. Here were found cheap bars specializing in girls hustling drinks, pornographic movie houses, strip joints, pinball arcades, and bookshops that sold magazines you couldn't buy in the suburbs. Today these areas are dying, partially because of expressways and urban renewal, and partially because they no longer perform an exclusive function. For example, it is no longer necessary to sit in a dirty movie house to see pornographic movies; they can be seen in major theaters in Times Square. Such patterned distribution of commercial vice was clearly noted by the sociologists of the Chicago school during the 1920s.* Such a location offered easy access both to local residents and to visitors staying in the downtown hotels.

Until the period before World War I, every major city in the United States also had a clearly marked "red-light district" just off the central business district that devoted itself to servicing needs which were not met elsewhere. Among the most famous were Storyville in New Orleans, the Tenderloin in San Francisco, and the Levee in Chicago. A turn-of-the-century social reform tract, *If Christ Came to Chicago*, provided a detailed map of every brothel, gambling place, and saloon in the downtown area of that city. The intent was to document the amount of vice, but the map also probably proved useful to many visitors.

The term "red-light district" comes from the red lights which prostitutes put in their front windows to indicate that they were open for business. Numerous European cities such as Amsterdam and Hamburg still have clearly defined red-light districts—lights and all. These areas become quite congested during the evening and the lunch hours. American red-light districts were shut down by local societies for the suppression of vice around the turn of the century. As a result, displaced prostitutes set up business in apartments throughout the city, and the call girl replaced the brothel. With service only a telephone call away, public visibility was a disadvantage rather than an asset.

During the 1970s, a number of cities reintroduced a section of the city devoted to commercial vice, known officially as "adult

---

*See, for example, Walter C. Reckless, "The Distribution of Commercialized Vice in the City: A Sociological Analysis," *Publications of the American Sociological Society,* 20:164–176, 1926.

entertainment districts" but commonly called "combat zones." The combat zone was established in response to citizens' outcry over adult bookstores, pornographic movie houses, massage parlors, and gay pickup bars in residential areas. The Supreme Court has ruled that it is legal to restrict certain activities to a specified zone.

Contemporary combat zones are if anything more tawdry than the old red-light districts. In Boston's combat zone seemingly endless numbers of prostitutes offer their wares. "Nameless bookstores peddle cellophane-sealed magazines with titles like 'Bondage Trios, No. 4' and 'Animal Lovers,' while Pussy Galore's Stag Bar offers its TOTALLY NUDE COLLEGE GIRL REVIEW."†

As the term "combat zone" indicates, the contemporary "sporting life" areas are far from free of violence. Boston's combat zone has become notorious for its homosexual violence, and female prostitutes have been involved in attacks on "johns." A couple of years ago, a Harvard football player on the town with his buddies was stabbed and died as the result of an on-the-street attack by a prostitute. Contemporary combat zones have all the sleaziness but little of the life and color of a Storyville.

† *Newsweek*, December 6, 1976, p. 35.

Today commercial and retail functions in CBDs are losing importance, while the function of providing office space is increasing. (The changing functions of the CBD will be discussed in some detail later in this chapter.) Specialized retailing of nonstandardized goods is still found in the CBD, but with the emergence of large convenient suburban shopping centers sales of general merchandise in central business districts have declined. Some larger stores have remained because of the prestige traditionally associated with the location, but even this is changing. Standardized goods can be sold just as well by regional shopping centers as by downtown stores, and there is less inconvenience in terms of traffic and parking problems.

Chicago has even built an all-new downtown shopping center on Michigan Avenue, barely a mile from the Loop and State Street. The new shopping area centers on the seventy-four-story Water Tower Place housing Marshall Field, Lord and Taylor, and thirty other shops catering to affluent whites. The upper stories of the building are given over to the grande-luxe Ritz-Carlton Hotel. State Street, the old downtown, has in turn increasingly become a shopping center for blacks. Other cities have put all their efforts into reviving the traditional downtown.

On the other hand, office space in the CBD is still in demand. Offices thrive on concentration, which permits the rapid exchange of information. The high-rise office building is well suited to provide the necessary concentration since "within itself, provided an adequate set of elevators, the skyscraper benefits from a facility of traffic which would not be possible if the working area were distributed on ground floor."[12]

American cities have poured millions of dollars into CBDs during the past twenty years with the hope of maintaining them or changing them back into what they once were. Not everyone agrees that this makes sense. As one national authority on planning said, "Many activities are downtown just because they are there, or in response to linkages which disappeared years ago. Many could be served better elsewhere."[13]

Zone 2—the zone in transition—contained both older factory complexes, many from the last century, and an outer ring of deteriorating neighborhoods of tenements. The zone in transition was known as an area of high crime rates and social disorganization.

The zone in transition was where immigrants received their first view of the city. It was the point of entry. Immigrants settled here in the cheap housing near the factories because they could not compete economically for more desirable residential locations. As they moved up in socioeconomic status, they moved out spatially and were in turn replaced by newer immigrants. Thus, a nonrandom spatial structure or pattern emerged, with groups of lower socioeconomic status most centrally located. In Burgess's day, land in the zone of transition was being

---

[12]Jean Gottmann, "The Skyscraper Amid the Sprawl," in Jean Gottmann and Robert Harper (eds.), *Metropolis on the Move*, Wiley, New York, 1967, p. 137.
[13]Edward Ullman, "Presidential Address, The Nature of Cities Reconsidered," *The Regional Science Association Papers and Proceedings*, 9:21, 1962.

held for speculation by landlords who provided only minimum maintenance in the expectation that the CBD would eventually expand into the area. It didn't happen that way, and half a century later many of the same slums remain—others having only recently been destroyed by urban renewal. Chapter 6, City Life-Styles, discusses patterns of life in zones 2 and 3 in greater detail.

Zone 3 was the zone of working people's homes. This was the area settled by second-generation families, the children of the immigrants; it was the place where one moved when one could get out of the inner core. Physically it was (at least in Chicago, Burgess's model) a neighborhood of two-family houses rather than tenements, apartments, or single-family houses. Typically, the father of the family had a blue-collar job in the city. The children, however, planned to marry and move out of the old neighborhood, perhaps to live in tract suburbs (see Chapter 7).

Zone 4 was called the "zone of the better residences." The ring included the area beyond the neighborhood of the second-generation immigrants. This was the zone of the great middle class—small businesspeople, professional people, sales workers, and those holding white-collar jobs. However, even in the 1920s this zone was in the process of changing from a community of single-family houses to one of apartment buildings and residential hotels (that is, there was an invasion of new land-use patterns).

The final zone, zone 5, was the commuter zone. In the early 1920s zone 5, thanks to the commuter railroads and the private automobile, comprised the upper-middle-class and upper-class dormitory suburbs. Here were found the classic suburban life patterns—the husband leaving in the morning for the city and returning in the evening, the wife left to raise the children, maintain the house, and participate in civic affairs. Chapter 7, Patterns of Suburbanization, deals further with this outer zone, which today we call "suburbia."

Invasion and Succession

Change in the city and in community areas comes about through intrusion of a new land use into an area of another land use.

The history of the American city is the story of the invasion of one land use by another. The end result when one group or function finally takes the place of another is called "succession."[14] None of the patterns of land use within a city are permanently fixed, although some zoning laws attempt to fix them. As cities have grown, areas that were once characterized by single-family houses have been converted to apartment, commercial, or industrial use—this is succession. All too frequently such ecological processes are given overlays of values or morals. But the city, if it is viable, is always in the process of changing. Ecological patterns are

---

[14]The term 'function," as used by ecologists— not by most other sociologists—means recurrent patterns of activities which depend on other activities. "Structure," to the ecologist, is the orderly arrangements of the parts that make up the whole: the loci within which the functions or activities are performed.

dynamic rather than static. Changes, it is hoped, are for the benefit of the community. Cities that do not change become historical tourist attractions or stagnant backwaters.

Today the most spectacular instance of invasion and eventual succession is found in the racial changes taking place in the central city. Many whites fear the movement of blacks into a neighborhood because they believe it will threaten the stability of the area. By this they mean that their neighborhood will lose its middle-class character, the quality of the schools will decline, street violence will increase, and the area will generally deteriorate to the level of an inner-city slum. In spite of the evidence that blacks do not bring dilapidation and that the quality of a neighborhood is determined more by the age and condition of the housing and the incomes of the residents than by race, the inaccurate belief that the coming of blacks means the end of a community still persists.

One of the most surprising trends of the 1970s was the return flow of limited numbers of affluent young whites to the central city. The in-migration was not to areas of new housing, but rather to older neighborhoods in a state of some decline. This rehabilitation or "gentrification," of the central-city neighborhoods will be discussed in Chapter 12, Housing Programs and Urban Regeneration.

The process of economic succession, while less dramatic than population changes, can be of equally great long-term importance. Examples are the moving out of industry, the transition within neighborhoods from single-family to multiple-family dwelling units, and the change from residential to commercial land use. Students will note that the last two of these invasion-succession patterns can commonly be found in residential areas abutting growing colleges and universities. Such changes are frequently viewed in moral terms—for example, as the decline of family neighborhoods. Remember though, that a city, if it is viable, is always in a process of change.

The early sociologists of the Chicago school were particularly interested in the segregated areas resulting from the process of selective competition. The Chicago sociologists called these areas "natural areas." They were natural in that they were supposedly the results of ecological processes rather than of planning or conscious creation by any government unit. When zoning laws were established, they generally recognized such natural areas of apartment houses, single-family neighborhoods, commercial areas, warehouse districts, etc., so as to maintain existing land-use patterns. A number of minor sociological classics, such as Wirth's book, *The Ghetto* and Zorbaugh's book *The Gold Coast and the Slum*, deal with so-called natural areas.[15] Today, only a few urban neighborhoods possess sufficient social solidarity and identification to be considered natural communities. (The so-called "defended neighborhoods" discussed in Chapter 6, City Life-Styles, are perhaps a contemporary version of natural areas.)

[15]Louis Wirth, *The Ghetto*, University of Chicago Press, Chicago, 1928; and Harvey W. Zorbaugh, *The Gold Coast and the Slum*, University of Chicago Press, Chicago, 1929.

The Zonal Hypothesis: Criticism and Alternatives

Over the years there has been considerable debate about the adequacy of the zonal hypothesis in analyzing community spatial organization and growth. In the decades since its formulation, Burgess's hypothesis has come under severe criticism on both theoretical and empirical grounds. As Alihan pointed out, Burgess's zonal boundaries "do not serve as demarcations in respect to the ecological or social phenomena they circumscribe, but are arbitrary divisions."[16] This is an overstatement, but it is clear that Burgess's zones are not totally homogeneous units. When evaluating Burgess's theory, we have to keep in mind that he was proposing a "model" or "ideal type" of what American cities would look like if other factors did not intervene—but of course other factors do intervene. Burgess's own statements make it clear that he recognized the effects of distorting factors. He said:

> If radial extension were the only factor affecting the growth of American cities, every city in this country would exhibit a perfect exemplification of these five urban zones. But since other factors affect urban development (including) situation, site, natural and artificial barriers, survival of an earlier use of a district, prevailing city plan and its system of transportation, many distortions and modifications of this pattern are actually found. Nevertheless, so universal and powerful is the force of expansion outward from the city's core that in every city these zones can be more or less clearly delimited.[17]

The question, then, is not whether the zonal pattern is an exact description, for it obviously is not. The question is whether it or other models best describes the growth patterns of American cities.

Alternative Theories. There are two major alternatives to Burgess's hypothesis. Homer Hoyt suggested an alternative to the concentric-zone pattern which became known as the "sector theory."[18] Hoyt suggested that growth took place in homogeneous pie-shaped sectors which extended radially from the center toward the periphery of the city. Residential areas thus extended rapidly along established lines of travel where economic resistance was least. A pattern of land use was said to develop in which each use—industrial, commercial, high-income residential, or low-income residential—tended to push out from the city core in specific sectors or wedges that cut across concentric zones. Thus, high-income housing could radiate from the core in one wedge, a racial ghetto in a second, industrial firms in a third, and working-class residences in a fourth. Hoyt's theory was based on the movement of high-rent districts in 142 American cities between 1900, 1915, and 1936. Since Hoyt did not attempt to locate social influences on

---

[16]Alihan, op. cit., p. 225.

[17]Ernest W. Burgess, "Residential Segregation in American Cities," *Annals of the American Academy of Political and Social Science*, **140**:108, November, 1928.

[18]Homer Hoyt, "The Structure and Growth of Residential Neighborhoods in American Cities," U.S. Federal Housing Administration, Washington, D.C., 1939.

phenomena within the metropolitan area, some sociologists seeking a compromise have used Hoyt's theory to explain residential movement and Burgess's theory to explain social-spatial phenomena.

Another theory of spatial growth rejects the idea of a unicentered city altogether and instead holds that differing land uses have different centers. This "multiple-nuclei" theory was suggested by Chauncy Harris and Edward Ullman.[19] They argued that land-use patterns developed around what were originally independent nuclei. Four factors were said to account for the rise of the different nuclei:

1. Certain activities require specialized facilities. Retailing, for example, requires a high degree of accessibility, while manufacturing needs ample land and railroad service.
2. Like activities group together for mutual advantages, as in the case of the central business district.
3. Some unlike activities are mutually detrimental or incompatible with one another. For example, it is unlikely that high-income or high-status residential areas will locate close to heavy industry.
4. Some users, such as storage and warehousing facilities, which have a relatively lower competitive capacity to purchase good locations, are able to afford only low-rental areas.[20]

In many respects the multiple-nuclei hypothesis better describes the metropolitan area than the central city.

In addition to these three models there is the position that holds that there can be no pattern of common spatial growth. Maurice Davie argued, for instance, that "there is no universal pattern, not even an ideal type."[21] Davie suggested that rather than propping up inadequate hypotheses, sociologists should use their own powers of observation and analysis. He suggested that topographical features such as rivers, lakes, and hills interfere with or take precedence over social or geometrical patterns of growth. He maintained that level land attracts business; higher land and hills attract private residences; low land near water attracts industry; erratic street arrangement encourages central growth; and expressways expedite radial expansion. As Thomlinson points out, the difficulty with these statements is that they are a list of ad hoc descriptions, lacking any theory to bind them together into a compact system of generalizations.[22] Analysis without theory contributes little to knowledge, since it simple states what is While such statements have a surface appeal, particularly when the shortcomings of other

[19]Chauncy Harris and Edward Ullman, "The Nature of Cities," *The Annals of the American Academy of Political and Social Science*, **252**:7–17, 1945.
[20]Harris and Ullman, loc. cit.
[21]Maurice R. Davie, "The Pattern of Urban Growth," in George Murdock (ed.), *Studies in the Science of Society*, Yale University Press, New Haven, Conn., 1937, pp. 131–162.
[22]Thomlinson, op. cit., p. 151.

theories are considered, they provide no hypothesis to be tested and thus cannot be proven right or wrong.

Testing Burgess's Hypothesis. To date, empirical tests have both supported and failed to support Burgess's hypothesis.[23] Haggerty, for example, looked at changes in educational levels from 1940 to 1960 in census tracts in eight large cities, using the statistical technique of Markov analysis. He reported that there was a definite trend through time toward a direct association between an area's social status and its distance from the city center. This tendency toward higher status on the periphery held even in cities whose original or present pattern was for higher-status groups to be more centrally located. Thus, whatever the original pattern, over time there appears to be a movement toward a concentric-zone system.[24]

Schwirian and Matre, on the other hand, found a more mixed pattern in their study of Canada's eleven largest cities.[25] Major research carried out by Schnore for 200 urbanized areas in the United States supports the position that for the oldest and largest cities, there is the predicted pattern of higher socioeconomic status being found in peripheral suburban rather than central-city locations. However, newer and younger cities tend to have populations of higher socioeconomic status in the central city (the preindustrial model).[26] A follow-up study by Palen and Schnore found that for the black population, Burgess's pattern holds in the north and west but not the south.[27]

The internal spatial structure of black city neighborhoods is also related to socioeconomic status. There is a fairly regular progression upward in socioeconomic status as one moves outward from the city center. Schnore's study of social-class segregation within the black communities of twenty-four large cities confirms that the higher social classes disproportionately occupy the more peripheral locations.[28] Marston, however, suggests that his research on variation by socioeconomic status in sixteen American cities shows that in addition to decentralization or distance from the city's center, the age and prestige of the area being entered are of crucial importance. Simply put, black groups of higher socioeconomic status move toward newer areas and areas of higher prestige, even if they are located close to the city center.[29]

---

[23]Leo F. Schnore and Joy K. O. Jones, "The Evolution of City-Suburban Types in the Course of a Decade," *Urban Affairs Quarterly,* **4:**421–422, June, 1969; Joel Smith, "Another Look at Socioeconomic Status Distributions in Urbanized Areas," *Urban Affairs Quarterly,* **5:**423–453, June, 1970; and Lee J. Haggerty, "Another Look at the Burgess Hypothesis: Time as an Important Variable," *American Journal of Sociology,* **76:** 1084–1093, May, 1971.

[24]Haggerty, op. cit., pp. 1084–1093.

[25]Kent P. Schwirian and Marc D. Matre, "The Ecological Structure of Canadian Cities," in Kent P. Schwirian (ed.), *Comparative Urban Structure,* Heath, Lexington, Mass., 1974.

[26]Leo F. Schnore, "The Socioeconomic Status of Cities and Suburbs," *American Sociological Review,* **28:** 76–85, February, 1963.

[27]J. John Palen and Leo F. Schnore, "Color Composition and City-Suburban Status Differences," *Land Economics,* **41:**87–91, February, 1965.

[28]Leo F. Schnore, *The Urban Scene,* Free Press, New York, 1965, chap. 16.

[29]Wilfred G. Marston, "Socioeconomic Differentiation within Negro Areas of American Cities," *Social Factors,* **48:**165–176, December, 1969.

We now know that Davie was mistaken in stating that no clear pattern exists. Research shows that a rough version of Burgess's model does appear to hold, at least for larger and older American cities. As Schnore suggested, "An area might show a certain pattern of city-suburban status differences when it is relatively small and young but evolve toward another, predictable pattern of differences as it grows and ages."

> More specifically . . . (1) smaller and younger central cities in the United States tend to be occupied by the local elite, while their peripheral, suburban areas contain the lower strata; (2) with growth and the passage of time, the central city comes to be the main residential area for both the highest and lowest strata, at least temporarily, while the broad middle classes are overrepresented in the suburbs; and (3) a subsequent stage in this evolutionary process is achieved when the suburbs have become the semiprivate preserve of both the upper and middle strata, while the central city is largely given over to the lowest stratum. In a very rough fashion, of course, this last stage corresponds to the way in which the various social classes are arrayed in space according to the original Burgess (1924) zonal hypothesis.[30]

There is some evidence to support this view.

In a longitudinal study of 198 metropolitan areas, James Pinkerton suggested that the patterns that were true of larger metropolitan areas are increasingly being found in smaller areas as well. As Pinkerton puts it:

> I propose that a new stage is approaching in which the city-ring distribution of classes will no longer vary according to size and age of the metropolis: instead, all areas will house their lower status groups in the city.[31]

Urban Growth outside North America. The concentric-zone pattern of urban growth, which says that there is an increasing status gradient as one goes from city core to periphery, is far less useful in describing patterns of ecological growth outside North America. The zonal pattern has not been the typical pattern of growth in the nonindustrial cities of Asia, Africa, and Latin America.

In contemporary cities with a preindustrial heritage, there appears to be an inverse zonal hypothesis. That is, instead of the poor in the inner core and the elite farther out, the central core is occupied by the elite whereas the disadvantaged fan out toward the periphery.[32] In such cities, it is common to find a pattern in which upper-class and upper-middle-class groups occupy the city proper and poor in-migrants settle on the "suburban" periphery in squatter shantytowns. These *favelas, barriadas, gecekondulas,* or *bustees* can be found on the periphery of almost every major city in Latin America, Africa, and Asia. Several decades of

[30]Leo F. Schnore, *Class and Race in Cities and Suburbs,* Markham, Chicago, 1972, p. 72.
[31]James R. Pinkerton, "The Changing Class Composition of Cities and Suburbs," *Land Economics,* **49:** 468, November, 1973.
[32]Gideon Sjoberg, *The Preindustrial City,* Free Press, New York, 1960, pp. 97–98.

research on Indian, Latin America, and some European cities generally indicate an inverse zonal hypothesis.[33]

As Part Five, Worldwide Urbanization, will detail, cities in the third world differ from North American cities in a number of respects. First, American cities have a commercial industrial base not found in cities that grew primarily as administrative centers. Second, the American city is based upon a highly developed transportation technology which allows relatively rapid movement between central-city offices and suburban residences. Where inexpensive easy transportation is lacking, central-city location is more desirable. (Higher transportation costs are now contributing toward some return of upper-status groups to the city. This topic will be treated later in this chapter.) Finally, there is the inertia to change created by preexisting locational patterns and preferences. Without draconian measures, cities cannot rapidly change their physical characteristics.

Cultural differences also have to be taken into account. As Caplow has stated:

> The literature of urban geography and urban sociology has a tendency to project as universals those characteristics of urbanism with which European and American students are most familiar. Thus, since a large proportion of all urban research has concerned itself with Chicago, there was until recently a tendency to ascribe to all cities characteristics which now appear to be specific to Chicago and other communities closely resembling it in history and economic function. . . .
>
> In the United States, almost all urban growth has been characterized by the rapid and uncontrolled expansion of the community and by unregulated competition for land. To a lesser degree this has been true also of modern Europe.[34]

There is also reason to question just how applicable Burgess's theory is to European cities. Certainly the major cities of Europe that were established before the industrial revolution have an internal distribution of social and economic classes that does not easily fit Burgess's model.[35] In the older cities the elites preempted the prestigious central locations and the poor were forced to live in more peripheral locations. Manufacturing and commerce, when located within the city, were restricted to specific areas. Thus the East End of London was, before the bombing of World War II, composed of small factories, workshops, and poor homes surrounding the dock area. On the other hand, the central and western districts of Westminster, Marylebone, and Kensington have continued to retain their upper-class airs for two centuries in spite of their central location. Moscow, before the Russian Revolution, clearly had the urban structure of a preindustrial city with its inverse zonal pattern.[36]

---

[33]See, for example: Noel Gist, "The Ecology of Bangalore India," *Social Forces,* **35:**356–365, May, 1957; Surinder Mehta, "Patterns of Residence in Poona by Name, Education, and Income," *American Journal of Sociology,* **73:**496–508, March, 1968; Norman Haynes, "Mexico City—Its Growth and Configuration," *American Journal of Sociology,* **50:**295–304, Jafuary, 1945; and Theodore Caplow, "The Social Ecology of Guatemala City; *Social Forces,* **28:**113–135, 1949.

[34]Caplow, op. cit., p. 132.

[35]Francis L. Hauser, "Ecological Patterns of European Cities," in Sylvia F. Fava (ed.), *Urbanism in World Perspective,* Crowell, New York, 1968.

[36]Walter F. Abbott, "Moscow in 1897 as a Preindustrial City: A Test of the Inverse Burgess Zonal Hypothesis," *American Sociological Review,* **39:**542–550, August, 1974.

Within European cities with central land already filled, heavy industry was confined to "suburban" areas where there was sufficient land for the growing factories. Thus, Paris has a concentration of automobile and aircraft factories to the south and east of the city, and the population of such suburban areas is heavily working-class. The continuation of a preindustrial ecological pattern results in social-class distribution and political voting patterns that are quite different from those found in American cities. Some suburban areas of Paris, the so-called "red ring," provide major political support for the Communist Party, while the inner-city middle-class districts vote for the more conservative candidates, exactly the opposite of the American stereotype. For major political protests, protesters are bused in from the suburbs.

Gideon Sjoberg sees this pattern of indentification of high-status groups with central-city location as a persistence of a "feudal tradition" that is not present in American cities. In his view, "In many European cities, including those in the U.S.S.R., the persistence of the feudal tradition has inhibited suburbanization because high status has attached to residence in the central city."[37]

One can question whether a preference for central-city locations, is today "feudalistic" or part of a "feudal tradition." Manhattan doesn't have a feudal tradition, but it still has a pattern of the well-to-do locating in certain areas of the central city. Cosmopolites, whether in London, Paris, or New York, simply prefer to live where they can easily get to work, easily get a drink or a sandwich at 2:00 A.M. It can be argued that, particularly in Europe, upper-status urban populations live in the city because they feel it is an exciting and attractive place to live.

It is possible that the differences in land use between North American industrialized cities and nonindustrial cities elsewhere, particularly in the developing world, may be part of an evolutionary pattern. Leo Schnore suggests that Burgess's concentric-zone scheme as well as preindustrial land-use patterns can be subsumed under a more general theory of residential land uses in urban areas.[38] However, such a theory has yet to be fully developed.

ECOLOGICAL METHODOLOGY

Ecologists, by and large, collect their data in the same manner as other sociologists. What distinguishes them is their preference for operating on the group level rather than the individual level. Ecologists, concerned as they are with the behavior of groups, rely heavily on mass data and are most comfortable with so-called "hard data." Probably the most-used source of data is the United States Census, which provides a wealth of information on the social and economic characteristics of groups, their housing patterns, and their business activities. In the United States the decennial census is supplemented by the monthly Current Population Survey of households across the nation, which yields far more detailed

---

[37]Gideon Sjoberg, "Cities in Developing and in Industrial Societies: A Cross-Cultural Analysis," in Philip M. Hauser and Leo F. Schnore, *The Study of Urbanization*, Wiley, New York, 1965, p. 230.
[38]Schnore, *Class and Race in Cities and Suburbs*, p. 21.

information. The Current Population Survey provides up-to-date information on social and economic questions—detailed information no single researcher or group of researchers could afford to gather. The use of computers enables researchers to obtain previously unavailable information on the characteristics of neighborhoods or groups within urban areas while still protecting the anonymity of the respondents.

The human ecologist's interest is in the characteristics and behavior of groups rather than the attitudes, motivations, and personalities of the individual members of groups. As a result, ecologists use quantitative rather than qualitative data. Also, their use of nonsocial variables such as distance, transportation, and physical environment means that ecologists sometimes have more in common with economists than sociologists such as those doing behavioral studies in the social psychology of small groups.

For example, in a study of occupational stratification and residential location, the Duncans empirically demonstrated the relationship between what one does and where one lives. Spatial distances between occupational groups are closely related to their social distances, whether measured in terms of the conventional indicators of socioeconomic status (income, education, occupation) or in terms of differences in occupational origins. In accordance with accepted ecological theory, they found that the occupational groups most segregated physically were those at the very bottom and very top of the occupational scale. Likewise, residence in low-rent areas and residence near the center of the city were inversely related to socioeconomic status. However, near the middle of the socioeconomic scale, where blue-collar and white-collar clerical occupations meet, the pattern is less clear. Although white-collar clerical workers on the average have considerably lower income than blue-collar craftworkers, and line supervisors, they have a pattern of residential distribution more in common with other white-collar groups. It appears that social status, or prestige, is more important to clerical groups, although their relatively lower income level vis à vis other white-collar groups does set up cross-pressures, as is indicated by a high rent-to-income ratio for clerical workers.[39] A recent replication by Albert Simkus indicates that occupational segregation remains high.[40] Nonwhites in the highest occupational categories are becoming slightly less segregated from whites while those in the lowest occupational categories are becoming slightly more segregated.

Social-Area Analysis and Factorial Ecology

An increasing amount of research to identify urban subareas, how they differ, and how cities are spatially differentiated has been done by researchers using the techniques of social-area analysis or factorial ecology. Both approaches seek to

[39]Otis Dudley Duncan and Beverly Duncan, "Residential Distribution and Occupational Stratification," *American Journal of Sociology*, **60:**493–503, March, 1955.
[40]Albert A. Simkus, "Residential Segregation by Occupation and Race in Ten Urbanized Areas, 1950–1970," *American Sociological Review*, **43:** 81–93, February, 1978.

classify urban phenomena systematically. In some respects social-area analysis can be viewed as an attempt to empirically define "natural areas." The originators of social-area analysis, Eshref Shevky and Wendell Bell, differentiate the structure of urban subareas according to three variables: social rank, urbanization, and segregation.[41] These variables were chosen because they were believed to measure crucial factors distinguishing types of urban populations. The "social rank" index is derived from census-tract measures of occupation and education. The "urbanization" index now generally called "familism," or family form, is derived from measures of the ratio of children to women, the proportion of working women, and the percentage of single-family dwellings. The "segregation index" is now usually called "ethnicity," and is derived from the measurement of spatial isolation of ethnic groups. The assumption is that a larger number of variables can be reduced to the three factors of social rank (socioeconomic status), family status, and ethnic status and three scores produced. It was also assumed that in an industrialized society, these factors would be relatively independent of one another.

The objective is to classify small sections of the city on the basis of their social attributes. Thus the areas are not determined by spatial criteria but rather are established on the basis of the social characteristics of the residents, although the basic unit for analysis still remains the spatially defined census tract of roughly 4,000 persons. The technique is designed to get finer detail and a more accurate map of social space by giving social values to the various census tracts, and to create a picture of the city's pattern from the social areas. It differs from the more conventional ecological position, which first hypothesizes a given spatial-social pattern and then examines the data to discover the degree of fit. The nature of the clustering of variables and the relationships among them are taken as measuring "societal scale," or the degree of the division of labor and social integration. Proponents of the technique argue that it has proved itself valuable in directing attention to social rather than spatial concerns, more adequately delineating subcommunities with the urban area and facilitating comparative and longitudinal study of cities.[42]

Studies have generally tended to confirm that social status, family status, and ethnic status are reasonable factors on which to differentiate subareas of American cities. There is far less agreement on whether these factors are separate from one another.[43]

Social area analysis has not had an uncritical reception. It has been strongly criticized by some ecologists as lacking both a theoretical rationale and empirical utility. A major criticism is that abstract variables of social rank, urbanization, and ethnicity are said to be an arbitrary grouping of several census measures into

[41]Eshref Shevky and Wendell Bell, *Social Area Analysis,* Stanford University Press, Palo Alto, Calif., 1955.

[42]For a number of social-area studies, see Kent P. Schwirian, *Comparative Urban Structures: Studies in the Ecology of Cities,* Heath, Lexington, Mass., 1974.

[43]Maurice Van Arsdol, Jr., Santo F. Camileri, and Calvin F. Schmid, "The Generality of Urban Social Area Indexes," *American Sociological Review,* **23:** 277–284, 1958; and Theodore R. Anderson and Lee L. Bean, "The Shevky-Bell Social Areas: Confirmation of Results and a Reinterpretation," *Social Forces,* **40:**119–124, December, 1961.

another type of index, where the index gives less detail than the component parts from which it was created. Duncan also argues that the discussion of theoretical reasons for choosing particular index variables does not lead to a unique selection of variables or even to a useful criterion for selection, and that there is no clear theoretical relationship between the basic conceptual concepts and the variables used in the index.[44]

Bell and Greer in turn suggest that critics of social-area analysis have applied unreasonable standards, have been uncautious in making conclusions unsupported by data, and have reached different evaluations because of basic differences in intellectual approach.[45]

Thus it can be seen that social-area analysis has both strong supporters and vocal opponents. Its eventual position in urban research is still uncertain.

Factorial ecology differs from social-area analysis in that it does not preselect variables but rather allows them to emerge from the data. This is done through the use of the statistical technique of factor analysis, in which all variables are correlated with one another and are then clustered with other variables that statistically appear to be clustered with and measure the same common factor. A separate factor is said to underlie each cluster of variables.

Factor analysis is a strong statistical tool for reducing a large number of variables to a few factors. Scores of variables may be reduced to half a dozen or so. Factorial ecology is limited more by logical problems of interpretation than by technical problems. Once one identifies a cluster of variables it requires a logical leap to giving the factor a label and interpretation. Whether factorial ecology will be able to overcome this fundamental problem remains open to dispute.[46]

Urbanization and Environment

Our discussion of the ecology of the city would be incomplete without mention of the effect of cities on the physical environment and vice versa. The actual physical shape of cities has been modified by human design. Much of contemporary Boston, for instance, was under water at the time of the Revolution. One of the former underwater zones is known today as Back Bay. Chicago in similar fashion created an Outer Drive and lakefront park system out of filled land, as did New Orleans. In other cases the pumping out of subsurface groundwater and other fluids has led, as in parts of Houston and in Long Beach, California, to subsidence. In the latter case, from 1937 through 1962 some 913 million barrels of oil, 482 million barrels of water, and 832 billion cubic feet of gas were extracted, causing parts of this heavily urbanized area to sink as much as 27 feet.[47]

Cities, of course, are notorious for their effect on air pollution. London in 1952

---

[44]Otis Dudley Duncan, Review of "Social Area Analysis," *American Journal of Sociology*, 61:84–85, July, 1955; and Amos Hawley and Otis Dudley Duncan, "Social Area Analysis: A Critical Appraisal," *Land Economics*, 33:337–345, November, 1957.

[45]Wendell Bell and Scott Greer, "Social Area Analysis and Its Critiques," *Pacific Sociological Review*, 5: 3–9, 1962.

[46]Alfred E. Hunter, "Factorial Ecology: A Critique and Some Suggestions," *Demography*, 9:107–117, February, 1972.

[47]Donald Eschman and Melvin Marcus, "The Geologic and Topographic Setting of Cities," in Thomas Detwyler and Melvin Marcus (eds.), *Urbanization and Environment*, Buxbury Press, Belmont, Calif., 1972, p. 46.

had a disastrous temperature inversion which kept an ever-deadly smog over the city for a week. The smog was so dense that after landing, an airliner was unable to find the terminal, and a vehicle sent out to lead it in also became lost in the smog. More serious was the effect on persons with lung conditions; some 4,000 Londoners died of smog-related causes before the smog lifted. (Today London has strict air pollution controls; the air is actually getting cleaner, and the city has more days of sunshine.)

Cities also create atmospheric changes. Buildings and paved streets retain heat, and urban areas become heat islands, as anyone who has spent a hot summer day in the central city knows. What is less well known is that the condensation nuclei produced by activity in cities increase cloudiness and precipitation over cities.[48]

By covering the ground with buildings, paved roads, and parking lots, urban development in effect waterproofs the land surface. Rainfall cannot be normally absorbed into the soil; instead, storm runoff must be handled by massive systems of storm sewers. The paving over of city and suburban areas, by preventing water absorbtion, actually increases the risk of severe flooding.[49] The relationship between urban residents and their physical environment is much closer than most city dwellers or suburbanites recognize.

[48]Reid Bryson and John Ross, in Detwyler and Marcus, op. cit., p. 63.
[49]Robert Kates, Ian Burton, and Gilbert F. White, *The Environment as Hazard,* Oxford University Press, New York, 1978.

PART THREE

URBAN LIFE

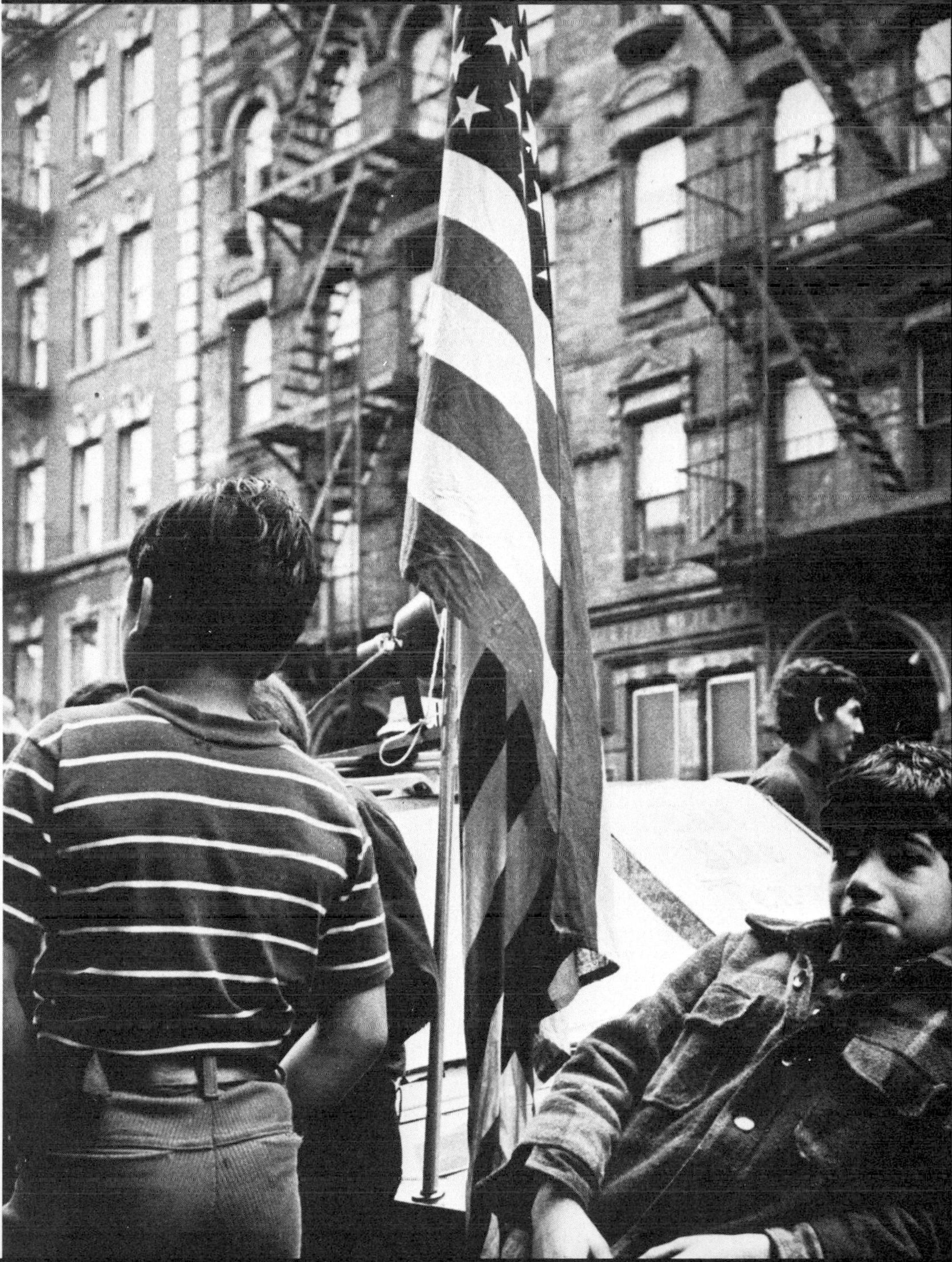

CHAPTER

6

CITY LIFE-STYLES

The city has many attractions
But think of the vices and sins.
When once in the vortex of fashion
How soon the course downward begins

A. Alden, 1887

INTRODUCTION

Life in the city is different. Cities differ from towns and rural areas not only in their size and patterns of economic activities, but also in their tone, texture, and pace. Heterogeneity, variety, and change are assumed, as is a potpourri of different occupations, social classes, cultural backgrounds, and interests. As William Munro expressed it half a century ago:

> The city has more wealth than the country, more skill, more erudition within its bounds, more initiative, more philanthropy, more science, more divorces, more aliens, more births and deaths, more accidents, more rich, more poor, more wise men and more fools.[1]

One of the major questions—if not the major question— confronting urban sociologists and other urban scholars throughout this century is explaining why cities are not only quantitatively larger than towns and villages, but also qualitatively different in terms of life-style. As expressed by the sociologist Louis Wirth:

> The central problem of the sociologist of the city is to discover the forms of social action and organization that typically emerge in relatively, permanent compact settlements of large numbers of heterogeneous individuals.[2]

Certainly urban densities offer an unparalleled number of contacts with others. It has been calculated that in Nassau County, a suburb of New York City, a person can meet 11,000 others within a ten-minute radius of his or her office by foot or car. In Newark one can meet 20,000 persons within this radius; and within midtown Manhattan, 220,000. In such places it is also quite possible that a person would not know a single one of these thousands of others. On the other hand, it is quite unlikely that someone in a small town could walk downtown for ten minutes without running into several persons he or she knew.

The potentialities of urban interaction quite frequently remain unfulfilled. Nor do most urban dwellers seek to realize these potentialities. As Anthony Downs has expressed it:

> It is true that some people want themselves and their children to be immersed in a wide variety of viewpoints, values, and types of people, rather than a relatively homogeneous group. This desire is particularly strong among the intellectuals who dominate the urban planning profession. They are also the strongest supporters of big-city life and the most vitriolic critics of suburbia. Yet I believe their viewpoint— though dominant in recent public discussions of urban problems— is actually shared by only a tiny minority of Americans of any racial group. Almost everyone favors at least some exposure to a wide variety of viewpoints. But experience in our own society and most others shows that the overwhelming majority of middle-class families choose residential locations and schools precisely in order to provide the kind of value-reinforcing experience described above. This is why most Jews live in

---

[1]William B. Munro, "City," in *Encyclopedia of the Social Sciences*, Macmillan, New York, 1930, p. 474.
[2]Louis Wirth, "Urbanism as a Way of Life," *American Journal of Sociology*, **44:**10, July, 1938, p. 9.

predominantly Jewish neighborhoods, even in suburbs; why Catholic parents continue to support separate school systems; and partly why so few middle-class Negro families have been willing to risk moving to all-white suburbs even where there is almost no threat of any harassment.[3]

It should be noted that while it might be reasonable to argue that most upper-middle-class and middle-class families chose "people like us" as neighbors, it is not reasonable to imply that the poor and minorities have similar choices regarding residence in ghettos.

The contrast between urban and rural ways of life was very much a part of urban studies and writings before World War II. The terms used to define the dichotomy sometimes differed, but the underlying content remained remarkably similar; the country represented simplicity, the city complexity .Rural areas were typified by stable rules, roles, and relationships, while the city was characterized by innovation, change, and disorganization. The city was the center of variety, heterogeneity, and social novelty, while the countryside or small town represented tradition, social continuity, and cultural conformity. The stereotype also included a view of city people as possessing greater sophistication but less real warmth and feeling.

Implicit and sometimes explicit in this viewpoint was that modern mass society was destroying close attachments to kin and community. In their place were being substituted uprooted, isolated, and alienated individuals who were free of traditional bonds, but alone in the big city. The best statement of this view is perhaps Charlie Chaplin's classic film *Modern Times,* in which the helpless worker is literally chewed up and spit out by the faceless factory.

Here we won't debate the inherent biases that occur when emotionally loaded terms such as "warmth," "friendliness," and "community" are associated with small places, while terms such as "anonymity," "alienation," and "isolation" appear to be reserved for large cities. What is important for our purposes is to understand the influence such beliefs have had on traditional and contemporary views of urban life.

THEORETICAL FORMULATIONS

Earlier Formulations

The specter of the city as the source of isolation and alienation for the individual, and social problems and collapse for the society, is far from new. It is not a consequence of the urban riots of the 1960s or the urban financial crisis of the 1970s. In attempting to explain emerging forms of social organization, descriptive studies of the 1920s and 1930s were at least implicitly responding to the various ideas that had been propounded by European social theorists as explanations for

---

[3]Anthony Downs, "Alternative Futures for the American Ghetto," in John Walton and Donald E. Carns (eds.), *Cities in Change: Studies on the Urban Condition,* copyright © 1973 by Allyn and Bacon, Boston, pp. 668, 669.

Isolation in the modern city is a recurrent (and probably overworked)
theme in contemporary literature. (Charles Gatewood/ Magnum.)

the momentous social changes which seemed to accompany urbanization.
Classical social theorists such as Ferdinand Tönnies, Karl Marx, Emile Durkheim,
Max Weber, and Georg Simmel all discussed the decline of local attachments and
the rise of mass urban society. The changes were frequently presented in terms of
logical constructs, which sociologists refer to as "ideal types." Among the most
noteworthy of these dichotomies, in terms of its impact upon later urban research,
was Tönnies's elaborate description of the shift from *gemeinschaft*—a community
where ties were based upon kinship—to *gesellschaft*—a society based on
common economic, political, and other interests. Equally important was the
division formulated by the German social theorist Max Weber between "traditional society" and "rational society"—that is, the substitution of formal rules and
procedures for earlier, more spontaneous methods. The prime ideal type of
rational behavior was institutionalized bureaucracy.

Emile Durkheim distinguished between societies based on "mechanical
solidarity" and those based on "organic solidarity." For Durkheim, the old
mechanical social order was one in which all had similar interests and carried out

similar tasks. Organic solidarity of urban places was by contrast based on the division of labor. Durkheim's distinction—which describes the difference between societies based on shared sentiments and tasks and those based on the integrating of complementary but different economic and social functions—has probably had the greatest impact on urban theory.[4] Karl Marx also discussed the dichotomy between the urban and the rural (as quoted in Chapter 1). For Marx, the emergence of urban-based capitalism meant destruction of the older agrarian-based social order. Market-based relations replaced feudal relationships, and industrial capitalism encouraged the exploitation and alienation of urban workers. Eventually this would result in the workers' developing a class consciousness and uniting to overthrow their capitalist oppressors. The workers' new unity was based, though, on common interest rather than being a commonality based on residing in similar areas.

Commonly, comparisons had an implicit time frame in which rural areas represented the past—sometimes in a glorified form (the "good old days")—and the city represented the future, with its technology and division of labor.

Later Formulations

One of the better-known formulations of the dichotomy between urban and rural places and the characteristics common to each was that of the anthropologist Robert Redfield, based upon his study of the differences between what he called "folk" and "urban" societies in Latin America. Redfield never did define "urban life," saying simply that it was the opposite of folk or peasant society. He characterized peasant society thus:

> . . . small, isolated, non-literate, and homogeneous, with a strong sense of group solidarity. The ways of living are conventionalized into that coherent system which we call "a culture." Behavior is traditional, spontaneous, uncritical, and personal; there is no legislation, or habit of experiment and reflection for intellectual ends. Kinship, its relationships and institutions, are the type categories of experience and the familial group is the unit of action. The sacred prevails over the secular; the economy is one of status rather than market.[5]

A few years later (1954) Redfield and Milton Singer developed a more elaborate typology of urban forms that distinguished between cities whose economic institutions were subordinate to religious and traditional norms and those where change and the economic marketplace played major roles. In cities of the first type, the moral order was defined by a literate hierarchy that was guided by tradition. The function of the "orthogenetic" city was administrative and political-religious, with an emphasis on refining and embellishing existing modes of life. Cities of the second type played a "heterogenetic" role, which emphasized rationality, technical criteria, and the economic demands of the marketplace;

---

[4]For a discussion of this and related points, see Paul Wheatley, "The Concept of Urbanism," in Peter Ucko, Ruth Tringham, and G. W. Dimbleby (eds.), *Man, Settlement, and Urbanism,* Schenkman, Cambridge, Mass., 1972, pp. 602–637.
[5]Robert Redfield, "The Folk Society," *American Journal of Sociology,* **52:**53–73, 1947.

tradition and custom were subordinate. These two types of cities are identical in basic characteristics to what are more commonly defined as preindustrial or industrial cities. Redfield and Singer said that the change and conflict which were central to the heterogenetic role led to painful discontinuities between past and future, and to anomie and alienation among the population.[6]

The Limitations of Logical Constructs

The problem with such logical constructs is that they are of only limited utility in empirical research. The opposed categories are so all-encompassing that they tend to result in considerable oversimplification. A related problem is that we often forget that ideal types are created by abstracting certain elements and deliberately heightening their significance, while other elements or factors are ignored. Unfortunately the constructs are sometimes treated not as theoretical formulations but as if they actually existed.

Real life is more complex than such constructs, as research on developing countries amply testifies. It is quite possible for city dwellers to base their economic decisions on modern economic theory and principles while at the same time controlling family life according to established traditional principles. Real people rarely fall into neat all-or-nothing categories.

The Chicago School

American urban scholars were influenced at least implicitly by the previously mentioned European theorists, as well as by the changes they saw occurring in the cities where they lived. The so-called "Chicago school" of sociology developed out of a particularly active group of scholars assembled during the 1920s at the University of Chicago who were concerned with change induced by urbanization. They focused particularly on the way urban life disrupted traditional ties to kin and community. Some of their writings on such diverse phenomena as juvenile delinquency, organized vice, ethnic community ghettos, and the nature of the city's ecological growth have become sociological classics. Writings of the 1920s such as *The Ghetto* (Wirth), *The Gold Coast and the Slum* (Zorbaugh), and *The Polish Peasant in Europe and America* (Thomas and Znaneicki) are descriptive gems giving insights into this unique period in the urbanization of the United States.[7]

Writers of the Chicago school such as Wirth were especially influenced by Georg Simmel's earlier vision of the social-psychological consequences of city life—a life-style where calculated sophistication would replace close and meaningful relationships.[8] Simmel suggested that the pace of city life and the

---

[6]Robert Redfield and Milton Singer, "The Cultural Role of Cities," *Economic Development and Cultural Change,* 3:53–77, 1954.
[7]Louis Wirth, *The Ghetto,* University of Chicago Press, Chicago, 1928; Harvey W. Zorbaugh, *The Gold Coast and the Slum,* University of Chicago Press, Chicago, 1929; William I. Thomas and Florian Znaniecki, *The Polish Peasant in Europe and America,* 5 vols., University of Chicago Press, Chicago, 1918–1920.
[8]Georg Simmel, "The Metropolis and Mental Life," *The Sociology of Georg Simmel,* Kurt H. Wolff (trans.), Free Press, Glencoe, Ill., 1950.

overwhelming number of stimuli in the city result in a state of mental overstimulation and excitement.

Simmel said that there is a constant nervous stimulation produced by shifting internal and external situations and that city dwellers have difficulty in maintaining an integrated personality in a social situation where the reference points are constantly changing: as a result they seek to protect themselves by anonymity and sophistication. Calculating expediency takes the place of affective feelings and personal relationships. One is forced to become blasé in the urban environment in order to protect his or her psyche from overstimulation.

> If so many inner reactions were responses to the continuous external contacts with innumerable people as are those in the small town, where one knows almost everybody one meets and where one has a positive relation to almost everyone, one would be completely atomized internally and come to an unimaginable psychic state.[9]

Contemporary reformulations of Simmel's belief that the city produces "nervous stimulation" among its inhabitants, and of the socially disorganizing and disruptive effects of urbanism as a way of life, can be found in Alvin Toffler's popular and much overrated book *Future Shock* and in Stanley Milgram's use of the concept of "psychic overload."[10] The term "overload" comes from systems analysis, where an overload is said to occur when a system cannot process inputs because they are coming too fast or because there are too many of them. Under such circumstances, adaptations are said to occur. This is essentially Simmel's argument of seventy years earlier, restated using a contemporary analogy.

"Urbanism as a Way of Life"

The classic formulation of how urbanization fosters innovation, specialization, diversity, and anonymity is Louis Wirth's essay "Urbanism as a Way of Life."[11] According to Wirth, the city created a distinct way of life—called "urbanism"—which is reflected in how people dress and speak, what they believe about the social world, what they consider worth achieving, what they do for a living, where they live, whom they associate with, and why they interact with other people.

Wirth further suggested that urbanization and its components— size, density, and heterogeneity—are the independent variables which determine urbanism, that is, urban life-styles. Moreover, the relationship is linear: the larger, denser, and more heterogeneous the city, the more prevalent is urbanism as a way of life.

As a way of life, urbanism was viewed by Wirth (and others) as economically successful but socially destructive:

> The distinctive features of the urban mode of life have often been described sociologically as consisting of the substitution of secondary for primary contacts, the

---

[9]Ibid., p. 415.
[10]Alvin Toffler, *Future Shock*, Random House, New York, 1970; Stanley Milgram, "The Experience of Living in Cities," *Science*, **167**:1461–1468, March 13, 1970.
[11]Wirth, "Urbanism as a Way of Life," op. cit.

weakening of bonds of kinship, the declining social significance of the family, the disappearance of the neighborhood, and the undermining of the traditional basis of social solidarity. All of these phenomena can be substantially verified through objective indices.[12]

Some characteristics of the urban way of life as described by Wirth are:

1. An extensive and complex division of labor replacing the artisan who participated in every phase of manufacture.
2. Emphasis on success, achievement, and social mobility as morally praiseworthy. Behavior becomes more rational, utilitarian, and goal-oriented.
3. Decline of the family (increased divorce) and weakening bonds of kinship, with previous family functions transferred to specialized outside agencies (schools, health and welfare agencies, commercial recreation).
4. Breakdown of primary groups and ties (neighborhood) and substitution of large formal secondary group-control mechanisms (police, courts). Traditional bases of social solidarity and organization are undermined, leading to social disorganization.
5. Relation to others as players of segmented roles (bus driver, shop clerk) rather than as whole persons; i.e., there is a high degree of role specialization. Utilitarian rather than affective relationships with others. Superficial sophistication as a substitute for meaningful relationships leading to alienation.
6. Decline of cultural homogeneity, and diversity of values, views, and opinions. The emergence of subcultures (ethnic, criminal, sexual) that are at variance with the larger society. Greater freedom and tolerance, but also decline in sense of common community.
7. Spatial segregation into disparate sections on the basis of income, status, race, ethnicity, religion, and so on.[13]

Not surprisingly, many of these read like a catalog of contemporary ills.

The effect of urbanism on institutions such as the family can be severe. As Neil Smelser has put it:

> One consequence of the removal of economic activities from the family-community setting is that the family itself loses some of its previous functions and becomes a more specialized agency. As the family ceases to be an economic unit of production, one or more members leave the household to seek employment in the labor market. The family's activities become more concentrated on emotional gratification and socialization. . . .
>
> The social implications of these changes in family life are enormous. The most fundamental of these implications—imposed mainly by the demands for mobility of the family—is the individuation and isolation of the nuclear family. If the family has to move about through the labor market, it cannot afford to carry all of its relatives with it, or even to maintain close, diffuse ties with extended kin. Thus the ties with

[12]Ibid., p. 21.

[13]For a discussion of Wirth's and others' views on community, see Dennis E. Poplin, *Communities,* 2d ed., Macmillan, New York, 1979, pp. 27–47.

collateral kinsmen begin to erode; few generations live in the same household; newly married couples set up new households, and leave the elders behind.[14]

Cultural Lag

William F. Ogburn suggested that the changes Wirth saw taking place, particularly the social disorganization, were due to a "cultural lag" in adjustment of values and beliefs, etc.—that is, the group's social heritage.[15] Difficulty and disorganization, Ogburn suggested, occur when changes in the technical material parts of society outpace those of the nonmaterial culture.

In industrial society, technology and technological problem solving increase at a far faster rate than in the nonmaterial culture. Some elements of the social culture adapt to new technologies fairly easily, but others change only slowly or resist change. The result is a period of maladjustment, conflicting pressures, strain, and psychological disorder. The weakness of the cultural-lag theory is the assumption that technology is always the first to change. Changing social beliefs and practices (e.g., Supreme Court decisions) can have considerable impact on a society.

REEVALUATION OF URBANISM AND SOCIAL DISORGANIZATION

Given the momentous changes taking place in the growing, immigrant-crowded, industrializing cities of the first part of this century, it is not surprising that writers on the city tended to emphasize the negative rather than the positive aspects of urban change. The alienation, atomization, and social isolation of the city were stressed in studies dealing with juvenile delinquency, suicide, mental illness, and divorce; and a whole subfield was developed in sociology under the value-loaded title "social disorganization."

We now know that the sociologists of Wirth's day (the 1930s), in their fascination with the socially disorganizing aspects of urban life, largely overlooked the role of the city as a social integrator and underestimated the strength of traditional ways of life. William F. Whyte's excellent study of street life in an Italian slum of Boston just before World War II was one of the very few to stress the sociocultural continuity and the vitality of traditional culture.[16] More than forty years later, we are still predicting the imminent disappearance of these same traditional life-styles. For example, the ethnic affiliations that were supposed to have vanished long ago, and are continually being pronounced dead, seem somehow to be constantly reviving. Ethnic identification is currently undergoing a revival.

Wirth's essay, "Urbanism as a Way of Life," like Simmel's earlier work, suffers from a failure to recognize the degree to which Wirth's generalizations were limited both by historical time and by the differing composition and variety

---

[14]Neil J. Smelser, *Sociology: An Introduction*, Wiley, New York, 1967, pp. 720–721.
[15]William F. Ogburn, *Social Change*, Viking Press, New York, 1938.
[16]William F. Whyte, *Street Corner Society*, University of Chicago Press, Chicago, 1943.

Neighborhood and community life is not a thing of the past—a street fair in Boston. (J. R. Holland/Stock, Boston.)

of urban areas. Herbert Gans questions Wirth's diagnosis of the city as producing anomic, goal-oriented, segmented role relationships on three grounds. First, Gans says, "Since the theory argues that all of society is now urban, *his analysis does not distinguish ways of life in the city from those in other settlements within modern society.*"[17] He suggests that Wirth's "urbanite" is a depersonalized and atomized member of a mass society, a representative of urban-industrial society

---

[17]Herbert J. Gans, "Urbanism and Suburbanism as Ways of Life: A Re-evaluation of Definitions," in J. John Palen and Karl Flaming (eds.), *Urban America,* Holt, Rinehart and Winston, New York, 1972, p. 185.

A Note on Density

Urban crowding and high density have long been seen as the cause of social pathology. Historically, high density and crowding have been cited as a cause of epidemics, contagion, crime, and moral degradation.* The engravings of Hogarth, the novels of Dickens, and primitive health statistics all tell the same unfortunate tale—high density means disorganization and disease. As graphically expressed by Charles Dickens:

> They walked on, for some time, through the most crowded and densely inhabited part of the town; and then, striking down a narrow street more dirty and miserable than any they had yet passed through, paused to look for the house which was the object of their search. The houses on either side were high and large, but very old, and tenanted by people of the poorest class: as their neglected appearance would have sufficiently denoted, without the concurrent testimony afforded by the squalid looks of the men and women who, with folded arms and bodies half doubled, occasionally skulked along. A great many of the tenements had shop-fronts; but these were fast closed, and mouldering away; only the upper rooms being inhabited. Some houses which had become insecure from age and decay, were prevented from falling into the street, by huge beams of wood reared against the walls, and firmly planted in the road; but even these crazy dens seemed to have been selected as the nightly haunts of some houseless wretches, for many of the rough boards which supplied the place of door and window, were wrenched from their positions, to afford an aperture wide enough for the passage of a human body. The kennel was stagnant and filthy. The very rats, which here and there lay putrefying in its rottenness, were hideous with famine.†

More recently almost every social evil—air pollution, the loss of community, the lack of response of neighbors to cries for help—has been attributed to urban density and overcrowding.‡

Experimental animal studies tend to support the view that high density and crowding produce a long list of physical and behavioral pathologies. At present we probably know more about the behavior of rats under conditions of crowding than we do about that of city dwellers. John Calhoun's now-famous article "Population Density and Social Pathology" indicates that in experiments with Norway rats, pathological states develop under conditions of crowding even when there is an abudance of food and freedom from disease and

---

*See A. D. Biderman, M. Louria, and J. Bacchus, *Historical Incidents of Extreme Overcrowding*, Bureau of Social Science Research, Washington, D.C., 1963.
†Exerpt from Charles Dickens, *The Adventures of Oliver Twist*, Chapman & Hall, Ltd., London, pp. 42–43.
‡See James Q. Wilson, "The Urban Unease," *The Public Interest*, 12:25–39, 1968; James A. Swan, "Public Responses to Air Pollution," in Joachim F. Wohlwill and Daniel H. Carson, *Environment and the Social Sciences*, American Psychological Association, Washington, D.C., 1972, pp. 66–74; Robert Buckout, "Pollution and the Psychologist: A Call to Action," in Joachim F. Wohlwill and Daniel H. Carson, *Environment and the Social Sciences*, pp. 75–81; and B. Latane and J. M. Darley, *The Unresponsive Bystander: Why Doesn't He Help?* Appleton-Century-Crofts, New York, 1970.

predators.§ In Calhoun's experiment, a behavioral sink developed in which infant mortality increased, females didn't build proper nests or carry infants to term, and homosexuality and even cannibalism occurred. When the experiment was terminated, the rat population was well on the way to extinction.

Unfortunately, there is a tendency to try to transfer findings from animal studies, where they apply, to human populations, where they do not. Sometimes there is even an assumption that what holds for Norway rats automatically applies to humans. For example, one writer suggests:

> The implications of animal and human studies are clearcut. Just as the offspring of frustrated mother rats, part of whose pregnancy was spent trapped in problem boxes with no exits, carried an emotional disturbance throughout their own lives, so too many children of frustrated human mothers, trapped by urban slums, show behavioral manifestations of emotional disturbance.¶

This analogy repeats the "commonsense" view of the effects of density and crowding.

The problem is that the commonsense view is both simplistic and inaccurate. A considerable body of sociological and psychological research on density indicates that it does *not* have any clear and definite association with human pathology.** Density research is a classic case: What everyone "knows to be true" is simply not being supported by the data.

What is clear is that one's social background and experiences play a major role in how "high-density" is defined. Upper-middle-class populations, for example, have been socialized to view crowding as a problem, and space and separation as natural and necessary. Community studies of working-class populations indicate, on the other hand, that residents of city neighborhoods often view high density as a positive sign of community vitality rather than an indication of social disorganization.†† Contact with others is viewed positively, as a sign of belonging, rather than negatively, as a sign of crowding. Inner-city youngsters from such areas are more comfortable being with others than being alone. Gans reports how social workers in the West End of Boston were forced to abandon an

§John B. Calhoun, "Population Density and Social Pathology," *Scientific American*, **206**:139–148, February, 1960.

¶Shirley Foster Hartley, *Population Quantity vs. Quality*, Prentice-Hall, Englewood Cliffs, N. J., 1972, p. 76.

For an overview of available research, see Claude Fischer, Mark Baldassare, and Richard Olshe, "Crowding Studies and Urban Life: A Critical Review," *Journal of the American Institute of Planners*, **41:406–418, November, 1975; and Jonathan Freedman, *Crowding and Behavior*, Viking, New York, 1975. For one of the best recent studies, see Harvey M. Choldin and Dennis Roncek, "Density, Population Potential, and Pathology: A Block Level Analysis," *Public Data Use*, **4**:19–30, July, 1976.

††Herbert J. Gans, *The Urban Villagers*, Free Press, Glencoe, Ill., 1962; Gerald Suttles, *The Social Order of the Slum*, University of Chicago Press, Chicago, 1968; and Michael Young and Peter Willmott, *Family and Kinship in East London*, Penguin Books, Baltimore, 1962.

experimental summer program that gave inner-city boys a chance to spend a vacation exploring nature at Cape Cod.‡‡ The boys could not understand why anyone would want to visit, much less live in, such a lonely spot. The boys were accustomed to, and thrived on, crowded and noisy street life. They wanted to be where the action was and were emotionally unprepared for wide vistas and open unused space.

The difference between the perceptions of middle-class and working-class populations can also be seen in how the two groups orient themselves to a common spatial feature, such as streets. For working-class and lower-class urban groups, much daily activity takes place in the streets; streets are seen as living space, a place to congregate and gather with others in the neighborhood. Streets serve a vital social function. Middle-class groups, on the other hand, are far less likely to see the streets as performing a social function. In their view streets are corridors to be used to travel from place to place; and they think that people should be kept off the streets, lest they interfere with rapid movement.

To residents of crowded and lively central-city areas, suburbs often appear to be cold and unfriendly places, where one does not easily and spontaneously meet friends and neighbors.

Contrary to the common assumption, density or crowding does not necessarily have either a negative or positive impact on urban life. It all depends on how the level of crowding is *socially* defined. As a side note, urban densities have been decreasing for fifty years, but there has been no corresponding decrease in urban social problems.

‡‡Gans, op. cit.

rather than of the city itself. Second, there isn't enough evidence to either prove or deny the posited relationship between size, density, heterogeneity, and social disorganization. Third, even if the causal relationship exists, many city dwellers are effectively isolated from it. Gans suggests that Wirth's characterization of urban life applies only to some inner-city residents, while other city dwellers— such as cosmopolites and suburbanites—pursue a different way of life. Residents of the outer city, Gans suggests, have a life-style that resembles the life-style of suburbanites far more than the behavior patterns of inner-city residents. These outer-city neighborhoods, and even most inner-city populations, consist "mainly of relatively homogeneous groups, with social and cultural moorings that shield [them] fairly effectively from the suggested consequences of number, density, and heterogeneity."[18]

Research done in San Francisco by Wendell Bell found that for many city dwellers, family and kinship bonds were far from dead, and relatives continued to be a significant source of socializing and support.[19] In his view, impersonal secondary-group contacts have not supplanted neighborhood and kin, but rather primary-group and secondary-group contacts both continue to exist. Mental health also appears to be better in urban than in rural areas.[20]

DIVERSE LIFE-STYLES

While cities generally have the highest rates of social problems, this is not the same as saying that all central-city populations or areas have high rates of alienation and disorganization. Some groups thrive in central-city locations. Inner-city working-class ethnic groups, for instance, live lives that, far from being disorganized, are probably more organized and integrated than those of other city dwellers. Characterizations of depersonalization, isolation, and social disorganization simply do not fit. Gans suggests that inner-city populations can be grouped in five classifications:

1. "Cosmopolites"
2. Unmarried or childless people (singles)
3. "Ethnic villagers"
4. The "deprived"
5. The "trapped" and downwardly mobile[21]

As you read the following pages, keep in mind that these classifications or categories are not descriptions of any particular person but rather "ideal types" or

[18]Ibid., p. 186.
[19]Wendell Bell, "The City, the Suburb, and a Theory of Social Choice," in Scott Greer et al. (eds.), *The New Urbanization*, St. Martin's Press, New York, 1968, pp. 137–143; and Thomas Drabek. et al.. "The Impact of Disaster on Kin Relationships," *Journal of Marriage and Family*, 37(3): 481–484, August, 1975.
[20]See Leo Srole's comments in Tim Hacker, "The Big City Has No Corner on Mental Illness," *New York Times Magazine*, December 16, 1979, p. 136.
[21]Gans, op. cit., p. 186.

logical constructs useful for purposes of comparison. Also remember that we are speaking of the inner city rather than the city as a whole; in the city as a whole, the middle class is the largest population group. For our purposes the last two categories—the "deprived" and the "trapped"—can be combined into one: "outcasts."

Cosmopolites

Cosmopolitan urbanites in larger cities often choose to remain in the city because of its convenience and cultural benefits. They include artistically inclined persons such as writers and artists, as well as intellectuals and professionals, who are attracted to the center of the city. They tend to be single, or if married, childless. The numbers in this group were augmented during the 1970s by the flow of some young and reasonably affluent whites returning to revitalized central-city neighborhoods. Demographically, such newcomers tended to be young married adults, childless or with preschool children, white, employed in managerial-level positions, and making middle- or upper-middle-class incomes. Cosmopolites or those choosing to return to the city hardly fit the stereotype of the anomic and isolated central-city dweller. (For a discussion of the revitalization of central-city neighborhoods, see Chapter 12, Housing Programs and Urban Regeneration.)

Singles

Another population group that is in the central city voluntarily is young singles. The unmarried and childless between the ages of roughly twenty and thirty remain in the city because it is both convenient to their jobs and, most important, is where other singles are found. Community roots and local ties of kinship are relatively rare among singles. Their stay in the city does not usually represent a decision to settle permanently in a neighborhood, but rather a reflection of a stage in the life cycle. The city was where they resided after completing their education and before they married, had children, and became suburbanites. The unanswered question today is what percentage of young singles will choose to remain in revitalized city neighborhoods rather than move to the suburbs.

In addition to younger singles, central-city locations have an attraction for those somewhat older who are divorced or who chose not to marry. Subcommunities of gays also almost invariably chose central-city locations.

The singles scene is supposedly composed of endless numbers of would-be Joe Namaths and "fly me" stewardesses who nightly crowd the city's singles bars and discos looking for one-night stands without any emotional commitments or hangups. But the realities of single life in the city are more humdrum. Each year colleges turn out large numbers of more or less similar young graduates who are more or less committed to a career. The marriage market removes some, who settle in apartment areas or move directly to the suburbs. Others follow the available job opportunities to the city. Singles in cities are trying to cope with the everyday problems of making friends, getting some satisfaction from their jobs, finding a decent place to live, and at the same time finding social partners and eventually a mate. They are far from being social or economic radicals. They are trying to achieve essentially middle-class happiness and essentially middle-class material goals without being able to rely on many of the usual institutional supports for their activities.

"Singles only" apartment complexes emerged first in California and then elsewhere to meet the housing and social needs of this group. In most places, buildings supposedly for young singles contain a good proportion of residents who are neither single nor young. But life in the complexes still has an almost self-conscious quality something like that of a college dormitory. Observers have commented on the desire to remain at the adolescent stage in which there are few duties or responsibilities. Some singles doubtless see the complexes as a welcome escape from the encounters and perhaps failures to be faced outside.

Joyce Starr and Donald Carns conducted some seventy semistructured face-to-face interviews with singles in their early twenties or mid-twenties who had opted to come to Chicago to work.[22] Most single people do not live in singles complexes, and the Chicago data indicate that housing and neighborhood are not significant in establishing meaningful social interaction, either friendships or dating relationships. Neighbors do not get to know one another; the idea of "turf" or territory, while it is crucial to the understanding of some urban minorities, "is not a useful concept in understanding the lifestyles of this large and growing urban subpopulation."[23] An exception appears to be housing complexes built particularly for singles. Research by Gerda Wekerle at Chicago's Carl Sandburg Village indicates that in an age-segregated environment where people also share a similar social class and life-style, residents do come to get acquainted and interact with each other.[24]

Singles bars and discos, according to some reports, serve as substitutes for a community. Here liberated men and women establish the highly transitory relationships that are said to characterize the singles world. Available data, however, indicate that this idea is considerably exaggerated. Interest in, and attendance at, singles bars evidently decreases with the time one spends in the city.[25]

Most singles have few community roots. They do not belong to organizations and view membership in organizations as a poor way of meeting possible mates, since many of the organization's members are likely to be married. Where most people do meet others, make friends, and meet potential mates is on the job. One's work takes up most of the day; it is the place where one is most likely to meet others of similar background and interests in a setting that facilitates easy familiarity. Of course, one may not meet others of the same age and marital status on the job, but if one does, the odds are that friendship will develop. The workplace provides the most frequent institutional setting for meeting friends and possible mates.

[22]Joyce R. Starr and Donald E. Carns, "Singles and the City: Notes on Urban Adaptation," in John Walton and Donald E. Carns (eds.), Cities in Change, Allyn and Bacon, Boston, 1973, pp. 280–292.

[23]Ibid., p. 291.

[24]Gerda R. Wekerle, "Vertical Village: Social Contacts in a Singles High-Rise Complex," paper presented at a 1975 meeting of the American Sociological Association, San Francisco.

[25]Starr and Carns, op. cit., p. 288.

The disappearance of ethnic neighborhoods has been predicted for over half a century, yet they continue to persist. The Chinatown pictured is in New York City. (Jim Cron/Monkmeyer.)

Ethnic Villagers

Among the various inner-city residents, the working-class ethnic populations probably lead the most highly organized lives. Far from being characterized by depersonalization, isolation and social disorganization, working-class neighborhoods, particularly when they are dominated by a single ethnic group, often exhibit a high degree of social interaction among residents. Those living in such organized inner-city neighborhoods have been referred to as "urban villagers" or "urban provincials."[26] Such names are used to suggest that they are in, but not of, the city; they are urban in their residential patterns but not in their thought processes. Such areas, whatever their predominant group, embody more of the

[26]See Herbert J. Gans, *The Urban Villagers*, Free Press, Glencoe, Ill., 1962.

family- and peer-oriented provincialism of a tight, homogeneous small town than the attitudes of an impersonal large city. An unresolved question is whether these tight ethnic urban neighborhoods are only anachronistic survivals from earlier times or are representative of contemporary urban life.

Ethnic villagers, although they live in the city, try to isolate themselves from what they consider to be the harmful effects of urban life, preferring to live in their own tight-knit ethnic neighborhoods. They desperately resist the encroachment of other ethnic or racial groups. Such primarily working-class neighborhoods place heavy emphasis on kinship and primary-group relationships and resent the secondary formal control mechanisms of the larger city. Some of these Italian, Puerto Rican, Mexican, or eastern European enclaves are no larger than a census tract, but some are quite extensive. Chicago and Detroit both claim the largest Polish population outside Warsaw; Cleveland's Hungarian population is said to be second only to that of Budapest.

To some people, urban villagers represent only "bypassed preindustrial locals" who have been left behind by modern society. As put by Melvin Webber: "Here in the Harlems and South Sides of the nation are some of the last viable remnants of preindustrial societies where village styles are nearly intact."[27]

Outsiders sometimes mislabel such areas as "slums" because the buildings are old and may not appear from the exterior to be in good condition. Often the area is in better condition than it appears when viewed from the window of a passing automobile on the suburban-bound expressway, but even when an area is physically deteriorated, its social fabric may still be strong.[28] Urban villagers are not committed to urban living. Rather, they remain in older neighborhoods in spite of the obvious physical limitations and conditions of the housing because moving to the suburbs would mean leaving the tight-knit social neighborhood. If they could take neighbors and social atmosphere with them, they would happily become suburbanites. Since they can't, they voluntarily remain inner-city residents. The mother of six children living in the Near West Side of Chicago clearly expressed the affection working-class urban villagers have for their neighborhoods:

> I got everybody on this block that would do something for me. If one of my children were sick, I wouldn't feel any compunction of waking up the man across the street to take me to the hospital. He expects this. He would expect me to do this for him.
>
> One night I took my daughter to the hospital at eleven o'clock at night. Next morning, at least eight people on my way to work asked me how my daughter was. When I got home it was worse than that. It took me an hour to get home. Because everybody wanted to know about Christine. Did the doctors do anything? Did I need anything? I get a cheery hello from everybody. Old ladies, when I get dressed to go out or to work: "Oh, how nice you look." Old and young blend together here. I have friends who live in the suburbs, they wouldn't dare be out in the dark.
>
> I know friends of ours, who've moved away from here, who bitterly lament their predicament now. They've got beautiful homes—I guess the city planners would say

---

[27]Melvin M. Webber, "The Post-City Age," in J. John Palen (ed.), *City Scenes*, Little, Brown, Boston, 1977, p. 314.
[28]See, for example, William F. Whyte, op. cit.; and Gerald D. Suttles, *The Social Order of the Slum*, University of Chicago Press, Chicago, 1968.

they've done better for themselves. Their plumbing works, their electricity is good, their environment is better—supposedly. If you're a type of person who considers a mink stole and a fountain in your living room and big bay windows, front lawn beautifully kept, all these things mean something to you, well . . . to me, we're more concerned about people.[29]

The next pages will spend some time on working-class neighborhoods and norms. Use this material to compare the type of neighborhood described with neighborhoods with which you are personally familiar.

Neighborhood Characteristics. *Territoriality.* Inner-city neighborhoods generally have a strong sense of territory. Studies of inner-city working-class areas often find that the residents, although living near the center of a large metropolis, still manage to remain physically, socially, and psychologically isolated from the rest of the urban area.[30] The city outside the neighborhood is viewed as a foreign land—and a potentially hostile one—into which one ventures only when necessary. Even in cosmopolitan New York there are people living in Brooklyn who have never been to Manhattan and have no real desire ever to go there.

Ecologically settled ethnic areas are usually characterized by *ordered segmentation.* That is, each ethnic group carefully and specifically defines its territory. Boundaries between different ethnic groups, while invisible to the outsider, are well known and respected by the local residents. Gerald Suttles in his study of the Taylor Street area of Chicago points out that the Italian, Mexican, Puerto Rican, and Black groups living in the area have their own provincial enclaves and conduct their daily lives within these known borders.[31] Within these territorial units, one is safe and comfortable. Outsiders are made to feel unwelcome unless they are there as guests. The use of community facilities such as churches and parks is exclusively for one group. The movement of one ethnic or racial group into what is known as the social area of another is likely to lead to violence or the threat of violence.

Awareness and concern over territory are not limited to public or semipublic facilities. Business establishments—particularly bars, but even grocery stores—are viewed by local inhabitants as being the exclusive property of a single minority group. In the words of Suttles:

> When someone from outside the area or from another ethnic group enters, the proprietor and regular customers view them with great suspicion and, in some cases, use *ad hoc* measures to insure their safety. Sometimes they will simply wait for the intruder to get his bearings and leave. If that fails the proprietor may eventually get around to asking what he wants. In the meantime, everyone in the store stops and stares. The treatment of regular customers, of course, is exactly the opposite. Commercial relations with these people are intimate and all economic transactions are buried in the guise of friendship and sentiment. In large part this is the reason

---

[29]Quoted in Studs Terkel, *Division Street: America,* Pantheon Books (Avon ed.), New York, 1967, p. 198.
[30]For an examination of how urban workers view their own lives and achievements, see Richard Sennett and Jonathan Cobb, *The Hidden Injuries of Class,* Vintage Books, New York, 1973.
[31]Suttles, op. cit.

Categories of Local Communities

A number of types of local communities have been defined in the professional literature, among which are:

1. The defended community
2. The community of limited liability
3. The expanded community of limited liability
4. The contrived or conscious community*

1. The defended neighborhood is an area in which local residents feel threatened by external change—be it an invasion of another ethnic or racial group, or an attempt to prevent destruction by external forces, such as urban renewal or an expressway through the neighborhood.† "Functionally, the defended neighborhood can be conceived of as the smallest spatial unit within which co-residents assume a relative degree of security on the streets as compared to adjacent areas."‡ The defended neighborhood thus is the place where people feel safe and secure. As such, it may or may not have a name or be recognized by government. Those within the defended neighborhood assume a common residential identification and identity.

2. The community of limited liability was first described by Morris Janowitz and later elaborated on by Scott Greer.§ The concept of the community of limited liability emphasizes the voluntary and limited involvement of residents in the local community. The amount of emotional investment in the area, or investment of time or resources, is dependent on the degree to which the community meets the needs of individuals. If the needs are not met, the individual might withdraw psychologically and socially, if not physically. Communities of limited liability usually have names and boundaries which are recognized by local planning agencies and government. Local organizations and particularly the local community press have a vested interest in maintaining the identity and boundaries of the area. The community of limited liability thus is defined by commercial interests and government agencies rather than coming from internal community awareness, as with the defended neighborhood.

3. The expanded community of limited liability is more fragmented

---

*For information and discussion of types of communities, see Dennis E. Poplin, *Communities*, 2d ed., Macmillan, New York, 1979.
†For an example of how a Boston neighborhood fought off such destruction, see Alan Lupo, Frank Colcord, and Edmund P. Fowler, *Rites of Way*, Little, Brown, Boston, 1971.
‡Gerald Suttles, *The Social Construction of Communities*, University of Chicago Press, Chicago, 1972, p. 57.
§Morris Janowitz, *The Community Press in an Urban Setting*, University of Chicago, Chicago, 1952; and Scott Greer, *The Emerging City*, Free Press, New York, 1962.

and diffuse than the community of limited liability. The expanded community may take in whole sections of the city such as the east side or the north side. As such, it has little real cohesion as an actual unit.

4. Contrived or conscious communities are areas—new or developing—in which builders, financers, public agencies, and residents alike set out to consciously create a community image. Boundaries are clearly laid out, and the housing in the area may even be identical—e.g., all apartments or all townhouses or all public housing. The name of the area is usually given by the builder rather than emerging from the community. Conscious communities tend to be more homogeneous than other communities. Residents in the development may all be young singles, family types, or elderly. Ethnic and racial conformity or similarity of social class is also common in both urban and suburban conscious communities.

they cannot tolerate the presence of strangers from another ethnic group. Among themselves the customers set aside their public face and disclose much of their private life to one another.[32]

Private information is too intimate to be revealed to potentially hostile strangers. In establishments such as small snack shops that may be near the boundary line between different ethnic groups, the problem of privacy may be solved by taking turns. One group of teenagers will not enter while another is inside. Rather, they will wait until the other ethnic group leaves.

Peer-Group Orientation. The primary integrative mechanism of stable inner-city ethnic neighborhoods is the peer group—that is, a group made up of members of the same age and sex who are at the same stage of the life cycle. As Gans says, "The peer group society continues long past adolescence, and, indeed, dominates the life of the West Ender [Boston] from birth to death."[33] It goes without saying that these peer groups occupy fixed physical as well as social space within the community. The peer group, be it a gang of adolescents or a clique of married friends and relatives of the same sex, provides a vital buffer between the individual and the larger society.

Gans has described the relationship of the peer-group society to the larger world as follows:

> . . . The life of the West Ender takes place within three interrelated sectors: the primary group refers to that combination of family and peer relationships which I shall call the *peer group society*. The secondary group refers to the small array of Italian institutions, voluntary organizations, and other social bodies which function to support the workings of the peer group society. This I shall call the *community* . . . The outgroup, which I shall describe as the *outside world*, covers a variety of non-Italian institutions in the West End, in Boston, and in America that impinge on his life—often unhappily to the West Ender's way of thinking.[34]

The peer group sets standards for behavior and acts as a filter through which one can obtain information. It provides psychological support in that it serves as a sounding board against which one can bounce ideas and receive confirmation of values. It reduces anonymity and tells the individual that he or she belongs. Frequently this in-group membership is signified by a distinctive way of dressing and locally distinctive speech patterns.[35] Whyte's classic treatment of a peer-group society, *Street Corner Society*,[36] deals extensively with the conflict in values between locally oriented "corner boys" and neighborhood adolescents who were success and object-oriented, the so-called "college boys." Peer groups of "corner boys" discouraged striving and emphasized personal relationships. If someone

[32]Ibid., pp. 48–49.
[33]Herbert J. Gans, *The Urban Villagers*, p. 37.
[34]Ibid., pp. 36–37.
[35]Suttles, op. cit., chap. 4.
[36]Whyte, op. cit.

got a job and made some money (this was during the late depression), he was expected to share his good fortune with his friends. Being a good guy was socially rewarded, while putting on airs of social striving was negatively sanctioned. On the other hand, the college boys were oriented toward the achievement values of the outside world, saved rather than shared their money, and constantly sought to "better themselves." The more recent studies of Boston's West End and the Addams area indicate that little has changed over the years: the priority of personal relationships over goal-oriented relationships remains. The absence of material wealth and luxurious consumer goods is rationalized: these goods are associated with the outside world and a cold, impersonal, friendless way of life.

Family Norms. Family life in settled ethnic working-class areas is generally adult-oriented. Children are frequently not planned, and once out of infancy, they are expected to accommodate and adjust themselves to a world run by adults. The child is not the center of the family as in many middle-class and upper-middle-class families, where everything is adjusted to avoid conflict with the child's needs, schedule, and general "development." The role of children is to stay out of the way and behave, at least around the home, like miniature adults. When girls reach eight or nine, they are expected to start helping their mothers around the home, frequently by caring for younger siblings. Boys are given a great deal more freedom to roam the streets. Children soon pick up the notion that the home is the preserve of the mother. Leisure activities for males often focus on the local tavern, which is the major neighborhood institution for many blue-collar workers.[37]

Sociability for married adults does not revolve around occupation or involve a search for new or different friends. The basis for gathering with others is kinship or long-standing friendship and association. Brothers, sisters, cousins, and local friends get together on a more or less regularized basis one or more times a week. Parties in the middle-class sense—gatherings for which specific invitations are issued and at which you expect to meet some people you do not know—are not part of the local life-style. As one West Ender put it: "I don't want to meet any new people. I get out quite a bit all over Boston to see my brothers and sisters, and when they come over, we have others in, like neighbors. You can't do that in the suburbs."[38] Usually the same people come the same days of the week. There are no formal invitations; these are used only for major family events such as a christening, graduation, or wedding. Husband and wife are not expected to be as close or to communicate as extensively as in the middle-class family model. Bott's description of this phenomenon among English families applies equally well to American cities:

> Husband and wife have a clear differentiation of tasks and a considerable number of separate interests and activities. They have a clearly defined division of labor into

---

[37]E. E. LeMasters, *Blue Collar Aristocrats,* University of Wisconsin Press, Madison, 1975; and William Kornblum, *Blue Collar Community,* University of Chicago Press, Chicago, 1974, p. 80.
[38]Gans, *The Urban Villagers,* p. 75.

male tasks and female tasks. They expect to have different leisure pursuits, and the husband has his friends . . . the wife here.[39]

To date the women's movement has not seriously altered this pattern

One difference between American and English studies is that in the United States interaction is primarily with relatives of the same generation. In the East End of London, the interaction may focus on the family matriarch, "Mum." Mum is the one who settles family quarrels, lends money, and looks after the grandchildren. It is at her house that the family gathers, and if a married daughter does not live in the same building, she will be within a short distance.[40] Family ties in the United States are more likely to be horizontal as well as vertical, with greater importance given to cousins and other relatives of the same age.

Housing. Housing often does not have the same meaning in established ethnic working-class neighborhoods that it has in suburban middle-class areas. For the middle class, how one decorates one's home is viewed as an extension of one's personality. The home is a reflection of one's tastes and style of life. The working-class home, on the other hand, is not viewed as a status symbol. Homes are old but quite comfortable. Rents are usually well below the average for the city.

Exteriors of buildings are not always in the best repair. However, inside the apartments everything is clean and in good order. To have more than one's neighbors is perceived as trying to be "better than you are," "snooty," or "stuck-up." Social closeness among neighbors is encouraged by the tendency of local landlords to rent apartments to their married children, relatives, and friends. The goal is a "respectable enough" neighborhood in which neighbors are of the same general ethnic, religious, and economic background. For the upwardly mobile working class hopeful of moving into the middle class, the home frequently is a symbol of one's "respectability." Cleanliness and order are emphasized, with the furniture carefully protected by plastic seat covers and the carpeting by plastic runners.

Imagery and Vulnerability. Blue-collar ethnic neighborhoods, although physically a central part of the city, manage to maintain a psychological distance between themselves and other areas. Their negative images of major urban institutions are remarkably similar to those of small-town dwellers, who also feel powerless in face of the large urban institutions and organizations that control much of their lives. The urban provincials may be city dwellers, but they think of the city as something removed from themselves and their neighborhood. Their area is perceived as being different from the big city outside. Thus the neighborhood is considered friendly, but the city is cold and hostile.

The peer-group orientation of working-class urban neighborhoods leaves

[39]Elizabeth Bott, *Family and Social Network*, Tavistock Publications, London, 1957, p. 53.
[40]Michael Young and Peter Willmott, *Family and Kinship in East London*, rev. ed., Penguin Books, Baltimore, 1962.

them vulnerable to change induced from the outside. The emphasis within the community on personal relations makes residents ill-equipped to participate in large-scale formal organizations or community-wide activities. One learns from the peer group how to get along with others, but not how to deal effectively with an outside bureaucracy.

This means that the community as a whole is rarely able to respond effectively as a unit to threats to its existence, such as urban renewal or an urban expressway that cuts it apart. A traditional distrust of politicians and a lack of knowledge about how to lobby on the level of city government further handicap the working-class neighborhood. Suburban upper-middle-class groups are by training and inclination well equipped to organize ad hoc committees for any purpose under the sun. Working-class people are used to working within an environment of limited size, oriented toward persons more than organizations. Except in cases where a powerful community-wide ethnic church exists, there is no large-scale organization that has the power both to organize and to speak for the neighborhood in its dealings with the larger city. A peer-group society based on ethnicity, age-grading, dominance of a single sex, and limited territoriality is at a considerable disadvantage when it necessarily comes into contact and confrontation with large-scale, complex bureaucratic middle-class society.

Urban provincials do not turn to outside bureaucratic structures in time of trouble. They distrust the city hall bureaucracy and that of the courts. They don't understand the system and feel that whatever happens they are going to lose. They are right, and their lack of knowledge of how to fight the system makes it all the easier for city hall and other outside interests to have their way. Piven and Cloward similarly argue that the poor are victimized because they lack the organization to be part of the conventional political pressure-group system.[41]

The Outcasts

Our final urban population group is the "outcasts." Descriptions of the negative consequences of urban ways of life best fit life in unstable inner-city slums. For the 15 to 20 percent of the overall population who are the bottom in terms of social status (unskilled manual workers, people with unstable and erratic work histories, and people on welfare, particularly if they are minorities), the slum has the character more of an urban jungle than an urban village. Such areas have high rates of residential instability, with the transient population sharing little but the physical area.

Unstable slums house the outcasts of society—the very poor, the old, and the unadjusted. This group, below the manual blue-collar workers, is not simply poorer, although that is also the case—it is in many ways cut off from the social system that includes both the rich and the manual workers. Unstable slums are the slums of despair, for their residents are for all practical purposes excluded from the economic and social life of the larger society. Working-class parents can

---

[41]Frances Fox Piven and Richard A. Cloward, *Regulating the Poor*, Pantheon, New York, 1971, pp. 147–148.

sacrifice to raise the level of their children, but for those of the urban underclass there is little realistic hope of moving from the slum to something better. Life in such an environment is not an attempt to maximize advantages but rather an attempt, frequently unsuccessful, to minimize the harsh negative realities of everyday life.

Those on the bottom, sometimes called the "disreputable poor" by the larger society, have been left behind by that society—people who are downwardly mobile, frequently because of drugs, alcoholism, or mental problems. The "disreputable poor" also includes newer in-migrants to the city who arrive lacking marketable skills or knowledge of urban ways and who, because of this lack and sometimes because of their educational and emotional liabilities, are virtually excluded from modern economic life.[42] They are in many respects America's "untouchable" caste.

Those in the urban underclass frequently find themselves victimized by other, more experienced and cleverer, slum dwellers. Additionally, some old people and handicapped people drift into unstable slums because they are not wanted elsewhere and are powerless to prevent the downward slide.

Everywhere one turns, one is beset by a bewildering variety of difficulties. Slum dwellers are never able to find enough money to have a style of life which both they and society would define as reasonable. They are also surrounded by others who are out to exploit them whenever possible. They are considered fair game by everyone from landlords to hustlers.

Survival Strategies. For those locked into lower-class status, it is unrealistic to have long-range goals. Success is measured in terms of developing strategies for day-to-day survival, not in terms of long-range goals. Even those with jobs usually are not on a track that will lead to a better job. For example, a dishwasher in a restaurant who works hard isn't going to become a chef or restaurant manager.[43] The job leads nowhere, and so long-range planning is meaningless. (See Chapter 10, Stratification and Power in Urban America, for further details.)

Life at the Bottom. For a welfare mother with children living in a high-rise public housing project, the problem is not whether there will be enough money in ten years to send a child to college, but whether the family can scrape together enough money to pay current bills and expenses. There is also a constant threat of violence. The extremely high rates of assault, mugging, robbery, and rape in unstable slums further isolates people. Their situation does not encourage openness and easy interaction with others in the area. Rather, it fosters wariness, anonymity, noninvolvement, and impersonality. Protection from hostile others has to take first priority. Lower-class individuals try, with only slight success, to isolate themselves from the violence of their world.

---

[42]David Matza, "The Disreputable Poor," in Neil J. Smelser and Seymour M. Lipset (eds.), *Social Structure and Mobility in Economic Development*, Aldine, Chicago, 1966, pp. 310–339.

[43]Elliot Liebow, *Talley's Corner*, Little, Brown, Boston, 1967.

Housing for the poor living in unstable slums is not a matter of self-realization or self-expression; it is a matter of providing a place of security safe from the physical and emotional dangers of the outside. The middle class may view housing as an extension of one's personality, and the working class may see the house as a place of comfort, but for the urban underclass the house is a place of refuge.

Urban poor, particularly those stored in public housing projects, have to be constantly on guard against violence against themselves and their possessions. Assaults, robberies, and muggings are a constant danger in stairwells, corridors, laundry rooms, and even apartments. In addition to physical violence, symbolic violence on the part of building supervisors, social workers, and others who perform caretaker services for the lower classes is also endemic in slums and public housing. Lower-class persons protect themselves from such symbolic violence and shaming by avoidance, sullenness, and feigned stupidity when contact cannot be avoided.[44] Certainly the image of lower-class life as presented on television to the slum dweller's children is one that demeans the slum dwellers and emphasizes their isolation from the larger society.

To the extent that the world is seen as consisting of dangerous others, the very act of making friends involves risks for the lower-class person. A friend could turn out to be an enemy and might report one to the housing authorities or cause other problems. Lower-class persons are constantly being exploited, and thus it is not surprising that they view the world as threatening. In the words of Lee Rainwater, "To lower class people the major causes stem from the nature of their own peers. Thus a great deal of blaming goes on and reinforces the process of isolation, suspiciousness, and touchiness both blaming and shaming."[45] Such patterns of distrust and recrimination make it difficult to establish any type of organization for cooperation in solving problems.

For the outcast poor, life is not getting better. As of 1950, the poorest fifth of the nation's population received 4.5 percent of the total national income; twenty years and an infinite number of poverty programs later, the poorest fifth received only 5.5 percent of total national income.[46] Today for the very poor, life is sometimes getting worse in absolute as well as relative terms.

Poor Blacks. The situation is particularly severe for the black poor, who find themselves increasingly separated and alienated from middle-class blacks. (See Chapter 9 for the divisions in the Spanish-speaking community.) Until recently blacks, regardless of their economic or educational achievements, were relegated to racial ghettos. Now middle-class blacks are beginning to cash in on the American dream. What aggregate figures on the black population mask is an increasingly sharp division between the affluent middle-class blacks who are making it and the deprived group remaining behind. (See Chapter 8 for detailed

---

[44]Lee Rainwater, "Fear and the House-as-Haven in the Lower Class," in J. John Palen and Karl H. Flaming (eds.), *Urban America*, Holt, Rinehart, and Winston, New York, 1972, pp. 311–321.
[45]Ibid., p. 319.
[46]U.S. Bureau of the Census, "Consumer Income," *Current Population Reports*, series P-60, no. 80, October, 1971, p. 28.

data on this point.) A consequence of the selected upward mobility of some blacks is that core neighborhoods are losing successful residents so that their percentage of families headed by women and by the aged is increasing—and these two groups have the most limited economic potential. Currently seven out of ten poor black families are headed by women. Forty-one percent of all black families are maintained by women, up from 30 percent in 1970.[47]

With those having economic strength or potential fleeing unstable slums, the isolation of those who are left behind locked into poverty increases. Decreases in discrimination *heighten* the isolation between the very poor and other strata of blacks. Poverty and economic instability lock the urban underclass at the bottom as effectively as discrimination once did. Certainly the feeling of being ignored and bypassed while all around others rise can lead to explosions of frustration—or worse, despair—not only for oneself but also for one's children. The bondage of unstable slums is made doubly oppressive by the relative prosperity of those outside their boundaries.

Increasingly, the major problem for the future is not the emergence of two Americas, one white and one black, but the emergence of two Americas, one economically viable and one a permanent poverty class. It is not unreasonable to foresee certain areas of cities, or even entire cities, serving essentially as ghetto reservations for the deprived underclass. A few once-viable cities such as Newark already exhibit major characteristics of urban reservations for the welfare poor.[48]

COMMUNITY

Thus far, the term "community" has been used but not really defined. Unfortunately, there is no single or even "most common" usage.[49] Anthropologists dealing with localized semi-isolated populations generally find the concept of "community" more useful than sociologists doing research in contemporary urban areas, where the boundaries between distinct groups or patterns of activities become blurred. Today the term "community" has lost much of its descriptive preciseness and efficiency. It is applied arbitrarily to everything from one block in a neighborhood to the international "community."

Contemporary urbanites can, in Weber's terms, have "community without propinquity" (nearness). On the other hand, "community," as used by ecologists, can be defined as a territorially localized population which is interdependent with regard to daily needs. Thus, this usage implies a territorial unit, as opposed to other uses of the term such as "community of scholars" or "religious community."

In the writings of the Chicago school, the term "community" was often a

[47]U.S. Bureau of the Census, "Social and Economic Characteristics of the Metropolitan and Nonmetropolitan Population: 1977 and 1970," *Current Population Reports*, Special Studies, series P-23, no. 75, Washington, D.C., November, 1978, p. 8.

[48]For more on this, see George Sternlieb, "The City as Sandbox," in J. John Palen (ed.), *City Scenes*, op. cit.; and Joseph M. Conforti, "Newark: Ghetto or City," *Society*, **9**:20–32, September-October, 1972.

[49]Some ninety definitions of community are listed by G. A. Hillery, "Definitions of Community: Areas of Agreement," *Rural Sociology*, **20**:111–123, 1955.

synonym for "urban neighborhood." However, two of the most important pre-World War II community studies focused on small cities as the unit of analysis. Robert and Helen Lynd's *Middletown* and *Middletown in Transition* focused on the transformation of life in Middletown (Muncie, Indiana) as a result of absorption into an industrially oriented community.[50] The Lynds documented the decline of control by the community over its own destiny. However, in spite of the economic shocks of the depression, Middletown residents did not become radicalized, but retained complacency and belief in traditional values. A major restudy of Middletown in the late 1970s indicates that while the city is no longer economically in control of its destiny and is heavily beholden to the federal government, the traditional values and normative structure still persist. To a remarkable degree, Middletown still thinks of itself as it did half a century ago.[51]

The second major study, W. Lloyd Warner's *Yankee City* (Newburyport, Massachusetts), dealt with the degree to which the movement from craft work by individuals to mass industrial production led to a breakdown of a sense of community.[52] Local power and control, Warner suggested, had gone from ownership and control by local family-owned firms to large outside corporations. Accompanying this, he also suggested the rigidification of the social structure and decreased social mobility among workers. The historical accuracy of the latter points, however, has been strongly challenged by Stephen Thernstrom.[53]

There is currently no consensus on the significance of community in modern social life. Some, such as Suzanne Keller and Claude Fischer, suggest that urbanites engage in activities on the basis of interests rather than propinquity, and that the neighborhood serves only minimal functions.[54] One might borrow eggs or a cup of sugar from neighbors, or call on them in an emergency, but for everyday life, local attachments are seen as being quite limited. Those taking this view would agree with Roland Warren that the strengthening ties of community units to extracommunity systems orient them in important and clearly definable ways toward larger systems outside the community, making the model of a somewhat delineated, relatively independent, and self-sufficient community less and less relevant to the modern scene.[55] Others, such as Albert Hunter, see urban neighborhoods continuing to sometimes play a significant if changing role.[56]

[50]Robert S. Lynd and Helen Merrell Lynd, *Middletown,* Harcourt Brace, New York, 1929; and *Middletown in Transition,* Harcourt Brace, New York, 1937.
[51]A session of the 1978 annual meeting of the American Sociological Association was devoted to papers on the restudy of Middletown, including Theodore Caplow, "Changing Patterns of Inequality in Middletown, 1920–1970"; C. Bradford Chappell, "Intergenerational Occupational Mobility of Working Women in Middletown"; Geoffrey K. Leigh, "Family Life Cycle and Kinship Interaction"; and Bruce Chadwick, "Convergence or Diverging Life Styles of Working and Business Class Families in Middletown, 1920–1977."
[52]W. Lloyd Warner, *Yankee City,* Yale University Press, New Haven, Conn., 1963.
[53]Stephen Thernstrom, "Yankee City Revisited: The Perils of Historical Naivete," *American Sociological Review,* **30:**234–242, April, 1965.
[54]Suzanne Keller, *The Urban Neighborhood,* Random House, New York, 1968; and Claude S. Fischer, *The Urban Experience,* Harcourt, Brace, Jovanovich, New York, 1976.
[55]Roland L. Warren, *Perspectives on the American Community,* Chicago, Rand McNally, 1966, p. vi.
[56]Albert J. Hunter, *Symbolic Communities: Persistence and Change in Chicago's Local Communities,* University of Chicago Press, Chicago, 1974.

CHAPTER 7

PATTERNS OF SUBURBANIZATION

The early romantic suburb was a middle-class effort to find a private solution for the depression and disorder of the befouled metropolis: an effusion of romantic taste but an evasion of civic responsibility and municipal foresight.

Lewis Mumford

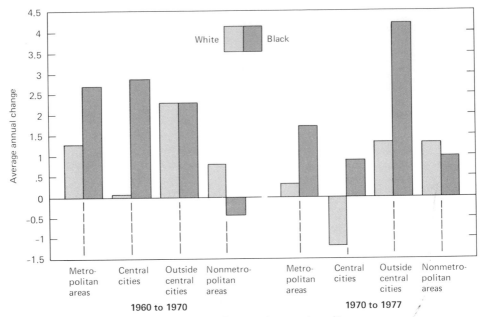

Figure 7-1. Population change in metropolitan and nonmetropolitan areas by race: 1960 to 1970 and 1970 to 1977. (*Source:* Population Reference Bureau and Bureau of the Census.)

SUBURBAN GROWTH

Writing at the end of the nineteenth century, Adna Weber concluded that the most hopeful sign in American urbanization was the "tendency . . . toward the development of suburban towns," for "such a new distribution of population combines at once the open air and spaciousness of the country with the sanitary improvements, comforts, and associated life of the city."[1]

This expresses what is in many ways still a dominant theme in American urbanization. The image of the suburb as a green or pleasant oasis with its single-family homes, neighbors, children, dogs, and ten-speed bikes—all within commuting range of the city—is one that still has force. Intellectuals may scorn "suburbia," but scorned or not, suburbs have transformed the landscape demographically, organizationally, and in life-style.

We have been a nation of suburbanites for a decade. The 1970 census showed that for the first time suburban areas of Standard Metropolitan Statistical Areas (SMSAs) exceeded their central cities in population size and growth rate (Figure 7-1). Suburban areas had 76 million persons, while central cities had 64 million and the areas outside SMSAs had 63 million.[2] By 1977, 58 percent of the national metropolitan population lived in suburban areas. (Remember, though,

[1]Adna Ferrin Weber, *The Growth of Cities in the Nineteenth Century,* Macmillan, New York, 1899, pp. 458–459.
[2]Conrad Taeuber, "Population Trends in the 1960's," *Science,* **176:**774, May 19, 1972.

that "suburban" as defined by the Bureau of the Census means that territory inside the SMSA which is outside the central city. Some of this area and its population would not ordinarily be considered "suburban.") Thus, the United States is now technically a nation of suburbs rather than a nation of cities. There are now four suburbanites for every three city dwellers. Suburbs actually have been growing faster than central cities since the 1900s.[3] The lack of new construction during the 1930s and 1940s for a time masked the extent of potential suburban growth.

The data document the recency and magnitude of the exodus to the suburbs. In 1920 only 17 percent of all Americans were suburbanites (18 million persons). The percentage was only 19 percent by 1930 and only 20 percent by 1940. The percentage increased to 24 in 1950, and then shot up to 33 percent in 1960 and 37 percent in 1970. Today population growth in metropolitan areas is all but synonymous with suburban growth. For the last 50 years virtually all population growth in metropolitan areas has occurred in the suburban rings. This chapter will begin by discussing the emergence of suburbs, then discuss their organizational and demographic aspects, and finally, spend some pages on the question of suburbia as a way of life.

EMERGENCE OF SUBURBS

The Nineteenth Century

Residence on the city fringe is not new, but American suburbanization as we know it was a reaction to the congestion, crowding, and environmental deterioration of the city core. The suburb was to provide a rural refuge from the clamor of the city. As advertised by a promotional piece of a century ago:

> The controversy which is sometimes brought, as to which offers the greater advantage, the country or the city, finds a happy answer in the suburban idea which says, both—the combination of the two—the city brought to the country. The city has its advantages and conveniences, the country has its charm and health; the union of the two (a modern result of the railway), gives to man all he could ask in this respect. The great cities that are building now, all have their suburban windows at which nature may be seen in her main expressions—and these spots attract to them cultured people, with their elaborate and costly adornments.[4]

As this quotation suggests, the first suburbs were generally upper-class villages of substantial country homes. The quotation also notes the importance of the railroad. In the absence of a reliable transportation technology, one could venture no farther from the railway station than one could conveniently walk, or at least be taken by one's driver. Suburbs were thus strung out along the rail lines

---

[3]John D. Kasarda and George Redfearn, "Differential Patterns of Urban and Suburban Growth in the United States," *Journal of Urban History*, 2:43–66, November, 1975.
[4]"North Chicago: Its Advantages, Resources, and Probable Future," reprinted in Charles N. Glaab, *The American City*, Dorsey, Homewood, Ill., 1963, pp. 233–234.

like beads on a string. Only those who could "afford" the costs in both time and money could combine an urban occupation with a rural residence.

Electric Streetcar Era

The rapid adoption of the electric streetcar allowed the middle class to move out to the new suburban developments springing up along the streetcar corridors. As noted in Chapter Five, Ecology and Structure of the American City, the streetcar changed the spatial configuration of American urban areas from that of a compact city to that of a star-shaped urban area. Development, both residential and commercial, occurred along the fingers of the electric streetcar tracks, while the interstitial spaces remained empty and undeveloped. This influence of street railways on Dorchester, Roxbury, and West Roxbury as early streetcar suburbs of Boston has been detailed by Sam Bass Warner.[5]

New housing developments on the edges of the cities, such as Hyde Park and Kenwood in Chicago, began as separate legal areas but were later annexed to the central city. Before the twentieth century, areas on the periphery of central cities often fought to get into the central city rather than stay out of it. Suburbs sought to be annexed by the city in order to benefit from its superior fire protection, schools, and roads; gain access to its water supply; and pay its lower taxes. However, by the turn of the century the pattern had generally reversed: suburbs increasingly actively sought "home rule" and opposed annexation. In the twenty-five metropolitan districts defined by the census of 1910, the pattern for the future was emerging. A full quarter of the metropolitan population already lived outside the core city. In some cases, the desire for suburban autonomy was directly linked to the desire to remain free of the graft, corruption, and the control by ethics of the central city. The desire to keep control over land use and particularly taxes was also important, as was influence over the local schools. The fragmentation of governmental units within the metropolitan area thus became part of the American system.

The Era of the Automobile

The widespread adoption of the automobile greatly accelerated the pattern of turning the city inside out. Car registrations, which had been 2 ½ million in 1915, took a jump to 9 million in 1920, and then skyrocketed to 26 ½ million in 1930. The car was no longer a plaything of the rich. Henry Ford's assembly lines were doing more than producing cars; they were bringing a revolution that was changing the face of the nation. The automobile meant that previously inaccessible land was open for suburban development. No longer was it necessary to be located along a railroad line; commuters who were willing to pay the costs in money and time could drive their own cars to work and live where they pleased.

Popular upper-middle-class suburbs of this era—the Grosse Pointes, Shaker Heights, and Winnetkas—established an image of suburbs as places of

[5]Sam B. Warner, Jr., *Streetcar Suburbs,* Harvard and M.I.T. Presses, Cambridge, Mass., 1962.

The automobile gave families a degree of mobility unknown to previous generations. (Culver Pictures.)

substantial single-family houses surrounded by lawns free of crabgrass, populated mainly by white Anglo-Saxon Protestants of upper-middle-class income and educational levels. Voting Republican was frequently included in this image.

These pre-World War II suburbs had the advantage of appealing to the long-standing antiurbanism of Americans—suburbs were supposedly closer to nature and thus better places to live, while at the same time close enough to the city to have all the advantages of the urban life that the suburbanite didn't really want to abandon. Many suburban houses built during this period reflect the romanticism of their owners. Styles were wildly eclectic; houses half-timbered in the grand English Tudor sytle were built next to pillared Georgian colonial houses and Spanish-Moorish villas. To their owners, these homes were far more than mere housing; they represented the romantic idealization of an earlier nonurban era. "A man's home was his castle," where he could live, if not as a lord, at least as a latter-day country gentlemen—and all without being isolated from the advantages of twentieth-century city life.

To real estate developers, the adoption of automobiles was a boon for it meant that unbuilt land lying between the rail and streetcar axes was now open for residential development. The mostly middle- or upper-middle-class character of this development meant that American cities were assuming a spatial configuration in which movement out was increasingly being associated with movement up. By the depression, the social distinction between cities and suburbs was set.[6]

The Era of Mass Suburbanization

The pent-up demand for housing that had been frustrated first by the depression and then by World War II gained momentum during the 1950s—a momentum that has carried to the present day. Some 60 percent of suburban housing units have been constructed since 1950, compared with 37 percent of city units, most of which have been public housing projects.[7] After World War II, the exodus from the city included not only the rich and well-to-do but also large numbers of middle-class families and even blue-collar families. As noted in Chapter 4, suburbanizing families were rapidly followed by retailers who discovered that retail shopping centers were more lucrative in suburban locations than in the declining central business districts. Industry was similarly leapfrogging to the suburbs in order to benefit from newer plants, increased space, lower taxes, and access to freeways.

The rapidity with which farmers' fields were converted to single-family housing developments is well known. Using mass production techniques, builders of tract developments of the Levittown type transformed huge areas of rural land into instant suburbia. One of the largest of these developments, Lakewood Village, south of Los Angeles, housed over 100,000 persons in 16 square miles. Most developments were, of course, far smaller.

The esthetic vapidness of these tracts of "little boxes" has been justly condemned. On the other hand, it should be kept in mind that the city neighborhoods from which many middle-class and lower-middle-class people migrated were far from being architectural gems. Suburbs have no monopoly on drabness and look-alike uniformity.

The titles of many suburban subdevelopments built after World War II—Rolling Meadows, Apple Orchard Valley, Oak Forest Estates—are really epitaphs for what has been destroyed by the housing developments that carry on the names. This author once lived for two years in a suburban apartment complex of several hundred units named Seven Oaks Farm. The farm had been plowed under by the housing project, and there were only three oaks—mere saplings hardly 3 feet tall. Country names are used to suggest an openness and rural nature which—if they ever existed—are certain to vanish as soon as the subdivision is built. But, of course, suburban developments called Congested Acres Estates or Flood Plains Hollow, while perhaps more accurately named, wouldn't have the same sales appeal.

[6]The existence of another type of suburb—the industrial suburb—was conveniently overlooked.
[7]Peter O. Muller, "The Evolution of American Suburbs: A Geographical Interpretation," *Urbanism Past and Present*, **4:8**, Summer, 1977.

CAUSES OF SUBURBANIZATIONS

The "cause" of expansion of the suburbs is frequently equated in the popular press with the decline of cities. Elements in this decline are certain to be the deterioration of central-city services, poorer-quality schools, higher crime rates, and, of course, the influx of minorities, especially blacks, into city neighborhoods. Whatever the force of such factors today— and they tend to be overrated—it is clear that they are inadequate to explain the massive suburbanization that occurred before the 1960s, when these explanations became fashionable. Suburban growth represents more a movement *toward* values associated with suburbanization—privacy, space, cleanliness, and other amenities—than a movement *from* perceived central urban ills.[8] The massive postwar suburban exodus has more to do with government subsidies for suburban housing and postwar fertility than with a simple "flight" from the city.

Four factors largely account for the postwar suburban boom. First, in the eastern and northern sections of the country, all or almost all the land within the legal boundaries of the city had already been developed by the 1950s. Without annexation, additional growth of the urban area would, by definition, *have* to be suburban growth. The depression years of the 1930s saw little building, and during the 1940s there was a war. Thus by the 1950s there was a tremendous pent-up demand for new metropolitan housing, and the available open land was, by definition, suburban.

Second, government lending policies—whether by intent or not—acted to directly subsidize suburban growth. After World War II, programs of the Federal Housing Authority (FHA) and the Veterans Administration (VA) provided government-guaranteed housing loans for new homes in the suburbs. Young veterans could purchase a suburban home with nothing or perhaps $500 down and with interest rates below those for conventional mortgages. As a consequence, young families moved to suburbs not just for "togetherness" or safety, but because houses in suburban subdevelopments were frequently cheaper than housing in the city. FHA and VA mortgages with low down payments could be obtained easily on new suburban homes; to buy older homes in the city required larger down payments. To new families just becoming economically established, this was a major consideration. The FHA program will be discussed in some detail in Chapter 12.

Overall, suburban costs were initially lower than costs in central cities. Suburban developers often did not include "extras" such as sewers, sidewalks, street lighting, parks, and, of course, schools. Thus, in the early years at least, taxes in the suburbs were generally lower than in the central city. As recently as the 1960s, the initial costs of housing were frequently lower and easier to finance in the newer "package" suburbs than in the central city.

Third, prosperity and the return of veterans created a "marriage boom" that

---

[8]Amos H. Hawley and Basil Zimmer, *The Metropolitan Community: Its People and Government,* Sage Publications, Beverly Hills, Calif., 1970, pp. 31–33.

was quickly followed by a "baby boom." In the decade after the war, some 10 million new households were created. Housing in cities was simply not adequate to absorb large numbers of additional families and children. New city housing had not been built since before the war; existing housing was badly overcrowded, and landlords were not inclined to be tolerant of young children. Young couples with children were, to a degree, forced toward the suburbs, since they were not welcome as renters in city apartments and could not afford to purchase city houses. The suburban "baby boom" children (born between 1947 and 1959, the "baby boom" years) created a need for new and larger houses—a need that suburban developers delighted to fill.

Finally, survey data show decisively that most Americans prefer the type of newer single-family house on its own lot that is most commonly found in the suburbs. Planners and architects may feel that such housing defiles the landscape, but despite such views, most people overwhelmingly prefer suburban sprawl to high-rise luxury apartments or even townhouses. This is true even of those without children. Given a choice, North Americans would rather live in

To many people suburbia still represents the image of the good life, with nice houses and friendly neighbors. (Bill Owens/ Jeroboam Inc.)

single-family housing outside the city. Most families residing in apartment buildings view their tenancy as a temporary step before moving to a single-family house.[9]

Among other things, this means that people are getting pretty much what they want in housing design. Look-alike suburban tract developments succeed while urban developments seek tenants because even when alternatives are open, most people prefer suburban locations. The fact that most professional urbanologists and architects deplore the "little boxes all in a row" has had little impact on the mass of the population. Residents, despite the moans of the architects, perceive individuality and differences even in large subdevelopments.[10]

CONTEMPORARY PATTERNS

Suburbia today is remarkably diverse. Affluent commuter suburbs have been joined by working-class suburbs, suburbs of condominiums, and industrial-park suburbs. Historically, suburbs were considered "sub" because they were not economically self-supporting but rather were appendages of the central city, serving as dormitories. Suburban residents had to commute to the central city in order to earn their livelihood. That no longer holds; suburbs are increasingly becoming major centers of employment. Census figures reveal that as of 1970, in the fifteen largest metropolitan areas a full 72 percent of workers who lived in the suburbs also worked in suburban areas. This meant that only 28 percent still commuted from the suburbs to the central city. Even in the New York area, the legendary citadel of the commuter, only 22 percent of the suburban workers actually commuted into New York City. Our image of the suburbs, obviously, has not caught up with reality.

Today in the nation's fifteen largest metropolitan areas, over one-half the jobs are located in the suburbs. In 1960, central cities, by contrast, held two-thirds of the metropolitan-area jobs. Even in Washington, D.C., with its heavy concentration of government employment, over 55 percent of all jobs are now in the suburbs. As a result of suburban employment opportunities, reverse commuting is becoming more common. One may now live in Dallas, Los Angeles, New York, or Chicago while working beyond the city limits.

The shift of new jobs to suburban locations has been well documented. Between 1947 and 1967 the sixteen largest cities of the northeast and north central states lost an average of 34,600 manufacturing positions each, while the suburban rings gained an average of 83,400 positions. In contrast, sun belt cities gained an average of 19,800 positions, but the suburban rings grew over three times faster, adding an average of 65,000 positions.[11] As discussed in Chapter 11, The Crisis of

---

[9]William Michelson, *Environmental Choice, Human Behavior, and Residential Satisfaction,* Oxford University Press, New York, 1977.
[10]Herbert J. Gans, *The Levittowners,* Vintage Books, New York, 1967.
[11]Brian J. L. Berry and John D. Kasarda, *Contemporary Urban Ecology,* Macmillan, New York, 1977, p. 235.

the Cities, figures such as these don't necessarily signal the "death of the city," although they definitely do indicate the increasingly diversified notion of suburbia. The image of the suburb as an exclusive area of single-family homes has to undergo revision. Even putting aside the questions of commercial and industrial construction and examining only residential building, it is clear that suburbs are increasingly high-rise, and apartment units—whether rental or condominiums—for young singles and the elderly have become increasingly commonplace. Suburbs are still primarily made up of single-family homes, but 1972, perhaps, represented the trend to come—in that year for the first time more multiunits than private houses were built.

Categories of Suburbs

Suburbs can be differentiated in many ways: old versus new, rich versus poor, incorporated versus unincorporated, ethnic versus WASP (white Anglo-Saxon Protestant), growing versus stagnant. Suburban settlements are so diverse that no single typology can adequately encompass them all.

Suburbs also differ systematically with regard to housing characteristics. Residential suburbs have the highest proportion of new housing, the highest percentage of owner-occupied units, and the highest percentage of single-family units; the employment suburbs were lowest on these measures.

Probably the most useful typology is the distinction between those suburbs which function essentially as dormitories—"residential" suburbs—and those which are basically manufacturing or industrial areas—"employment" suburbs. A third type—which combines characteristics of the other two—can also be delineated. Leo Schnore has empirically demonstrated the differences among these types of suburbs in terms of their social and economic characteristics.[12] Schnore used one sample of 74 suburbs surrounding New York City and a second sample of 300 suburbs found within the nation's twenty-five largest urbanized areas. He discovered that there were systematic differences in age and ethnic composition, fertility and dependency, socioeconomic status, population growth, and housing characteristics in residential, mixed, and employing suburbs. Employing suburbs contain higher proportions of both foreign-born inhabitants and nonwhites than residential suburbs, with "mixed" suburbs in the middle.

The percentage of nonwhites in residential suburbs was only 2.4, notably smaller than in the other types of suburbs. Interestingly, the highest fertility ratios and the highest proportion of married couples with children under six years of age are found in the mixed type of suburbs; in the two other types, these figures are lower. Socioeconomic status was highest in the residential suburb, as were the percentage having completed high school, the percentage employed in white-collar occupations, and at the median income level. The intermediate type of

---

[12] Leo F. Schnore, "The Social and Economic Characteristics of American Suburbs," *Sociological Quarterly*, 4:122–134, 1963.

suburb was in the middle. Residential suburbs were also likely to outstrip the growth of industrial suburbs. Three out of ten of the employing suburbs actually lost population during the decade before the census of 1960. Older residential suburbs are now also losing population as birthrates and family size declines.

Robert Lineberry suggests that suburbs be distinguished on the basis of life-style, separately from legal definition as a suburb.[13] Old industrial suburbs, all-black suburbs, and ethnic suburbs, for example, don't fit the conventional image of suburban life-style, yet they are legally suburbs. On the other hand, a place such as River Oaks, inside Houston, is very suburban in life-style but is legally within the city.

The pollster Louis Harris, using the criteria of income level and rate of growth, classified suburbs into four categories:

1. *Affluent bedroom:* Affluent bedroom communities—e.g., New Canaan, Connecticut; Leawood, Kansas; and Sausalito, California—come closest to the traditional stereotype of suburbia. They rank at the top in income, home ownership, and proportion of professionals and managers.
2. *Affluent settled:* Affluent settled communities— e.g., Oak Park, Illinois; Fairfield, Connecticut; and Arlington, Virginia—are less likely to be growing and today may even be losing population. Census figures for 1970 showed that 131 of the suburbs surrounding the nation's ten largest cities lost population over the preceding decade. Population decreased in forty-two of the suburbs near St. Louis, thirty-nine outside Philadelphia, and twenty-four surrounding New York. Since this land is developed, there cannot be a building boom as in more distant suburbs with vacant land. Declining birthrates, plus a pattern of young adults and the elderly living in separate households, also result in fewer people living in each household. Affluent settled communities are more self-sufficient and less likely to be dormitories than are affluent bedroom suburbs.
3. *Low-income growing:* Low-income growing communities are often the home of upwardly mobile blue-collar workers. These communities—e.g., El Monte, California; Sylvania, Ohio; and Millerica, Massachusetts— are far less likely to resemble sterotypical suburbia.
4. *Low-income stagnant:* Low-income stagnant suburbs— e.g. East Orange, New Jersey; McKeesport, Pennsylvania; and Joliet, Illinois—are suburban in name but not in life-style. Such places resemble satellite cities, and in fact are likely to have the full range of problems associated with central cities.[14]

Suburban growth, then, is not as chaotic as it might seem. Typologies, such as Harris's indicate that while suburbs may vary in many respects, there is a predictable pattern to the variation. There are persistent systematic differences which contribute to predicting the evolutionary development of suburban areas.

[13]Robert L. Lineberry, "Suburbia and Metropolitan Turf," *The Annals of the American Academy of Political Reports,* **442:**1–9, November, 1975.
[14]Louis Harris, as described in *Time,* March 15, 1971, p. 15.

Persistence of Characteristics

Since the 1920s many neighborhoods within central cities have undergone profound changes in terms of the characteristics of the residents and often even the physical sturctures. A one-time prosperous neighborhood may have declined and then been razed and rebuilt as an upper-income area or perhaps as public housing. Yet research done by Reynolds Farley and by Avery Guest indicates that there is considerable persistence over time in the suburbs.[15] Farley's research on 137 suburbs of twenty-four central cities suggests that although we tend to see the suburbs as experiencing a rapid rate of change, there is considerable consistency at least among older established suburbs. The socioeconomic status of individual suburbs in 1960 was generally the same as it had been twenty or forty years earlier. In fact, a sound prediction of the educational level of a suburb can be made if one knows the school-attendance rate of the high-school-age population of forty years earlier. Guest's later research indicates that suburban persistence was most pronounced in the more recent 1950–1970 period. Population growth of high-status suburbs enhanced their high position.

Individual suburbs thus have changed far less than the central cities. For example, Wilmette, north of Chicago, and Chevy Chase, just outside Washington, occupy positions of social status remarkably similar to the positions they occupied in 1920. Farley suggests that suburban persistency may result because a suburb originally establishes a distinct composition, so that the people who tend to move to it have socioeconomic characteristics similar to those of people already there.

The area, in effect, creates its own self-perpetuating characteristics. Although the entire suburban area is remarkably diverse, individual suburbs tend to be homogeneous in characteristics and do retain these characteristics over time. While the persistence of social and economic characteristics over, say, fifty years is commonplace in European cities, the same has not been true on this side of the Atlantic. Most of us would be hard-pressed to name central-city neighborhoods that have retained their characteristics for as long as a half century.

Characteristics of Suburbanites

The distinction between city and suburb is, of course, basically legal rather than sociological. While local municipal boundaries are significant in many ways— including financing, taxing, and provision of public services and schools— other social, organizational, ecological, and demographic criteria could be used, such as population density, the proportion of single-family dwellings, and distance from the center of the city. However, none of these alternative schemes have gained anywhere near the acceptance of the traditional city-suburb division. The city line is commonly viewed as a social, economic, and racial boundary.

---

[15]Reynolds, Farley, "Suburban Persistence," *American Sociological Review*, **29**:38–47, 1964; and Avery M. Guest, "Suburban Social Status: Persistence or Evolution," *American Sociological Review*, **43**, 1978.

Suburbs have long been associated with familism, and in 1977 one in every three households in cities was maintained by unrelated individuals compared with one in five in suburbs.[16] Nonetheless, in spite of the child-oriented image of suburbia, there are only minor differences between suburbs and cities in the number of families with children under eighteen living at home (57 percent as opposed to 54 percent in cities). There are no differences between cities and suburbs in size of families and average number of children. One family area in which there is a substantial difference, though, is the proportion of families headed by women. Twice as many central-city as suburban families are maintained by women (21 percent versus 11 percent). This is largely a reflection of the racial composition of cities, since 41 percent of all central-city black families are now headed by women.

The image of the suburban husband as a white-collar worker is also a misconception. Just under half (47 percent) of suburban men are white-collar workers, not far different from the 44 percent of men in cities. Suburbs are obviously no longer dominated by those of higher occupational status. However, although blue-collar workers have been suburbanizing in large numbers, the suburbs have not totally lost their selectivity. Levels of socioeconomic status in the suburbs are, on the average, higher than those of the central cities. Bureau of the Census data indicate that in 1976 dollars median family income in suburbs was $17,101, while the figure for central cities was $13,952. Sixteen percent of the urban population and 7 percent of the suburban are below the poverty level. Educationally, 72 percent of adults in suburbs had completed high school, compared with 63 percent in cities.

The most pronounced difference between cities and suburbs is in their racial composition. Suburbs remain overwhelmingly white, while cities are becoming increasingly black. The number of blacks living in suburbs increased 34 percent between 1970 and 1977, but suburban blacks still constitute only one-fourth of all metropolitan-area blacks and only 6 percent of the national suburban population. The Spanish-origin population, on the other hand, is more evenly distributed within metropolitan areas, with 41 percent living in suburbs. (See Chapter 9 for further details.)

THE MYTH OF SUBURBIA

It has become an article of popular faith that cities house the poor, the elderly, minorities, and the dispossessed while suburbia is the home of the affluent middle-class, families and, of course, whites.

Physically, the central city—again according to the popular wisdom—is in a state of deterioration and decay, barely able to stave off economic catastrophe. Suburbs, on the contrary, are said to be experiencing growth, rapid appreciation of real estate values, and an expanding tax base.

---

[16]Lineberry, op. cit.

Over the years suburbs have become more than mere places of residence. Suburbia has become endowed with a long list of physical and even psychological attributes: ranch-style houses, neat lawns, station wagons and car pools, uptight parents, and togetherness. It is the place where one supposedly finds

> ... a home of one's own, a small piece of real estate on which to practice yeoman's skills, good schools, plenty of land for recreation, clean and traffic free neighborhoods, a small town atmosphere, Christmas lights, a Fourth of July parade, a homogeneous community without social tensions. . . .[17]

This caricature has been called by some sociologists the "myth of suburbia," the myth being the belief that there is, in fact, a uniquely suburban way of life.[18] According to the myth of suburbia, people living in suburbs are, or become, somehow different from those who remain in the city. They are supposedly middle- and upper-class nonethnic whites who have fled the central city. Stereotypes of suburbia are frequently less than complimentary. The suburban way of life is one of wide lawns and narrow minds in which family life is child-oriented rather than adult-oriented. Critics have described the suburban family as surrendering all individuality and creativity. The late Margaret Mead characterized suburban life as consisting of "a living room or recreation room which often resembles a giant playpen into which the parents have somewhat reluctantly climbed."

In terms of life-style suburbanites, particularly those in the newer suburbs, are said to be gregarious. Numerous cocktail parties are interspersed with extensive informal visiting or neighboring. Togetherness is a way of life. Organizationally, suburbanites are said to be hyperactive joiners, with hobby groups, bridge clubs, neighborhood associations, and church-related social activities taking several nights a week. On top of this, there is a proliferation of women's groups, scout troops, and kaffeeklatsches. Husbands are said to spend their weekends cutting grass, watching football games, picking up the kids, going to parties, going to parties, going to church, and watching more football games.

Suburbanites are also charged with being highly status-conscious. Even the home is said to be a status symbol rather than a place to relax—as much a showcase for family goods as a place to unwind.

While the "myth of suburbia" is something of a straw man, it is unfortunately true that suburbs have not received enough study. For all the talk, the study of suburbs has not been a popular topic during the last decade. During the 1960s, "urban research" came to mean the study of inner-city poverty or minority groups. The vacuum left by the absence of hard research on suburban life-styles was filled with a plethora of popular books and articles dealing with suburban conformity, adultery, alcoholism, divorce, and plain boredom. Even the best of the popular writing on suburban life (e.g., *Bullet Park* and *The Man in the Grey*

---

[17]Robert Lineberry and Ira Sharkansky, *Urban Politics and Public Policy,* Harper and Row, New York, 1971, p. 34.
[18]Bennett M. Berger, "The Myth of Suburbia," *Journal of Social Issues,* 17:38–49, 1971; Herbert J. Gans, "Urbanism and Suburbanism as Ways of Life: A Re-Evaluation of Definitions," in Arnold Rose (ed.), *Human Behavior,* Houghton Mifflin, Boston, 1962.

Flannel Suit) painted a highly selective, if not downright inaccurate, picture. The best known of the early works was William H. Whyte's influential book *The Organization Man.*[19] Unfortunately, many of his imitators were not as careful.

Three problems with the early suburban studies can be cited. First, the problem with most of the postwar suburban studies was not so much that they were inaccurate but that they were selective of one type of suburb. Attention was focused on the large tract developments for young families, while little attention was given to industrial suburbs, working-class suburbs, or even older established suburbs. The end result was that the image of suburbia was loaded by emphasizing middle-class tract suburbs with their culture of backyard barbecues, picture windows, and station wagons. Generalizing from these studies, which presented a loaded sample, to all suburbanites is not scientifically valid, but it was nonetheless done by many writers of the period. Some of the studies are also an example of the ecological fallacy of generalizing from characteristics of an area to characteristics of individuals. Second, it is possible that some of the communities chosen for study were selected precisely because they were in some respects atypical and thus presumably more interesting. Third, many of the observations were based on a single look at a suburb immediately after the first wave of settlement. It is highly likely that another look five or ten years later, after the community had "matured," would show changes in the pace of life.[20]

Differences—Real or Not?

Do suburbanites differ from city dwellers in their behavior and attitudes? The overall answer appears to be no. Differences that do emerge tend to be minor, with high social-class level appearing to be more important than suburban location per se.[21] Suburbanization does not, for example, promote "hypersociability," or mass joining of organizations, as suggested by the myth of suburbia.[22] Suburbanization is usually associated with greater involvement with neighbors, although there is no agreement among researchers on why this is so.[23] Perhaps it is simply a reflection of the fact that greater congeniality is likely in an area where people have similar incomes, education, and occupational backgrounds.

Research done by Scott Greer on the metropolitan St. Louis area suggests that suburbs do foster somewhat greater political participation:

> In general, it seemed that the familistic neighborhoods, with their dense networks of neighboring and voluntary organizations, did produce more involvement and informed political action. However, the size of the municipality made a difference: the kind of people who were local political actors in the suburbs were much less likely to be so in the City of St. Louis. So, organizational type of neighborhood and political unit had independent effects. In general, the type of sub-area (urbanism-familism)

---

[19]William H. Whyte, *The Organization Man,* Doubleday (Anchor), Garden City, New York, 1956.
[20]On this point, see S. D. Clark, *The Suburban Society,* University of Toronto Press, Toronto, 1966.
[21]Claude S. Fischer and Robert Max Jackson, "Suburbs, Networks and Attitudes," in Barry Schwartz, *The Changing Face of the Suburbs,* University of Chicago Press, Chicago, 1976, pp. 279–307.
[22]S. Donaldson, *The Suburban Myth,* Columbia University Press, New York, 1969.
[23]Fischer and Jackson, op. cit.

predicted the proportion of local actors, but their *political* activity was affected by the organization of the polity.[24]

It has also been suggested that persons who opt to live in a suburban setting have deliberately chosen a life-style that emphasizes "familism" and deemphasizes alternative life-styles such as "careerism" and "consumership."[25] Data supporting this view, however, are lacking. If it were the case, it would mean that suburbanites put family values above achievement in their careers and the accumulation of consumer goods. David Riesman, for instance, has suggested that suburbanism is a form of escapism whereby men devote their time to family roles when they could be—and should be—participating in the public affairs of the city. He believes that the suburban emphasis on lawn and Little League robs the city of men with the skills and natural ability to act as leaders in addressing city problems.[26] Riesman's emphasis on the role of men as achievers, by the way, was obviously the product of an era when attention had not yet been given to the value of women as leaders in public life.

The belief that suburbanites have different personalities or are more prone to depression than city dwellers is not supported by research. Those who live in suburbs have minor differences in tastes, e.g., preferring gardening over cultural affairs.[27] There is no evidence, however, that suburbanites as individuals make less use of city museums, art galleries, theaters, and concerts than city residents. In many cities suburbanites provide the major support for cultural activities. Thanks to expressways, suburbanites can reach downtown facilities and events such as concerts and plays in little more time than a city resident living in one of the outer neighborhoods. Suburbs also frequently have their own community playhouses, theater groups, and festivals, which indicate interest in the arts. Popular culture (dinner theaters, sports stadiums, and first-run movies) are increasingly located *outside* the central city.

Some suburbs are indeed cultural wastelands, but so again are many city

[24]Scott Greer, *The Urbane View*, Oxford University Press, New York, 1972, p. 97.

[25]Wendell Bell, "The City, the Suburb, and a Theory of Social Choice," in Scott Greer, Dennis L. McElrath, David W. Minar, and Peter Orleans (eds.), *The New Urbanization*, St. Martin's Press, New York, 1968, pp. 132–168.

[26]David Riesman, "The Suburban Sadness," in William M. Dobriner (ed.), *The Suburban Community*, Putnam, New York, 1958, pp. 375–408.

[27]Joseph Zelan, "Does Suburbia Make a Difference?" in Sylvia Fleis Fava (ed.), *Urbanism in World Perspective*, Thomas Crowell, New York, 1968, pp. 401–408.

neighborhoods. Manhattan may be the center of the nation's theater, ballet, and opera, but very little of it seems to have rubbed off on the Bronx or Queens. Many suburbanites do not make use of the central city's cultural facilities, but there is no evidence to suggest that they supported or attended cultural activities even when they were city residents. It remains to be proven that suburbanites differ from city dwellers of similar socioeconomic status in their interest in, and support of, cultural activities.

The similarity between city dwellers and suburbanites is not surprising when one takes into account the fact that in terms of family composition suburbs are becoming increasingly heterogeneous.[28] Thus differences that may have existed in the 1950s, when suburbs had fewer unmarried singles or elderly people, are unlikely to be as noticeable today. Also, it should be recalled that middle-class city residents in outlying city neighborhoods lead lives essentially similar to those of suburbanites. Commenting on his study of Levittown (to be discussed presently), Gans states:

> The findings or changes and their sources suggest that the distinction between urban and suburban ways of living postulated by the critics (and by some sociologists as well) is more imaginary than real. Few changes can be traced to the suburban qualities of Levittown, and the source that did cause change, like the house, the population mix, and newness, are not distinctively suburban. Moreover, when one looks at similar populations in city and suburb, their ways of life are remarkably alike. . . .[29]

Less Affluent Suburbs

In predominately blue-collar suburbs the supposed suburban "involvement syndrome" may not occur at all. Bennett Berger looked at the working-class suburb of Milpitas, California, into which many automobile workers moved when the Ford Motor Company closed its plant in Richmond, California.[30] Two and a half years after the move, 70 percent did not belong to a single club, organization, or association other than their union. Visiting was rare unless relatives lived nearby. There had been none of the supposed suburban "return to religion"; half went to church rarely or not at all. Nor had the move to the suburbs affected their political affiliations; they still voted 81 percent Democratic. Finally, they had no expectations or illusions regarding their social mobility; they had no great hopes of getting ahead in their jobs. They overwhelmingly viewed the suburb not as a transitional stop on the career ladder but rather as a permanent place of settlement. The move from the city to the suburb did not affect the life-style of these workers. Although it definitely improved the quality of their homes, it did not change their behavior patterns. No magical transformation in social customs took place. Working-class norms, attitudes, and behavior persisted with little modification.

[28]Larry H. Long and Paul C. Glick, "Family Patterns in Suburban Areas: Recent Trends," in Schwartz, op. cit., pp.
[29]Gans, *The Levittowners*, p. 288.
[30]Bennett M. Berger, *Working Class Suburbs*, University of California Press, Berkeley, 1960.

Differences between blue-collar urbanites and blue-collar suburbanites were explored further by Albert Cohen and Harold Hodges, Jr., in their study of approximately 2,600 male family heads living in the San Francisco Bay area. They found no significant differences between urban and suburban blue-collar workers in areas such as self-concept, concern over status, familial loyalty, and sex norms.[31] Furthermore, there do not appear to be any changes in involvement with unions, according to a study of forty-six urban and suburban dwellers in New Jersey done by William Spinrad.[32] There were some differences, but these were not great or systematic.

A CASE STUDY: LEVITTOWN

Probably the most thorough case study of a suburban community is Herbert Gans's study of the social organization of Levittown, New Jersey, during the first two years of its existence.[33] The various Levittowns were prototypes of the postwar "package suburbs" that can now be found near all of the country's larger cities. Levitt and Sons, Inc., originally built for a lower-middle-class market, but over the years the size of their houses and their prices have increased considerably.

Gans's findings were based upon interviews with two sets of Levittowners and his own observations, made while he lived in Levittown for two years. Gans suggests that the sociability found within the community is a direct result of the compatibility or homogeneity of the backgrounds of the residents. Homogeneity was most evident in terms of age and income. But diversity in regional backgrounds, membership in ethnic groups, and religious beliefs provided variety for the community. Even the similarity in income did not indicate as much homogeneity as the statistics indicated, for one family might be headed by a skilled worker at the peak of earning power, another by a white-collar worker with some hope of advancement, and a third by a young executive or professional just at the start of a career. Active sociability emerged only when neighboring residents shared common tastes and values, were similar with regard to race and class, and shared similar beliefs regarding child-raising practices.[34] Family togetherness was seen by the residents as a positive attribute of the community. Parents and children all felt that they spent more time together as a family. Even commuting did not have the often-alleged negative effect on family activities. Most Levittowners did not really mind commuting unless it involved a trip of over forty minutes.

Gans's research indicated that residents of the mass look-alike suburb were generally content with their housing, life-style, and general environment. Although the popular literature is rather heavy with criticism of suburban anomie

[31]Albert Cohen and Harold M. Hodges, Jr., "Characteristics of the Lower Blue-Collar Class," *Social Problems*, 10:307, Spring, 1963.
[32]William Spinrad, "Blue-Collar Workers as City and Suburban Residents—Effect of Union Membership," in A. Shostak and W. Gomberg (eds.), *Blue-Collar World*, PrenticeHall, Englewood Cliffs, N.J., 1964, pp. 215–224.
[33]Gans, *The Levittowners*.
[34]Ibid.

(normlessness) and malaise, boredom was not a serious problem in Levittown. Depression and loneliness appeared if anything to be less common than in the city. Almost all the emotional difficulties were concentrated among working-class women who were for the first time cut off from their parents, and wives with husbands whose jobs kept them on the road and away from the family. Those most likely to find the community lacking were upper-middle-class people who had tried Levittown's organizational life and found it wanting.

Adolescents also had a hard time. The community was particularly deadly for teenagers owing to the lack of recreational facilities and even places to go. It was designed for families with young children, not adolescents. Thus, bedrooms were small and lacked the privacy or soundproofing necessary to allow teenagers to have their friends visit. Shopping centers were designed for adults who owned cars, and discouraged adolescents who hung around and made only marginal purchases. Even the high school discouraged its students from using its facilities after school hours because of the school administrator's fear of increasing maintenance costs.

Overall, Gan's description of Levittown shows a community that was not overly exciting but that generally met the needs of its residents. The worst thing that can be said about the community is that for anyone with cosmopolitan tastes, it is rather dull. But then, Levittowns weren't built for cosmopolites.

EXURBANITES

Beyond the built-up suburbs surrounding the very largest cities there is a special class of suburbanites who have become known as "exurbanites." These are the people who have achieved success in their professions—frequently the communications industry, advertising, and publishing, and have moved farther out to get away from the rat race.[35] Their work may allow them to use their own offices at home several days a week and avoid daily commuting. Thus, if their base is New York, they can live as far out as Fairfield, Bucks, and Winchester counties.

Unfortunately, the best-known study of exurbia, *The Exurbanites*, is a caricature of hyperactive, upwardly mobile, creative people all living in their trilevel houses. The picture is of people desperately trying to find meaning in their lives, people who find that moving out of the city doesn't reduce the anxiety of working in extremely competitive industries where the standards for judging performance are highly subjective and fickle. Since living in the country is a strain on the budget, there is also often the pressure of having to maintain a standard of living that one can't afford. Living in exurbia supposedly also puts considerable pressures on wives, who find themselves locked into a schedule of maintaining a house and providing a station-wagon shuttle service for children and commuting husbands while they remain isolated from the city.

This general outline has, of course, served as the framework for dozens of

[35]A. C. Spectorsky, *The Exurbanites*, Berkeley, New York, 1958.

novels, television dramas, and movies. Unfortunately, it is sometimes taken to be a scientifically valid reflection of reality, rather than inventive fiction. Although solid research is scarce, there does not appear to be evidence that exurbanites are significantly different from suburbanites. In fact, exurbs have a way of turning into suburbs as more and more people with the same background move into the same area—all seeking to get away from it all.

BLACK SUBURBANIZATION

Suburbs after World War II lost some of their social class exclusiveness, but not their racial exclusiveness. Blacks in suburbs have been noticeable by their absence. The general conclusion of researchers appears to be that black suburbanization is increasing, but only marginally.[36] Census figures for 1960 indicated that suburbs were 4.2 percent black; during the decade of the 1970s the rate increased only slightly, to 4.7 percent.

Taeuber in particular has pointed out that the social and economic character of some of the areas entered by suburbanizing blacks can be better typified as older, working-class, industrial towns rather than stereotypical suburbs.

Older ring suburbs, particularly in the northeast and midwest, often differ little in character and housing quality from central-city neighborhoods, and such suburbs increasingly serve as a point of suburban entry for blacks and other minorities. In such cases, suburbanization occurs because the extremities of the black ghetto extend across city-suburban legal boundaries. In such cases, black suburbanization can hardly be equated with racial integration.

Changes

The above analyses reflect the situation as of the 1970 census, but there is increasing evidence that this is changing. Between 1970 and 1977 some 1.2 million blacks became suburbanites, compared with 800,000 blacks during the period 1960–1970. Thus, since 1970, the total number of black suburbanites has increased from 3.4 to 4.6 million. Between 1970 and 1977 the rate of black suburbanization was 34.5 percent, compared with a 9.8 percent white increase. Moreover, census figures indicate that black migration to suburbs accelerated in the last half of the decade.[37]

Suburban blacks now represent one-fifth (19 percent) of the nation's black population and one-fourth (25 percent) of all blacks living in metropolitan areas. Nonetheless, blacks still constitute only 6 percent of the suburban population (as compared with 12 percent of the total national population). This is because whites have continued to flood to the suburbs. Between 1960 and 1977, some 22 million

---

[36]George Sternlieb and Robert W. Lake, "Aging Suburbs and Black Home-Ownership," *The Annals of the American Academy of Political and Social Science,* **422:** 105–117, 1975; Karl E. Taeuber, "Racial Segregation: The Persisting Dilemma," *The Annals of the American Academy of Political and Social Science,* **422:**87–96, 1975; and Leo F. Schnore, Carolyn D. Andre, and Harry Sharp, "Black Suburbanization 1930–1970," in Schwartz, op, cit., pp. 69–94.

[37]"Social and Economic Characteristics," op. cit., p. 5.

Black middle-class suburbanization, which was an unusual occurrence until recently, will become more commonplace during the 1980s. (Ray Ellis/Photo Researchers, Inc.)

whites became suburban residents. So long as the white exodus to the suburbs continues, suburban areas will retain their pale complexion regardless of how many blacks move in.

The very magnitude of the white suburban drive in recent decades suggests some diminution of the movement during the 1980s. White suburbanization may be at a somewhat less hectic pace since upper-class and middle-class whites desiring to suburbanize have in substantial part already done so. Remaining central-city whites are increasingly those who—either by choice or because they lack a down payment for a house in the suburbs—will remain city folk. Middle-class suburbanization also is no longer automatically lily-white. In the case of Washington, D.C., the majority of current movers from city to suburb are black. The 1980s will show whether this is an exception or the vanguard of a new urban pattern.

Causes

The traditional absence of blacks in suburbs is a reflection of racial discrimination more than economics. A decade ago one-third of black urban families had middle-class incomes; it is clear, then, that blacks are not suburbanizing at the rate one would expect on the basis of economics alone. Some degree of this segregation of more affluent blacks is doubtless by choice; much of it is not. Whatever the cause, the result is that, overwhelmingly, suburbs are de facto racially segregated areas.

Overall, suburbanizing blacks are generally younger (in their late twenties and early thirties) and have higher levels of income, education, and occupation than blacks remaining in the city. Blacks moving into particular suburbs can generally be said to have the same social and economic characteristics as other residents of the community. Middle-class blacks move into middle-income suburbs and rich blacks into upper-income suburbs.

As put by an Urban Coalition spokeswoman in a *New York Times* article: "Middle-class whites want a good education for their children; so do middle-class blacks. Middle-class whites want safe neighborhoods; so do middle-class blacks."[38] Also, like their white neighbors, middle-class black suburbanites are opposed to having poor people of any color in their neighborhood.

Suburbanization of blacks should not automatically be equated with racial integration. In some metropolitan areas as has been noted, black suburbanization represents not integration but rather the natural growth of the ghetto until it overflows city boundaries. Black suburbanization in this case is not integration but more of the same, although in the suburbs the housing is better. These black "gilded ghettos" are becoming a common feature of larger American cities. A ghetto that expands across a city boundary is still a ghetto; only the name of the town is different. Additionally, as noted earlier, many suburban blacks live in either industrial suburbs or relatively small segregated ghettos within older suburbs. "Black only" suburbs are also found surrounding many of the largest cities.

Older inner-ring suburban areas directly abutting the central city are the best candidates for absorbing the overflow from city ghettos. Many of these communities are essentially urban in character and have been for many years. Communities such as Yonkers have densities approaching those of the central city, while an older racially changing suburb such as Evanston, outside Chicago, already is composed heavily of multiple dwellings.

WHITE FLIGHT?

City-to-suburb population transfer is often discussed in highly emotional terms. Central-city mayors in particular often speak as if moving to a home in the suburbs was a desertion—as if the middle class had a "duty" to remain in the central cities. Mayors, of course, are reluctant to lose taxpaying citizens. The term "white flight" reflects the conventional wisdom that, particularly since the urban riots of the late 1960s, whites have fled central cities as these cities have become increasingly black, crime-ridden, dirty, and expensive.

[38]Sarah Austin, vice-president, Urban Coalition, *The New York Times*, January 4, 1976, p. 40.

Is this the case? Has flight to the suburbs occurred because of increases in the black central-city population and increases in city crime? A case can be made that some of the movement immediately after World War II was racially motivated. As noted earlier in this chapter, there was a substantial pent-up housing demand, but in addition the black invasion of previously all-white city neighborhoods, coupled with discriminatory housing practices, acted to selectively move whites to the suburbs. As put by William Frey:

> Since both market and non-market discriminatory practices effectively guaranteed movers all-white neighborhoods in the suburbs, an undeterminable portion of white postwar suburbanization can be attributed to racial motivations. . . .[39]

More recently, however, the end of major black migration to cities and more tolerant racial attitudes among whites—at least in principle—have acted to dampen rapid racial turnover.[40] While school desegregation potentially can motivate some flight, this is generally limited to those central-city residents who have school-age children in public schools.[41] Much of the city population is unaffected by such changes. In spite of all the rhetoric, very little is really known about the effects of busing.

The question, then, is whether contemporary suburbanization is based more on "push" factors from the central city such as changes in racial composition, racial disorders, and crime, or whether current suburbanization is based largely on "pull" factors such as open land, inexpensive government-subsidized financing, lower taxes, and newer housing.

The data tend to support the latter view. William Frey, in his statistical examination of the migratory movement of white and black residents in thirty-nine large metropolitan areas, found that the concept of "white flight" was not supported.[42] Racial factors do have some influence on the dislocation of those who are moving. However, the question of whether whites move or not is very responsive to differences between city and suburbs with regard to taxes, and to the extent to which suburbanized.

Another study, by Thomas Guterbock, had similar findings.[43] Guterbock examined whether SMSAs with large or increasing black populations and high or rising crime rates were suburbanizing more rapidly than other SMSAs. He found that the push effect of minorities was small and statistically nonsignificant.[44]

[39]William H. Frey, "Central City White Flight: Racial and Nonracial Causes," Center for Demography and Ecology, University of Wisconsin, Madison, Paper 77–11, 1977, p. 5.

[40]For data on racial changes, see Thomas F. Pettigrew, "Attitudes on Race and Housing," in Amos Hawley and Vincent Rock (eds.), Segregation in Residential Areas, National Academy of Sciences, Washington, D.C., 1973.

[41]In support of the theory that desegregation of schools has a major impact, see James Coleman, Sara D. Kelly, and John A. Moore, Trends in School Segregation, 1968–1973, The Urban Institute, Washington, D.C., 1975. For the opposing view, see Thomas Pettigrew and Robert Green, "School Desegregation in Large Cities: A Critique of Coleman's 'White Flight' Thesis," Howard Educational Review, 46:1 53, 1976.

[42]Frey, op. cit., p. 29.

[43]Thomas M. Guterbock. "The Push Hypothesis: Minority Presence, Crime, and Urban Deconcentration," in Schwartz, op. cit., pp. 137–161.

[44]For data from the Detroit Area study suggesting that white flight plays a more important role, see Bud Wurlock, "The Role of White Flight in Neighborhood Racial Transition," a paper presented at the April 1978 meeting of the Midwest Sociological Society. Wurlock's findings are discussed further in Chapter 8, Urban Diversity: White Ethnics and Black Americans.

There is indeed a rush to the suburbs, but it is just as common in SMSAs with few black newcomers.

While some "white flight" has indeed occurred, "pull" factors in general appear more important. Suburbs have been growing faster than central cities throughout this century, long before major racial changes or economic crises came to the cities. Movement to the suburbs has long been more a movement *toward* better housing and amenities than a flight from racial change.[45]

MAINTAINING RACIAL DIVERSITY IN SUBURBS

Attempts by some suburbs to maintain racial diversity have raised a debate that will probably be settled only by the Supreme Court. The eventual outcome will have profound effects on the racial makeup of metropolitan areas for decades to come.

An Example: Park Forest South

Park Forest South, a suburb carved in the early 1970s out of cornfields 30 miles south of Chicago, is a case in point. Park Forest South made every attempt to follow the spirit as well as the letter of open housing laws; as a consequence, the proportion of blacks grew rapidly (it is currently over one-third) while neighboring Homewood and Flossmore remained, respectively, 1 percent and 2 percent black. Park Forest South, concerned that real estate practices were resulting in resegregation, in 1977 passed a so-called "affirmative marketing" ordinance to prohibit real estate solicitation that acted against attracting whites.

The real estate industry challenged this as reverse steering and argued that the village's counseling of blacks to move into white rather than already black areas was preventing blacks from living where they wanted. The ordinance was later withdrawn, but the controversy over whether communities can or should take action to remain integrated rather than turning all-black is still hotly debated. The issues are complex, with differences even among civil rights groups. The Chicago chapter of the NAACP and the Southern Christian Leadership Conference have joined with their old enemy, the real estate industry, in denouncing as racist both efforts to keep the suburb integrated by controlling realtors and attempts to attract whites. On the other hand, local open-housing groups and the national NAACP support efforts to attract whites. The director of housing programs for the national NAACP calls the efforts of Park Forest South and other integrated communities "legitimate" and says that it is "tragic" that the town rescinded its affirmative market ordinance.[46]

Further complicating the local picture, the head of the Chicago NAACP and most members of its board are also real estate brokers. Members of the board

---

[45]Amos H. Hawley and Basil Zimmer, *The Metropolitan Community: Its People and Government,* Sage Publications, Beverly Hills, Calif., 1970, pp. 31–33.

[46]Robert Reinhold, "Nation Watching Outcome of Racial Puzzle in Illinois," *New York Times Service,* April 15, 1979.

interviewed on a television show ("60 Minutes"), have denied any conflict of interest, but others have noted that the black real estate firms they own profit directly from racial turnover. Still to be resolved by the Supreme Court is whether integration per se is important enough to justify attempts by communities to attract whites and discourage all-black enclaves. With the local and national NAACP split on the issue, it is obvious that opinion differs.

Managed Integration: Oak Park

Given the economic and social pressures, is it possible for racially integrated neighborhoods to survive? Or is integration simply the interval between the arrival of the first black family and the departure of the last white family? As Chapter 8, Urban Diversity: White Ethnics and Black Americans, points out, racial residential turnover can occur without white flight. All that is necessary is that an area attract more black than white newcomers. To keep an area integrated, it is necessary to maintain an influx of whites.

The suburban Chicago community of Oak Park is a working example of how older neighborhoods can be integrated and preserved. Once the home of Frank Lloyd Wright, and with many architecturally interesting homes, Oak Park by the late 1960s was a prime candidate for disinvestment and change. It is an old suburb of 60,000 with half its population in rental units. More important, it directly abuts Chicago's lower-class West Side ghetto. The adjacent Austin section of Chicago, a prime area a score of years ago, has experienced rapid deterioration. Austin is now 98 percent black.

What makes Oak Park unique is that most of its residents, instead of picking up and fleeing, decided to face integration head on. Their efforts have been so successful that Oak Park is currently one of the metropolitan area's most desirable housing areas, particularly for young white home buyers. The reason for Oak Park's success is a tightly managed community. The community both quickly intervenes to halt building deterioration and encourages racial diversity. The community enforces housing codes, and virtually controls all the activities of realtors.

Ten percent of every apartment building's flats are inspected every year, and every apartment must be inspected and the building brought up to code before selling. A new shopping mall and village hall brighten up the community, while local lending institutions have been persuaded to keep open funds for mortgages and remodeling. Several million dollars has also gone into low-interest loans for upgrading of apartments. House-to-house solicitation by real estate companies and the posting of "For Sale" or "For Rent" signs are banned to prevent panic selling. After some pressure, all real estate companies now report all sales or controls twice a week to the Oak Park Community Relations Department. To further discourage panic selling, the community initiated "moral homeowners' insurance." Homeowners who sign up for the insurance and stay in the community at least five years are guaranteed that they can sell their homes for 80 percent of the difference between the appraisal value and the selling price. The major reason for the homeowners' equity insurance is psychological rather than economic. It is meant to forstall any fears of declining housing values. Actually, the program, which went into operation in 1978, has had few takers, since property values in the suburb have not been declining but appreciating rapidly.

Currently Oak Park is 10 percent minority. Emphasizing diversity, the community actively welcomes minority residents, with a housing center providing listings of available apartments to prospective renters. The most controversial aspect is the encouragement of dispersal of all races throughout the suburbs. Thus whites are encouraged to move into integrated areas, and potential black buyers or renters are encouraged to look at properties in white sections rather than concentrating in areas that are already heavily black. Landlords are strongly discouraged from having one-race buildings.

Oak Park, with its affluent middle-class to upper-middleclass residents, is not typical of many urban areas faced with blockbusting. Nor do many communities exhibit such a strong sense of community involvement. There is no question that Oak Park manages its housing and rental market to an extent not found elsewhere. The community is integrated racially but not economically. Poor families are not desired.

Still, Oak Park's prosperity indicates that older areas— even when abutting a lower-class ghetto—can both integrate racially and upgrade physically. Outside observers are sometimes critical of the extent of housing controls in the community, but for Oak Park, managed integration works.

THE SUBURBAN POOR

The myth of suburbia has so permeated our unconscious thinking that we automatically associate poverty with city slums or marginal rural areas. Yet as of 1977, 7 percent of the suburban population—compared with 16 percent of the central-city population—was below the poverty line. Suburban poor are unseen poor, and thus their needs remain largely unmet. After all, the feeling goes, if they can afford to live in the suburbs, why should they get sympathy? "Suburban" equals "middle-class" in the thinking of most people. Core areas of central cities are expected to have poverty; suburbs are not. It would be difficult to imagine Congress, for instance, considering, much less passing, any bill to alleviate poverty in the suburbs.

An extreme example of how little "suburban" a suburb can be is Kinloch, outside of St. Louis. Kinloch is the second-largest black suburb in the nation, but it can be aptly described as a poverty area.[47] It is a desperately poor community surrounded by affluent white suburbs. Kinloch's single-family homes are in various stages of deterioration; its streets are largely unpaved; at the same time it has the highest rate of school taxes in the county, the lowest tax base, and the worst schools.

[47]John Kramer, "The Other Mayor Lee," in John Kramer (ed.), *North American Suburbs*, Glendessary Press, Berkeley, Calif., 1972, pp. 185–200.

Kinloch survives as a community simply because no other area is willing to absorb it and its problems. Meanwhile everything is done to isolate the black suburb from its wealthier neighbors. Roads from the next community, Ferguson, actually stop 1 foot before Kinloch's borders, and while a full-scale wall like that in Berlin has not been constructed around the community, the northern community of Berkeley has built a chain link fence all along Kinloch's border.

It should be noted that significantly increased lower-class suburbanization—white or black—simply is not on the horizon. Suburban housing costs of over $100,000 are no longer an exotic phenomenon restricted to southern California. Environmental and energy requirements such as larger lot sizes, increased insulation, and sanitary sewer systems drive costs up further. The virtual absence of public transportation systems in most new suburban communities mandates at least one car, and generally two cars, per family.

The consequences are clear; the poor are excluded from newer suburban housing. This is unlikely to change without radically altered and expanded federal subsidy programs. In the wake of Proposition 13, such programs have become increasingly unlikely. The least affluent are thus in practice restricted to older inner-ring suburbs—that is, to the suburbs that most closely approximate the central city.

PROGNOSIS

Suburbanization continues as a major trend in American urbanization. The overall rate of suburbanization may decline somewhat, and black middle-class suburbanization may increase; but for the immediate future most suburban subdevelopments will continue to be middle-income and white. Racial changes in the housing industry, or a massive commitment by Congress to a national housing program, could change this, but the odds are strongly against any such occurrence.

Escalating costs for land, labor, and building materials have dramatically driven up housing costs during the past decade. Rampant inflation and gasoline prices have similarly increased the cost of suburbanization. Substantial lower-class suburbanization will have to await both subsidization of housing costs and changes in restrictive zoning practices, neither of which appears particularly likely at this point in time. An increasingly attractive alternative for many young people may become revitalizing central-city neighborhoods. (This is discussed in detail in Chapter 12, Housing Programs and Urban Regeneration.)

CHAPTER

8

URBAN DIVERSITY:
White Ethnics and
Black Americans

INTRODUCTION: URBAN MINORITIES

A minority group comprises people who are singled out for special treatment, lack power, and are systematically discriminated against by other groups. In short, they are denied full participation in the society.

As Louis Wirth put it:

> We may define a minority as a group of people who, because of their physical or cultural characteristics, are singled out from the others in the society in which they live for differential and unequal treatment, and who therefore regard themselves as objects of collective discrimination. The existence of a minority in a society implies the existence of a corresponding dominant group with higher social status and greater privileges.[1]

Minority status is a social, not a statistical, condition. Patterns of discrimination, not size, make a minority. In South Africa, for example, blacks far outnumber whites, yet blacks are still considered a minority group. Likewise, in North America women are sometimes considered a minority, although they are numerically in the majority. Actually, it would be more logical to refer to black South Africans and American women as "subordinate" groups rather than minorities. However, the term "minority" is commonly used to designate any group that suffers discrimination, regardless of its size. Therefore it will also be used, with reservations, in this book.

In this chapter and Chapter 9, attention will be concentrated on ethnic and racial minorities whose futures are closely bound to the urban scene: white ethnics, black Americans, Mexican Americans, Puerto Ricans, and Native Americans. These groups differ from one another in numerous respects; what they have in common is that, compared with other Americans, they are relatively recent newcomers to the urban scene and, most important, they are deprived minorities encountering problems of acceptance and adjustment. White ethnics, blacks, Hispanics, and Native Americans have different histories and cultures, but, until very recently, all have been dismissed as unimportant or marginal to the mainstream of urban America.

These two chapters will examine the economic and social position of the deprived minorities in America's urban society as well as their degree of assimilation and whether they wish their future to be culturally and socially distinct or part of mainstream WASP society. This chapter will deal with white ethnics and blacks; Chapter 9 will continue the discussion for Mexican Americans, Puerto Ricans, and Native Americans. A note is also included on Japanese Americans—less than forty years ago a despised minority and today a respected and successful community.

---

[1]Louis Wirth, "The Problem of Minority Groups," in Ralph Linton (ed.), *The Science of Man in World Crisis,* Columbia University Press, New York, 1945, p. 347.

WHITE ETHNICS

Immigration

There is a story (possibly apocryphal) that President Franklin Roosevelt enraged the Daughters of the American Revolution (DAR) during the 1930s by addressing them as "Fellow Immigrants." If so, he was only stating what is frequently forgotten. That is, all groups—including Indians—were once newcomers. The only difference is in time of arrival. Indians came perhaps 15,000 to 20,000 years ago, while Europeans first came in significant numbers less than 400 years ago. Substantial numbers of blacks have been here for three centuries, while many of the most recent arrivals have been Hispanics, many of whom are first- or second-generation newcomers. Thus, it is impossible to discuss American urban patterns and life without discussing the role played historically—and in the present day—by the newcomer to the American city.

It is a cliché to state that America is a nation of immigrants, but it is sometimes forgotten that the American inmigration was the largest mass migration in the history of the world. Precise data are lacking, but it is possible that some 30 to 45 million immigrants have arrived in the United States since 1820; we will never know the exact number or distribution. In some cases overworked immigration officials automatically listed all newcomers on a ship from Hamburg as German, while first-class passengers usually weren't even included in the immigration figures until this century.

Generally there is a clear pattern of association between the social status of an ethnic group and the time its first ancestors landed on these shores. (The exception is the black population, who in spite of their early arrival remained a separate caste excluded from mobility in American society.) At the time of the Revolutionary War some nine-tenths of the new nation's white population traced their ancestry to the British Isles: English, Scotch, or Northern Irish (called Scotch-Irish to distinguish them from Catholic Irish).[2] Even cosmopolitan New York was dominated by English customs, laws, values, and mores. Protestantism in various forms was in effect the national religion.

The founding fathers strongly supported free and open migration. New immigrants were not welcomed, though, without reservations. George Washington's views were that

> The bosom of America is open to receive not only the Opulent and Respectable Stranger, but the oppressed and persecuted of all Nations and Religions, whom we shall welcome to participation of all our rights and privileges, if by decency and propriety of conduct they appear to merit the enjoyment.[3]

Washington was more liberal in his admission criteria than many of his contemporaries (his Federalist successor, John Adams, lengthened the waiting

---

[2]David Ellis et al., *A Short History of New York State,* Cornell University Press, Ithaca, N.Y., 1957, p. 64.
[3]Quoted in the President's Commission on Immigration and Naturalization, *Who Shall We Welcome?* U.S. Government Printing Office, Washington, D.C., 1953.

period for citizenship), but even Washington's statement has a final clause that says in effect, "if we think they behave themselves."

Old Immigrants

The Irish fleeing the potato famine in the mid-1840s were the first of the mass immigrant groups. The famine caused over a million deaths by starvation in Ireland; and another million or so impoverished Irish peasants immigrated to America. The Irish were closely followed by the Germans, and somewhat later the Scandinavians. These groups are collectively called the "old immigrants" to distinguish them from the early settlers— overwhelmingly of British origin—who were here first.

The Germans, in spite of the fact that they played cards and insisted on drinking beer on Sunday—shocking some bluenoses—fared rather well. They earned a reputation for industriousness, thrift, and orderly living—although they rioted in Chicago in 1855 when the mayor banned the sale of beer on Sunday. Easing assimilation was the fact that the majority of Germans were Protestant.

The Irish had greater problems, for not only were they viewed as recalcitrant, papist rowdies, but they were the poorest of the poor. Irish, rather than slaves, were used in hard or hazardous work. As it was explained by a riverboat captain to a famous visitor, "The niggers are worth too much to be risked here; if the Paddies are knocked overboard or get their backs broke, nobody loses anything."[4] Irish labor built the nation's railroads, and a saying of the time was, "An Irishman is buried under every tie." Confronted by discrimination —"No Irish Need Apply" was common in help-wanted ads—the Irish organized themselves. For the immigrant Irish, the route to social mobility was said to be through becoming one of the three P's, "priest, politician, or policeman"; and by the latter part of the nineteenth century, the Irish controlled the city halls in cities where they lived in significant numbers. Stereotypes also softened as more and more of the Irish became skilled workers. By the 1880s it was a common saying that "a good worker does as much as an Irishman."[5]

New Immigrant Groups

Sources of the "New Immigration." While the ethnic groups of the "old immigration" came from northern and western Europe, those of the "new immigration" came heavily from southern and eastern Europe (Figure 8-1). After 1880, increasing, numbers of immigrants had a Slavic, Polish, Jewish, Italian, or Greek heritage.[6] During the 1860s less than 2 percent of all immigrants came from southern or eastern Europe; by the 1890s southern and eastern Europeans were a

---

[4]Frederick Law Olmstead, *The Cotton Kingdom*, Modern Library, New York, 1969, p. 215.
[5]John Higham, *Strangers in the Land*, Atheneum, New York, 1977, p. 28.
[6]For an excellent account of the life of the newcomers, see Irving Howe, *World of Our Fathers*, Touchstone, New York, 1976.

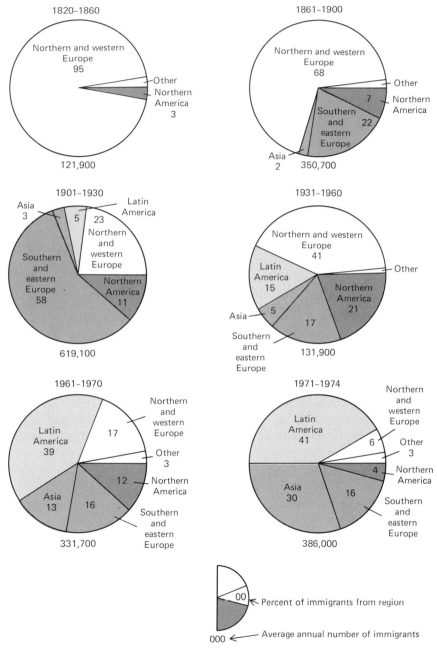

Figure 8-1. Immigrants to the United States by region of origin: 1820 through 1974. (*Source:* Population Reference Bureau.)

majority (52 percent) of all immigrants; and by the first decade of this century seven out of 10 immigrants came from southern or eastern Europe. Today all European migration is much reduced, with the major stream into the country consisting of illegal undocumented aliens from Mexico (see Chapter 9).

Concentration in Cities. The "new immigrants" faced a tide of rising nativist sentiment. To ethnocentric Americans, the new immigrants were alien races about to overwhelm American institutions and cities. First, they were coming from what were considered the most backward areas of Europe—regions that did not have self-government and thus by implication were incapable of self-government. Second, their customs and even food habits differed greatly from the Anglo-Saxon-Teutonic norm of earlier settlers. Third, their religion was different. They were more likely to be Catholic, Orthodox, or even Jewish than Protestant. Finally, they were concentrated in the cities and thus were highly visible. Well into the twentieth century, the majority of the urban population was foreign-born or first-generation American. As of 1900, only half (51 percent) the country's population was native white and of native parentage. In eastern seaboard cities such as New York and Boston, over three-quarters of the population was of foreign stock (foreign-born or second-generation). The negative reaction of WASP rural

Immigrants traveling steerage had to undergo physical examinations at Ellis Island. There was no such requirement for first-class passengers. (Culver Pictures.)

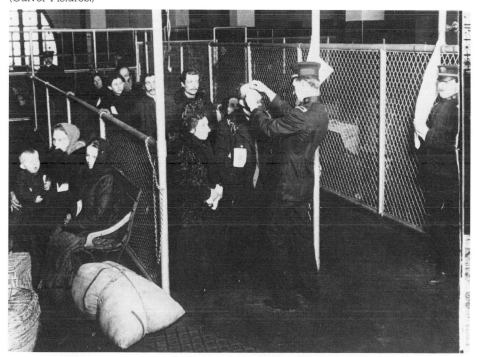

and small-town America to the nation's cities was closely linked to the perceived "foreignness" of the cities. Cities were cesspools of "rum, Romanism, and rebellion."

In the nineteenth century, writers and preachers such as Josiah Strong raised the clarion call against the menace of cities teeming with foreigners:

> The City has become a serious menace to our civilization. . . . It has a peculiar attraction for the immigrant. . . .
>
> While a little less than one-third of the population of the United States was foreign by birth or parentage, sixty-two percent of the population of Cincinnati was foreign, eighty-three percent of Cleveland, sixty-three percent of Boston, eighty percent of New York and ninety-one percent of Chicago. . . . Because our cities are so largely foreign, Romanism finds in them its chief strength. For the same reason the saloon, together with the intemperance and the liquor power which it represents, is multiplied in the city.[7]

As noted in Chapter 3, The Rise of Urban America, middle-class attempts to remove the bosses and reform the city generally meant removing power from the central-city immigrants.

By the time the new immigrants arrived, the frontier had closed and the good farmlands were taken. Of necessity the new immigrants became industrial factory workers. Easy assimilation of the immigrants was retarded not only by their overwhelming numbers but also by their concentration in ethnic ghettos—in the inner-city zone of transition. Residence in central-city tenements reflected an economic necessity, but it also reflected the desires of the immigrants to have their own communities where they could follow traditional customs free from Anglo-Saxon hostility. The consequence was the development of ethnic neighborhoods which were isolated as far as possible from the larger city. The social organization of one such neighborhood, with its strong peer-group relationships, is described in William F. Whyte's *Street Corner Society*.[8]

"Racial Inferiority" and Immigration

Before the turn of the century, arguments to restrict immigration were largely based upon (1) the ethnocentric assumption of the superiority of American ways and (2) the assumption that American industrial society represented a higher evolutionary form than the backward regions of Europe. Nonetheless, "the wretched refuse of your teeming shore" were felt to be convertible into the American mainstream. As the *Philadelphia Press* commented in 1888: "The strong stomach of American civilization may, and doubtless will, digest and assimilate ultimately this unsavory and repellent throng. . . . In time they catch the spirit of the country and form an element of decided worth."[9]

---

[7] Josiah Strong, *Our Country*, rev. ed., Baker and Taylor, New York, 1891, chap. 11.
[8] William F. Whyte, *Street Corner Society*, University of Chicago Press, Chicago, 1943. See Chapter 6, City Life-Styles, for a review of material on inner-city communities.
[9] Quoted in Higham, op. cit., p. 63.

However, a new argument, that of racial inferiority, was later added to the argument for exclusion. (The term "race" meant ethnicity or nationality rather than color, so that such terms as the "Polish race" and the "Italian race," were used. Various "experts" of the time agreed that the new immigrants were genetically inferior to the Anglo-Saxons who, combined with Germans, Scandinavians, and other "old immigrants," had formed the "American race." Discovering genetics, they jumped to the conclusion that not only hair color, size, and bone structure were genetically transferable, but also disposition, creativity, criminality, poverty, illiteracy, and all social behavior. Blood would tell—and what they believed it told was that Anglo-Saxon America was genetically committing suicide by allowing in unrestricted numbers of inferior races such as Poles, Italians, Slavs, and other eastern and southern Europeans. The conclusion seemed clear to opponents of immigration. "To admit the unchangeable differentiation of race in its modern scientific meaning is to admit inevitably the existence of superiority in one race and of inferiority in another."[10] According to E. A. Ross, a prominent sociologist of the time, even the appearance of the American population was likely to deteriorate: "It is unthinkable that so many persons with crooked faces, coarse mouths, bad noses, heavy jaws, and low foreheads can mingle their heredity with ours without making personal beauty yet more rare among us than it actually is."[11] While this sounds absurd today, the importance of the genetic argument cannot be overstressed. These genetic beliefs were held not by a lunatic fringe but by major scholars with national influence.

In the United States, the effect of the genetic argument was seen in the restrictive immigration laws of 1921 and 1924, the National Origins Act of 1929, and the McCarran-Walter Act of 1952. (President Truman vetoed the latter as discriminatory, but Congress passed it over his veto.) Southern and eastern Europeans were reduced from 45 percent of all immigrants under the already restrictive law of 1921 to 12 percent under the law of 1924. Northern and western Europeans were welcome— particularly if they were Protestant. About 85 percent of the quota went to northwest Europe, and roughly half the total quota went to three countries: England, Germany, and Ireland. Eastern and southern Europeans were given minimal quotas. Not until 1968 were the "racial" quotas eliminated.

White Ethnics Today

The days of mass European migration are past, but we still have a substantial foreign-born population, and that population is overwhelmingly urban. As of 1970 there were still 9.6 million foreign-born whites in the United States, 91 percent of whom resided in urban places. Cities such as Boston, New York, Chicago, Detroit, Milwaukee, San Francisco, and Los Angeles still have substantial ethnic colonies; "Little Italys," "Greektowns," "New Polands," and "Chinatowns" remind us of the heterogeneity of the metropolis. The majority of the whole ethnic population has

[10]Madison Grant, *The Passing of the Great Race,* Scribner, New York, 1921, p. XXVIII.
[11]E. A. Ross, *The Old World in the New,* Century, New York, 1914, p. 287.

been dispersed outward from segregated ethnic neighborhoods.[12] Today, ethnic neighborhoods, as described in Chapter 6, City Life-Styles, are viewed by some as simply historical remnants of bypassed ways of life.[13] New ethnic areas, though, continue to be formed, particularly among Mexican American and Puerto Rican groups.

There is still debate about the accuracy of the view of America as a melting pot blending diverse groups. Instead of a melting pot, cultural pluralists suggest that there is continued separation of national-origin groups, so that a nation is really a mosaic of ethnic blocks. For instance, Glazer and Moynihan, in *Beyond the Melting Pot,* a study of the enduring importance of ethnicity in New York City, found continuing cultural pluralism: "The point about the melting pot is that it did not happen. At least not in New York, and, mutatis mutandis, in those parts of America which resemble New York."[14] On the other hand, the urban sociologist Scott Greer maintains that the melting pot was effective, and that the result is a common American culture.[15]

Writers on white ethnicity such as Michael Novak and Andrew Greeley reject the view that the melting pot eventually dissolves distinct cultural traits. They charge that social scientists have been too quick to reject the importance of ethnicity.[16] Some of this rejection, Greeley goes so far as to suggest, may be "the unconscious guilt social scientists may feel for having left behind their own ethnic groups."[17] Whether or not this is indeed the case, it is true that there is a tendency to underplay the role of ethnicity. It should also be noted that the argument over melting pot versus pluralism need not be—and in real life isn't—an either-or situation.

In discussing the question of assimilation, it helps to remember Milton Gordon's often-quoted distinctions between cultural assimilation and structural assimilation. "Cultural assimilation" is said to occur when the newcomers adopt the dress, food habits, and cultural habits of the dominant group. Partially because of exposure through public schools and common media, cultural assimilation of new groups has been relatively rapid in America.

"Structural assimilation" is far more comprehensive, since it involves acceptance into the primary groups, cliques, and institutions of the dominant group. Structural assimilation is thus a more gradual process; ultimately it means intermarriage. "Once structural assimilation has occurred. . . . all other types of assimilation will necessarily follow."[18] Richard Alba's research, using a random

---

[12]Stanley Lieberson, *Ethnic Patterns in American Cities,* Free Press, New York, 1963; and Avery M. Gireot and James A. Weed, "Ethnic Residential Segregation: Patterns of Change," *American Journal of Sociology,* **81:** 10088–1111, March, 1976.

[13]Melvin M. Webber, "The Post-City Age," in J. John Palen (ed.), *City Scenes,* Little, Brown, Boston, 1977, pp. 307–319.

[14]Nathan Glazer and Daniel Patrick Moynihan, *Beyond the Melting Pot,* M.I.T. Press, Cambridge, Mass., 1963, p. v.

[15]Scott Greer, "The Faces of Ethnicity," in Palen, op. cit., pp. 147, 157.

[16]Michael Novak, *The Rise of the Unmeltable Ethnics,* Macmillan, New York, 1972; and Andrew M. Greeley, *Ethnicity in the United States,* Wiley, New York, 1974.

[17]Greeley, op. cit., p. 8.

[18]Milton M. Gordon, *Assimilation in American Life,* Oxford University Press, New York, 1964, p. 81.

sample of the national Catholic population, found that one measure of structural assimilation—intermarriage—had proceeded farther than had been commonly acknowledged.[19] Excepting the Hispanic and French Canadian populations, intermarriage was extensive, particularly in the English, Irish, and German populations. Scott Greer goes further in suggesting that ethnicity has lost real meaning when increasing proportions of the population have mixed ancestry and thus can choose whether to identify themselves as, for example, Italian, Irish, or Polish. He believes that "The romantic idealization of the ethnic bond persists, despite the difficulty many Americans have in deciding which ethnic background is the right one."[20]

No one challenges the upsurge in interest in ethnicity and family heritage. What continues to be debated is the strength and depth of the ethnic revival. Is the ethnic interest simply a romantic revival, or does it have deeper significance? Does it extend deeper than a "Polish Power" button, drinking green beer on St. Patrick's Day, or occasionally visiting Little Italy to purchase ethnic food? Does ethnicity make a difference in the attitudes, values, or life-style of second- and later-generation whites now living in the suburbs? For most social scientists, knowing one's social class is far more useful than knowing one's ethnicity.

BLACK AMERICANS

The following pages review the past and present status of black Americans. While reading this material, keep the following points in mind.

First, Afro-Americans did not come to American shores voluntarily, seeking a new way of life. Almost all were brought here in bondage, as slaves, and this has left a profound social-psychological imprint that both blacks and whites must overcome.

Second, major white immigration to the industrializing cities occurred during the nineteenth century, when the number of unskilled jobs was expanding. Black immigration to urban areas, on the other hand, occurred most heavily in the twentieth century, a period during which long-term industrial opportunities for the unskilled and poorly educated have been contracting.

Third, and most important, those who are visibly nonwhite are immediately subject to racist classification. White ethnics who suffered from discrimination or the imposition of quotas could, and often did, change their names as well as their life-styles, adopting the attitudes and customs of WASP America. But this choice is not open to most blacks and other nonwhites. Unlike ethnicity, color is a difference that cannot be denied. Table 8-1 shows the black population of the United States from 1790 to 1980.

[19]Richard D. Alba, "Social Assimilation among American Catholic National-Origin Groups," *American Sociological Review*, **41**:1030–1046, December, 1976.
[20]Greer, op. cit., p. 156.

TABLE 8-1
Black Population in the United States by Numbers and Percent, 1790 to 1980

Year	Number	Percent of total population
1790	757,000	19.3
1800	1,002,000	18.9
1850	3,639,000	15.7
1900	8,834,000	11.6
1930	11,891,000	9.7
1940	12,866,000	9.8
1950	15,042,000	10.0
1960	18,860,000	10.6
1970	22,672,570	11.2
1980	25,969,000	11.8

Source: U.S. Bureau of the Census: Fifteenth Census Reports, *Population*, vol. II; Sixteenth Census Reports, *Population*, vol. 11, part I; *U.S. Census of Population: 1950*, vol. II, part 1; *U.S. Census of Population: 1950*, vol 1; U.S. Bureau of the Census, *Current Population Reports*, series P-25, nos. 367, 416, 441, and 460.

Historical Patterns

Blacks, numbering some 25 million—or more than the population of Canada—are unique among American minorities in that they alone have experienced out-and-out slavery. Indians were removed from their lands and subjected to starvation; the first Mexican Americans became part of the United States by conquest; and during World War II, Japanese Americans on the west coast were rounded up and placed in internment camps. But no other group of people have been so systematically deprived of their very humanity as the blacks. The notorious pre-Civil War Dred Scott decision put even the Supreme Court on record as ruling that blacks were not persons but property.

The first blacks in the American colonies were not slaves but indentured servants. That meant that they had to serve for a given time—usually seven years—in bondage or indentureship before they became legally entitled to own property. However, this system—particularly in the south, where plantations required large labor forces—rapidly evolved into one of perpetual servitude. In 1661 Virginia passed a law allowing perpetual slavery, and two years later the Maryland colony declared that "all Negroes or other slaves within the province, to be hereafter imported, shall serve during life."

The fundamental conflict between America's social and political philosophy of freedom and equality on the one hand, and the practice of social inequality on the other was aptly characterized by Gunnar Myrdal as the "American dilemma."[21] Two centuries earlier, Thomas Jefferson (who owned slaves while

[21]Gunnar Myrdal, *An American Dilemma,* Harper and Row, New York, 1944.

opposing slavery) had referred to it as justice in conflict with avarice and oppression.[22]

Population Changes

At the time of the first census in 1790, blacks made up 19 percent of the total population. In spite of a high rate of natural increase, the proportion of blacks in the population declined during the nineteenth century because of heavy European inmigration. European immigration was restricted by the immigration laws of the 1920s; thus, since 1930, blacks have been increasing as a proportion of the population. They currently constitute 12 percent of the population.

The black population was—until this century—overwhelmingly rural and southern. Despite the Civil War and the extensive political and social upheavals of Reconstruction, there was but slight change in this pattern. As recently as 1910, nine out of ten blacks still lived in the south, and 73 percent of blacks were rural. Today half (52 percent) live in the south, and 22 percent are rural, with only a minority of the latter being farmers.

Slavery in Cities

Slavery was basically a rural institution, founded upon the plantation economy, but there was urban slavery as well. By 1820 about 20 percent of the people in the major southern cities were slaves.[23] Slavery in southern cities differed fundamentally from slavery on the plantations, so much that plantation owners vigorously opposed the use of slaves in urban manufacturing, fearing that it would undermine the south's "peculiar institution." As a consequence, slavery drastically declined in the large cities by 1860. (Richmond's iron works were an exception.) The reason was not economic but social.

On the plantation, slaves were totally dependent upon the white overseer and could, if necessary, be controlled through fear or repression. Some might try to run away, but pursuit by specially trained tracking dogs and professional slave hunters made successful escapes difficult. In urban areas, on the other hand, slaveholders had far less mastery:

> While plantation slaves were typically field hands or house servants, urban slaves engaged in a wide variety of occupations, skilled as well as unskilled, in addition to those who worked as domestic servants for their owners. A very large number of slaves were hired out to work for others, the arrangement being made either by the slave owners or the slaves themselves.[24]

The system of slaves being "hired out" or hiring themselves to others and sharing the income with their owners meant that the slave was, in Frederick Douglass's

[22]Ulrich B. Philips, *American Negro Slavery,* Louisiana State University Press, Baton Rouge, 1969, p. 122.
[23]Richard C. Wade, *Slavery in the Cities: The South 1820–1860,* Oxford University Press, New York, 1964.
[24]Thomas Sowell, *Race and Economics,* David McKay Company, New York, 1975, p. 12.

words, "almost a free citizen."[25] In effect, the slave and owner entered into an informal contract in which the slave, through the sharing of his or her earnings, "purchased" some degree of freedom. Escaping from slavery was far easier and more common in the cities; therefore, to prevent the loss of large capital inventments, urban slaveholders had to rule with a lighter hand.

The fact that urbanism undermined the traditional slave-master relationship did not escape plantation owners. Therefore, they were constantly making new restrictions and laws to govern urban slavery. Many nineteenth-century southerners saw city life as a direct threat to the southern way of life, and they were right.

"Free Persons of Color"

Nor were all urban blacks slaves. By the eve of the Civil War, roughly one out of eight blacks was a "free Negro," and most of these lived in cities—usually in border states. This growing population of "free persons of color" created serious problems for the slave states, for although they faired poorly in economic terms, they were still free men and women, and thus a threat to the system.

Until fairly recently, descendants of free Negroes—those who were not slaves at the time of the Civil War—dominated leadership roles in the black urban community. While Booker T. Washington was indeed "up from slavery," few other leaders were. W. E. B. DuBois and most other founders of the NAACP, for example, had never been slaves.

> Only in the post-World War II period did black students descended from the masses of those freed by the Civil War predominate in black colleges, and their arrival forced wholesale changes in the general character of these institutions. Descendants of the ante-bellum free persons of color similarly dominated Negro leadership at the local and national level a generation ago.[26]

Jim Crow Laws

It should be noted that segregation of public facilities was not characteristic of the pre-Civil War south. Jim Crow laws, which established separate railway cars, dining areas, rest rooms, and even doorways for blacks, were largely a product of the years between 1890 and 1910.[27] Grandfather clauses, literacy tests, and poll taxes disenfranchised blacks, while segregation laws were passed to separate the races in schools and public facilities. Crucial to segregation was the 1896 case of *Plessy v. Ferguson,* in which the Supreme Court ruled that separate racial facilities were legal if they were equal. The pernicious doctrine of "separate but equal" was not finally eliminated until the famous 1954 case of *Brown v. Board of Education of Topeka,* in which the Supreme Court ruled that "separate educational facilities are inherently unequal."

---

[25]Wade, op. cit.
[26]Sowell, op. cit., p. 41.
[27]C. Van Woodward, *The Strange Career of Jim Crow,* Oxford University Press, New York, 1966.

Blacks were evicted from houses in white areas after the Chicago race riot
of 1919. (Chicago Historical Society.)

Movement North

Significant migration of blacks out of the south began with World War I. When the
war cut off the tide of European immigrant labor and flooded industries with war
orders, a new source of labor had to be found. Soon labor recruiters were scouring
the south, encouraging Negroes to migrate north to "the promised land." In some
cases, one-way railroad tickets were even provided. Recruiters "stirring up the
negros" were unwelcome guests in southern communities. A licensing regulation
in Macon, Georgia, required each labor agent to pay a $25,000 fee and obtain
recommendations from ten local ministers, ten manufacturers, and twenty-five
merchants. Elsewhere, methods were more direct and recruiters were shot or
tarred and feathered.

The pull of northern industrial jobs, combined with the boll weevil's

Leavin' the South

". . . When I drove into town that next Saturday after I quit at Bonds,
I ran into this fella's son, Henry Bonds. He was a big stout
guy—wanted to know why I left his dad. I told him, "I can get
more money." He said, "If you don't come back to Dad by Monday,
we'll do away with you."

I knew what that meant. He and his brothers were gonna get me if
I drove for Asa Lever on Monday. I didn't dare argue with him,
cause maybe he'd got me right then.

Quite a few left to come into Tennessee. From there they'd go to St.
Louis, Murphysboro, some to Detroit, in fact all over the East. None
went as fast as I did though.

I was in danger of my life when I left Macon. It seemed like it was
a period when white folks was angry. The Negroes were leaving out,
and they were leaving out by numbers. They were comin' north
because jobs were open. They may not have been the best, but they
were far better than we had there.

They were rough in that period. They beat up a lot of our people,
left 'em out on the road. The flies got in some of 'em before the
people found 'em. Just because they were trying to better their
condition. It was awful rough in that time.

When they began to leave, if you owed these fellas a quarter, you
daren't talk about leavin'. They'd say, "You owe me money." And
they'd make it whatever they want to, and you dare not leave. So, I
beat the rap by gettin' out of there that Sunday night."*

*Interview by Clem Imhoff with Reverend D. W. Johnson, "The Recruiter," *Southern Exposure,* **4:** 83–87,
1976.

destruction of cotton and the mechanization of agriculture, encouraged migration. Cotton production was shifting out of the old south to the west and southwest, and field-hand labor was no longer so necessary. Between 1910 and 1920 the five states of the deep south—South Carolina, Georgia, Alabama, Mississippi, and Louisiana—lost 400,000 blacks through out-migration. (Whites were also out-migrating at this time.) There were three major migratory streams. The first was from the Carolinas, Georgia, and Florida up the east coast to key locations such as Washington, Philadelphia, New York, and Boston. The second was from Mississippi, Arkansas, and part of Alabama into the midwestern cities of St. Louis, Detroit, Chicago, and Milwaukee. The third stream was from Texas and parts of Louisiana to Los Angeles and the west coast.

The depression of the 1930s cut off employment opportunities in the north and stemmed the flow of in-migrants to the cities. But the resurgence of industry during World War II again accelerated the pace of migration, and it continued into the 1950s and 1960s. Mississippi's black population declined more than 100,000 during the decade 1960–1970, and there were also absloute losses (in spite of high birthrates) in Alabama and South Carolina.

This was an extremely substantial migration, but it should be kept in perspective—particularly since there is a tendency to exaggerate it. Between 1910 and 1960 somewhat under 5 million blacks left the south, largely for the big cities of the north. This is a great number of people but hardly compares with the waves of European immigrants that inundated American shores during the first years of this century. For example, a total of 8.8 million European immigrants entered the United States between 1901 and 1911 alone. Even today in urban areas there are far more foreign immigrants than blacks in-migrating. In fact, there are not enough rural southern blacks left to have all that great an impact, even if they all migrated out. Foreign immigrants, on the other hand, continue to flow into the United States at a pace of approximately 400,000 a year. (On top of this there are perhaps 1 million illegal immigrants—largely from Mexico—each year.) Thus in-migration of southern blacks to the cities should be kept in perspective.

As a result of the great northern migration, Chicago as of the 1970s housed more blacks then all of Mississippi, and the New York metropolitan area had more blacks than any state of the old south.[28]

End of Mass Migration

The period of mass migration from the south is now history. This movement contained the seeds of its own destruction, for as blacks moved to the cities, there were fewer persons left behind to become migrants in the future. Today most black movement is from one urban area to another. Increasingly, urban blacks are second- and third-generation urban residents. The image of the Negro as a southern rural sharecropper migrating to the big city is a picture out of another age and time. Today, while just over half of all blacks still live in the south, blacks

[28]Thomas F. Pettigrew, *Racially Separate or Together?*, McGraw-Hill, New York, 1971, p. 3.

are now one of the most urban segments of the total population. Blacks are more concentrated in the large cities and SMSAs than whites. Over half of all blacks (55 percent) now live in central cities of metropolitan areas (this is down from 59 percent in 1970), and one of five (19 percent) resides in suburbs.[29] Of whites, one-fourth (24 percent) live in central cities and 42 percent in suburbs. Blacks make up the majority of the population in four major American cities: Atlanta, Gary, Newark, and Washington, D.C. In nine other cities—Baltimore, Birmingham, Charleston, Detroit, New Orleans, Richmond, Savannah, St. Louis, and Wilmington—more than 40 percent of the population is black. When discussing racial change, however, it must be remembered that the prophecy of black majorities in most major American cities is demographically impossible. To put it simply, there are not enough blacks for this to occur. Blacks are only 12 percent of the total population, and three-quarters of all blacks are already urban. Because of somewhat higher birthrates among blacks the black population of central cities is still increasing slowly, but only by 0.9 percent a year. It was a much higher 2.9 percent per year during the 1960s.

Moving South

For the first time since the Civil War, there now are more blacks leaving than entering northern central cities. According to Bureau of the Census figures, between 1975 and 1977, some 104,000 more blacks aged two years and older moved out of the northeastern states than moved in, while in the north central states the numbers of blacks moving in and out were approximately equal. Blacks, like whites, are now more likely to be moving south and west than moving north. Black migration patterns increasingly resemble white migration patterns.

Urban Segregation Patterns

Amount of Segregation. Segregation of racial and ethnic groups into ghettos is not new to American life. Anti-immigrant and anti-Catholic political movements, from the Know-Nothing Party of the nineteenth century to the Klu Klux Klan of the 1920s, attempted to keep newcomers "in their place" socially and physically. Their "place" was the old and overcrowded housing in the central area near the factories. As members of ethnic groups prospered, they often moved out of the ghetto into outlying neighborhoods with better-quality housing, and so residential segregation decreased.[30] Blacks also started in the poorest central-city ghetto neighborhoods, but to a far greater degree, they remained restricted to such "black belts."[31] For blacks, until very recently, race automatically overrode economics.

The landmark study of changing patterns of racial segregation was that of

---

[29]U.S. Bureau of the Census, "Social and Economic Characteristics of Metropolitan and Nonmetropolitan Population: 1977 and 1970," *Current Population Reports*, series P-23, no. 75, Washington, D.C., November, 1978, table F.

[30]Lieberson, op. cit.,; and Gireot and Weed, op. cit.

[31]For an excellent study of ghetto life during the 1930s, see St. Clair Drake and Horace Cayton, *Black Metropolis*, Harcourt, Brace, New York, 1945.

Karl and Alma Taeuber, in which they compared segregation indexes for American cities for 1940, 1950, and 1960.[32]

Their segregation index, called the "index of dissimilarity," used the computer to analyze census data for blacks and save an index figure representing the proportion of nonwhites that would have to move to another block in order to have a complete balance of the races. For example, in a city where 10 percent of the population is black, the index would have a value of zero if one-tenth of the households on each block were black and a value of 100 if there was total segregation. Thus, the index has a theoretical range of 0 to 100, with 100 representing complete segregation.

According to the Taeubers' findings, the average segregation index for 207 of the largest cities in the United States was 86.2 in 1960. This means that 86 percent of all nonwhites would have had to change the block on which they live in order to produce an unsegregated pattern. Of the 207 cities in the sample, each having a population of 50,000 or more, the value of the segregation index ranged from a high of 98.1 in Fort Lauderdale to a low of 60.4 in San Jose. Thus, they found that a high incidence of segregation was virtually universal.

Extensive segregation of southern cities is a modern rather than a long-standing trend. In the south of days gone by, social segregation was so rigid that spatial segregation was unnecessary. Especially in the older southern cities, whites frequently lived in the big house on the street while blacks lived in the smaller house in the alley behind. Black servants lived on the premises. More recently, however, with the social distance between blacks and whites decreased by legislation, the south has been adapting northern racial patterns and substituting spatial distance for social distance. As of 1940, the *least* spatially segregated city of the 109 cities for which data are available was Charleston, South Carolina, the "birthplace of the Confederacy."[33] As of 1960 the segregation index of Charleston had increased almost 20 points, to 79.5.

As a rough generalization one could say that in the south it was acceptable for blacks to live close to whites but not to rise to the levels of white social classes. In the north, on the contrary, it was all right to move up but not to move next door. As the old folk saying went, "Down South, it's 'Nigger, you can live close but don't move up'; while up North, it's 'Nigger, you can move up, but don't get too close.'"

More recent research based on a sample of 109 cities indicated decreasing segregation levels in all regions of the country, including the south.[34] Overall segregation indexes for 1970 were below those for 1940. Another study of 237 metropolitan areas as of 1970, however, notes the very gradual decline in segregation during the decade of the 1960s and the slow response to more favorable racial attitudes.[35]

---

[32]Karl E. Taeuber and Alma F. Taeuber, *Negroes in Cities: Residential Segregation and Neighborhood Change,* Aldine, Chicago, 1965.
[33]Ibid., p. 45.
[34]Annemette Sorenson, Karl E. Taeuber, and Leslie J. Hollingsworth, Jr., "Indexes of Racial Residential Segregation for 109 Cities in the United States, 1940 to 1970," *Sociological Focus,* April, 1975, pp. 125–142.
[35]Thomas Van Valey, Wade Clark Roof, and Jerome E. Wilcox, "Trends in Residential Segregation: 1960–1970," *American Journal of Sociology,* 82:826–844, January, 1977.

Racial Turnover. The fact that racial segregation in cities is decreasing is now established. The question is whether this reflects changes in racial attitudes or reflects only the period of integration occurring between the in-migration of the first black and the out-migration of the last white to the suburbs. White flight and black suburbanization were discussed extensively in Chapter 7, Patterns of Suburbanization, and so that material will not be repeated here. Suffice it to say that the data indicate that whites were and are moving more *toward* perceived suburban advantages than *from* problems created by minorities, and black suburbanization increased more dramatically during the 1970s than expected.

Racial turnover of central-city areas does not require massive flight by white residents. Approximately one out of every five American households changes location each year; and even without panic by out-migration, an area will change from white to black if all or most of the newcomers are black. Harvey Molotch examined the process of racial transition in the South Shore neighborhood, where he found that in spite of attempts to create an intergrated area, the neighborhood became resegregated as an all-black area.[36] This was not because of whites fleeing, but rather because the dwelling units within the area, as they became vacant, were less likely to be filled by whites. The area thus turned over not because of white flight but because of a lack of white in-migration.

On the other hand, a study done in Cleveland suggested that "white flight was a factor in household turnover in a few neighborhoods."[37] Also, an examination of Detroit suburbs by Reynolds Farley indicated that white preference for all-white areas strongly contributes to residential segregation.[38] Farley suggested that blacks are willing to enter mixed areas, but whites are not. Thus, there is a "ratchet effect"—the more blacks there are in a neighborhood, the less likely it is that whites will move in. As whites move out, they are replaced by blacks, making the area even less appealing to whites. Building on this idea, Bud Wurdork has further suggested that data from the Detroit Area study indicated that the blacker a neighborhood becomes, the more likely it is that whites will move out for racial reasons.[39] It is hypothesized that once a threshold of "blackness" is reached, the "ratchet" process of whites moving out and blacks moving in begins.

However, an unanswered question is whether the Detroit area is typical of metropolitan patterns nationwide. The data presented in Chapter 7 would seem to suggest that white flight is less significant nationally. What is clear is that while legally enforced segregation is a thing of the past, most blacks, by choice or necessity, continue to reside in predominately black areas. The major cause of such segregation is racial rather than economic differences. As Karl Taeuber

[36]Harvey Molotch, *Managed Integration,* University of California Press, Berkeley, 1972.

[37]Avery A. Guest and James J. Zuiches, "Another Look at Residential Turnover in Urban Neighborhoods," *American Journal of Sociology,* **77:** 457–467, November, 1971.

[38]Reynolds Farley, Howard Schuman, Susanne Bianchi, Diane Colansanto, and Shirley Hatchett, "Chocolate City, Vanilla Suburbs," a paper presented at the August 1977 meeting of the American Sociological Association, Chicago.

[39]Bud Wurdock, "The Role of White Flight in Neighborhood Racial Transition," a paper delivered at the April 1978 meeting of the Midwest Sociological Society.

bluntly says, "I have concluded from my own research and a review of the work of others that the prime cause of residential segregation by race has been discrimination both public and private."[40] (For a discussion of governmental real estate practices see Chapter 12, Housing Programs and Urban Regeneration.)

Social-Class Distribution. As regards spatial distribution by social class, blacks tend to follow the same pattern as whites. The larger and older cities of the north are much more likely to have status differentials favoring suburban over central-city residence.[41] Within cities, there is commonly an increase in the level of socioeconomic status for blacks with distance from the city center. Marston suggests that areas that are changing to black residency are always of higher status than established black neighborhoods, regardless of where they are located in the urban area.[42] However, Rose did not always find this to be true. In his research, transitional areas closer to the city were sometimes lower-class or working-class, but transitional areas in more peripheral locations were areas of higher status than all-black areas.[43]

Middle-class blacks live in areas which are far more mixed in terms of socioeconomic composition than those inhabited by middle-class whites. A study done in Chicago indicates that the black middle class may be isolated from public housing, but middle- and upper-class black people live, on the average, closer to lower-class blacks than middle-class whites live to lower-class whites.[44]

Diversity among Blacks

The old stereotype of the poor uneducated black just up from the southern cotton fields to the big city is ludicrously out of touch with contemporary social and economic reality. This is not to say that blacks as a group are not economically deprived when compared with whites; there are still substantial, if lessening, differences between the two groups as aggregates. As of 1977 the median family income of blacks as a group was only 57 percent of the income for whites.

Such aggregate figures, although frequently quoted, present a misleading picture. There is in reality an increasing division into two black populations: one that is increasingly becoming middle-class and one that is increasingly being locked into poverty as a semipermanent urban underclass. If one concentrates attention on the first group, the inescapable conclusion is that blacks are cashing in on the American dream. If the focus is on the second group, it is just as obvious that blacks are slipping ever further behind.

[40]Karl E. Taeuber, "Racial Segregation: The American Dilemma," *The Annals of the American Academy of Political and Social Science,* **422:**91, November, 1975.
[41]J. John Palen and Leo Schnore, "Color Composition and City-Suburban Status Differences," *Land Economics,* **41:**87–91, February, 1965.
[42]Wilfred C. Marston, "Socioeconomic Differentiation within Negro Areas of American Cities," *Social Forces,* **48:**165–176, December, 1969.
[43]Harold M. Rose, "The Spatial Development of Black Residential Subsystems," *Economic Geography,* **48:**43–65, January, 1972.
[44]Brigitte Mach Erbe, "Race and Socioeconomic Segregation," *American Sociological Review,* **40:**801–812, December, 1975.

The Black Middle Class. Half (46 percent) of black husband-wife families as of 1977 were making over $15,000 a year. (Note that these are 1977 dollars and do not reflect the rapid inflation of the last years.) By any reasonable standard these families were middle-class or better. (The comparable figure was 61 percent for white husband-wife families.[45] Census figures indicate that the income gap has essentially disappeared for younger (under thirty-five) intact black families outside the south. As long as a decade ago, the 1970 census indicated that income for such younger families was 96 percent of white income.[46] When younger families in which both the husband and wife work were compared, the black families outside the south earned 104 percent of what comparable whites earned. Note, however, that what is being compared is younger intact families. For older blacks and for families without a male head, affirmative action programs have had little impact; they continue to bear the scars of exclusion.

Care has to be taken, though, not to automatically associate being a black woman with being a victim of perpetual poverty. Although families headed by women on welfare are indeed poor, black women who work make about as much money as white women who work. In fact, in the higher job categories, black women do better than their white counterparts. Black professional women in 1973 made 111 percent of what white women earned, and black women in managerial positions made 143 percent of what white women in similar jobs were paid.[47] (Both groups, however, made less than white males.) As expressed by the Bureau of the Census: "Overall black women earned about as much as their white counterparts in almost every occupational category for which earning differentials could be shown." On the other hand, "earning levels of black men were substantially below those of whites in nearly every occupational category."[48] Overall, then, if present trends continue—and there are signs that they will—intact black families will continue to develop an income structure identical to that of their white counterparts.

Scholars are increasingly documenting the extent to which class factors are supplanting those of race. William Wilson argues that the growth of corporate and government sectors has resulted in a segmented labor market in which poorly educated and trained inner-city blacks, particularly black teenagers, are restricted to low-wage jobs. "On the other hand, talented and educated blacks are experiencing unprecedented job opportunities . . . at least comparable to those of whites with equivalent qualifications."[49]

---

[45]U.S. Bureau of the Census, "Population Profile of the United States: 1978," *Current Population Reports,* series P-20, no. 336, Washington, D.C., 1979, table 28.

[46]For a fuller discussion of changes in the income levels of blacks, see Ben J. Wattenberg and Richard M. Scammon, "Black Progress and Liberal Rhetoric," *Commentary,* 55(4):35–44, April, 1973.

[47]U.S. Bureau of the Census, "The Social and Economic Status of the Black Population in the United States, 1974," *Current Population Reports,* Washington, D.C., 1975, p. 3.

[48]Ibid., p. 58.

[49]William Julius Wilson, *The Declining Significance of Race,* University of Chicago Press, Chicago, 1978, p. 151.

The Black Underclass. For the black underclass at the other end of the spectrum, the picture is much grimmer. Here we find the elderly who are scarred by previous racial experiences and the young who by accident of birth—illegitimacy, poverty, the absence of the father—are unable to take advantage of the new opportunities. They are stationary, or making only minimal progress, and thus are slipping relatively farther behind not only white society but middle-class blacks as well.

Currently, over three-quarters of poor blacks reside in female-householder families. As put by the Bureau of the Census:

> The increase in the number of poor families with a female householder, no husband present, (from 1.8 million to 2.6 million), was one of the most significant changes in the poverty population between 1969 and 1977. This rise was coupled with a decline in the number of poor families with a male householder, resulting in an increase in the proportion of poor families with a female householder . . . they accounted for 71 percent of poor black families in 1977, compared to 54 percent in 1969.[50]

The relationship between black poverty and female householders is likely to increase during the 1980s. As of 1950 only 18 percent of all black families were headed by women. By 1970 this figure had increased to 28 percent, and as of 1980 it was 41 percent. (During the same three decades the increase in white families headed by women was from 9 to 12 percent.)

For blacks growing up in inner-city poor families, the future is far from bright. Unemployment among black central-city youths has remained around one-third despite recessions or prosperity. Civil rights enforcement and minority job programs have had little impact on those with minimal skill levels. The departure of business and industry to the suburbs has further isolated these central-city youth. For black teenagers the old hiring hall dictum still has force: "If you're white, all right; if you're brown, stick around; if you're black, stay back."

The Future

In conclusion, it should be restated that there is no uniform "black population." For those at the bottom of the occupational structure, the future is grim. The urban underclass—black and white—is increasingly becoming a reservation population residing in inner-city welfare islands. The black middle class on the contrary, shows every sign of having economically entered the American mainstream. The future may show the black population becoming divided into two societies: one reasonably comfortable and affluent, the other increasingly locked into semipermanent poverty.

[50]U.S. Bureau of the Census, "Characteristics of the Population Below the Poverty Level: 1977," *Current Population Reports,* series P-60, no. 119, Washington, D.C., 1979. p. 3.

CHAPTER

9

URBAN DIVERSITY:
Mexican Americans,
Puerto Ricans,
Native Americans,
and Japanese Americans

SPANISH-ORIGIN POPULATION

Hispanic Americans constitute the most rapidly growing segment of the urban population (Table 9-1). The nation's 12 million persons of Hispanic origin account for 5.6 percent of the national population, and this figure excludes the estimated 7½ million illegal aliens. If present immigration—legal and illegal—continues, the Spanish-origin population may outnumber blacks within a score of years. The Spanish-origin population is more concentrated in metropolitan areas than either the whites or blacks, with 84 percent living in such areas. Within metropolitan areas the Spanish-speaking population is more evenly distributed than the black population. Some 41 percent of metropolitan-area Hispanics reside in suburbs (35 percent of all Spanish-speaking Americans live in suburbs).[1] Figure 9-1 shows the poverty status of Spanish-origin families in the United States.

The Spanish-speaking population is now quite diverse, including 6.5 million Mexican Americans and 1.7 million Puerto Ricans, plus Cubans, Dominicans, and other Latin Americans. Mexican Americans and Puerto Ricans—the two largest groups—are discussed below.

Mexican Americans

Mexican Americans—like the Indians—originally became a minority not by voluntary or involuntary migration from Europe or Africa but by being militarily conquered.[2] They are one of the nation's oldest minorities while at the same time, somewhat contradictorily, being the newest minority in terms of numbers of immigrants from Mexico and in-migration to the cities.

The stereotype of Mexican Americans as agricultural workers—an image strengthened by Cesar Chavez's successful struggle to organize California farm workers—is quite erroneous. Ninety percent of California's almost 3 million persons of Mexican descent are urban residents. Los Angeles today has well over 1½ million Mexican Americans, without counting the "undocumented aliens" in the Spanish-speaking East Los Angeles area. There are now more Hispanics than blacks in Los Angeles.

Housing Patterns. The crowded *barrios* of California and Texas are where new arrivals are most likely to settle. (Approximately five-sixths of all Mexican Americans live in Texas or California.) Poverty is common in the urban *barrios*, or ghettos, and Chicano gangs remain a serious problem. Gang-related drug use and crime are a way of life in the *barrios*.[3] Los Angeles County is estimated to have 13,000 gang members and scores of gang murders yearly.

---

[1] U.S. Bureau of the Census, "Social and Economic Characteristics of the Metropolitan and Nonmetropolitan Population: 1977 and 1970," *Current Population Reports,* Special Studies, series P-23, no. 75, Washington, D.C., November 1978, pp. 5, 7.

[2] There is no generally accepted term used by Americans of Mexican ancestry to describe the ethnic group. "Mexican American," "Spanish American," "Latino," and, among younger activists, "Chicano," are all used, and the preferred term differs from place to place. For convenience, we will generally use the term "Mexican American."

[3] For a study of Chicano gangs and the role of drugs, see Joan W. Moore, *Homeboys: Gangs, Drugs and Prison in the Barrios of Los Angeles,* Temple University Press, Philadelphia, 1978.

TABLE 9-1
Hispanic-Origin Population by Type of Origin, for the United States: 1976

Type of Spanish origin	Number (in thousands)	Percent
Total, Spanish origin	11,117	100.0
Mexican	6,590	59.3
Puerto Rican	1,753	15.8
Cuban	687	6.2
Central or South American	752	6.8
Other Spanish origin	1,335	12.0

Source: U.S. Bureau of the Census, "Persons of Spanish Origin in the United States," *Current Population Reports,* series P-20, no. 310, Washington, D.C., March, 1977.

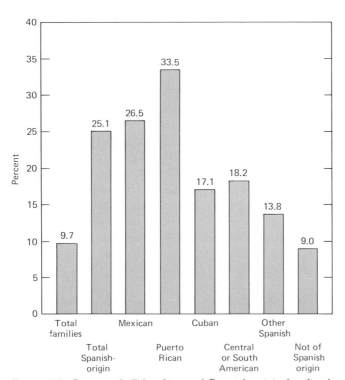

Figure 9-1. Percent of all families and Spanish-origin families by poverty status: 1975. (*Source:* Bureau of the Census, *Current Population Reports,* P-20, No. 310.)

For Mexican Americans, unlike blacks, there are wide variations in patterns of physical segregation. Outside of the border states, economics plays a larger part than discrimination in determining residential patterns. In the southwest there is a long history of prejudice against Mexican Americans, but elsewhere in the country (excepting cities such as Chicago) there is a general unawareness of Mexican Americans as a group—a situation with positive as well as negative aspects. There is a failure to know of, and appreciate, the richness of Mexican culture, but at the same time, there are no long-accepted patterns of discrimination against and segregation of Mexican Americans. Although segregation and discrimination do occur, they are not institutionalized to the extent that they are in the relationships between blacks and whites.

Socioeconomic Position. The majority of the present Mexican American population are fairly recent immigrants. The immigrants came north because there was a lack of economic opportunities in the labor-heavy Mexican economy and a demand for temporary farm workers in the United States. Particularly after World War II, the economic boom in the United States, coupled with the inability of the Mexican industrial economy to absorb all of its workers, led to both legal ("green-carders") and illegal migration northward to supply the shortage in American agricultural labor. During World War II some 300,000 to 500,000 Mexican Americans served in the armed forces, and others left the farms for the booming war industries of southern California. Few returned to the farms after the war. Today the agribusiness enterprises in California and Texas are replacing human workers with machines, a process that is likely to accelerate.

Economically, the Spanish-speaking population is as a whole somewhat better off than blacks. The median income level is some $2,000 higher. This general comparison, however, masks wide variations among those of different Spanish-speaking backgrounds. Puerto Ricans make slightly less than blacks, Mexican Americans make slightly more, and Cuban Americans—many of whom left Cuba with marketable skills—make considerably more.

In spite of the considerable diversity among the Mexican American population, it is often negatively stereotyped by other Americans as poor, complacent, fatalistic, not goal-oriented, emotional, superstitious, and traditional. "Anglo" (non-Mexican) society tends to assume, because there are so many lower-class Mexican immigrants, that all persons of Mexican descent are poor.

Some 22 percent of Mexican American families are below the poverty line (the figure for blacks is 31 percent), while only seven percent have incomes above $25,000 in 1977 dollars.[4] This represents some economic gain (even with inflation), since only .05 percent of all Mexican American families had incomes over $25,000 as of the 1970 census.

Contributing to the low economic position of Mexican Americans are generally low levels of education. Among adults, only one-third have completed high school and only four percent are college graduates. Since in the United States lack of a high school diploma means virtual exclusion from much of

---

[4]U.S. Bureau of the Census, "Persons of Spanish Origin in the United States: March 1977," *Current Population Reports*, series P-20, no. 329, Washington, D.C., 1978.

contemporary industrial life, many Mexican Americans are employed in the so-called "secondary" labor market of marginal jobs and illegal enterprises.

Problems of Adjustment. Unfortunately, inferior social status and economic position have sometimes led Mexican Americans to internalize some of the negative stereotypes of the majority culture. Surveys of San Antonio, Los Angeles, and Albuquerque indicate that Mexicans often accept the self-depreciatory stereotypes as well as the more positive ones: e.g., laziness and volatility as well as a special warmth for life.[5] For example, more than 80 percent of those interviewed in Los Angeles and San Antonio felt that Mexicans are more emotional than other Americans. This can result in what sociologists call a "self-fulfilling prophesy," where a false or incomplete premise is believed and invokes a response that makes it come true. An example would be the belief by a teacher that Mexican American children cannot cope with abstract concepts: if the teacher, because of this belief, organizes his or her teaching to avoid abstract concepts, the result will be educational deficiencies.

Mexican Americans have, in fact, had serious problems with the formal education systems of North America. In all states, Mexican Americans have lower median levels of education than blacks. American schools have been ill-equipped to deal with students who are not fluent in English, and have frequently shunted them aside as if they were poor learners or deficient in intelligence. Bilingual education programs are only now becoming accepted. Frequent moving of families also disrupts some childrens' education. The comparatively lower value placed on education in the traditional lower-class Mexican family is also a factor, particularly as regards the education of women.

Movement to Cities. The problem of adequate schooling and other problems of adjusting to the larger Anglo society have become more acute with the rapid urbanization of the Mexican American population during the last two decades. Traditional isolated towns and villages in New Mexico and other southwestern states have been losing population, while the Mexican American population of cities such as Albuquerque, San Antonio, and Los Angeles has been increasing.

In the border states, only about one-fifth of the Mexican American population still lives in rural areas.[6] Today Los Angeles has more people of Mexican ancestry than any other city in the Americas, except Mexico City and Guadalajara. Clearly, the Mexican American's future is an urban future. The geographical movement out of the southwest is not only migration out of a region; it is a symbol of the inevitable change from rural to urban residence and rural to urban ways of life.

Mexican Americans have as a group attracted less attention to themselves than other minorities such as blacks. The relative quiet of Mexican American city dwellers can be partially attributed to the fact that despite low-level income, housing, and services, cities in the United States are still infinitely superior to the destitute barrios of the Mexican *municipios*. The United States offers relative

---

[5]Joan W. Moore, *Mexican Americans*, Prentice-Hall, Englewood Cliffs, N.J., 1976, p. 8.
[6]Moore, *Mexican Americans*, pp. 55–56.

opulence compared with the poverty of the suburban squatter barrios of Ciudad Juárez—the latter sometimes without electricity or water. And even in these Mexican border slums, the per capita income is two or three times higher than in other regions of Mexico.[7] Moreover, some persons of Mexican ancestry in the United States are illegal immigrants and thus do not seek attention in any way. Official figures place the number of Mexican immigrants entering the United States at roughly a quarter of a million a year; unofficial estimates place the number of illegals at roughly 1 million.

Differences between Mexican Americans and Anglos. Mexican Americans, as a rule, put heavier emphasis on familism than Anglo society does—although the difference in the cities is lessening. Women are still expected to fill traditional roles as wives and mothers. Even in northern cities like Chicago, the patriarchal ideal is still prevalent.[8] Higher education and careers for women are still frequently discouraged, although this pattern is far stronger in the southwest than in northern cities.

It is, however, easy to exaggerate the extent and depth of Mexican American traditionalism. The overwhelming majority of Mexican Americans identify themselves as Roman Catholic, for instance, but at the same time an increasing proportion of Mexican American women use means of birth control disapproved of by the Catholic church. Of course, some differences do persist. Fertility rates among Mexican Americans are still extremely high, with an average family of four children in 1980. Only American Indians, another poor minority, have larger families. Increasing urbanization and urbanism, plus socioeconomic mobility, should bring fertility rates of Mexican Americans more in line with those of the larger society over the next decade.

Today the Mexican American population is a young population. High fertility rates and the large number of young immigrants have resulted in a population much younger than the national population. The median age of the Mexican-origin population is 20.8 years, well below the median age of 29.9 years for Americans as a whole.

Internal Diversity. A previously noted, the Mexican American population is remarkably diverse. Traditionally, Mexicans (and Anglos) made a broad distinction between the upper-class "Spanish" of "pure blood" untainted by Indian ancestry and the lower-class "Mexicans." "Spanish" ancestry has traditionally been considered more prestigious than "Mexican" ancestry, and "Indian" ancestry is at the bottom. This attitude is not a reaction to the racial situation in the United States, but rather has roots deep in the early colonial history of Mexico under the Spanish Crown. (The Spanish colonial social system is discussed further in Chapter 16, Latin American Cities.)

The gracious Spanish grandee on his California rancho typifies the first stereotype. Mexicans, by contrast, were stereotyped as lazy and cowardly. The

---

[7]Ellwyn R. Stoddard, *Mexican Americans*, Random House, New York, 1973, p. 31.
[8]See, for example, Gerald Suttles, *The Social Order of the Slum*, University of Chicago Press, Chicago, 1968.

lesson of the Alamo was clear: "One Texan was worth ten Mexicans." Particularly disparaged are the most recent Mexican immigrants. Often residing in the country as undocumented aliens and serving in menial jobs, they constitute one of the poorest-educated and least skilled segments of the population.

The division into "Spanish" and "Mexican" serves the sociological function of allowing the former to be accepted into the businesses, homes, and even families of Anglo society, while discrimination and exploitation of lower-class Chicanos continues.

Mexican Americans are underrepresented in the halls of political power. In spite of their numbers, there are no Mexican Americans on the Los Angeles city council or the Los Angeles County board of supervisors. (By contrast, Mayor Bradlee is black). Low levels of voter participation restrict political influence. Signs point to greater political activity among Mexican Americans in the future. The Chicano movement has awakened the Mexican American community, and particularly the young, to the potential of united community action. ("Chicano" is a contraction and corruption of "Mexicano"; it originally was a term of derision for one who was unsophisticated, but now means one who has soul.) Perhaps the greatest achievement of the movement is the instilling of pride in one's Mexican heritage.

Radical Chicanos developed during the late 1960s a loose ideology that rejected the striving of the Anglo society and glorified the special virtues of *la raza* (a term which implies ethnic identity and separateness). Middle-class Mexicans were labeled "Tío Tacos" or "Tío Tomases"—the equivalent of "Uncle Toms." Assimilated middle-class Mexican Americans in turn often resist being labeled as part of a minority group. The Mexican American appointed vice mayor of Los Angeles lamented: "The trouble is the Chicanos never developed a cadre of legitimized leadership such as the blacks had in the NAACP or the Urban League. All efforts to develop such leadership always end with the question, 'Who appointed you leader?' "[9]

On a more positive note, political awareness is increasing and class division and rhetoric are more muted than a decade ago. Economically successful Mexican Americans are moving out of the *barrios* while still retaining their Hispanic heritage. Their places are being taken by ever more newcomers attracted by the promise of life in urban America.

Puerto Ricans

General Characteristics and Conditions. Puerto Ricans constitute the second-largest Hispanic minority in the United States. Puerto Ricans differ from the other Spanish-speaking people in several significant respects. First, Puerto Ricans have been American citizens since 1917. Thus, there is no question regarding their legal right to live on the mainland. Second, most Puerto Ricans are first-generation

---

[9]Manny Aragon, quoted in the *New York Times,* November 24, 1974.

With the emphasis on urban problems there is a tendency to overlook the vitality found in central-city neighborhoods. (© James H. Karales/Peter Arnold, Inc.)

migrants, the bulk of Puerto Rican migration having occurred since World War II. Third, Puerto Ricans are almost totally urban. Some 96 percent of mainland Puerto Ricans reside in metropolitan areas. Finally, Puerto Rican family income in 1976 was only $7,700, and four out of ten (39 percent) Puerto Rican families were living in poverty.[10] Puerto Ricans, thus, are even more hard pressed than blacks.

As with blacks, but not other Hispanics, there is a high proportion of female-headed families. Over one-quarter (28 percent) of all Puerto Rican families are headed by a woman without a husband present, and six out of ten families in poverty have no adult male.[11] Compared with Mexican women, Puerto Rican women are relatively independent. Single or divorced women find life far more liberating in New York than in Puerto Rico. The majority of mainland Puerto Ricans reside in the New York area, which houses approximately 1.3 of the 1.7 million mainland Puerto Ricans. Here they are heavily concentrated in the tenements of Spanish Harlem, the Lower East Side, and Brooklyn's Williamsburg ghetto.

Mainland Puerto Ricans have a very young age structure, with half the population under twenty. Educational levels are the lowest among the Spanish-origin population, with only 31 percent of the adults having completed high school and one in five (19 percent) having less than five years of schooling.[12] As of the 1970 census, only 2 percent had finished college.[13] Today the number is only 2.5 percent.

[10]"Persons of Spanish Origin," Figures 7 and 8.
[11]U.S. Bureau of the Census, "Consumer Income: 1974," *Current Population Reports,* Washington D.C., 1975, table 16.
[12]"Persons of Spanish Origin," figure 4.
[13]Jose Hernandez et al., *Social Factors in Educational Attainment among Puerto Ricans in U.S. Metropolitan Areas,* Aspira, New York, 1979, pp. 1–2.

Chicago's Street Gangs

Mention Latino street gangs and many people immediately think of *West Side Story* or, if they are middle-aged, the youth gangs of the 1950s. In Chicago, though, gangs are not something out of a past era. Nor are they the stuff of musicals. Groups such as the Latin Kings and the Insane Unknowns accounted for over two dozen murders in 1979—a fact the newspapers play down to avoid encouraging even greater violence.

Today, Chicago's gang violence is concentrated in the Hispanic and black slum and project areas of the North Side and West Side. (Gang activity is far more subdued in the older black ghettos of the South Side, partially because the leaders of the Blackstone Rangers who were powerful there a decade ago are now almost all either dead or in prison.) Blacks in the massive Cabrini-Green housing project and Hispanics in the surrounding neighborhoods join the gangs as "peewees" (ages nine to eleven) and then graduate to "juniors" (age twelve to sixteen or so) and eventually "seniors." Girls form auxiliaries and also wear the gang colors. Gang members join for a variety of reasons including protection or even boredom, but the major reason is self-respect. As put by a gang member who has been in and out of jail since he was twelve:

> I was a little gang-banger. That means like a rumble—we call it gang-banging though. We used to fight with bricks and sticks and chains, now they use bats and guns. But when I was little I used to fight the other groups, and go to parties and get drunk and get high, get away from my house, go to jail.
>
> I don't really know how I got into all that. I just grew up with it, you know, it was in my neighborhood and I grew up into it. . . . I am tired of being a nobody.
>
> On the other hand, once you put on a sweater with the gang colors, you become somebody. You are a person of status—a King, an Unknown, a Lord:
>
> A sweater represents the gang you're in. You feel like you've got power wearing that sweater. You say yes, these are my colors and I've got all these guys behind me, and they're backing me up 100 percent.
>
> I never did no real big gang-bang except take away sweaters, that's what I like to do, you know. I thought it was fun and games. It was just like playing a sport. They got a sweater, you try to take it away from them. We've got sweaters and they try to take it away from us. To see who could hang on to your sweater, you know.
>
> It was just a game—until they started to shoot. Then I said wait a minute, this ain't no game. This is for keeps. This is for your life.*

Today righting a slight comes not through rumbles (gang fights) as in the 1950s, but through hit squads being sent out to open up on rivals from a moving car. Sometimes contracts are even put out. The murderers are often only fourteen or fifteen, since it is believed—with justification—that if caught they will be treated only as delinquent juveniles. Police crackdowns have had little except publicity value;

*BUILD descriptive material, Chicago, undated.

they only alienate the community. Police have shown little sensitivity to the community or ability to distinguish between hard-core gang leaders and people just hanging around a corner.

Because of this difficulty, traditional community organizations such as the YMCA and Boys Clubs have dropped out of youth gang work. Gang members often don't go to school or work—the gang is their whole life. This is a dangerous and frustrating situation. As put by Hank Bach, one of the co-founders of BUILD, the only organization actively working with gang members in the streets:

> We're talking about young people who are very easily frustrated. We're dealing with the kids that have the poorest attitudes, the kids whose behavior is very violent and very aggressive in many instances. The problem so often is the time that they've got to spend on the street corner without anything else going on. That's part of the problem just the whole concept of time. If you occupy time, then you're minimizing the things they'll be getting into. We're talking about active young people, and we're saying, "What are the most active kinds of ways of getting them involved?" So we use the athletic situation and we use the social recreational situation to develop money in the bank. We're establishing a relationship based on those short-term objective activities, and that relationship can then help carry the kids into other more demanding programs which have greater long-range benefits. Education and employment—the type of programs that the kids might back away from.†

BUILD workers, most of whom live within the community, stay on the street with the gangs. This organization has little formal office space, figuring that where its people belong is on the street. Many are former members or dropouts who are now back in school working part-time with the organization. The goal of BUILD is to show gang members that there are alternatives. Particular attention is given to gang leaders, since members will usually follow where they are led. BUILD offers help to dropouts in completing high school and provides guidance, training, placement, and advice on how to get and hold a job. Many of the gang youth have few skills for legitimate employment. Most, until they are taught, cannot even fill in the standard employment application properly.

In all cases the emphasis is on dealing with the youth realistically. No one is promised a free ride. Because they are former dropouts who are now making it, the street workers provide successful noncriminal role models. As such they are more likely to be listened to than formally trained social workers. Generally BUILD has been reasonably successful. While it has not eliminated the gangs—and it cannot change the massive unemployment that underlies so much of the communities' problems—it can and does provide these youths an alternative to gang warfare. It shows them how to achieve status as individuals outside the gang structure by itself a considerable achievement.

†Ibid.

Drastic upgrading of educational levels is essential if Puerto Ricans are to move ahead. New York's former deputy mayor for education, Herman Badillo, himself a Puerto Rican, is not optimistic about the schools' accomplishments with Puerto Rican youngsters. He estimated the dropout rate at 85 percent. "We have plenty of jobs in skyscrapers of midtown Manhattan," he says, "The problem is that kids can't spell."[14]

Central cities such as New York are losing the entry-level blue-collar jobs filled by immigrants. Newcomer Puerto Ricans can't sell their muscles the way the earlier Germans and Italians did. Today economic advancement strongly favors those having white-collar skills and levels of education. For Puerto Ricans, political involvement tends to be low compared with that of previous immigrant groups. In part, this is due to the availability of flights back to Puerto Rico. If things get difficult, it is sometimes easier just to return to the island.

The New Generation. The picture just sketched overwhelmingly reflects experiences of first-generation mainland Puerto Ricans. Thus it may be unduly pessimistic for the new generation. The median age of Puerto Ricans born in the mainland United States is only 9.3 years; the second generation is just beginning to make its impact.[15] Indications are that second generations are far more Americanized than their parents. Thus the educational and occupational levels of young Puerto Ricans will be far higher than those of their parents (although still below the average for all whites). Family patterns are also changing. First-generation Puerto Ricans have larger-sized families than the national average, while second-generation Puerto Ricans born in the United States have fewer children than the national average.[16] Thus, while the first generation is among the nation's most deprived citizens, the fate of the mainland-born may be far brighter.

NATIVE AMERICANS

By omission, we have in essence denied that the American Indian has a heritage other than that portrayed in old John Wayne movies on late-night television. Only recently have there been popular books telling history from the Indian's side, such as *Bury My Heart at Wounded Knee.*[17] Such works have helped to restore our perspective, but valuable as they are, they do not confront one basic problem: our tendency always to refer to Indians in the past tense, as if they had disappeared with the buffalo and the frontier. They didn't disappear; they were simply ignored and forgotten.[18]

[14]Quoted in *Time,* October 16, 1978.

[15]U.S. Commission on Civil Rights, "Puerto Ricans in the United States: An Uncertain Future," Washington, D.C., 1976, p. 36.

[16]Ibid.

[17]Wounded Knee was the final episode of the Indian wars. Here 300 Sioux were massacred by the army in 1890. It was also the site of an unsuccessful militant political occupation by Indians in 1973. See Dee Alexander Brown, *Bury My Heart at Wounded Knee,* Holt, Rinehart, and Winston, New York, 1971.

[18]American Indians—from Cherokee to Sioux to Algonquin—are heterogeneous in patterns of social organization and in their world view. The only justification for subsuming such diversity under the generic term "Indian" is that the white society has consistently done this for several centuries and has responded similarly to all groups it has labeled "Indian." Only in this sense can we speak of Indians as a unitary group.

As noted in Chapter 3, The Rise of Urban America, the first colonists saw Indians as part of the environment, to be mastered and tamed like the forests and wild animals. The Indians' antiurban orientation—they lived in nomadic bands or small villages—left them particularly vulnerable to exploitation. Indians were systematically exterminated by Indian wars, destruction of the buffalo, and epidemics of European diseases against which they had no immunity. By 1890, when the first federal census of Indians was taken, their population had been reduced to 250,000 most barely surviving on government reservations. Today Native Americans number approximately 1 million—less than .05 percent of the national population.

Chances in Life. Indians were our first minority, and despite dramatic recent improvements, they remain our most deprived. Infant mortality, for example, is still about 20 percent higher among Indians than among other Americans.[19] A decade ago, it was 44 percent above the national average.[20] Life expectancy for the average Native American is now sixty-five years. This is six years below the national average but far better than the shockingly poor life expectancy of only two decades ago: forty-six years.

In spite of higher mortality, the extremely high birthrate of American Indians indicates that the "vanishing red man" is vanishing no more. A birthrate almost double that of the whole population ensures continued growth. The Indian population doubled (51 percent increase) between 1960 and 1970, but part of the increase was due to less undercounting by the Bureau of the Census. Rural Indians have an average of five children per family—the highest fertility rate in the country.

Roughly one-third of Native Americans live in poverty. Educational attainment among Native Americans is also poor—particularly on reservations. The average adult educational level is tenth grade, with only one-third having completed high school as of 1970. At present, 95 percent of all Indian children are attending school, but the quality of the education, particularly in reservation schools, is suspect.[21]

Movement to Cities. Indians are increasingly deserting the reservations for the cities, since the reservations offer only a future of illiteracy, poverty, and alcoholism, all too frequently terminated by an early death. For today's Indians, anything more than bare survival means migration to the city. Reservations are devoid of opportunity and hope. The Bureau of Indian Affairs has also been urging Indians to leave their reservations and resettle in urban areas.

Between 1930 and 1980, the minority group that experienced the greatest degree of urbanization was not, as is commonly thought, blacks but rather American Indians. As of 1930, only 10 percent of the Indian population lived in

[19]Population Reference Bureau, *Interchange,* **4:2**, November, 1975.

[20]*Indian Health Trends and Services,* Program Analysis and Statistics Branch of the Indian Health Service, Dept. of H. E. W., Washington, D.C., 1969.

[21]Report of the U.S. Commission on Civil Rights, *The Navajo Nation: An American Colony,* Washington, D.C., 1975, p. 60.

Educational opportunities for younger Indians are better than those available to their parents, but still insufficient. (Staffan Wennberg/Black Star.)

metropolitan areas, and as recently as 1960, seven out of ten Indians were estimated to be rural. Today, roughly half of the Native American population is urban. A majority of the Native American population lives in cities at least part of the year.[22] Precise figures are unavailable, since for a variety of reasons the censuses have never adequately enumerated the Indian population. Indians have been moving to cities in general rather than to any one city. A dozen cities in the country have more than 10,000 Indians each, but in no large city do Indians account for more than 5 percent of the population. The largest Indian populations are found in Los Angeles, Chicago, Minneapolis, Milwaukee, Phoenix, Albuquerque, and Oklahoma City.

The common pattern of shuttling between city and reservation gravely hinders effective urban organization. Tribal differences and lack of stable urban Indian populations have worked against the creation of tight ethnic social communities such as those of European immigrants. Shuttling back and forth also

[22]Elaine M. Neils, *Reservation To City: Indian Migration and Federal Relocation,* University of Chicago, Department of Geography Research, Paper no. 13, Chicago, 1974.

interferes with holding stable city jobs. In the words of a sympathetic writer, the reservation is still necessary, since it "functions as an outpost and haven from the urban scene where the adult battle for survival really takes place."[23]

Life in the city may not be grand, but it is superior to the cycle of acute poverty that is the lot of Indians on the reservation.

The principal source of income on reservations is the government: over half the Indians who have jobs are employed—often at minimum wages—by the government. However, only about one-third of the men have permanent employment, while four out of every ten do not have any type of employment.[24] As a result, government welfare payments (ADC, etc.), surplus-food programs, and the Public Health Care programs play a major, if not dominant, role in the economic health of Indians on reservations. From the standpoint of the Indians, little has changed since the last century, when corrupt officials of the Indian Agency stole the funds Congress had appropriated for food for Indians on the reservations. Today Congress continues to appropriate money, but it still has trouble filtering down to those who need it. The federal government now spends over 1 billion dollars a year on reservation programs. However, the grossly overstaffed and inefficient Bureau of Indian Affairs manages to spend much of its funds before any money gets to the Indians. According to one generous estimate, "a maximum of 20 percent of the total grants for many governmental programs ever reaches the reservations."[25]

On the Pine Ridge Reservation in South Dakota—where an unsuccessful uprising by militants took place in 1973—more than 40 percent of the full-blooded Indian families had incomes below $1,000 per year. The income levels of urban Indians are only fractionally higher than those of blacks.[26] The fact that Native Americans have an extremely high rate of alcoholism and a suicide rate twice that of other Americans is perhaps not surprising. In sociological terms, it is a classic example of retreatism from both white society's goals and the institutionalized means to achieve them.[27]

Urban Native Americans generally live in poorer central-city neighborhoods, much as European immigrants did. However, not all Native Americans live in such areas. Persons whose ancestry is Indian but who have been assimilated into middle-class America may not identify themselves as Indians except under particular circumstances, such as the distribution of funds from selling tribal estates. These people have Indian ancestry, but in their behavior, attitudes, and daily life, they are indistinguishable from their neighbors of European ancestry. These culturally assimilated Indians are sometimes referred to by other Indians as "apples"—"red on the outside and white on the inside." More than one-third of Indians now marry non-Indians.

[23]Jeanne Guilhemin, *Urban Renegades*, Columbia University Press, New York, 1975, p. 150.
[24]Calvin A. Kent and Jerry W. Johnson, *Indian Poverty in South Dakota*, Bulletin 99, Business Research Bureau, School of Business, University of South Dakota, 1969, p. 112.
[25]Ibid.
[26]Alan L. Sorkin, *The Urban American Indian*, Lexington Books, Lexington, Mass., 1978, p. 14.
[27]Robert K. Merton, *Social Theory and Social Structure*, Free Press, Glencoe, Ill., 1957.

Urban ways can produce culture shock for Native Americans. Many (but not all) Indian cultures stress cooperation and noncompetitiveness over competition and achievement. Indian heritages are thus often at variance with the larger American culture, with its emphasis on hard work and economic success. Militant Native Americans are caught in a dilemma: they want educational and employment opportunities and at the same time want to live according to Indian ways that make it difficult to take advantage of such opportunities.[28]

The problem of being pulled between two cultures is, of course, not unique to new groups to the American city. The antiurban orientation of most Native American cultures, however, gives special sharpness to the issue of cultural separateness versus assimilation. Policy makers in Washington have also vacillated: they seem unable to decide whether Indians should be encouraged to remain tribal nations, with separate cultures, or whether Indians are better served by detribalization and urban relocation. At present, ideology favors the former idea, while the latter is more commonly practiced.

A NOTE ON JAPANESE AMERICANS

Whenever one starts making generalizations about minorities, one is brought up short by the example of the Japanese Americans. For the Japanese Americans, who only three decades ago were possibly our most hated minority, are now accepted, successful, and prosperous citizens. According to the sociologist William Petersen:

> Barely more than twenty years after the end of war-time camps, this is a minority that has risen above every prejudiced criticism. By any criteria of good citizenship that we choose, the Japanese Americans are better than any other group in our society, including native-born whites. They have established this remarkable record, moreover, by their own almost totally unaided effort. Every attempt to hamper their progress resulted only in enhancing their determination to succeed.[29]

Figures for California, where about 60 percent of the mainland Japanese Americans (i.e., Japanese Americans outside Hawaii) live, show that they have the highest educational levels of any group in the state and that their income levels are far higher than those of any other minority and second only to those of whites. Additionally, Japanese Americans have remarkably low rates of delinquency, crime, and even mental illness.

Obviously, Japanese Americans have been notably successful in adapting to the values, behaviors, and expectations of the American system. Harry Kitano suggests that the statement "Scratch a Japanese American and find a white

---

[28]Bruce Chadwick and Joseph Strauss, "The Assimilation of American Indians into Urban Society, The Seattle Case," paper presented at the meeting of the American Sociological Association, San Francisco, August, 1975, pp. 33–34; and John S. Morris, "Education and the Urban Indian," in Vine Delorio (ed.), *Indian Education Confronts the Seventies*, vol. 5, American Indian Resource Associates, Oglala, South Dakota, 1964, p. 154.

[29]William Petersen, "Success Story: Japanese-American Style, " *The New York Times Magazine,* January 9, 1966, p. 20. © 1966 by the New York Times Company. Reprinted by permission.

TABLE 9-2
Japanese Immigrants to Mainland United
States, 1861–1940*

Period	Number	Percent of all immigrants
1861–1870	218	0.01
1871–1880	149	0.02
1881–1890	2,270	0.04
1891–1900	27,982	0.77
1901–1907	108,163	1.74
1908–1914	74,478	1.11
1915–1924	85,197	2.16
1925–1940	6,156	0.03

*Not including migrants from Hawaii after its annexation. The use of the term "immigrant" is not clear even in official statistics. The above table is for "immigrants" who intended to settle permanently as opposed to "nonimmigrants" who did not.
Source: William Petersen, *Japanese Americans*, Random House, New York, 1971, p. 15. Calculated from U.S. Bureau of the Census, *Historical Statistics of the United States*, U.S. Government Printing Office, Washington, D.C., 1960, Series C-88, C-104; Yamato Ichihashi, *Japanese Immigration: Its Status in California*, Marshall Press, San Francisco, 1915, p. 9.

Anglo-Saxon Protestant" is generally accurate.[30] What makes all this the more remarkable is that Japanese Americans have had to overcome severe discrimination—discrimination which included being forcibly driven from their homes and businesses during World War II and being incarcerated behind barbed wire in "relocation camps."

The Issei and Nisei

The first significant Japanese immigration to the United States occurred during the 1890s. Before then, there were little more than 2,000 immigrants. Immigration developed slowly and never grew large by comparison with the mass migrations from Europe. The total immigration to 1900 was slightly over 30,000; from then to the Gentlemen's Agreement of 1908 with Japan, 110,000; and from 1908 until World War I, about 75,000. After the passage of the Immigration Act of 1924, the number of arrivals averaged 385 per year.[31] By 1970 there were 591,000 Japanese Americans, 217,000 of whom lived in Hawaii. (See Table 9-2.)

The emotional impact of the immigration was far more severe than its numbers might imply. The Issei, or first-generation Japanese Americans, were viewed by many on the west coast as a threat. Organized labor was particularly vicious in its attack, since its members saw the orientals as threatening their jobs. Samuel Gompers, the head of the American Federation of Labor (AFL) and himself

[30]Harry H. L. Kitano, *Japanese Americans: The Evolution of a Subculture*, Prentice-Hall, Englewood Cliffs, N.J., 1976, p. 3.
[31]William Petersen, *Japanese Americans*, Random House, New York, 1971, p. 16.

an immigrant, told a convention of the AFL in 1904 that "the American God is not the God of the Japanese." A pamphlet against the Chinese he had coauthored in 1902, *Some Reasons for Chinese Exclusion: Meat vs. Rice, American Manhood Against Asiatic Coolieism—Which Shall Survive?* was reworked when the Japanese were perceived as the new threat. It called for barring the Japanese by law, or, if that failed, by force of arms.

As a result of anti-Japanese agitation in California and panic over the "yellow peril," the United States and Japan agreed that Japan would voluntarily cut back Japanese immigration. California also passed anti-Japanese land laws which denied to all persons ineligible for citizenship the right to own agricultural land or lease it for more than three years. Since federal law until 1952 denied those born in Japan the right to become American citizens, the California legislation was designed to take land away from the successful Japanese American garden farmers. Many Issei responded by putting the title to their land in the name of their American-born children. This second generation is known as the "Nisei." In 1920, California closed the loopholes in the 1913 law in a further attempt to prevent Japanese Americans from owning land. This law was upheld by the Supreme Court on the ground that since there was no treaty stipulating aliens' rights, each state could make its own laws. The Immigration Act of 1924, by excluding aliens ineligible for citizenship, effectively barred all further Japanese immigration to the United States.

The Internment Camps

The entry of the United States into World War II on December 7, 1941, resulted in anti-Japanese hysteria. It was popularly believed that a Japanese fifth column existed, conducting sabotage on orders from Tokyo. Interestingly, considering their later political development, such well-known liberals as the late Earl Warren and Walter Lippmann were among the most vocal against the Japanese, while one of the few public officials to denounce the rumors of sabotage as "racist hysteria" was J. Edgar Hoover, the director of the FBI.

The public clamor for action was met in February 1942, when President Roosevelt, on the recommendation of advisors, signed Executive Order 9066. The order designated military areas from which military commanders could exclude persons because of national security. The order also authorized the construction of inland "relocation centers." It was quickly implemented. On March 2, 1942, General De Witt, commander of the Western Defense Area, a man noted for his antioriental feelings, ordered all persons of Japanese ancestry to be evacuated from the three western coastal states and part of Arizona. He summed up his feelings with the statement, "Once a Jap, always a Jap." The evacuation order included children with as little as one-eighth Japanese ancestry. Two-thirds of those ordered to leave their homes were citizens of the United States. They were each allowed to take one suitcase with them as they were herded by army troops into assembly centers and then shipped to one of ten inland relocation camps.

At the outbreak of World War II Japanese Americans on the west coast were rounded up and placed in internment camps. (United Press International.)

More than 110,000 of the 126,000 Japanese in this country were put in these concentration camps—regardless of their citizenship.

Interestingly, no such action was taken against those of German and Italian ancestry on the east coast, nor was any action taken against the Japanese on the strategic island of Hawaii, where the Japanese made up a full 37 percent of the population. Long after the war, it was officially admitted that no Japanese American had committed a single subversive act anywhere within the United States. But for as long as three years many Japanese Americans lived in dismal tar-paper shacks in deserted, inhospitable areas of California, Arizona, Idaho, Wyoming, Utah, and Arkansas, surrounded by barbed wire and machine guns. The inmates were let out only on "seasonal leaves"—which was an euphemistic way of saying that they were used as cheap labor on local farms. Jobs in the camps paid from $16 to $19 a month. In 1942 the Federal Reserve Bank of San Francisco estimated the Japanese Americans' financial loss—abandoned or cheaply sold stores, farms, and businesses—at $400 million. The United States government eventually paid settlement claims at the rate of 5 to 10 cents on the dollar.

Life in the camps radically changed the structure of Japanese American society. The second-generation Nisei, who spoke English and were citizens, quickly filled most of the local leadership positions, displacing the older Issei. Ironically, because there were no whites in the camps, the Nisei could fill a host of leadership positions which anti-Japanese discrimination on the west coast would have made unavailable to them on the outside. After the way many Nisei chose to move east, where their skills and abilities had a better chance of recognition, rather than back to the more ghettoized west coast.

One of the many paradoxes of this period was that the 442d Regimental Combat Team—the most-decorated American unit in World War II—was composed of Japanese Americans. More than 1,000 of the men in the 442d had enlisted directly from the internment camps to fight for the country that had forcibly removed them from their homes and livelihood. The 442d's war cry, "Go for Broke," is a part of American history. Less well known is the fact that the average IQ of the unit was very high (119) and that the 442d had more college graduates than any other comparable unit in the armed forces. The Nisei earned, in blood, the grudging respect of other GIs. In action in Italy and France, the unit suffered 9,486 casualties—or over 300 percent of its original infantry strength.

Japanese Americans Today

Thirty-five years after the war and the internment camps, the second-generation Nisei have an unparalleled record of upward mobility. In 1940 over a quarter of all Japanese Americans were laborers; by the 1970s this figure was down to only a few percent. Among all nonwhite groups the Japanese rank first in income and education. The "Sansei," or third generation, born since World War II, has become almost totally acculturated. Compared with other college students, they tend to be retiring and reticent, but not as conforming as their Nisei parents. Their fierce desire for success and upward mobility is often reflected in the choice of safe and secure professions such as engineering and business administration.

Compared with other Americans, Japanese Americans, particularly on the west coast, still live largely in cohesive ethnic communities with a strong sense of group responsibility and group "image." The sense of group identity is reflected in the low delinquency and crime rates—rates that are rising as "American" behavior patterns replace those of the tightly bound ethnic community. The structural factors that led to the isolation of the Japanese American community continue to change, moving it in the direction of the larger society.

Soon after arrival the Japanese Americans lost almost all knowledge of the Japanese language, and over the years many of the less functional Japanese customs have been abandoned in favor of the more efficient American models. Another sign of change has been the number of marriages outside the group. Marriage of Sansei out of the ethnic community has become more common, particularly away from the more traditional ethnic communities in California.

The breakdown of distinctive ways of life is a mixed blessing. On the positive side, Japanese Americans now participate fully in all aspects of national life. However, it would be sad and more than a little ironic if in an urban world that is seeking a sense of community the Japanese Americans, who persevered and prospered because of their strong community and their cohesive family system, would now allow their distinctive culture to be eroded or abandoned.

CHAPTER
10
STRATIFICATION AND POWER
IN URBAN AMERICA

The rich man in his castle,
The poor man at his gate,
God made them, high or lowly,
And order'd their estate.

From a Church of England hymn,
"All Things Bright and Beautiful"

Social stratification is not a uniquely urban phenomenon, but it is so important that any treatment of the city and city life-styles that did not include it would be incomplete. Today, the stratification system of metropolitan areas largely determines the pattern for all of American society.

In the city there has always been an association between one's address and one's social status. Knowing where people live tells a great deal about how they live. Certain addresses—Park Avenue in New York, Beacon Hill in Boston, Georgetown in Washington, North Michigan in Chicago, and Nob Hill in San Francisco—have traditionally signified not only spatial location but also an upper-class life-style. Similarly, Cleveland's Shaker Heights, Washington's Chevy Chase, and San Francisco's Marin County have come to be almost stereotypically identified with the professional and managerial upper middle class. At the other end of the spectrum, areas such as Hough in Cleveland, Back of the Yards in Chicago, and East Los Angeles and Watts have a more proletarian image. The point is that there is often a clear relationship between urban space and social class.

Burgess, it will be recalled, suggested that the social status of the various urban populations is correlated directly with their distance from the center of the city; the lowest-status ethnic immigrants are found in the zone immediately surrounding the central business district, while people having the highest levels of income, education, and occupation are located in the suburbs.[1]

This hypothesized relationship between spatial location and social-class level was for several decades accepted as fact. More recently, as documented in Chapter 5, Ecology and Structure of the American City, sociologists have been systematically examining the patterns of status distributions in American cities and suburbs. A study by Schnore (1963) based on a comparison of central cities and their suburbs looked at 200 urbanized areas and compared levels of socioeconomic status using median family income, percent completing high school, and percent in white-collar occupations as variables.[2] He found that the older and larger urbanized areas exhibited the expected pattern: The suburbs had higher socioeconomic status than the central cities. However, this became less true as city size and age decreased. In the smallest Urbanized Areas the status of city residents tended to be higher than that of suburbanites. Statistically, the age and size of the urban area were the best predictors of its status pattern.

A follow-up study by Palen and Schnore added two other variables: race of the population and region of the country. Comparisons were made for 180 Urbanized Areas for whites and 131 areas for nonwhites. For the white population, it was found that regardless of the region of the country, the larger and older the city, the more likely that its suburbs possessed higher levels of income, education, and occupation. For nonwhites, on the other hand, the pattern of higher status in

[1]Ernest W. Burgess, "The Growth of the City: An Introduction to a Research Project," *Publications of the American Sociological Society,* 18:85–97, 1924.
[2]Leo F. Schnore, "The Socioeconomic Status of Cities and Suburbs," *American Sociological Review,* 28:76–85, February, 1963.

suburbs was found only in the north and west. In the south, the persistence of traditional patterns—poor blacks living on the city's periphery—meant that there was no consistent pattern of higher-status blacks' being located either in the city or in the suburbs.[3]

Additional research has used census-tract data to study in detail status patterns of black ghettos in twenty-four large cities. These studies showed that Burgess's hypothesis that levels of socioeconomic status increase with distance from the center of cities clearly held true in the north; but in the south four out of five cities displayed a different pattern: socioeconomic status of blacks rose as one moved from the center of the city and then declined.[4] Further research has tended to support this general picture.[5]

DIMENSIONS OF CLASS

We like to think of ourselves as a relatively classless society, or at least one with social mobility. Our national mythology suggests that anyone who works hard enough and gets a few breaks can make it to the top. A few extreme cases, plus slight upward mobility for many more, provide just enough experiential data to maintain the myth. In actual practice, we recognize clear differences between groups of persons. Social inequality exists in America, as it does in all complex human societies. We have a class system—that is, an ordering of social positions and the roles (social expectations) associated with each one. The inequalities are not random; they are systematic and organized into patterns that are generally recognized by society.

Within the urban area, we rank others in categories on a scale of superiority–inferiority. While there are no universal criteria for evaluation, the standards for grouping persons into social classes in the United States usually include these factors: income, education, type of occupation, race, family background, and general life-style.[6] Some sociologists also distinguish between class position and status position. "Class position" is the resources, particularly economic, which one controls in the marketplace. "Status position" refers to the more intangible prestige or honor that is attached to a position. The impoverished aristocrat, a classic and much overworked fictional character, is a clear example of one having a higher status position than class position. A Mafia leader in Chicago would, conversely, have high power but low status. However, in sociological usage the distinction between class and status frequently becomes blurred, and the terms are often used interchangeably.

[3]J. John Palen and Leo F. Schnore, "Color Composition and City-Suburban Status Differences," Land Economics, 41:87–91, February, 1965.
[4]Leo F. Schnore, The Urban Scene, Free Press, New York, 1965, chap. 16.
[5]Joel Smith, "Another Look at Socioeconomic Status Distributions in Urbanized Areas," Urban Affairs Quarterly, 5:423–453, June, 1970.
[6]See, for example, W. Lloyd Warner, The Social Life of a Modern Community, vol. 1 of Yankee City Series, Yale University Press, New Haven, Conn., 1941.

MEASURING SOCIAL CLASS

There are a number of ways to measure social class. The most common measures of socioeconomic status (SES) are income, education, and occupation. Income and education are easy to rank—college is obviously higher than high school—but occupation presents greater problems. One solution is to use the classification of the Bureau of the Census, which places occupations under the following headings:

1. Professional, technical, and kindred workers
2. Managers, officials, and proprietors, except farm
3. Clerical and kindred workers
4. Sales workers
5. Craft workers, line supervisors, and kindred workers
6. Operatives and kindred workers
7. Private household workers
8. Service workers, except private household workers
9. Laborers, except farm and mine workers
10. Farmers and farm managers
11. Farm laborers and farm supervisors

For urban research, categories 1 through 4 are frequently combined to create the category "white collar"; categories 5 through 9 are combined to create the category "blue collar." Another measure of occupational prestige is provided by the studies of the National Opinion Research Center, which rank the relative prestige of some ninety occupations on a five-point scale by taking a national sample. A much-abbreviated example of the scale is provided in Table 10-1. A comparison of the rankings in 1947 and 1963 showed virtually no change. The correlation between the two samples was .99, or virtually perfect—a rare occurrence in social science.[7] While occupation cannot be matched directly with class, the scale continues to be used as an indicator of class because it provides the best available approximate index in complex urban societies. Comparisons with other countries also show a high degree of similarity, with agreement being greatest among western countries such as Great Britain, New Zealand, Germany, and the United States.

Another method of determining social class is to have families assign other families to social-class levels according to their reputation in the community. This is the technique Hollingshead used in his study *Elmtown's Youth* (Morris, Illinois).[8] Since this method is based upon respondents' personal knowledge of others, it is inappropriate for urban research, except where the unit of study is a relatively small homogeneous neighborhood.

A combination of objective and subjective methods was used in perhaps the

[7]Robert W. Hodge, Paul M. Siegel, and Peter H. Rossi, "Occupational Prestige in the United States: 1925–1963," *American Journal of Sociology*, 70:297, November, 1964.
[8]A. B. Hollingshead, *Elmtown's Youth*, Wiley, New York, 1949.

TABLE 10-1
Occupational Prestige Scale—1963

Occupation	Prestige score	Rank
U.S. Supreme Court justice	94	1.0
Physician	93	2.0
Scientist	92	3.5
Cabinet member in the federal government	90	8.0
Lawyer	89	11.0
Psychologist	87	17.5
Mayor of a large city	87	17.5
Civil engineer	86	21.5
Banker	85	24.5
Sociologist	83	26.0
Owner of a factory that employs about 100 people	80	31.5
Musician in a symphony orchestra	78	34.5
Official of an international labor union	77	37.0
County agricultural agent	76	39.0
Farm owner and operator	74	44.0
Newspaper columnist	73	46.0
Radio announcer	70	49.5
Insurance agent	69	51.5
A local official of a labor union	67	54.5
Traveling salesperson for a wholesale concern	66	57.0
Playground director	63	62.5
Owner-operator of a lunch stand	63	62.5
Truck driver	59	67.0
Clerk in store	56	70.0
Restaurant cook	55	72.5
Dockworker	50	77.5
Coal miner	50	77.5
Farmhand	48	83.0
Clothes presser in a laundry	45	85.0
Garbage collector	39	88.0

Source: Modified from Robert W. Hodge, Paul M. Siegel, and Peter H. Rossi, "Occupational Prestige in the United States, 1925–1963," *American Journal of Sociology,* 70:290-292, November, 1964, table 1.

most famous study of social stratification, *Yankee City.*[9] Yankee City—actually Newburyport, Massachusetts—was studied from top to bottom by a team of researchers under Lloyd Warner's direction during the mid-1930s. While the methodology is not always clear, families were apparently weighted for status on the basis of four seven-point scales: occupational level, source of income (inherited, profits, salary, wages, relief), type of residence, and area of the

[9]W. Lloyd Warner (ed.), *Yankee City,* Yale University Press, New Haven, Conn., 1963.

John D. Rockefeller, one of the nation's ruthless robber barons, achieved notoriety in later life by eccentrically dispensing part of his great wealth in nickels for young children and dimes for those older. (NYT Pictures.)

community. Income level was given a weight of four, source of income and housing each a weight of three, and area a weight of two. Such elaborate procedures are hardly possible in more modest studies, particularly where social class is not the major focus of the study. As a result, the objective categories as defined by the Bureau of the Census are the measure most frequently found in the professional literature.

Warner, on the basis of his data, divided the American population into six classes, a system that has come to be the standard. According to Warner, each class has its own behaviors, values, and style of life. They can be briefly sketched as follows:

1. *Upper upper class.* This group includes the families of old wealth who have had money for several generations. The members sit on boards of directors. Emphasis is put upon reverence for the past and gracious living. Members of this elite class have enough security to allow a person to be an individualist or even a bit of a character. Aside from their money, what sets the established rich apart is not so much what they do as the style in which they do it. Community service is often a characteristic of the second generation and later generations. Religious affiliation is almost always to traditional Protestant denominations such as Episcopalian and Presbyterian.

2. *Lower upper class.* This group is generally even richer than the upper upper class, but their money is newer, and families are not as socially prominent. While the new rich may never achieve full acceptance by the upper upper class, their children, if they go to the right schools and achieve the proper polish, may be socially accepted. Acceptance into the upper upper group is dependent as much on knowing how to spend money properly as on knowing how to make it.

3. *Upper middle class.* The key word for the upper middle class is "career." While the upper groups are generalists, the upper middle class consists of specialists. These are successful business and professional people who live in large homes in the better suburbs. Education, particularly for the professionals is extremely important, and graduate education is common. These are the people who run community organizations, but they do not make top decisions. Family life-style, not lineage, is important.

4. *Lower middle class.* This group includes small business-people, lower-level government bureaucrats, most teachers, and the more successful blue-collar workers, such as electricians, plumbers, and line supervisors. Respectability is of paramount importance to this class. Today they are high school graduates with perhaps some further training. Homes are in the less affluent suburbs or perhaps in the city. A characteristic of this and the next class is home-centeredness (recall Chapter 6, City Life-Styles).

5. *Working class.* In the past this group was sometimes referred to as the "upper lower class." Those in this class have factory jobs or other semiskilled jobs and work for wages rather than salary. They make adequate incomes, but there is little hope of substantial social or economic advancement. Union contracts

Skid Row

Near but not in the central business district of almost every major city there exists an area consisting of bars, flophouses, cheap restaurants, pawnshops, and rescue missions. This is skid row—the quarantined section of the city given over to meeting the needs of the down-and-outer.* Skid row's population is almost exclusively one of homeless males, living lives marked by poverty and personal problems. In the public mind, skid row is often synonymous with "drunken bum." This is an inaccurate stereotype. Studies have found that approximately one-third of those on skid row are heavy drinkers, one-third drink moderately, and the remaining third drink little or abstain. † While most are not problem drinkers, the proportion of people with alcohol problems is higher than in any other area of the city.

In the United States there are more than 150 skid rows, but the number and size of such enclaves are decreasing. One authority estimates that yearly declines may be as high as 7 percent.‡ The record of the past decade suggests that the inhabitants of skid row are a dying breed, and skid row itself faces extinction. There are two principal reasons. First, the economic system no longer requires large masses of unskilled migratory workers; second, the land occupied by skid rows is being converted by speculators for office buildings and other uses. The beginning of the end of Chicago's skid row on West Madison Street came over a decade ago, when across the street from the cheap bars and flophouses a new Holiday Inn was erected. Similar processes are occurring from New York to San Francisco.

Down-and-Outers. In his study of Chicago's skid row, Donald Bogue found that the three characteristics which distinguish skid row occupants from other urbanites are their homelessness (living outside a private household), poverty, and acute personal problems. Not everyone on skid row had all these characteristics, but skid row had the highest concentration in the city of people with such problems.§ Poverty is a major determinate of almost all aspects of life on skid row, but not all the people on skid row are bums. At any given time, between one-third and one-half are employed, usually at day labor. The amount of employment is linked to the health of the economy; during recessions unemployment increases.

---

*The term "skid row" comes from the skid road the lumberjacks used in Seattle to transport logs. The lodging houses where the lumberjacks lived and the bars they got drunk in were near the "skid road."

†Howard M. Bahr, *Skid Row,* Oxford University Press, New York, 1973, p. 103.

‡Ibid., p. 9.

§Donald J. Bogue, *Skid Row in American Cities,* University of Chicago, Community and Family Study Center, Chicago, 1963, p. 2.

The New Inhabitants of Skid Row. As old skid rows die out, newer skid rows inhabited not by old winos but by young migratory dropouts—referred to in the early 1970s as "street people"—have emerged. The term "street people" originated in Berkeley to describe those who slummed near the university—living hand to mouth and sleeping in parks and doorways or crashing with anyone who would take them in.

Although the media and the middle-aged sometimes referred to street people as "hippies," the street people were socially quite dissimilar from hippies. The now-defunct hippie movement of the late 1960s was heavily populated by philosophically alienated, middle-class white youths. During a period of high employment, they rejected jobs, a money culture, and a work ethic—although even their alienation was often supported by monthly checks from worried parents. With the death of the hippie movement, a few moved on to political radicalism, communes, or alternative life-styles, and the great mass blended back into the middle class whence they had come.

The new skid row inhabitants, who number over 1 million, differ from the hippies of the late 1960s in several important respects. They are older, have low educational levels, have few marketable skills, are more likely to be black or brown as well as white, and come predominantly from blue-collar homes.¶ They have not dropped out from the mainstream of American society; they have been pushed out and can't find their way back in.

In terms of job qualifications and histories, street people resemble older skid row inhabitants. Baumohl and Miller surveyed 305 street people in Berkeley and found that one-third had not finished high school and only 23 had completed college.** Eighty-six percent were unemployed, and those who worked generally had only menial part-time jobs as dishwashers, gardeners, or domestics.

In terms of mental health, street people also have characteristics of young skid row inhabitants. Twenty-two percent of the Berkeley respondents had been hospitalized at least once for psychiatric reasons. The actual figure is even higher, since the most disturbed could not fill out questionnaires, and others probably were reluctant to reveal such information about their past.

In other ways street people differ from the traditional skid row

¶Celeste MacLeod, "Street People: The New Migrants," *The Nation,* 217:395–397, October 22, 1973.
**Ibid., p. 397.

inhabitants. Unlike the older skid row derelicts, they didn't drift down over a period of years. They are already misfits and down-and-outers before reaching middle age. Second, street people include both sexes. Nineteen percent of those in the Berkeley study were female. Exploitation of the females is commonplace. One-third of the female street people report being raped at least once. Young runaway girls are particularly vulnerable. Trading sex for room and board is a common form of semiprostitution.

Finally, the most important common denominator of street people is not alcohol but drugs. In the Berkeley sample, virtually all used marijuana, 87 percent had taken LSD, and 37 percent used heroin. One-fifth admitted to past or present addiction, usually to heroin or barbiturates.†† To outsiders the drug-oriented street people represent at worst moral deprivation, and at best local color. Stripped of external trappings, what remains is a skid row for society's young rejects.

††Ibid.

frequently determine the pace of economic advancement. Homes are clean but not fancy. Non-WASP backgrounds are overrepresented.

6. *Lower class.* This group consists of people with irregular work histories and the poorest-paying jobs. Poverty-level families on welfare fall into this category. Education is rarely much beyond the legal minimum. Housing is rented, not owned, and residence in public housing projects is widespread.

In the midwest, southwest, and west, categories 1 and 2 are frequently combined, since there is not usually an established class of old families as in parts of the east and the old south. Family history is generally more important in smaller cities, where local inhabitants know each other's family history and react appropriately. In bigger cities families are more anonymous, and money alone makes more of a difference.

More recently Richard Coleman and Lee Rainwater examined how residents of the Boston and Kansas City metropolitan areas classified themselves and each other. Based on 900 in-depth interviews, they identified seven categories:

The Success Elite. These are people whom others feel have really made it. It includes the old rich and the "celebrity rich," and the "run-of-the-mill rich" such as physicians. Inherited money earns the highest social standing. Minimum family income would be approximately $60,000 in 1980 dollars. [Readers should adjust figures appropriately to account for inflation.]

People Who Are Doing Very Well. Those at this level are dentists, engineers, business managers, and the like. They live in eight-room houses, have two cars, travel about at company expense, and can send their children to good state universities without undue strain. Minimum family income is over $40,000 a year.

Middle-American Good Life. These families have what those below consider the good life. They own their own three-bedroom homes, have two cars including a station wagon or camper, and take a three-week vacation. Minimum income level is $25,000 a year.

Average Person—Comfortable. Families at this level are managing to pay the bills but have only modest savings. They own their own six-room homes in one of the less prestigious suburbs. Minimum income level is $20,000.

Just Getting Along. Those just getting along probably started work just after high school and now work in a factory or office. When possible both adults work. They are most likely to rent a small home or a five-room apartment and have an older car in good repair. Income level is $12,000.

Having a Hard Time. These families are just above welfare and proud to say they work. They work at low-prestige jobs such as janitor or domestic, and rent a flat in an older building showing some deterioration. For entertainment they watch a lot of television. Minimum income is $7,000.

The Poor. Those in the bottom group are heavily dependent on welfare. They have few job skills and live in inner-city tenements or projects. Family income level is below $7,000 a year.[10]

While it would be absurd to suggest that all members of a class hold similar attitudes or have an identical style of life, it is nonetheless true that social class has a more pervasive effect than Americans, with their lip service to equality, always recognize. We take it for granted that the upper class makes more money than the middle and lower classes, and perhaps we even recognize that they obtain better medical care and live longer. However, the upper class has a pronounced advantage in other areas as well. As an example, the upper class has more marital stability (related to marrying at a later age and to greater financial stability)—23 percent of low-income white males in the age group 25–34 have had one or more broken marriages, as compared with 10 percent for the middle-income group, and only 6 percent for the upper-income group.[11] Even being overweight is correlated with social class—52 percent of low-income women have problems with obesity, compared with 43 percent of middle-income women and only 9 percent of high-income women.[12] (While this may seem an unimportant difference, it directly affects life expectancy and quality of life.) There is also substantial evidence indicating an inverse relationship between class and a number of psychiatric conditions. However, the relationship between class and mental illness is extremely complex; we certainly cannot say that as one goes up the class scale, mental health improves.[13]

The break between white-collar and blue-collar workers has traditionally been considered culturally significant; but on many issues—such as family behavior, religion, political and economic attitudes, and intergroup attitudes—the difference between professionals and businesspeople are almost as large as the differences between the lower white-collar and the skilled blue-collar groups.[14]

STATUS CONSISTENCY

Particularly within urban areas, as noted earlier, it is possible for an individual to be high on status measures such as income and residence, while being low on other measures such as occupation and ethnic background. Urban upper-class blacks with a superior education have had, particularly in the past, status inconsistency of this sort. George Washington Carver was once forced to ride in a service elevator to get to a banquet at which he was the principal speaker. More

---

[10]Richard Coleman and Lee Rainwater, *Social Standing in America: New Dimensions of Class,* Basic Books, New York, 1978.
[11]Richard J. Udry, "Marital Instability by Race and Income Based on 1960 Census Data," *American Journal of Sociology,* **72:**673, 1966.
[12]Robert Burnight and Parker Marden, "Social Correlates of Weight in an Aging Population," *Milbank Memorial Fund Quarterly,* **45:**75–92, 1967.
[13]A. B. Hollingshead and Fredrich Redlich, *Social Class and Mental Illness,* Wiley, New York, 1958.
[14]Norval Glenn and Jon Alston, "Cultural Distances among Occupational Categories," *American Sociological Review,* **33:**365–382, June, 1968.

recently, urban blue-collar workers in certain building trades have enjoyed a very high income as against low educational background and occupational rank. Such status inconsistency is said to be a source of stress for individuals and leads to such dissimilar reactions as supporting political parties advocating change, and higher incidences of psychosomatic illness.[15]

Empirical study of status consistency is usually associated with the research of Gerhard Lenski, who, working with a probability sample in the Detroit area, tested the hypothesis that "individuals characterized by a low degree of status crystallization differ significantly in their political attitudes and behavior from individuals characterized by a high degree of status crystallization, when status differences in the vertical dimension are controlled."[16] (Lenski uses the term "status crystallization" rather than "status consistency" to refer to a situation in which all statuses are equally high or equally low.)

It has already been mentioned that one reaction to status inconsistency may be political support for liberal or even radical rather than conservative political policies. An example might be the support of affluent, well-educated urban Jews for the Democratic Party. Another reaction to status inconsistency is the tendency to blame others for one's problems and to strike out at those who appear threatening. For example, lower-middle-class groups living in ethnic enclaves may seek to block the aspirations and expectations of those below them in order to protect what position they have. "Let them do it the way we did," is the cry. If the class division is also a racial division—and this is frequently the case—the hostility is all the greater. To those groups not yet secure in their own grip on a decent income and quality of life, an aggressive and demanding group immediately below them is a threat to their own position. Paradoxically, those who have experienced poverty and discrimination themselves are frequently hardest on those lower down.

As a blue-collar worker expressed it:

> The blacks have had a hard time. I don't deny that a minute. But they're always complaining and wrecking things and goofing off. Not all, but a lot of them. The way I see it, they've gotten a lot in the last years. They've moved into the cities, like into my neighborhood, and taken them over. They've moved up into all the top jobs. They're in the offices and the plants. They've done a hell of a lot better than I have—or my family—or people like me. Everybody's getting ahead but us.[17]

It was not accidental that Martin Luther King said that he felt the greatest hatred toward blacks was not in the south but in the lower-middle-class white ethnic neighborhoods of Chicago.

[15]Gerhard E. Lenski, "Status Inconsistency and the Vote: A Four Nation Test," *American Sociological Review*, **32**:298, April, 1967; and Elton Jackson, "Status Consistency and Symptoms of Stress," *American Sociological Review*, **27**:469–480, August, 1962.

[16]Gerhard E. Lenski, "Status Crystallization: A Non-Vertical Dimension of Social Status," *American Sociological Review*, **19**:405–406, August, 1954.

[17]Patricia Cayo Sexton and Brendan Sexton, *Blue Collars and Hard Hats*, Vintage Books, a Division of Random House, Inc., New York, 1971, p. 54.

Status inconsistency should, however, be kept in proper perspective. Urban life, because it emphasizes and rewards change and innovation, has built into it a certain degree of status tension, and most urban dwellers expect this as a part of urban life. Many persons prefer this inconsistency and the potential mobility it suggests to the more static and consistent structure of smaller communities.

MOBILITY

Myths and Reality

The mythology of social mobility in nineteenth-century and early twentieth-century America emphasized the rags-to-riches urban careers of unlettered persons of low origins, such as Andrew Carnegie and Henry Ford. On the other hand, the actual data paint a somewhat less spectacular picture. There are very few examples of members of the industrial elite who rose from childhood poverty by their own pluck and luck. What consistently is shown by the various studies done on the entrepreneurs at the very top of the social and economic order is that the best way to become rich is to be born to rich parents.[18] William Miller, after studying the careers of just under 200 of the leaders of early-twentieth-century corporations, concluded that among these powerful financiers, corporation officials, and railroad and utility executives one could find hardly any who started as poor immigrants. In fact, 95 percent of his sample came from native upper-class or at least middle-class families.[19]

The findings of Frances Gregory and Irene Neu are substantially similar. They carefully studied the careers of the business leaders in railroads, steel, and textiles in seventy-seven large firms as of the 1870s. The sample included the president, vice-president, and general manager of the seventeen largest railroads, the general managers of thirty steel mills, and the treasurers and agents of thirty very large textile mills. Gregory and Neu found that the typical industrial leader in their sample was male, American-born, Protestant, and of upper-class origin. Moreover, he was most likely to have been raised in an urban environment and to have been well educated for the times. Examining the occupations of 194 men, they found that only sixteen of them (8 percent) were the sons of workers. They therefore concluded that there was little evidence to support the belief that the top-level businessman of the late 1800s had worked his way from rags to riches.[20]

On the other hand, Herbert Gutman found that in the case of urban Paterson, New Jersey, during the years 1830 to 1880, the rags-to-riches promise was not mere myth. All the thirty-odd entrepreneurs he studied had started as apprentices and

---

[18]See Seymour M. Lipset and Richard Bendix, *Social Mobility in Industrial Society*, University of California Press, Berkeley, 1959.

[19]William Miller, "American Historians and the Business Elite," in William Miller (ed.), *Men in Business, Essays on the Historical Role of the Entrepreneur*, Harper and Row, New York, 1962, pp. 309–328.

[20]Frances W. Gregory and Irene D. Neu, "The American Industrial Elite in the 1870s, Their Social Origins," in Miller, op. cit., pp. 193–211.

later went on to open shops of their own.[21] Unfortunately, the data are not sufficient to let us generalize from these findings. Available data do suggest, however, that mobility was probably most likely in industries that required only limited initial outlays of capital. Mobility was probably also most likely in the newer, rapidly expanding cities.

When one moves away from examining elite groups such as railroad presidents and factory owners and looks at the social mobility of lower-status urban groups, the data are far more scanty. Lloyd Warner in his famous studies of Yankee City emphasized that mobility had been possible for working men during the nineteenth century but had decreased by the twentieth century. Warner suggested that between the nineteenth century and the twentieth there had been a hardening of the social structure. This he attributed to the change, brought by industrialization, from craft work to mass assembly-line production.[22]

Stephen Thernstrom's research on the class system of nineteenth-century Newburyport indicates that social mobility in Newburyport during the nineteenth century was actually far less than Warner had assumed.[23] Thernstrom looked at the career patterns of nearly 300 day laborers in Newburyport between 1850 and 1880. He found a good deal of geographical mobility out of the town, but the most common form of social mobility was advancement within rather than out of the working class. There was no rags-to-riches mobility: "In the substantial sample of workers and their sons studied for the 1850–1880 period not a single instance of mobility into the ranks of management or even into a foremanship position was discovered."[24]

However, on the basis of later and more extensive research, Thernstrom suggests that the minimal mobility of Newburyport was an exception to the general pattern in nineteenth-century urban America.[25] Newburyport, it is evident, had notably lower upward mobility than other communities: Thernstrom attributed this to the city's relative economic stagnation in the late nineteenth century and the preponderance of Irish of low mobility in the sample.[26]

Research does not support the view that the coming of industrialization made class lines more rigid. Thernstrom's study of social mobility in Boston indicates that as traditional skilled callings became obsolete, there was an enormous expansion of other skilled trades, and that many craft workers moved rapidly into these positions.[27]

[21]Herbert G. Gutman, "The Reality of the Rags-to-Riches Myth," in Stephen Thernstrom and Richard Sennett (eds.), *Nineteenth-Century Cities,* Yale University Press, New Haven, Conn., 1969, pp. 98–124.

[22]Warner, *Yankee City.*

[23]Stephen Thernstrom, "Yankee City Revisited: The Perils of Historical Naivete," *American Sociological Review,* 30:236–242, April, 1965.

[24]Ibid.

[25]Stephen Thernstrom, *The Other Bostonians: Poverty and Progress in the American Metropolis, 1880–1970,* Harvard University Press, Cambridge, Mass., 1973, p. 247.

[26]Ibid.

[27]Stephen Thernstrom, "Urbanization, Migration, and Social Mobility in Late Nineteenth-Century America," in Alan Trachenberg, Peter Neill, and Peter C. Bunnell (eds.), *The City: American Experience,* Oxford University Press, New York 1971, pp. 99–111.

Intergenerational Mobility

Data on intergenerational mobility of male workers for the past century suggest several things. First, there were clear and definite rigidities in the occupational structure which gave strong preference to those of higher social class. Sons of professional men and substantial businessmen were four times as likely as children from low-status white-collar families to attain upper-status white-collar levels. When compared with the sons of skilled workers they were six and a half times as likely to reach upper levels, and twelve times as likely as sons of unskilled or semiskilled laborers.[28] Second, while few men from laboring households achieved positions of power and high income, there was a substantial amount of short-distance upward mobility of laborers into skilled and minor white-collar posts. In Boston, for example, "an average of 4 in 10 of the sons in families on the lowest rung of the occupational ladder found their way into middle-class jobs of some kind, and a significant proportion of the remainder— roughly 1 in 6—entered a skilled trade."[29]

Similarly, Natalie Rogoff's data on urban occupational mobility across generations of men in Indianapolis indicated that the sons of displaced artisans were likely to move into other skilled trades or white-collar occupations rather than down the ladder.[30]

In another study by Thernstrom, the career mobility of native-born white men was compared with that of foreign-born immigrant men during the last half of the nineteenth century. Consideration of movement between manual and nonmanual callings revealed that regardless of their fathers' occupational level, men of foreign birth—and even those of native birth but foreign parentage—were handicapped vis-à-vis old-stock Americans of similar class origins.[31] Thernstrom also discovered that there were important differences in the experiences of newcomers of various national backgrounds. Some groups, such as the British and the eastern European Jews, were dramatically successful, while others, such as the Irish and Italians, were slower in entering the American middle-class mainstream.[32] The tradition-oriented social systems and religion of the Irish and Italians in the past set them apart from the "official" Protestant work ethic of the nation. It is instructive to note that while over 80 percent of all Catholics are urban—compared with roughly 60 percent of all Protestants—Catholics are still much underrepresented in fields such as banking, financing, and corporate control. Catholics were also long absent from scholarly careers, but that pattern has been reversed.[33] However, it is in the realm of political control that the Catholic ethnic groups have been most successful.

---

[28]Thernstrom, *The Other Bostonians*, p. 257.
[29]Ibid., p. 245.
[30]Natalie Rogoff, *Recent Trends in Occupational Mobility*, Free Press, Glencoe, Ill., 1953.
[31]Stephen Thernstrom, "Immigrants and WASPS: Ethnic Differences in Occupational Mobility in Boston, 1890–1940," in Stephen Thernstrom and Richard Sennett (eds.), *Nineteenth-Century Cities*, Yale University Press, New Haven, Conn., 1969, p. 148.
[32]Ibid.
[33]Andrew M. Greeley, "The 'Religious Factor' and Academic Careers: Another Communication," *American Journal of Sociology*, **78**:1247–1255, March, 1973.

Sources of Mobility

Traditionally there have been four principal causes for American social mobility:

1. *Individual or career mobility.* This is the type of mobility most familiar to the average individual. It occurs when some people slip down or move up and thereby make room for others to move up.
2. *Technological mobility.* Over the past century there has been a constant upgrading of the occupational distribution, which has been outdating unskilled and manual jobs at the bottom of the occupational structure and replacing them with higher-level technical and administrative positions. The space industry, for example, was virtually nonexistent thirty years ago, and much the same can be said about computer data processing.
3. *Reproductive mobility.* At least in the past, the upper classes had smaller families than those at lower levels, and this made room at the top. The old cliché about marrying the boss's daughter implies that the boss does not have sons to inherit the business.
4. *Immigration mobility.* Before the 1920s, when immigration was legally restricted, hundreds of thousands of immigrants yearly came to the United States, and the vast majority started at the bottom as semiskilled or unskilled workers. By taking blue-collar manual jobs, they pushed earlier ethnic groups up a rung. A not uncommon pattern at the turn of the century was for the boss to be Anglo-Saxon, the supervisor Irish, and the workers from southern or eastern Europe. A generation earlier, the Irish had been the workers. Today blacks or Hispanics occupy the bottom rungs, while those of eastern European background are now the supervisors or skilled workers.

Examining changes in the male work force between 1920 and 1950, Kahl estimated that two-thirds of the work force was intergenerationally mobile—that is, sons were in different occupations from their fathers. In discussing these changes, he attributed 43 percent to individual mobility in both directions, the same percentage to technological mobility, 13 percent to reproductive mobility, and 1 percent to immigration mobility.[34] However, because of the methodological problems involved in this type of research, Kahl's figures were basically educated assumptions.

More recent research by Robert Hauser et al. shows that within this century there has been no change in the relative mobility of men having fathers in different occupations.[35] Change in the occupational structure (technological mobility) is the major factor affecting mobility patterns. Thus, while relative mobility has remained the same, there has been a massive transformation from an agrarian to a metropolitan technological society. The resulting changes over

[34]Joseph Kahl, *The American Class Structure*, Holt, Rinehart and Winston, New York, 1957, particularly chap. 9, pp. 251–298.
[35]Robert M. Hauser, John N. Koffel, Harry P. Travis, and Peter J. Dickinson, "Temporal Change in Occupational Mobility," *American Sociological Review*, 40:279–297, 1975.

time in occupation distribution have produced upward occupational mobility.[36]

In brief, mobility comes from changes in social structure rather than from individual efforts and achievement.

One of the more elaborate studies of social mobility (again, among fathers and sons), that by Blau and Duncan, come up with the following findings and generalizations:

1. In terms of movement among occupational groups, there are three broad occupational classes in the United States: white-collar workers, including managerial and professional workers; blue-collar workers; and farm workers.
2. A small fourth class is made up of self-employed professionals such as doctors, lawyers, dentists, and other professionals. Mobility into this group is very difficult, and occupational inheritance from father to son is the highest of any group.
3. Social-class boundaries are more of a barrier to downward than to upward mobility. For example, white-collar workers or their offspring only rarely move down into blue-collar positions.
4. Social mobility appears to be increasing, with most mobility being for relatively limited social distances. The evidence is not clear, but it is possible that downward mobility is more common than it was in the past.
5. Physical geographical migration (spatial mobility) and social mobility are related. Those who move spatially are more successful than those who do not, and those who are downwardly mobile are likely to be geographically immobile.
6. The most successful migrants are those from one urban area to another urban area. Farm migrants are usually the least successful, doing worse than nonmigrants. Those migrating from the south, whether black or white, are less successful in terms of social mobility.
7. Blacks with equal educational and family background are less socially mobile than comparable whites. Occupationally, blacks suffer from restricted occupational mobility.
8. Immigrant whites do not suffer any handicap to occupational mobility. Their occupational levels, although lower than those of the total native population, are nonetheless equal to the occupational levels of natives with similar education and family background.[37]

The study also found that only four factors account for 50 percent of a person's chances for mobility: education, first job held, occupation of father, and education of father. Note that these factors all reflect one's background at least as much as one's abilities, and two of them refer to the father's characteristics rather than the child's. Individual achievement and mobility are possible for many, but they are

[36]Robert M. Hauser and David L. Featherman, "Trends in the Occupational Mobility of U.S. Men 1962–1970," *American Sociological Review*, **38**:302–310, 1973.
[37]Peter M. Blau and Otis Dudley Duncan, *The American Occupational Structure*, Wiley, New York, 1967.

In spite of all the rhetoric about aiding the disadvantaged, many of the poor aren't being trained to go anywhere. (Jeff Albertson/Stock, Boston.)

most likely if one has the good fortune to be born to an economically successful father. Revisionist educational historians and sociologists are increasingly questioning the role of the schools per se in allowing the poor to enter the economic mainstream.[38]

The size of the community in which a person spends childhood and adolescence is also of importance in determining the probable mobility of the children of manual workers.[39] This is apparently because the larger cities offer a youngster far greater exposure, through both education and general experience, to a wide range of possible occupations. Those from smaller communities are less likely to be aware of all the occupational alternatives. But size of community does not appear to influence the mobility of middle-class children whose fathers are in white-collar positions. This is probably because middle-class children learn about alternatives and pick up aspirations within the family.

William H. Sewell, in his research on the effect of place of residence, intelligence, and social class on educational and occupational aspirations of young people, found that the size of the community did indeed have a profound effect on aspirations to go to college. Seven out of ten city boys of high intelligence, but only four out of ten farm boys of high intelligence, planned to go on to college.

[38]Colin Greer, *The Great School Legend*, Viking Press, New York, 1972; and Michael Katz, *Class, Bureaucracy and Schools: The Illusion of Educational Change in America*, Praeger, New York, 1975.
[39]Lipset and Bendix, op. cit.

Sewell describes his findings this way:

The results of the statistical analysis show that there are sizable differences in the college plans of rural and urban youth which are not artifacts of the sex, intelligence, and socioeconomic (class) composition of the sample. Many factors would probably help to account for this finding. At the most general level, the opportunity structure provided by the more rural communities is clearly very limited both in its educational and occupational dimensions. . . . Greater access to higher education in urban areas, however, is not the only education factor that encourages the higher aspirations of urban youth. Urban schools generally provide a more academically stimulating climate than rural schools because of their better trained faculties, superior facilities, and more varied and challenging curricula.

Equally obvious is the fact that urban communities offer a much wider and more varied range of occupational opportunities than do rural communities. Many of these occupations require a minimum of college training for entry. While rural high school seniors are probably not completely unaware of either the rewards or the entrance requirements of many of the high-prestige professional, managerial, and technical positions available in urban communities, they are certainly less likely to have had first-hand exposure to most of them.[40]

Intergenerational Mobility of Women

Until the last decade little systematic attention was given to the social mobility of women or their part in the process of social stratification. As Joan Acker expressed it, "Sex has rarely been analyzed as a factor in stratification processes and structures, although it is probably one of the most obvious criteria of social differentiation. . . ."[41] This is now changing, and a number of scientific articles have appeared researching the intergenerational mobility of women.

Men's mobility is studied through analysis of the father's occupation compared to that of the son. Early studies of women's mobility frequently contrasted a woman's status as measured by her father's occupation with her status as measured by her husband's occupation. Marriage mobility was used, since in the past most women were not in the labor force, and the jobs held by those who were did not reflect social status. Most women tended to drop out of the labor force when they had children, or to be relegated to lower-status, poorer-paying jobs. Much of the latter was due to discrimination, but it was also a consequence of sporadic and part-time participation in the labor force by women. Only during the past decade have over half the women of childbearing age been in the labor force, and the majority (59 percent) of women who work still do so on a part-time basis. As Alice Rossi stated, "What a man does defines his status, but whom she marries defines a woman's."[42] This has now changed as more and more women develop long-term career patterns.

[40]William H. Sewell, "Community of Residence and College Plans," *American Sociological Review*, **29**:35, February, 1964.

[41]Joan Acker, "Women and Social Stratification: A Case of Intellectual Sexism," *American Journal of Sociology*, **78**:936, 1973.

[42]Alice Rossi, "Women in Science: Why So Few?" in C. F. Epstein and W. J. Goode (eds.), *The Other Half*, Prentice-Hall, Englewood Cliffs, N.J., 1971, p. 110.

Tyree and Treas found differences in the intergenerational occupational mobility of men and women—some to women's advantage, some not. Intergenerational mobility through marriage was more similar between the sexes than mobility from father's to daughter's occupation.[43]

An elaborate study by Chase using a nationally representative sample found that women have greater mobility (both upward and downward) through marriage than men do through occupation.[44] Men are more likely to "inherit" their fathers' status, while women are more likely to cross status lines in terms of both occupation and marriage. Physical and social attractiveness facilitates the upward mobility of some lower-status women.[45] Greater upward mobility among lower-class women than among lower-class men thus is the expected pattern.

Further research has indicated that in those cases where both mother and father have occupations outside the home, the mother's occupation is the best predictor of the daughter's occupation.[46]

International Differences

The most commonly held positions is that the overall pattern of social mobility is much the same in western industrialized countries.[47] However, some sociologists disagree, believing that Americans are more mobile than those in other industrial nations. A comparative study of national samples in the United States, Australia, and Italy indicated that when mobility from father to son was examined, the United States had the greatest upward mobility of manual workers: 36 percent of the sons were mobile, Australia had 31 percent mobile, and Italy had only 20 percent mobile.[48] This would indicate that social mobility is somewhat more common in the United States than in other industrialized countries. However, these findings are far from definitive.

COMMUNITY DECISION MAKING

The questions of who has power in metropolitan areas and how this power is exercised are of major interest to both sociologists and political scientists. Do the formal governmental mechanisms really indicate how community decisions are made, or are there more important informal mechanisms? During recent decades the field has experienced vigorous growth and considerable controversy on how

[43]Andrea Tyree and Judith Treas, "The Occupational and Marital Mobility of Women," *American Sociological Review,* **39:**292–302, 1974.

[44]Ivan D. Chase, "A Comparison of Men's and Women's Intergenerational Mobility in the United States," *American Sociological Review,* **40:**483–505, 1975.

[45]Glen H. Elder, Jr., "Appearance and Education in Marriage Mobility," *American Sociological Review,* **34:**519–533, 1969.

[46]Rachel A. Rosenfeld, "Women's Intergenerational Occupational Mobility," *American Sociological Review,* **43:**36–46, 1978.

[47]Seymour M. Lipset and Hans Zetterberg, "Social Mobility in Industrial Societies," in Lipset and Bendix, op. cit., pp. 60–64.

[48]Leonard Broom and F. Lancaster Jones, "Father-to-Son Mobility: Australia in Comparative Perspective," *American Journal of Sociology,* **74:**333–342, January, 1969.

urban decision making is accomplished. Although the concern has sometimes been with the attributes of the individuals wielding power, a social-psychological approach, the main issue is the structure of decision-making processes.

Research before the mid-1960s focused on case studies and asked the question "Who governs?" Two general schools of thought have emerged—one more closely associated with sociology and the other with political science. The first school, made up heavily of sociologists, has suggested that power is concentrated in an elite. Those who support this view argue that community power structures are frequently pyramidal, and that businesspeople or economic elites most commonly dominate the top positions, with elected political officials having secondary importance as decision makers. The second school of thought, usually associated with political science, suggests that power is widely distributed and that community power structures, to the degree that they exist at all, are highly pluralisitc, with political officials playing a leading role and exerting considerable influence.

Elitists

Empirical study of community decision-making processes began in effect during the 1950s with Floyd Hunter's study of the "community power structure" in "Regional City" (actually Atlanta, Georgia).[49]

Hunter's basic thesis was that in Atlanta the important community decisions were made by a group of about forty men who constituted a "power elite." This pyramidal power structure was dominated by an economic elite (mostly business-men) who set policy. Under this group there was a larger group of several hundred who had some influence but basically carried out the wishes of those at the top. Elected and appointed public officials such as the mayor were in this secondary group, not at the top.

Hunter's method of research was to ask a panel of knowledgeable judges to rank individuals "who in your opinion are the most influential . . . from the point of view of ability to rank others." Forty persons influential in the areas of civic affairs, business, government, and social status were selected, of whom twenty-seven were interviewed and asked to rank the influence of those on the list and add other names when appropriate. This has come to be known as the "reputational" method. Hunter found that when the respondents were asked to name the ten on the list who were top "leaders that nearly everyone would accept," the same names continually reappeared. Of these ten key people, only one (the mayor) was not a business executive. Not only were elected political leaders relatively unimportant, but Hunter found that the top influential individuals made the major policy decisions within their own crowd and only then exposed them to public discussion through associations, newspapers, and the like.

[49]Floyd Hunter, *Community Power Structure*, University of North Carolina Press, Chapel Hill, 1953, p. 258.

Hunter's portrait of how community decisions were made by economically dominant people immediately came under attack from political scientists who felt that his overall picture was inadequate on both methodological and ideological grounds. Critics of Hunter's results noted that the reputation for power and the exercise of power are different things, and that the reputational technique appeared to measure opinions about power rather than power itself. The technique was said to identify not those who had power and exercised it, but rather those who merely had the potential for such power. The technique was also criticized for starting with the assumption that there is a power structure and asking how individuals fit into it, rather than asking if any sort of power structure exists.[50]

Strong arguments were made that what was needed was a study of actual issues and how and by whom they were resolved. However, even more than the methodology, the underlying assumptions of an elitist model of power deeply upset those who held that community decision making was pluralistic and that the mayors and political officials were indeed important.[51]

Pluralists

Pluralists, as those opposed to the theory that economic dominants controlled urban decision making came to be called, held that American communities were composed not of a single elite but rather of a series of competing elites. On any given issue ad hoc coalitions form, so that a group may win on one issue and lose on others.

Coalitions are constantly in flux, with the composition of the group varying with the issue at hand. Moreover, people who are powerful may decide not to take any action at all and thus not affect the decision in any way. Pluralists tend to work by analyzing who participated in resolving particular issues; thus, their method is called the "positional" or "decision-making" approach.

The best-known of the studies by the pluralists is Robert Dahl's extensive research on how decisions were made in New Haven, Connecticut, in three areas: urban development, public school officials and policy, and nominations for mayor. Dahl defined his elite on the basis of their leadership positions (e.g., president or vice-president of a large corporation) or their personal assessed wealth. Two hundred and thirty-eight economic notables were defined in this fashion. Additionally, a separate group of social notables were defined on the basis of their having been invited to the New Haven Assemblies (231 families).

The finding of the New Haven study was that there was very little overlap between the various types of notables. Only twenty-four economic notables were

[50]Nelson W. Polsby, "How to Study Community Power: The Pluralist Alternative," *Journal of Politics*, 22:474–484, August, 1960.
[51]See Robert A. Dahl, "A Critique of the Ruling Elite Model," *American Political Science Review*, 52:463–469, June, 1958; Nelson W. Polsby, "The Sociology of Community Power: A Reassessment," *Social Forces*, 37:232–236, March, 1959; and Thomas J. Anton, "Power, Pluralism, and Local Politics," *Administrative Science Quarterly*, 7:425–457, March, 1963.

also identified as social notables. More important, neither the economic nor the social notables participated in significant numbers in the three areas of issues noted above. Dahl found that there was virtually no participation by notables in the public schools or the mayoral nomination. They participated somewhat more in urban renewal, but even here only one out of five notables was involved. Dahl concluded that there was little support for the belief in the economic elites that dominate all community issues.[52] Rather, there were many special-interest groups which combined on various issues to form temporary power groupings.

Dahl's study, though, had some substantial methodological weaknesses. Two of the three issues—the school board and the mayoral nominations—were hardly crucial for Dahl's economic notables, since they lived in the suburbs and none of their children attended New Haven city schools.

Unfortunately, unless one can commit time and resources to a long-term longitudinal study, it is difficult to choose key issues, since there are few objective indexes. Even an analysis of the space that the local newspaper gives to various issues may be misleading, because publishers are generally part of the elite. Thus if an elite does exist, the only issues that would surface in the newspapers would be those upon which the elite itself had some disagreement. Real community issues such as poverty and segregation might not, according to this view, be publicly discussed, while questions such as where a new highway should be built might receive great attention.

Dahl's study thus identified not economic influentials but rather a pool of those who had the potential to become powerful if they so chose. Thus whether participation by one out of five in the issue of urban renewal is a high or low rate of participation is largely a matter of professional judgment. Also weakening Dahl's case is the fact that New Haven is highly atypical in the area of urban renewal. At the time of the study, New Haven had received more funds per citizen than any other city in the nation. Statistically, New Haven was eight standard deviations above the mean, which raises serious question as to whether it is a typical city.[53]

Variation among Communities

By the late 1960s case studies of scores of communities had been completed, but the generalizability of their disparate findings was far from clear. Atlanta, New Haven, and other cities differed in size, age of the physical city, regional location, economic base, importance of absentee ownership, presence of ethnic groups, type of civic government, class composition, and race. Thus in order to discern major patterns, comparisons were made of the available studies. Two such studies of the studies have been done.

John Walton, examining thirty-nine studies dealing with sixty-one communities, found that particularly in the northeast and midwest older cities tended to

[52]Robert A. Dahl, *Who Governs?*, Yale University Press, New Haven, Conn., 1961.
[53]Michael Aiken and Paul E. Mott. *The Structure of Community Power*, Random House, New York, 1970, p. 198.

have more pluralistic or dispersed power structures, while newer cities and suburbs tended toward the pyramidal model.[54]

In an additional attempt to identify some of the structural attributes of communities that are associated with their power structures, Michael Aiken examined a sample of fifty-seven communities that have been the subject of community decision-making studies. He reported:

> A large number of community characteristics—location in the north, a high degree of absentee ownership, non-reform political structures, heterogeneous population, lower socioeconomic status of the population—are found to be consistently, although not strongly, related to dispersion of community power.[55]

While Walton and Aiken do not agree on all points—Aiken sees regional location as being of greater importance, for example—studies of the available research literature indicate that there are systematic differences among types of cities. For example, the more diversified the economic base and the more heterogeneous the city in terms of class, ethnicity, and race, the more diversified the power structure. Large cities, particularly in the north, depend heavily upon federal funds and local elites; their wishes control only a limited part of the city's resources. As Sally Ward has demonstrated, communities that have extensive ties to the larger society are more likely to be involved in, and have resources from, social programs that are national in origin.[56]

Today, with the debate between pluralists and elitists fading, the questions are "Who rules?—in what kinds of communities; when; under what conditions; and with what effects? How do decisions affect policy outputs and impacts?"[57]

Middletown

One of the most interesting studies of power and stratification in a community was done long before the current debate over methodology and its effects on findings. This was the remarkably productive Middletown studies by Helen and Robert Lynd.[58] In their first book, the Lynds studied the effects of industrialization on a small city which would "be as representative as possible of American life" and at the same time "compact and homogeneous enough to be manageable."[59] Middletown (Muncie, Indiana) remarkably reflected the white, Protestant "middle America" of the 1920s, and there is a significant correspondence between the

---

[54]John Walton, "The Structural Bases of Political Change in Urban Communities," paper presented at the American Sociological Association meeting, August, 1973; and "A Systematic Survey of Community Power Research," in Michael Aiken and Paul E. Mott (eds.), *The Structure of Community Power*, Random House, New York, 1970, pp. 443–464.

[55]Aiken and Mott, op. cit., p. 407.

[56]Sally K. Ward, "Community Interdependence, Decentralization, and Policy Outputs: A Comparative Analysis of American Cities," paper presented at the American Sociological Association meeting, September, 1977.

[57]Terry Nichols Clark, "Community Power," in Alex Inkeles (ed.), *Annual Review of Sociology*, Annual Reviews, Palo Alto, Calif., 1975, p. 271.

[58]Robert Lynd and Helen Lynd, *Middletown*, Harcourt, Brace, New York, 1929; and Robert Lynd and Helen Lynd, *Middletown in Transition*, Harcourt, Brace, New York, 1937.

[59]Lynd and Lynd, *Middletown*, p. 7.

sociological study of Middletown and the socially aware novels of the period, such as Sinclair Lewis's *Babbitt.*

The later book, *Middletown in Transition,* explored the effects of the depression on the community and on the attitudes of its people. The most specific change was the overwhelming dominance in 1935 of every aspect of the community's life by the X family (the Ball family), who owned a plant that manufactured glass jars for household canning and thus continued to profit during the depression while other factories were closing. The depression brought into bold relief the economic dominance of this family and their control over the political and social as well as economic life of the city. As it was put in 1935 by one local citizen:

> If I'm out of work I go to the X plant; if I need money I go to the X bank, and if they don't like me I don't get it; my children go to the X college; when I get sick I go to the X hospital; I buy a building lot or house in an X subdivision; my wife goes downtown to buy clothes at the X department store; if my dog strays away he is put in the X pound; I buy X milk; I drink X beer, vote for X political parties, and get help from X charities; my boy goes to the X Y.M.C.A. and my girl to their Y.W.C.A.; I listen to the word of God in X-subsidized churches; if I'm a Mason I go to the X Masonic Temple; I read the news from the X morning newspaper; and, if I am rich enough, I travel via the X airport.[60]

As others had gone under in the depression, the X family had expanded their influence to the point where in addition to having their own glass factory, they also controlled the only bank, the only department store, the newspaper, the school board, the college, and a wealthy subdivision, and they had co-opted all the prominent lawyers and other sources of potential opposition in the city.

The picture of the community power structure was thus Marxist: a small number of economic dominants controlled all major economic, political, social, and religious organizations. However, this pattern of consolidation of power ended with the depression, for two major reasons. First, the depression itself was a unique, temporary situation; as business began to revive, other economic influentials reasserted themselves. General Motors, for example, reopened its Muncie plant, which was under absentee ownership and control. Second, the older members of the X family, who had devoted their interests to Muncie, were passing from the scene, and their eastern-educated children had far less concern with local affairs. Their interests were statewide, or larger. Moreover, generalizing from Muncie to larger cities is difficult, for there is no evidence that Muncie is typical of larger cities.

Although the depression changed or brought into focus the economic dominance of the community by a small self-serving elite, it had small effect on the attitudes of the community. Economic crisis did not lead to Marxian revolt or even to much heightening of class consciousness. The old ideology and its slogans continued to be mouthed, although they were less applicable than ever. "Middletown, capitalism, and progress" was still the official ideology—and it was

---

[60]Lynd and Lynd, *Middletown in Transition,* p. 74.

shared by many workers. Unionism came to Muncie, but because of changes outside the community rather than because of local militancy. "Getting ahead" was still the goal and central value, in spite of the loss of the means to do so. The desire for security was modifying the old system, but only gradually. The economic collapse of the system did not result in a radical divorce from its basic goals, values, and ideology.

The recent restudy of Middletown by Theodore Caplow et al. (discussed in Chapter 6, City Life-Styles) indicates that while Muncie is now economically tied to federal programs and outside economic forces, it still retains to a remarkable degree many of its traditional values and attitudes.[61]

Black Powerlessness

Studies of power in communities have provided relatively little information on participation by blacks in community decision making.

In a study of the powerlessness of blacks in Chicago it was found that blacks occupied only 285 of the 19,997 top policy-making positions in the Chicago area—2.6 percent.[62] Black representation in Chicago was greatest in the elected public sector, welfare and religious voluntary organizations, and industrial unions. In the words of the Chicago study:

> The sectors and individual groups in the Chicago area with the highest Negro representation were those with Negro constituency-elective offices, supervisory boards, labor unions, and religious and welfare organizations.[63]

Blacks were virtually unrepresented in the policy-making positions of private institutions such as business corporations, banks, insurance companies, universities, and professional organizations.

A replication and extension of this research examined the degree to which blacks were found in key policy-making positions in the Milwaukee, Wisconsin, metropolitan area. At the time of the study the city was 12 percent black and the county was 9 percent black. In this study a total of 4,930 policy-making positions in the sectors of business, public government, education, and voluntary organizations were identified and the number of blacks holding such policy-making positions was identified.[64] A total of 1,867 policy-making positions in the private sector were surveyed. Business and industrial concerns, law firms, banks, stock brokerage firms, insurance companies, and hospitals, were included. The results are shown in Table 10-2.

Only *one* black occupied any of the 1,867 key positions in the business sector. The all-but-total absence of blacks in these critical positions was a major handicap to black entrepreneurship. Blacks fared somewhat better in the sector of

[61]Theodore Caplow et al., in a session devoted to the restudy of Middletown at American Sociological Association meetings, August, 1978.

[62]H. M. Baron et al., "Black Powerlessness in Chicago," *Trans-Action*, November, 1968, p. 28.

[63]Ibid., p. 29.

[64]Karl H. Flaming, J. John Palen, et al., "Black Powerlessness in Policy-Making Positions," *Sociological Quarterly*, 13:126–133, Winter, 1972.

TABLE 10-2
Percentage of Blacks in Policy-Making Positions in
the Private Sector

Selected areas	Number of positions	Number of blacks	Percent of blacks
Business and industrial concerns	622	0	0.0
Law firms	399	0	0.0
Banks	413	0	0.0
Stock brokerage		0	0.0
Insurance firms	145	0	0.0
Hospitals	220	1	0.5
Total	1,867	1	0.05

Source: Karl H. Flaming, J. John Palen, et al., "Black Powerlessness in Policy-Making Positions," *Sociological Quarterly*, 13:131, Winter, 1972, table 1.

public government. There, twenty blacks held 42 of the 856 policy-making positions (4.9 percent) in the city and county. The picture was similar in the academic sector: of a total of 553 policy-making positions, blacks held 21, or 3.8 percent.

The highest degree of representation of Negroes was found in the voluntary sector. Blacks were highly visible in programs and organizations primarily concerned with minority groups and problems of poverty. Of the 472 policy-making posts in the voluntary service organizations, 125 (26.5 percent) were held by blacks. However, the majority of these voluntary organizations, such as the Urban League, had only limited influence in the community. Blacks were most visible in organizations dealing directly with minority-group problems. On the other hand, it is noteworthy that in civic associations (Association of Commerce, Bar Association, Board of Realtors) as opposed to service organizations, only 2 of the 121 posts were held by blacks. However, the degree to which this situation has been modified or changed over the decade is unknown. Replication is badly needed.

Women and Power

In examining the research of recent decades on community power, it is difficult to find more than a cursory mention of the status, prestige, or even presence of women in power structures. This is because in sociological research, as elsewhere, women have been largely overlooked as a separate group. This situation is changing radically, but one result of past inattention is a virtual lack of solid data on participation by women other than the obvious counts of women in Congress and the Senate, as state governors, as local mayors, etc.

One exception is a study done by Babchuk and others of the role played by women in the voluntary civic associations of a large northeastern city. They found that while women participated extensively on the Council of Social Agencies and

Community Chest boards—522 of the 1,937 memberships were held by women—there were substantial differences between participation by men and by women.[65]

Agencies were classified according to their function and according to whether they were "instrumental," "instrumental-expressive," or "expressive." "Instrumental" agencies as a group provided a service or produced a good—for example, a Council of Social Agencies or a hospital. "Expressive" agencies provided a framework in which actions were immediately gratifying—for example, a settlement house. "Instrumental-expressive" agencies included both instrumental and expressive activities consciously exercised. It was hypothesized that agencies with instrumental functions would have the greatest status, the largest budgets, and correspondingly the fewest women. It was expected that women would be more likely to be members of boards with expressive functions and smaller budgets.

The findings were as predicted. The authors of the study concluded that the more vital, high-status boards were overwhelmingly dominated by men. The researchers found:

> Of the 222 board members of the agencies ranked as most vital, 198 or 89 percent, were men. Only 147 of the 240 members, or 61 percent, of the boards of agencies ranked as least vital were men. Thus, while men tend to dominate the boards of both types, they are most likely to be represented on boards of agencies ranked as most vital. . . .
> Of the 25 members of the most vital boards only one was a woman.[66]

It is reasonable to assume that research currently in progress will indicate that the numbers and percentage of women in positions of community power are increasing and will continue to do so as women achieve economic as well as legal and social equality with men. "Sisterhood" has already made some progress at city halls. As of 1980, women served as mayors of Chicago, San Francisco, Phoenix, Oklahoma City, and San Jose.

---

[65]Nicholas Babchuk, Ruth Morsey, and C. Wayne Gordon, "Men and Women in Community Agencies: A Note on Power and Prestige," in Nona Glazer-Malbin and Helen Youngelson Waehrer (eds.), *Women in a Man-Made World,* Rand McNally, Chicago, 1972, pp. 248–253.
[66]Ibid., p. 25.

PART FOUR

URBAN PROBLEMS
AND PLANNING

CHAPTER

11

THE CRISIS OF THE CITIES?

Through me the way into the doleful city,
Through me the way into eternal grief,
Through me a people forsaken.

Inscription over the gate of hell in Dante's *Inferno*

THE "URBAN CRISIS"

As recently as 1930 a planner could exult over the harmonious combination of urban and rural elements in Los Angeles and describe the city as "a federation of communities coordinated into a metropolis of sunlight and air."[1] No one makes such claims today. All around, one hears that the city is not only going to hell but going to hell at an ever more rapid pace. It is an accepted cliché that we live in an age of urban crisis. Crime, violence, pollution, ugliness, congestion, and alienation are all attributed in one degree or another to urban life. Certainly there is no lack of prophets to passionately catalog our urban ills. As Lewis Mumford says:

> Nobody can be satisfied with the form of the city today. Neither as a working mechanism, as a social medium, nor as a work of art does the city fulfill the high hopes that modern civilization has called forth—or even met our reasonable demands.[2]

Are cities, particularly large cities, doomed? During the 1960s and 1970s voices were raised everywhere proclaiming the inevitable decline, if not death, of the city. Over and over we heard of the doleful state of the city.[3] A conference of large-city mayors in 1977 proclaimed that what was at stake was not only "the survival of our cities" but the survival of the American way of life as we have known it. The chairman of the New York Real Estate Board states: "American cities are collapsing. This peril to the nation, and in consequence to over 200 years of experiment in democracy, is no overstatement."[4]

This view is shared by many urban scholars. Philip Hauser contends that "the stark facts indicate that the worst still lies ahead. The urban crisis will grow worse before it grows better.[5] Similarly, George Sternlieb pessimistically suggests that "the Newarks of America are forecasts of things to come, and if we want to understand the probable future that faces many of our older cities, then we will first have to get clear on what is happening—has happened—in places like Newark."[6] Sternlieb contends that the older cities have lost their economic function, particularly as areas of entry for newcomers, and have become simply "sandboxes." People in the sandbox occasionally get new toys (federal programs), but these don't allow the underclass to move into the larger world—they just keep the people in the sandbox from being bothersome to the rest of society.

In this view, cities are having their vital signs maintained by external life-support systems, with the federal government making the judgment about whether to pull the plug. To those holding such views, shrinkage in city size is

---

[1] R. M. Fogelson, *The Fragmented Metropolis: Los Angeles 1850–1930*, Harvard University Press, Cambridge, Mass., 1967, p. 163.
[2] Lewis Mumford, *The Urban Prospect*, Harcourt Brace Jovanovich, New York, 1968, p. 108.
[3] See *U. S. News and World Report*, April 5, 1976, pp. 49–64.
[4] Seymour B. Durant, "Laetrile for the Urban Crisis: 'Planned Shrinkage' and Other Dangerous Nostrums," *Journal of the Institute for Socioeconomic Studies*, 4:68, Summer, 1979.
[5] Philip M. Hauser, "Chicago—Urban Crisis Exampler," in J. John Palen (ed.), *City Scenes*, Little, Brown, Boston, 1977, pp. 15–25.
[6] George Sternlieb, "The City as Sandbox," *The Public Interest*, 4:(25):00, Fall, 1971.

inevitable.[7] Not surprisingly, most discussions regarding the future of urban areas have focused not on what will occur, but rather on questions of the degree and timing of the collapse.

Certainly central cities no longer dominate demographically the way they did as recently as three decades ago, when the CBD was still economically dominant and mass suburbanization was still in the future. During the decade of the 1960s, the percentage of the population living in the nation's fifty largest cities declined 2 percent, and twenty-two of these cities lost population. This trend accelerated during the 1970s, with central cities losing 5 percent of their population. At the same time suburban areas grew by 12 percent and nonmetropolitan areas, reversing a long trend, gained 10 percent. Of the nation's twenty-five most populous cities, eighteen acutally lost population.

The greatest losers were Cleveland and St. Louis, which each lost 17 percent of their residents; Atlanta, which was down 14 percent; and Detroit, which lost 13 percent. Among the other population losers were New York, down 6 percent; Chicago, down 9 percent; Baltimore, down 9 percent; and Washington, D.C., down 7 percent. New York's 1978 population of 7,443,000 was its lowest since the 1930s.

Those cities registering gains were mainly sunbelt cities still containing space for development. Major gainers were Houston, with an 18 percent increase (partially due to annexing areas); San Diego, with a 13 percent increase; San Antonio, with 20 percent; Phoenix, with 17 percent; and San Jose, with 24 percent.

Keep in mind, though, that population decline cannot necessarily be equated with a decline in the quality of life. City boosters in the past always equated quantitative growth with qualitative improvement. Thus, when the Bureau of the Census first noted declines a couple of decades ago, the announcements were often treated as insults to the cities' honor. The late Mayor Daley of Chicago was outraged to hear that his city was losing people.

We are now beginning to mature in our attitudes and to realize that lessening population pressures may provide real opportunities to improve the amenities of urban life, but the old idea that "bigger is better" dies slowly. As a further note, it has to be remembered that while the urban population may be declining, that of the suburban fringe is not. Thus there remains the necessary population base to support the cultural, entertainment, and professional sports activities of the central city.

THE CITY RESURRECTED?

The fact that some cities will inevitably continue to falter economically as well as demographically is generally acknowledged, but in many cities the last few years have witnessed a rebirth of hope. Just as continued decline seemed inevitable, signs of hope began appearing. The media discovered that the city was not only

---

[7]Roger Starr, "Making New York Smaller," *New York Times Magazine*, November 19, 1976, pp. 32–33, 99–106.

A Marxist View

One cannot discuss the urban crisis without the perspective provided by the new Marxist urban sociology.* Marxist sociologists hold that cities cannot be examined separately from the political, historical, and, particularly, economic system of which they are a part. Manuel Costells argues, for example, that not only is the crisis of the cities real, but the decay of the central cities, their fiscal insolvency, and flight to the suburbs are inevitable and necessary consequences of a capitalistic economic system.† He says that the quest for ever-greater profits by large monopolistic companies led to government policies such as government-insured mortgages and subsidies for expressways. The corporations—and their wealthy managers—thus could move to the suburbs, where land costs and taxes were lower, while still maintaining the economic benefits of being near the central city. The fiscal crises of cities such as New York were not the consequence of excessive services, public service jobs, and welfare, as the elites argue. Rather, New York's "bankruptcy" is the result of the corporations' rejection of increased taxes to pay for these social services. The result is the abandonment—and destruction—of largely poor areas of the city, while corporations concentrate on issues important to themselves such as downtown redevelopment. Social movements by the poor are either repressed or bought off. The consequence is said to be a future where the urban crisis is sharpened and mass repression and control become inevitable adjuncts of an exploitative metropolitan model.‡

* See, for example, Manuel Costells, *The Urban Question: A Marxist Approach*, Alan Sheridan (trans.), M.I.T. Press, Cambridge, Mass., 1977.
†Manuel Costells, "The Wild City", *Kapital State*, 4–5:2–30, Summer, 1976.
‡Ibid.

Houston, the so-called "silver buckle on the sun belt," is booming. Cries about the death of the city have to be evaluated in terms of what type of city is meant and where it is located. (United Press International.)

alive but healthy.[8] Only a few large cities (e.g., New York and Cleveland) are said to still show signs of fiscal stress, and the employment gap between cities and suburbs is closing. Particularly in the south and west, we are told that cities are "now generating new jobs twice as fast as the nearer suburban centers."[9] Suddenly we hear that the "urban crisis" has left town, and the slumming of the suburbs is the new problem.[10] Meanwhile, the central cities have bottomed out and are now experiencing an urban renaissance. Revitalized downtowns are showing economic vigor, while affluent whites are rediscovering the city as a place of residence and are rehabilitating inner-city areas. (This will be discussed in detail in Chapter 12, Housing Programs and Urban Regeneration.)

What is the case? Readers, understandably, may be confused by the contradictory claims. Just as they have come to accept the urban crisis as part of

[8]Horace Sutton, "America Falls in Love with its Cities—Again," *Saturday Review,* August, 1978, pp. 16–21; and "A City Revival," *Newsweek,* January 15, 1979, pp. 00.
[9]T. D. Allman, "The Urban Crisis Leaves Town," *Harpers,* December, 1978, p. 5.
[10]Ibid., pp. 41–56.

American life, they are told, "Never mind; the crisis is over." This section will attempt to evaluate the various claims and counterclaims; but as you read the material, keep in mind that these are the judgments of this author, and others might draw different conclusions. The discussion focuses on two aspects of the urban situation: the central business district and the urban fiscal crisis.

Changing Central Business Districts

In evaluating what is occurring in cities, it is helpful to distinguish between what is occurring in the economic heart of the city—the central business district (CBD)—and what is happening in residential neighborhoods.

Discussions of the decline of downtowns often focus on the weakening position of the CBD as a center of retail trade. As shopping centers, downtowns have been declining both in absolute terms and in terms of a percentage of metropolitan-area sales. Aging downtown stores have not been able to compete effectively with suburban shopping malls.

On the other hand, the CBD has been far more successful in retaining business and government administrative offices. Economically, the downtowns of most large cities are experiencing new business construction. From the mid-1960s to early 1970 alone there was over a 50 percent increase in office space in older cities such as New York and Chicago, while Houston doubled its office space. Downtown Los Angeles is undergoing a building boom.[11]

Chicago has over $1 billion in new skyscrapers planned or under construction, and New York is experiencing a major influx of foreign capital—including reinvested oil money. Even in riot-devastated Detroit, the downtown is growing, crowned by a $350 million business-hotel-shopping complex called "Renaissance Center." New downtown cultural centers, sports arenas, and convention facilities are common. For CBDs the worst may be over. The presuburban era will not return, but most cities are in the process of stabilizing at a moderate but reasonable level of economic activity.

Overall, downtown stores will never again have the dominance of retail trade they exhibited during the centralizing era of the streetcar and subway; but so long as the downtown is a major white-collar employment center, the CBD will be a solidly profitable location for retail sales. Moreover, downtown remains the location of choice for insurance firms, financial and legal services, government, and administrative headquarters of all sorts. One visible consequence of this change from retail trade to office space is that the crowded CBD of working hours often becomes a virtual wasteland after 5:00 P.M., when offices close.

However, there is a catch to this development of the CBD. Central-city offices provide new jobs—but only for those possessing specific white-collar skills. City factories and manufacturing plants continue to move to the suburbs—or beyond.

---

[11]Gerald Manners, "The Office in the Metropolis: An Opportunity for Shaping Metropolitan America," *Economic Geography,* 50:93–110, 1974.

From 1960 to 1970, cities experienced a 13 percent reduction in blue-collar jobs but a concurrent 7 percent increase in white-collar jobs.[12] This pattern accelerated during the 1970s.

There is a mismatch between people and jobs. Stagnant or declining manufacturing and factory sectors offer scant employment opportunities for those with limited educational backgrounds and job experience. Poor minority-group members have not been able to follow manufacturing jobs to the suburbs. The consequence is that cities often have high unemployment and welfare rolls at the same time that white-collar opportunities are expanding. Depending on where the emphasis is placed, one can make a case that things are either much better or much worse.

Fiscal Crisis of the Cities

During the 1970s it was common knowledge that the cities were in financial trouble. The middle class with its tax dollars was flowing to the suburbs while central-city expenses were skyrocketing.

Declining populations meant greater costs to those who remained. As middle-class taxpayers departed, municipal payrolls and public assistance expenditures usually increased rather than declined. Growing numbers of poor residents needing services raised costs while depressing revenues. Aging city properties also required more fire and police protection, and older street, lighting, and sewer systems required more maintenance.

Today there is less talk of the fiscal crisis of the cities. Most cities are meeting their day-to-day expenses. According to a major financial study, only four of sixty-six cities studied suffered serious financial stress.[13] Terry Clark et al. have similarly showed that cities vary dramatically in their fiscal health.[14] In their study, debt-ridden New York City was an extreme case of high expenditures—some, such as free city college tuition, not even found in most other cities—and poor financial management.

The major reason for the improved municipal fiscal picture is a massive increase in direct and indirect federal aid to cities. However, the fact that cities can meet their payrolls does not mean that they are in robust financial health. Federal revenue sharing has provided temporary relief but has not resolved long-term problems. Cities are still squeezed between growing expenditures and a declining tax base. The larger the city, the greater the financial burden. Per capita debt is more than twice as high in cities of over 1 million as in smaller cities.[15]

---

[12]John Kasarda, "The Changing Occupational Structure of the American Metropolis," in Barry Schwartz (ed.), *The Changing Face of Suburbs,* University of Chicago Press, Chicago, 1976, p. 122.

[13]"Urban Fiscal Stress," a report by Touche Ross and Co. and the First National Bank of Boston, 1978. This report is challenged by the Department of Housing and Urban Development in "The Urban Fiscal Crisis: Fact or Fantasy?" Office of Policy Development and Research, Washington, D.C., March, 1979.

[14]Terry N. Clark, Irene Sharp Rubin, Lynne C. Pettler, and Erwin Zimmerman, *How Many New Yorks? Comparative Study of Community Decision-Making,* Research Report no. 72, University of Chicago, Chicago, 1976.

[15]*U.S. News and World Report,* April 6, 1976, p. 51.

Deterioration of the cities' physical infrastructure is actually a far more serious problem than potential default. In New York, bursting water mains and collapsing streets have become commonplace, yet little is being done. At the present level of construction, it would take over 200 years to replace New York City's streets and water mains and 300 years to replace its sewers.[16] Nor is New York alone; Philadelphia's sewers are falling apart, while Boston and Houston are plagued by hemorrhaging water mains.

What Should Be Done?

Not surprisingly, there is dispute over what should or even can be done to improve CBDs and deal with urban fiscal problems. Paul R. Porter has been one of the strongest advocates of a Marshall Plan for cities and regeneration of the central city as a place of residence for those who work in the CBD.[17] Decentralization of manufacturing and employment should not be discouraged; rather, federal aid should be used to resettle inner-city residents near outlying sources of employment. Others dispute whether a Marshall Plan for cities would have the anticipated result, pointing out that even accounting for inflation, the federal government is now devoting to American cities ten times the amount given for postwar European recovery.

At the opposite pole from those who contend that the city has become a sandbox or dumping ground for the unwanted and unfit is Edward Banfield's contention that things not only are not going to hell but are actually improving. According to Banfield:

> Most of the "problems" that are generally supposed to constitute "the urban crisis" could not conceivably lead to disaster. They are—some of them—important in the sense that a bad cold is important, but they are not critical in the sense that a cancer is critical. They have to do with comfort, convenience, amenity, and business advantage, all of which are important, but they do not affect either the essential welfare of individuals or what may be called the good health of society.[18]

Banfield says that banes such as traffic congestion could be largely alleviated by staggering office hours, since commuting constitutes the bulk of the traffic problem. Even the fiscal problem of cities is relatively rapidly resolvable, he argues, given the political will to do so. Only in a few cities such as Newark are residents unable to pay more taxes. Rather, the problem is that city dwellers "do not want to pay more simply because other people have moved away."[19] The obvious solutions are redrawing city boundary lines to include all metropolitan residents, or charging nonresidents for use of services. Banfield suggests that these actions aren't taken because the political cost is too great. Thus the problem

[16]"City Fiscal Time Bomb—Decaying Facilities," *New York Times,* January 29, 1979.
[17]Paul R. Porter, *The Recovery of American Cities,* Sun River Press, New York, 1976.
[18]Edward Banfield, *The Unheavenly City Revisited,* Little, Brown, Boston, 1974 p. 4.
[19]Ibid., p. 8.

isn't all that serious, for if it were, the disadvantages of not taking action would outweigh those of doing something.

Banfield suggests that the real problem is not that cities are getting worse, but that they are improving at a rate slower than our expectations. For example, the proportion of the population in poverty has decreased, and urban housing stock, including that of inner-city areas, has been improving. He argues that while "things have been getting better absolutely, they have been getting worse *relative to what we think they should be.*"[20] Thus, solutions always seem to fall short of expectations. Banfield suggests that the federal government really does not know how to make things better, the best approach is to not make things worse by charging aimlessly ahead. In other words, he advocates "benign neglect" for the cities. Needless to say, such a view infuriates large-city mayors who feel they are beset with ever deepening problems and need all the assistance they can get. They believe that Banfield's views are used to legitimize a "do nothing and let them sink" attitude.

OVERVIEW: THE FUTURE OF CITIES

The overall future of the cities remains clouded. On the positive side, the short-term urban crisis appears to be winding down. Cities have not defaulted. The state of the cities is fiscally and—perhaps more important—psychologically healthier than a decade ago. Bright new office buildings and refurbished shopping centers are a sign of hope. There are also clear if limited signs of middle-class movement into city neighborhoods.

On the debit side, the long-term indicators are still grim. There is still an outflow of tax dollars; older cities continue to lose manufacturing jobs; and the cost of services is soaring. Physically some neighborhoods are experiencing regeneration, but deterioration of the physical infrastructure (e.g., water mains) remains an expensive if often unseen problem. The political climate favors tax cutbacks rather than new urban programs.

Not all cities are going to experience similar situations. Declines in size may reflect only deterioration, or may spur the development of new roles as cultural and service centers. Cities such as Newark and Cleveland may well continue their declines regardless of valiant efforts to reverse the process. Old cities such as Boston and Baltimore appear to be on the threshold of an urban renaissance. Others such as Denver, Dallas, Seattle, and Phoenix show signs of increasing problems but also retain considerable vigor. Ironically, there is widespread acceptance of the thesis of inevitable and irreversible urban decay, just as the data indicate renewed urban vitality and regeneration.

---

[20]Ibid., p. 22.

SELECTED CURRENT PROBLEMS

Redlining

The poor, and particularly the minority poor, are also still victimized by redlining. "Redlining" is the practice of banks' and savings and loans associations' writing off an area as undesirable for mortgage loan investment. Financial institutions thus in effect draw a "red line" around a neighborhood that has been defined as a bad risk for "responsible" investment. Redlined areas most frequently are within the ghetto or in abutting racially changing neighborhoods. Once the financial institution determines that a neighborhood is likely to turn over racially, the lending institution either outright refuses loans or subtly discourages whites from purchasing in the area. The latter might be done through charging higher interest rates, demanding higher down payments, or cutting down the length of the mortgage.

Redlining is now illegal, but the process of "disinvesting" in certain communities obviously continues. Redlining creates a self-fulfilling prophecy of neighborhood decline. Without conventional mortgages and home improvement loans, newcomers are forced to purchase land contracts or use government loans, while existing residents can't get money for home improvement. As a consequence, the neighborhood declines, thus justifying the "wisdom" of the lending officials who by their actions virtually assured this outcome, and perhaps even the eventual abandonment of the neighborhood.

Abandonment of Buildings

During the 1970s the problem of abandoned housing in central-city neighborhoods worsened severely. Nationally there are 150,000 abandonments a year. In New York City, abandonments have reached epidemic proportions, with 40,000 units a year being abandoned (housing starts, by comparison, have averaged only 6,000 units annually for the last five years). The city brought foreclosure actions for nonpayment of taxes against 33,000 properties in 1978, and presently owns well over 35,000 apartments, half of them walk-up tenements 60 to 100 years old.[21] It is feared that by the mid-1980s the number will rise to 75,000.[22] These figures don't include the larger number of buildings that have been razed.

To keep the city from going bankrupt by maintaining all this run-down housing, the Carter administration allowed New York to set aside $100 million in federal community development funds to help pay for running the buildings. The

[21]Durant, op. cit., p. 72.

[22]Some conservative scholars argue that abandonment can occur because there is a housing surplus in some cities. See William Gorham and Nathan Glazer, *The Urban Predicament*, The Urban Institute, Washington, D.C., pp. 129–130.

The south Bronx has come to symbolize the worst possible case of urban decay and abandonment. (Barbara Pfeffer/Peter Arnold, Inc.)

goal of the city is to transfer the ownership to tenant and community groups and return some of the buildings to the tax rolls.

How is it that usable buildings are being abandoned? The answer lies in the economics of the private housing market. Being a slumlord traditionally was a lucrative business, but by the 1960s things had begun to change. Tenants, often urged on by community organizers, began to militantly demand improvements in their buildings. Sometimes these demands were accompanied by rent strikes. At about the same time, some cities began to actually enforce housing codes and even order that illegally converted units be returned to original occupancy (that is,

Discrimination in Housing

For years it has been assumed that blacks are discriminated against in the sale and rental of housing. The extent is documented by a major national study done by the National Committee Against Discrimination in Housing under contract from HUD.* Forty metropolitan areas were randomly selected from 117 SMSAs having large central cities and large central-city black populations. During the spring of 1977 approximately 300 whites and 300 blacks in matched pairs shopped for the same housing units advertised in local metropolitan newspapers.

The housing to be audited was selected by random sample. In five areas selected for "in-depth" study—Atlanta, Boston, Dallas, Milwaukee, and Sacramento—some 80 real estate and 120 rental visits were conducted by each pair of couples. In the thirty-five other sites, thirty to fifty visits each were conducted. In all, some 3,264 real estate agencies and apartment-rental complexes were visited by both couples.

With regard to an index of housing availability—the most important of the measures of discrimination—27 percent of the rental agents and 15 percent of the sales agents discriminated. The effect on housing searches may be cumulative; that is, if 15 percent of sales agents discriminate, a black who visits four agents can expect to encounter one or more instances of discrimination 48 percent of the time. Discrimination treatment as measured by other indexes exhibited smaller but still significant differences. Rental housing discrimination was uniformly high in the north central, southern, and western regions, while incidents of discrimination in housing were approximately three times higher in the north central region than in the northeast, south, and west.

Not surprisingly, these estimates of discrimination have been challenged by the housing industry as being too high and by civil rights groups as being too low. Nonetheless, the study will most likely become the landmark against which further progress can be judged. Overall, it indicates that efforts to combat racial discrimination have not been completely successful, although blacks are not longer totally excluded from the housing market. Potential black purchasers in particular are in the great majority of cases treated no differently from potential white purchasers.

*Ronald E. Wienk, Clifford E. Reid, John C. Simonson, and Frederick J. Eggers, *Measuring Racial Discrimination in American Housing Markets: The Housing Market Practice Survey,* Office of Policy Development and Research, Department of Housing and Urban Development, Washington, D.C., 1979.

increase the number of rooms per apartment and decrease the number of paying renters). The interest of absentee landlords declined dramatically further with the urban riots of the late 1960s, increasing vandalism, and the rapidly escalating heating costs of the 1970s. Slumlords simply found that housing the poor was no longer a paying proposition, particularly in cities with rent controls. The cost of owning buildings was rising faster than rental income.

When landlords see no long-term economic potential in their property, improvements and even necessary maintenance are allowed to slip. As a last type of profit taking, the landlord invariably stops paying property taxes. (Cities traditionally did not begin foreclosure action until there were three years of tax arrears. Some states such as New York have now shortened the period to one year.) An area with a sharp spurt in tax delinquencies is almost always on the verge of abandonment.

Finally, when landlords see no more economic potential, they default on their mortgages and simply abandon their buildings. Under the law action can be taken by the city to take possession of the property, but no action can be brought against the slumlords themselves. Once the landlord abandons a building, services are cut off and the tenants move to other housing. Vandals and professional looters strip the building of anything of value. They pull up with trucks and rip out plumbing and heating systems and whatever else can be sold. (In St. Louis the face bricks are sometimes stripped off buildings.) Fires set by vandals or others are common in such abandoned buildings.

A case in point is the Woodlawn area of Chicago, which was organized in the early 1960s by Saul Alinsky to force landlords to maintain their property. Woodlawn is now pocketed with empty lots where apartments once stood. After the riots of 1968, the Woodlawn section experienced wholesale abandonment of buildings and a series of fires that displaced half the population—some 30,000 persons. By 1973 over 20 percent of the community's housing had been abandoned.[23] The population that remained was largely poor, unemployed, and on welfare. Continuing abandonment of central-city property is a visible example of the inability of the private housing market to house the poor adequately.

The Army is currently considering a New York City proposal that Army troops be used to demolish abandoned hulks and clear out the rubble. There are some 10,000 buildings in the city considered beyond salvage—3,000 of them in the South Bronx alone—that are currently open invitations to arson.

Burning for Profit

Arson is a growing phenomenon in the older cores of central cities. Exact figures are difficult to determine, partially because a good arsonist destroys the evidence and partially because there are an inadequate number of fire investigators to officially categorize suspicious blazes as arson. In the United States as a whole, it

[23]Winston Moore, Charles P. Liversmore, and George Galland, Jr., "Woodlawn: The Zone of Distruction," *The Public Interest*, **30**:44–59, Winter, 1973.

is estimated that the arson rate has tripled in the last fifteen years to roughly 15,000 cases annually.[24] The chief of operations of the New York City Fire Department estimates that 25 to 40 percent of the building fires in that city are deliberately set.

Many of these fires are set by slumlords or businesspeople who burn their buildings for the insurance money. Some are entrepreneurs who buy decrepit buildings in order to set profitable fires. Others are "building strippers" who "torch" old buildings in order to gain access and strip the building of plumbing and other items that can be sold for scrap. In New York, slum residents have been known to ignite their own apartments to get the relocation allowance of up to $2,000. Those who are burned out also obtain a higher priority for public housing vacancies. There are also youngsters who, even if they are not paid to torch a building by the owner, will do it for the sheer excitement.

New York State is trying to take some of the profit out of arson by permitting the city to deduct unpaid taxes and other payments from landlords' insurance settlements. There also have been sporadic attempts in New York and elsewhere to indict persons for arson fraud, but so long as urban decay and building abandonments continue in inner cities, arson will also be an urban problem.

Crime in the City

Finally, it is impossible to discuss urban problems without some discussion of crime. Crime remains one of the most serious problems for urban residents in general and for inner-city residents in particular. As of the mid-1970s, in one survey 56 percent of those in cities of over 1 million, and over three-quarters of the women (77 percent), said they were afraid to walk the streets at night in their own neighborhoods.[25]

Whether crime rates in the city are currently increasing or decreasing is difficult to determine, since the major source of data, the *Uniform Crime Reports,* is far from uniform. Only crimes known to the police are reported—which means that almost all homicides are reported, but many burglaries and larcenies are not, since victims sometimes feel that it is futile to complain. At best only half the actual crime is reported.[26] However, the opinion of most authorities is that over recent decades crime has generally been increasing. Perhaps more important, the *belief* of the general population that it is increasing has led in some cities to paralyzing fear and a siege mentality. This is particularly true among vulnerable groups such as the aged.

Crime Rates and Age. Crime is an activity of the young. Some 45 percent of crimes excepting murder are committed by people under eighteen, and three-quarters are committed by those under twenty-five. The most likely age for being

[24]Joseph P. Fried. "Arson. A Devastating Big-City Crime," *New York Times,* August 14, 1977.
[25]Gallup Poll, Field Enterprises, July 28, 1975.
[26]P. H. Ennis, *Criminal Victimization in the United States: A Report of a National Survey,* U.S. Government Printing Office, Washington, D.C., 1967.

arrested is sixteen; fifteen, seventeen, and eighteen are the next most likely ages. (White-collar crimes and crimes which require training or skill such as embezzlement, fraud, and counterfeiting are most likely to be committed by older persons.)

Between the mid-1960s and mid-1970s the proportion of males aged fifteen to twenty-five grew 32 percent (30 percent for whites and 55 percent for blacks). Now that is reversed. The children of the "baby boom" are now over twenty-five, and with birthrates down, there are fewer youngsters in the high-crime ages. Even without improved police efficiency, better rehabilitation programs, or an improved moral climate, street crimes committed by the young should decrease during the 1980s.

The Racial Question. The question of urban crime is frequently overlayed by racial fears. Urban crime rates are much higher for blacks than whites, particularly for violent street crime. The National Commission on the Causes and Prevention of Violence reports that arrests of blacks are ten to eleven times higher than arrests of whites for assault and rape, and sixteen to seventeen times higher for robbery and homicide. Some of this difference occurs because blacks are more likely to be arrested on suspicion.[27] The result, though, is that middle-class whites often see crime as a matter of black against white—that is, a question of race rather than crime.

In actuality blacks are more fearful of crime than whites. According to the Gallup poll blacks feel less secure than whites both walking the streets and in their homes. This is, in fact, reasonable, since blacks are more likely to be the victims of crime. Over 85 percent of all crimes committed by blacks are against black victims. Robbery is the only heavily interracial crime, with 45 percent involving a black offender (almost always a young male) and a white victim (usually an older white male). Given their high victimization rate, it is not surprising that middle-class blacks are more "hard line" against street crime than middle-class whites.

Blacks have low arrest rates for white-collar crimes such as tax evasion, embezzlement, and price-fixing. This probably reflects occupational discrimination, which has kept blacks out of policy-making white-collar jobs. A reasonable hypothesis would be that as blacks' incomes improve and their occupational levels rise, street crime by blacks will decline and white-collar crime will increase.

Differences within the City. Crime rates within urban areas generally reflect Burgess's hypothesis, discussed in Chapter 5. That is, the highest crime rates are found in inner-city neighborhoods and decrease as one moves toward the periphery. (White-collar crime, on the other hand, is more concentrated in suburban populations.) Research done half a century ago by Shaw and McKay demonstrated this high concentration in the central city—a phenomenon they

---

[27]Donald J. Black, "Production of Crime Rates," *American Sociological Review*, **35**:753, August, 1970; and Edward Green, "Race, Social Status and Criminal Arrest," *American Sociological Review*, **35**:476–490, June, 1970.

attributed to the "social disorganization" of such areas, as typified by high poverty and welfare rates, low levels of education, broken homes, and other social ills.[28] Since that time the concept of social disorganization has largely been superseded by other explanations, but the pattern of decreasing crime rates as one moves toward the urban periphery has been confirmed.

Interestingly, the pattern has held while the occupants, and even the physical characteristics, of the area have changed completely. This consistency does not mean that these neighborhoods or their locations somehow create crime. Rather, it suggests that the inhabitants of these areas—whether European immigrants at the turn of the century, blacks after World War II, or Mexicans and Puerto Ricans today—have been subject to the same pressures.

As Chapter 6, City Life-Styles, pointed out, not all central city neighborhoods have gone through the cycle of invasion and reinvasion by new groups—a process which hinders the development of social control by family, peers, and neighbors. Inner-city areas that have not been successively invaded by disadvantaged newcomers are often among the most stable areas in the city.

Suburban Crime. As newspaper stories document, crime rates in the suburbs are increasing faster than those in the central cities. This can be misleading, though, because the suburban increase is applied to a much smaller base. The amount of crime thus remains smaller. As of 1975, for example, there were 52.1 crimes per 1,000 persons in central cities but only 36.1 in suburbs. (Rural areas were lower yet at 15.9)

Suburban crime also tends to be much less violent than city crime. Someone living in the city of Chicago, for instance, is six times more likely to be murdered and seven times more likely to be robbed than a suburban resident.[29] The most frequently reported single crime in suburbs is bicycle theft—a problem if it's your expensive ten-speed that is stolen, but not equivalent to being mugged.

Within suburbs, crime is not randomly distributed, but rather concentrated in those low-income suburbs whose character most closely approximates the central city. Older inner-ring suburbs generally have higher rates than outlying areas. Around Chicago ten suburbs accounting for 15 percent of the suburban population account for 40 percent of the murder and a majority of the armed robberies, assaults, and rapes. These suburbs have burglary rates three times as high as the richest ten suburbs of Chicago, indicating that "them that hasn't gets taken." High-crime suburbs tend to have low-income or minority residents. Suburbs with large shopping centers and industrial parks also have more crime, particularly automobile theft. While overall crime rates are lower, some suburbs are beginning to develop the same fear of crime found in larger cities.

[28]Cliford R. Shaw and Henry D. McKay, *Juvenile Delinquency in Urban Areas,* University of Chicago Press, Chicago, 1942.
[29]*Chicago Tribune,* January 6, 1975, p. 37.

12

HOUSING PROGRAMS AND URBAN REGENERATION

We shape our buildings, and afterwards our buildings shape us.
Winston Churchill

Chapter 11 focused on city problems. This chapter will concentrate on past and present governmental housing-related programs. The United States government's official housing policy was formulated in 1949. It states that it is the aim of the government to:

1. Eliminate substandard and other inadequate housing through clearance of slums and blighted areas.
2. Stimulate housing production and community developments sufficient to remedy the housing shortage.
3. Realize the goal of a decent home and a suitable living environment for every American family.[1]

However, in the over three decades that this has been official policy, no one has taken these to be guidelines for clear and decisive action; rather, they have been viewed as goals or objectives to be sought. Today, as when the policy was written into law, safe, decent, and sanitary housing at affordable prices within a suitable living environment remains but a dream for all too many Americans.

Housing in America has traditionally been considered a private rather than a public concern, and the whole concept of involvement by the federal government in the housing of its citizens is fairly recent in the United States. The concept of government support for housing is far from universally accepted in the United States—a situation unlike that in northern European countries, for example.

THE BEGINNINGS OF GOVERNMENT INVOLVEMENT

The United States government first became involved in housing during World War I, when it built housing for defense workers. This involvement was temporary. It took the massive economic collapse of the great depression of the 1930s to involve the government permanently in the question of housing. During the depression, residential construction dropped by 90 percent and downtown skyscrapers stood vacant. Even the prestigious Empire State Building in New York City was unable to fill its many offices. Franklin D. Roosevelt's administration came into office committed to reviving the economy through federal intervention, a new and radical approach at that date. In order to get a sick housing industry on its feet and encourage "builders to build and lenders to lend" the government engaged in extensive "pump-priming" in the housing area.

The Housing Act of 1937, for example, established a slum-clearance program and created the United States Housing Authority, which built some 114,000 low-rent public housing units before the program was ended during World War II. However, it was never clear whether the goal of the programs of the 1930s was to put people to work or to provide new housing for those lacking "standard" dwellings. Whatever the purpose, the result was that several deteriorating slums were cleared, and every substandard unit of housing that was cleared was replaced with a standard unit.

[1] Martin Anderson, *The Federal Bulldozer*, M.I.T. Press, Cambridge, Mass., 1964, p. 4.

The program of the 1930s differed from later efforts in at least two respects: first, only public housing was built on the cleared land, not shopping centers or office buildings; second, the housing projects were by and large successful— many of them are still well maintained today. Their success can be attributed both to their design (few were over four stories high, giving the buildings the atmosphere of family apartment buildings where people knew each other) and to the fact that residents initially were largely workers and artisans on WPA or other fill-in jobs. Projects at this time did not house the very poor on welfare.

FEDERAL HOUSING ADMINISTRATION (FHA) SUBSIDIES

In order to get bankers to invest in mortgages during the depression, the government, through the Housing Act of 1934, created the Federal Housing Administration to insure home loans. After World War II, the Veterans Administration also made loans (VA loans) guaranteed by the government to veterans. Under such schemes, private lending institutions still decide who will get loans—the FHA or VA in effect insures the bank against loss if the buyer defaults. The theory is that this system encourages lending institutions to make loans to buyers whom they would otherwise reject.

After World War II, the FHA and the VA became active in issuing mortgages to working-class and lower-middle-class families who wanted to buy homes.

FHA loans can be made for the purpose of new construction, purchase, or rehabilitation of homes, but originally the program concentrated on financing the construction of new homes. About a third of the houses built in the first decade of the program (1934–1944) had FHA assistance. Since the FHA was interested only in gilt-edge collateral to back up its mortgages, these homes were substantially middle-class; and since there was little vacant land in the cities, houses insured by the FHA were built in the suburbs. From the 1930s to the present an indirect effect of the FHA program has been to subsidize suburbanization. The suburban tract developments that surround all our larger cities would have been impossible without the federal mortgage-insurance programs that in effect paid middle-class whites to desert the central cities for newly built government-insured houses with low interest and low down payments in the suburbs. The FHA program encouraged and subsidized white suburbanization. At the same time the urban renewal program, which will be discussed presently, was designed to hold these same middle-class white families in the central city. The government was thus simultaneously trying to hold the middle class in cities while subsidizing them to leave.

Suburbs (with FHA encouragement) were zoned to exclude blacks and other "undesirables" who might lower property values and threaten the FHA's investment. Until 1950 FHA regulations expressly forbade issuing loans that would permit or encourage racial integration.

From 1935 to 1950, the federal government insisted upon discriminatory practices as a prerequisite to government housing aid. The Federal Housing Administration's official manuals cautioned against "infiltration of inharmonious racial and national groups," "a lower class of inhabitants," or "the presence of incompatible racial elements" in the new neighborhoods. . . . Zoning was advocated as a device for exclusion, and the use was urged of a racial covenant (prepared by FHA itself) with a space left blank for the prohibited races and religions, to be filled in by the builder as occasion required.[2]

Government policy thus directly encouraged "white-only" suburbs and held blacks in the inner city. Overt discrimination is now illegal, but racial "steering"—where blacks are shown homes only in black or integrated areas— still continues, though at a far lower level than previously. Civil rights legislation and policies since the 1960s have placed the federal government in the forefront of attempts to eliminate remaining de facto housing discrimination.

In the United States today we have anything but a laissez-faire housing policy. Almost all financing for new houses or apartments involves the federal government in one way or another. The federal government pours over $20 billion a year into direct and indirect subsidies of the housing market. Included in this figure are appropriations for urban renewal, public housing, interest on mortgage loans, and subsidy programs. Included in the indirect subsidies are the funds provided by the FHA and VA mortgage-guarantee programs. About half the outstanding mortgage debt on single-family homes is insured by either the FHA or the VA.[3] Most of the balance is financed through savings and loan associations or banks whose deposits are insured and whose investments are regulated by federal laws. Additionally, the American tax system (unlike that of Canada) provides for tax deductions on money paid for interest on mortgages.

In terms of upgrading the housing stock, and enlarging the access of the middle class to single-family homes, the FHA and VA programs have been extremely successful. Two-thirds of all housing units in the United States are owner-occupied; at the end of World War II, by contrast, over half were occupied by renters. The amount of space and level of amenities are also extremely high, even when the United States is compared with other developed nations.

URBAN RENEWAL

Since World War II a variety of programs have been implemented to upgrade cities in general and improve housing stock in particular. After the war it was widely recognized that cities were headed for trouble if the federal government didn't intervene. Housing was in poor shape, and downtowns were showing age and wear. Problems were particularly acute on the deteriorating fringe areas of CBDs. Land was being used only for warehouses or slum housing, but was nonetheless extremely expensive. Compared with costs on the city's edge, the expense of buying, tearing down, and rebuilding in the inner city was not economically feasible for private developers.

[2]Charles Abrams, *The City in the Frontier*, Harper and Row, New York, 1965, p. 61.
[3]Bernard Weissbroud, "Satellite Communities," *Urban Land*, 31:6, October, 1972.

Liberals and conservatives in Congress had radically different ideas of what government should do. The eventual result was a classic American compromise, the Housing Act of 1949. The act contained both a public housing section, which the liberals had lobbied for, and an urban development section, which some conservatives and businesspeople had sought. The section on urban redevelopment helped overcome resistance to the section on public housing, and vice versa.

Commercial and financial interests in the central cities supported urban renewal because they saw the renewal areas as providing the downtown area with a buffer or *cordon sanitaire* against encroachment by slums. Moreover, the occupants of the urban renewal housing were expected to be families with substantial purchasing power and thus able to help stimulate retail trade. Urban renewal was seen as being both good for business and good for the city. The purpose of urban renewal was not to rebuild the area for the old residents but rather to change land-use patterns.

The urban redevelopment section of the Urban Renewal Act was a radical break with past housing policies in that it provided for the use of public funds to buy, clear, and improve the renewal site, after which the ownership of the land would revert to the private sector. When the renewal area was approved, the authorities were given the power to buy properties at market prices and, in cases where the owner refused to sell, to have the property condemned and compensation paid through the government's right of eminent domain. The Supreme Court ruled five to four that this exercise of the right of eminent domain was constitutional.

Once the city acquired all the land in the renewal area, the existing buildings were destroyed (or rehabilitated under later modifications of the act) and the land was cleared. New streets, lights, and public facilities were then installed, and finally the land was sold to a private developer who agreed to build in accordance with an approved development plan.

The developer paid about 30 percent of what it had cost the local government to purchase, clear, and improve the land. This so-called "write-down" was the difference between what the land had cost the public and what it was sold for to the private developer. Two-thirds of the city's loss was made up in a direct cash subsidy from the federal government. Thus, the control of the program was basically local, while most of the funds were federal.

Rehabilitation

The Housing Act was revised in 1954 to provide a more workable program. No longer did an area have to be a slum in order to qualify. It could be "blighted"—that is, a potential slum. The earlier act had, in effect, made it necessary to level everything. In order to qualify for federal funding, a city had to demonstrate that it had a "workable program" which contained items such as a housing code setting adequate to minimal standards, a plan for relocating those displaced, and some provision for participation by citizens. The 1954 act also allowed funds to be used for projects that were not predominantly residential.

Rehabilitation of existing structures theoretically made it possible for at least some of the original residents to remain in a renewal area. In practice, it frequently worked differently. Many of the poorer families within the area to be redeveloped were buying their homes through land contracts— a type of contract in which the buyer has fewer rights than a mortgagee and must pay higher interest—and were investing a sizable percentage of their monthly income in housing. This was and is particularly true of blacks. As a result, these families had little financial flexibility. They were not able to invest additional funds in their homes to bring them up to the rigorous standards required by the redevelopment agency, even when loans for improvements could be obtained at low interest. The end result was that the house was sold to a middle-class or upper-middle-class person who could better afford the cost of rehabilitating the property. Thus, though the houses remained, the tenants frequently changed.

Since the purpose of urban redevelopment is to change patterns of land use for the benefit of the city as a whole, there is no requirement that housing which is destroyed has to be replaced with housing for people with a similar income level. In fact, once the dwelling units within the renewal area have been demolished and cleared, the land can be used for a shopping center, a park, or an office building. When urban renewal ended in the early 1970s, over one-third of the federal funds were being used for largely nonresidential projects.

Most of the housing built in renewal areas has been high-income or upper-middle-income apartments rather than apartments with low or moderate rent. This has been done with the intent of holding in the city, or luring back into the city, upper-middle-class whites, with their spendable—and taxable— incomes. Low-income housing has been either excluded or minimized because it would usually house the poor and possibly blacks, and their presence in the renewal area would discourage more affluent groups from moving into the high-rent units.

Relocation and New Housing

The most glaring weakness of urban renewal programs is the displacement of large numbers of low-income families without adequate provision for their relocation. Until criticism built up to a point where it could no longer be ignored, little had been done to rehouse those who were forced to move from a renewal area. There is considerable dispute as to whether area residents displaced by urban renewal are able to find adequate housing elsewhere. It is generally agreed that during the first years of the urban renewal program, residents were dispossessed and ejected from their homes in a fashion that can only be characterized as ruthless. The residents of the West End of Boston, for example, found themselves bulldozed out of their old Italian community virtually before they knew what was happening. Far from being encouraged to participate in planning for the area, local residents were actively discouraged, since it had already been decided that the existing low-rent area would be far more valuable to the city as an area of expensive high-rise apartments.[4] The result was

---

[4]Herbert J. Gans, *The Urban Villagers*, Free Press, New York, 1962.

essentially similar when removal was for the purpose of construction of expressways.

In early urban renewal projects relocation programs were given the very lowest priority. As one housing authority put it: "There was a tendency to give families a few dollars and tell them to get lost."[5] Certainly, funds were not lavished on those who had to move. For instance, in the West End of Boston each family received $100 for moving expenses. Between 1949 and 1964 only 0.5 percent of all federal expenditures for urban renewal went to families and individuals; and this figure increases to only 2 percent if businesses are included.[6]

Defenders of rehousing policies point to a survey made in 1964 by the Bureau of the Census of 2,275 families displaced by urban renewal in 135 cities. The survey showed that 94 percent had "standard housing." Robert C. Weaver has said that this survey refutes "frequent charges of widespread failure by urban renewal to meet its rehousing obligations for those it displaces." Coming from a black authority on housing who served as secretary of the Department of Housing and Urban Renewal, such a statement has to be given considerable weight.

Nonetheless, critics continue to make valid points. Even in the study by the Bureau of the Census, a reading of the definitions indicates that 9 percent of the units defined in the special study as "standard" were also regarded, under regular census criteria, as "deteriorating."[7] Moreover, the study of by the Bureau of the Census appears to overrepresent small towns, where housing problems are generally less severe.[8]

Data from the West End of Boston illustrate the controversy over what happens to those who have to move. According to the official figures, 97 percent of those relocated from the West End were properly rehoused in standard housing. On the other hand, a careful study by outside researchers found that only 73 percent were properly rehoused, and the researchers suggested that the figure was that high only because those being relocated were white and thus found it easier to obtain alternative housing.[9]

From 1949 to 1965 a total of 311,197 dwelling units were demolished on urban renewal sites, with only 166,288 units built or planned to take their place.[10] Federal law required that priority be given in any low-rent units to be constructed to those who were displaced. There was, however, no requirement that low-income housing be provided on the renewal site, and in fact very few renewal sites have been used for low-income housing. The theoretical priority was a meaningless commitment, for the new building usually took over five years to construct, and there was no requirement that any units be available for occupancy before a

[5]Jeanne R. Lowe, *Cities in a Race with Time,* Random House, New York, 1967, p. 206.
[6]Herbert J. Gans, *People and Plans,* Basic Books, New York, 1968, p. 263.
[7]"The Housing of Relocated Families," in J. Bellush and M. Hausknecht (eds.), *Urban Renewal: People, Politics, and Planning,* Doubleday (Anchor), Garden City, New York, 1967, p. 356.
[8]Chester W. Hartman, "A Rejoinder: Omissions in Evaluating Relocation Effectiveness Cited," *Journal of Housing,* **23:**157, 1966.
[9]Chester Hartman, "The Housing of Relocated Families," *Journal of the American Institute of Planners,* **30:**266–286, November, 1964.
[10]Lowe, op. cit., chap. 6.

family was displaced. Nor was there any guarantee that the units available would be of the right size for the families being displaced. In practice, the implicit goal of renewal was to move the old residents out so that they could be replaced by middle-class or upper-middle-class groups.

Even when low-income housing was originally included in the renewal plan, it was not uncommon for it to disappear somewhere in the inevitable replanning before construction. For example, one of the projects—the successful and racially integrated Hyde Park–Kenwood project on Chicago's South Side, adjoining the University of Chicago—included 600 units of low-income housing in the original proposal. However, by the time the plans were finally approved, this had shrunk bit by bit to zero units. Hyde Park consciously made the decision to integrate racially but not economically, and this was agreed upon by the upper-middle-class blacks in the area. As beautifully put by the comedians Mike Nichols and Elaine May, both one-time residents of Hyde Park, "Here's to Hyde Park–Kenwood, where Negro and white stand shoulder to shoulder against the poor." There is more than a little truth in this, for while it has sometimes been charged that urban renewal is "black removal"—70 to 80 percent of the displaced families are black—it probably is more accurate to say that it is "poor folks' removal."

Critique

One of the more scholarly critiques of urban renewal is provided by Scott Greer. He contends that much of the confusion and downright contradiction in present urban renewal programs were a result of the mixture of three different goals. These were increasing low-cost housing while eliminating slums, revitalizing the central city, and (this last is the most recent goal) creating planned cities through community renewal programs.[11] There is no question that urban renewal has done little to increase low-income housing. As Greer put it: "At a cost of three billion dollars the Urban Renewal Agency (URA) has succeeded in materially reducing the supply of low-cost housing in American cities."[12] Greer maintains that any program for improving housing must include public housing, and it must include open occupancy in practice as well as theory so that blacks can move anywhere in the city and not simply be channeled into transitory areas which then become new black ghettos.

> Aside from CBD development, the "gray areas" of the city are far too vast to be developed profitably. Nor, in general, is there any reason why they should be; they constitute a huge supply of housing, markedly better in quality than the neighborhoods where most of the Negroes and poor live in contemporary cities.[13]

Finally, it is only fair to say that the urban renewal program has had some notable successes, such as the comprehensive renewal effort in New Haven, the Southwest Project in Washington, D.C., the Western Addition in San Francisco,

[11]Scott Greer, *Urban Renewal and American Cities*, Bobbs-Merrill, Indianapolis, Ind., 1965, p. 165.
[12]Ibid., p. 3.
[13]Ibid., p. 176.

and Society Hill in Philadelphia. Also, very few of the renewal sites were originally active, attractive communities; the majority were blighted, dilapidated, filthy slums which no one wants to bring back. Even critics of urban renewal concede that the grossest mistakes were made by the earliest projects and that as the program matured, it profited from earlier errors.

PUBLIC HOUSING

Public housing was originally designed to provide standard-quality housing for those who could not afford decent, safe housing on the private market. One of the basic unwritten assumptions of the program was that by changing a family's residence you could also change the way they lived and the way they behaved.

Advocates of social planning originally supported public housing as a means of social uplift and betterment. The tearing down of slum housing was seen as a way of destroying the crime, delinquency, drunkenness, and lax morals that were considered to be associated with the slum housing. Once again, technology was going to solve social problems—a naive belief of long standing in America. This can be characterized as a "salvation by bricks and mortar" approach.

Public housing erected during the 1930s was built as much to give workers jobs as to eliminate slums. Projects were filled mainly with lower-middle-class families who were there because, owing to the depression, family heads could not get regular work and could not find adequate housing elsewhere.

After World War II, with other housing becoming more plentiful, those who were working their way into the middle class sought new housing. As these families moved out, the projects gradually lost their sound working-class image.

In many cities working-class households were replaced by new, unskilled, and frequently minority households. Increasingly, families living in projects were headed by women without a husband present, and were on welfare without any reasonable expectation of moving into the middle class. The lack of education and training of the newer project residents, coupled with regulations that placed low limits on how much a family could earn and still qualify for public housing, meant that those who could be upwardly mobile moved on, while those who were not mobile stayed. The policy, now reversed, of evicting the successful also meant that in the largest projects successful adult role models are virtually nonexistent. This has disastrous results for children, who have few images of successful adults who aren't dope pushers, policy operators, or pimps.

Public housing is concentrated in relatively few, usually black neighborhoods. This is because "aldermanic courtesy" traditionally allows aldermen and women to veto public housing in their own wards, and white neighborhoods don't want blacks in public housing. Attempts to disperse public housing to suburban locations have met with intense opposition from suburbanites.

The consequence is that too many inner-city projects have today become the residence of last resort for the permanently poor. Under the circumstances, it is not at all surprising that public housing has become associated in the public mind with crime, welfare, and vice. The public has become disillusioned with the whole concept of public housing, since it obviously isn't remaking the present-day poor into middle-class citizens. Once professionals thought that if they could get problem families out of the slums, then fathers would stop drinking, mothers would stop fooling around, and kids would stop doping and stealing. It didn't work; as caustically expressed by one professional in urban affairs, "they're the same bunch of bastards they always were."[14]

Public housing, in its present form, has few supporters, liberal or conservative, black or white, well-to-do or poor. Without conscious intent, we have designed a public housing program that almost ensures its own failure.

Pruitt-Igoe: Profile of Failure

In 1951, *Architectural Forum* featured an article entitled "Slum Surgery in St. Louis" which described a public housing project "of 11 story apartment houses, which even unbuilt have already begun to change the public housing pattern." The complex of twenty-six or more buildings was to be laid out on a fully landscaped site incorporating the latest principles of design, which would "save not only people, but money."[15] The project, known as Pruitt-Igoe, was supposed to pave the way for a bright new era in public housing.

The central feature of the design was a "skip-stop" elevator system that would stop only at every third floor, which would have an open gallery containing laundry facilities and storage bins. The galleries were to be "vertical neighborhoods," providing, in addition to the laundry and other facilities, a "close, safe playground." In order to increase neighborliness, no more than twenty families would use a gallery. The floors in between the galleries would consist only of apartments. The entire complex was to be located on a large site (57 acres) with a "river of green running through it, and no through streets."

Pruitt-Igoe was completed in 1955, with thirty-three buildings of eleven stories each. A few changes had been made. The plan to mix some townhouses in with the high-density units was rejected on the basis of a cost-benefit analysis done by the Public Housing Authority. There were also other economies, such as eliminating the landscaping, not painting the cinder-block galleries and other public areas, eliminating public washrooms on the ground floor, leaving steam pipes uninsulated, and not providing screens for the gallery windows. Although the project won an award in 1958 for architectural design, very serious problems were beginning to emerge. The economies listed above had some unexpected consequences: children urinated in hallways, burned themselves on exposed pipes, and fell out of gallery windows.

The project had been designed for a racially mixed population—one-third white and two-thirds black—but a heavy influx of hard-core poor families with numerous social problems soon drove out all who could escape. Demographically,

---

[14]Michael Stegman, "The New Mythology of Housing," *Trans-Action,* **7:**55, January, 1970.
[15]"Slum Surgery in St. Louis," *Architectural Forum,* April, 1951, pp. 128–135.

the project soon became inhabited mainly by black households headed by women, with a large number of children—five to twelve per household—and on welfare. Of the 10,736 people living in Pruitt-Igoe in 1965, there were only 900 men—many of them elderly—but over 7,000 children, of whom 70 percent were under twelve years of age.

During the 1970s, Pruitt-Igoe became a symbol of all that is wrong with public housing projects, with elevators battered and out of order, stairwells with lighting fixtures ripped out, galleries unused and unsafe, and laundry rooms that invited robbery and rape. Laundry rooms, stairwells, and halls in Pruitt-Igoe were used by adolescents for sex. Making many "conquests" was one of the few ways for a boy there to achieve status with his peer group, and the girls viewed sex as a way of achieving popularity and maturity. The mean age for becoming sexually active was thirteen, and half the girls in the project became pregnant at least once before age eighteen.[16] Mothers found it practically impossible to supervise children. They feared to go out of their apartments; and this was a reasonable fear: a survey of residents disclosed that 41 percent of the adults had been robbed, 20 percent physically assaulted, and 39 percent insulted by teenagers.[17] The absence of resident men and the physically unsafe design features, such as the skip-stop elevators and the open galleries, resulted in a constant threat of mugging or rape for female inhabitants.

By 1972, only the most desperate of the poor remained in the dangerous, foul-smelling buildings. Occupancy was down to a total population of only 2,788 persons. One by one, the buildings were simply abandoned by their tenants. Even the most down-and-out welfare recipients were unwilling to tolerate the degradation and the constant threat of personal danger. Rehabilitating the buildings to make them fit for human habitation, it was estimated, would cost more than $40 million, and then there was no guarantee that addicts and vandals would not destory and terrorize the buildings again.

In the fall of 1972, the Housing Authority took the drastic action of blowing up the two worst buildings and began dynamiting the top seven stories off others in order to convert them into more manageable four-story buildings. It was hoped that the resulting low-rises would be easier for the tenants to control against outsiders and would provide some sense of defensible space and physical security. This effort was not successful, and in 1973 the Housing Authority began to demolish the remainder of the buildings. Today Pruitt-Igoe is a wasteland.

If there is a lesson to be learned from Pruitt-Igoe and numerous similar projects across the country, it is that public housing all too frequently removes "nonhuman" problems such as leaking roofs, faulty electricity, and rats at the cost of isolating the residents from the rest of society and frequently increasing the human problems. Designs based on low-rise buildings or townhouses provide greater defensible space and make possible surveillance by adults, which can

---

[16]Lee Rainwater, *Behind Ghetto Walls,* Aldine, Chicago, 1970, p. 309.
[17]Ibid., p. 103.

Pruitt-Igoe was dynamited in the 1970s, bringing to full cycle the history of a housing project that was designed to "change the public housing pattern." (Paul Ockrassa.)

reduce crime rates and give residents an important sense of territory.[18] This point is discussed more fully in Chapter 13. However, architecture can never solve the basic problem of an economic system that creates an underclass and effectively isolates it from the rest of society. Until this is changed, we are merely attacking symptoms rather than the disease. The ultimate problem is not housing but poverty.

The Controversy over Title 235

By the mid-1960s, it was apparent that public housing projects were not providing safe, clean, and well-maintained housing for the poor. The answer was thought to be providing subsidies so that the poor could become homeowners. Thus they would have a stake in both the upkeep of their own homes and the quality of the

[18]Oscar Newman, *Defensible Space*, Macmillan, New York, 1972.

neighborhood in general. The 1968 Housing and Urban Redevelopment Act thus provided direct subsidies for low-income families so that they could purchase homes under the so-called "Title 235" program; a companion "Title 236" program provided for rent subsidies enabling the poor to afford to rent apartments rather than go into public housing. Both programs have had a checkered history.

Much of the controversy regarding the Title 235 program was the result of bureaucratic sloppiness in the way the program was administered, permitting criminal collusion between real estate speculators and FHA and VA employees. The 1968 act directed the Department of Housing and Urban Development (HUD) to relax standards so that low-income buyers could obtain mortgages. In practice, in cities such as Detroit and Chicago it provided a massive ripoff opportunity for real estate speculators. Huge profits were made by selling at big mark-ups supposedly rehabilitated properties that in fact had only cosmetic improvements. As expressed by the director of HUD's Chicago office: "Every unethical, unscrupulous real estate broker and lender, many of them so slimy they crawled out from under a rock, looked at this program and said, 'What a gold mine out there.' "[19]

The poor, as always, were the victims. The scheme worked like this: A real estate speculator bought a run-down, inner-city home at a low price and then put in at most cosmetic repairs. A qualified low-income buyer was then found, and the appraiser was bribed to considerably overvalue the house. The FHA or VA then insured the mortgage at the higher price, and the speculator made a fast profit, minus the bribe.

William Keye, for example, thought he was getting a good deal when he bought a house for $22,500 from Conteco in Chicago and financed it with a loan insured by the Veterans Administration.[20] He soon discovered that the furnace was totally inoperable, the house needed a new roof, and the indoor-outdoor carpeting in the kitchen covered a large hole rotted through the floor. Research revealed that Conteco had purchased the home for $12,000. Another home purchased from HUD for $500 was later sold for $19,000. Not surprisingly, most such properties are eventually abandoned by the low-income homeowners. The mortgage is then foreclosed by the bank, which gets it money, and the government finds itself owning another house that no one wants, in an area where no one will buy. Thus the federal government in effect finances the creation of urban blight.

The Title 235 program has also been used unofficially by speculators to turn areas over racially for profit. Once an area is redlined and marked for transition, realtors stop showing homes to potential white buyers, and banks refuse to make conventional loans. The goal is to frighten white owners into selling out at giveaway prices to the real estate firms. The cheaply bought properties are then sold at huge mark-ups through the FHA or VA programs. The ideal buyer from the speculators' viewpoint is one who is so economically marginal that he or she will default so that the bank can foreclose and get its guaranteed money from the FHA

---

[19]Gregory Gordon and Albert Swanson, "Evaluation of a Ghetto," *Milwaukee Journal,* December 15, 1976.
[20]*United Press International,* September 19, 1976.

or VA. Until some minor tightening in 1975, even those on welfare could purchase such homes. The subsidy program now has a minimum 5 percent interest rate for mortgages and requires a larger (but still low) down payment. This program was designed to save the cities, but it was exploited in some cities to encourage neighborhood turmoil and abandonment while providing windfall profits for speculators. Problems were especially serious in Detroit, but the fact that several hundred persons have been convicted of fraud will not help the poor who bought decaying homes. Nor will it bring back the abandoned neighborhoods. Callous greed seriously undermined what potentially was a good program.

Section 8

Housing subsidies are the nation's fastest-growing welfare program. In 1974 subsidies cost $2 billion. By 1979 the figure had risen to $5 billion, and, according to the Office of Management and Budget, in 1984 the figure will be $10 billion. This is more than the federal Aid to Families with Dependent Children program and almost as much as food stamps. There are two main housing subsidy programs—public housing and the less well known Section 8 program.

The current Section 8 Housing Assistance Payments Program is essentially a housing allowance program for renters. It allows a developer to build or substantially rehabilitate subsidized rental units for qualified low-income renters. No tenant pays more than 25 percent of his or her income for rent. HUD sets what is called a "fair rental value" and gives the landlord the difference between this and what the tenant actually pays. Generally, those whose adjusted income does not exceed 80 percent of the median income in the area are eligible for Section 8 housing.

Not surprisingly, landlords think that a program that guarantees their being paid most of a tenant's rent directly from the federal coffers is a great idea. Section 8 is in a long tradition of programs that ostensibly are meant to aid the poor, but in reality subsidize the affluent.

Experimental Housing Allowance Program

The concept of direct housing assistance to tenants (rather than through landlords) has been debated for years, but until the Experimental Housing Allowance Program (EHAP) began in the early 1970s under the direction of HUD, there was little data on what would occur.[21] Who would participate, how many would move to better housing, and whether landlords would get most of the benefits by raising rents were unanswerable questions.

The EHAP experiments were extremely elaborate, involving a substantial number of cities and the comparison of different types of payments. For example, some received assistance payments (averaging about $70) limited to use for housing payments, some received assistance payments not limited to use for

---

[21] *A Summary Report of Current Findings from the Experimental Housing Allowance Program,* Office of Policy Development and Research, U.S. Department of Housing and Urban Development, Washington, D.C., April, 1978.

housing, and control groups received no assistance (they received $10 a month for providing monthly information). In Pittsburgh and Phoenix, some 1,250 renter households received aid in each city while 550 similar but unassisted families served as controls.

Initial findings indicate that about one-half of the eligible renters and two-thirds of the eligible homeowners chose not to participate in receiving housing assistance. If assistance is not specifically designated for housing, 90 percent of those eligible will participate. However, only about 10 percent of that assistance will go for housing.

Contrary to expectations, neither housing assistance nor unconstrained assistance seemed to affect rates of mobility. Those receiving assistance do not move any more often than those not receiving assistance. (Over one-quarter of low-income renters move each year.) It was also assumed that housing assistance would increase demand for acceptable housing units, and thus rents would inflate, with landlords being the major beneficiaries. This did not occur; rents were not inflated by the program. The EHAP housing assistance programs thus did not have as large an impact on the housing of lower-income participants as was expected. Where the program did have unexpected impact was in boosting the rate of family dissolution among participants. The reasons for the increased divorce rates are not known with certainty, but it is certain that the results have cooled support for the program. Few members of Congress want to be on record as having voted for programs that appear to encourage family dissolution.

RECENT DEVELOPMENTS

Conversion to Condominiums

Across the country rental apartments are being converted to condominium units, where the occupant of an apartment owns the unit. "Condo fever" has been particularly strong in Washington, D.C., and Chicago; Washington has even issued a temporary moratorium on conversions. As the gap between operating cost and rental income has narrowed, apartment owners have increasingly converted their units to condominiums. Fear of rent control, which has spread rapidly in California and elsewhere, has also depressed the building of new rental units. Currently there is an annual shortfall of 50,000 new apartments, which is aggravated by the conversion of thousands of existing units.

The apartment shortage and increased rental costs are real problems to the poor and to "young mobiles" who are not yet prepared to make a commitment on a house. However, if the trend continues, those who will suffer most are the working poor who are unable to qualify for public housing or subsidies, but also unable to compete with the more affluent for scarce apartments. If "condo fever" becomes a nationwide pattern during the 1980s, working-class families will increasingly find themselves priced out of the apartment market, as they already have been out of the market for new single-family homes. On the other hand, those able to obtain financing for condominium purchases gain the advantages of property appreciation as well as the tax advantages that come with home ownership.

Tax-Exempt Mortgage Bonds

In the late 1970s cities came up with a new way to hold the middle class in the cities: below-market interest rates for homes. Cities discovered that they could attract home purchasers by offering lower interest rates on city homes. The lower interest rates resulted from the cities' using their credit to issue tax-exempt bonds to raise money for mortgages. The mortgages in turn pay off the bonds to the banks. Thus the program is virtually costless to the cities. The use of home bonds more than tripled between 1975 and 1978, with $7.5 billion issued in 1978.

However, not everyone is happy with this scheme. While the bonds have helped the cities, and the new home buyers are delighted, the federal government is losing money. The Urban Institute estimates that each $1 billion of bonds costs the federal government $30 million in lost tax revenue. President Carter, as of this writing, is supporting controversial legislation to stop cities and states from issuing tax-exempt bonds to raise money for mortgages. The administration focuses its public argument not on the major issue that the bonds are draining the Treasury, but rather the politically more appealing claim that the programs provide government-supported housing for upper-income families. In fact, while there have been cases of families making more than $50,000 a year using the programs, most cities place limits on the mortgages to prevent the program from being exploited by the wealthy. There is no question, though, that middle-class buyers are being provided low interest rates. The whole intent of the programs is to do just that, and thereby to encourage home purchases in the city rather than the suburbs. By holding middle-class home buyers the city also both improves the quality of its housing stock and increases its tax revenues. The interest of the cities and the direct financial interest of the federal government are thus at loggerheads on this issue. In the larger sense, the nation as well as the cities benefits by having more middle-class people remain in the cities.

Urban Homesteading

How can government, particularly the federal government, aid cities in housing their populations? Public housing, the answer of the 1950s, is bankrupt; today few people argue for more projects. Urban renewal, the remedy of the early 1960s, and Model Cities, that of the late 1960s, similarly have few remaining backers. One idea of the 1970s that has caught on, though, is "urban homesteading." Homesteading programs turn over abandoned and foreclosed homes to those who agree to stay for at least three years and bring the homes up to code standards within eighteen months.

Urban homesteading programs conjur up the image of the handy pioneers, who, under the 1862 Homestead Act signed by President Lincoln, were given 160 acres of western land if they could stick it out for five years. Urban homesteaders,

Urban homesteading often demands "sweat equity" from those rehabilitating the property. (Photo courtesy of the Baltimore Department of Housing and Community Development.)

on the other hand, are not supposed to build on the land but to rebuild inner-city neighborhoods. The first urban homesteading program (and still one of the most active) began in Wilmington, Delaware, in 1973. As expressed by Wilmington's mayor, who pushed the program, "We are not trying to provide housing for people. We are trying to provide people for (abandoned) housing."[22] Offering homes at nominal fees such as $10 or $100, urban homesteading programs implicitly recognize that by definition there is no market for abandoned property. Thus it is given away to those who agree to improve and use it. The Housing and

[22]Quoted in Wiltram G. Conway, "People Fire in the Ghetto Ashes," *Saturday Review*, July 23, 1977, p. 15.

Community Development Act of 1974 got the federal government into the business of transferring residential properties to local governments for homesteading.

So far, the record of urban homesteading has been mixed. While the concept sounds ideal, there are some major limitations.

First, it is only a relatively small program. The program to date is, indeed, only a drop in the bucket, with under 10,000 homes having been rehabilitated by the homesteading mechanism. (By comparison, 150,000 inner-city homes and apartments are abandoned annually.)

Second, and perhaps most serious, by the time government action is taken, most abandoned properties are beyond the point of economic rehabilitation. As noted earlier, professional and amateur looters strip homes to the core, and vandals deface what isn't taken. Fires are also common, and no one wants to rehabilitate a burned-out hulk.

Third, there is the cost factor. Title to the property may come cheap, but rehabilitation costs big money. Even when owners use "sweat equity" (i.e., their own labor) rehabilitation loans commonly run from $20,000 to $60,000. Thus urban homesteading is definitely not the answer for the urban poor.

Fourth, as a home rehabilitation program, urban homesteading does not affect multifamily apartments, where the bulk of the poor are housed.

Fifth, for loans, of course, lenders are necessary, and thus far financial institutions have been reluctant to invest in rehabilitating abandoned slum properties. Thus low-interest municipal loans or loans guaranteed by the municipality appear to be essential. Also necessary are changes in municipal tax policies. While cities invariably say that they are in favor of urban homesteading, most are unwilling to change policies that raise taxes when improvements are made. Without some form of tax moratorium, those who upgrade abandoned buildings are rewarded by the municipality with higher taxes.

Finally, there is no point in rehabilitation of one home if the remainder of the neighborhood consists of vandalized burned-out buildings. There has to be an overall change in the neighborhood, with a substantial number of homes being simultaneously redone and reasonable public services and police protection provided. Homesteading, therefore, is likely to be most successful in areas where only a few homes have been abandoned.

Nonetheless, urban homesteading has had a psychological as well as physical impact on cities ranging from Baltimore to Pittsburgh to Oakland. HUD evaluations suggest that early urban homesteading programs have been successful. However, urban homesteading must be transformed from a catchy slogan to a substantial program. A start in this direction was taken by HUD in 1979, when pilot projects were begun to repair and seel some 100 houses in the Roseland neighborhood of Chicago and 75 homes in the Buckeye-Woodland and Union-Miles areas of Cleveland. During the 1980s urban homesteading may become an important, if still limited, contributor to the upgrading of neighborhoods.

Neighborhood Revival

For decades there has been talk of a "back to the city" movement, but the talk has not been followed up by actual movement.[23] As Chapter 7, Patterns of Suburbanization, documents, the movement has long been outbound rather than directed toward the central city. The assumption has been that those having the choice (i.e., white middle-class home buyers) would shun the central city for the suburbs. As noted in Chapter 6, a 1972 Gallup poll supported the view of suburban preference, with only 13 percent of those interviewed preferring city residence to residence in suburbia or a small town.

However, there is now a limited but symbolic countermovement toward residence in the central city. Ironically, the movement is not to leveled and rebuilt urban renewal areas, but to older neighborhoods that are recycling from a period of decay. Middle-income and upper-middle-income whites (and some blacks) are buying and restoring old homes and new houses—a process commonly known as "neighborhood regeneration" or "gentrification."

"Gentrification" is a recent phenomenon, with the majority of activity occurring since 1975. Also, revitalization is not occurring in all city neighborhoods but is thus far limited largely to areas having substantial residences with historic or architectural merit. While the homes in these neighborhoods may be in disrepair when purchased by the "urban pioneer," they were originally constructed to standards generally unavailable in new suburban houses. Revitalizing areas are also generally well located in terms of accessibility, transportation routes, and overall physical location.

Middle-class in-movement to older central-city neighborhoods challenges traditional theories of growth. According to the classical Burgess model (discussed in Chapter 5) or the filtered-down economic model, this in-movement should not be occurring. Rather, older central-city residences should be abandoned to the economically marginal. Also, according to the original Burgess model, central-city residential property is vacated for commercial or industrial usage. Today, the pattern is more often the reverse; in some cities, formerly commercial buildings such as warehouses are being rehabilitated as residences. The SoHo section of New York, for instance, contains numerous older commercial structures which have been transformed into homes.[24] Other cities provide similar examples. Commercial-to-residential transformations may become more common during the next decade, but most of the regeneration will occur in older residential neighborhoods. Neighborhoods such as Ansley Park in Atlanta, the Fan in Richmond, New Town in Chicago, Five Points in Denver, Montrose in Houston, the Mission District in San Francisco, and Capitol Hill in Washington, D.C., are physically more robust than they were a decade ago.

---

[23]The purpose of the urban renewal programs of the 1950s and 1960s was to rebuild the cities' inner cores in order to encourage middle-class residency in such areas. As we will see in this chapter, the effort was largely unsuccessful.
[24]James R. Hudson, "Changing Land-Use Patterns in Soho: Residential Invasion of Industrial Areas," unpublished paper, Pennsylvania State University, 1978.

Role of Government. Urban regeneration has not occurred as a consequence of federal, state, or municipally funded programs. To date, urban regeneration has been funded almost entirely by the private sector. Nonetheless, government, particularly municipal government, has played a role in urban regeneration—a role different from what one might imagine. The most common role of local governments has been to provide a body against which the neighborhood can unite in common cause. Whether it is failure to enforce building codes, inadequate police protection, poor garbage collection and sanitation, nonmaintenance of parks, streets, and sidewalks, or just general neglect of the area, residents are often brought together in opposition to city hall. The common cry is, "They can't do that to us."

Thus municipal governments have unintentionally been influential in serving as a catalyst to bring neighbors together. It will be interesting to see whether communities can maintain the same level of commitment once they start winning their battles with city hall.

Who Is Moving In? Although one commonly hears the phrase "return to the city," most in-movers actually come from other areas of the city.[25] Thus they are perhaps better described as "urban stayers" than "urban in-movers."

While it is a misconception to suggest that those moving into or staying in the city are largely childless professionals, it is true that young adults have been in the vanguard of the return to older neighborhoods. Donald Bradley in his study of the Virginia-Highlands area of Atlanta found that newcomers were generally young, childless, married adults, white urban-bred, well-educated, employed in professional or managerial positions, and earning middle-class to upper-middle-class incomes.[26] Newcomers also tend to be socially active, with an intense commitment to "their" neighborhood.

Explanations for Return. Three principal reasons can be given for the return movement.

The first is economic. With suburban housing costs skyrocketing, the relatively depressed prices of city real estate are appealing. Of course, once a neighborhood passes the takeoff phase prices escalate dramatically, but even so they are quite competitive for the value received. The rising cost of gasoline is an ever more important social factor. A central-city location can be a particularly strong advantage when both husband and wife are employed at central-city jobs. In the city, with its public transportation, two cars are not as necessary as in the suburbs.

---

[25]Denis Gale, "The Back to the City Movement Revisited: A Survey of Recent Homebuyers in the Capitol Hill Neighborhood of Washington, D.C.," paper published by George Washington University, Department of Urban and Regional Planning, 1977.

[26]Donald J. Bradley, "Neighborhood Transition: Middle-Class Home Buying in an Inner-City, Deteriorating Community," paper presented at the annual meeting of the American Sociological Association, Chicago, September, 1977.

Second, demographic changes increase interest in revitalizing areas. The baby-boom generation is now in its mid-twenties to mid-thirties and thus is seeking housing. However, the low birthrates of these people mean that they have less desire for suburban housing and yards than their parents' generation. The continuing low quality of many central-city schools also has little impact on the residential decisions of those without children.

Finally, there are social-psychological factors—that is, factors having to do with life-styles. To earlier generations "new" was automatically assumed to be better. Everyone knew that the this year's car was better than last year's and a new house was better than an old house. Upper-middle-class values have undergone a transformation in this regard during the past decade. Today older is often assumed to be better. Older homes, with their real plaster walls, oak woodwork, leaded glass, and solid brass fixtures, offer qualities unavailable in new suburban housing. For example, new construction usually lacks even hardwood floors—the carpeting or tile is laid over plywood sheeting.

Revitalized neighborhoods are popular not only because they make sense economically but because they have the convenience and culture urban young adults seek. It is now considered to be a very "in" thing to be an "urban pioneer." Taste in housing, like taste in other consumer goods, undergoes changes. Twenty years ago prestige was likely to be associated with a suburban residence. Such areas still have high general status, but among some young professionals, suburban residence is definitely déclassé and a refurbished townhouse is more prestigious. However, whether this prourban bias will spread from some young elites to other segments of the population is still problematic.

Displacement of the Poor? Urban regeneration, however, does not have only positive effects. There are two common worries regarding the return of the white middle class. The first concern is that not enough affluent whites will return to make a difference. Not all central-city neighborhoods have housing worth renovating. Many inner-city areas were originally constructed during the last century for working-class populations, and such areas have little appeal to middle-class home buyers of the late twentieth century.

The second concern is that too many well-to-do whites will return and force poor and minority residents from their current neighborhoods. Rapid gentrification, it is feared, will result in the displacement of those unable to absorb the increasing rents and property taxes of the upgrading neighborhoods. The National Urban Coalition fears that the poor will become "urban nomads" priced or pushed out of their neighborhoods.[27] The Department of Housing and Urban Development has also popularized the idea of displacement. HUD has recently become very concerned over the plight of inner-city residents who live in upgrading neighborhoods. (Unfortunately, this concern over the future of those living in declining neighborhoods remains unfashionable, perhaps because the

---

[27]National Urban Coalition, *Displacement: City Neighborhoods in Transition,* Washington, D.C., 1978.

issue is so difficult.) Mayor Barry of Washington, D.C., has even supported hefty luxes to discourage housing speculation and gentrification.

The hand-wringing over too-rapid upgrading has a bit of an "Alice in Wonderland" quality to it. Many of the people who are most vocal about the consequences of middle-class return to the city have also been the most eager to condemn middle-class flight from the city. It seems ironic that some officials now are complaining that housing is being upgraded and the property tax base being augmented too fast. The conflict of varied political-interest groups creates a situation in which someone is always unhappy.

Fortunately, the belief that upgrading speeds residential mobility and creates a special class of "urban nomads" is yet to be supported by empirical evidence. The widely quoted National Urban Coalition study, for example, didn't actually study a single neighborhood or interview a single displaced resident. Rather, questionnaires were sent to city planners, housing specialists, and realtors, asking them their opinions on what they thought was occurring in their cities. Such reports, while interesting, should not be confused with rigorous social science research.

The Bureau of the Census's Annual Housing report studied eighteen selected cities and found that fewer than 100 or 200 households a year were displaced in most large cities. Their study found far more people being displaced by housing abandonment and urban disinvestment than by renovation.[28]

In a study of the Ramsey Hill section of St. Paul, Sonia Sands found that the widely held assumption that the displaced inevitably end up worse off was not the case.[29] A startling 87 percent of the 112 households surveyed found their new homes either similar to or better than those they left behind. Moreover, housing costs did not go up significantly, with most of the increases caused by inflation. Whether Ramsey Hill is typical of other renovating neighborhoods has to be determined by further studies, but obviously, caution is needed. We just don't know much yet about revitalization and displacement. One of the most important questions is the extent of the revitalization movement and whether it will spill over into working-class city neighborhoods during the 1980s.

[28]"U.S. Study Finds Displacement of Poor in Slums Is Minimal," *New York Times,* February 14, 1979.
[29]Sonia Mattson Sands, "Population Change Due to Housing Renovation in St. Paul's Ramsey Hill Area," unpublished masters thesis, Center for Urban and Regional Affairs, University of Minnesota, Minneapolis, June, 1979.

CHAPTER

13

URBAN PLANNING:
Western Europe
and Socialist Countries

Let there be one man who has a city obedient to his will, and he might bring into existence the ideal polity about which the world is so incredulous.

Plato
The Republic

INTRODUCTION: HISTORICAL BACKGROUND

The Bible, in Genesis 11:4, tells of one of the earliest attempts at urban planning:

> It came to pass as they journeyed to the East that they found a plain in the land of Shinar and they dwelt there. . . . And they said, "Come let us build us a city, and the tower the top of which may reach unto heaven; and let us make ourselves a name, lest we be scattered upon the face of the whole earth. . . .

As we all know, the Tower of Babel was not noticeably successful as a form of urban planning in spite of the fact that it did have full citizen participation. The hope is that some of our more modest attempts will be more successful.

Ancient Greece and Rome

Ancient cities, as was indicated in Chapter 2, were rarely based on a plan or even a general concept of what the city should be. The Greeks, who appreciated organization and structure in other aspects of their lives, gave little attention to the physical arrangement of the communities in which they lived. In classical Greek cities the main thoroughfares were generally planned as processional avenues, but residential development was undisciplined and chaotic. Rhodes, with its avenues radiating from a center, was something of an exception. What planning did take place was limited to the central municipal area, containing the principal monuments, temples, and stately edifices. Greek colonial cities, such as Priene in Asia Minor, show far more concern for planning than the Greek mother cities, with their meandering lanes and mazelike paths that followed no discernable pattern or higher logic.

Aristotle tells us that Hippodamus of Miletus, who lived in the fifth century B.C., was an early city planner. According to Aristotle,

> Hippodamus, son of Euryphon, a native of Miletus, invented the art of planning and laid out the street plan of Piraeus. . . . He planned a city with a population of 10,000 divided into three parts, one of the skilled workers, one of farmers, and one to defend the state. The land was divided into three parts: sacred, public, and private supporting in turn the worship of the gods, the defense of the state, and the farm owners. . . .[1]

Note that provision was made for farming within the city walls, a most necessary consideration during periods when the city was under siege.

The Romans were somewhat more successful than the Greeks at planning their towns. Rome itself showed limited evidence of planning, but provincial Roman towns, with their central square and gridiron pattern of residences, established a model that can be seen in most American communities today. The provincial cities of western Europe were modeled after the pattern of encampment developed by the Roman legions. Since the provincial towns were initially military outposts, civilian buildings followed the pattern of the military camp, particularly since much of the planning was done by military engineers. It has been said that

[1] Aristotle, *Politics, Book VII, ii, 8,* B. Jowett (trans.), 1932 ed.

these outpost towns were so similar that if a Roman centurion was dropped in the middle of any one of them, he could not tell which town he was in. The largest of the planned Roman cities was Constantinople, the "Rome of the East," which the emperor Constantine built to glorify his reign and escape the fate of previous emperors at the hands of the Roman Senate and street mobs.

Medieval and Later Developments

The fall of the Roman empire in the west meant the death of urban planning for virtually a millennium. However, even during the Middle Ages, when gradual organic growth was most likely to be the rule, some of the newly reviving towns built by French, Italian, and German princes followed the planned pattern of the earlier Roman colonial settlements—a grid layout and a central square with a market.[2]

The Renaissance revived cities and thinking about cities, but few of the planners' conceptions for total communities ever became more than academic exercises. Since these conceptions were rather fanciful and artificial, and bore virtually no relationship to the haphazard but vital cities then in existence, it is perhaps just as well that they were rarely executed. Star-shaped cities were especially popular; Vincenzo Scamozzi designed a utopian city shaped as a twelve-pointed star and actually built a small city, Palma Nova, in the shape of a nine-pointed star in 1593. The star shape was not entirely fanciful, however, since in the age of cannons and gunpowder the points of a star could serve as bastions for directing the defenders' enfilading fire.

Planners usually designed unrealistic static communities that completely ignored the needs of the inhabitants, as well as basic considerations such as topography. Stylized form rather than naturalness was the goal. The epitome of this insistence on symmetrical perfection was Versailles, the magnificent home of the French kings, whose gardens, palaces, and town were planned as a unit.[3]

The English also made their own attempts, largely unsatisfactorily, at town planning. In 1580 Queen Elizabeth proclaimed restrictions on London's growth that were designed to give the city a green belt of open land and thus prevent crowding and poverty.[4] This policy—which foreshadowed the twentieth-century green-belt towns discussed later in this chapter—failed, although it was backed by royal statute. Probably the most noteworthy master plan was that designed by Christopher Wren for the rebuilding of London after the disastrous fire of 1666. His plan was, unfortunately, not adopted in the rush to rebuild the city.

During the nineteenth century, the changes in the physical organization of Paris must be listed among the more successful attempts at planning. Contemporary Paris, with its broad avenues and magnificent squares, is the result of seventeen years of rebuilding directed by Baron Haussmann under the sponsor-

---

[2]Howard Saalman, *Medieval Cities*, Braziller, New York, 1968, p. 114.
[3]Ralph Thomlinson, *Urban Structure*, Random House, New York, 1969, p. 205.
[4]Daniel R. Mendelker, *Green Belts and Urban Growth*, University of Wisconsin Press, Madison, 1962, p. 27.

Planned Capitals

Twentieth-century planned capital cities have been mixtures of success and failure. Canberra, Australia, which was begun in 1918, is pleasing to the eye; but is it difficult to go anywhere in Canberra without using a car, owing to the strict segregation of the city into governmental, residential, and commercial areas. Canberra is sometimes referred to as the world's most inconvenient suburb.

Brasilia, the capital of Brazil, located 600 miles inland from Rio de Janeiro, has a different problem. Brasilia, begun in 1957 and inaugurated as the capital in 1960, did not just grow; rather, it was designed from the ground up, primarily by Lucio Costa. The city was designed for the age of the automobile, and it is characterized by massive superblocks of concrete and glass.

Brasilia is grand and impressive, but the visitor finds it hard to escape the feeling that it is not really meant to be lived in. Separate centers for government, commerce, and recreation are clustered along one axis of the city, while housing occupies the other main axis (creating monumental twice-daily traffic jams). Although Brasilia is proving successful in encouraging the economic development of the center of the country and infusing national spirit, it is less successful in generating that perhaps indefinable human response we experience in the great cities of the world. Brazilian government officials and bureaucrats resist being transferred to Brasilia, and those who are assigned there fly back to the far more lively Rio de Janeiro as often as they can afford to. Brasilia lacks Rio's human warmth and livability. While the design is unquestionably bold and creative, it is also somewhat stark and abstract. The city is a remarkable monument, but monuments are not always comfortable places in which to live.

An unanticipated problem has been the continuing influx of poor workers into the so-called "satellite cities" and the favelas (unplanned peripheral slums) at a rate of over 10 percent a year. The superblocks of the central city—known as the "plano piloto" (pilot plan)—house the upper and middle classes, while the slum settlements are mostly hidden from view miles from the center of the city.

Too much may have been expected of the utopian city. As the designer, Costa, replies to critics:

> Things are done differently here. You have to accept the country for what it is. Of course, half the people in Brasilia live in favelas. Brasilia was not designed to solve the problems of Brazil, it was bound to reflect them.[*]

Perhaps the Brazilian spirit will, with the passage of time, convert Brasilia if not into another Rio, at least into a more comfortable and livable city.

[*]"Brazil's Dream City Has Flaws," *United Press International*, August 19, 1973.

ship of Napoleon III (1852–1870). The beauty of Paris today is not accidental but the result of Haussmann's genius. Boulevards were cut through festering slums, and the city was planned for separate industrial and residential areas. However, the rationale for the changes was not solely aesthetic; the broad boulevards provided excellent fields of fire for cannon and divided the city into districts which could be more easily controlled and isolated in times of civil insurrection.

Unfortunately, under recent French governments the skyline of Paris has been disfigured by some of the worst-designed skyscrapers in Europe. The controversial skyscraper complex of La Defense is an example: its insurance company building blots out the view of the Arc de Triomphe.

URBAN PLANNING IN WESTERN EUROPE

Europe has a tradition of urban planning for the community welfare that goes back many years. Europeans, lacking the land resources of the United States, have been more concerned with conserving their resources and preventing unlimited growth. The tendency toward compactness and public ownership also means that the desires of the individual builder are more subject to the criteria of the public welfare.

The United States, by contrast, has yet to formulate a national or even regional land-use policy.[5] In the United States, plans concentrate on the local level. (Ironically, those who most oppose national land-use controls as "socialistic" are often the strongest supporters of stringent local controls in their suburbs. Some opponents of a national land-use policy live in suburbs that regulate matters such as lot sizes, home sizes, the placement of fences, and even whether residents can park a trailer in the driveway.)

In North America, urban rebuilding almost invariably means the tearing down of older buildings and rebuilding using modern architectural designs and materials. In Europe, rebuilding has sometimes had quite a different effect. Much of the rebuilding of German cities after World War II has consciously attempted to return the destroyed areas to the same appearance that they had before the war. Urban renewal need not mean changing existing patterns: this decision is one for us to make. Poland, after considerable thought and debate, rejected a modern glass-and-concrete design for rebuilding the center of Warsaw after its total destruction. The Poles consciously reproduced the appearance of this section of Warsaw during the period of its medieval glory. Brick by brick, the medieval section has been replicated. The fact that in North America renewal has taken place in one direction does not mean that there are not other alternatives; it means, rather, that we have become locked into one way of viewing urban renewal and rebuilding.

[5]William K. Reilly (ed.), *The Use of Land: A Citizen's Guide to Urban Growth*, Rockefeller Brothers Fund, Thomas Crowell, New York, 1973.

Control of Land

One advantage enjoyed by some European communities is control over their own municipal lands. Stockholm began buying land in 1904 outside the city limits, with the goal of providing both green space and room for future garden suburbs. Most of this land has since been annexed to the city, so that Stockholm is now in the favorable position of owning about 75 percent of the land within its administrative boundaries. The city rarely sells its land; instead, it leases the land on sixty-year renewable leases to both public and private developers. The money earned from the leases pays off the cost of the loan used to buy the land; and the municipality has the additional advantage of profiting directly from increases in land values. The public, rather than private land speculators, thus profits from the increased value of the land. If the city wants the land after the sixty-year lease is up, it must go to court and prove that the land is needed for the public interest, and then pay the leaseholder the value of any buildings on the property.

Since World War II, the city-owned land in Stockholm has been used to develop a system of subcenters or "mini-cities," built one after another along rapid-transit lines extending in five directions from the old city center. Each subcenter contains between 10,000 and 20,000 inhabitants and is served by its own community services, schools, and shops. Unlike the British new towns, these subcenters emphasize easy access to the center city. Blocks of flats, frequently high-rises, are built 550 yards from the transit station; detached and terrace-style housing is built beyond up to about 1,000 yards from the station. Cars are routed through green areas surrounding the living areas.

Along each string of subcenters, "main centers" are built at appropriate intervals. Each main center, with a larger shopping mall, theaters, and a major transit station, has a supporting population of between 50,000 and 100,000 persons within ten minutes by automobile or public transit.

Housing

Everywhere in Europe the housing shortage has been chronic since World War II and the "baby boom" that followed it. Today, France, Germany, Holland, and Sweden all build more housing units per 1,000 population than the United States. The rate in Sweden is nearly double the rate in the United States. Nonetheless, even in Sweden there is an undersupply of housing. The housing squeeze is compounded by rising standards of demand—more room, modern bathrooms, etc.—and the changing nature of the family structure that is swelling the demand for housing. In the Netherlands the average number of persons per housing unit has dropped from 5.6 in 1900 to 2.9 in 1970, and it is still going down. The same trend is taking place elsewhere in Europe: aged persons and young single people now have their own housing units so that the need for additional units is increasing.

There is a positive side to the situation in Europe: most new residential building there is subsidized in one way or another in order to hold down costs and maintain quality. German and the Netherlands have elaborate programs for loans to nonprofit housing organizations; Great Britain has rent rebates for the poor; and Sweden has an annual housing allowance for all families with two or more children.

Urban Growth Policies

While the United States does not have a national land-use or growth policy, several European countries have explicit growth policies. Great Britain, France, Italy, the Netherlands, and Sweden are all seeking to disperse national population and stem migration to the largest centers. While the measures haven't been entirely successful, they have slowed the movement from smaller to larger places.

In Britain the goal has been to stem the so-called "drift to the south"—out of Scotland and Wales and into the area centering on London. In France the goal has been to lessen the domination of Paris; in Italy, to develop the economy of the depressed south, or Mezzogiorno; in the Netherlands, to save the remaining green areas; and in Sweden, to halt the flow out of more northern areas into Stockholm and the south.

The basic tool has been to provide manufacturers with economic incentives to invest in depressed areas needing growth. Subsidies in terms of capital grants are provided by the national government. In addition, controls are increasingly imposed upon adding factories or offices to places where growth isn't wanted. For example, to build a factory or office building in the London area, the developer must show that the enterprise cannot be developed elsewhere. The Netherlands also puts higher taxes on buildings in the cities of Amsterdam, Rotterdam, and The Hague. Another policy is to relocate government offices to areas where growth is desired. Sweden is relocating one-quarter of its government offices outside of Stockholm—a policy that definitely does not appeal to the government bureaucrats who have to move.

It is difficult to see any such urban growth and redistribution policy being implemented in the United States. There is no clamor for a program administered out of Washington, and programs by individual states are unlikely to be effective. If one state imposed sanctions, a company could—and probably would—simply up and move to another state that did not. Thus, while European programs for dispersion of growth have been reasonably successful, they are unlikely to be copied in North America, with our stronger opposition to decision making by the central government.

Rents are subsidized and in most countries take less than 20 percent of a family's income: this is excellent by American standards. In the Netherlands and Germany, rents frequently do not exceed 15 percent of family income. The extreme is found in the Soviet Union, where the rent for a small apartment for a family of four would absorb only 3.5 percent of the average monthly income of an industrial worker. Utilities would cost another 3.5 percent on the average. The drawback in the Soviet Union is that owing to a severe housing shortage the current "housing norm" (rationing of space) is only 7 square meters (approximately 21 square feet) per person.[6]

The Dutch Approach: An Example of Planning in Western Europe

Americans who fear that certain regions of the United States are turning into unrelenting megalopolises should find it instructive to see how the Dutch are coping with similar problems. The Netherlands is a small country with a population of 14 million and a population density of over 410 persons per square kilometer. If the United States had this population density, it would have a population of over 3½ billion, or roughly the present population of the world. The problem in the Netherlands is aggravated by the fact that the majority of the Dutch population is found in a megalopolis about 100 miles in diameter, including Amsterdam, Rotterdam, and The Hague. This conurbation is known as the *randstad,* or "rim city."

Nonetheless, it is possible to reach the open countryside in half an hour's time from the center of any of the cities in the *randstad.* In spite of considerable population growth and a housing shortage since World War II, the Dutch lead remarkably uncluttered lives. Urban sprawl such as that found in the United States is virtually unknown. The line between town and country is sharply drawn. When a city such as Amsterdam stops, it stops abruptly. It is quite common at the city's edge to see massive blocks of high-rise apartments overlooking cows peacefully grazing in totally open fields. By building upward rather than outward, the Dutch have kept their towns compact; and valuable woods, lakes, and fields are kept as a reserve for the use of all.

The Dutch have been able to save much of their environment, and at the same time provide for an ever-expanding demand for housing, by building tall multiple-unit residential buildings. The use of high-rises is dictated by the shortage of land and the necessity to keep down costs of land. Almost without exception, single-family houses are built in rows.[7] Many families in the Netherlands, particularly those with small children, prefer single-family houses; and the privately financed dwellings now being built are substantially of this type. However, only the more affluent segment of the population can afford the high building costs. The government in effect subsidizes both rents and building costs for those not able to carry the full cost. The Dutch feel that every family, regardless of income level, is entitled to reasonable housing. As a result, rents are low by comparison with those in the United States. After deduction for taxes and social insurance, the average Dutch family pays only about 10 percent of its income on

---

[6]Leon M. Herman, "Urbanization and New Housing Construction in the Soviet Union," *American Journal of Economics and Sociology,* 30:216, April, 1971.

[7]*The Netherlands: Current Trends and Policies in the Field of Housing, Building, and Planning During the Year 1968,* Ministry of Housing and Physical Planning, The Hague, 1970, p. 18.

rent.[8] This is a result of the government's policy of rental subsidies and loans for building new dwellings. The average rent of a new dwelling financed with a state loan is roughly 15 or 16 percent of the average gross income of an industrial worker.[9] Subsidies and rent supplements are periodically readjusted so that the poor and the working classes will not be priced out of the housing market.

The Dutch also believe in public ownership of urban land; about 70 percent of Amsterdam is now owned by the city. In The Hague the policy is somewhat different: only about 20 percent of the land is owned by the city, but it is strategically located so that it can be used to set the pattern of real estate prices for the city. The third major city of the Netherlands, Rotterdam, saw its downtown area reduced to rubble by Nazi dive bombers in 1940. Rotterdam began to reconstruct after the war, with the core of the city as a commercial, cultural, and administrative center. Dutch officials now concede that it was a mistake to rigidly segregate commercial and residential areas. The Lijnbaan, the downtown shopping mall which has received much praise, contains fine shops, sidwalk cafes, and several apartment buildings without vacancies. Rotterdam's land policy is somewhere between that of Sweden and that of the United States. The city retains ownership of industrial and commercial land, with the land being leased and rents reviewed every three to five years. Land to be used for housing, on the other hand, is sold outright after it has been determined that the land use is in conformity with the overall development plan for the city.

A system of local, regional, and—finally—national controls prevents unwanted urban sprawl. New buildings simply cannot be constructed unless they conform to the detailed development plan prepared by each municipality. Plans for development are drawn up by the city, but they must be approved by provincial authorities, who have certain limited powers of review and veto. If a local development is in conflict with the regional plan, and if the difference cannot be resolved at that level, the question then goes to the national level for a decision. There is no national plan, as such; rather, there are national guidelines which influence the regional plans and the detailed city development plans. An attempt is made to avoid rigidity, and plans are constantly being modified—within the national guidelines—to meet new situations and needs. Without some controls, the remaining green space between The Hague, Rotterdam, and Amsterdam would soon be filled, and a megalopolis would become inevitable.

EASTERN EUROPEAN PATTERNS

The Soviet Union

Any discussion of socialist cities should begin with the Soviet Union, which has set the pattern for eastern Europe. In contrast to western Europe or the United States, the Soviet Union is still undergoing rapid urbanization. Fifty years ago, it

---

[8]Ibid., p. 14.
[9]Ibid.

had only two cities of over 1 million (Moscow and Leningrad) and no cities between 500,000 and 1 million. Today over 60 percent of the Soviet population is urban, with thirteen cities of over 1 million people and twenty-nine cities of between 500,000 and 1 million.

Cities. Contemporary Soviet cities are the product of a number of distinctive forces, of which the most influential have been (1) the unprecedented destruction of housing stock during World War II, (2) the rigidity and massiveness of "socialist realist" architecture of the Stalin era, (3) national emphasis on developing heavy industry rather than housing, and (4) the attempts to build a "socialist city."

Land Use. Under the Soviet system the use of land is determined not by market values (the underpinning of the tradition of the Chicago school discussed in Chapter 5) but by government policy. According to Szelenyi, socialist urban developments were expected to look different from western cities because (1) the western mechanisms of land values couldn't prevail, (2) most urban housing is built by the state, and rents are highly subsidized, thus replacing the housing market by a redistribution of national income through the housing system, and (3) state-owned enterprises have a monopoly in the construction industry, trade, and servicing.[10]

Housing. Housing its people remains the most critical urban problem faced by the Soviet Union. (This is a problem on which only limited data were available in the west until recently.) Under the tsars much of the population was ill-housed, and conditions did not improve after the communist revolution. Stalin followed a policy of "industry first; cities be damned" which has been difficult for leaders coming from that era to break.[11] Nonetheless, in recent decades great efforts have been made. For the last twenty-five years the Soviet Union has built 2.3 million housing units a year.[12] Most of these units are in huge, identical slablike complexes, and the units fall far short of western standards in quality and size. Less than half the urban dwellers have the official housing norm of 9 square meters of living area, and approximately 40 percent of Soviet families still share kitchens, bathrooms, or whole apartments with another family. The problem is not that nothing is being done, but that after half a century during which housing needs were virtually ignored, the housing problem has become so massive that only exceptional measures can reduce the deficit.

City governance. Actual city governance in the Soviet Union is only partially in the hands of local officials. Mayors and city officials, particularly outside the largest cities or the state capitals, have far more responsibilities than authority to

[10] Ivan Szelenyi, "Urban Sociology and Community Studies in Eastern Europe," *Comparative Urban Research*, 4(213):11–20, 1977.
[11] William Taubman, *Governing Soviet Cities: Bureaucratic Politics and Urban Development in the USSR*, Praeger, New York, 1973, p. 18.
[12] Alfred John Di Maio, Jr., *Soviet Urban Housing Problems and Policies*, Praeger, New York, 1974.

The Soviet government builds almost all its current housing using preformed sections assembled at the construction site. (Tass/Sovfoto.)

carry them out.[13] Managers of large factories often have direct responsibility for municipal services such as housing, electricity, water supply, or even running the streetcars. But factory managers are judged by their superiors on how well they meet production quotas, not on how they maintain city services. As a consequence, the need for services is often indifferently met. William Taubman suggests that it is the local Communist Party officials who often lobby for increased services and environmental improvements such as reducing industrial pollution. Factory directors, by contrast, are more likely to oppose change, since improvement in city services and amenities will in effect be an added "cost" of production. Ironically, business directors and factory managers in the Soviet Union often have more direct control over local affairs than their counterparts in capitalistic systems do.

[13]Taubman, op. cit.

Social-Class Distribution in Socialist Countries

Theoretically, socialist countries have largely abolished social segregation. Low state-subsidized rents mean that the upper class can't outpurchase other groups. Housing is allocated on the basis of need, family size, and the possession of key job skills. Nonetheless, while a free market in which the upper class can get the best housing by paying higher rents does not exist, the upper strata still get the best housing. Rather than a market system, a system of social rewards applies. Political, military, scientific, academic, and cultural elites receive special consideration *before* those on the allocation list. With consumer goods limited, housing is the major symbol of social status.

The elites receive priority for the newest and largest housing. "Thus the group that are most advantaged become the beneficiaries of redistributed social wealth by living in units that are the most highly subsidized by the state."[14]

> All the available data from Poland, Czechoslovakia and the G.D.R. (German Democratic Republic) suggest that the inhabitants of heavily subsidized state rental housing are of higher social status than the owners of the less subsidized family-built dwellings. Workers with lower qualifications build their own houses, workers with higher qualifications and professionals receive new state housing.[15]

Thus, in eastern European socialist countries housing inequalities resulting from market inequalities have been replaced with housing inequalities as a consequence of the systems of social rewards. East or west, the upper strata still get the best.

There are, however, some real differences between socialist countries and other countries. For example, the pattern of cities and suburbs found in North America is largely reversed in the Soviet Union and eastern European countries. With city housing in extremely short supply, and permits to move to the city difficult to obtain without influence, poor workers often must live in the country while working in the city. The "suburban" commuter from Moscow, Warsaw, or Budapest is most likely to be a blue-collar worker living in a peripheral slum community. In Hungary, for example, 70 percent of the cities' unskilled workers and half the industrial workers commute into the cities.[16] Thus, in direct contrast to the cities of the developing world, to be discussed in Chapters 15–18, eastern European cities have more employment and industry than housing for workers.

The best housing areas are often the new housing developments located on the near edges of the city. Since in socialist countries the price of land isn't taken into account, there is no economic incentive for renewal of inner-city areas for occupancy by the upper class. The consequence is that in socialist countries the location of newer state housing rather than the market affects the social status of areas. Government planning thus plays a direct—if unintentional—role in socially segregating the city.

---

[14] Morton, p. 45.
[15] Szelenyi, op. cit., p. 19.
[16] Ibid., p. 15.

NEW TOWNS

Throughout the centuries, humans have had visions of creating new towns free from the fads and foibles of older cities. The term "utopia" originated as the title of a book (1516) by Thomas More which gave his version of how a new land of towns should be organized. Here the emphasis is on new towns that have actually been built, beginning with the world-renowned English new towns program and then discussing other European alternatives. In Chapter 14, all these will be compared with the experience in the United States.

British New Towns

The British new town movement owes its origins to Ebenezer Howard (1850–1928), an English court stenographer who proposed the building of whole new communities. His ideas appeared in a book called *To-morrow, A Peaceful Path to Real Reform* (1898), which was soon reissued under the title *Garden Cities of To-morrow* (1902). Howard's new towns, which were called "garden cities," were not to be simply another version of suburbs. Rather, they were to be self-contained communities of 30,000 inhabitants which would have within their boundaries

Howard's Garden Cities were designed to be self-sufficient and self-contained communities. Note that the railroads were not to enter the city proper but would remain within the manufacturing belt on the town periphery. (Ebenezer Howard, *Garden Cities of To-morrow*, London: Faber & Faber, 1902, p. 52.)

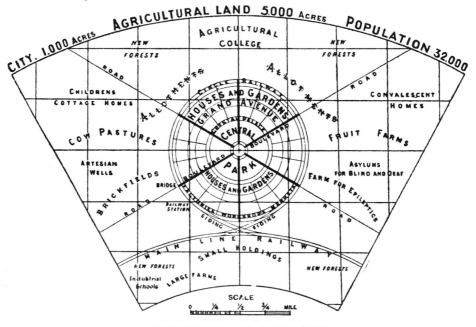

GARDEN CITY AND RURAL BELT

ample opportunities not only for residence but also for employment, education, and recreation. The towns were to be completely planned, with all land held in public ownership to prevent speculation.

Howard's garden cities were essentially a reaction against the urban abuses of the industrial revolution in England. His new towns were not to be extensions of the morally and socially polluted city but self sufficient towns with all necessary amenities, where one could enjoy the benefits of a healthful country life. In Howard's words:

> There are in reality not only, as is so constantly assumed, two alternatives—town life and country life—but a third alternative in which all the advantages of the most energetic and active town life, with all the beauty and delight of the country, may be secured in perfect combination.[17]

This combination would in turn spur "the spontaneous movement of the people from our crowded cities to the bosom of our kindly mother earth, at once the source of life, of happiness, of wealth, and of power." Thus the garden city was fundamentally antiurban in its basic conception. It was to solve the problem of the great cities largely by abandoning them and starting over with a fresh environment.

Frederick Osborn, one of the major proponents of new towns, described them as follows:

> Howard's Garden City is to be industrial and commercial with a balanced mixture of all social groups and levels of income. Areas are worked out for the zones: public buildings and places of entertainment are placed centrally, shops intermediately, factories on the edge with the railway and sidings. Houses are of different sizes, but all have gardens and all are within easy range of factories, shops, schools, cultural centers, and the open country. Of special interest is the central park and the inner Green Belt or Ring Park, 420 feet wide, containing the main schools with large playgrounds and such buildings as churches.[18]

However, the most distinctive feature of the garden cities was that beyond the city itself, there was an encircling "green belt" of natural fields and woodlands which were owned by the town and could never be sold. This green belt could not be encroached upon for housing, business, industry, or even farming—although it could be used for pasturage. Because of this feature, garden cities are also known as "green-belt cities." The green belt not only provided a way for the residents to enjoy nature, it also was intended to prevent the city from growing beyond its planned limit of 30,000 inhabitants.

Nor was the internal design of the garden city left to chance. The whole town, including its pattern of roads, was planned with both the quality and the basic design of buildings controlled. The central 5 or 6 acres were to contain civic buildings, a library, lecture halls, and theaters. Stores and shops were nearby. This core was surrounded by rings of houses, each with its own yard.

---

[17]Ebenezer Howard, *Garden Cities of To-morrow*, Faber and Faber, London, 1902, pp. 45–46.
[18]Frederick J. Osborn, *Green-Belt Cities*, Schocken, New York, 1969, p. 28.

Neighborhood schools and churches were scattered throughout the city, and small parks connected the various neighborhoods. The outermost ring of the city was to contain industries and warehouses with direct access to rail lines. The rail lines did not penetrate the center of the city proper.

The town was totally planned, and strict zoning was central to Howard's basic scheme. The residential city was divided into five neighborhoods or wards, each with approximately 5,000 residents. Each was to have its own centrally located school and community subcenter, and every attempt was to be made to keep all houses within walking distance of factories, schools, churches, shops, and, of course, the open country.[19]

The whole site, including agricultural land, was to be under quasi-public or trust ownership to ensure planning control through leasehold covenants. When the population outgrew the prescribed size and area, another new town was to be created with its own sacrosanct green belt. As with the ancient Greeks, problems of growth were to be handled by colonization rather than by extending city boundaries.

First Towns. The concept of garden cities would have gone the way of other utopian plans had Howard not been an activist as well as a visionary. In 1902, with the aid of the newly formed Garden City Association, he established the first garden city at Letchworth, some 30 miles north of London.[20]

This initial venture was plagued by many difficulties, the principal one being that the site selected was poor. Another problem was the difficulty of finding investors for a project that limited dividends to a maximum of 5 percent per year. In fact, it was twenty years before the shareholders received any dividends at all.[21]

The understandable reluctance of industry to move out to the new town meant that residents became commuters to London—a situation directly opposed to Howard's conception of a town that would provide its own employment. Howard was emphatically against the green-belt towns' becoming commuter suburbs.

Despite these problems, while the first garden city was still not out of the financial woods, a second, Welwyn Garden City, was begun in 1920. It too suffered financial crises for many years, but it eventually surmounted them. Today it is a pleasant and prosperous community of 44,000 residents about twenty-five minutes by rail from London.

Government Invovement. Were it not for World War II, Howard's garden cities would probably have remained a quaint experiment. However, World War II, with its extensive destruction in the heart of London, led Patrick Abercrombie to formulate a Greater London Plan of 1944, with decentralization as one of its major aims.

The new towns were to be one part of a four-part policy. The policy included:

---

[19]For a detailed discussion of the community's organization, see Osborn, op. cit.
[20]Frank Schaffer, *The New Town Story*, MacGibbon and Kee, London, 1970, p. 4.
[21]Lloyd Rodwin, *The British New Towns Policy*, Harvard University Press, Cambridge, Mass., 1956, pp. 12–13.

(1) a green belt around London to halt continuous metropolitan growth, (2) new towns to house the expanding urban population, (3) redevelopment of inner-city areas, conforming to higher standards than had existed previously, and (4) an attempt to control the location of employment and to prevent everyone from building in London.[22]

The British government became directly involved in the building of new towns through the New Towns Act of 1946. Advocates of new towns had long argued that they would provide a healthier, cleaner, safer, and more democratic environment. In the back of everyone's mind was also the fact that London had suffered grievously from bombing during the war and that new towns would disperse both population and industry at numerous smaller nodes rather than create one massive target in London. Furthermore, it was considered undesirable to rebuild badly damaged areas of London, such as the East End, at the old unsatisfactory population densities; new towns would help to absorb the surplus population. Government involvement in new towns meant that building on a grand scale was now possible, as a result of government financing. Compulsory purchase of land from private owners for building the town was also available.

The involvement of the British government, however, meant that the new towns would differ in significant ways from Howard's original scheme. First, the development corporation was appointed by and answerable to the central government, not to the town. Second, the size range was pushed upward—first to 60,000; and some towns plan for ultimate populations of up to 250,000 in cluster cities. This is far from Howard's limit of 30,000. Third, no provision was made for nearby land to be used only for agriculture. "As far as access to the countryside is concerned the new towns do not differ from most other settlements in Britain."[23] Finally, the concept of a city providing all its own employment was also abandoned, in practice if not in theory. Although the new towns are certainly not designed to be commuter suburbs, they are basically manufacturing centers, with approximately half the population in industry and the other half in trade, the services, and the professions.

The first of the English government-sponsored new towns, Stevenage, was begun in 1947. Among other innovations, it had the first pedestrian shopping mall in Britain and neighborhoods designed to separate pedestrian walkways from contact with automobile and truck traffic. Today Stevenage is a pleasant and economically self-supporting community of 66,000.

Houses and apartments built by the local new towns development corporations are not distributed on a first-come, first-served basis. Rather, priority is determined by a number of criteria, including employment by local or incoming industries and previous residence in one of the more crowded inner-city areas of London. Originally, following Howard's plan, almost all dwellings were rented, but successive British governments have been moving toward increasing the number of owner-occupied homes. As a means of encouraging home ownership, present renters were being offered the option of purchasing the property in which they lived for 20 percent below the market value.[24]

As of 1977, thirty-one new towns had been completed in Great Britain, with a total investment of over $4 billion. It should be pointed out that only 5 percent of Britain's housing construction after World War II has taken place in new towns. Still, the British are well pleased with their new towns program. By the end of the 1980s, they expect to have nearly 4 million persons living in new towns.

New Towns on the Continent and in Eastern Europe

Not only England but other European countries, including Sweden, Finland, the Netherlands, and the Soviet Union, built new towns after World War II. The Soviet Union has probably founded more new towns than any other nation—more than 800 between 1926 and 1963 alone. About one-third of these were established in totally undeveloped areas. The Soviets' development of new towns has been generally explained as part of broad schemes for national development and the decentralization of industry. Many of their earlier new towns were connected with hydroelectric power projects and then expanded into manufacturing centers.[25]

In the Soviet Union, as in England, the new towns were planned to be separate from existing urban centers although related to them. Local industry was to provide sufficient employment so that few, if any, residents would be required to commute to the large city. Generally, these communities were originally designed to house a maximum of 60,000 to 100,000 people. These new communities were not a consequence of the garden city concept, as were the British new towns. Rather, they were closer to company towns. The goal was not to build more humane environments but to provide housing for the workers in the factories.

In Sweden and the Netherlands, the new communities were designed to be closely tied to the central city, and to serve as residential—not employment— areas. Scandinavian new towns such as Vallingby, Farsta, and Täby are basically residential and shopping areas. Unlike the British new towns, they are constructed along rapid-transit lines so that they will be an integral part of the city's life; they are not designed to be independent and self-contained employment units.[26] It is expected that most residents will work in the central city; consequently, rapid transit to the core of the central city is a basic feature of the design of these towns. Zoetermeer, a Dutch new town of 100,000 inhabitants 7 miles from The Hague, will be able to speed its residents to the center of The Hague in less than twenty minutes. Such new towns are really extensions of the older city into the countryside rather than attempts to create new rural utopian communities.

All European new towns have in common the fact that they were initiated, planned, and financed by the government. While there has occasionally been some financing from cooperatives, unions, or even private sources, the land and

---

[24]For this and other information on policy, I am indebted to Mr. Frank Schaffer, Secretary of the Commission for the New Towns.

[25]J. Clapp, *New Towns and Urban Policy—Planning Metropolitan Growth*, Dunellen, New York, 1971, p. 28.

[26]For a description of urban planning in Sweden, see Goran Sidenbladh, "Stockholm: A Planned City," in *Cities: A Scientific American Book*, Knopf, New York, 1965.

The Swedish new town ot Täby is located on a transit line and has rapid access to the center of Stockholm. (Swedish Information Service.)

the facilities built on it have been owned either directly by the local government or by quasi-public corporations chartered by the national government to build and administer the town. Dutch planners also have the advantage that, since much of the land for new towns was drained from marshes, there is little dispute as to how the land is to be used.

Throughout Europe high-rise apartment buildings are generally used, not only because land costs are high but also to avoid suburban sprawl and to provide open spaces for recreation and enjoyment of the natural environment. In Sweden, Finland, and the Netherlands over 80 percent of the units are in blocks of flats. English new towns, on the other hand, have over 80 percent single-family homes.[27] Everywhere automobiles remain a problem. Every attempt is made to put parking lots underground or otherwise out of sight to preserve the environment. The increasing number of cars, however, seems to constantly outrun the planners' ideas about where to put them all. Still, by building compactly the planners ensure that much open space is left for woods, sports areas, and lawns.

[27]Pierre Merlin, New Towns, Methuen, London, 1971, p. 250.

Generally there is satisfaction with the new towns, although they lack the excitement of the central city.

Since the housing in new towns is constructed first and amenities follow, there is a problem of boredom and its consequences. Not everyone can adjust to the absence of night life and city excitement. Sweden's planned communities, for example, have had problems with alcohol and drugs—although these problems are hardly unique to new towns.

Although Swedish new towns such as Vallingby and Farsta were constructed in the 1950s to deliberately high densities (only 8 percent of the former and 13 percent of the latter are single-family homes), the communities have an openness and closeness to nature that residents find appealing. While there are no private yards as in the North American model, there are many walkways, trees, and common open spaces.

More recent Swedish new towns have a far more negative image among Swedes.[28] The brick-sided walk-up apartments characteristic of Vallingby have been largely replaced with six- to eight-story concrete-slab buildings—many more than a block long. Such slab cities have been criticized as "inhuman environments" and social disaster areas. Built in parallel rows, they present a very sterile and uninviting appearance. Only the color of the buildings distinguishes one group from another. The relative lack of popularity of such buildings has resulted in their having a high concentration of younger persons with lower incomes and being identified in the popular mind with social problems—drug addiction, alcoholism, and crime. Some of the newest housing areas also have high concentrations (25 percent or more) of foreign workers—groups often poorly integrated with Swedish society.

On the other hand, in the better-designed new towns there is a high degree of satisfaction among residents.[29] Recreational facilities and services surpass those of most American cities and suburbs. Of particular importance to the many working mothers are the extensive neighborhood systems of day-care centers for children and youth centers for those over age thirteen.

American new towns are discussed in Chapter 14, Urban Planning: United States.

[28]David Popenoe, *The Suburban Environment,* University of Chicago Press, Chicago, 1977, especially chap. 9.
[29]Ibid., chaps. 3 and 4.

CHAPTER

14

URBAN PLANNING:
United States

Make no little plans,
they have no magic
to stir men's blood.

Daniel Burnham

City planning in the United States is usually regarded as a twentieth-century development, but as early as 1672 Lord Ashley Cooper instructed that Charles Town be laid out "into regular streets for be the buildings never so mean and thin at first, yet as the town increases in riches and people, the void places will be filled up and the buildings will grow more beautiful." The town was designed to form a narrow trapezoid four squares long by two squares wide, fronting on the Cooper River. Philadelphia was also laid out according to the gridiron pattern. Today, the area surrounding Independence Hall once again shows the original pattern as William Penn intended. North American colonial cities as disparate as Quebec in the north and James Oglethorpe's Savannah in the south began their existence as planned enterprises.

However, as is indicated in Chapter 16, Latin American Cities, planning was developed furthest in the Spanish colonies. The sixteenth-century Laws of the Indies, promulgated by the Spanish Crown, clearly specified how the conquistadores should construct their cities. Every new town was to have a wide central plaza (the *plaza mayor*) bordered by the major religious and administrative buildings, which were to radiate outward from the *plaza mayor* according to a gridiron plan. Better residences were located near the center of the city; the poor lived on the periphery. The effect of the Spanish town-planning ordinances can be seen to this day in Latin American cities. The patterns thus established are almost the reverse of Burgess's pattern, which was by and large typical in the development and growth of North American cities.

EIGHTEENTH AND NINETEENTH CENTURIES

Washington, D.C.

There is little that can be said for North American town planning during the eighteenth and nineteenth centuries. Pierre L'Enfant's plan for Washington, D.C., is one of the few bright spots in the picture of urban planning after the Revolutionary War. L'Enfant's original design, produced in 1791, called for broad sweeping diagonal boulevards overlying a basic gridiron pattern with major monuments or buildings gracing capacious squares at the intersections of major avenues. Economic realities soon forced the effective abandonment of L'Enfant's overall plan, and L'Enfant himself was removed in 1792, after numerous disputes. His contention that his plan was "most unmercifully spoiled and altered" is largely accurate. For example, he planned a broad boulevard along the river to be lined with gardens; but this have never been seen except on his own detailed maps. He even had a plan to divert the river, making it flow toward the Capitol, whence it would be routed over a 40-foot waterfall and then back to its original course.[1] It was probably fortunate, however, that this particular feature was never constructed.

[1]Charles N. Glaab and A. Theodore Brown, *A History of Urban America*, Macmillan, New York, 1967, p. 253.

Salt Lake City's streets were planned to be wide enough for a team of oxen to be turned around. (National Archives.)

For much of the nineteenth century Washington remained, in Charles Dickens's words, "a city of magnificent intentions." Washington's oppressively hot, unhealthful summers did not encourage year-round residence. At the time that Lincoln assumed the Presidency, Washington was still a half-finished quagmire, packed with members of Congress, lobbyists, job seekers, prostitutes, gamblers, and hangers-on while Congress was in session, and deserted when it was not. Only near the end of the century did a revival of interest in L'Enfant's original plans give us the neoclassical style of government buildings found in the capital today.

One of the city's most notable legacies from L'Enfant is the numerous traffic circles. Any tourist who has ever had the folly to drive into the city is not likely to forget the traffic circles, which disorient even the most experienced drivers.

Nineteenth-Century American Towns

During the nineteenth century little creative energy went into the design of the rapidly multiplying new towns. New western settlements merely replicated older urban traditions. Communities were built as if God had intended that streets be laid out in a grid, at right angles to each other. This was in fact a fairly useful model in the midwest and on the prairie, but it was applied even when it was grossly inappropriate. If hills got in the way, for example, as in San Francisco, streets were simply cut up one side and down the other rather than following the natural contour of the land.

The gridiron pattern, in which plots could easily be divided, was well suited to the feverish speculation that accompanied the nation's early growth; most promoters of sites were speculators whose major interest in the new communities was quick profit. The Federal Land Ordinance of 1785 also encouraged the gridiron pattern, since it divided all lands west of the Appalachians in the public domain into units of 1 square mile to facilitate their sale to settlers.[2] A gridiron pattern was also good for fire protection.

[2]Edmund K. Faltermayor, *Redoing America,* Harper and Row, New York, 1968, p. 17.

Roads and the way they divide land are another strong influence on the pattern of development of a city. A circular pattern, with roads leading from the center like the spokes of a wheel, focuses attention on the center of the city. It is a system "beloved by chieftains, emperors, priests, and popes."[3] Washington, D.C., and Detroit, Michigan, were both designed on modified circular patterns. The gridiron system, with its square lots, has always facilitated subdivision and thus is the model used in industrial and other economically oriented cities in the United States and elsewhere (Johannesburg is an example outside the United States). According to Christopher Tunnard, "the open lot and speculation have always gone hand in hand."[4] This was certainly true of the development of North American cities.

It is interesting to note that by the early twentieth century the rectangular grid, although also used for newer additions to European cities, had come to be identified with the American city.

> It is in America that the persistence of uniform right-angled streets has been most marked. Here the universality of the plan's adoption, and the rigidity of adherence to it, has been such that Europeans, forgetting the long history of rectangular street planning refer to it now as the American method.[5]

In the new frontier towns, housing was as predictable as the pattern of streets. The same American businesspeople who prided themselves on their originality and inventiveness in business created towns that were dull and drab.

Planned Communities

Totally planned communities fared little better. Lowell, Massachusetts, for all its early promise as an idealistic, paternalistic community, quickly deteriorated into just another New England mill town. Pullman, Illinois, was designed in the late nineteenth century as an experiment in both well-managed labor relations and town planning. In the words of its founder and sole owner, George Pullman, "With such surroundings and such human regard for the needs of the body as well as the soul the disturbing conditions of strikes and other troubles that periodically convulse the world of labor would not be found here."[6] But the town of Pullman proved to be socially unexciting and architecturally monotonous. Although when it was built in 1880 it had been well outside the city of Chicago, by the turn of the century it had been surrounded by the expanding city. Pullman is today best known because of a bitter strike which took place there in 1894 and was finally put down by the National Guard.

Planned urban communities tended to quickly become satellites and then suburbs of the nearest central city, since, on their own, they lacked both the economic and the social diversity necessary to keep them viable. Of the new communities organized around religious doctrines—New Harmony and Oneida,

[3]Christopher Tunnard, *The City of Man*, Scribner, New York, 1953, p. 121.
[4]Ibid., p. 77.
[5]C. M. Robinson, *City Planning*, Putnam, New York, 1916, p. 16.
[6]Stanley Buder, *Pullman*, Oxford University Press, New York, 1967, p. vii.

for example—only Salt Lake City has grown and prospered, possibly because it had, under Brigham Young, a very tight social organization, plus an excellent environmental situation along the trail to the California gold fields.

Parks

One of the brightest aspects in the rather discouraging story of nineteenth-century urban planning is the work of Frederick Law Olmstead. In 1857, after much controversy, he began the building of Central Park on 843 acres of wasteland on the outskirts of New York City. The site was hardly promising, for, as Olmstead described it, much of it was a swamp "seeped in the overflow and mush of pigsties, slaughterhouses, and boneboiling works, and the stench was sickening." Central Park not only served the function of providing "lungs" for the city, but it inspired other cities to copy New York's successful plan. Parks were built across the country, and some of them, such as Lake Park in Milwaukee, Wisconsin—which was also designed by Olmstead—have become invaluable assets of their cities.

The City Beautiful

The movement that had the most pronounced effect on the design of American cities was the "city beautiful" movement that more or less emerged from the Chicago Columbian World Exhibition of 1893. The Columbian exhibition gave Chicago a chance to show the world that it was no longer a ramshackle town

The World Columbia Exposition of 1893 impressed virtually all who saw it. Its emphasis on monumental grandeur influenced American public architecture for decades. (Culver Pictures.)

surrounding stockyards, but a booming modern metropolis; and the city leaders were determined to make a good impression.

Daniel Burnham was placed in charge of assembling the nation's leading architects and landscape designers to create for the exposition the famous White City. In order to produce an impression of magnificence, a uniform cornice line was set, and all the buildings—with the exception of the Transportation Building, designed by the great architect Louis Sullivan—were classical in style. The classical buildings of White City, combined with harmoniously planned lagoons and grounds, created an overwhelming impact even to the architecturally sophisticated.

The classical ancestry and majestic size of such public buildings neatly meshed with the optimistic and expansionist mood of the country at the turn of the century. Strong, powerful buildings were a way of expressing the fever of imperialism and material success then sweeping the land. The United States had easily humiliated Spain in a short war and was (it believed) blessed by God with a "manifest destiny" to rule.

White City, with its magnificence and grandeur, started a trend; it became customary to design all government buildings in neoclassical or pseudoclassical style. As a result of the "city beautiful" movement, there is not a city in the nation without at least one building—a city hall, court, or library—designed to resemble a Greek temple. The influence of this movement on the architecture of the federal government has been even more pronounced. For fifty years after the Colombian exposition, almost every large post office was designed as a Greco-Roman temple. Many of these buildings were poor imitations of the classical style, but among the better products of the neoclassical revival are the famous civic center in San Francisco and the Benjamin Franklin Parkway in Philadelphia, which terminates at a majestic neoclassical art museum. It must be pointed out that the "city beautiful" movement paid attention almost exclusively to city centers; there was little concern for housing or neighborhoods.

Parks, which have already been discussed briefly, were related to—though not an integral part of—the "city beautiful" movement: a number of elaborate park systems, tied together by attractive boulevards, were developed. The excellent parks of Chicago, Kansas City, and Washington are largely a result of the early-twentieth-century trend for planned public, if not yet private, development.

At the request of Chicago's civic businesspeople, Daniel Burnham drew up a master plan for that city which included a massive civic building program; a central feature of this plan was an extensive network of city parks tied together by a system of grand, tree-shaded boulevards. Burnham captured the mood of the age when he ordered his staff to "make no little plans." The nation's capital also profited from the new emphasis on planning. L'Enfant's long-neglected design for Washington, D.C., was revived, and the appearance of the Capitol was greatly improved by the removal of the Pennsylvania Railroad tracks from the Mall in front of it. Burnham and other architects prepared plans for the beautification of Washington from which have been developed the present-day "federal triangle" group of government buildings and the Mall between the Capitol and the Lincoln Memorial.

The "city beautiful" movement may of course be criticized on aesthetic grounds, but it did have a concept of the city as an integrated whole and a vision of what it could be. It was a solid and sincere attempt to consciously improve the urban environment. Perhaps the greatest weakness of the "city beautiful" movement was that it almost totally ignored the problem of the slums.

Tenement Laws

The end of the nineteenth century also saw a movement by social reformers to improve the quality of life in inner-city slums by enforcing building codes and passing model tenement laws to correct some of the worse abuses of the design and construction of older tenements. To reformers such as Jacob Riis, the slum was the enemy of the home and of basic American virtues. To quote Riis:

> Put it this way: You cannot let men live like pigs when you need their votes as freemen; it is not safe. You cannot rob a child of its childhood, of its home, its play, its freedom from toil and care, and expect to appeal to the grown-up voter's manhood. The children are our to-morrow, and as we mould them to-day so will they deal with us then. Therefore that is not safe. Unsafest of all is any thing or deed that strikes at the home, for from the people's home proceeds citizen virtue, and nowhere else does it live. The slum is the enemy of the home. Because of this the chief city of our land [New York] came long ago to be called "The Homeless City." When this people comes to be truly called a nation without homes there will no longer be any nation.[7]

The answer at that time appeared clear: Destroy the slum and you will destroy the breeding ground of social problems. Symptoms of social disorganization such as alcoholism, delinquency, divorce, desertion, and mental illness were to be cured, or at least greatly reduced, through the provision of better housing and more open spaces for the young. This belief in salvation by bricks and mortar fit in neatly with the American belief in the unlimited potential of technology.

Many greatly needed improvements in housing were made as a result of the campaigns of the turn-of-the-century reformers; but crime, violence, and alcoholism were not banished as a result. The relationship between housing and social behavior is complex and not amenable to simplistic solutions.

TWENTIETH CENTURY

The City Efficient and Zoning

The golden age of concern with, and reform of, urban social life, esthetics, and politics died with the entry of the United States into World War I. Wholistic visions of the city's future such as had been provided by the "city beautiful" movement

[7]Jacob Riis, *The Children of the Poor*, Scribner, New York, 1892.

ran contrary to the laissez-faire atmosphere of the 1920s. As a result, the emphasis was gradually shifted from the "city beautiful" to the "city efficient," and urban planning was replaced by city engineering. During the 1920s, the city was viewed as an engineering problem, and planners became technicians concerned with traffic patterns, traffic lights, and sewer systems. The city was viewed as a machine, and the goal was to keep the machine running smoothly.

The concept of the city as an evolving organic unit was also overshadowed by the development of a new planning tool, zoning. Zoning, which became a force in the United States with the New York City Zoning Resolution of 1916, was originally seen as a device to "lessen congestion in the streets" and to "prevent the intrusion of improper uses into homogeneous areas."[8] "Improper" use of land meant not only industrial and commercial establishments, but also lower-class housing. It was an attempt, largely successful, to segregate land use and freeze "noncompatible" uses out of upper-middle-class neighborhoods.

The effect of the first weak zoning laws was mainly negative—that is, to keep unwanted types of buildings from being constructed. Zoning laws had little retroactive effect. (Zone boundaries in many cases recognized the existence of "natural areas" described by the early human ecologists, and then went a step farther and tried to prevent further change in these areas.) The 1921 Standard State Zoning Enabling Act, which was issued by the federal government, advised state legislatures to grant the following power to the cities:

> For the purpose of promoting health, safety, morals, and the general welfare of the community, the legislative body of cities and incorporated villages is hereby empowered to regulate and restrict the height, number of stories, and size of the buildings, and other structures, the percentage of the lot that may be occupied, the size of the yards, courts, and other open spaces, the density of the population, and the location and use of buildings, structures, and land for trade, industry, residence, or other purpose.[9]

Today Houston, Texas, is the only major city in the country without zoning laws. Houston does not look noticeably different from other cities because the market mechanism allocates the downtown land to business and commercial usage while outlying land is used for residential purposes. It is not economically feasible to deviate from the normative pattern of land use. Restrictive covenants on land use are a functional equivalent of zoning in many cases.

Master Plans

The idea of the "city efficient" was also evidenced in the master plans for city development that became the hallmarks of the city-planning agencies created in the largest metropolises. The purpose of the master plan was to coordinate and regulate all phases of city development; but in practice the preparation of the plan frequently became an end in itself, since the planners rarely had any real authority over the nature and direction of urban development.

---

[8]Dennis O'Harrow, "Zoning: What's the Good of It?" in Wentworth Eldridge (ed.), *Taming Megalopolis*, Doubleday (Anchor), Garden City, New York, 1967, p. 762.
[9]Newman F. Baker, *Legal Aspects of Zoning*, University of Chicago Press, Chicago, 1927, p. 24.

The Approach of Jane Jacobs

Among the critics of urban planning practices, Jane Jacobs is the best known.* She is diametrically opposed to zoning and other planning tools as they are currently applied.

Using as an example her own beloved area of Greenwich Village in New York City (she now lives in Toronto), Jacobs argues that the mixed housing and commercial usages and the resulting congestion, factors which orthodox planners are said to deplore are the very reason why the area has retained its buoyancy and unique character over time. Cities, she suggests, are natural economic generators of diversity and incubators of new enterprises, and attempts by planners to zone various activities into distinct areas only work toward dullness and eventual stagnation both economically and socially.†

Jacobs says that four conditions are indispensable if diversity and liveliness are to be generated in a city:

1. The district, and indeed as many of its internal parts as possible, must serve more than one primary function; preferably more than two. These must insure the presence of people who go outdoors on different schedules and are in the place for different reasons.
2. Most blocks should be short; that is, streets and opportunities to turn corners must be frequent.
3. The district must mingle buildings that vary in age and condition, including a good proportion of old ones so that they vary in the economic yield they must produce. This mingling must be fairly closegrained.
4. There must be a sufficiently dense concentration of people, for whatever purposes they may be there. This includes dense concentration in the case of people who are there because of residence.‡

Thus she sees the physical environment of the city directly affecting city life, and argues for a mix of social activities and a heterogeneous population to increase neighborhoods' vitality.

By providing a mixture of functions—residence, work, place of entertainment—a district ensures that eyes are constantly on its streets, maintaining safety. This diversity of use further means that uniquely urban specialty shops can operate profitably, since there is considerable traffic past their doors. Short city blocks provide for alternative routes and use of different streets—with the result that a cross section of the public passes the doors of the smaller specialty

---

*For a retrospective analysis of Jacobs's views, see Harvey M. Choldin, "Retrospective Review Essay: Neighborhood Life and Urban Environment," *American Journal of Sociology,* 48:457–463, September, 1978.
†Jane Jacobs, *The Death and Life of Great American Cities,* Random House, New York, 1961.
‡Ibid., pp. 150–151.

operations. Old buildings are needed, since, as Jacobs puts it, "Old ideas can sometimes use new buildings. New ideas must use old buildings." New buildings are limited to enterprises that can support the high costs of construction and rent. Old buildings not only provide space for new enterprises; they also break the visual monotony, and they can house cozy stores that provide gossip and a place to leave your keys as well as merely selling goods. Finally, the dense concentration of people in an area contributes to its vitality and liveliness. Jacobs suggests that it is not accidental that the district in San Francisco with the highest dwelling density is the popular North Beach–Telegraph Hill section. High building density does not, of course, necessarily mean crowding. Medium-density areas fail to provide liveliness and safety, and they have none of the advantages of low-density, semisuburban areas.

In Jacobs's view, the population and environmental characteristics of a neighborhood shape its social character:

> Great cities are not like towns, only larger. They are not like suburbs, only denser. They differ from towns and suburbs in basic ways, and one of these is that cities are, by definition full of strangers. . . . Even residents who live near each other are strangers, and must be, because of the sheer number of people in small geographical compass. The bedrock attribute of a successful city district is that a person must feel safe and secure among all these strangers. He must not feel automatically menaced by them. A city district that fails in this respect also does badly in other ways and lays up for itself, and for its city at large, mountains on mountains of trouble. §

A valid criticism of Jacobs is that her preoccupation with street safety makes her oblivious to other urban problems and values. She views the city as a place where people will do violence to one another unless restrained. One of her most knowledgeable critics, Louis Mumford, suggests that Jacobs puts so much emphasis on the necessity for continued street life because her ideal city is mainly an organization for the prevention of crime.

Mumford points out that according to Jacobs's view, "the best way to overcome criminal violence is to create a mixture of economic and social activities such that at every hour of the day the streets will never be empty of pedestrians and that each shopkeeper, each householder, compelled to find both his main occupations and his recreations on the street, will serve as watchman and policeman, each knowing who is to be trusted and who not. . . ."¶ Mumford points out that London of the eighteenth century, violent and crime-ridden, met these prescriptions. Furthermore, the benefits of

§Ibid., p. 300
¶Lewis Mumford, "Home Remedies for Urban Cancer," in Louis K. Loewenstein (ed.), *Urban Studies,* Free Press, New York, 1971, pp. 392–393.

high density, pedestrian-filled streets, cross-lines of circulation, and a mixture of primary economic activities can be found in Harlem—where they do not reduce street or other crime. On the other hand, a dispassionate observer would have to concede that whatever else Harlem is, it is certainly not dull.

Mumford also argues that the emphasis on safety blinds Jacobs to other values in an urban environment. Convenience, beauty, the absence of the noise of trucks crowding the street, the minimizing of the effects of pollution   all these factors are made subservient to safety.

Jacobs can also be criticized for not dealing with the question of racial change in the city. Nonetheless, the importance of her work should not be underemphasized. Partially because of her influence, the planners of today are far more conscious of the social impact of design and planning decisions. The message that cities are for people is finally affecting urban policies.

The fact that master plans were seldom carried out was generally beneficial to the public, for they were often static and stylized, without any solid relationship with the real city. The plans adorning the walls of city planning agencies rarely defined neighborhoods, for instance, on the basis of established social-class and ethnic composition unless these happened to coincide with pronounced differenc-

The retirement community of Sun City, Arizona, is an extreme case of a socially as well as physically planned community. Among other restrictions, children under age eighteen are not allowed in the community except as short-term visitors. (Georg Gerster/Photo Researchers, Inc.)

es in type of housing. Physical criteria were almost exclusively used. Transportation lines and physical boundaries were all too frequently used to determine the units into which the planners divided the city. In the words of Herbert Gans:

> The ends underlying the planners' physical approach reflected their Protestant middle-class view of city life. As a result, the master plan tried to eliminate as "blighting influences" many of the land uses and institutions of lower class and ethnic groups. Most of the plans either made no provision for tenements, rooming houses, second hand stores, and marginal loft industry, or located them in catch-all zones of "nuisance uses," in which all land uses were permitted. Popular facilities that they considered morally or culturally undesirable were also excluded. The plans called for many parks and playgrounds but left out the movie theater, the neighborhood tavern, and the clubroom; they proposed churches and museums, but no night clubs and hot dog stands.[10]

Case studies of the actual planning process indicate that planners often made their recommendations on the basis of arbitrary considerations without fully examining or understanding the consequences.[11] The death blow for many a master plan was the upsurge of urban renewal and other development plans after World War II. These development schemes were frequently put forward by interest groups in business or government that had no concern for the master plan as such. Conflicts between the static master plan and specific development proposals with available funding were almost always resolved in favor of the specific proposals. Today planners themselves are questioning the utility of creating more master plans, unless the plans are directly related to, and can have influence on, the future development of the city.

Experiments with New Towns

Government-Built New Towns. Today, when European governments have directly taken the responsibility for planning and financing new towns, it is almost forgotten that during the 1930s the United States government also designed, financed, built, and for a decade managed three of the world's first green-belt towns for middle-class and lower-middle-class groups. The United States, however, has never had a national program for developing new towns as such. The building of these towns reflected specific measures that were being taken to combat the depression of the 1930s. The government had three main objectives:

1. To demonstate a new kind of suburban community planning which would combine the advantages of city and country life
2. To provide good housing at reasonable rents for moderate-income families
3. To give jobs to thousands of unemployed workers which would result in lasting

---

[10]Herbert J. Gans, "Planning, Social: II. Regional and Urban Planning," in David Sills (ed.), *International Encyclopedia of the Social Sciences,* Crowell Collier and Macmillan, New York, 1968, vol. 2, p. 130.
[11]Martin Meyerson and Edward C. Banfield, *Politics, Planning, and the Public Interest,* Free Press, Chicago, 1955.

economic and social benefits to the community in which the work was undertaken

The three American green-belt towns were Greenbelt, Maryland, outside of Washington, D.C.: Green Hills, Ohio, near Cincinnati; and Greendale, Wisconsin, just south of Milwaukee. They were basically experimental or demonstration projects. The towns were to have their own industry, as in the British model, but first a shortage of funds and then World War II kept them basically commuter suburbs. After World War II, the private housing industry was able to convince Congress that having the government involved in the building and renting of low-rent homes was socialistic and dangerous to the free-enterprise system. As a result of Public Law 65 of 1949, all the homes built by the government were sold. The green belts surrounding the towns—which with the expansion of the central cities had become valuable land—were converted to other uses. Much of Greendale's green belt, for example, is now occupied by privately developed housing tracts and a large shopping center. It is more than a little ironic that when much of the world was trying to save its remaining green space surrounding cities, we were busy converting an existing green belt into a shopping center.

Privately Built New Towns. Although the business of building cities is the largest single industry in the United States, we still construct our cities on a largely ad hoc basis. Thousands of small enterprises build our towns and cities, with little planning and even less research.

Privately built new towns were a phenomenon of the years after World War II. According to the Department of Housing and Urban Development, sixty-four new communities have been completed or substantially begun in the United States since World War II; forty of these were constructed during the 1960s.[12] These new towns are located in eighteen states, but half of them are in California, Florida, and Arizona. Four-fifths are within metropolitan areas; the remainder are mainly retirement communities for the elderly.

The best known of the American new towns are Reston, Virginia, just west of Washington, D.C., and Columbia, Maryland, near Baltimore on the way to Washington, D.C. Both Reston and Columbia are financed privately rather than by the government.

Reston, which was the brainchild of the developer Robert E. Simon, was taken over by Gulf Oil Corporation in 1967 because the town was not returning a profit. Economically, the town is now healthy, although some residents say that there has been some slippage in the quality of architecture. Reston, like other privately financed new towns, and unlike the earlier ventures by the government, has a distinctly upper-middle-class character. Studies revealed that the average buyer in Reston was between thirty and forty years old, was the head of a family

---

[12]National Committee on Urban Growth Policy, *The New City*, Praeger, New York, 1969, p. 114.

High- and low-rise structures blend harmoniously along the shores of Lake
Anne in the new town of Reston, Virginia. (Gulf Reston, Inc.)

with two children, and had an annual income over one-third higher than the
national average. Reston, however, does have several hundred units of federally
subsidized housing. Although Robert Simon had attempted to integrate the
community economically by placing middle-income and more expensive houses
side by side, the new management abandoned this practice as not being
economically sound. Mixed-income housing is desirable for social reasons, but it
is apparently a drain on profits.

Columbia, Maryland, the second new town, is 20 miles from Washington,
D.C. Architecturally it is less successful; it resembles an ideal supersuburb,
largely because the builders of the various sections were given a relatively free
hand and built a mixture of their best-selling models. For example, a buyer can
choose a standard interior and then decide whether the facade is to be Cape Cod,
Nordic, or Georgian colonial. Columbia is, however, a pleasant and well-planned
community. Wooded areas and pathways run throughout the town.

Columbia, developed by the Rouse Company in a joint venture, covers 15,600
acres and will eventually house 110,000 people. When complete, it will represent
an investment of over $2 billion. Like most new towns, it is organized into
neighborhoods. Each neighborhood has some 900 houses, and each has its own
elementary school and recreational facilities, including a swimming pool, a
neighborhood center, and a convenience store. Four neighborhoods are combined

to form a "village" of about 3,500 units, which has an intermediate or middle school, a meeting hall, and larger and more varied shops plus a supermarket. These are all designed to cluster around a small plaza with benches and a fountain. There is also a larger shopping center for the whole community in the downtown city center, which contains office buildings and larger department stores. Other innovations include a community college and a comprehensive full-care medical program in conjunction with the Johns Hopkins Medical School.

Socially, Columbia has made a conscious effort to be a racially integrated community; roughly one-fifth of the residents are black. Income integration has generally not been as successful. Subsidized units have not been as clustered as in Reston but are spread over five different sites to avoid the creation of a low-income ghetto. Nonetheless, when a ten-speed bicycle is stolen, it is the low-income residents who are usually blamed. Within the community, use of automobiles is discouraged by providing walkways and bicycle paths that are both more direct and not in physical contact with the highways. Nonetheless, the parking lots of the shopping centers are generally filled, and the corporation has had to discontinue the minibus service within the city because it did not attract enough customers.

All in all, residents seem pleased with new towns, although they are not significantly more satisfied than residents of other suburban communities. Raymond Burby and Shirley Weiss compared responses of 7,000 residents in fifteen new towns and fifteen conventional suburbs of similar location, age, size, and income level.[13] Ninety percent of the respondents from the new towns thought their community a good place to live—but then so did 86 percent of those in conventional suburbs. New towns per se had little effect on social behavior or perceptions.

Enthusiastic about the idea of new communities free from urban blight or suburban sprawl, Congress during 1968 and 1970 passed legislation to spur the development of new towns. The legislation offered federal funds and technical aid to developers and—most important—guaranteed up to $50 million worth of each developer's bonds plus the interest on the bonds. This was done because a new town is an inherently risky financial venture and requires front-end outlays for land purchase and infrastructure well before the first house is build or sold. The Nixon administration, however, opposed the program and withheld all funds for planning grants and technical assistance. The processing of applications was deliberately ensnarled in red tape.[14]

By 1974, twelve projects had issued bonds for a total of $252 million in federally guaranteed debentures. At this critical point the program was hit with

---

[13]Raymond J. Burby III, et al., *New Communities U.S.A.*, Lexington Books, Lexington, Mass., 1976.

[14]Helen V. Synookler, "Administrative Hari Kari: Implementation of the Urban Growth and New Community Development Act," *Annals of the American Academy of Political and Social Science*, **422:**131–132, November, 1975.

the energy crisis and a depressed housing market, and developers found themselves caught between expensive front-end costs (one developer spent $13,000 a day just for interest and taxes) and no customers. While established towns such as Reston and Columbia were able to weather the crisis, brand-new towns still in the infrastructure-building stage were not. At this point (1975) the Ford administration announced that it would accept no further applications for loan guarantees. In effect, the new towns were cut loose to sink or swim. Many—such as Johathan in Minnesota and Riverton in New York—didn't make it. Soul City, North Carolina, the dream of the civil rights activist Floyd McKissick, which went under in July 1979, was the eighth and most recent of the new towns to be foreclosed by the Department of Housing and Urban Development. HUD assumed ownership of Soul City in 1980.

Overall, the new town program cost $149 million in losses. Critics charge that much of this loss was the government's own doing, since it deliberately underfunded the towns and then pulled back at a critical juncture. By contrast, the British do not anticipate that their government-built new towns will be self-supporting for the first decade and a half. There is at present no sign that the United States government is willing to make such a commitment. Economically, new towns, except for the affluent, cannot be expected to stand alone financially in their early years.

Limits to Growth

One of the newest planning concerns in rapidly growing communities is the question of limiting growth. For years it was part of the American creed that bigger is better. City boosters, as a matter of course, bragged that their town or city was growing faster than neighboring places. Now that is changing, and rapidly growing communities from St. Petersburg, Florida, to Boulder, Colorado, to San Diego are seeking ways of limiting growth. Similarly, Governor Ariyoshi of Hawaii has stirred up considerable controversy by seeking to slow down Hawaii's exploding population by limiting in-migration from the other forty-nine states.

Those favoring control, such as the Sierra Club, generally argue that uncontrolled sprawl has destroyed the physical and cultural environment, and believe that indiscriminate gobbling up of land by developers has to be controlled. Opponents of control, such as the National Association of Home Builders and the National Association for the Advancement of Colored People, on the other hand, say that the real question is whether those already in the area can infringe on what they see as a constitutional right to settle where one chooses. They deplore a "pull up the gangplank" approach on the part of established communities who resist change in their way of life or level of amenities. Not all opponents have similar reasons for opposition. The home-building industry is concerned about the effect of building restrictions on the profits of developers; the NAACP, on the other hand, is concerned that setting minimum lot sizes and imposing environmental protections (e.g., requirements for municipal sewers and water hookups rather than septic systems and wells) will drive up prices and exclude minorities.

While the debate goes on, the legal issue has been resolved for the moment by a case involving the farming center of Petaluma, a city of some 32,000 roughly 35 miles north of San Francisco. A new freeway allowed commuters to discover Petaluma, and by 1971 growth had reached 18 percent a year; schools were in double session, and the water and sewage systems were strained to the maximum. It was clear that in a few years the entire pleasant valley would be covered with wall-to-wall subdivisions of look-alike homes. In desperation, the city instituted a plan limiting development to 500 new dwelling units a year. Developers and builders challenged the limits in court. In 1976, the Supreme Court, by refusing to hear the case, let stand the decision by the Court of Appeals that the traditional responsibility of local communities for public welfare was sufficiently broad to allow Petaluma to preserve its small-town character and open spaces. The court of appeals rejected the developers' argument that limits to growth unconstitutionally restricted people's right to travel and live where they please.

Now Petaluma is dealing developers another blow. Forced with the limitations on property taxes set by Proposition 13, the city is charging developers a fee to pay for the public services needed by new homes. The fee (a maximum of $700 per unit) is largely passed on to home buyers. The idea is that new residences should not be a financial burden to existing taxpayers. (A study in Denver in 1972 indicated that each new residence cost taxpayers $21,000 for items such as streets, water, sewer and electric lines, schools, and parks.)

To date, only a limited number of communities, usually in areas in the south and west which are environmentally attractive, have actually put lids on growth. However, decisions by the courts seem to indicate that while a town can't simply ban all growth, it can control its future. However noble the purpose, the consequence of limits, if widely adopted, would be to increase housing costs and thereby exclude not only the poor but also many middle-class home buyers.

The Use of Space

As noted in Chapter 6, City Life-Styles, physical space often has different meanings to different groups. Understanding the symbolic uses of space can certainly be of practical use to architects and planners who want to use sociological information to increase the adequacy of their designs.

Public housing projects in particular can be designed to minimize rather than maximize feelings of deprivation and isolation from the community at large. Traditional high-rise projects too often are designed to be not only dull and monotonous but also dangerous to the inhabitants. Large open areas outside the projects frequently become "no man's lands" after dark, while within the buildings the corridors, washing rooms, and even elevators are unsafe. Residents are helpless to prevent muggings and rapes and feel that the only area they can control, and thus feel safe in, is the space within their own apartments. (See the section on unstable slums in Chapter 6 and Chapter 10.)

Architectural design can do a great deal to increase the security and livability of projects. One of the simplest changes is to build low-rise buildings (six stories at most) where no more than a dozen families share the same stairwell and thus know who should or should not be present. Oscar Newman suggests that some other elements which can help in providing security are:

1. The territorial definition of space in developments reflecting the areas of influence of the inhabitants. This works by subdividing the residential environment into zones toward which adjacent residents easily adopt proprietory attitudes.
2. The positioning of apartment windows to allow residents to naturally survey the exterior and interior public areas of their living environment.
3. The adoption of building forms that avoid the stigma of peculiarity that allows others to perceive the vulnerability and isolation of the inhabitants.
4. The enhancement of safety by locating residential developments in functionally sympathetic urban areas immediately adjacent to activities that do not provide continued threat.[15]

The effect of proper planning can be seen in a comparison of the Brownsville and Van Dyke housing projects in New York, which are separated only by a street (see Table 14-1). The low-rise Brownsville buildings, although older, have significantly fewer problems of crime and maintenance than the high-rise Van Dyke buildings. This is in spite of the fact that the average density per acre of the two projects is virtually identical. The Brownsville projects, with their six-story buildings and three-story wings, are humanly manageable and controllable to a far greater degree than the thirteen- and fourteen-story Van Dyke projects across the street.

Internal space can also be designed to decrease alienation. Architects define spaces inside apartments usually in terms of the functions they serve: kitchens for cooking, bedrooms for sleeping, dining rooms for eating, and windows for letting in light and air. Urban residents, however, often have their own ideas of the functions of space. Windows, for example, are not only for air and light but also for observing and communicating with the street; living rooms may not be viewed as an area for entertainment but as sacred space to be used for formal family occasions.

In one experiment, Puerto Rican residents of tenement buildings in East Harlem, a local community group, and an architect jointly redesigned apartments according to the needs of the residents.[16] On the basis of what they learned from

---

[15]Oscar Newman, *Defensible Space,* Macmillan, New York, 1972, p. 9.
[16]John Zeisel, "Symbolic Meaning of Space and the Physical Dimension of Social Relations," in John Walton and Donald E. Carns (eds.), *Cities in Change,* Allyn and Bacon, Boston, 1973, pp. 252–263.

TABLE 14-1
Van Dyke and Brownsville: Some Comparisons

Comparison of crime incidents

Crime incidents	Van Dyke	Brownsville
Total incidents	1,189	790
Total felonies, misdemeanors and offenses	432	264
Number of robberies	92	24
Number of malicious mischief	52	28

Source: New York City Housing Authority Police Records, 1968.

Comparison of maintenance

Maintenance	Van Dyke (constructed 1955)	Brownsville (constructed 1947)
Number of maintenance jobs of any sort (work tickets) 4/70	3,301	2,376
Number of maintenance jobs, excluding glass repair	2,643	1,651
Number of nonglass jobs per unit	1.47	1.16
Number of full-time maintenance staff	9	7
Number of elevator breakdowns per month	280	110

Source: New York City Housing Authority Project Managers' Bookkeeping records.

A comparison of physical design and population density

Physical measure	Van Dyke	Brownsville
Total size	22.35 acres	19.16 acres
Number of buildings	23	27
Building height	13–14 story 9–3 story	6 story with some 3 story wings
Coverage	16.6	23.0
Floor area ratio	1.49	1.39
Average number of rooms per apartment	4.62	4.69
Density	288 persons/acre	287 persons/acre
Year completed	1955 (one building added in 1964)	1947

Source: New York City Housing Authority Project Physical Design Statistics.

Source: Oscar Newman, *Defensible Space*, Macmillan, New York, 1972, pp. 46–48, tables 5, 6, and 7.

interviewing the residents and from their own observations, they designed the apartments to avoid the large areas of undifferentiated space so desired by middle-class whites. The residents wanted a design where the apartment entrance would not open directly into the sacred space of the living room and where the kitchen, contrary to middle-class preference, could be closed off from the rest of the house by a solid wall with a door. This is what the families themselves wanted in their homes.

Unfortunately, this experiment was a rare occurrence. Working-class and lower-class people are seldom asked what they want in housing. Perhaps some of the horrible mistakes in public housing projects could have been avoided if someone had bothered to talk with those for whom the apartments were being designed.

PART FIVE

CHAPTER

15

LESS DEVELOPED COUNTRIES:
Overview and
Common Problems

He that will not apply new remedies must expect new evils;
for time is the greatest innovator.

Sir Francis Bacon

URBANIZATION IN THE THIRD WORLD

Large-scale urbanization in Europe and North America was a process that spanned more than a century and involved massive economic and social change. Industrialization spurred in-migration from rural hinterlands. As documented in Chapter 2, Emergence of Cities, urban places in Europe and America, with their high death rates, were able to grow only because of massive inflows of rural population.

The context of contemporary urbanization in less developed countries differs from that of North America and western Europe in several respects. First, the extent—and rapidity—of the urban increase in less developed countries (LDCs) is outpacing anything that occurred in the west. Second, industrialization rather than providing a spur for urbanization, often trails far behind the rate of urban growth. Third, cities in LDCs differ from the western model in having continued high rates of growth by natural increase as well as migration. Modern public health and vaccination programs mean that contemporary third world cities are not the "graveyards of countrymen" as developing western cities were. Cities in developing countries may appear unhealthful by contemporary western standards, but they are, nonetheless, often more healthful than the rural alternatives. The consequence often is traumatic urban growth.

Common or Divergent Paths?

A crucial question regarding cities in less developed countries is whether such cities will in rough fashion repeat the North American socioecological patterns of growth (as detailed in Chapters 4 and 5), or whether developments in the third world will follow entirely different paths. If there is a rough evolutionary process based on an ecological model which is in turn based on land values and competition for scarce space, urban planning can predict what will occur. The belief that such patterns exist is sometimes referred to as "convergence theory." As you may recall, such a pattern was suggested by Leo Schnore (see Chapter 5).[1]

If, on the contrary, there are divergent paths, because of fundamentally different processes, cultures, and historical and religious factors, making plans and policies on the basis of what has occurred in the west could be disastrous. Brian Berry argues for such different growth patterns.[2] To date there is no consensus about the pattern of the future; some believe that third world cities will converge toward the western model, and some believe that there will be divergent paths of development. Most scholars probably incline toward the latter view.

The chapters in Part Five, because of limited space, necessarily focus on what is common to third world cities rather than on their unique differences. Readers should keep in mind, though, that particular cities may differ from the general pattern. Instructors who are familiar with specific cities or cultures may

[1]Leo F. Schnore, *Class and Race in Cities and Suburbs*, Markham, Chicago, 1972, p. 72.
[2]Brian J. L. Berry, *The Human Consequences of Urbanization*, St. Martin's Press, New York, 1973.

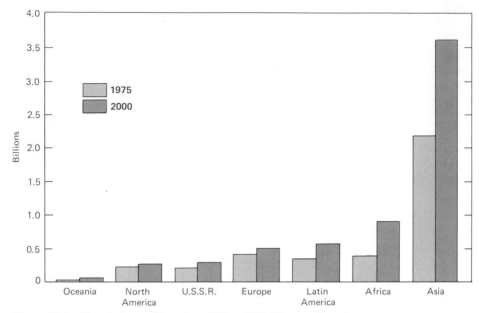

Figure 15-1. Growth by world region: 1975 to 2000. (*Source:* Based on estimates by the Population Reference Bureau.)

wish to expand on the influence of particular historical, cultural, geographic, religious, or economic factors.

The process of urbanization, Schnore argues, produces three changes in a nation.[3] First, it modifies the behavior of the population as they adopt urbanism as a way of life. Second, it shifts the economic and social structure of the nation from agriculture to industrialization. Third, it accelerates both the proportion of urban dwellers in the nation and the rate of urban population growth. These three factors will be discussed in this section in roughly reverse order.

Urban Population Explosion

A common characteristic of cities of the developing world is the explosion of their populations (see Figure 15-1). By the end of the century, more than two-thirds of the world's total urban population will be living in less developed countries. While the developing world is still heavily rural, it already contains over one-third of the world's urban population and many of the world's largest cities. As of 1950 only 16 percent of the people in less developed countries lived in cities. Today the figure is about 30 percent, and the United Nations estimates that it will reach 43 percent by the year 2000.[4]

[3]Leo Schnore, "Urbanization and Economic Development: The Demographic Contribution," *American Journal of Economics and Sociology,* **23**:37–48, 1964.
[4]United Nations Population Division, "Trends and Prospects in the Population of Urban Agglomerations 1950–2000, as Assessed in 1973–75," United Nations, New York, November, 1975.

TABLE 15-1
Population in Selected Cities, 1950, 1975, and 2000

Africa	1950	1975	% increase 1950–1975	2000	% increase 1975–2000
Cairo (Egypt)	2,377*	6,932	(192%)	16,398	(137%)
Lagos (Nigeria)	288	2,064	(617%)	9,437	(357%)
Kinshasa (Zaire)	164	2,049	(1149%)	9,112	(345%)
Latin America					
Mexico City (Mexico)	2,872	10,942	(281%)	31,616	(189%)
Sao Paulo (Brazil)	2,450	9,965	(307%)	26,045	(161%)
Lima (Peru)	614	3,901	(535%)	12,130	(211%)
Asia	1950	1975	% increase 1950–1975	2000	% increase 1975–2000
Calcutta (India)	4,446	8,077	(81%)	19,633	(143%)
Jakarta (Indonesia)	1,565	5,593	(257%)	16,933	(203%)
Teheran (Iran)	1,041	4,435	(326%)	13,785	(211%)
Europe					
Paris (France)	5,441	9,189	(69%)	12,293	(34%)
Milan (Italy)	3,641	6,030	(66%)	8,267	(37%)
London (U.K.)	10,247	10,711	(5%)	12,693	(19%)
Other Industrialized Countries					
Moscow (U.S.S.R.)	4,841	7,609	(57%)	10,623	(40%)
Tokyo-Yokohama (Japan)	6,737	17,317	(157%)	26,128	(51%)
New York-N.E. New Jersey (U.S.)	12,340	17,013	(38%)	22,212	(31%)

*In thousands.
Source: United Nations Population Division, WP 58.

The change can be grasped more easily by looking at the impact on an individual city. Mexico City, for example, had one-quarter of New York's population in 1950 (2.9 million compared with 12.3 million). Currently Mexico City has 14 million inhabitants, and it will have 31.6 million by the year 2000 if the city's current growth rate of 4.4 percent continues.[5] This will make Mexico City the world's largest urban area—half again as large as New York and 2½ times as large as London or Paris.

The overall figures for cities in developing areas (Table 15-1) tell an astonishing tale of growth. In the half century between 1950 and 2000, the urban population of less developed countries will increase eight times, while that of developing countries will grow only marginally (2.4 percent). The consequence is that by the year 2000 almost two-thirds of the world's urban population of 3.1 billion will live in developing countries.[6] The United Nations estimates that 264 (63 percent) of the world's anticipated 414 cities of over 1 million will be in less

[5]Ibid.
[6]George J. Beier, "Can Third World Cities Cope?" *Population Bulletin,* **31**:3, December, 1976.

developed regions.[7] The impact of this urban explosion on cities of the developing world is difficult to overexaggerate. Some cities in less developed countries already top 10 million; with current growth rates, they will double their population in a decade (London or Tokyo, by contrast, will grow less than 1 percent). While each city is in some ways unique, they generally share common problems of unemployment, poverty, and crowding in slums and squatter settlements.

Recently publicity has been given to the fact that the worldwide rate of population increase has begun to show declines. Today's growth rate of 1.8 percent is likely to continue falling during this decade and may reach 1.5 percent by the year 2000. This, however, emphatically does not mean that world population will be declining, since today's growth rates are being applied to a base population of over 4 billion. This translates into nearly 200,000 persons being added to the world's population each day; and even with declines in fertility, 1 billion persons will be added during the 1980s and another 1 billion during the 1990s.

An awesome 90 percent of this increase will be in less developed regions. Cities of LDCs will add some 1.3 billion persons between 1975 and 2000.[8]

Problems of Growth

Increases of this magnitude are certain to create almost unbearable pressures for food, better living conditions, more education, and more employment.

Zero population growth may be a potential reality in Europe, the United States, and Japan; but it is still only a slogan in the developing world, where the combined population of the various countries is currently increasing by more than 50 million a year. This means an additional 50 million persons a year who must be fed, clothed, housed, and otherwise provided for before the developing countries can even begin to improve the quality of life for those already present.

Much of the present population explosion, with its yearly national population increases of 2½ and even 3½ percent (2 percent doubles a population in only thirty-five years; 3½ percent, in less than twenty years) can be traced to the importation of modern sanitation, public health, and medicine. After World War II, death rates were reduced drastically and at little cost, but were often only slowly accompanied by other changes in the social or economic fabric of the societies. Malaria, for example, was largely eradicated in Sri Lanka (Ceylon) by the decision of a handful of officials in government ministries to spray DDT from airplanes. This achieved declines in the death rates that took half a century in the west. The result was a population explosion. In contrast to reducing death rates, the decision to restrict the number of births must be made by millions of individual couples. Even when a society favors small families, there is a time lag in implementation.

The resulting population increases greatly exacerbate already serious

---

[7]"Trends and Prospects," op. cit.
[8]U.S. Bureau of the Census, "Illustrative Projections of World Population to the 21st Century," *Current Population Reports,* series P-23, no. 79, Washington, D.C., 1979.

problems, including problems of economic development. Funds that should be devoted to economic development are instead consumed in providing minimal subsistence and service to an ever-increasing number of people. Rather than investing capital, some developing nations are forced to spend it in order to meet, even marginally, the needs of their growing populations. Less developed countries have 35 to 45 percent of their population under age fifteen, as contrasted with a maximum of 25 to 30 percent in the industrialized countries. The consequence is that the cities of LDCs are filled with dependent children and young people who must be educated and otherwise provided for. The problem is not just that there are more people, but that LDCs have an age structure in which much of the population consists of dependents who have yet to make any contribution to the economic well-being of their families or nation.

The accepted rule of thumb is that the percent of national income which must be invested merely to keep productivity from declining is some three times the annual percent rate of increase in the labor force.[9] In other words, if the labor force is growing by 3 percent a year, it will take a net investment of 9 percent of the national income just to keep productivity from declining. It is the difference between the rate of increase of the population and the rate of increase of industrial production that tells whether real progress is being made. By this measure the picture in developing countries is not very optimistic.

In addition to the economic demands put on developing countries by new mouths to feed, there are also increasing demands from those already present. This "revolution of rising expectations" occurs because increasing numbers of people in developing countries—and particularly in the cities—become aware that their condition of poverty is not the immutable natural order of life everywhere. Developments in communication technology—first radio and now even television—have exposed the urban underclasses to the existence of higher standards of living. The urban populations, with their greater exposure to alternatives and their greater awareness of nontraditional ways of life, have expectations for themselves and their children; and governments that ignore these expectations do so at their own risk.

RICH COUNTRIES AND POOR COUNTRIES: SOME DEFINITIONS AND EXPLANATIONS

Less developed countries vary in their rates of development, but they all suffer in varying degrees from common problems such as low industrial output, low rates of savings, inadequate housing, poor roads and communication, a high proportion of the labor force engaged in agriculture, insufficient medical services, inadequate school systems, high rates of illiteracy, poor diets, and sometimes malnutrition. The developing countries contain two out of three of the world's people, but they

[9]Ansley J. Coale, "Population and Economic Development," in Philip M. Hauser (ed.), *The Population Dilemma*, Prentice-Hall, Englewood Cliffs, N.J., 1969, p. 70.

account for only one-sixth of the world's income, one-third of the food production, and one-tenth of the industrial output.[10]

It is thus quite clear that the term "developing country" is a euphemism. Various other terms, such as "modernizing country," "third world country," and "noncommitted country," have been used, and they sometimes reflect ideological differences, but essentially they are all polite ways of saying "poor country." The current preferred term is "less developed countries." While the difference between the developed and the underdeveloped countries is usually phrased less harshly, the major distinction is that one category includes the "haves" and the other the "have-nots."

This rich-poor classification cuts across conflicting ideological systems. Developed nations, whether capitalistic or communistic, whether in Europe, Asia, or the western hemisphere, all have urban-industrial economies.

Jack Gibbs and Walter Martin strongly reject the idea that the level of urbanism is tied to any ideology such as capitalism or socialism.[11] Less developed countries are so named because of their relationship to the economic power of the developed countries, which are used as the standard of comparison. "Development" is thus a relative rather than an absolute state. Newly developing countries are underdeveloped in the context of an economic comparison with Europe, the United States, or the Soviet Union. Whether the indigenous economic organization of a developing country is simple or complex—and in many cases it is extremely complex—it is invariably a traditional system and not a modern industrialized urban economy.

Economically, the developing nations of Asia, Africa, and Latin America find themselves locked into a system where prices for the raw products they produce remain relatively stable while the cost of imported goods skyrockets. Such nations are seeking to achieve industrial development while the marketplace in which they must operate is largely controlled by the developed nations. The major exception to this statement, of course, is the countries of the Organization of Petroleum Exporting Countries (OPEC), which, largely for historical reasons, are commonly classified as developing countries. In actuality, they should be classified as rich nations.

Much of the underdevelopment of third world countries, then, is due not to traditionalism or internal problems but to a worldwide system of structural dependency and unequal exchange. Increasing oil prices during the past decade have increased this dependency. Data indicate that for many developing nations the status of "underdevelopment" may become relatively permanent; while the poor nations are not getting poorer—as a whole—the rich nations are certainly getting richer. As a result, the gap between the developed and developing nations is increasing rather than decreasing. A survey of 150 nations by the Department of

---

[10]Irwin Isennberg, *The Developing Nations: Poverty and Progress:* Columbia University Press, New York, 1969, p. 13.
[11]Jack P. Gibbs and Walter T. Martin, "Urbanization, Technology, and the Division of Labor: International Patterns," *American Sociological Review,* **27:**677, 1962.

Social and Economic Affairs of the United Nations shows that in the decade 1960–1970 the per capital output of the developed countries rose 43 percent, compared with an increase of only 27 percent in the less developed countries. The same pattern occurred in the 1970s.

It should be kept in mind, however, that there are variations and changes through time among the countries to which the label "LDC" is applied. Singapore, for example, is clearly moving toward the "developed" category, while, just as clearly, Upper Volta is not. An "LDC" such as Mexico may also change categories rapidly if oil production increases as projected. As noted earlier, OPEC nations have become dramatically richer during the past decade, while oil-importing LDCs have become relatively poorer. Sometimes the distinction between countries that are developing and countries that are not is expressed in terms of the third world and the "fourth world." The following chapters will detail some of the differences between LDCc; here the emphasis is on their general similarities.

CHARACTERISTICS OF THIRD-WORLD CITIES

Employment and Industrialization

Of all the common problems faced by the cities in developing countries, the problem of providing employment is, next to that of population growth, the most severe. The situation is quite different from that faced by the economically advanced western countries during their earlier periods of urban-industrial expansion. In the era of western industrialization during the nineteenth century, farmers and peasants were drawn to the city because of the economic opportunities it offered. Entry-level jobs, both in manufacturing and in services, were generally available; and there was a solid demand for unskilled, if low-paid, workers. This was true both in Europe and in North America.

The experience of the developing countries has been quite different. Workers flood into the cities not because of the availability of jobs but because of the lack of opportunity in the rural areas and small villages. Recent data for twenty-seven Asian and Latin American nations presented by Firebaugh show that high agricultural density and plantation-type agriculture spur urbanization regardless of the rate of economic development.[12] The consequence is "subsistence urbaniza-tion," in which the ordinary citizen has only the bare necessities for urban survival.[13] Urban unemployment rates commonly exceed one-quarter of the work force.

Many, if not most, urban workers in less developed countries are employed in the informal sector of the economy—that is, small enterprises without access to credit, banks, or formally trained personnel. Nonetheless, the informal sector

[12]Glenn Firebaugh, "Structural Determinants of Urbanization in Asia and Latin America, 1950–1970," *American Sociological Review,* 44:195–215, April, 1979.
[13]Gerald Breese, *Urbanization in Newly Developing Countries,* Prentice-Hall, Englewood Cliffs, N. J., 1966, p. 5.

commonly provides most of the consumable food products and much of the services, trade, transportation, and construction.[14]

In the vast majority of developing countries, the modern or formal sector of the economy is only a small portion of the whole. In spite of some gains in industrial productivity and some increases in the gross national income, the rate of unemployment remains high. Industrialization starting from the low base found in the developing world has only a marginal effect on employment even when the *rate* of industrialization is relatively high.[15] Modern industrialization, unlike that in the United States during the latter part of the nineteenth century, does not require tremendous numbers of unskilled laborers.

Nor do public works necessarily benefit those most in need. Public funds also tend to be invested in projects such as multilane highways for the automobiles of the rich and universities for their offspring, while slums still have mud roads and the very poor receive minimal schooling.

Squatter Settlements

The population growth of virtually all cities in LDCs has outrun the capacity of municipalities to house them.[16] Decaying central-city slums and new squatter settlements house one-third of the entire urban population in developing countries. The present squatter population of Mexico City exceeds 4 million, and squatters in both Seoul and Calcutta number over 2 million. With shantytowns mushrooming at 15 percent a year (doubling their size in six years), the squatter population of poorer cities is certain to increase.[17]

Squatter or peripheral settlements are called *barriedas, favelas, bustees, kampongs,* or *bidonvilles* in various countries; but everywhere their function is the same—to house those who have the least resources and nowhere else to go. In the squatter settlements shanties and shacks are built in random fashion out of whatever refuse material the builder can salvage. Old packing crates, loose lumber, and odd pieces of metal are somehow patched together to provide a shelter. Since shantytowns almost by definition are "illegally" occupying the land on which they are built, they cannot demand city services. Streets, police, and fire protection, and—most important—sanitary services are usually nonexistent. Water almost always has to be carried from the nearest public tap. Schools are rare. Electricity is the most commonly found utility, since wires can easily be strung from shack to shack.

Public services such as running water and schools are first provided to those with economic clout. Shanty dwellers in Lima, for instance, pay ten times as much for water carried on private trucks as the middle class pays for plumbing in its

[14]S. V. Sethuraman, "The Informal Urban Sector in Developing Countries: Some Policy Implications," in Alfred de Souza (ed.), *The Indian City,* South Asia Books, New Delhi, India, 1978, pp. 1–15.

[15]Gunnar Myrdal, *Asian Drama,* vol. 2, Pantheon, New York, 1968, pp. 1174–1175.

[16]For information on third world housing patterns with emphasis on Delhi, see Geoffrey K. Payne, *Urban Housing in the Third World,* Routledge & Kegan Paul, Boston, 1977.

[17]Estimate by the United Nations.

Squatter settlements such as these climbing the hillside outside of
Caracas, Venezuela, are a common feature of developing cities. (Alain
Keler/Editorial Photocolor Archives.)

homes. Health problems are exacerbated by the crowding, by the lack of proper
disposal for sewage and refuse, and by the fact that the settlements are frequently
built on the least desirable terrain, such as city dumps, marshlands, or hillsides.

Attempts by the government to remove squatters are invariably unsuccessful:
if one slum is destroyed, another is built overnight with the refuse from the earlier
settlement. When no other city housing is available, there is little alternative. As
one authority confesses, "We have learned that we cannot hope to provide
'standard' housing for all, or even most of the urban poor in the developing
countries in this century, almost no matter how one defines 'standard.' "[18]

Demolishing settlements and relocating the urban poor in new fringe
settlements is sometimes disastrous for the poor. It often impoverishes families
who not only lose what they have invested in the demolished squatter shack, but
also are faced with increased transportation costs. Women in particular tend to
become unemployed because of the increased distance to their traditional places
of work. The poor who were forcibly removed from squatter settlements in Delhi

[18]Maurice Kilbridge, "Some Generalizations on Urbanization and Housing in Developing Countries," *Urban Planning, Policy Analysis, and Administration,* Policy Note P. 76–1, Harvard University Press, Cambridge, Mass., 1976, p. 13.

during the 1970s and moved to outlying areas now spend one-fifth of an unskilled worker's daily wage on bus transportation to the city. For the very poor a location near work is more important than the quality of the shelter. The same was true of the nineteenth-century American poor, who crowded into tenements near central-city factories.

Density and Economic Development

It should be noted that there is no clear relationship between density per se and the level or rate of economic development. High agricultural density is usually seen as a sign of underdevelopment, but high urban densities may or may not be desirable, depending on the level of economic development.

High densities of rural, and particularly agricultural, labor indicate inefficient agricultural production and a surplus of personnel which is either unemployed or underemployed. In closed extractive economies—such as farming, lumbering, and mining—the employment of a high proportion of the labor force in such pursuits means smaller average holdings. India, for example, employs about 70 percent of its labor force in agriculture, with an average holding of about 2 acres for every person of working age (fifteen to sixty-five years of age). In Asia over 83 percent of the available acreage is already under cultivation; thus increases in rural population will necessarily mean less land per person. Rural out-migration thus will continue to be a major force into the foreseeable future.

In developed countries, where nonextractive industries dominate and a large volume of trade is possible, density is frequently an advantage rather than a liability. The industrial ring cities of the Netherlands and the Rhine River urban complex of Germany both have extremely high densities and high standards of living. Hong Kong provides an even more extreme example. Hong Kong has a population of over 4 million crowded on a land area of 398 square miles: this comes out to over 10,000 persons per square mile. Nonetheless, Hong Kong has for years managed to increase its GNP at a rate far in excess of the rest of the world. Hong Kong has practically no natural resources, but it is blessed with a literate, energetic, and trained labor force. Its extremely high population density has not prevented Hong Kong from achieving one of the highest levels of per capita income in Asia, although much exploitation of workers remains.

This in no way suggests, of course, that high densities automatically result in high income levels and economic expansion. However, high density *can* be an advantage to a highly organized and heavily industrialized economy. The city concentrates large numbers of people in one place and thus minimizes what has been called "the friction of space." Production can be concentrated in one place; the city itself is a massive factory. Technological breakthroughs in transportation and communication also are means of overcoming the friction of space, and allow the city to export both to its rural hinterland and to other urban areas.

In the noneconomic sphere, population concentration also permits and encourages specialized educational, cultural, and scientific organizations. Accumulations of personal and capital resources necessary for the emergence of such organizations can be found only in the city. The requirements of urban living also produce new problems, such as housing, sanitation, and the prevention of crime; and the necessity of dealing with these problems can lead to an emphasis on innovation and rational problem solving.

The requirements of contemporary urban life and those of industrialization complement one another. Both emphasize the importance of adapting to changing conditions. Urbanization and industrialization are not the same thing, but it is not surprising that industrialism in the third world is directly associated with the growth of urban areas and the spread of urban ideas.

Overurbanization

Closely related to the question of density is that of overurbanization. The term "overurbanization" generally implies the belief that a particular developing country has too high a proportion of its population residing in cities, at densities detrimental to health, morals, and general well-being. Most important, "overurbanization" commonly is taken to mean that the urban population of a nation is too large in relation to the extent of its economic development—in short, that there are too many people for the available jobs, housing, schooling, medical services,

Cairo, without the benefit of oil monies, has an overworked bus system where people hang on the bus roofs or from the windows. (United Press International.)

etc. Egypt, for instance, is far more urbanized than its degree of economic development would lead one to expect: indeed, it is more urbanized than France or Sweden, both industrial nations. Some urbanists refer to Egypt, therefore, as being overurbanized.[19]

While there has been some attempt to keep the term "overurbanization" free of any connotation of values, the concept usually does have negative connotations: it suggests that overurbanization is both artificial and harmful to economic growth. As one United Nations publication expressed it:

> Thus the recent rapid rate of urbanization visible in Asian countries does not bespeak of a corresponding growth of industry but of a shift of people from low productive agricultural employment to yet another section marked by low productivity employment, namely handicraft production, retail trading, domestic services in urban areas.[20]

However, the whole picture is not as glum as the term "overurbanization" suggests, for the productivity of the rural in-migrants is higher in the city than in the rural areas, and per capita incomes in cities are almost universally higher than in rural areas.[21] If the concept of overurbanization is meant to suggest the undesirability of rapid urbanization in developing countries, the argument is difficult to prove. Certainly the data do not support the belief that rapid urbanization slows or impedes economic development. Life may be difficult in the city, but it is not better in the countryside; and in the city there is at least always hope and the possibility of something better. Experts may debate the issue, but all over the world peasants are voting with their feet in favor of city life. It is an intellectual and rational decision for most in-migrants.

It can be argued that the rapid growth of cities is a positive sign of the social and economic development of an area.[22] The city is not only the first area to reflect change, but also is a source of change. City growth is correlated with the change from agriculturalism to industrialism, with economic rationality, with lower birth rates and death rates, with increased literacy and education—in short, with the whole process of modernization. Insofar as urbanization is associated with the development of a modernized mode of life, the problem in much of the developing world, one could argue, is not overurbanization but underurbanization. As expressed by one expert, "The continued growth of a metropolis is evidence that, on balance, the positive aspects continue to outweigh the negative."[23]

[19]See, for example, Kingsley Davis and Hilda Hertz Golden, "Urbanization and the Development of Pre-Industrial America," *Economic Development and Cultural Change,* 3:6–26, October, 1954.

[20]*Urbanization in Asia and the Far East,* Proceedings of the Joint UN/UNESCO Seminar held in Bangkok, August 8–18, 1956, UNESCO, Calcutta, 1957, p. 133.

[21]N. V. Sovani, "The Analysis of Over-Urbanization," *Economic Development and Cultural Change,* 12:113–122, January, 1964.

[22]See, for example, Kingsley Davis and Anna Casis, "Urbanization in Latin America," *Milbank Memorial Fund Quarterly,* 24:186, April, 1946.

[23]Slaneslaw H. Wellisz, "Economic Development and Urbanization," in Jacobson and Prakash (eds.), *Urbanization and National Development,* Sage Publications, Beverly Hills, Calif., 1971, p. 42. Not all agree that "overurbanization" and primate cities are not a problem. See, for example, Antony J. La Greca, "Urbanization: A Worldwide Perspective," in Kent P. Schwirian (ed.), *Contemporary Topics in Urban Sociology,* General Learning Press, Morristown, N. J., 1977.

Primate Cities

A characteristic common to most developing countries is the "primate" city. A primate city is a principal city overwhelmingly large in comparison with all other cities in the country. In many countries, the primate city is frequently the only city of note.[24] Commonly, within developing countries there is no hierarchy of cities of various sizes such as that found in developed nations. Ethiopia, for example, is 95 percent rural and has few towns; but its capital city, Addis Ababa, has over 1 million inhabitants. Bangkok, with over 3 million people, is the most extreme case, being thirty-three times larger than Thailand's second-largest city.[25]

Most primate cities owe their origin and development to European colonialism. Cities such as Accra, Nairobi, Saigon, Hanoi, Singapore, and Hong Kong do not have long histories as urban places but rather were created consciously by colonial powers in order to establish bases from which they could exercise administrative and commercial control. They were established as little "Europes-in-Asia" or "Europes-in-Africa." Thus, they were usually located along the coasts in order to facilitate communication with, and transportation of raw material to, the mother country. From the very first, the orientation of the primate city was toward other cities in the developed countries rather than toward its own hinterland, and this pattern of commerce and culture coming from the outside has largely endured to this day. Government elites, particularly in Africa and Asia, may also be more oriented to the outside than to their own hinterland or "bush."

Primate cities are most likely to be found when any one of three circumstances exists. First, they occur in countries that were political and economic dependents of other countries. Second, they may occur in countries which now are small but once had extensive areas (examples are Vienna, Austria, which once controlled the Austro-Hungarian Empire; and Dakar, which was until the early 1960s the administrative center for French West Africa). Third, they occur in countries where the extent of economic development does not require cities of middle size.[26] A study based on worldwide data found the existence of primate cities to be associated with a number of other circumstances. These were: (1) dense populations in small areas, (2) low per capita income, (3) export-oriented and agricultural economies, (4) a colonial history, and (5) a rapid population growth.[27]

The concentration of population and economic activity in primate cities presents some typical features throughout the developing world:

1. In the earlier stages, the economies of such cities were primarily export-oriented, and the cities also specialized in political and administrative

[24]Mark Jefferson, "The Law of the Primate Cities," *Geographical Review*, **29:**226–232, April, 1939.

[25]Ralph Thomlinson, "Bangkok: Beau Ideal of a Primate City," *Population Review*, **16:**32–38, January-December, 1972.

[26]Brian J. Berry, "City Size Distribution and Economic Development," *Economic Development and Cultural Change*, **9:**573–581, July, 1961.

[27]Arnold S. Linsky, "Some Generalizations Concerning Primate Cities," *Annals of the Association of American Geographers*, **55:**506–513, September, 1965.

activities. Today, manufacturing and services are the primary economic activities.

2. Economic advantages result from the concentration of industry. Thus, income from peripheral areas finds its way to the metropolitan area. The higher rate of return attracts more capital; and this in turn leads to more enterprises, particularly services.

3. The concentration of industrial activities—and above all the accompanying services—increases employment. Skilled workers are attracted from peripheral locations. Thus, the city represents an advantage in terms of quality as well as quantity.

4. Concentration of population and economic activities goes hand in hand with the centralization of administrative activity. The decision-making power of the primate city increases, while that of outlying cities and towns decreases. The center thus receives the lion's share of the available investment funds.

5. The basic infrastructure of the nation is heavily determined by the requirements of the major city. This in turn encourages further concentration.[28]

Growth and economic development lead to further concentration, which in turn leads to further growth. Without anyone's really planning it that way, the primate city comes more and more to dominate the rest of the country economically, politically, and socially. Government, education, and commerce all are located in the principal city, and this concentration produces further concentration. Urban-bred civil servants and teachers are reluctant to give up the advantages of the relatively cosmopolitan city for the backward rural hinterland. The new political independence of former colonies has only accelerated this trend, for the capital of a new nation takes on additional symbolic significance, and political officials and hopefuls now concentrate there.

A number of negative effects of such concentration have been noted. Hoselitz notes that these cities are called "parasitic" because they (1) rob the countryside of valuable personnel, (2) consume all available investment funds, (3) all but prevent the development of other cities, (4) dominate the cultural pattern and lead to the breakdown of the traditional culture, and (5) tend to have a high rate of consumption as opposed to production.[29]

While some of this may be true, the overall impression is a distortion. Many smaller developing countries simply cannot support more than one major city at their present state of development. Regional balance is viewed as desirable by many planners, but even if it were economically feasible, few governments have the power to effectively control the movement of their people.

Incomplete data indicate that the influence of the largest city over other

---

[28]Based on information in "Some Regional Development Problems in Latin America Linked to Metropolitanization," *Economic Bulletin for Latin America,* United Nations, New York, 17:58–62; 1972.

[29]Bert F. Hoselitz, "The City, The Factory, and Economic Growth," *American Economic Review,* 45:166–184, May, 1955.

Dependency Theory
and Modernization Approaches

An increasingly popular perspective on development and underdevelopment is provided by dependency theory. Modernization approaches stress the importance of "modern" attitudes and values (e.g., openness to innovation, planning, faith in science and technology).* Dependency theory, by contrast, views the economic stagnation of much of the third world as a direct consequence of the process of capitalist expansion.† Industrial growth in the developed western nations is seen as a result of the exploitation and subordination of a third world periphery from which raw materials and surplus are extracted.‡ Thus, world trade patterns ensure the continued dependency of some nations. Underdevelopment is seen not as a passing state but as a consequence of a capitalist world economy. Much of the writing on dependency theory has focused on the question of foreign penetration and control of the economies of Latin America.¶

Dependency theory has often been criticized as a catchall for explaining everything that is wrong with third world societies. Alejandro Portes, an important proponent of dependency theory, replies that this was true of the earliest and crudest versions, but concedes that the "theory of dependency does not represent a system of logically interrelated propositions."§ Rather, it is a historical model. Portes further emphasizes that in spite of the confusion of many of its own theorists, contemporary dependency is much different from external foreign domination. It also involves the locally dominant classes who defend their own privileged position at the expense of the masses of the nation as a whole.

---

*Alex Inkeles, "Making Men Modern: On The Causes and Consequences of Individual Change in Six Countries," *American Journal of Sociology*, 75:200–225, September, 1969.

†Alejandro Portes, "On the Sociology of National Development: Theories and Issues," *American Journal of Sociology*, 82:55–85, July, 1976.

‡Immanuel Wallerstein, *The Modern World System—Capitalist Agriculture and the European Economy in the Sixteenth Century*, Academic Press, New York, 1974.

¶Ronald H. Chilcote, "Dependency: A Critical Synthesis of the Literature," in Janet Abu-Lughad and Richard Hay, Jr., (eds.), *Third World Urbanization*, Maqroufa Press, Chicago, 1977.

§Portes, op. cit.

urban places and rural areas is increasing rather than declining. This is true not only in Asia and Africa but also in Latin America. In Latin America, even in countries such as Colombia which formerly possessed some degree of regional balance, there is a clear trend toward concentration in a single metropolitan area.[30] In Chile, the primate city of Santiago has grown in spite of a national policy of decentralization.

In time a structure of intermediate-size cities will no doubt emerge in less developed countries, but meanwhile there frequently is no alternative to the primate city. Whatever its faults, the primate city is the center of economic and social change. The movements for independence received their ideas and their support from the urban population; and the present governments, even in rural countries, are overwhelmingly led and staffed by urban dwellers. The very idea of a civil service is an urban concept.

CONCLUSION: THE FUTURE

This chapter concludes with a number of observations regarding the most likely patterns for the remainder of this century. The reader should keep in mind, though, that what follows are this author's views; the opinion of others may differ.

First, cities in the developing world are going to continue to grow, and to grow at a rapid rate. In some cases the rate will exceed 15 percent a year. Growth will occur in spite of government policies to the contrary. For example, Jakarta was unsuccessful in becoming a "closed city," and China has been unable to halt city growth. India's new policies of directing growth to smaller places will be equally unsuccessful. Natural increase as well as in-migration will spur city growth.

Second, given such growth, squatter settlements, which currently hold one-third of the urban population, are unavoidable. Official disapproval will not make them go away. Thus, it is best to accept and legalize them, and provide at least minimal community services.

Third, urban infrastructure will inevitably remain inadequate. For example, attempts to provide "standard housing" are probably doomed to failure, though countries experiencing new wealth (as from oil), or highly organized states such as Singapore, will be an exception. Western-style industrialization will lag behind population growth and thus will not provide necessary jobs. A secondary informal labor market will remain a fact of life.

Fourth, the factors just noted suggest that political instability will be a serious problem in some countries. Rising expectations, widespread problems, and the availability of mass media will enable charismatic leaders to exploit anger and frustrations. (Iran is not a unique case but rather an example of the conflicts accompanying industrialization.)

---

[30]"Some Regional Development Problems in Latin America Linked to Metropolitanization," *Economic Bulletin for Latin America*, United Nations, New York, 17:77, 1972.

Urban growth and urban industrialization are not gradually transforming traditional societies throughout the world; rather, they are bursting such societies asunder and upsetting traditional attitudes, beliefs, customs, and behaviors. Scholars and politicians can debate whether these changes are for the better, but it is certain that urban industrial growth means change—a great deal of change.

CHAPTER
16
LATIN AMERICAN CITIES

Gazing on such wonderful sights, we did not know what to say or whether what appeared before us was real, for on one side in the land there were great cities and in the lake ever so many more, and the lake itself was crowded with canoes, and in the causeway there were many bridges at intervals, and in front of us stood the great City of Mexico, and we . . . we did not even number four hundred soldiers.

Bernal Diaz, *The True History of the Conquest of New Spain*, 1568

Any discussion of urbanization in less developed countries (LDCs) invariably points out that most third world cities are the result of conscious decisions by European colonial powers, and that as a result most of the cities are relatively new—having been founded during the expansionist period of the late nineteenth century.[1] But while this pattern may fit Africa and Asia, it most certainly does not apply to the situation in Latin America. Latin America already had grand cities at the time the Pilgrims were beginning to learn from the Indians how to raise corn. In fact, all the Latin American metropolitan areas that had more than 1 million inhabitants in 1960—except Montevideo—were founded in the sixteenth century.[2]

SPANISH COLONIAL CITIES

The Spanish designed their colonial cities to be remarkably similar in both ecological plan and functional purpose. Growth and development over the centuries have blunted many of the original similarities, but elements of the first cities still remain. The purpose of the cities was to serve as administrative centers and garrison posts for the Spanish military forces. The city was the center from which the mining or agricultural hinterland was to be controlled and the funnel through which wealth was to flow to the mother country. The Spanish Crown discouraged commercial or manufacturing activities that would make the colonial city any less dependent on Spain.

Spanish colonial cities did not enjoy the virtual independence of most of the early English towns in North America. Administrative decrees were promulgated from Spain.

Socially and commercially, the city looked toward Spain rather than toward its own hinterland. Cities were placed on the land; they did not grow out of it. Control and wealth were concentrated in the city. Before the period of independence (about 1825), there was little change in the social or economic organization of the colonial cities. None of them developed into manufacturing centers. The limited manufacturing and processing that did exist, such as the production of syrup and molasses and the spinning and weaving of cotton and woolen cloth, took place on the *haciendas* and other large landed estates.

The decrees governing the colonies were written in Spain by the Council of the Indies; home rule was unknown. These policies had two objectives, according to Smith: "(1) to make the colonies into producers of gold, silver, and precious stones; and (2) to limit their consumption of manufactured goods strictly to those produced in Spain, shipped in convoys from Spanish ports, and destined for a few strongly fortified seaports, of which the principal ones were Vera Cruz, Cartagena, and Callao."[3] The effect of all this was a throttling of trade and commerce as a

---

[1]See, for example, William A. Hance, *Population, Migration, and Urbanization in Africa,* Columbia University Press, New York, 1970.
[2]Jorge E. Hardoy, *Urbanization in Latin America: Approaches and Issues,* Doubleday (Anchor), Garden City, New York, 1975, p. viii.
[3]T. Lynn Smith, "The Changing Functions of Latin American Cities," *The Americas,* 25:74, July, 1968.

The traditional center, as in the Plaza de los Armos in Lima, Peru, was dominated by the Catholic church. (Alain Keler/Editorial Photocolor Archives.)

basis for urban life in Latin American cities under Spanish domination. The merchant, who enjoyed such a prominent position in the social structure of New England, did not have influence in the Spanish colonies. The seaports were heavily fortified entrepots for receiving the manufactures of Spain in the annual convoys and assembling the treasure that was to be shipped to Spain on the return voyage. The impact of this pattern can be seen today; only in Mexico and Colombia are metropolitan areas of over 1 million found other than on the coastline.[4]

Physical Structure

Regulations of Charles V and Philip II, eventually codified into the famous Laws of the Indies, specified how cities were to be laid out. For example, cities were to follow a rectangular plan and be founded near rivers in a manner permitting expansion. However, as Hardoy points out, "legislation only formalized a situation already perfectly defined in practice."[5] The existence of indigenous cities, of course, modified the plans, as did various practical considerations such as topography.

[4]The planned city of Brasilia is also an exception to the rule.
[5]Hardoy, op. cit., p. 30.

Nonetheless, most Spanish settlements adhered to the classical model of a central *plaza mayor*. Around the central plaza was the cathedral and major government buildings. The *solares*, or house lots, were of uniform shape, and the city was laid out in a grid with intersections at right angles. Houses and grounds were to be surrounded by walls, and because of this the early cities frequently appeared to be more heavily inhabited than was actually the case. Since the cities were to serve as fortified strong points performing administrative functions for the surrounding hinterland, they were not always ideally located from the standpoint of transportation; Mexico City was located on an island in the middle of a lake. Political rather than economic considerations often weighed heavily in the location of cities. Even the legal rank of a city was a matter decided in Spain rather than in the new world.

The Spanish government did everything possible to retain a rigid class system. One edict even reserved all the top administrative, religious, and political positions for *peninsulares*, or those born in Spain. Those born in the colonies, regardless of their wealth or family position, were relegated to a secondary status—a factor that directly motivated local leaders to instigate the rebellion against Spain.

Colonial Spaniards had little interest in the countryside. Newcomers preferred to remain in the cities with their fellows. The frontier settlement or agricultural village held little of interest for the Spaniards. Farming was left to the Indians while the Spanish landlords resided in the colonial cities.

Fortunately, the grid layout of the cities offered considerable flexibility; the boundaries could be expanded as more room was needed. Additional grids were easily added by extending the straight streets and adding more identical blocks. The focus on the central plaza meant that there were no markets, walls, or storehouses at the periphery of the city to impede expansion.[6] The large lots (which the law required be enclosed by walls) initially resulted in a relatively low population density. Later, subdivision of lots occurred, and this—and the cutting of new streets midway between existing streets—allowed the city to increase its density with relative ease.

Brazilian cities differed considerably from the model just described in that they were not built to any standard plan such as that provided by the Laws of the Indies. Cities in Brazil were few, with little influence, since the Portuguese, unlike the Spaniards, preferred to live a semifeudal existence on their estates in the country. Portuguese policy also kept towns such as Santos, Bahia, and Recife relatively small. Their splendid natural ports were open only to ships from Portugal, and this trade was not sufficient to turn these towns into real cities. By the nineteenth century Rio de Janeiro was the undisputed political, economic, and cultural center of Brazil.

---

[6]Ralph A. Gakenheimer, "The Peruvian City of the Sixteenth Century," in Glen H. Beyer (ed.), *The Urban Explosion in Latin America*, Cornell University Press, Ithaca, N. Y., 1967, p. 50.

Policy and Traditions

The differences in ecological patterns between the North American and South American cities are frequently attributed to Spanish colonial policy as typified by the Laws of the Indies.[7] However, Leo Schnore suggests that factors more powerful than "Iberian values" were apparently at work: "The fact of the matter is that the 'traditional Latin American pattern' could be observed in cities of the New World prior to the Spanish conquest."[8] He cites historical and archeological evidence that among the pre-Colombian Aztec and Maya civilizations the elites tended to live in the centers of the great cities. According to Bishop Landa's account, first published in 1566,

> The fundamental unit of the town settlement, with its core of civic and religious buildings, is dominant in all periods and in all but the most remote and inaccessible localities. Landa's classic description of the town of Yucatan can be applied with only minor variations to most of the known archeological history within the area of high culture in Meso-America: "Before the Spaniards had conquered that country, the natives lived together in towns in a very civilized fashion. . . . In the middle of the towns were their temples with beautiful plazas, and all around the temples stood the houses of the lords and the priests, and those of the most important people. Thus came the houses of the richest and of those who were held in the highest estimation next to these, and at the outskirts of the town were the houses of the lower class.[9]

Apparently, the pattern of spatial distribution by social class was set well before the Spaniards arrived. The pattern conforms to that suggested by Gideon Sjoberg for all preindustrial cities.[10] (See Chapter 2, Emergence of Cities.)

EVOLVING PATTERNS

Before the introduction of modern transportation technology, and before industrialization contaminated central areas with its noise, noxious fumes, and congestion, the central area of the city was the most pleasant and the most convenient area. This is where the elite built their homes, frequently with extensive grounds and almost always behind high walls that effectively isolated the home from the confusion of the streets and markets outside.

The pattern of high socioeconomic status in the center has also been found in North American cities before industrialization, particularly in the old south. Heberle gives a clear account of the development of these cities:

> It seems to be characteristic for the older, smaller cities in the South that the homes of the socially prominent families were to be found just outside the central—and

---

[7]See George A. Theodorson (ed.), *Studies in Human Ecology*, Row, Peterson, Evanston, Ill., 1961, pp. 326–327.

[8]Leo F. Schnore, "On the Spatial Structure of Cities in the Two Americas," in Philip Hauser and Leo Schnore (eds.), *The Study of Urbanization*, Wiley, New York, 1965, p. 369.

[9]Quoted in Edwin M. Shook and Tatiana Proskouriakoff, "Settlement Patterns in Meso-America and the Sequency in the Guatemalan Highlands," in Gordon R. Willey (ed.), *Prehistoric Settlement Patterns in the New World*, Wenner-Gren Foundation for Anthropological Research, New York, 1956, pp. 93–100.

[10]Gideon Sjoberg, *The Preindustrial City: Past and Present*, Free Press, New York, 1960, pp. 96–98.

only—business districts. . . . As the city grew and as wealth increased, the "old" families tended to move toward the periphery—following the general fashion of our age. . . . The old homes are then converted into rooming houses and "tourist homes."[11]

A review of seven of the most prominent sociological studies of Latin American cities indicates that the "traditional" model, with its central plaza and with groups of higher socioeconomic status occupying the center rather than the suburbs, is true of all but the newest cities of Latin America.[12] According to Leo Schnore, the data suggest that the residential structure of cities evolves in a predictable direction and that this pattern is observable both in North America and, more recently, in Latin America:

> Given growth and expansion of the center, and given appropriate improvements in transportation and communication, the upper strata might be expected to shift from central to peripheral residence, and the lower classes might increasingly take up occupancy in the central area abandoned by the elite. Despite mounting land values occasioned by the competition of alternative (nonresidential) land uses, the lower strata may occupy valuable central land in tenements, subdivided dwellings originally intended for single families, and other high-density "slum" housing arrangements.[13]

"POET"

The previously discussed ecological complex of *population, organization, environment,* and *technology* (POET) helps us understand these changes. A population has to reach a certain size before highly segregated patterns of land use can be expected to develop. Sorting out people by socioeconomic status into separate neighborhoods and functional specialization can occur only when there is a large total population. The rate of growth is also significant; stagnant or slowly growing centers are not likely to resemble rapidly expanding cities. Variations in the racial and ethnic composition of a population can also affect spatial distribution, independent of economic factors. In growing cities subpopulations that are being augmented by new in-migrants can be expected to be more distinct than groups that are more socially and economically assimilated.

While the four broad factors mentioned above (POET) interact, we are most interested here in regarding social organization as being dependent on the other three. Preindustrial cities are generally segregated into homogeneous communities based upon ethnic, religious, linguistic, and tribal criteria. Anyone observing the cities of developing countries is struck by the segmented nature of urban life, with different areas remaining socially—and sometimes occupationally— isolated from one another. Organizationally, the city itself is not the operating unit; rather, the city provides an umbrella for many relatively self-contained

---

[11] Rudolf Heberle, "Social Consequences of the Industrialization of Southern Cities," *Social Forces,* October, 1940, pp. 34–35.
[12] Schnore, op. cit., p. 366.
[13] Ibid., pp. 373–374.

subsystems. Even when there are no physical walls and gates between areas of the city, there are lines of demarcation known to every resident.

Economic organization is also of great importance. The introduction of industrialization almost invariably leads to the development of separate factory districts, and the nature of industrialization determines the residential character of surrounding land. Industrialization also changes the "traditional" class system of rich and poor associated with preindustrial cities, and the growth of a middle class clearly affects the spatial distribution of residential populations within the city.

Environmental factors, such as the presence or absence of highlands or bodies of water, clearly affect the spatial development of cities. However, while unique physical features have obviously shaped the growth and development of some cities, there is a surprising degree of uniformity in spatial structure from country to country, culture to culture, and continent to continent.

Technology is the variable that has done most in recent times to change the configuration of cities. As was indicated earlier, railroads and steam power did much to produce the nineteenth-century American city. Since the 1920s the automobile has permitted a form of population dispersion that was impossible earlier. The telephone and other advances in communication technology have meant that interrelated functions can be spatially separated without loss of contact and control. In Latin American cities, the elite preempted the more central areas for their residences, since these were the most accessible sites in an era of primitive transportation technology. Technological changes—automobiles, good roads, extension of power and sewage lines—have drastically reduced the attractiveness of the central city as a place of residence. Upper-class suburbanization is now found in Latin America on the pattern of North America.

Early Social and Economic Structure

As previously noted, in colonial Latin America the pattern was one of creating deliberate dependency. Political independence from Spain and Portugal did not end economic dependency. Independence, if anything, increased the dependence of the new republics upon European powers and the United States.[14] Cities remained tied to external markets while virtually ignoring their hinterlands. Until this century geography also set limits on penetration of the interior and fostered a pattern of external dependence.

The absence of an entrepreneurial middle class stunted the economic growth of the cities. Merchants and businesspeople were looked down upon socially; for membership in the elite, one's income was expected to come from land holdings rather than manufacture or trade. As a result, the city—in contrast to cities in North America—was a political rather than an economic center:

> Political considerations and motivations, rather than economic or social, have historically controlled urbanization in Latin America. The city has, therefore, often

---

[14]Hardoy, op. cit., p. viii.

emerged as an imposition, an appendage, tucked onto a relatively underdeveloped agricultural countryside—the military centers of the Aztecs, the political centers of the Incas, the political towns of the Spaniards, the political capitals of the nineteenth century republican cities of Latin America. Not only has the city not grown out of the economic needs or in relation to the socioeconomic development of its surrounding area; it has until very recently been divorced from the national reality.[15]

The growth of the middle class in the nineteenth century, when it did occur, was due in large part to the technological changes in transportation and to immigration. The railroad and later the highway opened up new territories— territories that could be developed with the newly emerging agricultural technology. Also, in the latter years of the nineteenth century, waves of European immigrants brought about the formation of new urban institutions. Simultaneously, a new professional middle class and an urban bureaucracy began to develop.

However, this middle class, the most important group in economic growth and industrial development, usually weakened its possible influence by allying itself with the upper classes and against the urban proletariat. Upper-middle-class professional groups have often become so involved with the establishment that they cease to be a force for political change. The urban middle class, which so dominates political life in North America and Europe, still has relatively little influence on national policy in most Latin American nations.

RECENT DEVELOPMENTS

Urban Growth

The Latin American cities of today are far from the sleepy towns of the turn of the century. Urbanization in Latin America is currently proceeding at a phenomenal rate. As recently as 1950, 39 percent of the population lived in places of 20,000 or more, but this figure had risen to 50 percent in 1960. Currently Latin America is 61 percent urban.[16]

Most North Americans still think of Latin America as a basically rural continent. Certainly they don't consider it to be as urbanized as Europe, but that is in fact the case. Data compiled by the United Nations indicates that in 1970 the extent of urbanization in South America was 54 percent, or just above the figure of 53 percent for Europe (the figure for North America was 64 percent).[17] Latin American cities are growing at an annual rate of 4.5 percent a year, compared with a much slower rural growth rate of only 1.4 percent a year. Every year between 1985 and the year 2000 over 11 million new persons will live in Latin American cities, if present trends continue.

To put it another way, in 1930 Latin America had only one city of over 1 million

---

[15]James Scobie, quoted in Beyer, op. cit., p. 63.
[16]Population Reference Bureau, "1979 World Population Data Sheet," Washington, D.C., 1979.
[17]Western Europe is more heavily urbanized than Latin America; eastern Europe is less urbanized.

It is predicted that by the turn of the century Mexico City will be the most populated city on the globe. (© Paolo Koch/Rapho/Photo Researchers, Inc.)

persons (Mexico City); as of 1980 the number is twenty-six. The greatest growth has been in the very largest cities. Latin America is a continent of primate cities, with 20 percent of its population in cities of over 100,000 inhabitants.

Within the period of a lifetime, Latin America is being transformed from a rural, agriculturally oriented continent to one that is predominantly urbanized and urban-oriented. The process of urbanization, which took over a century in North America, is being compressed into a few short decades.

Figures for the entire continent, of course, cloud variations among nations. The range of urbanization in Latin American countries is great. Haiti has under 10 percent of its population in places of 20,000 or more, while Argentina, Chile, Venezuela, and Uruguay are among the most urbanized nations in the world. At 83 percent, Uruguay is the most highly urbanized; half its population lives in the capital city of Montevideo.

The complex and rapid growth of Latin American cities has not been accompanied to date by equal growth in industrialization. Because European and North American countries with equal levels of urbanization have much higher indexes of industrialization—such as per capita consumption of energy, percent of the labor force in nonagricultural employment, level of education, and per capita income—it is sometimes maintained that Latin America is "overurbanized" for a developing region.

Taken as a whole, Latin America is considerably more urbanized than other third world regions. It is far more urbanized than Asia and Africa, and during the

1950s it surpassed all regions except Oceania (Australia, etc.) in both rate of growth and size of the urban increment to the population.[18] The rate of growth is now probably higher in African cities, but the urban population explosion in Latin America has not slowed. Latin American cities, and particularly the largest primate cities, are growing at a rate that considerably outpaces their ability to provide urban services and employment.

The explosive growth of the cities comes from two sources. The first is natural increase. Cities in Latin America currently have low death rates, owing to the utilization of modern programs of public health, sanitation, and vaccination. Birthrates, while decreasing, are still high, leading to a natural increase of urban population.

The second source of growth is in-migration from rural areas. The contribution of migration varies from country to country, but it accounts for as much as half the urban growth in countries such as Brazil and Venezuela.[19] In spite of out-migration to the cities, rural populations are still increasing, and the rural economy simply cannot support the increased numbers. Rural industrialization is further decreasing the number of farm laborers required.

As has been noted before, rural dwellers are often more pushed from the land than drawn to the cities by opportunities for employment. Rural unemployment is simply being transferred to the cities. The annual increase in the rural population of Latin America is such that each year jobs on the land should be found for over half a million new workers.[20] The chance of finding employment for so many workers in the already overloaded agricultural sector is, however, minimal. There is already a considerable surplus in the rural labor force. According to one expert:

> Under-employment in Latin American agriculture is so evident to anyone with first-hand knowledge of the agrarian situation that it is difficult to take seriously the academic debates about whether or not it exists. The CIDA studies showed that, by any common-sense definition of under-employment, from one-fifth to over one-third of the workers in Latin American agriculture are practically surplus.[21]

Economically, it probably does not make sense to try to hold the peasants in the country or in small towns. It is sometimes argued that if rural life can be made more attractive, people will be less likely to abandon rural areas for the opportunities and advantages of the city. However, the costs of modernizing the rural sector are prohibitively high, particularly when the cities also need modernization. Rural electrification, for example, is far more expensive than providing electricity for urban slum dwellers. The same amount of money can do more for more people if it is spent in the city than if it is spent in the country. Because funds are limited, "community development" is more effectively directed

[18] John D. Durand and Cesar A. Pelaez, "Patterns of Urbanization in Latin America," in Gerald Breese, *The City in Newly Developing Countries*, Prentice-Hall, Englewood Cliffs, N. J., 1969, p. 184.

[19] Louis J. Ducoff, "The Role of Migration in the Demographic Development of Latin America," *Milbank Memorial Fund Quarterly*, 43:203, October, 1965.

[20] *Estudio Economico para America Latina*, ECLA, United Nations, 1966, pp. 41–51.

[21] Solon L. Barraclough, "Rural Development and Employment Prospects in Latin America," in Arthur J. Field (ed.), *City and Country in the Third World*, Schenkman, Cambridge, Mass., 1970, p. 106.

toward urban populations, who by their very presence in the city have already indicated a willingness to make the changes required by the modernization process.

Characteristics of Urban Inhabitants

Latin America is typical of the third world in that half or more of the inhabitants of its largest cities are migrants from elsewhere. According to the Colombian census, half the inhabitants of Bogota and two-fifths of the inhabitants of other cities are in-migrants.[22] Half the residents of Santiago are in-migrants. In Latin America, migration to cities tends to be more permanent and less seasonal than in other developing regions.[23] The city-bound migrants, like those elsewhere in the world, tend to be largely young adults. Older people are less prone to leave villages or rural areas for the opportunities and bright lights of the city.

This heavy migration of young persons, plus the population explosion—which, of course, adds only young people to the population—means that there are proportionately few people over the age of forty in the urban population. The impression of outsiders that "everyone seems so young" is borne out by the empirical data: some 42 percent of the Latin American population is under fifteen years of age. This pattern will change somewhat as birthrates drop.

In Latin America, the pattern of sex distribution in urban areas differs from that of other developing regions. Most developing countries have an excess of males over females; Latin America has more females than males. In this respect, it is more similar to economically developed western areas. While there is general agreement that there are more females, there is no agreement why this is the case. Perhaps the greater degree of urbanization and economic development in Latin America, compared with developing countries elsewhere in the world, accounts for the difference.

Squatter Settlements

Squatter slums ring all the great cities of Latin America, but there is no universally accepted view of this phenomenon. Some observers emphasize the squalor and disorganization of the squatter settlements (this is the majority view); some argue that these settlements are in effect evolving into reasonable low-income suburban housing areas (this is the minority position). Frequently, it seems that what a writer describes is not shaped as much by what he or she sees as by the writer's philosophy and political beliefs. There is no unanimity, as the next pages will indicate.

What is agreed upon is that the peripheral slums grow like mushrooms (in Chile they are called *poblaciones callampas*, which means "mushrooms") because of the population explosion and the migration of peasants from the land

---

[22]"Some Regional Development Problems in Latin America Linked to Metropolitanization," *Economic Bulletin for Latin America,* United Nations, New York, 1972, p. 70.
[23]Philip M. Hauser (ed.), *Urbanization in Latin America,* UNESCO, Paris, 1961, p. 45.

These squatters in Rio de Janeiro at least are compensated by a magnificent view of the city and mountains behind. (Hans Mann/Monkmeyer.)

in search of a better life. For instance, the total population of Lima was estimated to be 4,994,788 persons as of 1975, of which 1,217,700—24.3 percent—lived in *barriadas*.[24] In Caracas, the capital of Venezuela, over 35 percent of the total metropolitan popluation is living in squatter settlements, while in Bogota, Colombia, more than half the population lives in neighborhoods still considered

[24]Estimates from Peruvian national figures, 1970.

"clandestine" by officials. Over one-third of Mexico City's inhabitants live in slums and squatter settlements, many in the aptly named "lost cities" surrounding Mexico City.

In spite of sporadic resettlement programs, it is clear that shantytown squatter settlements will be part of the Latin American urban scene for the foreseeable future. As long as the urban population continues to increase because of high birthrates and migration to the cities, the cities will continue to add more people than they can house. The Peruvian government has been more candid than most in admitting that it is unable to reduce the urban housing deficit because public investment must be directed toward developing national objectives, but the situation elsewhere is similar.

Social upheavals and mob violence are likely to become more common in marginal settlements. Clashes between squatters and police appear inevitable in places such as Mexico City, where landlords, as land prices escalate, increasingly attempt to evict squatters who previously were ignored. Leftist attempts to organize the vast but largely still silent urban proletariat have had some limited success. But in-migrant squatters and slum dwellers, in contrast to better-off university students, are generally more interested in day-to-day survival than Marxist theory.

For the future, an undercurrent of resentment and the seeds of social conflict are being sown by governments whose policies continue to favor the "haves" over the "have-nots." Urban guerrilla movements should become more common during the 1980s.

Settlements as Squalor. A description of daily life in squatter shantytowns is provided by the supposed diary of a dweller in a *favela* outside São Paulo, Brazil (there is some doubt about its authenticity). The following are excerpts from her diary for one day in July:

> July 16 I got up. . . . I went to get the water. I made coffee. I told the children that I didn't have any bread, that they would have to drink their coffee plain and eat meat with *farinha*. I was feeling ill and decided to cure myself. I stuck my finger down my throat twice, vomited, and knew I was under the evil eye. The upset feeling left and I went to Senor Manuel, carrying some cans to sell. Everything that I find in the garbage I sell. He gave me 13 cruzeiros. I kept thinking that I had to buy bread, soap, and milk for Vera Eunice. The 13 cruzeiros wouldn't make it. I returned home, or rather to my shack, nervous and exhausted. I thought of the worrisome life that I led. Carrying paper, washing clothes for the children, staying in the street all day long. Yet I'm always lacking things, Vera doesn't have shoes and she doesn't like to go barefoot. For at least two years I've wanted to buy a meat grinder. And a sewing machine.[25]

The picture conjured up by such accounts is one of fecund, festering slums filled with dirty shacks and having no sanitary facilities, no garbage collection, and no hope of improvement.

One graphic account describes the notorious *barridas* of Lima as:

> . . . so bestial, so filthy, so congested, so empty of light, fun, color, health, or comfort, so littered with excrement and garbage, so swarming with barefoot children, so reeking of pitiful squalor that just the breath of it makes you retch.[26]

A former official of the United Nations has described squatter settlements as a "spreading malady" and "plague" of "excessive squalor, filth, and poverty, fostering mounting social disorder and tension."[27]

Squatter Settlements as Transitional Settlements. On the other hand, John Turner suggests that while there is some truth in the conventional image, and while some inhabitants of squatter settlements are indeed wretchedly poor, there are "many squatter settlements that are socially developing and physically self-improving suburbs rather than slums.[28] William Mangin's description of the same areas surrounding Lima, described above as "bestial" and "filthy" is far more optimistic.

> At worst a *barriada* is a crowded, helter-skelter hodge-podge of inadequate straw houses with no water supply and no provision for sewage disposal; parts of many are like this. Most do have a rough plan, and most inhabitants convert their original houses to more substantial structures as soon as they can. Construction activity usually involving family, neighbors, and friends is a constant feature of *barriada* life and, although water and sewage usually remain critical problems, a livable situation is reached with respect to them.
>
> For most of the migrants the *barriada* represents a definite improvement in terms of housing and general income, and Lima represents an improvement over the semi-feudal life of the Indian, *cholo,* or lower-class mestizo.[29]

Subgroups. In generalizing it has to be remembered that squatter settlements differ markedly not only in their physical appearance but in the subgroups inhabiting them. Some settlements are disorganized and crime-ridden; others, usually those which have existed longer, are highly organized "slums of hope."

Contrary to conventional assumptions, not all squatters own their own shacks. As areas become more settled, the proportion of squatter renters often increases. Charles Abrams has noted several squatter types.[30] On the basis of his analysis, we can identify the following subgroups:

1. *Owner squatters* are the "typical" squatters who own their own shack, but not the land on which it stands.

[26]James Morris, *Cities,* Harcourt Brace Jovanovich, New York, 1964, p. 227.

[27]Morris Juppenlaty, *Cities in Transformation: The Urban Squatter Problem in the Developing World,* University of Queensland Press, Australia, 1970.

[28]John F. C. Turner, "Squatter Settlements in Developing Countries," in Daniel P. Moynihan (ed.), *Toward a National Urban Policy,* Basic Books, New York, 1970, pp. 256–257.

[29]William P. Mangin, "Mental Health and Migration to Cities: A Peruvian Case," *Annals of New York Academy of Sciences,* 84:911–917, 1960.

[30]Charles Abrams, "Squatting and Squatters," in Janet Abu-Lughod and Richard Hay, Jr., (eds.), *Third World Urbanization,* Maaroufa Press, Chicago, 1977, pp. 297–298.

2. *Squatter tenants* are new in-migrants who pay rent to another squatter. Landlord's profits are often considerable, since landlords pay no taxes or upkeep.
3. *Speculator squatters* see holding property as a way to make a profit. They view squatting as a sound business venture, expecting eventually to obtain title to the land.
4. *Store or business squatters* open businesses, catering to the needs of other squatters. They often live on the premises. Most are marginal operators; but some, in the absence of rents or taxes, make substantial profits.
5. *Semisquatters* build their huts on private land but eventually come to some sort of terms with the owner. Strictly speaking, semisquatters are perhaps better classified as tenants.

A casual observer, however, is unlikely to be conscious of these differences. While all squatter settlements have in common the fact that dwellers don't own their own land, and most are terribly poor and without municipal amenities, it has to be remembered that settlements differ in condition, services, and social composition. Some are self-upgrading communities; many are horrendous.

Urban Adjustment. Authorities differ when discussing the lives lived by the inhabitants of shantytowns. One view is that these inhabitants are set apart from the other city residents not only by their poverty but by their traditional rural orientation. Their rural backgrounds and continued rural ties mean that they remain essentially peasants, but peasants who by force of circumstance live in what is defined as an "urban" area. They are in but not of the city. The implicit, if not explicit, assumption here is that the problem is how to integrate these nonurban people into a complex modern economic system.

A second position is that the rural character of the immigrants is considerably overemphasized, and that problems of adjustment are far less severe than is commonly supposed.

The view of the city as a disorganizing force is part of an intellectual tradition going back to the "Chicago school" of sociology and its concern with problems of assimilating immigrants into the inner-city slums of North America.

Louis Wirth—as you recall from Chapter 6—defines "urbanism" as the mode of life of people who live in cities and are subject to their influences. These influences, it is said, act to destroy primary groups, weaken family ties, loosen the bonds of kinship, and lessen neighborliness. The result is impersonality, superficiality, anonymity in personal relations, and the substitution of large secondary organizations for the declining role played by kith and kin. Disruption of family life, rejection of traditional religion, delinquency and alienation among the young, and a generally fragmented social world were some of the consequences associated with life in the slums of North American industrial cities. The newcomers—whether Irish, Italian, Polish, Jewish, or black—went through a period of disorganization in which old ways were shed and new urban ways were acquired. The move to the city was frequently not easy. Many families and individuals were not able to withstand the emotional as well as physical wrenching and tearing.

Sociologists such as Wilbert Moore and Philip Hauser in their various writings—in particular, those done for the United Nations—have suggested that urban newcomers in the third world are in similar circumstances.[31] The general position is that urban migrants find themselves in a marginal position in the city. Economically, they almost always enter the labor force at the bottom, and here they are in competition with thousands of others possessing the same low level of skills. More important, the migrants are socially cut off from others not only by lack of a job but by clothes, language, and customs. Emotional stress is built into a situation where the migrants must decide which traditional practices to preserve and which to discard. Moreover, they are provided with few criteria for making such decisions. The resulting tension and strain are considered to be associated with antisocial behavior such as alcoholism, crime, drug addiction, and mental illness.[32]

The family is also modified severely by urban life, according to this view. Customarily, it is claimed that there is an inevitable deterioration and disruption of traditional family life and a continual erosion of control by the family over individual members.[33]

Politically, slum dwellers are said to sell their vote to whoever delivers the greatest favors. The whole electoral process is said to be so remote from their lives that they are unlikely to perceive constitutionalism as a whole as having any relevance to them. Their lives are so close to the edge of disaster that gradualist and abstract orientations toward the future are not likely to develop.[34] According to this view, in-migrant slum dwellers are ruralities awash in an urban sea—and they don't swim very well. When they can pick up work, they work; when they can't, they hustle, beg, or steal. While they dream of success, their real goal is simply to get by for another day.

Culture of Poverty. A different view, stressing the nonintegration of the poor into the major institutions of society but denying that newcomers are disorganized, was developed by the late social anthropologist Oscar Lewis. While accepting the cultural distinctiveness of the *favela* and barrio populations, Lewis took issue with the generalization that these squatters and recent arrivals from the country had the same characteristics—personal isolation and social disorganization—that were associated with newly arrived North American slum dwellers. Lewis's studies described a "culture of poverty," with the poor having a provincial, locally oriented culture, whether they live in the country or in the city. Being severely deprived, slum dwellers have little ability to defer gratification, are strongly

[31]See Bert F. Hoselitz and Wilber E. Moore (eds.), *Industrialization and Society*, UNESCO, Mouton, Paris, 1963; and Hauser, op. cit.

[32]Wilbert E. Moore, "Industrialization and Social Change," in Bert F. Hoselitz and Wilbert E. Moore, op. cit., p. 343.

[33]For a summary emphasizing the negative effects of urban life on the individual and the family, see Gerald Breese, *Urbanization in Newly Developing Countries*. Prentice-Hall, Englewood Cliffs, N. J., 1966, pp. 86–90.

[34]See Daniel Goldrich, "Toward the Comparative Study of Politicalization in Latin America," in D. Heath and R. N. Adams (eds.), *The Contemporary Cultures and Societies in Latin America*, Random House, New York, 1965, p. 369.

oriented to the present, and exhibit fatalism and resignation. Physically, they live in the urban area, but actually they are "enclaves within the city," isolated from the larger society.[35]

The idea of a "culture of poverty" with a strong orientation to the present rather than to the future is said to explain why even slum dwellers who strike it rich by winning national lotteries seldom remain well off. Rather than invest their windfall conservatively to provide for the future, they frequently spend it to live like kings until it is gone, and then return to life in the shanty slum.

Describing his own research in Mexico City, Lewis summarized his findings as follows:

1. Peasants in Mexico City adapted to city life with far greater ease than one would have expected judging from comparable studies in the United States and from folk-urban theory.
2. Family life remained quite stable and extended family ties increased rather than decreased.
3. Religious life became more Catholic and disciplined, indicating the reverse of the anticipated secularization process.
4. The system of *Compadrazgo* [close ties between a child's natural father and the child's godfather] continued to be strong, albeit with some modifications.
5. The use of village remedies and beliefs persisted.[36]

Testing these findings several years later in an inner-city slum area only a short walk from the central square of Mexico City, Lewis found support for his earlier conclusions. Lower-class residents showed much less personal isolation or anonymity than one would expect on the basis of the common North American model. People moved their residences only within a very restricted area. Lifetime friendships and day-to-day contact with the same people were common. A high proportion of the residents of any particular housing settlement were related by ties of kinship or friendship. Extended family ties were strong, particularly in emergencies, and most marriages occurred within the neighborhood unit.

The *vecindad,* or housing settlement, acted as a shock absorber for new rural in-migrants "because of the similarity between its culture and that of rural communities."[37] The family structure, diet, dress, and systems of belief differed little between people of rural origins and those of urban origins:

> The use of herbs for curing, the raising of animals, the belief in sorcery, and spiritualism, the celebration of the Day of the Dead, illiteracy and low level of education, political apathy and cynicism about government, and the very limited membership and participation in both formal and informal associations were just as common among persons who had been in the city for over thirty years as among recent arrivals.[38]

[35]Oscar Lewis, "Urbanization Without Breakdown: A Case Study," *The Scientific Monthly,* **75:**31–41, 1952; and Oscar Lewis, "The Culture of Poverty," *Scientific American,* **215**(4):19–25, 1966.
[36]Oscar Lewis, "The Folk-Urban Ideal Types," in Philip Hauser and Leo Schnore, *The Study of Urbanization,* Wiley, New York, 1965, pp. 494–495.
[37]Lewis, in Hauser and Schnore, op. cit., pp. 495–496.
[38]Ibid.

Thus, in Lewis's view, the urban-born and the rural-born slum dwellers share a common culture of poverty. One researcher has said that *barriada* residents "differ from the rest of the urban population more in the degree of their poverty than in their origins."[39]

Criticisms of the Culture of Poverty. Critics such as Charles Valentine content that traits of the so-called "culture of poverty"—such as unemployment, lack of education, consensual marriage, low aspirations, and hostility toward authority—are structural rather than cultural.[40] Other traits, such as child-raising practices and illegitimacy, may be cultural or may be attempts to carry out the goals of the larger society within the severe limitations of poverty.

Other researchers insist that the culture of the squatter slum dwellers is not rural at all, but essentially urban in its adaptation to the confusion, inequality, and lack of opportunity they experience in the city at large. Such researchers explicitly reject concepts such as "the culture of poverty." For example, on the basis of their work in Rio de Janeiro and Lima, Anthony and Elizabeth Leeds are extremely critical of what they refer to as the "myth of urban rurality." They maintain that the rural migration into the cities is not simply a movement of primitive peasant farmers. Rather, the in-migrants include people who have lived in large towns and villages, who have been in the army, who have worked abroad, and who have skills, trades, and experience in providing personal services which are needed in the city. The Leedses suspect that many of the so-called "rural values," including things such as "peasant shrewdness," also have considerable utility in an urban setting. They reject any explanations which assume that rural values persist unchanged:

> Interviews with the few people we identified as having come specifically from rural village areas of Brazil or Portugal directly contradict these assumptions more often than they confirm them. In a number of cases, the person in question appears to have adapted exceedingly rapidly to the urban and favela ambivalence and grasped vigorously what it offered. Thus, for example, the "rural" president of one favela association who had gotten training in electrical work, plumbing, and other construction skills had carried out a clever embezzlement once in office and stayed in a full term to boot, and had invested in land in the State of Rio De Janeiro where land values are appreciating rapidly.[41]

Four factors are said to operate in the selection of persons out of the total population to live in *favelas:* (1) true marginality, (2) stress, (3) economizing, and (4) taste.[42] "True marginality" refers to situations in which persons are unable to manage in the legal or, in some cases, the illegal economy of the city. Particularly

[39]Andrew C. Frank, "Urban Poverty in Latin America," *Studies in Comparative International Development,* 2:76, 1966.
[40]Charles A. Valentine, *Culture of Poverty: Critique and Counter-Proposals,* University of Chicago Press, Chicago, 1968.
[41]Anthony Leeds and Elizabeth Leeds, "Brazil and the Myth of Urban Rurality: Urban Experience, Work, and Values in 'Squatments' of Rio de Janeiro and Lima," in Arthur J. Field (ed.), *City and Country in the Third World,* Schenkman, Cambridge, Mass., 1970, p. 233.
[42]Ibid., p. 243.

in times of economic recession, those who are marginal to the labor supply find that they cannot get work. Robbery and thefts increase at such times, but not everyone can be successful even as a criminal. Some people are only able to survive somehow by begging and handouts.

"Stress" refers to situations resembling true marginality but in which the person involved is better able to manage because of greater internal or external resources. However, unpredictable situations such as loss of a job, the loss of the breadwinner, or prolonged sickness can put a family in a serious bind.

"Economizing" refers to situations in which stable but limited resources have to be spread to take care of many needs. In order to achieve a goal such as moving oneself or one's children up the socioeconomic scale, the decision may be made to remain in a squatter shack (paying no rent or taxes) and to save one's money for other uses. Money can thus be saved, or even invested, rather than being eaten up by housing costs. In the *favela* it is also possible to raise garden vegetables and even some chickens. This pattern of economizing is part of the family history of the European immigrant groups who settled North America.

Finally, "taste" refers to the situation in which someone simply prefers to live in a squatter settlement. The squatter settlement may be preferred because it is a place where one can be comfortable and free from the stresses of middle-class life. For example, a man with a common-law wife or wives may prefer not to live in an area where there would be social pressures. Also, those engaged in marginal occupations such as prostitution or petty crime find the *favela* more hospitable than other areas of the city. Finally, people who would be nobodies elsewhere in the city might prefer to remain in a slum where they can have some importance.

Leeds and Leeds provide a useful counterweight to the more common view of the squatter slum as continuing an essentially rural cultural pattern. However, they do tend to glorify squatter settlements somewhat and to overstress the urban character of their inhabitants.

As the differences of opinion noted above indicate, the squatter settlement, like North American suburbs, can be many things to many people. Descriptions of such areas are probably most useful if viewed as logical constructs in which certain characteristics of an area (poverty, for instance) can be emphasized in order to compare and contrast the ideal construct with an actual existing locality.

In Conclusion: Squatter Settlements. There is little question that the move from the country to the city has a considerable impact upon the migrant's way of life. However, what strikes many observers living in developing countries is not the difficulty of the adjustment to urban life, but rather the speed and facility with which the rural migrant becomes a city slicker. It is easy to forget that the urban dwellers with whom we are comparing the new migrant were quite likely migrants themselves. Half the population of many Latin American cities were originally migrants, and this figure is higher for many African and Asian cities. Within a few months of his or her arrival, it is often very difficult to tell the migrant from someone who has spent years in the city. A balanced picture must include both the problems, adjustments, and disorientation confronting the migrant and the reasonably successful adjustment most migrants make to their new surroundings.

A more serious question is how the squatter or slum dweller, after the initial period of adjustment, will respond to his or her relative deprivation, compared with affluent city dwellers. Will the slum dweller accept semipermanent poverty? Recent events suggest not. During the 1980s internal upheavals and revolutions, possibly led by charismatic leaders who can direct aggression toward unpopular scapegoats, will in all likelihood become more common.

17

AFRICAN AND MIDDLE EASTERN URBANIZATION

There is always something new out of Africa.

Pliny the Younger (A.D. 62–113)

AFRICA

Africa is currently the least urbanized of the continents. As of 1980, only one out of four people in Africa 25 percent—lived in urban places. At the same time, however, Africa is the continent with the highest rate of increase in urban population (4.9 percent).[1] Some African cities are growing even more rapidly, with yearly population increases of 10 or more percent—growth rates that would severely tax the capabilities of even the most economically advanced countries.

The population of the continent as a whole, which is estimated to be 457 million, is increasing at an overall rate of 2.9 percent a year—up from 2.6 percent a decade earlier.[2]

This overall rate—although it is only three-fifths of the rate of increase in the cities alone—is still sufficient to double the population of the continent by the year 2000. The rate of increase is this high because birthrates are among the highest in the world while death rates (although still high) are falling. As death rates continue to decline faster than birthrates, it is quite likely that Africa's rate of natural increase will go up rather than decline. Currently, only Latin America—which has high birthrates and already low death rates—shows a higher rate of natural increase. Family-planning programs are still minuscule in sub-Saharan Africa, with the exception of Ghana and Kenya. Existing programs are small and poorly funded, since population growth is still not seen by most governments as an important factor in economic development. More visible economic development projects are given a higher priority than population control. Indeed, a few African nations still have official policies encouraging more rapid population growth.

Regional Variations

Africa has some fifty separate nations, and African cities vary greatly; the major regional distinction is between the cities of north Africa and those of sub-Saharan Africa. North Africa is the most urbanized of the African regions. All the countries bordering the Mediterranean Sea have between two-fifths and three-fifths of their population in places of 20,000 or more inhabitants. This is not at all surprising when one considers the great civilizations this region has produced and its superior location for the development of trade centers. Also, away from the coast much of the land of north Africa is either mountainous or arid desert and hardly suited for urban growth (the Nile Valley being the obvious exception). Thus the population is highly concentrated in a limited area.

West and central Africa lie in the middle range of African urbanization—ranging between 4 percent in Upper Volta to 40 percent in the Peoples' Republic of the Congo. (By world standards those would be considered low levels of urbanization.) The larger cities are located along, or within easy access to, the

---

[1] *The World Population Situation in 1970,* United Nations, New York, 1971, p. 65.
[2] *Demographic Handbook for Africa,* United Nations Economic Commission for Africa, Addis Ababa, 1971, p. 12; and Population Reference Bureau, *1979 World Population Data Sheet,* Washington, D.C., 1979.

coast. Their founding and development can almost always be tied to their role as colonial entreport cities. Of the west African countries, oil-rich Nigeria is the largest and has by far the most cities.

East Africa is the least urbanized part of the continent.[3] It does not have a tradition of cities: only Zimbabwe (Rhodesia) and Zambia has as much as one-eighth of their populations in cities over 20,000. Tanzania, for example, has roughly 7 percent of its population in cities, and only 2½ percent in cities of 100,000 or more—in this case, the capital city of Dar es Salaam.

It should be noted that virtually none of what can be said regarding the rest of sub-Saharan Africa applies to white-ruled southern Africa. The Republic of South Africa is easily the most industrialized nation on the continent, with nearly half (48 percent) of its population in urban places. In terms of economic position South Africa, with its gold reserves and industrial base, is a world economic power.[4] In South African cities the government policy of *apartheid,* or forced racial segregation, has resulted in a conscious division of the major cities into African, European, Indian, and "Coloured" (mixed-race) areas. Each of the populations is allotted specific areas in which, and only in which, they can purchase property. For South Africa, race overrides all other criteria in determining the spatial development of the city.[5]

Early Cities

One sometimes hears a great deal of nonsense about African cities before the nineteenth-century colonial period. Until a decade or two ago, a reading of the literature gave the impression that there were few, if any, indigenous African cities south of the Sahara. This was due partially to a colonial mentality which did not admit the possibility that "backward natives" were capable of building cities, and partially due to a lack of serious research on African history.

Scholars from Muslim Africa also have been prone to minimize the contributions of black Africa. For instance, one writer suggests that "historic (or ancient) capitals are confined to Arab Africa" and "Native" (or Medieval) capitals are in fact a transition between the historical and colonial capitals. . . . Culturally, they are universally associated in one way or another with intrusive, alien influences, mainly Arab and generally Asian."[6]

More recently, the pendulum has been swinging in the opposite direction. Trading centers such as Timbuktu (whose current population is approximately 6,000) have been elevated to the status of major metropolises, a position they occupied for only relatively short periods of time, if at all. One the other hand the region did produce cities, some of which had considerable importance, especially during the Ghana, Mali, and Songhay empires of west Africa (roughly the eleventh to late sixteenth centuries after Christ).

[3]Edward Soja, "Spatial Inequality in Africa," *Comparative Urbanization Studies,* University of California School of Architecture and Urban Planning, Los Angeles, 1976.
[4]Lutz Holzner, "Urbanism in Southern Africa," *Geogorum,* **4:**75–90, 1970.
[5]Leo Kuper, Hilstan Watts, and Ronald Davies, *Durban: A Study in Racial Ecology,* Jonathan Cape, London, 1958.
[6]G. Hamdan, "Capitals of the New Africa," *Economic Geography,* **40:**239–241, July, 1964.

Of all African cities, those of north Africa have the longest urban traditions. Alexandria was founded by its namesake, Alexander the Great, in 332 B.C., but settlements on that location go back at least another 1,000 years. The north African city of Carthage, until it was destroyed, was the greatest rival of Rome. During the height of the Roman Empire, north Africa was dotted with important cities, some of which may have contained as much as 25 percent of the population of their regions.[7] With the decline of the Roman Empire these cities suffered the same fate as Roman cities in Europe. Over time, most of them disappeared—although, again as in Europe, newer cities now sometimes sit over the ancient ruins.

Elsewhere in Africa, many cities were first built during the peak of Muslim power. The revival of trade in the tenth century benefited not only north African cities such as Fez and Algiers but also sub-Saharan towns, including Kano in northern Nigeria. The Yoruba towns of southwest Nigeria also emerged at about this time, as did caravan centers such as Timbuktu. During the following centuries a number of primarily west African kingdoms created capitals, but most of these capitals had short histories. Segou in Mali, Labe in Guinea, Zinder in Niger, and Kumasi in Ghana all rose and fell. These cities served their kingdoms primarily as market and trade centers.

Then as now, east African cities were less numerous, with only a few Muslim towns, found generally along the coast of the Indian Ocean. Present cities such as Mogadishu in Somalia and Mombasa in Kenya prospered as Muslim trading centers. These towns served almost until the present century as centers for the trading in goods, and slaves from the interior, for shipment to Arabia.

The Colonial Period

European Influence. During the sixteenth century, the Portuguese founded the first European settlements, which were little more than fortified trading posts where goods from the interior could be collected and stored for shipment to Europe. Attempts by the Portuguese to extend their influence inland were unsuccessful. Their early successes in Ethiopia, for example, were short-lived, and Portuguese missionaries and traders were later expelled from that country.

Until the late nineteenth century, Europeans showed little interest in colonization. Cape Town in the Republic of South Africa, for example, was established by the Dutch East India Company only as a station to provide meat, fresh produce, and water to the Dutch ships on the way to the Indies.[8]

The seizure of land in black Africa by Europeans accelerated during the last quarter of the nineteenth century. Britain, France, Germany, Belgium, and Portugal all rushed in to carve up the continent into colonies. The important African cities of the present are largely the products of this colonialism, since each colony had to have an administrative capital. The major cities, founded during the colonial

[7]William A. Hance, *Population, Migration, and Urbanization in Africa,* Columbia University Press, New York, 1970, p. 211.
[8]H. M. Robertson, *South Africa,* Cambridge University Press, London, 1957, pp. 3–4.

Even a decade ago, when this photograph was taken, Government Square in Nairobi, Kenya, presented an ultramodern appearance. The circular building is that ever-present symbol of western influence, the Hilton Hotel. (Editorial Photocolor Archives.)

period, with the dates of their founding, are: Accra, Ghana (1876); Abidjan, Ivory Coast (1903); Port Harcourt, Nigeria (1912); Brazzaville, Congo (1883); Kinshasa, Zaire (formerly Leopoldville, Belgian Congo) (1881); Yaounde, Cameroon (1889); Kampala, Uganda (1890); Nairobi, Kenya (1899); and Johannesburg, South Africa (1886). Of the major new towns founded during this period, only Addis Ababa in Ethiopia (1886) and Omdurman in Sudan (1885) were indigenous creations.

Most of the cities of Africa are in actuality far newer than the dates mentioned above would indicate, for rapid increases in the populations of sub-Saharan African cities did not begin until a little over thirty years ago. Until World War II, most African cities were relatively small. Nairobi, one of the most pleasant of all African cities, had a population of only 20,000 in 1920 and only 33,000 in 1930. The population jumped to 200,000 in the 1950s, and today it is in excess of 1 million. The pattern is similar, and in many cases even more spectacular, in other African cities. Kinshasa, for instance, has tripled its population in the last two decades. In spite of these increases, Africa still remains—as has been noted—the least urbanized of the world's major regions.

Colonial Cities. The colonial cities founded by Europeans did not grow out of the local culture. Rather, the layout of the city, its social and political organization, and even its architectural styles came from Europe. The government housing in Accra, Ghana, with its wide lawns and large single-family houses, looks like nothing so much as Victoria England. The centers of colonial cities were for the use and residence of Europeans. Nighttime curfews frequently prevented the entry of Africans into the European sections, and the entry of Europeans into the African sections.

The colonial city was organized around the central business district, which in addition to stores and other business offices also included the administrative offices of the colonial government. Streets were usually wide and crossed at right angles in a grid pattern. A description of Stanleyville (now Kisangani) is typical:

> The physical layout of the town could be seen as both an expression and a symbol of the relations between Africans and Europeans. European residential areas were situated close to, and tended to run into, the area of administrative offices, hotels, shops, and other service establishments, while African residential areas were strictly demarcated and well removed from the town centre.[9]

Spatial location thus reflected social power within colonial society.[10] Without significant industrialization, central residence was preferred. Africans who worked in the European center were in effect commuters from suburban locations—although, in this case, the suburbs were high-density indigenous communities. This is, of course, the complete reverse of the pattern in American industrial cities.

Indigenous Cities. Indigenous cities often were located next to colonial developments, but in other cases they were almost completely separate developments. In west Africa the most noted cities of strictly African origin are the Yoruba cities of Nigeria. Many of these cities have fairly large populations, although there is a continuing scholarly debate whether these were and are true cities or extremely large agglomerations of basically agricultural villages. These are referred to in the literature as "rural cities," "city villages," or "agrotowns." In any case, the Yoruba cities had the largest populations in sub-Saharan Africa before the colonial period. Ibidan as of 1850 had roughly 70,000 inhabitants; the Nigerian census for 1963 showed ten Yoruba towns with populations exceeding 100,000. In east Africa many of the functions of towns, such as markets, took place at permanent sites—although residence was not one of the functions.[11]

Ecologically indigenous cities are not as sharply differentiated as western

[9]V. G. Pons, cited by A. L. Epstein, "Urbanization and Social Change in Africa," *Current Anthropology*, 8:(4)277, 1967.
[10]Goeffrey K. Payne, *Urban Housing in the Third World*, Routledge & Kagan Paul, Boston, 1977, p. 53.
[11]D. R. F. Taylor, "The Concept of Invisible Towns and Spatial Organization in East Africa," *Comparative Urban Research*, 5:44–70, 1978.

cities. In the indigenous city the main focus was and is the central market, which is commonly quite large and frequently out of doors rather than housed in buildings. Nearby are the quarters of the chief or ruling prince. The main mosque is also centrally located in Muslim cities. Historically, surrounding this central core were the quarters of the lesser chiefs and nobles. These areas contained not only the nobles but also their retainers, soldiers, and followers. Each quarter was a self-contained city within the larger city. Much of this legacy persists today in cities such as Addis Ababa.

Frequently, quarters are divided on the basis of tribal or religious affiliation. Walls and gates sometimes separate the quarters from one another. Within a quarter, there was no overall plan or scheme. Streets wind in an irregular pattern and are suitable only for walking or animal traffic, since the lanes are narrow and buildings come right up to the passageway. Structures are rarely more than two stories high and are constructed of local materials. Congestion is common and sanitation facilities are minimal.

As these indigenous towns came under the control of colonial powers, a new administrative area on the European style was frequently appended to the periphery of the old city, and a major road or two would be cut through the old city to connect its center with the offices of the colonial administrators. Rarely did the indigenous city and the colonial city blend. Each was a separate entity; and though existing side by side, they frequently even followed different laws, with western legal systems applying only in the European quarters. In time, the European quarters expanded to include modern commercial and business districts. In a few cases, the modern city came to completely surround the old city. The Casbah in Algiers, for example, has long been completely enclosed by a modern city largely created by the French. Rail lines went only into the European quarter.

Contemporary Patterns

At the time of independence (in the majority of cases the 1960s) the political, administrative, commercial, and industrial centers of the new nations were centered in the old colonial city, now the new capital. These cities, with a local elite replacing the Europeans, have retained much of their orientation toward the outside world rather than their own hinterlands.

Primate Cities. The term "primate city" is clearly appropriate to the pattern of urbanization found in the independent black nations of sub-Saharan Africa. The cities—and most particularly the capital cities—are the dominant economic force, the seats of government, the cultural centers, and the hubs of transportation and communication networks. The primate city is the manufacturing center, the break-of-bulk transportation node, the major market, and the financial center.

The dominance of the primate cities is easy to document. Dakar, which has only 16 percent of the population of Senegal, consumes 95 percent of all the

A Case Study of One Indigenous City

Indigenous cities are most common in north and west Africa. In east Africa the most notable indigenous city is Addis Ababa, Ethiopia. Although founded in 1886 at the height of European colonial expansion, the city was an authentically African creation.[*]

Addis Ababa (the name means "new flower") was not originally intended to be a permanent city. Rather, it was founded by Emperor Menelik II as a temporary capital. Having no urban tradition, the Ehtiopian emperors moved their capital from time to time as military factors, weather, or exhaustion of local resources (food and firewood) dictated. Addis Ababa—which was Menelik's eighth capital—was laid out as an armed camp. The emperor chose for his *guebi*, or palace, a hill above the northern thermal springs and then allotted various surrounding quarters, known as *sefers*, to his leading nobles. Social organization was strongly feudalistic. Each *sefer*—literally, "camp"—included the residence of an important noble plus all the noble's warriors, troops, retainers, and slaves and their families. No distinctly upper- or lower-class areas were initially developed, as was the case in cities founded by Europeans. The effect of this original organization as an armed camp can still be clearly seen in the city's social, economic, and ethnic arrangements.

Early visitors to Addis Ababa universally commented that it resembled a large straggling village more than a city.[†] Further contributing to this impression of a large floating camp were fluctuations in the city's population. The normal population around 1910 was roughly 60,000; during the rainy season, it sometimes dropped to as low as 40,000.[‡] When important chiefs came to the capital, they brought their entire armies and households with them. There are reports of chiefs who brought 100,000 to 150,000 people with them, and even as late as 1915 it was not unusual for a governor to bring 30,000 to 50,000 people along as a personal guarantee of safety.

As the city grew, its eastern side surrounding the palace gradually developed into the administrative center, while the western zone surrounding the old marketplace, or *mercado*, became the commercial center. Because the ruling Amhara tribe despised any type of commercial activity or trade, business activities were relegated to subordinate tribes. The Amhara concentrated their attentions on

[*]J. John Palen, "Urbanization and Migration in an Indigenous City: The Case of Addis Ababa," in Anthony Richmond and Danial Kubat (eds.), *Internal Migration,* Sage Publications, London, 1976.
[†]Docteur Merab, *Impressions d'Ethiopie,* vol. 2, Leroux, Paris, 1921–1923, p. 11.
[‡]Richard Pankhurst, "Notes on the Demographic History of Ethiopian Towns and Villages," *The Ethiopian Observer,* 9:71, 1965.

ruling, farming, and mounting expeditions to the south to capture more slaves.

Haile Selassie I ruled the country, first as regent and then as emperor, from 1916 to 1973. He officially decreed the end of slavery in the early 1920s, but this was not observed to any large degree inside the city and virtually not at all outside. It is estimated that 25,000 of the 60,000 inhabitants of the city were slaves in 1910. Today slavery in the true sense is gone from all but the most remote areas. However, the descendants of slaves—the Shanquellas, Sidamo, Gurages, and some of the darker-skinned Gallas—still are at the bottom of the social ladder; the men serve largely as *zabanias* (guards for houses and walled compounds) and the women as domestic maids or *mamitas* (children's nurses).

The Italians occupied Ethiopia from 1936 to 1941. They envisioned Addis Ababa as the capital of their sub-Saharan African empire and engaged heavily in building, constructing the country's first road network—five roads radiating outward from the capital. These roads, which still make up the basic road network, ensured that Addis Ababa would become the transportation and administration center of the country. The Italians also constructed a new market area, known as the Piazza, east of the traditional market, and built a road from this new market to the small railway station at the southern end of the city. The southern end of the city, which is somewhat lower in altitude and thus warmer, was set aside as the Italian residential area. A southward movement has been characteristic of the city since this time. Most of the newer European-style villas and high-rise apartments that have been constructed during the past decade are in the southern area.

Today the radius of the city is about 4 to 5 miles, with the most heavily built-up area roughly in the center. Although its present population is over 1 million, Addis Ababa still essentially retains its nonurban character. Most of the housing units are still constructed of *chica*—a mixture of earth, straw, and water plastered around eucalyptus poles. The ever-present and fast-growing eucalyptus trees also serve to give the city a small-town appearance by masking the houses. The trees do a yeoman service, since they provide firewood for all heating and cooking, lumber for building, and wood for furniture. Even the leaves are used in baking the Ethiopian bread, called *injera*.

The rural feeling of the city is also partially due to the fact that Addis Ababa is a city of rural migrants. Three-quarters of the inhabitants were not born in the city, and the continuing warfare with Somalia and the Eritrean Liberation Front have encouraged greater movement to the city.

In terms of its functional base, Addis Ababa is still primarily a political and administrative center. All major Ethiopian government agencies, all foreign embassies, the United Nationa Economic Commission for Africa, and the Organization of African Unity are located in the capital. Recently there have been noticeable increases in several sectors: transportation, communications, manufacturing, and education. Industrialization is growing but is still, relatively speaking, in its infancy, with all capital goods being imported. Retail trade is also growing but is oriented largely to Addis Ababa itself. Traditional custom, which gives low status to those working with their hands, has inhibited the development of handicraft industries. Weavers, for example, are still believed by some to possess the evil eye.

Transportation to and from the city is still primitive, particularly for goods. With the sole narrow-gage railroad connecting Addis Ababa and the port of Djibouti often closed because of warfare, goods from the outside come largely by air. The large contingent of Cuban troops is brought in and supplied in similar fashion. Each day thousands of donkeys also bring wood, hay, and produce into the city from surrounding areas, but they are being supplanted by large, overloaded trucks.

Addis Ababa is both a feudal city and a modern city. It is an overgrown village and the headquarters of the prestigious United Nations Economic Commission for Africa. It has high-rise apartments, but still no sanitary sewers. For better or worse, it represents the future.

electricity in the country and accounts for three-quarters of its commercial and manufacturing workers and over half its employees in transportation, administration, and other services. Lagos, although it is only one of the cities of Nigeria and contains only about 1 percent of the nation's population, still manages to account for 46 percent of the electricity consumed, 56 percent of the country's telephones, and 38 percent of the registered vehicles.[12]

The importance of the primate cities is heightened by the economic separation of the major city from the surrounding countryside. Africa is noted for a sharp break between the modernizing city and the tribal "bush." Urban influences are concentrated in the cities themselves. There is little of the American pattern, in which the city gradually tapers off and becomes the countryside. Going a few miles into the bush can take someone not only away from built-up areas but also away from the major influence of modernization.

The physical size and structure of the primate city is the most visible sign of its dominance; but its social role as the breaker of the cake of custom is even more significant. The primate cities "are not merely the focal points where the break with tradition can be seen most clearly, but also the centers in which a major restructuring of African society as a whole is taking place."[13] Just how deep into the countryside major restructuring has penetrated is, of course, open to some dispute. But that change is taking place in the cities is accepted by all.

The association between the growth of cities and the rise of African independence movements has been commented upon by many observers. A political scientist has noted that "it is above all in these new urban societies that the characteristic institutions and ideas of African nationalism are born and grow to maturity."[14] In Africa the city is the incubator of social change. More than on any other continent, the city not only towers over the countryside but controls it economically, educationally, politically, and socially.

Squatter Slums. *Bidonvilles* ("tin-can cities") are a standard part of the "suburban" landscape of every growing African city. They house up to one-third of the total urban population. The rapid population growth of recent years, along with the push from the land, has resulted in an explosive expansion of the urban population—without a proportionate increase in city housing.

As a result, *bidonvilles* are a fact of city life, from Casablanca in the north (180,000 residents in shantytowns) to Lusaka in the south (90,000 in shantytowns). Most governments simply do not have the resources to engage in massive housing programs. Even a relatively affluent country such as the Ivory Coast has not been able to begin to meet the housing demand. Improvements in central-city housing act as magnets drawing ever more rural newcomers.

Compounding the problem is the inability of the increasing urban population to pay even the minimal rents that government-built housing would require. Food

---

[12]Hance, op. cit., pp. 209–210.
[13]Peter C. Gutkind, "The African Urban Milieu: A Force for Rapid Change," *Civilizations*, **12**:185, 1962.
[14]T. Hodgkin, *Nationalism in Colonial Africa*, Muller, London, 1956, p. 18.

and clothing generally absorb from two-thirds to nine-tenths of a newcomer's income.[15] That doesn't leave much for extras such as decent housing. Shantytowns with homes of packing crates, scrap metal, or mud and wattle thus will be part of the urban scene for years to come.

Lagos: An Example of Urban Growing Pains. Lagos, the booming capital of Nigeria, provides an example of the difficulties facing even relatively affluent metropolises. With its oil revenues, Lagos is far better off than most growing cities, but it is nonetheless unable to keep up with its need for roadways, sewers, housing, and efficient land government.

Some of the problems stem from the city's location. Lagos was originally founded on a narrow island close to the coast. This made considerable sense when the concern was defending a trading post; but today the island is the crowded center of the city, and the lagoon separating it from the mainland is a foul-smelling, polluted sewer. There are currently only two bridges connecting the island with the mainland. At peak traffic hours, it can take forty-five minutes just to get over the bridge. Urban problems apparently can be exported to developing countries more rapidly than urban solutions.

Population growth by in-migration is about 10 percent per annum, and the multiplicity of local state and federal governments and agencies often seem to work at cross purposes.[16] While new high-rise buildings are constructed, the open street drains continue to overflow, refuse collection is erratic, and big overloaded trucks continue to tear up colonial-era roads.

If comparatively economically affluent cities such as Lagos in Nigeria or Bidjan in the Ivory Coast are having growth pains, the problems of poorer countries are far more severe. Dar es Salaam in Tanzania, for instance, is quite visibly decaying. The run-down buildings emphasize the country's status as one of the world's twenty-five poorest. Unlike other countries, Tanzania's socialist government has virtually ignored the capital while emphasizing the total resettlement of the agricultural population in new communal agricultural villages.

The Economic Picture and the Urban Future. Colonialism may be dead, but the economic effects of exploitation linger on. Overdependence on a single crop or mineral resouce leaves many countries vulnerable to fluctuations in world market prices. Ghana was set back by almost a decade of depressed cocoa prices; Ethiopia is subject to fluctuations in the price of coffee; Liberia is subject to fluctuations in the price of crude rubber; Zambia depends on the price of copper. It is difficult to plan a development budget under such circumstances.

It is generally assumed that a developing country should expand economically at a rate of at least 3 percent a year. According to this minimum criterion, twenty-eight African countries, containing some 72 percent of the population of Africa, have been growing economically at a rate far too slow to be considered

---

[15]Hance, op. cit., p. 286.
[16]Rasheed Gbadamosi, "Growing Pains in Lagos," *Draper World Population Fund Report,* Spring, 1976, pp. 15–17.

even marginally satisfactory.[17] In fact, thirteen countries, accounting for 22 percent of the African population, have had *negative* economic growth rates.[18] Poor planning and excessive reliance on foreign capital, which is not always available, have contributed heavily to this unsatisfactory economic performance.

Agriculture still occupies a preeminent economic position in most African countries. It occupies about 77 percent of the economically active population. The growth in food production, however, has been disappointing. African food production grew at a rate of about 2 percent a year during the 1960s. However, owing to increases in the population, on a per capita basis there was actually a *decline* of 0.2 percent annually in available foodstuffs.[19] This stagnation in a crucial area is generally attributed to traditional and inefficient methods of farming. As a result, nations whose economies are based on agriculture find themselves in the unfortunate position of importing foodstuffs.

Industrial growth has also been slower than was hoped for a decade ago; but here the increases have been relatively steady, if unspectacular. Almost everywhere, the industrial base remains small, reflecting a colonial history of producing raw materials rather than finished manufactures. Industrialization is slowed by the smallness of internal markets, the shortage of skilled and experienced personnel, and the lack of capital. However, the picture differs from country to country. Nigeria, for one, has made major strides in developing its oil resources. Generally, the rate of industrial development is closely tied to the availability of investment funds.

The Organization of African Unity officially recognized the problem of lack of economic growth in 1979. Its report on Africa's economic development acknowledged that "Africa in particular is unable to point to any significant growth rate or satisfactory index of general well being" in almost two decades of independence.[20] It was noted that per capita income in Africa is still the world's lowest and infant mortality rates are among the world's highest.

The proposed solutions were the avoidance of the "narrow nationalism" that hinders regional development, and the establishment of an African common market to pool strength and avoid uneconomic duplication. However, given the political and economic realities, these are not likely developments. While it would be pleasant to predict a better future for all the developing African countries, the economic facts of life indicate that this is unrealistic. A decade ago, for example, Somalia overthrew a corrupt feudalistic regime and replaced it with a socialistic state intent on modernization. Unfortunately, this has really made little difference as far as economic development is concerned, since regardless of its form of government Somalia has virtually no resources. So long as its major export is bananas, Somalia is going to remain an impoverished country. Developing

---

[17] *Africa Social Situation: 1960–1970,* Prepared for the African Population Conference, Accra, Ghana, December, 1971, by the Economic Commission for Africa, p. 8.

[18] Ibid.

[19] Ibid., p. 11.

[20] Quoted in Leon Dash, "African Leaders Have Seen the Future and It Looks Bleak," *Washington Post Service,* July 29, 1979.

countries that have few natural or other resources are almost certain to see the gap between themselves and the developed world widen rather than close unless the present pattern and rate of investment and aid are radically increased. Furthermore, increases in the cost of importing necessary oil and gasoline, which have disrupted the economies of developed countries, have all but destroyed the economies of some developing nations, while a fortunate few have boomed. The real victims of ever-higher OPEC oil prices are the LDCs, which are being reduced to a permanent debtor class.

Regardless of the extent of economic growth, continued urban growth is clearly the pattern for as far into the future as anyone cares to project. There really is little alternative. Many of the semiarid agricultural and grazing areas of East Africa are already overused. Remaining in the area of one's birth, and further raising the density of the area, is not a reasonable alternative for those who hope to better their way of life. The opening up of new lands not previously used for settlement requires costs far out of proportion to the possible returns. The cost of providing necessary services—water, roads, schools, housing—would be extremely heavy. In east Africa it would also involve a political decision to destroy many of the remaining game parks and wildlife refuges, since there is little other land that is not already being used.[21]

The following description of the situation in Tanzania could be applied equally well to the social, political, and economic situation in other African countries.

> Death rates have fallen and the population is now estimated to be growing at 2.1 percent a year. This means that almost 45 percent of the population is under sixteen, and raises immediate political issues. The economy will have to expand in the industrial and cash-crop sectors if these people are not to be either unemployed workers in the cities or subsistence farmers. Many youths are migrating to the towns, producing a severe strain on the social services. Unemployed or semi-employed youth, loitering in the streets or waiting around TANU offices for small jobs, begin to be a political problem. Party leaders are aware of them; but harranguing against loiterers, telling unemployed youth to go and farm, and even restricting people's freedom to come to Dar es Salaam has not dissuaded youth from accumulating in the towns.[22]

Finding employment for the masses in the cities is an increasingly serious problem. Urbanization is clearly the wave of the African future, but whether it will mean economic development is still problematic.

Second only to employment, the most pressing problem in African cities is housing. Various approaches have been taken to reduce the number of shanty-towns and squatter slums surrounding the major cities, but none of these programs has come near to solving the problem.

[21]For a discussion of some of the problems in Kenya, see Dick Oloo (ed.), *Urbanization: Its Social Problems and Consequences,* Kenya National Council of Social Service, Nairobi, 1969.

[22]Henry Bienen, *Tanzania: Party Transformation and Economic Development,* Princeton University Press, Princeton, N. J., 1970, p. 265. Reprinted by permission of Princeton University Press.

Some west African governments have tried to stem the migrant tide by passing legislation providing for the repatriation of unwanted new workers back to their villages and setting stiff prison terms for those who return to the city. Repatriation has not proved successful: Workers either drift back to the city or are replaced by others. Other governments have tried to increase the attractiveness of rural villages and to settle unemployed urban populations in new, self-contained communal villages. Both of these approaches are quite expensive, and as a result seldom move beyond the planning or pilot-project stage. Such schemes have difficulty competing for scarce governmental funds. Moreover, the pressures driving younger people to the cities are social as well as economic and are not likely to be solved by such government programs as can be presently implemented.

The construction of low-cost houses or flats cannot come near to meeting the need for new housing. Abidjan in the Ivory Coast is doing better than most; it constructs roughly 1,200 government units annually, but the need is for between 6,000 and 8,000 units annually. As a result, governments are coming more and more to accept the idea of aiding in the construction of reasonably planned slums which at least have minimal urban amenities such as an available water supply, roads, and group sanitary facilities for the disposal of human waste.

Zambia is adopting the so-called "site and service" scheme, by which a township is laid out and a prospective builder is given a plot and a loan of $50 to by necessary building materials, such as cement for the floor or a corrugated iron roof. After that, the builders are for all intents and purposes on their own. The rationale underlying this approach is that the goal of the government should not be to build housing but to raise the standard of living. Slum dwellers don't need more prodding to improve their living conditions; what they need is more money. As shanty dwellers get decent jobs and begin to make some money, they being to improve their housing on their own.

Social Composition of Contemporary African Cities. The recent explosive growth of urban areas means that the majority of the adults in the cities were not born there but are in-migrants. The African city is a city of newcomers. In Abidjan, only 29 percent of the total population, and only 7 percent of those over twenty years of age, were actually born in the city. Research by the author shows that over three-quarters of the inhabitants of Addis Ababa over fifteen years of age were born outside the city and are thus migrants.

The sociologist Louis Wirth's view of the city as a place where social relations are dominated by the labor market and contacts with others are superficial, impersonal, and transitory is only partially accurate as a description of African urbanism. There is no question that many of the disorganizing aspects of urbanism posited by Wirth can be found in any large African city. Family life sometimes breaks down, and prostitution is common. The latter situation is partially due to urban sex ratios, which are typified by disproportionate numbers of males. The situation is reasonable in west Africa, where in the cities there is a ratio of roughly 95 females to every 100 males. However, in middle Africa there are only about 85 females per 100 males, and in parts of east Africa there are only 55 to 75 females per 100 urban males. The situation is most extreme in South Africa, where government policy prevents workers from bringing their wives to the cities with them. The resulting abnormal family situations encourage drunkenness, gambling, prostitution, and violent crime. The situation is not unlike that found in the towns of the American west before the arrival of the homesteaders with their families.

In the cities tradition and modern ways often blend. An example of such blending is the use of both courts and traditional agents to resolve conflicts.[23] Problems of psychological maladjustment appear as a rule to be far rarer than Wirth's thesis would suggest. The town may be a new experience, but since a major proportion of the townspeople were once migrants themselves, almost all newcomers know someone in the city who will take them in and who will help them adjust to urban life. Family ties and wider kinship ties are surprisingly strong and resilient to urban pressures. Relatives are expected to take the newcomers in and provide for their basic needs until they can get on their feet. A migrant who does get a job is then expected to contribute to providing for the family.

In most cases, far from being subject to indifference and social isolation, the migrant is quickly integrated into the life of the quarter—a place where there are numerous others of the same tribe, and probably even the same village. Outside observers are struck by the ebullience, gusto, and camaraderie found in African towns, particularly in west Africa. A description of Dar es Salaam fits other African cities equally well:

> It would be difficult to find a single African who arrived in Dar-es-Salaam knowing not a soul. . . . Almost every African who decides to come comes to a known address, where lives a known relation; this relation will meet him, take him in and feed him and show him the ropes, help him seek a job . . . until he considers himself able to launch out for himself and take a room of his own.[24]

This pattern is, if anything, more prevalent in west Africa.

Also aiding the migrant's adjustment is the African pattern of remaining in the city for months or even years and then returning to the countryside for a period of time before migrating back to the city. Migration out of the cities during rainy seasons or harvest seasons is common in some countries.

It is well to keep in mind that the pull of the town is not uniform for all groups. The Masai of Kenya, although pressured by the Kenyan government to rationalize their agriculture and adopt modern ways, have consistently rejected town life in favor of their traditional rural culture. The Ila of Zambia have also rejected

[23]Michael J. Lowy, "Me Ko Court: The Impact of Urbanization on Conflict Resolution in a Ghanaian Town," in George Foster and Robert Kemper (eds), Anthropologists in Cities, Little, Brown, Boston, 1974, pp. 153–177.
[24]J. A. K. Leslie, A Social Survey of Dar es Salaam, Oxford University Press—The East African Institute, London, 1963, p. 33.

urbanization and modernization. Both tribes seem to be an embarrassment to their national governments because they don't want to "modernize." The Kenyan government plans to divide up the Masai communal lands and give each family individual plots. A similar program was tried by the United States government to modernize the American Indians, with the result that many Indians lost their lands. There are indications that the same fate awaits the Masai. It is quite possible that by the year 2000 the self-reliant virtues and warrior strengths of the Masai will be praised in every local Kenyan schoolbook; but by then the Masai culture may have been effectively destroyed.

Tribal and Ethnic Bonds. Urbanization is supposed to weaken traditional bonds, but it can be argued that urbanization in Africa has strengthened rather than weakened tribal identification.[25] Some scholars maintain that the immigrant, rather than being "detribalized," is "supertribalized" as a result of coming into contact, for perhaps the first time, with people from other cultures. Tribal origin usually replaces kinship as a symbol of belonging. This is an expansion of identity from the parochial to the more general.

Gideon Sjoberg suggests that the role played by cultural or tribal subsystems in modernizing societies is analogous to that played by immigrant enclaves in the American city of several decades ago. Cultural, ethnic, tribal, class, or occupational groupings perform a number of functions not only for the newcomer but for the society at large. First, the tribal, ethnic, or other group introduces newcomers to others in the city and indoctrinates them into the ways of the city. Information on such matters as where to live, how to get a job, and how to avoid the police is transmitted to migrants in order to aid their adaptation to the city. Second, the subgroup, being originally itself a part of the rural culture, maintains within the city many rural customs and traditions. While learning the new ways, migrants will still have some contact with their past. Third, because migrants return to rural areas for periods of time, and because there is a pattern of visiting between rural villages and the city, the customs and ways of the city (urbanism) are spread to villages—so that patterns of urbanism are gradually being diffused throughout rural areas.[26]

Kinship and tribal affiliation provide bridges by which the migrant crosses into the urban arena. Being a member of a tribe gives a newcomer an immediate identification that is recognized by everyone. It tells the newcomer how to behave, and it provides a more or less ready-made group of associates, friends, and even drinking partners. While tribalism may have negative effects in a country seeking to develop national rather than tribal loyalties, on the individual level tribal membership eases the adjustment to city life.

[25]William John Hanna and Judith Lynne Hanna, *Urban Dynamics in Black Africa,* Aldine-Atherton, Chicago, 1971, p. 107.
[26]Gideon Sjoberg, "Cities in Developing and in Industrial Societies: A Cross-Cultural Analysis," in Philip M. Hauser and Leo F. Schnore (eds.), *The Study of Urbanization,* Wiley, New York, 1965, pp. 226–227.

Leaders often call for "detribalization" but do not always practice what they proach, if one can judge by the limited ethnic makeup of their own governments. It is among the educated young that the sense of national dedication is strongest.

Tribal Elders and New Elites. One way the city promotes social change is by undermining the position of rural-based tribal elders. A tribal background offers little precedent for confronting urban problems. A young person migrating to the city can frequently make more than a tribal elder, and rural patterns of communal sharing break down under a system of individual wages. The tribal elders may know little of how the urban social and economic order operates, and they can offer only minimal assistance to those entering city life; indeed, their advice may be dysfunctional for solving urban problems. Someone who is considered a person of status and prestige in the bush or village may be little more than another unemployed worker in the city. The strength of the traditional elite lies in the countryside; its influence in the city is minimal.

Very little of what has been said thus far applies to the African upper classes. Younger, well trained, and frequently critical of the past, they are the antithesis of the tribal elders. The schooling of the urban elite has often taken place abroad: at Oxford or Cambridge if the country was formerly British, in Paris if the country was formerly French. Members of this elite are trained as doctors, lawyers, teachers, and other professionals, and their backgrounds and their general life-style are distinctly cosmopolitan, with a European orientation. For example, while they may listen to the national radio station, they almost certainly get their daily news of the outside world from the BBC World Service.

Income differences between this urban elite and the African urban poor are even greater than in developed nations such as the United States and the Soviet Union. In west Africa, a university graduate just entering a government bureaucracy can expect to earn ten times more than an urban laborer.[27] A full professor in Nigeria earns almost thirty times as much.[28] Formal education, which may bear little relationship to governance, plays a heavy role in entry into civil service and military elites. Being strongly oriented toward the future, members of the urban elite seek to push their countries into the modern world and have little patience for the slow, older ways of the traditional tribal elites.

Status of Women. It is difficult to make generalizations about the position of women in Africa, since this varies from country to country and from one tribal and cultural group to another. Still, several overall statements can be made. It is generally safe to say that norms, attitudes, and values in Africa have a long history of strongly favoring male dominance. It is also clear that, regardless of

[27]P. C. Lloyd, *Africa in Social Change,* Penguin Books, Baltimore, 1967, p. 150.
[28]Josef Gugler and William G. Flanagan, *Urbanization and Social Change in West Africa,* Cambridge University Press, London, 1978, p. 158.

other factors, cities are far more equalitarian in practice than the countryside. Urban populations are young, new to urban life, and more flexible than their rural counterparts.

In Ghana "mammy wagons" (small buses) dominate local transporation. Ghanaian women are noted throughout the continent for their organizing skills. Ninety percent of the retailing of food and other goods is controlled and operated by women. Even in north African Muslim cultures, where the status of females has been traditionally inferior, changes are taking place in the education of women and participation by women in national life—Libya, with its strongly traditionalist internal policies, being the major exception.

Nonetheless, while the overall situation is improving, women have yet to attain equal status with men. Among the elites, western ideology—particularly Christian missions, with their doctrine of equality of marriage partners and schools open to both sexes—generally fostered equality.[29] However, no African nation at the time of this writing has a woman head of government or any women in the very top policymaking positions. Women are also underrepresented in the education system, with roughly two boys at school for every girl in most countries.[30]

In the bush and in rural villages, the position of women is set by custom; but in the city, with its new occupations and skills, the occupational structure is more flexible. Urban occupations may be so new that they are not yet sex-defined. Skills and professional training of all sorts are usually in short supply, so that the woman who has had the benefit of education and training can generally use her training. On the other hand, those females (or males, for that matter) without specific skills or abilities are likely to remain locked into poverty. While it is true that trained women participate in the social and economic life of the city to an extent unknown in the countryside, it is also true that for lower-class women without husbands there frequently is little alternative to prostitution and other marginal economic enterprises.

Further clouding the situation is the problem of distinguishing between the normative beliefs regarding the position of women and the actual practice in the cities. Laws based on western models may specify equality in the civil code while customary marriage practices continue.[31] On the other hand, in Muslim countries of north Africa, where the position of women may be legally inferior, the actual practice, for economic and social reasons, may be more equal.

Differences from the Western Pattern. The geographer William Hance has assembled a number of characteristics differentiating between urban growth in Africa and urban growth in the west during the nineteenth century. These

[29]Ester Boserup, *Women's Role in Economic Development*, St. Martin's Press, New York, 1970.
[30]Gugler and Flanagan, op. cit., pp. 136–137.
[31]Alain A. Levasseur, "The Modernization of Law in Africa with Particular Reference to Family Law in the Ivory Coast," in Philip Foster and Aristide R. Zolberg (eds.), *Ghana and the Ivory Coast: Perspectives on Modernization*, University of Chicago Press, Chicago, 1971, pp. 151–166.

differences are presented not so that "value judgments" can be made, but in order to highlight certain aspects of African urbanization that differ from the western experience. The points of difference Hance notes are as follows:

1. The rates of growth, particularly of the major cities, are much more rapid in Africa. Some have achieved their present position in one-fifth to one-tenth the time required in western Europe.
2. There is less correlation—association—between the cities' rate of growth and the measures of economic growth in their countries.
3. The growth of urbanization is often not paralleled by a comparable revolution in the rural areas.
4. A less favorable ratio of population to resources in rural areas means that the push factor is more important than it was in Europe. That is, people pour into the cities not because the city needs workers, but because the countryside is overpopulated.
5. The linkage of some cities with their domestic hinterlands is less developed, while the ties of these cities to the outside world and their dependence on it remain striking.
6. There is relatively less specialization in the African cities. The division of labor is less developed.
7. There are generally higher rates of unemployment. Here the European cities had the advantage of being able to drain off large numbers of people who might have become redundant, to the new world. The African cities have no such convenient safety valve.
8. Differences in outlook and values may slow the adjustment to the city and reduce the tempo of its economic life, as, for example, the reliance on the extended family for support and the absence of the Protestant Ethic with its emphasis on hard work, achievement, and success.
9. There is a dual tribal and western structure in many African cities.
10. Migrants to the town differ in several important respects: almost all are unskilled, their level of educational achievement is relatively lower though above average as far as the source areas are concerned, and almost all arrive without capital resources.
11. Heavier responsibility is placed on governments, local and national, to provide for the urban residents. In the west, private enterprise normally met the needs for new housing, while local governments had a tax base adequate to provide the public services. Not so in Africa, where the demands of government are far more onerous and almost none are capable of meeting them.[32]

The reference to a "dual structure" in point 9 has to do with the simultaneous existence of tribal customs and westernized ways of life. Generally, western ways tend to dominate in the economic sphere, while in the social and family sphere traditional customs retain their old strength. For instance, a man who has graduated from college may choose his job, but in many places his father still chooses his bride.

[32]Hance, op. cit., pp. 293–294.

In Conclusion: Contemporary African Cities. Discouraging overall figures regarding population growth, rural poverty, and economic stagnation must be applied with discretion. While urban growth is occurring virtually everywhere, some nations are coping with the transformation more adequately than others. In sub-Saharan Africa, Nigeria, Kenya, and the Ivory Coast appear to be on the road to national economic development, while other nations just as clearly appear to be mired in internal strife and economic regression. For the remainder of this century Africa will remain the world's least urbanized continent, while at the same time its major cities continue to mushroom.

THE MIDDLE EAST

The middle east is in many respects more a political than a geographical concept. Technically, most of what we call the "middle east" is in Asia Minor, with some overlap into north Africa (for example, Egypt). However, in terms of history, culture, and development, the middle east is a relatively distinct area.

The middle east is sometimes referred to as the "cradle of civilizations." This is not entirely an exaggeration, for the great ancient civilizations of Mesopotamia, Egypt, and the Levant all developed in this relatively small geographic area. The early development of this area was discussed briefly in Chapter 2. In this chapter, the emphasis will be on the cities of the middle east from the Islamic period to the present, for the social and spatial organization of present cities in the area is directly related to their preindustrial past. In terms of economic development as well as geography, the middle east occupies a position somewhere between the countries of western Europe and those of Asia and Africa, with the OPEC nations rapidly developing as economic forces.

Scholars agree that Islamic civilization has been predominantly an urban civilization.[33] In the words of Lapidus, "From the beginning of recorded history Middle Eastern cities and civilization have been one and the same."[34] The city was the center of political, social, and cultural activities. This was true in spite of the fact that many of the countries still are not unified and tribal factors are important.

Middle eastern cities differed in significant respects from the medieval corporate city and the autonomous city-state of the classical world. The medieval European city with which we are most familiar grew out of a feudal land-based system; its charter defined its rights vis-à-vis the rural manors which were the real centers of power. European medieval cities initially were only on the fringes of power and were forced to develop their own political structure because they did

---

[33]S. M. Stern, "The Constitution of the Islamic City," in A. H. Hourani and S. M. Stern (eds.), *The Islamic City,* Bruno Cassirer, Oxford, 1970, p. 25.
[34]Ira M. Lapidus, *Middle Eastern Cities,* University of California Press, Berkeley, 1969, p. v.

not fit into the dominant agriculturally based system. They had to evolve their own laws and customs, often in opposition to those of the countryside.

Islamic cities, by contrast, did not have distinct legal privileges of a charter—criteria, which Max Weber, using the legally autonomous European model, has suggested were necessary for a true city.[35] Under Islamic law all believers, whether in the city or the countryside, were equal. The laws of the city were those of the entire territory. Since laws were written in the cities, there was no need for autonomous laws and regulations for cities—and thus no independent group which could legally challenge the caliphate as the western middle class challenged its rulers by developing constitutional law. The city was not viewed as a rival of the hinterland: the city was superior and dominant. City authorities enforced the laws and collected the taxes. Thus there was no need for independent municipal governments of the type developed in western Europe. Rather, the middle eastern cities resembled Asian cities in lacking independent formal organizations.[36]

The city was not on the fringe of the system; it was the system. Cities in the east had traditionally been administrative or trade centers within large urban-oriented empires. The caliph, like the earlier Roman emperors, lived in the city, not in the countryside in fortified rural castles.

In the middle east, the peasants—many of whom actually lived within the protection of the city walls and cultivated adjacent lands—needed the technical skills, such as the canalizing and storing of water, and the military security, particularly from roaming nomads, provided by an urban population. Some cities, like Damascus, still have agriculturists living within the city and working the fields outside.[37] This is directly opposite to the American pattern of people living outside the city and working within it.

Physical and Social Considerations

Roughly four-fifths of the middle east is either desert or arid mountains, and this basic environmental fact greatly influenced, if it did not determine, the location of cities. In addition to the limitations of the environment, political and military considerations influenced the location of Islamic cities. During the Roman Empire and earlier, the great cities were almost always seaports—Alexandria, Antioch, and Carthage are examples. The Muslims did not follow this ancient pattern: they shunned the sea and instead built an inland empire. This was partly from choice—the origins of Islam were in the interior rather than on the more sophisticated coast—but also partly from military necessity. Arab armies were successful on land, but the Mediterranean Sea was controlled by others—first by

[35]Max Weber, *The City*, D. Martindale and G. Neuwirth (trans.), Free Press, New York, 1959, p. 88.
[36]J. Gernet, *"Note sur les villes chinoises au moment de l'apogee islamique,"* in Hourani and Stern, op. cit., pp. 77–85.
[37]Charles Issawi, *The Economic History of the Middle East.* University of Chicago Press, Chicago, 1966, p. 216.

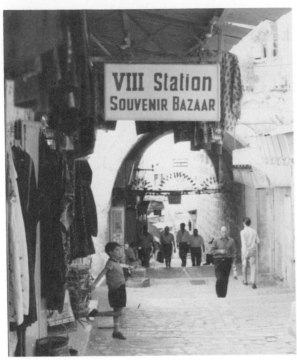

One of the stations of the cross in the old Arab section of Jerusalem. Note the narrow, enclosed street that can be used only by pedestrian or animal traffic. (Mary Doody.)

the hostile Byzantine Empire and later by the equally dangerous Italian city-states.

As a result, the Muslims built an interior empire, and previously great cities such as Alexandria shrank to the status of frontier outposts. The great Muslim cities, such as Damascus, Baghdad, Cairo, Tehran, Jerusalem, Mecca, and Medina, were all inland. Some, such as Kairouan and Fustat, were originally Arab camps at the edge of the desert; others, such as Damascus and Yazd, had been handling desert traffic for centuries; still others, such as Samarra, Baghdad, and Cairo, had once served as royal cities; and a few, such as Jerusalem and Mecca, were religious centers.

The holy city of Mecca in Saudi Arabia illustrates how social organization can sometimes override environmental conditions. Mecca is 40 miles from the Red Sea along a series of *wadis*, or gullies, flanked by steep granite hills. Summer temperatures reach 105°F, and there is an almost total lack of greenery and cultivation. Nonetheless, as the focus of prayer and pilgrimage for Muslims throughout the world—non-Muslims are forbidden to enter the holy city—Mecca prospered.

Traditionally, Islamic cities had a number of physical features in common. First, located in the most dominant natural defense position within the city would be the citadel. This was the military heart of the city, the place where, if necessary, a last-stand defense could be made.

Second, all cities had a central mosque which served as the focus of urban life. Around the mosque—which contained the religious school—could generally be found the main religious, civic, social, cultural, and even economic activities.

Third, there was the palace of the local ruler. Sometimes this was located in the very heart of the city, and sometimes on virgin land; but wherever it was placed, it invariably grew and absorbed surrounding properties. The compound contained not only the palace, treasury, and other directly related operations; it also was the center for all administrative offices. In addition, there were also barracks for the house guards and personal troops whose loyalty could be counted on in times of revolt or attempted coup.

Finally, there was the central market area or bazaar. The citadel and palace are now tourist sights, but the grand bazaars continue to serve an important commercial function. Various sections of the bazaar are devoted to specific goods or products: all the spice markets are found in one section, another specializes in shoes, another in clothing, and another in copper or brass metalwork. Silversmiths and goldsmiths also have their own special locations. The fabled Khanel Khalili bazaar of Cairo covers over a square mile of the city center.

Internally, Islamic cities have traditionally been divided into quarters that resemble village communities. Damascus in the sixteenth century had some seventy quarters.[38] Most of one's daily life would be lived within a quarter; there were relatively few institutional ties cutting across district lines to bind various quarters together. Guilds, merchant associations, and professional organizations, which were so important in medieval European cities, were all extremely weak.[39] What little organization that did cross the boundaries of quarters was created by the *ulma*, the learned religious elite that later came to exercise political and social power as well. The schools of law of the *ulma* were socially, religiously, and physically central.

Within the various quarters there were wide differences in social, economic, and political power. There were no specifically upper-class districts. Residence in quarters was based on adherence to particular religious or political positions. Ethnic minorities, specialized crafts, and even foreign merchants might have their own quarters. Some of the more suburban quarters were composed largely of people of recent village or nomadic origin—again, a contrast to the North American pattern.

---

[38]Ira M. Lapidus, *Muslin Cities in the Later Middle Ages,* Harvard University Press, Cambridge, Mass., 1967, p. 85.
[39]Lapidus, *Middle Eastern Cities,* p. v.

Contemporary Urban Trends

Most cities are growing at a rapid rate, with many doubling their population in a decade. Accurate figures are difficult to come by, since censuses are often viewed as political instruments. Saudi Arabia, for instance, will probably never release the results of its 1975 census because it would document that at most 8 million people live in an oil-rich country three times the size of Texas.[40]

In the oil-wealthy city of Kuwait as in Saudi Arabia, old sections have been virtually obliterated by new building. Air-conditioned steel, cement, and glass office buiildings tower over streets clogged with automobile traffic. Residential neighborhoods are filled with new villas and apartments, while garages are filled with Mercedes automobiles. Bare traces of the previous traditional—and often poverty-stricken—cities remain.

At the other extreme is Cairo, which is almost bereft of modern downtown office buildings. For twenty years there has been virtually no meaningful maintenance or repair of the city's streets, sewers, telephones, or housing. Building codes are not enforced. The city is notorious for its power outages, garbage-strewn porches and streets, and out-of-commission telephones. Egyptian residents, with, endless patience and tolerance, respond with an Arabic expression: *Molish* ("Never mind"). The housing crisis is so severe that landlords can charge $1,500 a month for an unheated apartment where the water may or may not run. The poor among Cairo's over 8 million residents fare much worse. People live on roofs and in the streets and even inhabit the aboveground tombs of the "city of the dead" or the road in from the airport. Still, the city has a magic allure for newcomers and remains one of the world's great cities.

Until the recent flood of oil wealth to some states, the industrial growth of middle eastern cities resulted from the imposition of a tiny modern sector upon the traditional society.[41] Since the major impetus and capital were provided by Europeans, the modern sector long remained isolated from the traditional economy. Estimates made from information provided by censuses indicate that even today over half the employed males in Cairo are within the traditional rather than the modern economy.[42] There has not been a gradual blending of the traditional into the modern; rather, modern fixed-price stores compete with nearby traditional markets where prices are the result of bargaining.

There is no pattern of economic and social change common to all middle eastern cities. Tel Aviv, for example, differs enormously from Baghdad, Damascus,

---

[40]According to a story that may be true or apocryphal, former King Saud commissioned a national sample during World War II. In making his report to the king, the western demographer confidently said that the monarch had some 3 million subjects. The king, with some upset, replied that he had at least 7 million subjects, The expert countered that there might be 4 million. The king demanded 6 million; the expert said that perhaps there might be 5 million. "So be it," the king declared.

[41]Janet Abu-Lughod, "Varieties of Urban Experience: Contrast, Coexistence and Coalescence in Cairo," in Ira M. Lapidus, *Middle Eastern Cities*, p. 164.

[42]Ibid., p. 166.

or even Jerusalem. The development of Tel Aviv as a primate city can be explained in great part by the emergence of Israel as a nation-state. Founded in 1909 as a Jewish "garden city" separated from the Arab city of Jaffa, Tel Aviv grew rapidly, particularly after World War II. Its reservoir of trained professional and managerial talent aided its transformation into a major industrial commercial center. Tel Aviv has expanded its metropolitan area until now it encompasses numerous formerly independent surrounding towns. After Jerusalem came under Israeli administration as a result of the Six-Day War in 1967, Tel Aviv was no longer the only Israeli city, but its economic primacy remains.

Comparisons and Conclusions

In making comparisons with other regions of the world, and particularly with North America, certain differences should be remembered.

First, middle eastern cities are generally of moderate size compared with those of America or western Europe. The nation of Kuwait, for instance, for all its oil revenues, has just over 1 million inhabitants.

Second, middle eastern cities are not industrialized centers in the western sense. The cites are commercially oriented, but the way of life is far less bureaucratic than in industrialized states. Contacts count for more than formal rules. For example, *baksheesh* (the giving of bribes or gifts) is a culturally accepted way of doing business in the middle east.

Third, theories of urban ecological organization developed in America have little relevance to the middle east. If one looks at the ecology of Cairo, it is apparent that Burgess's concentric-zone theory has little utility there.[43] Contrary to the American pattern, in Cairo the areas of high social status are centrally located, and close to both the old and the new central business districts. Housing patterns still largely follow the traditional preindustrial model rather than the industrial model.

Fourth, because they are in-migrants, many city dwellers exhibit characteristics and behavior patterns that reflect their rural or village background. Families ties, kinship, ethnic groups, and primary groups still have a great deal to do with determining the nature of the life one will lead. In Cairo, more than one-third of the residents were born outside the city. Migrants do not simply pick up urban ways; they also, in effect, ruralize the cities. Many city dwellers are still tied to rural customs and culture, and migrants shape the city as much as the city shapes them. Overall evidence indicates that while migrants do suffer from social disorientation, it is not on the scale experienced by America's immigrants.[44]

---

[43]See, for example, S. S. Hassan, "The Ecology and Characteristics of Employed Females in Cairo City," paper presented at the Seminar on Demographic Factors in Manpower Planning in Arab Countries held at the Cairo Demographic Center, November, 1971; and Janet Abu-Lughod, "Testing the Theory of Social Area Analysis: The Ecology of Cairo, Egypt," *American Sociological Review*, 34:198–212, April, 1969.

[44]V. V. Costello, *Urbanization in the Middle East*, Cambridge University Press, Cambridge, 1977, chap. 5.

In the middle east, cafes serve as both business settings and social clubs.
(Marc Riboud/Magnum.)

Fifth, formal institutions, such as civic associations, labor unions, and charitable organizations, rarely play more than a minor role in adjusting the migrant to the city. Informal organizations or subsystems based on tribal, cultural, or ethnic identification are far more important. For instance, the role of the coffee shop is often central. Men conduct much of their social and business lives from the coffee shop. Frequently it is a place where news of the village can be exchanged and assistance can be given to newcomers. As such the coffee shop is more of a social than an economic institution.[45]

Finally, the existence of large cities should in no way be confused with the existence of an overall contemporary urban culture. Secular ways have not replaced traditional ways, even within the oil-rich cities which are physically most modern. External signs of western influence such as high-rise buildings, western automobiles, and western clothing styles, do not signify abandonment of traditional beliefs. For example, even in supposedly secular states the statements of traditional Islamic religious leaders can produce civil disorder and even bring down governments. The power of religious leaders in expressly religiously oriented states such as Saudi Arabia, Libya, and Iran is even greater. The urbanities of the middle east remain more traditional and less secular than those of Asia, Europe, or the Americas.

[45]For a description of this pattern in Cairo, see Janet Abu-Lughod, "Migrant Adjustment to City Life: The Egyptian Case," *American Journal of Sociology*, 67:22–2, July, 1961.

\

CHAPTER

18

URBAN PATTERNS IN ASIA

Woe to them that join house to house. Woe to them that lay field to field till there be no place.

Isaiah 5:8

INTRODUCTION: ASIAN CITIES

Of all the regions of the world, it is Asia about which one must be most careful when attempting to make generalizations on urbanization. Patterns of urbanization in China, Japan, India, and southeast Asia all have different historical roots and have developed in dissimilar cultures. These areas do, of course, have some things in common; but generalizations must be applied with some care to individual cities.

What can be said is that Asia has a great tradition of city life and numerous cities whose histories go back many centuries. In fact, until 200 years ago Asia contained more city dwellers than the rest of the world combined.[1] And if present demographic trends continue, by the year 2000 Asia will again have more city dwellers than any other continent. While precise data are hard to obtain—particularly on the size of Chinese cities—it is still clear that at least one-third of the total urban population of the world is found in Asia. Asia has more large cities and a larger number of people—but not a larger *percentage* of people—in cities than either Europe or America.

Despite this, the majority of Asia's population still consists of village-based agrarians; only a minority live in true urban places. Overall, some 27 percent of the population of Asia is urban.[2] This low level of overall urbanization places Asia just above Africa as regards the percentage of the population that is urbanized. The greatest degree of urbanization is found in the east Asian region (31 percent urban); this region includes Japan, which is three-quarters urban (76 percent).

All this means that while Asia is still predominantly rural, at the same time it has some of the world's largest cities. A relatively low proportion of the population lives in urban places, but these places are frequently immense. Tokyo has between 9 and 23 million people, depending upon whether one uses the most restrictive definition of the historic twenty-three wards of the city or the broad definition of the Tokyo agglomeration. The Asian cities of Shanghai, Peking, Calcutta, and Bombay also number among the world's ten largest.

It has been suggested that less developed Asian nations are in the position of being "overurbanized" while at the same time their momentum of urbanization is increasing. "Overurbanization," however, as we have suggested in Chapter 15, is a loaded term. The degree of overurbanization is measured against western industrial standards and western levels of per capita income, which are unrealistic standards of comparison for much of the world.

Indigenous Cities

Asian cities other than those founded and developed by westerners display a spatial organization having much in common with the preindustrial city (discussed in Chapter 2). Indigenous Asian cities of the past were predominantly

[1] Rhoads Murphey, "Urbanization in Asia," *Ekistics,* 21:8, January, 1966.
[2] Population Reference Bureau, *1980 World Population Data Sheet,* Washington, D.C., 1980.

political and cultural centers and only secondarily economic centers. The function of traditional capital cities was to serve as a symbol of the authority, legitimacy, and power of the national government. Administrative functions were everywhere more important than commercial or industrial functions.

Cities were located inland, near the centers of their empires, except in Japan and parts of southeast Asia, where this was not practical. Such inland cities were centers physically as well as socially and were also far safer from attack than coastal cities. Peking, Delhi, and Ankor are classic examples: they served as symbols of legitimate authority and were planned with monumental architecture, such as temples and palaces, that would emphasize this role. For example, Peking is famous for its Forbidden City Palace, Delhi for its magnificent Red Fort, and Ankor for its many fine temples. In China and sometimes in India the city was walled; in southeast Asia it usually was not; and in Japan walls rarely existed.

Colonial Cities

The history of western-type cities is quite different from that of indigenous cities. Western-type cities were imported to the east by European adventurers who entered the area seeking trade. These cities, in contrast to the traditional preindustrial cities, were primarily oriented toward exportation and commerce and thus were located along seacoasts in order to facilitate trade and communication with the mother country. Originally small trading sites, perhaps with a small fort for protection, these cities are now among the largest in the world. Hong Kong, Singapore, Shanghai, Calcutta, and Bombay all developed as foreign-dominated port cities.

The physical design of these cities clearly reveals their non-Asian origins. During the colonial period, Europeans and Asians were segregated into separate housing areas, with the European colonial sections clearly resembling western cities in their street development, architecture, and overall use of space. Asian quarters of the cities developed in more traditional ways and at considerably higher densities. While the overwhelming majority of the population was Asian, even during the height of the colonial period, the skylines and particularly the centers of these cities show the unmistakable hand of western influence.

Cities such as Shanghai, Singapore, and Hong Kong had model western economies that emphasized manufacturing as well as commerce. Although they occupied Asian soil, their real social and economic roots were in England. Urban institutions were transplanted from Europe, since the traditional society lacked the required economic and commercial organization. Today cities such as Hong Kong and Singapore are famous throughout the world for their industrial products and the experience and skills of their businesspeople.

Since it is impossible to fully describe the range of Asian cities in one chapter, we will have to content ourselves with a discussion of a limited number of places. This will, however, provide some understanding of the variations possible within this one geographic region.

INDIA

India is only 21 percent urban—but that means some 135 million city dwellers. Calcutta's 1979 population is estimated at 9 million, while that of Bombay is estimated by the municipality at 7.5 million.[3]

Since there is not space here to discuss all relevant aspects of Indian culture and their impact on urban life, we will limit our discussion basically to a description of some of the physical differences between Indian and western cities.

Land Use: Foreign and Indigenous Influences

Contemporary Indian cities are a combination of indigenous and foreign influences. However, even today these two cultures have remained distinct from one another, so that in Indian cities one can distinguish the European from the traditional sections by physical criteria. In the cities created by foreigners, such as Bombay and Calcutta, the differences may be seen within the various sectors of the city. Where a native city already existed, as was the case with Delhi, the British built their European city (in this instance, New Delhi) next to the existing city. During the British colonial period native sectors of the various cities were even administered differently. Bangalore, for instance, was divided for purposes of administration into Bangalore City on the west side and the Civil Station and Military Cantonment on the east side.[4]

Traditional Indian cities used their land quite differently from cities founded by Europeans. The indigenous cities of India have business districts, but these differ in both size and function from the western model. The business areas of the Indian cities are both spread throughout the city and quite small by western standards. Also, they are not highly specialized in only one or two functions, such as retailing and services, as is characteristic of the western model. The central area, which is made up of numerous small shops selling a variety of goods for personal or household use, is surrounded by streets specializing in specific merchandise such as goldware, brassware, furniture, and clothing. Intermixed throughout these streets are small hotels, small manufacturing plants, residences, moneylenders' shops, lawyers' offices, and even wholesale merchants. The CBD is given over to a variety of uses; particular activities are not concentrated in particular locations. Western models do not apply.

The colonial city, on the other hand, was the location of the rich and powerful. As such it reflected not only western organization and values, but also the fact that it housed the upper-class "sahibs." British "civil lines" contained civil administrative headquarters and the homes of the British in the Indian civil service, while "cantonments"—military reservations—graciously housed the British officers (the troops themselves fared far worse).

[3]Population estimates from International Communications Agency, Delhi, India, 1979.
[4]Noel P. Gist, "The Ecology of Bangalore, India: An East-West Comparison," *Social Forces*, 35:357, May, 1957.

In contrast to the model typical in the United States, the military reservations occupied central land rather than being peripherally located. Much of the city of Poona, for instance, is still occupied by military cantonments reflecting that city's heritage as a headquarters for the British and then the Indian army. Even within New Delhi, military bases continue to occupy much prime land. Attempts to persuade the military to move to outlying areas have been notably unsuccessful.

The spacious houses of the colonial city, graciously separated by large lawns and trees, to a lesser degree also reflect the nineteenth century's lack of knowledge about causes of disease. Malaria was thought to be caused by bad air (*mala aria*), and so the British constructed their residential areas with ample space for circulation of air between homes.

Density figures clearly document the difference between the old and new areas. The gross density is 13.2 persons per acre in New Delhi, but 213.3 persons per acre in Old Delhi.[5] The high figure for Old Delhi, moreover, is not for an area of apartment buildings but for an area of one- and two-story buildings. (In parts of Old Delhi the density rises to 600–700 persons per acre, while in Calcutta the average density is 45,000 people per square kilometer.)[6]

Old Delhi, with its stores and homes right on the edges of its always crowded streets and lanes, is a world apart from New Delhi, with its lawns and boulevards. Old Delhi is also a remarkably lively and interesting place. Its heavily Muslim population successfully fought Indira Ghandi's plans to raze some of the area and resettle its inhabitants elsewhere. It is important to keep in mind that while indigenous cities often lack modern amenities, this may be more than compensated for in the eyes of residents by the areas' vitality and activity.

Since it is impossible in the space available to cover more than a feeling for Indian urbanization, we will focus on the nation's two largest cities—the economically developing city of Bombay and the more economically stagnant city of Calcutta.

Bombay

Bombay, India's traditional gateway to the west, is perhaps that nation's most dynamic city.[7] Yet even Bombay, with 7.5 million inhabitants, is showing signs of coming apart at the seams. The reason isn't difficult to understand. Bombay, built on a peninsula, can extend only northward along a narrow corridor of two rail lines; but it contains more people than it can reasonably service—and the situation is getting worse. Bombay gains 10,000 residents every day, and few cities anwhere could keep up with such an influx. Most come seeking not better employment, but any employment.[8] Sewage systems, housing, educational systems, and transportation systems are overwhelmed. For example, the city has

[5]Gerald Breese, *Urbanization in Newly Developing Countries*, Prentice Hall, Englewood Cliffs, N. J., 1966, p. 62.
[6]Alfred de Souza (ed.), *The Indian City*, South Asia Books, Columbia, Mo., 1978, p. xiv.
[7]This section is partially based upon discussions with officials of the Bombay Metropolitan Region Development Authority and the City of Bombay Industrial Development Corporation. The opinions are, of course, the author's.
[8]P. Ramachandran, *Pavement Dwellers in Bombay City*, Tata Institute of Social Sciences, Bombay, India, 1972, p. 18.

several hundred thousand "pavement people" who actually live on the street, without even a squatter shack in a bustees, or spontaneous settlement. In the area of transportation, commuter railways are so overpacked that riders even sit on the roofs of trains. An average of twelve commuters a day die as a result of losing their balance or other accidents.

A new satellite town, New Bombay, is being built across the bay, and it is intended eventually to house over 1 million residents. Thus far, however, New Bombay is more a hope than an actual community, owing to bureaucratic delays and the reluctance of industries and government offices to resettle there. The city numbered under 25,000 as of 1980. Few people want to leave the central city, with its excitement and vitality, for resettlement across the bay.

In Bombay, as elsewhere in the burgeoning cities of Asia, the poverty of the masses contrasts sharply with the wealth of a few. Row upon row of new high-rise apartment buildings, some with rents exceeding $1,000 a month, serve as reminders that the problem is as much distribution of rewards as unavailability of resources. For most city residents, the situation is getting worse rather than better. The city's social and physical facilities simply cannot cope with the strain of increased numbers. Bombay, like other Indian cities, is unable to limit its population to a size that can be adequately employed, housed, and cared for.

Calcutta

Across the subcontinent, Calcutta—India's largest metropolitan center—numbers over 9 million people in the metropolitan district and 3 million in the city proper. Calcutta's growth is slower than that of Bombay or Delhi; but, given the stagnation of its urban industrial economy and the poverty of its populace, any growth presents serious problems. Calcutta is losing its economic base. The once-active machine-shop industry, for example, is now too antiquated to compete with more advanced operations elsewhere in India. The important jute industry is also affected by a fluctuating market and obsolescence.[9] Nor has the national government been eager to invest its interest and funds in Calcutta—partially, perhaps, because the municipal officials are Marxists.

The city also has problems with a unique land-tenure system which virtually ensures nonmaintenance of slum properties. In the *bustee* one person owns the land, another then builds a hut upon it, and a third serves as tenant, paying a monthly rent without any claim to either the land or the hut. Under this system no one has any incentive to maintain the property. *Bustee* residents technically are not squatters but tenants. Since landlords can't legally raise the rent without the tenants' permission, buildings are literally left to rot until they tumble into the street.

Attempts by the Municipal Development Authority to upgrade the slums, and by the Municipal Corporation to maintain them (a major Indian problem), are

[9]Harold Cubell, *Urban Development and Employment: The Prospects for Calcutta*, International Labour Office, Geneva, 1974.

Rickshaw pullers remain a common form of transportation in Calcutta. (Photograph by the author.)

hampered by lack of funds. Meanwhile, people and the sacred cattle coexist in the *bustees.* As a form of recycling, cattle dung is collected by women and children and formed into circular patties that serve as fuel when dried.

Within the city, groups occupy geographical wards largely on the basis of religion (Hindu or Muslim), caste, and ethnic region of origin.[10] Occupations are also ethnically segregated. For example, Bengalis traditionally prefer white-collar jobs and avoid heavy labor, while the rickshaw pullers are mostly Bihari. Taxi drivers used to be largely Punjabi but now also include some Bengalis.

Three-quarters of the population of Calcutta is housed in crowded tenements and *bustee* huts. A large survey by the State Statistical Bureau revealed that 90 percent of the families lived in a single room with shared kitchen, privy, and bathing facilities.[11] These *bustee* dwellers are in some ways fortunate, for between one-third of a million and 1 million pathway dwellers—no one knows the exact figure—have no housing of any type. They work, eat, sleep, breed, and die on the streets without the benefit of any shelter.

As if the city did not have enough internal problems, it twice has been flooded by Bengali refugees from nearby Bangladesh, and nature produces its own yearly floods. The 1978 floods were among the worst ever recorded, covering the entire city to a depth of a couple of feet. The city is almost flat, so that there is

[10]Nirmal Kumar Bose, *Calcutta 1964: A Social Survey,* Larani, Bombay, India, 1968. See also Brian J. Berry and John D. Kasarda, *Contemporary Urban Ecology,* Macmillan, New York, 1977, pp. 134–157.
[11]K. C. Sivaramakrishnan, "The Slum Improvement Programme in Calcutta: The Role of the CMDA," in de Souza, op. cit., p. 134.

Some of Calcutta's over half a million pavement people sleeping in their
only homes, the pathways. (J. P. Lafonte/United Nations.)

no high ground to serve as a refuge from the flood. The flat terrain also severely
complicates waste problems, since sewers—which cover only a small portion of
the city in any case—quickly become clogged. Most of Calcutta's sewers are
currently inoperable.

The litany of Calcutta's ills seems endless, and the city's international
reputation as the epitome of urban problems is not without cause. Nonetheless,
Calcutta, even with all its social and physical problems, remains one of the
world's more vital cities. It is the active center of Bengali poetry and theater, and
few Bengali intellectuals would trade the city's excitement for all the fine
neighborhoods and homes of New Delhi.

Calcutta is also remarkably free of street crime. Residents fatalistically may
accept power outages, poor housing, malaria, cholera, antiquated transportation,

and constant strikes that close down municipal services, but they do not tolerate street crime against women. Bengalis pride themselves on the safety of women, and any violator risks the wrath of the ever-present street crowds. Indian women in Calcutta can walk even at night with a degree of safety unknown in New Delhi, London, or New York. Physically the city is in decay; socially it retains a vigor of life and pride that other cities might envy.

Programs to alleviate Calcutta's problems have been proposed by the United Nations, the Ford Foundation, and the Indian government. Unfortunately, the aid that Calcutta has received has not always met its real needs. For example, to solve the city's transportation problems, the national goverment is now building an expensive subway system. The system is being built in a city where all buses are ancient and constantly in disrepair, where the last new streetcar was purchased before World War II, and where 40,000 barefoot rickshaw pullers still provide transportation for people and goods. Despite this, despite periodic floods, and despite the certainty that subway stations inevitably will become a home for pavement people, it was decided for political reasons to build a subway to provide employment. The protests of state and municipal officials on the scene were of no avail.

Government Intervention

National Programs for Housing the Poor. India is currently engaged in various programs to build low-cost self-help homes on the urban periphery for the poor. Very basic homes to be furnished by the occupant are being built by development authorities for as little as $300. However, even this price is well beyond the reach of most squatters and pavement people. In relatively prosperous Delhi, for instance, half the people in the lowest-status "economically weaker section" have a monthly income under $50. Another quarter (23 percent) earn between $50 and $90 a month.[12] Elsewhere the monthly incomes are generally lower.

Increasing attention is thus being given to "site and service" projects, in which a housing site is provided with basic sewerage facilities and a shared water pump. Construction of the house over time is the responsibility of the resident. This is a good program, for while some Indian planners are still put off by the disorderly nature of the site and service areas, there is no reasonable alternative. Government-built public housing projects on the western model are too expensive and have been beset by massive maintenance and other problems.

Government Policy on Urban Places. Despite the pleas of urban officials and planners working in the cities, India's national government has yet to develop an effective policy for urban growth. (Responsibility for urban development technically rests with each state.) The legacy of Gandhi—an emphasis on rural and village

[12]Delhi Development Authority figures, March, 1979.

Urban and rural homes constructed by India's National Building
Organization. The construction cost for the rural house is approximately
$210 with self-help, and is $540 for the urban house. (Courtesy National
Building Organization.)

India—still prevails in policy making and attitudes reflect this antiurban heritage. Politicans are largely of rural origin themselves and depend upon rural support to stay in office. City dwellers, because they constitute but one-fifth of the population, remain politically underrepresented.

Current national policy is attempting to slow the growth of the larger cities and disperse their population. This is to be done through consciously limiting economic expansion in the largest cities. However, such attempts to divert the flow of migration toward smaller cities are unlikely to succeed. Prohibiting new industrial enterprises is unlikely to have a deterrent effect on in-migrants. On the other hand, limiting economic expansion in the cities is almost certain to further accelerate problems of jobs, housing, transportation, sewage, and schooling. Short of draconian measures—which no one is even suggesting—India's great cities will continue to grow with or without government approval.

India: Prognosis

Overshadowing all other Indian problems is that of how to cope with population growth. India now has some 676 million people and will top 1 billion by the year 2000. To put it in more understandable terms, each year India is adding 14 million persons, or the total population of Australia.

The eradication of smallpox, the partial eradication of malaria, and control of cholera have reduced infant mortality drastically. Life expectancy in the past four decades has been extended from twenty-six to fifty years. As a consequence, 41 percent of the population is still under fifteen years of age. When these young people come of age, it is problematic whether the necessary educational opportunities, jobs, and housing will be available. India for decades has had various birth control programs, but the population is already so large that even a moderate growth rate has a tremendous numerical impact. (India, with a 1.9 percent yearly increase, will double its population in only 36 years.) India is capable of feeding itself, and there are also very substantial nonagricultural resources. Economic growth, though, tends to benefit the elite and the middle class rather than the masses. (Nationally over two-thirds of the urban families must survive on monthly incomes of between $15 and $50.) Also, as a result of continual population growth, development is distorted: attention must be constantly focused on increasing the amount of foodstuffs available. Other problems such as education and housing necessarily receive lower priority. Questions of improving the quality of life and saving the environment receive much less attention.

Thus for the masses life cannot be expected to improve much. Short of a major national restructuring and effort, it is difficult to see how adequate housing, municipal services, and employment can be provided for the burgeoning urban population.

CHINA

China took its last national census in 1953; thus there is a lack of recent data on Chinese urbanization. What little is known refers more to the decade of the 1950s than to the most recent period.[13] Because of the lack of hard data, even the most general statements regarding the extent of urbanization may be subject to considerable error. It is not so much that the Chinese have been withholding data as that reliable statistical information for the decades since the 1950s often does not exist.

The Chinese census of 1953 indicated a total population of 583 million. The last official population figure released by the Chinese was 647 million in 1957. While there is agreement among experts that both birthrates and death rates have been dropping significantly in recent years, there is still disagreement as to the size of the total population. The Population Reference Bureau estimates the current population at 975 million.[14] Even with declining birthrates, roughly one out of every four children born this year will be Chinese.

The People's Republic of China has an area of about 3,800,000 square miles, with 96 percent of the population living on 40 percent of the land area.[15] The population of China is concentrated in the southern and eastern sections of the country. The greatest density is found in the Yangtze valley, where there are 2,000 to 2,500 persons per square mile.

Background

The first modern manufacturing and industrial cities of China were the western-dominated treaty ports. During the nineteenth century and the early twentieth century, the ports of Chinese coastal cities were at various times physically controlled and occupied by European, and later Japanese, administrators and troops.

The European powers forced the weak and ineffectual Manchu, or Ch'ing, dynasty to give foreigners substantial control over the economic life of the major Chinese cities. Europeans lived in separate, newer sections of the cities. The foreign concessions of Shanghai were even policed by European troops; nor could foreigners be tried for crimes in Chinese courts. In Shanghai, the largest and most prosperous of the treaty ports, the Chinese city was separated from the foreign section by a fine park. Signs at the borders of the park stated, "No Dogs or Chinese Allowed." Even the capital of Peking had its "legation quarter" for foreigners, near the central Imperial City, However, the number of foreign residents was never particularly large. In Canton, China's major southern city,

[13]Among the best overviews are M. B. Ullman, "Cities of Mainland China: 1953 and 1958," *International Population Reports,* series P-95, Washington, D.C., 1961; and John S. Aird, "The Size, Composition and Growth of the Population of Mainland China," *International Population Reports,* series P-90, Washington, D.C., 1961.

[14]Population Reference Bureau, *1980 World Population Data Sheet,* Washington, D.C., 1980.

[15]Aird, op. cit., p. 5.

foreigners at their height numbered only 894 out of a city population of over 1 million.[16]

The Nationalist government, which replaced the Ch'ing dynasty in 1911, was made up of an urban military and upper-class elite which continued the traditional practices of taxing and coercing the peasants to support the urban-based government. Landowners, many of whom lived in the cities, had little sympathy for the declining quality of life in rural China. The government continued to serve the landowners and disregard the plight of the peasants; land reform was ignored.

The communists also initially ignored the peasants and attempted to organize in the cities, but having failed at that, Mao Tse-tung redirected attention to the peasants. After decades of internal struggle and the civil war of 1947–1949, the communists achieved national dominance.

Current Urbanization Policies

Almost one-fourth of China's population is defined as urban by the People's Republic; using this definition, China currently has an urban population of 235 million. This would mean that China—although still three-quarters rural—has the world's largest national population of urban dwellers. For three decades China's policy under Mao was resolutely antiurban. This was in part a reaction to the treaty port cities' being seen (correctly) as the centers of western thought and influence. "The foreign presence (in China) was almost exclusively urban."[17] (Inland cities such as Tsinan were more successful in resisting foreign intervention.[18]) The initial failures of the communist cause in the cities further separated the cities from the original communist leadership. However, in spite of the discouraging of urban growth, between 1949 and 1956 some 20 million Chinese migrated from rural areas into the cities.

In 1963, following the economic crisis brought on by the failure of the "great leap forward" campaign, the government decided to stabilize the urban population at 110 million, which was considered a manageable figure.[19] In order to so this, it was decided to "rusticate," or return to the countryside, urban school graduates; this would lessen the pressure on the urban economy and help promote agriculture and indigenous industry in rural areas. During the "cultural revolution" of the 1960s, the government tried to reverse the flow to the cities and send surplus urban population into the countryside. Unemployed Red Guards, labor battalions, and those guilty of ideological sins were shipped by the trainload to the countryside. Many of these migrants made poor adjustments to their new surroundings and have drifted back into the cities.

---

[16]Ezra Vogel, *Canton Under Communism*, Harvard University Press, Cambridge, Mass., 1969.

[17]Rhoads Murphey, "The Treaty Ports and China's Modernization," in Mark Elvin and G. William Skinner (eds.), *The Chinese City between Two Worlds*, Stanford University Press, Stanford, Calif., 1974, p. 67.

[18]David D. Buck, *Urban Change in China*, University of Wisconsin Press, Madison, 1978.

[19]Pi-chao Chen, "Overurbanization, Rustication of Urban-Educated Youths, and Politics of Rural Transformation," *Comparative Politics*, April, 1972, p. 374.

During Mao's final years, as a result of the combination of extreme pressure and ideological conviction, many urban-educated youths volunteered for permanent resettlement in the countryside. These included all graduates of urban secondary schools and universities who had not been accepted at an educational institution at the next higher level or had not been assigned to a post in urban industry or service units.[20] In the words of a call by Mao Tse-tung in December 1968:

> It is very necessary for the educated youth to go to the countryside to be reeducated by the poor and lower-middle peasants. Cadres and other people in the cities should be persuaded to send their sons and daughters who have completed junior or senior middle school, college or university, to the countryside. Let us mobilize. Comrades throughout the country should welcome them.[21]

It is estimated that within two years of this call, between 10 and 15 million youths volunteered either by conviction or coercion to move permanently to rural villages.[22] Some estimates run as high as 25 million. If this is an accurate picture, the migration was one of the greatest in history. Most of the youths came from the largest industrial and educational centers, such as Peking, Tientsin, Shanghai, and Canton.

The present government is stressing modernization and industrial development, and has de facto largely abandoned the rural resettlement of urban youth.

Shanghai

Shanghai, China's largest city, grew as a treaty port built on western commercial enterprise. It was largely imposed upon the existing peasant civilization.[23] Within a decade of its opening to foreign trade in 1843, Shanghai's manufacturing sector had become a physical and economic embodiment of nineteenth-century European thought. In nineteenth-century Shanghai, with its extraterritoriality (foreigners having their own laws, police, and courts), foreign concessions, and foreign gunboats, the modern industrial world of European rationality came face to face with the traditional seclusionist ways of the Chinese Empire.

Today Shanghai, with an urban area population of over 12 million, is one of the world's largest cities. For Chinese planners, the physical development of Shanghai has been complicated by several factors. For example, in their attempts to plan the development of Shanghai, the Chinese have had to overcome the effects of the previous pattern of mixed foreign domination. Each of the foreign settlements had not only its own administration and police but also its own pattern and width of streets. Developing a uniform citywide street pattern has required widening existing streets as well as extending others by tearing down

---

[20]Ibid., p. 365.
[21]Ibid.
[22]Ibid., p. 369.
[23]For a description of Shanghai before communism, see Rhoads Murphey, *Shanghai—Key to Modern China*, Harvard University Press, Cambridge, Mass., 1953.

An intersection in downtown Shanghai. Note both the traffic control tower and the absence of private automobiles. (© 1979 Diane Rawson/Photo Researchers, Inc.)

buildings and houses. The total length of city streets has increased more than ten times—from 200 miles to over 2,000 miles—over the period from 1949 to 1972.[24]

Shanghai's dominant position as the industrial center of the nation has also complicated plans for industrial dispersion. Today Shanghai has more than 1.5 million industrial workers employed in industries such as steel, machine tools, shipbuilding, chemicals, motor vehicles, and textiles. Efforts to disperse industrial sites to outlying areas have been handicapped by shortages of transportation and capital. China's "opening to the west" is already having a major impact on Shanghai as the major port and industrial center.

With the mass of industrial activity located within the city proper, there is considerable pollution and transportation congestion. The pollution and congestion from automobiles is minimal, however, since there are no private automobiles on the streets. The absence of automobiles also limits the distance one can live from one's workplace. In order to get to work, the populace uses a crowded bus system—although not as overcrowded as that in Tokyo—and bicycles. There are perhaps 2 million bicycles in the city, but some families still do not own one, and the demand outruns the supply.

At the time of the revolution, Shanghai, like other Chinese cities, was faced with a massive housing problem. Years of war and turmoil had left the poor to

[24]Hung-Mao Tien, "Shanghai: China's Huge 'Model City,' " *Milwaukee Journal,* December 16, 1973.

exist in shacks and straw huts along the streets and the riverbank. These hovels are now gone, and some ninety-five residential villages have been constructed. Although the housing is crowded—from 43 to 48 square feet per person, according to Chinese officials—apartments are reported to be neat and well maintained.[25] Within the city, water, sewers, and electricity are available to virtually every family, and 300,000 families are reported to have gas stoves. An average working family pays only from roughly 4 to 8 percent of its income for monthly rent.[26] The major complaint voiced by foreign observers is that the cities of China are on the dull side, lacking the noisy vitality of other Asian cities.

Peking

Today Peking, which has been the capital of China almost continuously since A.D. 1267, has a population of over 6 million.[27] The city—China's second largest—is a combination of the ancient and the very modern, with the suburban districts being mostly farming villages that have been organized into communes. A factory sector is being developed in the eastern and southern suburbs. Because of the absence of private transportation on a large scale—although the city does have 1.5 million bicycles—every attempt is made to construct new factories near housing for the workers. Older housing is less satisfactory than new housing, which usually consists of brick buildings four to six stories tall. A family of four or five persons generally lives in an apartment consisting of two rooms plus a kitchen, a bathroom, and a small foyer. All the newer apartments have running water, water heaters, and flush toilets.[28] The shape of the future can be seen in housing development in Ho-p'inh-li, a suburb of Peking, which contains not only primary and middle schools, but also nurseries, hotels, and other facilities. Overall, however, the quality of life is still generally below that of Hong Kong, Singapore, or Taiwan.

Summary—China

China has been relatively successful in providing for its urban population. In many cities of the developing world, there is massive unemployment, sometimes in excess of 25 percent; but this does not appear to be a problem in China, partially because of rural resettlement. While life is highly regimented by western standards, it also is quite tolerable. The starvation and street begging that were a common sight in China before 1949 no longer exist. Great wealth and great poverty have both been abolished; and average workers, it is generally agreed, live better and more securely than ever before, although not as comfortably as many of their Asian neighbors. As China encourages technological development, trade, and industrialization, it can be expected to undergo many of the same problems faced by other nations in the throes of rapid urban industrial development.

[25]Ibid.
[26]Ibid.
[27]Hikotaro Ando, *Peking*, Dodansha International, Tokyo, 1968, p. 41.
[28]Arthur Galston, "Peking Man (and Woman) Today," *Natural History*, November, 1972, p. 28.

Hong Kong has very limited space for its growing population. Even the streetcars are double-deckers. (Photograph by the author.)

A Note on Hong Kong

The British Crown Colony of Hong Kong, although on the Chinese mainland, is most noted for its extremely laissez-faire economic structure. Hong Kong, including the New Territories which technically revert back to mainland Chinese ownership in 1997, totals only 404 square miles. Much of this land, however, is so steep and mountainous as to be incapable of development, or is located on scattered islands where development would be uneconomical. This, plus the strong desire of newcomers to remain in the city proper, means that Hong Kong's population is heavily concentrated in a narrow ring around the harbor. As a consequence densities in Hong Kong reach 6,500 persons *per acre,* the highest in the world,[29] The continued influx of refugees into this already overcrowded environment is further straining the city's resources.

In an attempt to provide public housing for all who need it, Hong Kong is developing several new towns. Tsuen Won, which was begun in 1973, already holds over 600,000 persons and eventually will have over 1 million. (Obviously the new towns are far larger than Ebenezer Howard's vision of self-contained communities of only 30,000.) Hong Kong's new towns (or cities) are being developed as self-sufficient entities, but in fact cannot yet meet their own

---

[29]Murray MacLehose, "Modern Urban Development in Hong Kong," paper delivered by the Governor to the Commonwealth Society, Honk Kong, November 28, 1977.

educational, retail trade, and entertainment needs, much less provide their own employment base.

Hong Kong is noted for having produced an economic miracle. What it has not produced is a means of equitably sharing that miracle. The profits largely go to a wealthy entrepreneurial elite, while the poor live in some of the most crowded slums in Asia. One reason new towns can be constructed rapidly is that construction workers labor for minimal pay, ten hours a day, seven days a week. The only break in the workers' routine occurs at the Chinese New Year holidays. Nonetheless, for the continuing flood of in-migrants, Hong Kong represents living standards and opportunities unavailable on the mainland.

JAPAN

Any discussion of Asian urban patterns must include Japan, the region's most urbanized large nation. Japan is not an urban newcomer; it has an urban tradition even longer than that of India as regards the role of the city in regional and national life. Japan's urban tradition goes back at least to the fifteenth century. The so-called "castletowns" formed a basic urban stratum upon which later cities were built. Edo, as Tokyo was then called, may have had 1 million people in 1700, while Osaka, the great trade center, and Kiyoto, the ancient capital, both had several hundred thousand inhabitants.[30]

The Extent of Urbanization

The forced opening of Japan to western influences in the nineteenth century, led to a boom in city building. Cities such as Tokyo, Nagoya, and Osaka grew, first as trading centers, and later as manufacturing and commercial cities. Industrialization and urbanization took place so completely that today Japan equals and in some cases surpasses western levels in these two areas. Today Japan is three-quarters urban (76 percent), a figure which is essentially the same as that for the United States.[31] Moreover, the urban population of Japan is remarkably concentrated, with an overall national density of over 300 persons per square kilometer and 45 percent of the total population occupying only 1 percent of the land area.

Current Patterns

In discussing contemporary Japanese urbanization it is important to remember that while Japan is an Asian country, its levels of urbanization and industrialization are far closer to those of Europe and North America than to those of the rest of Asia. The strengths and problems of Japanese cities are largely those of developed western metropolises. Japan, along with the small enclaves of Hong

---

[30] Edwin O. Reishauer, *The Japanese*, Belkhap Press, Cambridge, Mass., 1978, p. 25.
[31] Population Reference Bureau, *1980 World Population Data Sheet*, Washington, D.C., 1980.

Kong and Singapore, has both a level and a pattern of urbanization highly atypical of Asia in general.

Many current urban problems in Japan are a result of the decision of the Japanese after World War II to concentrate all their efforts on industrial production for export. Only minimal attention and resources were devoted to "social overhead" such as sewage systems, water systems, housing, pollution control, and urban transporation. The result is that today Japan has a massive backlog of demands for urban services.

The picture, however, is not as grim as these considerations alone would indicate, for while Japan has large problems, it also has great resources. Japan has the technology, the skilled personnel, and the financial resources to rebuild and remake its cities. What it now requires is the will to make the commitment. The problem is one of social organization rather than technology or resources.

Tokyo

Tokyo, the world's largest city, is to the western observer a series of contradictions.[32] Signs of prosperity are everywhere, from the streets clogged with new automobiles to futuristic new office buildings to luxury department stores unmatched in Paris, London, or New York. A shabbily dressed person is difficult to find. Few would disagree with the contention of President Isomura of Tokyo University that Japanese women are, as a group, better and more expensively dressed than women anywhere in Europe or the United States.

Yet Japan, in spite of its affluence, has not been able or willing to properly house its population and provide urban amenities taken for granted in other developed countries. Japan's cities reflect the emphasis on production for export rather than an attempt to upgrade the urban infrastructure. For example, housing conditions are extremely cramped and excessively expensive by American standards. Land prices are estimated to be ten times as high as in New York.[33] This means that a small plot of land within commuting distance that would cost the average American worker 45 days' wages to purchase would cost the average Tokyo worker 6½ years wages.[34] Again and again one hears that young people spend money on consumer goods and holidays, since, without major parental assistance, they are unable to purchase homes.

Exorbitant land costs have also resulted in structures being built wall to wall up to the lot lines. Unfortunately, within the Tokyo-Yokohama agglomeration, the traditional Japanese gardens exist only in memory or on the estates of the wealthy. Zoning regulations are minimal, and even they are frequently flouted. This absence of control over construction is notable in such a structured society.

There is also a lack of public services. Within the area of the Tokyo metropolitan government (the old city of twenty-three wards and the immediate

---

[32]Material in this section is based heavily on my own observations and conversations with Japanese planning officials.
[33]Peter Hall, *World Cities,* McGraw-Hill, New York, 1977, p. 227.
[34]Ibid.

Japan's rail system is good, but it cannot cope with the demand. Uniformed pushers are employed to shove additional people into already overcrowded cars. (© Minoru Aoki/Rapho/Photo Researchers, Inc.)

surrounding suburbs with a population of 11½ million), half (48 percent as of 1974) the population still has no sewerage or flush toilets.[35] Ironically, at the same time 98 percent of the homes in Tokyo have color television.

Tokyo-Yokohama is not only the world's largest metropolitan area; it is also possibly the world's most congested and polluted. Air pollution is so severe that it directly causes scores of deaths each year. Workers in some industries automatically use face masks. The level of water pollution was graphically demonstrated when a Tokyo newspaper printed on its front page a photograph that had been developed solely by dipping the negative in a chemically polluted river.

In the area of transportation, Tokyo has a remarkably clean and efficient subway system, but during rush hours it and commuter rail lines must employ an army of 700 pushers whose job it is to force additional passengers into the overcrowded cars. The record was set by the Chico line, which in 1972 carried 260 percent of its supposed capacity. Above ground, the roads are continually packed with wall-to-wall vehicles. Because space is at a premium, express roads are usually built above existing roadways, but they also are commonly clogged. The system is simply not adequate for a city half Tokyo's size.

During the final years of World War II much of Tokyo was leveled—the city

[35]Ibid., p. 228.

lost 56 percent of its housing stock—and Tokyo had the opportunity to rebuild itself with widened streets, open spaces, parks, and reasonable lot sizes. The fact that this was not even seriously considered is still seen as more of a tragedy by outsiders than by the business elites of Tokyo. These elites continue Japan's extremely successful emphasis on foreign exports and trade surpluses, while strongly resisting any meaningful national or municipal government spending on infrastructure. Thus far urban planning and development have taken a distinct back seat to unbridled laissez-faire economic growth.

Planned Towns

There are, of course, some major exceptions. Suma New Town, near Kobe, currently with a population exceeding 100,000 was built on reclaimed land. To provide land the tops of hills were literally blasted and bulldozed off, and the rock was then carried underground for miles to the sea on huge conveyer belts. The fill was then used to construct the artificial port and Rokko Islands in Kobe harbor. The inland project, which was officially dedicated in 1980, is estimated to have cost $2.5 billion.

Public housing, in new towns or elsewhere, is built for middle-class rather than low-income groups. The public Japan Housing Corporation, for example, is required by law to break even on the projects it constructs, and so rents are usually far more than the poor can afford. Limited public housing for low-income groups is built by the Metropolitan Housing Supply Corporation.

Suburbanization

Suburbanization has been a factor in Japan ever since the earthquake of 1923, which encouraged decentralization and until the last decade limited multistory dwellings to a height of 102 feet. The Japanese have a tradition of city living; and before World War II, the poor lived outside the municipal boundaries, particularly in marshy areas. A long commute to work in that era was a penalty of poverty rather than a prerogative of affluence as in the United States.

More recently, high land costs have resulted in heavy middle-class and even upper-class suburbanization. Since commuting to and from suburbs is done largely by rail, the greatest suburban development has been along the very profitable suburban rail lines. (The average commute is 1½ hours each way.) As land prices rise, the center of Tokyo is more and more given over to shops and commercial and business activities. The resident central-city population can be expected to decline further while suburban growth—some of it quite distant—accelerates.

SOUTHEAST ASIA

Urbanization is not part of the tradition of southeast Asia. Unlike China, India, or Japan, southeast Asia had few indigenous urban areas. Most cities there are a product of European colonial expansion, Chinese enterprise, or a combination of the two. "In almost every country in Southeast Asia, with its 220 million people of which about 25 million live in cities, there are large cities, but every one of these is the product of a merging of European colonialism with Chinese urbanness."[36] This is perhaps somewhat of an exaggeration, but the pattern holds true.

Cities in southeast Asia are relatively new. Few date back more than a century or so. Primate cities, particularly ports, are common. Most of the cities are clearly divided into western and nonwestern districts. Saigon (now Ho Chi Minh City) provides an example.

Saigon's urban history began in 1859, when the French captured a village of native huts, none of them permanent structures. On this site the French built Saigon as an administrative capital, laying out the streets in the grid pattern. The Chinese quarter and marketplace, known as Cholon, developed simultaneously with Saigon. Thus Saigon became the French colonial capital for Cochin China, later named Vietnam, while Cholon was the Asian city. Early growth in Saigon was orderly, while Cholon grew haphazardly. The two areas were merged by the French in 1932 for administrative purposes.

Before World War II, the largest population group in Saigon-Cholon was the Chinese.[37] From about 300,000 inhabitants in 1940, the population increased to an estimated 1,400,000 by 1953.[38] Roughly 60 percent of Cholon, and 30 percent of the entire city, was Chinese at this time. More recently the government of Vietnam has been expelling the Chinese, fearing that they dominate the economy and constitute a potential "fifth column" loyal to China. The great majority of the so-called Vietnamese "boat people" were in fact ethnic Chinese.

Singapore

The modern island Republic of Singapore is quite atypical of southeast Asia. Whether this is good or bad depends on the perspective of the observer. Economically there is no question that, in spite of the total absence of natural resources (Singapore even has to import sand for building), the country is prosperous. Singapore has some 2.4 million persons in an area of only 225 square miles (584 square kilometers), making it one of the most densely crowded areas on the globe. Officially Singapore is 100 percent urban, although some semirural areas remain.

What makes Singapore unique, though, is its strategy for control and development. Since 1960 the government has been involved in an ambitious program to replace virtually all of Singapore's previous housing with high-rise apartment buildings. Slums and squatter settlements have been eradicated, sometimes by the use of draconian measures. The old Chinese neighborhoods of street vendors and dilapidated overcrowded buildings so dear to the hearts of travelers have been replaced almost entirely by government-sponsored high-rise estates and new office buildings and hotels. Currently two-thirds of the population

---

[36]Norton S. Ginsburg, "Urban Geography and 'Non-Western' Areas," in Philip M. Hauser and Leo F. Schnore (eds.), *The Study of Urbanization*, Wiley, New York, 1965, p. 332.

[37]Norton S. Ginsburg, "The Great City in Southeast Asia," *American Journal of Sociology*, **60**:459, March, 1955.

[38]D. W. Fryer, "The Million City in Southeast Asia," *Geographical Review*, **43**:477, October, 1953.

resides in government-built high-rises.[39] By 1988, 75 percent of the population will live in high-rise structures. Singapore is also rapidly building several new towns—also of high-rises—the largest of which will be Woodlands New Town, with a population of 290,000.

The rapid transformation of Singapore into an ultramodern city is not however, without its critics. Some charge that too much of the traditional culture has been sacrificed to the god of efficiency. For example, once government planners decide to rebuild a district, the land is compulsorily acquired; and although compensation is paid, neither litigation by owners nor public protests by residents will stop redevelopment. If an ancient temple sits on land desired for redevelopment, the temple is either moved or rebuilt elsewhere.

Singapore's sharp break with the past has both advantages and disadvantages. While the high-rise structures are not as effective as the old *kampongs* and squatter settlements in fostering community ties and close human relationships, they do provide better housing and living facilities for the majority of the population.[40] Compared with high-rise housing projects in the United States, the buildings are well maintained. Perhaps this is because, as a result of government policy, more residents own than rent their flats.

Under the government's "home ownership for the people" scheme, residents can draw upon their mandatory 15 percent social security payments for the down payment and even monthly payments for their flats. Most apartments are still relatively small, but it is not uncommon for a family to spend a considerable amount upgrading and redecorating its flat. Currently the Housing and Development Board is starting to "thin out" some of the earlier projects by tearing down every second building. At the same time it is phasing out one-room flats by converting them to two-room units. Singapore is thus in the unique position of being in the process of "solving" its physical housing problems, insofar as government-built housing of standard quality is available to most residents.

Whether the high-rise projects can meet the social and community needs of the populace remains to be seen. Singaporeans enjoy one of the highest standards of living in Asia. Economic prosperity has resulted in so many automobiles that to control congestion and pollution, cars not having an expensive entry permit are banned from the center of the city during working hours. The city is also engaged in a major program of beautification by planting trees and bushes along the streets. (Because Singapore is near the equator, newly planted trees grow rapidly along the streets and around the housing projects.)

Overall, Singaporeans live in a tightly controlled society where efficiency ranks well ahead of participation by citizens in making decisions. Regulations, even on littering (a $50 fine), are enforced strictly. Today Singapore is a modern commercial city. If it isn't as quaint, colorful, and interesting as in the old days, that is a price most residents seem willing to pay.[41]

[39]Housing and Development Board, *Annual Report 1978–79*, Republic of Singapore, 1979.
[40]Peter S. J. Chen and Tai Ching Ling: *Social Ecology of Singapore*, Federal Publications, Singapore, 1977.
[41]"Progress Dooms Charm and Bustle of the Chinatown in Singapore," *Smithsonian*, 6:38–47, January, 1976.

Other Places

Space does not permit a discussion of all the cities of southeast Asia; my apologies to those whose favorite city has not been included. Any complete treatment would of course have to include the building boom of Seoul, the sprawling cities of Taipei and Manila, and the world-famous traffic congestion of Bangkok.

Finally, there is Australia, a country that is in, but not of, Asia. Australia's 14 million people are heavily concentrated in the cities of the southeastern corner of the nation. Six million people inhabit the two metropolitan areas of Melbourne and Sydney alone. Although Australia is demographically one of the most highly urbanized nations in the world, its physical appearance is far different from what one usually associates with urbanization. For example, it is not a nation of high-rises, as Singapore is. Four out of five Australian families own their own single-family houses, and Australian sociologists refer to their country as the "first suburban nation." Almost nothing that can be said about Australia applies to the rest of Asia, and vice versa.

CONCLUSION

Everywhere in Asia urbanization and urbanism are increasing rapidly, if not spectacularly. Even in China, where government policies strongly encourage birth control, the cities are inevitably going to grow, since the Chinese government is also encouraging industrial development and trade.

Individual cities are frequently immense, but the overall level of urbanization is still low in all moderate- or large-size Asian nations except Japan and Australia. This is certain to change. Looking at Asia as a whole, it is quite reasonable to assume that by the year 2000 four out of every ten Asians will be city dwellers. Asian cities will be booming for the remainder of this century.

Generalizing beyond this point for the entire region is impossible, since the outstanding characteristic of the area is its diversity. Many of the urban problems may be similar, but the solutions to date have differed widely both in content and degree of success.

Japan is by far the most urbanized of the large nations of Asia and has the greatest resources, both technical and economic, that can be brought to bear on specific problems such as housing, sanitation, and transportation. China has immense human resources but a far more limited technical base. Thus far it has managed potential urban problems by controlling urban population growth. Indian cities, by contrast, come closer to the old "teeming masses of Asia" stereotype. Rapid population growth has severely strained the physical capabilities of the cities to house, educate, and employ their residents. Indian cities, though, possess vitality, color, and even safety that other nations might envy.

It has to be kept in mind that everywhere in Asia the cities, even with all their very real problems, are not places of defeat and despair but of hope and life. Issues such as the "death of the city" have little meaning in the Asian context.

PART SIX

CONCLUSION

CHAPTER

19

TOWARD THE URBAN FUTURE

We will ever strive for the ideals and sacred things of the city, both alone and with many; we will unceasingly seek to quicken the sense of public duty; we will revere and obey the city's laws; we will transmit this city not only not less, but greater, better and more beautiful than it was transmitted to us.

Oath of the Athenian city-state

Urban life is, as mayors of large cities are constantly reminding us, in a state of turmoil, troubled, and transition. The city of the 1920s, 1930s, and 1940s is dying, and a new postindustrial urban form is being born. However, how fast this new urban society will emerge and what physical and social form it will take are matters of considerable doubt and dispute.

CHANGES IN THE CITY

Urban Growth

As has been indicated throughout this book, the world is presently urbanizing at a remarkable rate, with no end of the process in view. Today we live in an urban world, a massive change from the beginning of the nineteenth century, when only 3 percent of the world's population lived in places of 5,000 or more. Kingsley Davis suggested two decades ago that "there is no apparent reason why [the world] should not become as urbanized as the most urban countries today—with perhaps 85–90 percent of the population living in cities and towns of 5,000 or more and practicing urban occupations."[1] Today there is no reason to fundamentally question Davis's prediction.

In the United States downward trends in birthrates have apparently convinced some people that there is no longer any problem of population increase. This is a risky assumption for Americans, and even more so for the world in general. For example, assuming that the United States maintains only a replacement level of fertility, the population of the country will still continue to grow during all of our lifetimes and into the second half of the twenty-first century. The current net population increase, even with our present birthrates, is less than 1 percent a year, but that still means a yearly net increase of our 1¾ million people a year.[2] Declines in birthrates have been offset by rises in the number of women of childbearing years. According to projections by the demographer Norman Ryder, which are based upon the smallest ultimate population size compatible with a uniform number of future births, the population of the United States by the year 2000 will be 262.5 million. By 2060 the population would reach its maximum size—297.9 million, an increase of 46 percent over 1970.[3]

Thus growth is definitely part of the future of America. In fact, of the 35 million people—this is a minimum—that will be added to the American population between 1980 and 2000, approximately 80 percent will live in urban areas. This is an additional metropolitan population larger than the total 1980 populations of Sweden, Denmark, Holland, Luxembourg, Belgium, and Austria combined. The consequence of population growth coupled with increasing numbers of young

[1]Kingsley Davis, "The Origin and Growth of Urbanization in the World," *American Journal of Sociology*, 60:437, March, 1955.
[2]"Population Growth in the United States and Canada," *Statistical Bulletin*, 60:11, April-June, 1979.
[3]Norman B. Ryder, "The Future Growth of the American Population," in Charles F. Westoff (ed.), *Toward the End of Growth*, Spectrum Books, Prentice-Hall, Englewood Cliffs, N. J., 1973, p. 87.

people and the elderly having their own households is an increasing demand for housing.

Internal Migration

In the United States—except for the cities of the sun belt—central-city populations can be expected to stabilize in size or even show some decreases. For 200 years the combination of heavy immigration from abroad and internal movement from farm to city gave the city a growth rate far in excess of that of the countryside. Now that period is ended. As stated by Charles Tilly:

> We can expect the migrant from the farm—and even the small town—to virtually disappear. For a great many reasons it is unlikely that the rural migrant from overseas will replace him. A constantly mounting proportion of the new arrivals will be lifelong urbanites from other American metropolitan areas.[4]

Migration today is increasingly between one metropolitan area and another, with the poorer migrants more commonly going from central city to central city. The more affluent move from the suburbs of one metropolitan area to the suburbs of another metropolitan area without touching the cities themselves. Aggregate movement in the United States is toward the south and the west—particularly the southwest. The movement also is toward deep water—the Atlantic and Pacific oceans, the Gulf of Mexico, or the Great Lakes. Today more than two out of five Americans live in a metropolitan area abutting deep water. The effects of such concentration are already all too visible in parts of California and Florida. It would be tragic if the mistakes made after World War II, which produced urban sprawl, were unthinkingly repeated. But there is not a great deal of evidence that most community planning is taking place on other than a piecemeal, ad hoc basis.

Changes in Housing Trends

In spite of the need for additional housing, increased urban sprawl of the type described in Chapters 4 and 7 now seems less likely. High interest rates, rising costs of building and land, and soaring gasoline prices may do what planning was unable to achieve. Continued surburban and exurban sprawl has been constrained not by government fiat or planning, but by escalating costs.

An alternative to unguided metropolitan development might be a national commitment to a new towns program similar to the European programs discussed in Chapter 13. The National Commission on Urban Growth recommended such a commitment of 100 new towns of about 100,000 each and 10 new cities of 1 million each. However, unless there is a radical change in national will and commitment such a development is highly unlikely, for new towns clearly are not a current national priority.

---

[4]Charles Tilly, "Migration to American Cities," in Daniel P. Moynihan (ed.), *Toward a National Urban Policy*, Basic Books, New York, 1970, chap. 13, pp. 153, 165.

Ghirardelli Square in San Francisco first demonstrated how abandoned buildings could be transformed into vibrant shopping and restaurant areas. (Fred Kaplan/Black Star)

A more likely possibility is an acceleration of the last decade's trend toward central-city urban rehabilitation and regeneration. Changing life-styles and priorities and rising commuting costs have made residence in peripheral locations quite costly; for young adults and perhaps even the elderly the option of living in a restored central-city neighborhood may well become increasingly attractive. However, as Chapter 12 indicated, such a location does not appeal to all householders.

Changes in Racial Trends

Since World War II the population in central cities has become increasingly dark-skinned. However, as noted in Chapters 7 and 8, this process may be drawing to a close. Out-migration of blacks from the south to northern cities is no more. The growth of the black populations in these central cities is now dependent upon natural increase. During the 1980s birthrates among blacks can be expected to more closely approach those of the white population. At the same time white movement into regenerating central-city neighborhoods can be expected to accelerate, while more blacks suburbanize. The consequence in some cities may be decreases in the number and proportion of central-city blacks. This reversal of the historical pattern has already begun in Washington, D.C.

Middle-class black suburbanization may become more commonplace than predicted by scholars during the late 1970s.[5] As noted in Chapter 7, however, it is unlikely that black suburbanization will be randomly distributed across suburbia. Rather, black suburbanization will be disproportionately concentrated in the older—and generally less affluent—inner ring of suburbs. Thus while some black suburbanization will reflect true racial integration, the remaining suburbanization may only be a consequence of black ghettos extending across city-suburban legal boundaries. In any case, as long as whites continue to move or to remain in the suburbs, suburbia as a whole will retain its pale complexion.

Changes in the Energy Situation

The energy crunch has conjured up numerous scenarios—each grimmer than its predecessor. There are apocalyptic visions of the new housing market collapsing and of suburbs being abandoned. The "worst possible case" scenario sees virtually the entire northeast of the country becoming a disaster area.

In the long run the United States may move toward the pattern of other nations, where the poor reside on the metropolitan periphery. Such changes, though, would come relatively slowly. The best guess of scholars is that things are going to change, but not all that drastically. For the immediate future suburbs are not going to be abandoned. This is because Americans are reluctant to change their life-styles and—more important—because an immense investment has already been made in existing homes, office complexes, and industrial plants. Even expensive energy costs for heating and transportation are cheaper than rebuilding the economy.

Since, as Chapter 7 demonstrated, most suburbanites not only live but also work in suburban areas, these suburbanites have little incentive to move back to the city for reasons of employment. Moreover, there is a tendency to exaggerate the distance people commute to work. The median distance from home to work,

---

[5]For development of this point, refer back to Chapter 7. For a good article taking the opposite position, see Karl E. Taeuber, "Racial Segregation: The Persisting Dilemma," *Annals of the American Academy of Political and Social Science,* **422**:96, November, 1975.

according to Bureau of the Census data, is 7.6 miles.[6] In Philadelphia it is only 4.4 miles, in Chicago 6.6 miles, and in Dallas 6.2 miles. Even in the Los Angeles area, where one hears stories of 75-mile commuter trips, the average distance is under 9 miles. It might also be remembered that Europeans, with roughly double our gasoline costs, have not abandoned their automobiles. For better or worse we shan't either.

The most reasonable prognosis is for a series of slow adjustments rather than radical changes. With many jobs already decentralized, the greatest future demand for housing may come in inner-ring established suburbs. These suburbs represent a compromise: they provide residential neighborhoods of single-family homes without the necessity of long-distance commuting. If the relative attractiveness and property values of such suburbs increase dramatically, it would probably slow the movement of less affluent blacks toward such areas.

Changes in Federal Funding

Despite the deep public pessimism of the past decade, the older "frostbelt" cities of northeast and north central regions are not about to disappear. As documented in Chapters 11 and 12, in spite of all the wringing of hands, cities generally have not lost their economic function, and some are experiencing considerable social as well as physical resurgence. This does not mean that all is rosy. Growing municipal payroll and public assistance expenditures coupled with relative declines in locally generated revenues continue to plague older cities. Yet this has to be balanced against sharp increases in federal contributions to cities. For example, the federal contribution to Newark's general city revenue skyrocketed from a negligible 1.7 percent in 1967 to 55.2 percent in 1978.[7] Other cities have shown a similar pattern. A consequence of the opening of the federal coffers is that cities, with a few notorious exceptions, are economically solvent. Note that the successful mayor no longer boasts so much of the new industries he or she has brought to the city but of his or her role in increasing federal grants and programs.

Given the recency of these changes, the long-range implications are only beginning to be grasped. What is occurring, though, is that American cities are becoming part of a national system. Whether the myth of local independence can be maintained under the reality of external budget maintenance remains to be seen. Few communities are willing, or financially able, to indulge in the luxury of noncompliance with federal guidelines. The ambition of local mayors and officials to receive federal funds without federal controls is likely to be largely unsuccessful. The federal piper will most likely call the tune. The real unanswered question is what tune will be chosen.

---

[6]U.S. Bureau of the Census, "Selected Characteristics of Travel to Work in 20 Metropolitan Areas: 1976," *Current Population Reports*, series P-23, no. 72, Washington, D.C., 1978.
[7]J. John Palen, "The Urban Nexus: Toward the Year 2000," in Amos H. Hawley (ed.), *Societal Growth: Process and Implications*, Free Press, New York, 1979, p. 155.

PLANNING FOR THE CITY

To many people, urban planning almost automatically means physical planning; but physical planning is never free from social implications—the two are always intertwined. Moreover, our view of the future influences our contemporary behavior. As Scott Greer has expressed it:

It is my assumption that images of the future determine present actions. They may or may not determine the nature of the future—that depends on a much more complex set of circumstances. Buy willy-nilly much of our behavior is postulated upon images of a possible and/or desirable future.[8]

Ebenezer Howard's very livable "garden cities" have already been discussed in Chapter 13. Howard advocated a system of compact, self-contained cities of limited size that were designed to attract residents away from large cities such as London. Other planners have had different visions of utopia. Frank Lloyd Wright's model (1934) of a decentralized garden city called "Broadacres" was more explicitly antiurban than Howard's. Wright proposed that each individual in his "urban" model be allotted at least 1 acre, which he or she would be expected to farm. Significantly, his book *The Living City* ends with material excerpted from Ralph Waldo Emerson's "Essay on Farming."[9]

A different type of "city of tomorrow," and one that has had far more influence on American planners, is Le Corbusier's "radiant city." This was to be composed of a center of towering skyscrapers surrounded by parks and open spaces. Residences, similarly, would be tall, thin apartment superblocks surrounded by greenery.[10] Brasilia, the new capital of Brazil, although not designed by Le Corbusier, followed his general plan: it has a unified high-rise center and residential superblocks untied by a radial system of freeways. However, as was indicated earlier, Brasilia, while striking, is too uncomfortably monumental for most people, who prefer the chaos of a Rio de Janeiro.

Sometimes physical planning for the future takes on a fanciful, "brave new world" character. The vision of Buckminster Fuller is an example: it cuts our ties to the physical earth and to mundane things such as water mains and sewers by means of recycling packs that we could wear on our backs like the astronauts' life-support systems. The urban architectual critic Wolf von Eckardt has a more earthbound view of such a future:

The box regenerates our wastes and water and even reconditions our air and provides us with light and heat. If only we strap those little black boxes to our backs, he says, we can all disperse over the world's mountains and deserts, telecommunicate with each other, and dispense with crowded settlements. Fuller, needless to say, did not acquire his astounding, sophisticated knowledge from video screens on lonely

[8]Scott Greer, *The Urbane View*, Oxford University Press, New York, 1972, p. 322.
[9]Frank Lloyd Wright, *The Living City*, Mentor-Horizon, New York, 1958.
[10]Le Corbusier, *The Radiant City*, part I, Pamela Knight (trans.), parts II and VI, Eleanor Levieux (trans.), parts III, IV, V, VII, and VIII, Derek Coltman (trans.), Grossman-Orion, New York, 1967; this is a translation of the French version, *La Ville Radieuse*, 1933.

mountaintops. He acquired it in the lively bustle, the intellectual interchange, and the accumulation of wisdom that crowded human settlements stand for.[11]

The visionary and planner Constantinos A. Doxiadis's prescription for planning an organized community likewise is radically removed from the situation in contemporary cities. Doxiadis proposes a city of 2 million, organized into communities of 30,000 to 50,000—each within an area of 2,000 yards by 2,000 yards. Services, schools, stores, businesses, and parks would all be organized so that residents could walk to them; public transit and highways would be around the communities. Movement from community to community within the city would be by means of "deepways"—underground highways.[12]

Another fanciful model for future cities is architect Paolo Soleri's "arcology," a compact three-dimensional city. Soleri places heavy emphasis on building a city vertically, layer on layer, and on using "miniaturization," or a more compact form, which he believes is the rule of evolutionary development.[13] Instead of urban sprawl Soleri would have cities confined to a few square miles, with buildings 300 stories high. At present Soleri and volunteers are attempting to build in Arizona a small 3,000-person, twenty-five story prototype of the future named "Acrosanti."

Dantzig and Saatz take this idea of vertical compactness a step further and propose a compact vertical city that makes round-the-clock use of all facilities.[14] Such a city, though, would require immense amounts of energy and constant services. Strikes by municipal workers would paralyze such a compact high-rise city, and thus would have to be prohibited. It is easy to foresee such a city turning into a tightly monitored totalitarian state.

Planned utopias may challenge the imagination, but they also frequently appear rather sterile and lifeless. They often seem better suited to guided tours than to day-in, day-out habitation. To theorize about the future is one thing; to want to live in it is another. For example, Buckminster Fuller claims that plastic domes, similar to that covering the Houston Astrodome, can now be constructed, permitting a controlled climate and environment. Cities covered by domes could theoretically be built in otherwise hostile environments such as desert regions or even the smog-filled Los Angeles basin. Inside the domes, artificial light, controlled heating and cooling, and even synthetic grass can be provided. The question is whether we really want to live with synthetic lawns.

On the other hand, viewing the future as a lineal multiplication of the past is not only far less interesting but over the long run almost certain to be inaccurate. It would be rather depressing if our only dream for the future of the metropolitan area was of an endless growth of subdivisions and shopping malls. The choice for the future is not between planning and no planning—we will plan, even if it is

[11]Wolf von Eckardt, "Urban Design," in Moynihan, op. cit., chap. 9, p. 113.
[12]C. A. Doxiadia, Ekistics, Hutchinson, London, 1968.
[13]Paolo Soleri, Arcology, The City in the Image of Man, M.I.T. Press, Cambridge, Mass., 1969.
[14]George B. Dantzig and Thomas L. Saatz, Compact City: A Plan for a Liveable Urban Environment, Freeman, San Francisco, 1973.

only low-level planning of individual pieces of property or individual buildings. The question thus is not whether planning should be done, but rather on what level it should be done.

Planning for City Dwellers

Planners and social critics must get away from the all-or-nothing approach by which we exercise our imaginations either in grand fantasies or not at all. The trick is to find the line between speculative fancy and unimaginative extension of the past. This is another of those things which are far simpler in theory than in practice, for novel and innovative schemes are all too often considered unrealistic and dismissed out of hand. As Machiavelli accurately observed centuries ago, "There is nothing more difficult to carry out, nor more doubtful of success, nor more dangerous to handle than a new order of things."[15]

It is crucial to remember that whatever our formal plans for the city of the future, much of what will actually happen is the result of untold numbers of diverse decisions made by different individuals. As stated by Jane Jacobs:

> . . . most city diversity is the creation of incredible numbers of different people and different private organizations with vastly differing ideas and purposes, planning and contributing outside the formal framework of public action. The main responsibility of city planning and design should be to develop—insofar as public policy and action can do so—cities that are congenial places for this great range of unofficial plans, ideas and opportunities to flourish, along with the flourishing of the public enterprises.[16]

We need far more ideas and schemes of the middle range. An interesting architectural innovation in housing design, for example, is Moshe Safdie's "Habitat," erected for Expo '67 in Montreal. Safdie's design of modular boxes piled irregularly upon one another was originally hailed by some observers as the answer to the urban housing problem. The modular units were prefabricated and shipped to the construction site; the irregular placement of the units provided not only for variety but also for balconies and private space. The result was a rare combination of both privacy and a sense of community. Unlike most modern apartment buildings, Habitat gave the immediate impression of being concerned with human needs and designing buildings to meet these needs rather than simply stuffing people into space. Unfortunately, "Habitats" have turned out to be both more expensive and less practical than was hoped. In addition to the financial difficulties, there is also a less clearly expressed but nevertheless deep reluctance to try anything as different from conventional apartment buildings as Habitat.

In terms of transportation alternatives to the private automobile, a pet scheme of the author is the "borrow a bike" plan. A version was, in fact, proposed

---

[15]Niccolo Machiavelli, *The Prince*, W. K. Marriot (trans.), J. M. Dent, London, 1958, p. 29.
[16]Jane Jacobs, *The Death and Life of Great American Cities*, Vintage–Random House, New York, 1961, p. 241.

Habitat in Montreal was designed both to get away from slab-sided
high-rises and to provide private space for every apartment. (Monkmeyer)

in Amsterdam but rejected by conservative officials. The idea is quite simple: The
city would put up numerous clearly marked municipal bicycle racks and fill them
with city-owned bicycles. Anyone could use any bike from any rack, the only
requirement being that he or she eventually return it to one of the racks. The bikes
would be simple, straightforward, one-speed models painted a distinctive
common color. There would be little point in stealing them, since in any event they
would be freely available as transportation to anyone who wanted them. Some
people would undoubtedly lock their "own" bikes, but if enough bikes were
available, this would not be an important problem. Certainly some riders would
move on to purchase their own more elaborate models, so that the scheme would
probably increase rather than decrease sales by private dealers—just as Henry
Ford's cheap Model T spurred the purchase of more elaborate automobiles.
Bicycles could be manufactured and assembled at little cost by the city itself,
employing persons on public assistance who want jobs but have only minimal
skills.

Such a scheme would reduce pollution, reduce gasoline consumption, ease
traffic, and increase the physical—and probably emotional—health of the
population. Increasing public awareness of the importance of regular exercise
should contribute to the plan's success. The concept would have even greater
appeal in certain types of communities, such as university towns and sun belt
retirement villages. The possible disadvantages would be the initial cost of the
bicycles (although lower costs of repairing streets should more than compensate
for this over the long run) and the fact that in some cities the bikes would probably

not be used much through the winter months. Also, even if the plan saved the city money, some residents would no doubt complain that it was socialistic nonsense and that the city had no business giving people bicycles.

The "borrow a bike" plan is simply one example of how, without massive rebuilding or expense, we can make our cities more healthy and livable. If American city dwellers used bicycles as much as the residents of Amsterdam or Peking, there would be fewer problems with pollution and with energy crunches.

Planning Metropolitan Political Systems

Organizationally, metropolitan areas appear in a state of confusion and disorganization. Present home rule provides for local control at a substantial price. The political system itself becomes a major obstacle to effective planning. A multiplicity of city, suburban, county, township, regional, state, and federal bureaucracies all must intermesh if the metropolitan area is to be serviced effectively and at minimum cost, and this rarely works as well in practice as in theory. The interminable squabbling between city mayors and suburban political officials is one index of the ineffectiveness of the present system. The New York conurbation (admittedly an extreme example) includes people from three different states and some 1,400 different jurisdictions of one sort or another.

One alternative would be to abandon most local jurisdictions and move in the direction of one metropolitan-area government such as those found in Dade County, Florida (Miami) or Nashville, Tennessee. However, in spite of the generally favorable reports on this consolidations, there is little real agitation or political pressure in major American urban areas for adoption of this system.

Another approach is a two-tiered, or two-level, system which would move certain decision-making powers and organization to the level of a county or SMSA while other functions would be handled by dividing the entire area—including the central city—into political units the size of suburbs, which would handle local problems. Toronto, Canada, is a successful example of the two-tiered approach.

What is necessary, therefore, is to move in two directions. One is to create the kind of urban governmental mechanism that is capable of handling the major maintenance functions of a metropolitan aggregation, playing the coordinating role essential to a specialized and large-scale community, and guaranteeing the "openness" of the opportunity structure. The other is to establish local governmental units of such size that the individual will have meaningful opportunity to participate in and control those public activities which directly and immediately affect his neighborhood and his life style. The first objective will require the creation of a metropolitan or regional government with territorial jurisdiction over the entire urbanized area; the second will necessitate the division of the central city into smaller political units of 100,000 to 150,000 population, each with governmental structures and power similar to those of the suburban municipalities. Under this plan, the counties and all special districts within the urban region would be abolished as governmental entities; the other local units—the suburban municipalities and suburban school districts—would continue in existence as at present, although some industrial concentrations, because of their importance to the total community, would be placed under the jurisdiction of the larger government. Elections to the regional council would be by district, with the chief executive selected at large.[17]

Under the larger metropolitan unit would be placed functions common to the urban system as a whole, such as water supply, waste disposal, expressways and streets, control of air and water pollution, museums, public hospitals, and major recreational facilities. On the other hand, local matters such as education, enforcement of housing codes, and recreation would be left to the local community. As for education, there is no reason why local central-city areas should not have their own school boards and school policies, just as suburbs presently do. Given the present low quality of most central-city schools, more localized control could probably only improve the situation.

Police departments could also be organized on a local basis—with a common radio network and other specialized facilities—while fire protection should be provided on a metropolitan basis. It makes little sense for suburban fire departments to duplicate expensive equipment; furthermore, the area that a fire station services should be determined by the needs of a population rather than by political boundaries. Police officers, on the other hand, have a day-to-day contact with the community that firefighters do not. Small, locally administered departments such as those found in suburbs today are most likely to provide a setting in which the police and the community can come to know and respect one another. Large bureaucratic departments in which police are shifted from district to district seldom are able to establish rapport with citizens. This is especially true of many black inner-city areas, where the police are objects of overt hostility and are viewed by the residents as an occupying army. In such a situation, the police generally respond in kind. What would happen to the extremely high crime rates in these areas if locally controlled police forces replaced the present system? A new system would certainly be worth trying, in selected cities and as a closely monitored experiment.

However, dissatisfaction with past policies and practices has yet to create sufficient pressures for change. There is little chance that such new approaches will receive serious consideration by policy makers, particularly since some politicians would see their control diminish. City mayors have little interest in transferring authority to county officials. For the immediate future we appear to be doomed to continue with overlap and confusion; we can only hope that voluntary cooperation among the various governmental units within metropolitan areas will increase.

Social Planning

Three Approaches to Social Planning. Approaches to social planning and problem solving range from the use of existing social mechanisms in conventional ways to attempts to radically restructure the entire system. Three general

---

[17]Henry J. Schmandt, "Solutions for the City as a Social Crisis," in J. John Palen and Karl H. Flaming (eds.), *Urban America*, Holt, Rinehart and Winston, New York, 1972, p. 363.

TABLE 19-1
Strategies for Planning and Problem Solving

Assumptions regarding problem solving	General approach to planning	Resulting action taken
Most, if not all, problems can be solved by existing mechanisms	Conventional approaches (System needs minor modifications, fine tuning, or both)	New leadership, better administration shift in priorities, new legislation
Some problems cannot be solved by existing mechanisms	Reformist approaches (System needs some major modification; likely to see system itself as source of problems)	Mobilization of power bases outside existing party structures, quasi-legal protests, civil disobedience
Most, if not all, problems cannot be solved by existing mechanisms	Radical approaches (System needs major revision or replacement)	Rejection of societal goals, extreme counter-cultural movements, revolution, planned violence

Source: Based on J. John Palen and Karl H. Flaming, *Urban America,* Holt, Rinehart and Winston, New York, 1972, p. 335.

assumptions regarding problem solving and the resulting approaches to planning can be delineated: (1) conventional approaches, which assume that problems can be solved by existing mechanisms, (2) reformist approaches, which assume that the system needs some major modification, and (3) radical approaches, which assume that problems cannot be solved by the existing social system (see Table 19-1).

Conventional approaches to planning and problem solving assume that the system itself is not in question. Inadequacies are attributed to the failings of individuals. An example might be those who responded to the Watergate scandal by blaming it all on bad advisors and poor personal judgments made by a few individuals. The appropriate traditional response would thus be to replace the offending personnel with new faces. Reassessment of priorities would also be an essentially conventional response. Here, the emphasis is upon the allocation of resources and weighting of priorities within the system rather than upon structural modification of the system itself.

Reformist responses, as outlined in Table 19-1, are characterized by ideological commitment to the goals and ideals of the society but not by attempts to achieve them through conventional means. Reformers are more likely to see the system itself as the source of the problem and to have little faith in correcting it by traditional means. They accept quasi-legal methods falling outside the traditional system, as did some members of the civil rights movements of the 1960s the environmental movement of the 1970s.

Radical approaches differ from the conventional and reformist positions by rejecting, at least implicitly, the goals of the society as well as the means used to implement them. The existing system is judged to be so corrupt and repressive that the response is to destroy it and start over. Radical responses (most Marxist approaches, for example) are almost always overtly ideological in their vision of the new utopia.

Social Planning and Technology. One point upon which urbanists, including conservatives generally agree is that the core problems of the city are social problems.

The difficulty is that we are frequently unwilling to admit the existence of social problems until they reach serious proportions, and even then we seek solutions through other than social reforms in the naive belief that "technology saves." Public housing projects and freeways are perhaps the two best-known examples of how we have, with disastrous results for the cities, attempted to provide engineering solutions for social problems. For example, the technology exists for building mile-high apartment buildings. The real question should not be "Is it possible?" but rather "Is it desirable?" Still, the faith in the ultimate technical solution persists. Jeb Magruder, at one time a technology consultant for the Nixon administration, said:

> The cities have no place else to turn except to technical solutions. There is no political or social solution to providing more adequate energy, or waste disposal, or drug abuse. I want to see something better and technology can do it if we work at it.[18]

The answers even to questions about energy are, of course, far more social and political than technical. America's social orientation toward automobiles, its values concerning the environment, and even its political policies toward the oil monopolies determine whether the nation has an "energy crisis" far more than technology alone. The decision of an oil company not to build a needed refinery may be an economic or a political decision, or both, but it is not a technological decision. Of course, if one expects technology to solve all problems, even including drug abuse, there really isn't any need to even consider modifying or changing the social, economic, or political system.

THE "POSTCITY" AGE

Superterritoriality

Some futurists see us as inevitably moving toward immensely larger metropolises. Doxiadis, for example, viewed population increases resulting in a world where urban settlements covered an area not just seven to ten times larger than they now do, but as much as thirty, forty, or even fifty times as large. Moreover, he predicted that it is probable that all settlements will become interconnected to form a continuous system covering the inhabitable earth. In Doxiadis's opinion,

[18] *The New York Times,* July 29, 1972.

there is no possibility of halting or changing the growth of this ultimate megalopolis he calls "Ecumenopolis." He felt that stopping the trend toward Ecumenopolis is impossible for two reasons:

1. These are trends of population growth determined by many biological and social forces which we do not even understand properly, let alone dare countermand.
2. The great forces shaping the Ecumenopolis—economic, commercial, social, political, technological, and cultural—are already being deployed, and it is too late to reverse them.[19]

He further believed that the eventual creation of Ecumenopolis should be considered "an inevitability which we must accept." The challenge as he saw it is "to make the Ecumenopolis fit for Man."[20]

Fortunately, this prediction has little contact with empirical reality. Population growth is far from inevitable; and biological and social forces do not operate in response to mysterious and mystical "forces" beyond our knowledge. Whatever our urban areas become, they will be the result of our present and future actions—wise or unwise—not the result of unchangeable forces.

Nonterritoriality

Others see the traditional city as passing away. In recent years, we have come to think less in terms of the city versus the country and more in terms of a larger urban-dominated community that often includes rural sectors. This new unit, commonly called the "metropolitan community," has evolved rapidly in the United States during the past half century. Now some scholars believe that we are moving from metropolitan communities to a new "postcity" age. As Melvin Webber states this position, "We are passing through a revolution that is unhitching the social processes of urbanization from the locationally fixed city and region."[21] Webber maintains:

> A new kind of large-scale urban society is emerging that is increasingly independent of the city. In turn, the problems of the city place generated by early industrialization are being supplanted by a new array different in kind. With but a few remaining exceptions (the new air pollution is a notable one), the recent difficulties are not place-type problems at all. Rather, they are the transitional problems of a rapidly developing society-economy-and-polity whose turf is the nation. Paradoxically, just at the time in history when policy-makers and the world press are discovering the city, "the age of the city seems to be at an end."[22]

He suggests that we have failed to draw up a simple conceptual definition distinguishing between the spatially defined urban area and the social systems

[19]Doxiadis, op. cit., p. 430.
[20]Ibid.
[21]Melvin M. Webber, "The Postcity Age," *Daedalus,* **97**(4):1092, Fall, 1968.
[22]Webber, ibid., pp. 1092–1093. Reprinted by permission of *Daedalus,* Journal of the American Academy of Arts and Sciences, Boston, Mass., Fall, 1968, *The Conscience of the City.*

that are localized there. Because our cities have historically been spatially structured, we don't have the concepts or language to deal with the new situation. The resulting problems, Webber says, are serious ones, for we seek local solutions to problems that transcend local boundaries and are not susceptible to municipal treatment. Problems of poverty, crime, unemployment, and even transportation transcend any city or even cities in general.

Webber suggests that the future pattern can be discerned in the life-styles of the new cosmopolites who through frequent use of airlines and telephones have established new spatially dispersed networks of specialized knowledge. These cosmopolites are the producers of the information and new ideas that are transforming societies.

Like much of the "Chicago school" of sociology of half a century earlier, Webber assumes that movement from localized primary-group relationships to territorially unbounded secondary-group relationships is inevitable and irreversible. He states:

> At one extreme are the intellectual and business elites, whose habitat is the planet; at the other are the lower-class residents of city and farm who live in spatially and cognitively constrained worlds. Most of the rest of us, who comprise the large middle class, lie somewhere in-between, but in some facets of our lives we all seem to be moving from our ancestral localism toward the unbounded realms of the cosmopolites.[23]

This is far from certain. It *may* be true for segments of the upper middle class; but, as we have seen in earlier chapters, upper-middle-class professionals tend to consistently underrate both the strength and the utility of territorially bounded urban life-styles.

The Passing of the City?

Another reworking of the concept of the passing of the city is provided by John Seeley, who suggests that the western nations have reached their highest point of development and institutional practices. He goes on to say: "If the view is correct, there is something tragicomic about sitting around 'planning' to secure, extend, and improve what is to be shortly swept away. . . ."[24] In his view, the city as we know it will pass, to be replaced by a new and as yet undefined form:

> Very little will need planning—just enough control over the spread of cities and their ways to permit the conscience of the city to find itself chiefly outside these centers, to spread through the society which, by then, may be ready, having reached its fevered climax, to abandon its delirium and search out a new way. That new way, I am confident, will not be, cannot be, in content, organization, aim, or spirit, anything like a continuation or culmination of what we have hitherto nurtured and known.[25]

[23]Webber, op. cit., p. 1095. Reprinted by permission of *Daedalus*, Journal of the American Academy of Arts and Sciences, Boston, Mass., Fall, 1968, *The Conscience of the City*.
[24]John R. Seeley, "Remaking the Urban Scene: New Youth in an Old Environment," *Daedalus*, 97(4):1125, Fall, 1968.
[25]Ibid., p. 1139. Reprinted by permission of *Daedalus*, Journal of the American Academy of Arts and Sciences, Boston, Mass., Fall, 1968, *The Conscience of the City*.

Most urban sociologists, on the other hand, are extremely dubious as to whether this prophecy of the passage of the city will come to be. Nor would many social scientists accept the idea that planning for cities is unnecessary, futile, and perhaps even harmful. Even with all the limitations of planning, most of us prefer to plan our urban futures on the basis of empirical knowledge rather than soothsaying or speculation. To paraphrase Mark Twain's famous remark on being told that he had been reported dead, the reports of the death of the city have been greatly exaggerated.

BIBLIOGRAPHY

CHAPTER 1

Abu-Lughod, Janet: "Migrant Adjustment to City Life: The Egyptian Case," *American Journal of Sociology*, vol. 67, 1961.

Berry, Brian J. L.: "The Counterurbanization Process: Urban America Since 1970," in *Urbanization and Counterurbanization*, Urban Affairs Annual Reviews, vol. 11, Sage Publications, Beverly Hills, Calif., 1976.

Chandler, Tertius, and Gerald Fox: *3000 Years of Urban Growth*, Academic Press, New York, 1974.

Davis, Kingsley: *World Urbanization 1950–1970*, vol II: *Analysis of Trends, Relationships, and Development*, University of California, Berkeley, 1972.

Demographic Handbook for Africa, United Nations Economic Commission for Africa, Addis Ababa, 1968.

Durkheim, Emile: *The Division of Labor in Society*, George Simpson (trans.), Free Press, Glencoe, Ill., 1960.

Eldridge, Hope Tisdale: "The Process of Urbanization," in J. J. Spengler and O. D. Duncan (eds.), *Demographic Analysis*, Free Press, Glencoe, Ill., 1956.

Fischer, Claude S.: "Urban Malaise," *Social Forces*, vol. 52, December 1973.

Gerth, H. H., and C. Wright Mills (trans. and ed.): *Max Weber, Essays in Sociology*, Oxford University Press, New York, 1966.

Hauser, Philip, and Leo Schnore (eds.): *The Study of Urbanization*, Wiley, New York, 1965.

Hawley, Amos H.: *Human Ecology: A Theory of Community Structure*, Ronald Press, New York, 1950.

International Urban Research: *The World's Metropolitan Areas*, University of California, Berkeley, 1959.

Macura, Milos: "The Influence of the Definition of Urban Place on the Size of Urban Population," in Jack Gibbs (ed.), *Urban Research Methods*, Van Nostrand, New York, 1961.

Marx, Karl, and Friedrich Engels: *The German Ideology*, R. Pascal (trans.), International Publishers Company, New York, 1947.

Meadows, Paul, and Ephraim Mizruchi (eds.): *Urbanism, Urbanization, and Change: Comparative Perspectives*, Addison-Wesley, Reading, Mass., 1969.

Park, Robert E.: "The City: Suggestions for the Investigation of Human Behavior in the Urban Environment," in Robert E. Park, E. W. Burgess, and Roderick D. McKenzie (eds.), *The City*, University of Chicago Press, Chicago, 1925.

Redfield, Robert: "The Folk Society," *American Journal of Sociology*, vol. 52, 1947.

Schnore, Leo: "Urbanization and Economic Development: The Demographic Contribution," *American Journal of Economics and Sociology,* vol. 23, 1964.

Shaw, Clifford R.: *The Jack Roller,* University of Chicago Press, Chicago, 1930.

Srole, Leo: "Urbanization and Mental Health: Some Reformulations," *American Scientist,* vol. 60, September–October, 1972.

The State of World Population: 1978, United Nations, New York, 1978.

Stein, Maurice R.: *The Eclipse of Community,* Princeton University Press, Princeton, N.J., 1961.

Thomas, William I., and Florian Znaniecki: *The Polish Peasant in Europe and America,* 5 vols., University of Chicago Press, Chicago, 1918–1920.

Urbanization in the Second United Nations Development Decade, United Nations, New York, 1970.

Vidich, Arthur J., and Joseph Bensman: *Small Town in Mass Society,* Princeton University Press, Princeton, N.J., 1958.

Weber, Adna Ferrin: *The Growth of Cities in the Nineteenth Century,* Cornell University Press, Ithaca, New York, 1899.

Weber, Max: *Essays in Sociology,* C. Wright Mills, and H. H. Gerth (eds. and trans.), Oxford University Press, New York, 1966.

Wirth, Louis: *The Ghetto,* University of Chicago Press, Chicago, 1928.

————: "Urbanism as a Way of Life," *American Journal of Sociology,* vol. 44, July, 1938.

Zorbaugh, Harvey W.: *The Gold Coast and the Slum,* University of Chicago Press, Chicago, 1929.

CHAPTER 2

Adams, Robert M.: "The Origins of Cities," *Scientific American,* September, 1960.

Aristotle: *Politics,* Book VII, B. Jowett (trans.), 1932 ed.

Berry, Brian J., and John D. Kasandra: *Contemporary Urban Ecology,* Macmillan, New York, 1977.

Braidwood, Robert: "The Agricultural Revolution," *Scientific American,* September, 1960.

Carcoping, Jerome: *Daily Life in Ancient Rome,* Yale University Press, New Haven, Conn., 1940.

Chandler, Tertius, and Gerald Fox: *3000 Years of Urban Growth,* Academic Press, New York, 1974.

Childe, V. Gordon: "The Urban Revolution," *Town Planning Review,* vol. 21, 1950.

————: *What Happened in History,* Penguin Books, London, 1946.

Creel, H. G.: *The Birth of China,* Reynal and Hitchcock, New York, 1937.

Curwin, E. Cecil, and Gudmund Hart: *Plough and Pasture,* Collier Books, New York, 1961.

Davis, Kingsley: "The Origin and Growth of Urbanization in the World," *American Journal of Sociology,* vol. 60, March, 1955.

de Coulanges, Numa Denis Fustel: *The Ancient City,* Doubleday, Garden City, New York, 1956. (First published 1865.)

Deauz, George: *The Black Death,* Weybright and Talley, New York, 1969.

Duncan, Otis Dudley: "From Social System to Ecosystem," *Sociological Inquiry,* vol. 31, 1961.

George, Dorothy: *London Life in the Eighteenth Century,* Harper Torchbooks, New York, 1964.

Gibbon, Edward: *The Decline and Fall of the Roman Empire,* Dell, New York, 1879. (First published 1776.)

Glotz, Gustave: *Ancient Greece at Work*, Norton, New York, 1967.

Hammond, Mason: *The City in the Ancient World*, Harvard University Press, Cambridge, Mass., 1972.

Hawley, Amos H.: *Urban Society*, Ronald Press, New York, 1971.

Hiorns, Frederick: *Town Building in History*, Harrap, London, 1956.

Homblin, Dora Jane: *The First Cities*, Time-Life Books, Little, Brown, Boston, 1973.

Hoselitz, Burt F.: "The Role of Cities in the Economic Growth of Underdeveloped Countries," *Journal of Political Economy*, vol. 61, 1953.

Jacobs, Jane: *The Economy of Cities*, Random House, New York, 1969.

July, Robert W.: *A History of the African People*, Scribner, New York, 1970.

Lampara, Eric: "The Urbanizing World," in H. J. Dyds and Michael Wolfe (eds.), *The Victorian World*, Routledge and Kegan Paul, London, 1976.

Langer, William L.: "The Black Death," in *Scientific American: Cities: The Origin, Growth, and Human Impact*, Freeman, San Francisco, 1973.

Lee, Rose Hum: *The City*, Lippincott, Chicago, 1955.

Lenski, Gerhard: *Human Society*, McGraw-Hill, New York, 1970.

Mumford, Lewis: *The City in History, Its Origins, Its Transformations and Its Prospects*, Harcourt, Brace and World, New York, 1961.

Mundy, John H., and Peter Reisenberg: *The Medieval Town*, Van Nostrand, New York, 1958.

Petersen, William: *Population*, Macmillan, New York, 1969.

Piggot, Stuart: "The Role of the City in Ancient Civilization," in E. M. Fisher (ed.), *The Metropolis in Modern Life*, Doubleday, Garden City, N.Y., 1955.

Pirenne, Henri: *Economic and Social History of Medieval Europe*, Harcourt, Brace and World, New York, 1936.

——: *Medieval Cities*, Princeton University Press, Princeton, N.J., 1939.

Plato: *The Laws*, Book V, B. Jowett (trans.), 1926 ed.

Rice, Lee R.: *Man's Nature and Nature's Man: The Ecology of Human Communities*, University of Michigan Press, Ann Arbor, 1955.

Rörig, Fritz: *The Medieval Town*, University of California Press, Berkeley, 1967.

Russell, J.C.: *Late Ancient and Medieval Population*, The American Philosophical Society, Philadelphia, 1958.

Saalman, Howard: *Medieval Cities*, Braziller, New York, 1968.

Siegfried, Andre: *Routes of Contagion*, Harcourt, Brace and World, New York, 1965.

Sjoberg, Gideon: *The Preindustrial City: Past and Present*, Free Press, Glencoe, Ill., 1960.

——: "The Preindustrial City," *American Journal of Sociology*, vol. 60, March, 1955.

Trigger, Bruce: "Determinants of Urban Growth in Pre-Industrial Societies," in Peter Ucko, Ruth Tringham, and G. W. Dimbleby (eds.), *Man, Settlement, and Urbanism*, Schenkman, Cambridge, Mass., 1972.

Weber, Max: *The City*, D. Martindale and G. Neuwirth (trans.), Free Press, New York, 1958.

Wirth, Louis: "Urbanism as a Way of Life," *American Journal of Sociology*, vol. 44, July 1938.

CHAPTER 3

Blake, Nelson M.: *A History of American Life and Thought*, McGraw-Hill, New York, 1963.

Bogue, Donald J.: *The Population of the United States*, Free Press, Glencoe, Ill., 1969.

Bradford's History of Plymouth Plantation, William T. Davis (ed.), Scribner, New York, 1908.

Bridenbaugh, Carl: *Cities in the Wilderness*, Capricorn Books, New York, 1964.

Brown, Theodore, and Lyle W. Dorsett: *K. C.: A History of Kansas City, Missouri*, Pruett, Boulder, Colo., 1978.

Bryce, James: *The American Commonwealth*, Putnam, New York, 1959. (First edition 1888.)

Cassedy, James H.: *Demography in Early America*, Harvard University Press, Cambridge, Mass., 1969.

Chudacoff, Howard P.: *The Evolution of American Urban Society*, Prentice-Hall, Englewood Cliffs, N.J., 1975.

Cressey, Paul F.: "Population Succession in Chicago: 1898–1930," *American Journal of Sociology*, vol. 44, 1938.

Ford, P. L.: *The Works of Thomas Jefferson*, Putnam, New York, 1904.

Frame, Richard: "A Short Description of Pennsylvania in 1692," in Albert Cook Myers (ed.), *Narratives of Early Pennsylvania, West New Jersey, and Delaware*, New York, 1912. Reprinted in Ruth E. Sutter, *The Next Place You Come To*, Prentice-Hall, Englewood Cliffs, N.J., 1973.

Glaab, Charles N.: *The American City*, Dorsey, Homewood, Ill., 1963.

————, and A. Theodore Brown: *A History of Urban America*, Macmillan, New York, 1967.

Glazier, Willard: *Peculiarities of American Cities*, Hubbard, Philadelphia, 1884.

Green, Constance McLaughlin: *The Rise of Urban America*, Harper and Row, New York, 1965.

Hofstadter, Richard: *The Age of Reform*, Knopf, New York, 1955.

Hurd, Richard: *Principles of City Land Values*, Record and Guide, New York, 1903.

Jackson, Kenneth T., and Stanley K. Schutty (eds.): *Cities in American History*, Knopf, New York, 1972.

Lipscomb, Andrew A., and Albert E. Bergh (eds.): *The Writings of Thomas Jefferson*, vol. X, Thomas Jefferson Memorial Association, Washington, D.C., 1904.

McKelveg, Blake: *The Urbanization of America 1860–1915*, Rutgers University Press, New Brunswick, N.J., 1963.

Merton, Robert K.: *Social Theory and Social Structure*, Free Press, Glencoe, Ill., 1957.

Mumford, Lewis: *Sticks and Stones*, Liveright, New York, 1924.

Petersen, William: *Population*, Macmillan, New York, 1961.

Riis, Jacob A.: *How the Other Half Lives*, Scribner, New York, 1890.

Schlesinger, Arthur M.: *Paths to the Present*, Macmillan, New York, 1949.

————: "The City in American History," *Mississippi Valley Historical Review*, vol. 27, June, 1940.

Smith, John: *The General Historie of Virginia, New England, and the Summer Isles*, University Microfilms, Ann Arbor, Mich. (First published in London, 1624.)

Steffens, Lincoln: *The Autobiography of Lincoln Steffens*, Harcourt, New York, 1931.

Strong, Josiah: *Our Country: Its Possible Future and Its Present Crisis*, Baker and Taylor, New York, 1885.

Tocqueville, Alexis de: *Democracy in America*, Henry Reeve (trans.), New York, 1839.

Tunnard, Christopher, and Henry Hope Reed: *American Skyline: The Growth and Form of our Cities and Towns*, New American Library, New York, 1956.

U.S. Bureau of the Census: *Historical Statistics of the United States, Colonial Times to 1957*, Washington, D.C., 1960.

Warner, Sam Bass, Jr.: *The Private City: Philadelphia in Three Periods of Its Growth*, University of Pennsylvania Press, Philadelphia, 1968.

————: *The Urban Wilderness*, Harper and Row, New York, 1972.

————: *Streetcar Suburbs*, Harvard and M.I.T. Presses, Cambridge, Mass., 1962.

White, Morton, and Lucia White: *The Intellectual versus the City*, Harvard and M.I.T. Presses, Cambridge, Mass., 1962.

Zink, Harold: *City Bosses in the United States*, Duke University Press, Durham, N.C., 1930.

CHAPTER 4

Atchley, Robert C.: "A Size Function Typology of Cities," *Demography*, vol. 4, 1967.

Beale, Calvin L.: "A Further Look at Non-Metropolitan Population Growth Since 1970," paper presented at the Annual Meetings of the Rural Sociological Society, New York, 1976.

———, and Glen V. Fuguitt: "The New Pattern of Non-Metropolitan Population Change," Center for Demography and Ecology, University of Wisconsin, Center Paper 75-22, Madison, 1975.

Berry, Brian J. L., and John D. Kasarda: *Contemporary Urban Ecology*, Macmillan, New York, 1977.

Biggar, Jeanne: "The Sunning of America: Migration to the Sunbelt," *Population Bulletin*, vol. 34, March, 1979.

Bollens, John C., and Henry J. Schmandt: *The Metropolis*, Harper and Row, New York, 1970.

Coale, Ansley J.: "Population and Economic Development," in Philip M. Hauser (ed.), *The Population Dilemma*, Prentice-Hall, Englewood Cliffs, N.J., 1969.

Downs, Anthony: *Opening Up the Suburbs: An Urban Strategy for America,* Yale University Press, New Haven, Conn., 1973.

Duncan, Beverly: "Factors in Work-Residence Separation: Wages and Salary Workers, 1951," *American Sociological Review*, vol. 21, 1956.

Duncan, Otis D.: "Community Size and the Rural-Urban Continuum," in Paul K. Hatt and Albert J. Reiss (eds.), *Cities and Society*, Free Press, New York, 1957.

———, et al.: *Metropolis and Region*, Johns Hopkins Press, Baltimore, 1960.

Forstall, Richard L.: "Economic Classification of Places over 10,000," *Municipal Year Book: 1967*, International City Managers Association, Chicago, 1967.

Forstall, R. C.: "Trends in Metropolitan and Nonmetropolitan Population Growth Since 1970," Bureau of the Census, Washington, D. C., 1975.

Gold, Neil N.: "The Mismatch of Jobs and Low Income People in Metropolitan Areas and Its Implications for the Central-City Poor," in Sara Mills Mazie (ed.), *U.S. Commission on Population Growth and the American Future*, U.S. Government Printing Office, Washington, D.C., 1972.

Gottmann, Jean: *Megalopolis: The Urbanized Northeastern Seaboard of the United States*, Twentieth Century Fund, New York, 1961. (First published M.I.T. Press Paperback ed., February, 1964.)

Gras, N.B.S.: *Introduction to Economic History*, Harper, New York, 1922.

Hadden, Jeffrey K., and Edgar F. Borgatta: *American Cities*, Rand McNally, New York, 1965.

Harris, Chauncy: "A Functional Classification of Cities in the United States," *Geographical Review*, vol. 33, January, 1943.

———, and Edward L. Ullman: "The Nature of Cities," *The Annals of the American Academy of Political and Social Science*, vol. 242, November 1945.

Hawley, Amos H.: "Urbanization as Process," in David Street (ed.), *Handbook of Contemporary Urban Life*, Jossey-Bass, San Francisco, 1978.

———: *Urban Society: An Ecological Approach*, Ronald Press, New York, 1971.

———, and Vincent P. Rock (eds.), *Metropolitan America in Contemporary Perspective*, Holsted Press, New York, 1975.

———, Beverly Duncan, and David Goldberg: "Some Observations of Changes in Metropolitan Population in the U.S." *Demography*, vol. 1, 1964.

Humphrey, Craig, and Ralph Sell: "The Impact of Controlled Access Highways on Population Growth in Pennsylvania and Non-Metropolitan Communities, 1940–1970," *Rural Sociology*, vol. 40, 1975.

Jusenius, C.L. and L.C. Ledebur: *A Myth in the Making: The Southern Economic Challenge and Northern Economic Decline,* Economic Development Administration, Department of Commerce, Washington, D.C., November, 1976.

Manners, Gerald: "The Office in the Metropolis: An Opportunity for Shaping Metropolitan America," *Economic Geography,* vol. 50, 1974.

McCarthy, Kevin F., and Peter A. Morrison: "The Changing Demographic and Economic Structure of Non-Metropolitan Areas in the 1970s," Rand Corporation, January, 1978.

McKenzie, Roderic: *The Metropolitan Community,* McGraw-Hill, New York, 1933.

National Resources Committee: *Technological Trends and National Policy,* U.S. Government Printing Office, Washington, D.C., 1937.

Perry, David D., and Alfred J. Watkins (eds.): *The Rise of the Sunbelt Cities,* Sage Publications, Beverly Hills, Calif., 1977.

Reiss, Albert J., Jr.: "Functional Specialization of Cities," in Paul K. Hatt and Albert J. Reiss, Jr. (eds.), *Cities and Society,* Free Press, New York, 1957.

Sale, Kirkpatrick: *Power Shift: The Rise of the Southern Rim and Its Challenge to the Eastern Establishment,* Random House, New York, 1975.

Schnore, Leo F.: "Satellites and Suburbs," *Social Forces,* vol. 36, December, 1957.

Smith, T. Lynn, and Paul E. Zopf, Jr.: *Demography: Principles and Methods,* Alfred, New York, 1976.

U.S. Bureau of the Census: *Census of Population: 1970 General Social and Economic Characteristics,* Final Report PC(1)-C1, Washington, D.C., 1970.

U.S. Bureau of the Census, U.S. Department of Commerce and Agriculture: "Farm Population of the United States: 1977," *Current Population Reports,* ser. P-27, Washington, D.C., November, 1978.

U.S. Commission on Population Growth and the American Future: *Population Distribution and Policy,* Sara Mills Mazie (ed.), U.S. Government Printing Office, Washington, D.C., vol. 5, 1973.

U.S. Department of Commerce, Bureau of the Census: *Small Area Data Notes,* Washington, D.C., 1971, vol. 6.

The Use of Land, Rockefeller Brothers Fund, Crowell, New York, 1973.

Vernon, Raymond: "Production and Distribution in the Large Metropolis," *Annals of the American Academy of Political and Social Science,* vol. 314, 1957.

Weller, Robert H.: "An Empirical Examination of Metropolitan Structure," *Demography,* vol. 4, 1967.

Zimmer, Basil: "Suburbanization and Changing Political Structures," in Barry Schwartz (ed.), *The Changing Forces of the Suburbs,* University of Chicago Press, Chicago, 1975.

CHAPTER 5

Abbott, Walter F.: "Moscow in 1897 as a Preindustrial City: A Test of the Inverse Burgess Zonal Hypothesis," *American Sociological Review,* vol. 39, August, 1974.

Abu-Lughod, Janet: *Cairo: 1001 Years of the City Victorious,* Princeton University Press, Princeton, N.J., 1971.

Alihan, Milla A.: *Social Ecology,* Columbia University Press, New York, 1938.

Anderson, Theodore R., and Lee L. Bean: "The Shevky-Bell Social Areas: Confirmation of Results and a Reinterpretation," *Social Forces,* vol. 40, December, 1961.

Bell, Wendell, and Scott Greer: "Social Area Analysis and Its Critiques," *Pacific Sociological Review,* vol. 5, 1962.

Burgess, Ernest W.: "The Growth of the City: An Introduction to a Research Project," *Publications of the American Sociological Society,* vol. 18, 1924.

————: "Residential Segregation in American Cities," *Annals of the American Academy of Political and Social Science,* vol. 140, November, 1928.

Caplow, Theodore: "The Social Ecology of Guatemala City," *Social Forces,* vol. 28, 1949.

Davie, Maurice R.: "The Pattern of Urban Growth," in George Murdock (ed.), *Studies in the Science of Society,* Yale University Press, New Haven, Conn., 1937.

Duncan, Otis Dudley: "Social Area Analysis," (review), *American Journal of Sociology,* vol. 61, July, 1955.

————, and Beverly Duncan: "Residential Distribution and Occupational Stratification," *American Journal of Sociology,* vol. 60, March, 1955.

Eschman, Donald, and Melvin Marcus: "The Geologic and Topographic Setting of Cities," in Thomas Detwyler and Melvin Marcus (eds.), *Urbanization and Environment,* Buxbury Press, Belmont, Calif., 1972.

Firey, Walter: "Sentiment and Symbolism as Ecological Variables," *American Sociological Review,* vol. 10, 1945.

Gettys, Warner E.: "Human Ecology and Social Theory," in George A. Theodorson (ed.), *Studies in Human Ecology,* Row, Peterson, Evanston, Ill., 1961.

Gist, Noel: "The Ecology of Bangalore, India: An East-West Comparison," *Social Forces,* vol. 35, May, 1957.

Gottmann, Jean: "The Skyscraper amid the Sprawl," in Jean Gottmann and Robert Harper (eds.), *Metropolis on the Move,* Wiley, New York, 1967.

Haggerty, Lee J.: "Another Look at the Burgess Hypothesis: Time as an Important Variable," *American Journal of Sociology,* vol. 76, May, 1971.

Harris, Chauncy, and Edward Ullman: "The Nature of Cities," *Annals of the American Academy of Political and Social Science,* vol. 252, 1945.

Hauser, Francis L.: "Ecological Patterns of European Cities," in Sylvia F. Fava (ed.), *Urbanism in World Perspective,* Crowell, New York, 1968.

Haynes, Norman: "Mexico City—Its Growth and Configuration," *American Journal of Sociology,* vol. 50, January, 1945.

Hoyt, Homer: "The Structure and Growth of Residential Neighborhoods in American Cities," U.S. Federal Housing Administration, U.S. Government Printing Office, Washington, D.C., 1939.

Hawley, Amos, and Otis Dudley Duncan: "Social Area Analysis: A Critical Appraisal," *Land Economics,* vol. 33, November, 1977.

Hunter, Alfred E.: "Factorial Ecology: A Critique and Some Suggestions," *Demography,* vol. 9, February, 1972.

Kafes, Robert, Ian Burton, and Gilbert F. White: *The Environment as Hazard,* Oxford University Press, New York, 1978.

Marston, Wilfred G.: "Socioeconomic Differentiation Within Negro Areas of American Cities," *Social Factors,* vol. 48, December, 1969.

McKenzie, Roderick: *The Metropolitan Community,* McGraw-Hill, New York and London, 1933.

Mehta, Surinder: "Patterns of Residence in Poona by Name, Education, and Income," *American Journal of Sociology,* vol. 73, March, 1968.

Michelson, William H.: *Man and His Urban Environment,* Addison-Wesley, Reading, Mass., 1970.

Palen, J. John, and Leo F. Schnore: "Color Composition and City-Suburban Status Differences," *Land Economics,* vol. 41, February, 1965.

Park, Robert: *Human Communities,* Free Press, New York, 1952.

Pinkerton, James R.: "The Changing Class Composition of Cities and Suburbs, *Land Economics*, vol. 49, November, 1973.

Reckless, Walter C.: "The Distribution of Commercialized Vice in the City: A Sociological Analysis," *Publications of the American Sociological Society*, vol. 20, 1926.

Schnore, Leo: *Class and Race in Cities and Suburbs*, Markham, Chicago, 1972.

————: "The Myth of Human Ecology," *Sociological Inquiry*, vol. 31, 1961.

————: "The Socioeconomic Status of Cities and Suburbs," *American Sociological Review*, vol. 28, February, 1963.

————: *The Urban Scene*, Free Press, New York, 1965.

————, and Joy K. O. Jones: "The Evolution of City-Suburban Types in the Course of a Decade," *Urban Affairs Quarterly*, June, 1969.

Schwirian, Kent P.: *Comparative Urban Structures: Studies in the Ecology of Cities*, Heath, Lexington, Mass., 1974.

————, and Marc D. Matre: "The Ecological Structure of Canadian Cities," in Kent P. Schwirian (ed.), *Comparative Urban Structure*, Heath, Lexington, Mass., 1974.

Shevky, Eshref, and Wendell Bell: *Social Area Analysis*, Stanford University Press, Palo Alto, Calif., 1955.

Simkus, Albert: "Residential Segregation by Occupation and Race in Ten Urbanized Areas 1950–1970, *American Sociological Review*, vol. 43, February, 1978.

Sjoberg, Gideon: "Cities in Developing and in Industrial Societies: A Cross-Cultural Analysis," in Philip M. Hauser and Leo F. Schnore, *The Study of Urbanization*, Wiley, New York, 1965.

————: *The Preindustrial City*, Free Press, New York, 1960.

Smith, Joel: "Another Look at Socioeconomic Status Distributions in Urbanized Areas," *Urban Affairs Quarterly*, vol. 5, June, 1970.

Thomlinson, Ralph: *Urban Structure*, Random House, New York, 1969.

Ullman, Edward: "The Presidential Address, the Nature of Cities Reconsidered," *Regional Science Association Papers and Proceedings*, vol. 9, 1962.

Van Arsdol, Maurice, Jr., Santo F. Camilleri, and Calvin F. Schmid: "The Generality of Urban Social Area Indexes," *American Sociological Review*, vol. 23, 1958.

Wirth, Louis: *The Ghetto*, University of Chicago Press, Chicago, 1928.

————: "Urbanism as a Way of Life," *American Journal of Sociology*, vol. 44, July, 1938.

Zorbaugh, Harvey W.: *The Gold Coast and the Slum*, University of Chicago Press, Chicago, 1929.

CHAPTER 6

Bell, Wendell: "The City, the Suburb, and a Theory of Social Choice," in Scott Greer, *et al* (eds.), *The New Urbanization*, St. Martin's Press, New York, 1969.

Biderman, A. D., M. Louria, and J. Bacchus: *Historical Incidents of Extreme Overcrowding*, Bureau of Social Science Research, Washington, D.C., 1963.

Bott, Elizabeth: *Family and Social Network*, Tavistock Publications, London, 1957.

Buckout, Robert: "Pollution and the Psychologist: A Call to Action," in Joachim F. Wohlwill and Daniel H. Carson, *Environment and the Social Sciences*, American Psychological Association, Washington, D.C., 1972.

Calhoun, John B.: "Population Density and Social Pathology," *Scientific American*, vol. 206, February, 1960.

Caplon, Theodore: "Changing Patterns of Inequality in Middletown," *1978 Annual Meeting of the American Sociological Association*.

Chadwick, Bruce: "Convergence or Diverging Life Styles of Working and Business Class Families in Middletown, 1920–1977," *1978 Annual Meeting of the American Sociological Association.*

Chappell, C. Bradford: "Intergenerational Occupational Mobility of Working Women in Middletown," *1978 Annual Meeting of the American Sociological Association.*

Choldin, Harvey M., and Dennis Roncek: "Density, Population Potential and Pathology: A Block Level Analysis," *Public Data Use,* vol. 4, July, 1974.

Conforti, Joseph M.: "Newark: Ghetto or City," *Society,* vol. 9, September–October, 1972.

Dickens, Charles: *The Adventures of Oliver Twist,* Chapman S. Hall, Ltd., London, pp. 42–43.

Downs, Anthony: "Alternative Futures for the American Ghetto," in John Walton and Donald E. Carns (eds.), *Cities in Change: Studies on the Urban Condition,* Allyn and Bacon, Boston, 1973.

Drabek, Thomas, et al.: "The Impact of Disaster on Kin Relationships," *Journal of Marriage and Family,* vol. 37, no. 3, August, 1975.

Fischer, Claude S.: *The Urban Experience,* Harcourt Brace Jovanovich, New York, 1976.

————, Mark Baldassare, and Richard Ofshe: "Crowding Studies and Urban Life: A Critical Review," *Journal of the American Institute of Planners,* vol. 41, November, 1975.

Freedman, Johnathan: *Crowding and Behavior,* Viking, New York, 1975.

Gans, Herbert J.: "Urbanism and Suburbanism as Ways of Life: A Reevaluation of Definitions," in J. John Palen and Karl H. Flaming (eds.), *Urban America,* Holt, Rinehart and Winston, New York, 1972.

————: *The Urban Villagers,* Free Press, Glencoe, Ill., 1962.

Greer, Scott: *The Emerging City,* Free Press, New York, 1962.

Guest, Avery M.: "Suburban Social Status: Persistence or Evolution," *American Sociological Review,* vol. 43, 1978.

Hartley, Shirley Foster: *Population Quantity vs. Quality,* Prentice-Hall, Englewood Cliffs, N.J., 1972.

Hillery, G. A.: "Definitions of Community: Areas of Agreement," *Rural Sociology,* vol. 20, 1955.

Hunter, Albert J.: *Symbolic Communities: Persistence and Change in Chicago's Local Communities,* University of Chicago Press, Chicago, 1974.

Janowitz, Morris: *The Community Press in an Urban Setting,* University of Chicago Press, Chicago, 1952.

Keller, Suzanne: *The Urban Neighborhood,* Random House, New York, 1968.

Kornblum, William: *Blue Collar Community,* University of Chicago Press, Chicago, 1974.

Leigh, Geoffrey K.: "Family Life Cycle and Kinship Interaction," 1978 Annual Meeting of the American Sociological Association.

Latane, B., and J. M. Darley: *The Unresponsive Bystander: Why Doesn't He Help?,* Appleton-Century-Crofts, New York, 1970.

LeMasters, E. E.: *Blue Collar Aristocrats,* University of Wisconsin Press, Madison, 1975.

Liebow, Elliot: *Tally's Corner,* Little, Brown, Boston, 1967.

Lupo, Alan, Frank Colcord, and Edmond P. Fowler: *Rites of Way,* Little, Brown, Boston, 1971.

Lynd, Robert, and Helen Merrell Lynd: *Middletown,* Harcourt, Brace, New York, 1929.

———— and ————: *Middletown in Transition,* Harcourt, Brace, New York, 1937.

Matza, David: "The Disreputable Poor," in Neil J. Smelser and Seymour M. Lipset (eds.), *Social Structure and Mobility in Economic Development,* Aldine, Chicago, 1966.

Milgram, Stanley: "The Experience of Living in Cities," *Science,* vol. 167, March 13, 1970.

Munro, William B.: "City," in *Encyclopedia of the Social Sciences,* Macmillan, New York, 1930.

Ogburn, William F.: *Social Change,* Viking Press, New York, 1938.

Piven, Frances Fox, and Richard A. Cloward: *Regulating the Poor,* Pantheon, New York, 1971.

Poplin, Dennis E.: *Communities,* 2d ed., Macmillan, New York, 1979.

Rainwater, Lee: "Fear and the House-as-Haven in the Lower Class," in J. John Palen and Karl H. Flaming (eds.), *Urban America,* Holt, Rinehart and Winston, New York, 1972.

Redfield, Robert: "The Folk Society," *American Journal of Sociology,* vol. 52, 1947.

————, and Milton Singer: "The Cultural Role of Cities," *Economic Development and Cultural Change,* vol. 3, 1954.

Sennett, Richard, and Jonathan Cobb: *The Hidden Injuries of Class,* Vintage Books, New York, 1973.

Simmel, Georg: *The Sociology of Georg Simmel,* Kurt H. Wolff (trans.), Free Press, Glencoe, Ill., 1950.

Smelser, Niel J.: *Sociology: An Introduction,* Wiley, New York, 1967.

Starr, Joyce R., and Donald E. Carns: "Singles and the City: Notes on Urban Adaptation," in John Walton and Donald E. Carns (eds.), *Cities in Change,* Allyn and Bacon, Boston, 1973.

Sternlieb, George: "The City as Sandbox," in J. John Palen (ed.), *City Scenes,* Little, Brown, Boston, 1977.

Suttles, Gerald: *The Social Construction of Communities,* University of Chicago Press, Chicago, 1978.

————: *The Social Order of the Slum,* University of Chicago Press, Chicago, 1968.

Swan, James A.: "Public Responses to Air Pollution," in Joachim F. Wohlwil and Daniel H. Carson, *Environment and the Social Sciences,* American Psychological Association, Washington, D.C., 1972.

Terkel, Studs: *Division Street: America,* Avon, New York, 1967.

Thernstrom, Stephen: "Yankee City Revisited: The Perils of Historical Naivete," *American Sociological Review,* vol. 30, April, 1965.

Thomas, William I., and Florian Znaniecki: *The Polish Peasant in Europe and America,* 5 vols., University of Chicago Press, Chicago, 1918–1920.

Toffler, Alvin: *Future Shock,* Random House, New York, 1970.

U.S. Bureau of the Census: "Social and Economic Characteristics of the Metropolitan and Non-metropolitan Population: 1977 and 1970," *Current Population Reports,* Special Studies, series P-23, November, 1978.

————: "Consumer Income," *Current Population Reports,* series P-23, October, 1971.

Warner, W. Lloyd (ed.): *Yankee City,* Yale University Press, New Haven, Conn., 1963.

Warren, Roland L.: *Perspectives on the American Community,* Rand McNally, Chicago, 1966.

Webber, Melvin M.: "The Post-City Age," in J. John Palen (ed.), *City Scenes,* Little, Brown, Boston, 1977.

Wekerle, Gerda R.: "Vertical Village: Social Contacts in a Singles High-Rise Complex," paper presented at the 1975 Meetings of the American Sociological Association, San Francisco, Calif., 1975.

Wheatley, Paul: "The Concept of Urbanism," in Peter Ucko, Ruth Tringham, and G. W. Dimbleby (eds.), *Man, Settlement, and Urbanism,* Schenkman, Cambridge, Mass., 1972.

Whyte, William F.: *Street Corner Society,* University of Chicago Press, Chicago, 1943.

Wilson, James Q.: "The Urban Unease," *The Public Interest,* vol. 12, 1968.

Wirth, Louis: *The Ghetto,* University of Chicago Press, Chicago, 1928.

————: "Urbanism as a Way of Life," *American Journal of Sociology,* vol. 44, July, 1938.

Young, Michael, and Peter Willmott: *Family and Kinship in East London,* Penguin Books, Baltimore, 1962.

Zorbaugh, Harvey W.: *The Gold Coast and the Slum,* University of Chicago Press, Chicago, 1929.

CHAPTER 7

Bell, Wendell: "The City, the Suburb, and a Theory of Social Choice," in Scott Greer, Dennis L. McElrath, David W. Minar, and Peter Orleans (eds.), *The New Urbanization,* St. Martin's Press, New York, 1968.

Berger, Bennett M.: "The Myth of Suburbia," *Journal of Social Issues,* vol. 17, 1971.

————: *Working Class Suburbs,* University of California Press, Berkeley, 1960.

Berry, Brian J. L. and John D. Kasarda: *Contemporary Urban Ecology,* Macmillan, New York, 1977.

Clark, S. D.: *The Suburban Society,* University of Toronto Press, Toronto, 1966.

Cohen, Albert, and Harold M. Hodges, Jr.: "Characteristics of the Lower Blue-Collar Class," *Social Problems,* vol. 10, Spring, 1963.

Coleman, James, Sara D. Kelly, and John A. Moore: *Trends in School Segregation, 1968–1973,* The Urban Institute, Washington, D.C., 1975.

Donaldson, S.: *The Suburban Myth,* Columbia University Press, New York, 1969.

Farley, Reynolds: "Suburban Persistence," *American Sociological Review,* vol. 29, 1964.

Fischer, Claude S., and Robert Max Jackson: "Suburbs, Networks, and Attitudes," in Barry Schwartz, *The Changing Face of the Suburbs,* University of Chicago Press, Chicago, 1976.

Frey, William H.: "Central City White Flight: Racial and Nonracial Causes," Center for Demography and Ecology, University of Wisconsin Press, Madison, 1977.

Gans, Herbert J.: *The Levittowners,* Vintage Books, New York, 1967.

————: "Urbanism and Suburbanism as Ways of Life: A Reevaluation of Definitions," in Arnold Rose (ed.), *Human Behavior,* Houghton Mifflin, Boston, 1962.

Glick, Paul C., and Larry H. Long: "Family Patterns in Suburban Areas: Recent Trends," in Barry Schwartz, *The Changing Face of the Suburbs,* University of Chicago Press, Chicago, 1976.

Greer, Scott: *The Urban View,* Oxford University Press, New York, 1972.

Guest, Avery M.: "Suburban Social Status: Persistence of Evolution," *American Sociological Review,* vol. 43, 1978.

Guterbock, Thomas M.: "The Push Hypothesis: Minority Presence, Crime, and Urban Deconcentration," in Barry Schwartz, *The Changing Face of the Suburbs,* University of Chicago Press, Chicago, 1976.

Hawley, Amos H., and Basil Zimmer: *The Metropolitan Community: Its People and Government,* Sage Publications, Beverly Hills, Calif., 1970.

Kasarda, John D., and George Redfearn: "Differential Patterns of Urban and Suburban Growth in the United States," *Journal of Urban History,* vol. 2, 1975.

Kramer, John: "The Other Mayor Lee," in John Kramer (ed.), *North American Suburbs,* Glendessary Press, Berkeley, Calif., 1972.

Lineberry, Robert L.: "Suburbia and Metropolitan Turf," *Annals of the American Academy of Political and Social Science,* vol. 442, 1975.

————, and Ira Sharkansky: *Urban Politics and Public Policy,* Harper and Row, New York, 1971.

Michelson, William: *Environmental Choice, Human Behavior, and Residential Satisfaction,* Oxford University Press, New York, 1977.

Muller, Peter O.: "The Evolution of American Suburbs: A Geographical Interpretation," *Urbanism Past and Present,* vol. 4, 1977.

Ogburn, William F.: *Social Change,* Viking, New York, 1938.

Pettigrew, Thomas F.: "Attitudes on Race and Housing," in Amos Hawley and Vincent Rock (eds.), *Segregation in Residential Areas,* National Academy of Sciences, Washington, D.C., 1973.

————, and Robert Green: "School Desegregation in Large Cities: A Critique of Coleman's 'White Flight' Thesis," *Howard Educational Review,* vol. 46, 1976.

Riesman, David: "The Suburban Sadness," in William M. Dobriner (ed.), *The Suburban Community,* Putnam, New York, 1958.

Schnore, Leo F.: "The Social and Economic Characteristics of American Suburbs," *Sociological Quarterly,* vol. 4, 1963.

————, Carolyn D. Andre, and Harry Sharp: "Black Suburbanization 1930–1970," in Barry Schwartz, *The Changing Face of the Suburbs,* University of Chicago Press, Chicago, 1976.

Smelser, Neil J.: Sociology: An Introduction, Wiley, New York, 1967.

Spectorsky, A. C.: *The Exurbanites,* Berkley, New York, 1958.

Spinrad, William: "Blue-Collar Workers as City and Suburban Residents—Effect of Union Membership," in A. Shoslak and W. Gomberg (eds.), *Blue-Collar World,* Prentice-Hall, Englewood Cliffs, N.J., 1964.

Sternlieb, George, and Robert W. Lake: "Aging Suburbs and Black Homeownership," *The Annals of the American Academy of Political and Social Science,* vol. 422, 1975.

"Suburbia the New American Plurality," in J. John Palen (ed.), *City Scenes,* Little, Brown, Boston, 1977.

Taeuber, Conrad: "Population Trends in the 1960s," *Science,* vol. 176, 1972.

Taeuber, Karl E.: "Racial Segregation: The Persisting Dilemma," *The Annals of the American Academy of Political and Social Science,* vol. 422, 1975.

U.S. Bureau of the Census: "Social and Economic Characteristics of the Metropolitan and Non-metropolitan Population: 1977 and 1970," *Current Population Reports,* Washington, D.C., 1978.

Warner, Sam B., Jr.: *Streetcar Suburbs,* Harvard and M.I.T. Presses, Cambridge, Mass., 1962.

Weber, Adna Ferrin: *The Growth of Cities in the Nineteenth Century,* Macmillan, New York, 1899.

Whyte: William F.: *Street Corner Society,* University of Chicago Press, Chicago, 1943.

Whyte, William H.: *The Organization Man,* Doubleday Anchor, Garden City, N.Y., 1956.

Wurlock, Bud: "The Role of White Flight in Neighborhood Racial Transition," paper presented at April 1978 meeting of Midwest Sociological Society.

Zelan, Joseph: "Does Suburbia Make a Difference?" in Sylvia F. Fava (ed.), *Urbanism in World Perspective,* Oxford University Press, New York, 1968.

CHAPTER 8

Alba, Richard D.: "Social Assimilation Among American Catholic National-Origin Groups," *American Sociological Review,* vol. 41, December, 1976.

Drake, St. Clair, and Horace Cayton: *Black Metropolis,* Harcourt, Brace, New York, 1945.

Ellis, David, et al.: *A Short History of New York State,* Cornell University Press, Ithaca, N.Y., 1957.

Erbe, Brigitte Mach: "Race and Socioeconomic Segregation," *American Sociological Review,* vol. 40, December, 1975.

Farley, Reynolds, Howard Schuman, Susanne Bianchi, Diane Colansanto, and Shirley Hatchett: "Chocolate City, Vanilla Suburbs," paper presented at the August 1977 meetings of the American Sociological Association, Chicago, 1977.

Gireot, Avery M., and James A. Weed: "Ethnic Residential Segregation: Patterns of Change," *American Journal of Sociology,* vol. 81, March, 1976.

Glazer, Nathan, and Daniel Patrick Moynihan: *Beyond the Melting Pot*, M.I.T. Press, Cambridge, Mass., 1963.

Gordon, Milton M.: *Assimilation in American Life*, Oxford University Press, New York, 1964.

Grant, Madison: *The Passing of the Great Race*, Scribner, New York, 1921.

Greeley, Andrew M.: *Ethnicity in the United States*, Wiley, New York, 1974.

Greer, Scott: "The Faces of Ethnicity," in J. John Palen (ed.), *City Scenes*, Little, Brown, Boston, 1977.

Guest, Avery A., and James J. Zuiches: "Another Look at Residential Turnover in Urban Neighborhoods," *American Journal of Sociology*, vol. 77, November, 1971.

Higham, John: *Strangers in the Land*, Atheneum, New York, 1977.

Howe, Irving: *World of Our Fathers*, Touchstone Books, New York, 1976.

Lieberson, Stanley: *Ethnic Patterns in American Cities*, Free Press, New York, 1963.

Marston, Wilfred G.: "Socioeconomic Differentiation within Negro Areas of American Cities," *Social Forces*, vol. 48, December, 1969.

Molotch, Harvey: *Managed Integration*, University of California Press, Berkeley, 1972.

Myrdal, Gunnar: *An American Dilemma*, Harper and Row, New York, 1944.

Novak, Michael: *The Rise of the Unmeltable Ethnics*, Macmillan, New York, 1972.

Olmsted, Frederick Law: *The Cotton Kingdom*, Modern Library, New York, 1969.

Palen, J. John, and Leo Schnore: "Color Composition and City Suburban Status Differences," *Land Economics*, vol. 41, February, 1965.

Pettigrew, Thomas F.: *Racially Separate or Together?* McGraw-Hill, New York, 1971.

Phillips, Ulrich B.: *American Negro Slavery*, Louisiana State Press, Baton Rouge, 1969.

Rose, Harold M.: "The Spatial Development of Black Residential Subsystems," *Economic Geography*, vol. 48, 1972.

Ross, E. A.: *The Old World in the New*, Century, New York, 1941.

Sorenson, Annemette, Karl E. Taeuber, and Leslie J. Hollingsworth, Jr., "Indexes of Racial Residential Segregation for 109 Cities in the United States, 1940 to 1970," *Sociological Focus*, April, 1975.

Sowell, Thomas: *Race and Economics*, David McKay, New York, 1975.

Strong, Josiah: *Our Country*, rev. ed., Baker and Taylor, New York, 1891.

Taeuber, Karl E.: "Racial Segregation: The American Dilemma," *The Annals of the American Academy of Political and Social Science*, vol. 422, November, 1975.

———, and Alma F. Taeuber: *Negroes in Cities: Residential Segregation and Neighborhood Change*, Aldine, Chicago, 1965.

U.S. Bureau of the Census: "Characteristics of the Population Below the Poverty Level: 1977," *Current Population Reports*, Washington, D.C., 1979.

———: "Population Profile of the United States, 1978," *Current Population Reports*, Washington, D.C., 1979.

———: "Social and Economic Characteristics of Metropolitan and Nonmetropolitan Population: 1977 and 1970," *Current Population Reports*, November, 1978.

———: "The Social and Economic Status of the Black Population in the United States, 1974," *Current Population Reports*, Washington, D.C., 1975.

Van Valey, Thomas, Wade Clark Roof, and Jerome E. Wilcox: "Trends in Residential Segregation: 1960–1970," *American Journal of Sociology*, vol. 82, January, 1977.

Wade, Richard C.: *Slavery in the Cities: The South 1820–1860*, Oxford University Press, New York, 1964.

Wattenberg, Ben J., and Richard M. Scammon: "Black Progress and Liberal Rhetoric," *Commentary*, vol. 55, April, 1973.

Webber, Melvin M.: "The Post-City Age," in J. John Palen (ed.), *City Scenes*, Little, Brown, Boston, 1977.

Wilson, William Julius: *The Declining Significance of Race*, University of Chicago Press, Chicago, 1978.

Wirth, Louis: "The Problem of Minority Groups," in Ralph Linton (ed.), *The Science of Man in World Crisis*, Columbia University Press, New York, 1945.

Whyte, William F.: *Street Corner Society*, University of Chicago Press, Chicago, 1943.

Woodward, C. Vann: *The Strange Career of Jim Crow*, Oxford University Press, New York, 1966.

Wurdock, Bud: "The Role of White Flight in Neighborhood Racial Transition," paper delivered at the April 1978 meetings of the Midwest Sociological Society, 1978.

CHAPTER 9

Brown, Dee Alexander: *Bury My Heart at Wounded Knee*, Holt, Rinehart and Winston, New York, 1971.

Chadwick, Bruce, and Joseph Strauss: "The Assimilation of American Indians into Urban Society, The Seattle Case," paper presented at the meetings of the American Sociological Association, San Francisco, Calif., August 1975.

Guilhemin, Jeanne: *Urban Renegades*, Columbia University Press, New York, 1975.

Hernandez, Jose, et al.: *Social Factors in Educational Attainment Among Puerto Ricans in U.S. Metropolitan Areas*, Aspira, New York, 1979.

Ichihashi, Yamamoto: *Japanese Immigration: Its Status in California*, Marshall Press, San Francisco, 1915.

Kent, Calvin A., and Jerry W. Johnson: *Indian Poverty in South Dakota*, Bulletin 99, Business Research Bureau, School of Business, University of South Dakota, 1969.

Kitano, Harry H. L.: *Japanese Americans: The Evolution of a Subculture*, Prentice-Hall, Englewood Cliffs, N.J., 1976.

Merton, Robert K.: *Social Theory and Social Structure*, Free Press, Glencoe, Ill., 1957.

Moore, Joan W.: *Homeboys: Gangs, Drugs, and Prison in the Barrios of Los Angeles*, Temple University Press, Philadelphia, 1978.

————: *Mexican Americans*, Prentice-Hall, Englewood Cliffs, N.J., 1976.

Morris, John S.: "Education and the Urban Indian," in Vine Deloria (ed.), *Indian Education Confronts the Seventies*, American Indian Resource Associates, Oglala, S. Dak., vol. 5, 1974.

Neils, Elaine M.: *Reservation to City: Indian Migration and Federal Relocation*, University of Chicago, Department of Geography Research Paper, Chicago, 1974.

Petersen, William: *Japanese Americans*, Random House, New York, 1971.

Population Reference Bureau, *Interchange*, vol. 4, November, 1975.

Program Analysis and Statistics Branch of the Indian Health Service, Dept. of H.E.W.: *Indian Health Trends and Services*, Washington, D.C., 1969.

Report of the U.S. Commission on Civil Rights, *The Navajo Nation: An American Colony*, U.S. Government Printing Office, Washington, D.C., 1975.

Sorkin, Alan L.: *The Urban American Indian*, Lexington Books, Lexington, Mass., 1978.

Stoddard, Ellwyn R.: *Mexican Americans*, Random House, New York, 1973.

Suttles, Gerald: *The Social Order of the Slum*, University of Chicago Press, Chicago, 1968.

U.S. Bureau of the Census: "Persons of Spanish Origin in the United States: March, 1977," *Current Population Reports*, series P-20, Washington, D.C., 1978.

————: "Social and Economic Characteristics of the Metropolitan and Nonmetropolitan Population: 1977 and 1970," *Current Population Reports*, Special Studies, series P-23, Washington, D.C., November, 1978.

————: "Consumer Income: 1974," *Current Population Reports,* Washington, D.C., 1975.

————. *Historical Statistics of the United States,* series C-88 and C-104, Washington, D.C., 1960.

U.S. Commission on Civil Rights: "Puerto Ricans in the United States: An Uncertain Future," Washington, D.C., 1976.

CHAPTER 10

Acker, Joan: "Women and Social Stratification: A Case of Intellectual Sexism," *American Journal of Sociology,* vol. 78, 1973.

Aiken, Michael, and Paul E. Mott: *The Structure of Community Power,* Random House, New York, 1970.

Anton, Thomas J.: "Power, Pluralism, and Local Politics," *Administrative Science Quarterly,* vol. 7, March, 1963.

Babchuk, Nicholas, Ruth Morsey, and C. Wayne Gordon: "Men and Women in Community Agencies: A Note on Power and Prestige," in Nona Glazer-Malbin and Helen Youngelson Waehrer (eds.), *Women in a Man-Made World,* Rand McNally, Chicago, 1972.

Bahr, Howard M.: *Skid Row:* Oxford University Press, New York, 1973.

Baron, H. M., et al.: "Black Powerlessness in Chicago," *Trans-Action,* November, 1968.

Blau, Peter M., and Otis Dudley Duncan: *The American Occupational Structure,* Wiley, New York, 1967.

Bogue, Donald J.: *Skid Row in American Cities,* University of Chicago, Community and Family Study Center, Chicago, 1963.

Broom, Leonard, and F. Lancaster Jones: "Father-to-Son Mobility: Australia in Comparative Perspective," *American Journal of Sociology,* vol. 74, January 1969.

Burgess, Ernest W.: "The Growth of the City: An Introduction to a Research Project," *Publications of the American Sociological Society,* vol. 18, 1924.

Burnight, Robert, and Parker Marden: "Social Correlates of Weight in an Aging Population," *Milbank Memorial Fund Quarterly,* vol. 45, 1967.

Chase, Ivan D.: "A Comparison of Men's and Women's Intergenerational Mobility in the United States," *American Sociological Review,* vol. 40, 1975.

Clark, Terry Nichols: "Community Power," in Alex Inkeles (ed.), *Annual Review of Sociology,* Annual Reviews, Palo Alto, Calif., 1975.

Coleman, Richard, and Lee Rainwater: *Social Standing in America: New Dimensions of Class,* Basic Books, New York, 1978.

Dahl, Robert A.: "A Critique of the Ruling Elite Model," *American Political Science Review,* vol. 52, June, 1958.

————: *Who Governs?,* Yale University Press, New Haven, Conn., 1961.

Elder, Glen H., Jr.: "Appearance and Education in Marriage Mobility," *American Sociological Review,* vol. 34, 1969.

Flaming, Karl H., J. John Palen, et al.: "Black Powerlessness in Policy-Making Positions," *Sociological Quarterly,* vol. 13, Winter, 1972.

Glenn, Norval, and Jon Alston: "Cultural Distances among Occupational Categories," *American Sociological Review,* vol. 33, June, 1968.

Greeley, Andrew M.: "The 'Religious Factor' and Academic Careers: Another Communication," *American Journal of Sociology,* vol. 78, March, 1973.

Greer, Colin: *The Great School Legend,* Viking Press, New York, 1972.

Gregory, Frances W., and Irene D. Neu: "The American Industrial Elite in the 1870's; Their Social Origins," in William Miller (ed.), *Men in Business, Essays on the Historical Role of the Entrepreneur,* Harper and Row, New York, 1962.

Gutman, Herbert G.: "The Reality of the Rags-to-Riches Myth," in Stephen Thernstrom and Richard Sennett (eds.), *Nineteenth-Century Cities*, Yale University Press, New Haven, Conn., 1969.

Hauser, Robert M., John N. Koffel, Harry P. Travis, and Peter J. Dickinson: "Temporal Change in Occupational Mobility," *American Sociological Review*, vol. 40, 1975.

Hauser, Robert M., and David L. Featherman: "Trends in the Occupational Mobility of U.S. Men 1962–1970," *American Sociological Review*, vol. 38, 1973.

Hodge, Robert W., Paul Siegel, and Peter H. Rossi: "Occupational Prestige in the United States: 1925–1963," *American Journal of Sociology*, vol. 70, November, 1964.

Hollingshead, A. B.: *Elmtown's Youth*, Wiley, New York, 1949.

————, and Fredrich Redlich: *Social Class and Mental Illness*, Wiley, New York, 1958.

Hunter, Floyd: *Community Power Structure*, University of North Carolina Press, Chapel Hill, 1953.

Jackson, Elton: "Status Consistency and Symptoms of Stress," *American Sociological Review*, vol. 27, August, 1962.

Kahl, Joseph: *The American Class Structure*, Holt, Rinehart and Winston, New York, 1957.

Katz, Michael: *Class, Bureaucracy, and Schools: The Illusion of Educational Change in America*, Praeger, New York, 1975.

Katz, Michael: *Class, Bureaucracy and Schools:* The Illusion of Educational Change in *American Sociological Review*, vol. 19, August, 1954.

————: "Status Inconsistency and the Vote: A Four Nation Test," *American Sociological Review*, vol. 32, April, 1967.

Lipset, Seymour Martin, and Reinhard Bendix: *Social Mobility in Industrial Society*, University of California Press, Berkeley, 1959.

Lynd, Robert, and Helen Lynd: *Middletown*, Harcourt, Brace, New York, 1929.

————: *Middletown in Transition*, Harcourt, Brace, New York, 1937.

MacLeod, Celeste: "Street People: The New Migrants," *The Nation*, vol. 217, October 22, 1973.

Miller, William: "American Historians and the Business Elite," in William Miller (ed.), *Men in Business, Essays on the Historical Role of the Entrepreneur*, Harper and Row, New York, 1962.

Palen, J. John, and Leo F. Schnore: "Color Composition and City-Suburban Status Differences," *Land Economics*, vol. 41, February, 1965.

Polsby, Nelson W.: "How to Study Community Power: The Pluralist Alternative," *Journal of Politics*, vol. 22, August, 1960.

————: "The Sociology of Community Power: A Reassessment," *Social Forces*, vol. 37, March, 1959.

Rogoff, Natalie: *Recent Trends in Occupational Mobility*, Free Press, Glencoe, Ill., 1953.

Rosenfeld, Rachel A.: "Women's Intergenerational Occupational Mobility," *American Sociological Review*, vol. 43, 1978.

Rossi, Alice: "Women in Science: Why So Few?" in C. F. Epstein and W. J. Goode (eds.), *The Other Half*, Prentice-Hall, Englewood Cliffs, N.J., 1971.

Schnore, Leo F.: "The Socioeconomic Status of Cities and Suburbs," *American Sociological Review*, vol. 28, February, 1963.

————: *The Urban Scene*, Free Press, New York, 1965.

Sewell, William H.: "Community of Residence and College Plans," *American Sociological Review*, vol. 29, February, 1964.

Sexton, Patricia Cayo, and Brendan Sexton: *Blue Collars and Hard Hats*, Vintage Books, a Division of Random House, New York, 1971.

Smith, Joel: "Another Look at Socioeconomic Status Distributions in Urbanized Areas," *Urban Affairs Quarterly*, vol. 5, June, 1970.

"A Systematic Survey of Community Power Research," in Michael Aiken and Paul L. Mott (eds.), *The Structure of Community Power*, Random House, New York, 1970.

Thernstrom, Stephen: "Immigrants and WASPS: Ethnic Differences in Occupational Mobility in Boston, 1890–1940," in Stephen Thernstrom and Richard Sennett (eds.), *Nineteenth-Century Cities*, Yale University Press, New Haven, Conn., 1969.

————: *The Other Bostonians: Poverty and Progress in the American Metropolis, 1880–1970*, Harvard University Press, Cambridge, Mass., 1973.

————: "Urbanization, Migration, and Social Mobility in Late Nineteenth-Century America," in Alan Trachenberg, Peter Niell, and Peter C. Bunnel (eds.), *The City: American Experience*, Oxford University Press, New York, 1971.

————: "Yankee City Revisited: The Perils of Historical Naivete," *American Sociological Review*, vol. 30, April, 1965.

Tyree, Andrea, and Judith Treas: "The Occupational and Marital Mobility of Women," *American Sociological Review*, vol. 39, 1974.

Udry, Richard J.: "Marital Instability by Race and Income on 1960 Census Data," *American Journal of Sociology*, vol. 72, 1966.

Walton, John: "The Structural Bases of Political Change in Urban Communities," paper presented at the American Sociological Association meeting, August, 1973.

Ward, Sally K.: "Community Interdependence, Decentralization, and Policy Outputs: A Comparative Analysis of American Cities," paper presented at the American Sociological Association meeting, September, 1977.

Warner, W. Lloyd: *The Social Life of a Modern Community*, Yale University Press, New Haven, Conn., 1941.

————: *Yankee City*, Yale University Press, New Haven, Conn., 1963.

CHAPTER 11

Allman, T. D.: "The Urban Crisis Leaves Town," *Harpers*, December, 1978.

Banfield, Edward: *The Unheavenly City Revisited*, Little, Brown, Boston, 1974.

Black, Donald J.: "Production of Crime Rates," *American Sociological Review*, vol. 35, August, 1970.

Clark, Terry N., Irene Sharp Rubin, Lynne C. Pettler, and Erwin Zimmerman: *How Many New Yorks?, Comparative Study of Community Decision-Making*, Research Report 72, University of Chicago, 1976.

Costells, Manuel: *The Urban Question: A Marxist Approach*, Alen Sheridan (trans.), M.I.T. Press, Cambridge, Mass., 1977.

————: "The Wild City," *Kapital State*, vol. 4–5, Summer, 1976.

Durant, Seymour B.: "Laetrile for the Urban Crisis: 'Planned Shrinkage' and Other Dangerous Nostrums," *Journal of the Institute for Socioeconomic Studies*, vol. 4, Summer, 1979.

Ennis, P. H.: *Criminal Victimization in the United States: A Report of a National Survey*, U.S. Government Printing Office, Washington, D.C., 1967.

Fogelson, R. M.: *The Fragmented Metropolis: Los Angeles 1850–1930*, Harvard University Press, Cambridge, Mass., 1967.

Gorham, William, and Nathan Glazer: *The Urban Predicament*, Urban Institute, Washington, D.C., 1976.

Green, Edward: "Race, Social Status and Criminal Arrest," *American Sociological Review*, vol. 35, June, 1970.

Hauser, Philip M.: "Chicago—Urban Crisis Exampler," in J. John Palen (ed.), *City Scenes*, Little, Brown, Boston, 1977.

Kasarda, John: "The Changing Occupational Structure of the American Metropolis," in Barry Schwartz (ed.), *The Changing Face of Suburbs*, University of Chicago Press, Chicago, 1976.

Manners, Gerald: "The Office in the Metropolis: An Opportunity for Shaping Metropolitan America," *Economic Geography*, vol. 50, 1974.

Moore, Winston, Charles P. Liversmore, and George Galland, Jr.: "Woodlawn: The Zone of Destruction," *The Public Interest*, vol. 30, Winter, 1973.

Mumford, Lewis: *The Urban Prospect*, Harcourt Brace Jovanovich, New York, 1968.

Porter, Paul P.: *The Recovery of American Cities*, Sun River Press, New York, 1976.

Shaw, Clifford R., and Henry D. McKay: *Juvenile Delinquency in Urban Areas*, University of Chicago Press, Chicago, 1942.

Sternlieb, George: "The City as Sandbox," *The Public Interest*, Fall, 1971.

Wienk, Ronald E., Clifford E. Reid, John C. Simonson, and Frederick J. Eggers: *Measuring Racial Discrimination in American Housing Markets: The Housing Market Practice Survey*, Office of Policy Development and Research, Department of Housing and Urban Development, Washington, D.C., 1979.

CHAPTER 12

Abrams, Charles: *The City Is the Frontier*, Harper and Row, New York, 1965.

Anderson, Martin: *The Federal Bulldozer*, M.I.T. Press, Cambridge, Mass., 1964.

Bradley, Donald J.: "Neighborhood Transition: Middle-Class Home Buying in an Inner-City Deteriorating Community," paper presented at the annual meetings of the American Sociological Association, Chicago, September, 1977.

Gale, Denis: "The Back to the City Movement Revisited: A Survey of Recent Homebuyers in the Capitol Hill Neighborhood of Washington, D.C.," paper published by George Washington University, Department of Urban and Regional Planning, 1977.

Gans, Herbert J.: *People and Plans*, Basic Books, New York, 1968.

————: *The Urban Villagers*, Free Press, New York, 1962.

Greer, Scott: *Urban Renewal and American Cities*, Bobbs-Merrill, Indianapolis, Ind., 1965.

Hartman, Chester W.: "The Housing of Relocated Families," *Journal of the American Institute of Planners*, vol. 30, November, 1964.

————: "A Rejoinder: Omissions in Evaluating Relocation Effectiveness Cited," *Journal of Housing*, vol. 23, 1966.

"The Housing of Relocated Families," in J. Bellush and M. Hausknecht (eds.), *Urban Renewal: People, Politics, and Planning*, Doubleday (Anchor), Garden City, N.Y., 1967.

Lowe, Jeanne R.: *Cities in a Race with Time*, Random House, New York, 1967.

National Urban Coalition: *Displacement: City Neighborhoods in Transition*, Washington, D.C., 1978.

Newman, Oscar: *Defensible Space*, Macmillan, New York, 1972.

Rainwater, Lee: *Behind Ghetto Walls*, Aldine, Chicago, 1970.

Sands, Sonia Mattson: "Population Change Due to Housing Renovation in St. Paul's Ramsey Hill Area," masters thesis, Center for Urban and Regional Affairs, University of Minnesota, Minn., June, 1979.

"Slum Surgery in St. Louis," *Architectural Forum*, April, 1951.

Stegman, Michael: "The New Mythology of Housing," *Trans-Action*, vol. 7, January, 1970.

A Summary Report of Current Findings from the Experimental Housing Allowance

Program: Office of Policy Development and Research, U.S. Department of Housing and Urban Development, Washington, D.C., 1978.

The Urban Homesteading Catalogue: Office of Policy Development and Research, Department of Housing and Urban Development, Washington, D.C., vols. 1–4, August, 1977.

Weissbroud, Bernard: "Satellite Communities," *Urban Land,* vol. 31, October, 1972.

CHAPTER 13

Aristotle: *Politics,* Book VII, B. Jowett (trans.), 1932.

Clapp, J.: *New Towns and Urban Policy-Planning Metropolitan Growth,* Dunnellen, New York, 1971.

Di Maio, Alfred John, Jr.: *Soviet Urban Housing Problems and Policies,* Praeger, New York, 1974.

Herman, Leon M.: "Urbanization and New Housing Construction in the Soviet Union," *American Journal of Economics and Sociology,* vol. 30, April, 1971.

Howard, Ebenezer: *Garden Cities of To-morrow,* Faber and Faber, London, 1902.

Mendelker, Daniel R.: *Green Belts and Urban Growth,* University of Wisconsin Press, Madison, 1962.

Merlin, Pierre: *New Towns,* Methuen, London, 1971.

The Netherlands: Current Trends and Policies in the Field of Housing, Building, and Planning During the Year 1968, Ministry of Housing and Physical Planning, The Hague, 1970.

Osburn, Frederick J.: *Green Belt Cities,* Schocken, New York, 1969.

Popenoe, David: *The Suburban Environment,* University of Chicago Press, Chicago, 1977.

Reilly, William K. (ed.): *The Use of Land: A Citizen's Guide to Urban Growth,* Rockefeller Brothers Fund, Thomas Crowell, New York, 1973.

Rodwin, Lloyd: *The British New Towns Policy,* Harvard University Press, Cambridge, Mass., 1956.

Saalman, Howard: *Medieval Cities,* Braziller, New York, 1968.

Schaffer, Frank: *The New Town Story,* MacGibbon and Kee, London, 1970.

Sidenbladh, Goran: "Stockholm: A Planned City," in *Cities: A Scientific American Book,* Knopf, New York, 1965.

Szelenyi, Ivan: "Urban Sociology and Community Studies in Eastern Europe," *Comparative Urban Research,* vol. 4, 1977.

Taubman, William: *Governing Soviet Cities: Bureaucratic Politics and Urban Development in the USSR,* Praeger, New York, 1973.

Thomas, Ray, and Peter Cresswell: *The New Town Idea,* Open University Press, England, 1973.

Thomas, Wyndham: "Implementation: New Towns," in Derek Senior (ed.), *The Regional City,* Aldine, Chicago, 1966.

Thomlinson, Ralph: *Urban Structure,* Random House, New York, 1969.

CHAPTER 14

Baker, Newman F.: *Legal Aspects of Zoning,* University of Chicago Press, Chicago, 1927.

Buder, Stanley: *Pullman,* Oxford University Press, New York, 1967.

Burby, Raymond J., III, et al.: *New Communities U.S.A.,* Lexington Books, Lexington, Mass., 1976.

Choldin, Harvey M.: "Retrospective Review Essay: Neighborhood Life and Urban Environ-
    ment," *American Journal of Sociology,* vol. 48, September, 1978.
Faltermayor, Edmund K.: *Redoing America,* Harper and Row, New York, 1968.
Gans, Herbert J.: "Planning, Social: II. Regional and Urban Planning," in David Sills (ed.),
    International Encyclopedia of the Social Sciences, Crowell, Collier, and Macmillan, New
    York, 1968.
Glaab, Charles N., and A. Theodore Brown: *A History of Urban America,* Macmillan, New
    York, 1967.
Jacobs, Jane: *The Death and Life of Great American Cities,* Random House, New York, 1961.
Meyerson, Martin, and Edward C. Banfield: *Politics, Planning, and the Public Interest,* Free
    Press, Glencoe, Ill., 1955.
Mumford, Lewis: "Home Remedies for Urban Cancer," in Louis K. Loewenstein (ed.), *Urban
    Studies,* Free Press, New York, 1971.
National Committee on Urban Growth Policy, *The New City,* Praeger, New York, 1969.
Newman, Oscar: *Defensible Space,* Macmillan, New York, 1972.
O'Harrow, Dennis: "Zoning: What's the Good of It?," in Wentworth Eldridge (ed.), *Taming
    Megalopolis,* Doubleday (Anchor), Garden City, N.Y., 1967.
Riis, Jacob: *The Children of the Poor,* Scribner, New York, 1892.
Robinson, C. M.: *City Planning,* Putnam, New York, 1916.
Synookler, Helen V.: "Administrative Hari Kari: Implementation of the Urban Growth and
    New Community Development Act," *Annals of the American Academy of Political and
    Social Science,* vol. 422, November, 1975.
Tunnard, Christopher: *The City of Man,* Scribner, New York, 1953.
Zeisel, John: "Symbolic Meaning of Space and the Physical Dimension of Social Relations,"
    in John Walton and Donald E. Carns (eds.), *Cities in Change,* Allyn and Bacon, Boston,
    1973.

CHAPTER 15

Beier, George J.: "Can Third World Cities Cope?" *Population Bulletin,* vol. 31, December,
    1976.
Berry, Brian J.: "City Size Distribution and Economic Development," *Economic Develop-
    ment and Cultural Change,* vol. 9, July, 1961.
————: *The Human Consequences of Urbanization,* St. Martin's Press, New York, 1973.
Breese, Gerald: *Urbanization in Newly Developing Countries,* Prentice-Hall, Englewood
    Cliffs, N.J., 1966.
Chilcote, Ronald H.: "Dependency: A Critical Synthesis of the Literature," in Janet
    Abu-Lughod and Richard Hay, Jr., *Third World Urbanization,* Maaroufa Press, Chicago,
    1977.
Coale, Ansley J.: "Population and Economic Development," in Philip Hauser (ed.), *The
    Population Dilemma,* Prentice-Hall, Englewood Cliffs, N.J., 1969.
Davis, Kingsley, and Anna Casis: "Urbanization in Latin America," *Milbank Memorial
    Fund Quarterly,* vol. 24, April, 1946.
————, and Hilda Hertz Golden: "Urbanization and the Development of Preindustrial
    Areas," *Economic Development and Cultural Change,* vol. 3, October, 1954.
Firebaugh, Glenn: "Structural Determinants of Urbanization in Asia and Latin America,
    1950–1970," *American Sociological Review,* vol. 44, April, 1979.
Gibbs, Jack P., and Walter T. Martin: "Urbanization, Technology, and the Division of Labor:
    International Patterns," *American Sociological Review,* vol. 27, 1962.

Hoselitz, Bert F.: "The City, the Factory, and Economic Growth," *American Economic Review*, vol. 45, May, 1955.

Inkeles, Alex: "Making Men Modern: On the Causes and Consequences of Individual Change in Six Countries," *American Journal of Sociology*, vol. 75, September, 1969.

Isennberg, Irwin: *The Developing Nations: Poverty and Progress*, Columbia University Press, New York, 1969.

Jefferson, Mark: "The Law of the Primate Cities," *Geographical Review*, vol. 29, April, 1939.

Kilbridge, Maurice: "Some Generalizations on Urbanization in Developing Countries," *Urban Planning Policy Analysis and Administration*, Harvard University Press, Cambridge, Mass., 1976.

La Greca, Anthony J.: "Urbanization: A Worldwide Perspective," in Kent P. Schwirian (ed.), *Contemporary Topics in Urban Sociology*, General Learning Press, Morristown, N.J., 1977.

Linsky, Arnold S.: "Some Generalizations Concerning Primate Cities," *Annals of the Association of American Geographers*, vol. 55, September, 1965.

Myrdal, Gunnar: *Asian Drama*, Pantheon, New York, vol. 2, 1968.

Payne, Geoffrey K.: *Urban Housing in the Third World*, Routledge & Kegan Paul, Boston, 1977.

Portes, Alejandro: "On the Sociology of National Development: Theories and Issues," *American Journal of Sociology*, vol. 82, July, 1976.

Schnore, Leo F.: *Class and Race in Cities and Suburbs*, Markham, Chicago, 1972.

————: "Urbanization and Economic Development: The Demographic Contribution," *American Journal of Economics and Sociology*, vol. 23, 1964.

Sethuraman, S. V.: "The Informal Urban Sector in Developing Countries: Some Policy Implications," in Alfred de Souza (ed.), *The Indian City*, South Asia Book, New Delhi, 1978.

"Some Regional Development Problems in Latin America Linked to Metropolitanization," *Economic Bulletin for Latin America*, United Nations, New York, vol. 17, 1972.

Sovani, N. V.: "The Analysis of Over-Urbanization," *Economic Development and Cultural Change*, vol. 12, January, 1964.

Thomlinson, Ralph: "Bangkok: Beau Ideal of a Primate City," *Population Review*, vol. 16, January–December, 1972.

United Nations Population Division: "Trends and Prospects in the Population of Urban Agglomerations 1950–2000, as Assessed in 1973–75," United Nations, New York, November, 1975.

U.S. Bureau of the Census: "Illustrative Projections of World Population to the 21st Century, *Current Population Reports*, Series P-23, Washington, D.C., 1979.

Urbanization in Asia and the Far East: Proceedings of the Joint UN/UNESCO Seminar held in Bangkok, August 8–18, 1956, UNESCO, Calcutta, 1957.

Wallerstein, Immanuel: *The Modern World System—Capitalist Agriculture and the European Economy in the Sixteenth Century*, Academic Press, New York, 1974.

Wellisz, Stanislaw H.: "Economic Development and Urbanization," in Jacobson and Prakash (eds.), *Urbanization and National Development*, Sage Publications, Beverly Hills, Calif., 1971.

CHAPTER 16

Abrams, Charles: "Squatting and Squatters," in Janet Abu-Lughod and Richard Hay, Jr. (eds.), *Third World Urbanization*, Maaroufa Press, Chicago, 1977.

Barraclough, Solon L.: "Rural Development and Employment Prospects in Latin America," in Arthur J. Field (ed.), *City and Country in the Third World,* Schenkman, Cambridge, Mass., 1970.

Breese, Gerald: *Urbanization in Newly Developing Countries,* Prentice-Hall, Englewood Cliffs, N.J., 1966.

Ducoff, Louis J.: "The Role of Migration in the Demographic Development of Latin America," *Milbank Memorial Fund Quarterly,* vol. 43, October, 1965.

Durand, John D., and Cesar A. Palaez: "Patterns of Urbanization in Latin America," in Gerald Breese, *The City in Newly Developing Countries,* Prentice-Hall, Englewood Cliffs, N.J., 1969.

Estudia Economico par America Latina: ECLA, United Nations, 1960.

Frank, Andrew C.: "Urban Poverty in Latin America," *Studies in Comparative International Development,* vol. 2, 1966.

Gakenheimer, Ralph A.: "The Peruvian City of the Sixteenth Century," in Glenn H. Beyer (ed.), *The Urban Explosion in Latin America,* Cornell University Press, Ithaca, N.Y., 1967.

Goldrich, Daniel: "Toward the Comparative Study of Politicalization in Latin America," in D. Heath and R. N. Adams (eds.), *Contemporary Cultures and Societies in Latin America,* Random House, New York, 1965.

Hance, William: *Population, Migration and Urbanization in Africa,* Columbia University Press, New York, 1970.

Hardoy, Jorge E.: *Urbanization in Latin America: Approaches and Issues,* Doubleday (Anchor), Garden City, N.Y., 1975.

Hauser, Philip M. (ed.): *Urbanization in Latin America,* UNESCO, Paris, 1961.

———— and Leo Schnore (eds.): *The Study of Urbanization,* Wiley, New York, 1965.

Herberle, Rudolf: "Social Consequences of the Industrialization of Southern Cities," *Social Forces,* October, 1948.

Hoselitz, Bert F., and Wilbur E. Moore (eds.): *Industrialization and Society,* UNESCO, Mouton, Paris, 1963.

Juppenalty, Morris: *Cities in Transformation: The Urban Squatter Problem in the Developing World,* University of Queensland Press, Australia, 1970.

Leeds, Anthony, and Elizabeth Leeds: "Brazil and the Myth of Urban Rurality: Urban Experience Work and Values in 'Squatments' of Rio de Janeiro and Lima," in Arthur J. Field (ed.), *City and Country in the Third World,* Schenkman, Cambridge, Mass., 1970.

Lewis, Oscar: "The Culture of Poverty," *Scientific American,* vol. 215, 1966.

————: "The Folk-Urban Ideal Types," in Philip Hauser and Leo F. Schnore, *The Study of Urbanization,* Wiley, New York, 1965.

————: "Urbanization Without Breakdown: A Case Study," *Scientific Monthly,* vol. 75, 1952.

Mangin, William P.: "Mental Health and Migration to Cities: A Peruvian Case," *Annals of New York Academy of Sciences,* vol. 84, 1960.

Moore, Wilber E.: "Industrialization and Social Change," in Bert F. Hoselitz and Wilber E. Moore (eds.), *Industrialization and Society,* UNESCO-Mouton, Paris, 1963.

Morris, James: *Cities,* Harcourt Brace Jovanovich, New York, 1964.

Population Reference Bureau: "1979 World Population Data Sheet," Washington, D.C., 1979.

Schnore, Leo F.: "On the Spatial Structure of Cities in the Two Americas," in Philip Hauser and Leo Schnore (eds.), *The Study of Urbanization,* Wiley, New York, 1965.

Scobie, James: quoted in Glenn H. Beyer (ed.), *The Urban Explosion in Latin America,* Cornell University Press, Ithaca, N.Y., 1967.

Shook, Edwin M., and Tatiana Proskouriakoff: "Settlement Patterns in Meso-America and the Sequency in the Guatemalan Highlands," in Gordon R. Willey (ed.), *Prehistoric Settlement Patterns in the New World,* Wenner-Gren Foundation for Anthropological Research, New York, 1956.

Sjoberg, Gideon: *The Preindustrial City: Past and Present,* Free Press, New York, 1960.

Smith, T. Lynn: "The Changing Functions of Latin American Cities," *The Americas,* vol. 25, July, 1968.

"Some Regional Development Problems in Latin America Linked to Metropolitanization," *Economic Bulletin for Latin America,* United Nations, New York, 1972.

St. Clair, David (trans.): *Child of the Dark: The Diary of Carolina Maria De Jesus,* E. P. Dutton, New York, 1962.

Theodorson, George A. (ed.): *Studies in Human Ecology,* Row, Peterson, Evanston, Ill., 1961.

Turner, John F. C.: "Squatter Settlements in Developing Countries," in Daniel P. Moynihan (ed.), *Toward a National Urban Policy,* Basic Books, New York, 1970.

Valentine, Charles A.: *Culture of Poverty: Critique and Counter-Proposals,* University of Chicago Press, Chicago, 1968.

CHAPTER 17

Abu-Lughod, Janet: "Migrant Adjustment to City Life: The Egyptian Case," *American Journal of Sociology,* vol. 67, July, 1961.

———— "Testing the Theory of Social Area Analysis: The Ecology of Cairo, Egypt," *American Sociological Review,* vol. 34, April, 1969.

————: "Varieties of Urban Experience: Contrast, Coexistence and Coalescence in Cairo," in Ira M. Lapidus, *Middle Eastern Cities,* University of California Press, Berkeley, 1969.

Africa Social Situation: 1960–1970, prepared for the African Population Conference, Accra, Ghana, by the Economic Commission for Africa, December, 1971.

Bienen, Henry: *Tanzania: Party Transformation and Economic Development,* Princeton University Press, Princeton, N.J., 1970.

Boserup, Esther: *Women's Role in Economic Development,* St. Martin's Press, New York, 1970.

Costello, V. V.: *Urbanization in the Middle East,* Cambridge University Press, Cambridge, Mass., 1977.

Demographic Handbook for Africa: United Nations Economic Commission for Africa, Addis Ababa, 1971.

Gbadamosi, Rasheed: "Growing Pains in Lagos," *Draper World Population Fund Report,* Spring, 1976.

Gernet, J.: "Notes sur les villes chinoises au moment de l'apogée islamique," in A. H. Hourani and S. M. Stern (eds.), *The Islamic City,* Bruno Cassirer, Oxford, 1970.

Gugler, Josef, and William G. Flanagan: *Urbanization and Social Change in West Africa,* Cambridge University Press, London, 1978.

Gutkind, Peter C.: "The African Urban Milieu: A Force For Rapid Change," *Civilizations,* vol. 12, 1962.

Hamden, G.: "Capitals of the New Africa," *Economic Geography,* vol. 40, July, 1964.

Hance, William A.: *Population, Migration, and Urbanization in Africa,* Columbia University Press, New York, 1970.

Hanna, William John, and Judith Lynne Hanna: *Urban Dynamics in Black Africa,* Aldine-Atherton, Chicago, 1971.

Hassan, S. S.: "The Ecology and Characteristics of Employed Females in Cairo City," paper presented at the Seminar on Demographic Factors in Manpower Planning in Arab Countries held at the Cairo Demographic Center, November, 1971.

Hodgkin, T.: *Nationalism in Colonial Africa,* Muller, London, 1956.

Holzer, Lutz: "Urbanism in Southern Africa," *Geoforum,* vol. 4, 1970.

Issawi, Charles: *The Economic History of the Middle East*, University of Chicago Press, Chicago, 1966.

Kuper, Leo, Hilstan Watts, and Ronald Davies: *Durban: A Study in Racial Ecology*, Jonathan Cape, London, 1958.

Lapidus, Ira M.: *Middle Eastern Cities*, University of California Press, Berkeley, 1969.

————: *Muslim Cities in the Later Middle Ages*, Harvard University Press, Cambridge, Mass., 1967.

Leslie, J. A. K.: *A Social Survey of Dar es Salaam*, Oxford University Press–The East African Institute, London, 1963.

Levasseur, Alain A.: "The Modernization of Law in Africa with Particular Reference to Family Law in the Ivory Coast," in Philip Foster and Aristide R. Zolberg (eds.), *Ghana and the Ivory Coast: Perspectives on Modernization*, University of Chicago Press, Chicago, 1971.

Lloyd, P. C.: *Africa in Social Change*, Penguin Books, Baltimore, 1967.

Lowy, Michael J.: "Me Ko Court: The Impact of Urbanization on Conflict Resolution in a Ghanaian Town," in George Foster and Robert Kemper (eds.), *Anthropologists in Cities*, Little, Brown, Boston, 1974.

Merab, Docteur: *Impressions d'Ethiopie*, vol. 2, Leroux, Paris, 1921–1923.

Oloo, Dick (ed.): *Urbanization: Its Social Problems and Consequences*, Kenya National Council of Social Service, Nairobi, 1969.

Palen, J. John: "Urbanization and Migration in an Indigenous City: The Case of Addis Ababa," in Anthony Richmond and Donial Kubat (eds.), *International Migration*, Sage Publications, London, 1976.

Pankhurst, Richard: "Notes on the Demographic History of Ethiopian Towns and Villages," *The Ethiopian Observer*, vol. 9, 1965.

Payne, Geoffrey K.: *Urban Housing in the Third World*, Routledge & Kegan Paul, Boston, 1977.

Pons, V. G. cited by A. L. Epstein: "Urbanization and Social Change in Africa," *Current Anthropology*, vol. 8, 1967.

Population Reference Bureau: *1979 World Population Data Sheet*, Washington, D.C., 1979.

Robertson, H. M.: *South Africa*, Cambridge University Press, London, 1957.

Sjoberg, Gideon: "Cities in Developing and in Industrial Societies: A Cross-Cultural Analysis," in Philip M. Hauser and Leo F. Schnore, *The Study of Urbanization*, Wiley, New York, 1965.

Soja, Edward: "Spatial Inequality in Africa," *Comparative Urbanization Studies*, University of California School of Architecture and Urban Planning, Los Angeles, 1976.

Stern, S. M.: "The Constitution of the Islamic City," in A. H. Hourani and S. M. Stern (eds.), *The Islamic City*, Bruno Cassirer, Oxford, 1970.

Taylor, D. R. F.: "The Concept of Invisible Towns and Spatial Organization in East Africa," *Comparative Urban Research*, vol. 5, 1978.

Weber, Max: *The City*, D. Martindale and G. Neuwirth (trans.), Free Press, New York, 1958.

The World Population Situation in 1970: United Nations, New York, 1971.

CHAPTER 18

Aird, John S.: "The Size, Composition and Growth of the Population of Mainland China," *International Population Reports*, Series P-90, Washington, D.C., 1961.

Ando, Hikotaro: *Peking*, Dodansha International, Tokyo, 1968.

Berry, Brian J., and John D. Kasarda: *Contemporary Urban Ecology*, Macmillan, New York, 1977.

Bose, Nirmal Kumar: *Calcutta 1964: A Social Survey*, Lakvani, Bombay, India, 1968.

Breese, Gerald: *Urbanization in Newly Developing Countries*, Prentice-Hall, Englewood Cliffs, N.J., 1966.

Buck, David D.: *Urban Change in China*, University of Wisconsin Press, Madison, 1978.

Chen, Peter S. J., and Tai Chian Ling: *Social Ecology of Singapore*, Federal Publications, Singapore, 1977.

Chen, Pi-chao: "Overurbanization, Rustication of Urban Educated Youths, and Politics of Rural Transformation," *Comparative Politics*, April, 1972.

Cubell, Harold: *Urban Development and Employment: The Prospects for Calcutta*, International Labour Office, Geneva, 1974.

de Souza, Alfred (ed.): *The Indian City*, South Asia Books, Columbia, Mo., 1978.

Fryer, D. W.: "The Million City in Southeast Asia," *Geographical Review*, vol. 43, October, 1953.

Galston, Arthur: "Peking Man (and Woman) Today," *Natural History*, November, 1972.

Ginsburg, Norton S.: "The Great City in Southeast Asia," *American Journal of Sociology*, vol. 60, March, 1955.

————: "Urban Geography and 'Non-Western' Areas," in Philip M. Hauser and Leo F. Schnore, *The Study of Urbanization*, Wiley, New York, 1965.

Gist, Noel P.: "The Ecology of Bangalore, India: An East-West Comparison," *Social Forces*, vol. 35, May, 1957.

Hall, Peter: *World Cities*, McGraw-Hill, New York, 1977.

Hauser, Philip M., and Leo F. Schnore: *The Study of Urbanization*, Wiley, New York, 1965.

Housing and Development Board: *Annual Report 1978–79*, Republic of Singapore, 1979.

Lubell, Harold: *Urban Development and Employment: The Prospects for Calcutta*, International Labour Office, Geneva, 1974.

MacLehose, Murray: "Modern Urban Development in Hong Kong," paper by the Governor to the Commonwealth Society, Hong Kong, Nov. 27, 1977.

Murphey, Rhoads: *Shanghai—Key to Modern China*, Harvard University Press, Cambridge, Mass., 1953.

————: "The Treaty Ports and China's Modernization," in Mark Elvin and G. William Skinner (eds.), *The Chinese City Between Two Worlds*, Stanford University Press, Stanford, Calif., 1974.

————: "Urbanization in Asia," *Ekistics*, vol. 21, January, 1966.

Population Reference Bureau: *1980 World Population Data Sheet*, Washington, D.C., 1980.

"Progress Dooms Charm and Bustle of the Chinatown in Singapore," *Smithsonian*, Vol. 6, 1976.

Ramachandran, P.: *Pavement Dwellers in Bombay City*, Tata Institute of Social Sciences, Bombay, India, 1972.

Reischauer, Edwin O.: *The Japanese*, Belknap Press, Cambridge, Mass., 1978.

Sivaramakrishnan, K. C.: "The Slum Improvement Programme in Calcutta: The Role of the CMDA," in de Souza, *The Indian City*, South Asia Books, Columbia, Mo., 1978.

Ullman, M. B.: "Cities of Mainland China: 1953 and 1958," *International Population Reports*, Series P-95, Washington, D.C., 1961.

Vogel, Ezra: *Canton Under Communism*, Harvard University Press, Cambridge, Mass., 1969.

CHAPTER 19

Dantzig, George B., and Thomas L. Saatz: *Compact City: A Plan for a Liveable Urban Environment*, Freeman, San Francisco, 1973.

Davis, Kingsley: "The Origin and Growth of Urbanization in the World," *American Journal of Sociology*, vol. 60, March, 1955.

Doxiadia, C. A.: *Ekistics*, Hutchinson, London, 1968.

Greer, Scott: *The Urbane View*, Oxford University Press, New York, 1972.

Jacobs, Jane: *The Death and Life of Great American Cities*, Vintage–Random House, New York, 1961.

Le Corbusier: *The Radiant City*, Grossman-Orion, New York, 1967.

Machiavelli, Niccolo: *The Prince*, J. M. Dent, London, 1958.

Palen, J. John: "The Urban Nexus: Toward the Year 2000," in Amos H. Hawley (ed.), *Societal Growth: Process and Implications*, Free Press, New York, 1979.

———— and Karl H. Flaming: *Urban America*, Holt, Rinehart and Winston, New York, 1972.

"Population Growth in the United States and Canada," *Statistical Bulletin*, Vol. 60, April–June, 1979.

Ryder, Norman B.: "The Future Growth of the American Population," in Charles F. Westoff (ed.), *Toward the End of Growth*, Spectrum Books, Prentice-Hall, Englewood Cliffs, N.J., 1973.

Schmandt, Henry J.: "Solutions for the City as a Social Crisis," in J. John Palen and Karl H. Flaming (eds.), *Urban America*, Holt, Rinehart and Winston, New York, 1972.

Seeley, John R.: "Remaking the Urban Scene: New Youth in an Old Environment," *Daedalus*, vol. 97, 1968.

Soleri, Paolo: *Arcology: The City in the Image of Man*, M.I.T. Press, Cambridge, Mass., 1969.

Taeuber, Karl E.: "Racial Segregation: The Persisting Dilemma," *Annals of the American Academy of Political and Social Science*, vol. 422, November, 1975.

Tilly, Charles: "Migration to American Cities," in Daniel P. Moynihan (ed.), *Toward a National Urban Policy*, Basic Books, New York, 1970.

U.S. Bureau of the Census: "Selected Characteristics of Travel to Work in 20 Metropolitan Areas, 1976, *Current Population Reports*, Series P-23, Washington, D.C., 1978.

von Eckardt, Wolf: "Urban Design," in Daniel P. Moynihan (ed.), *Toward a National Urban Policy*, Basic Books, New York, 1970.

Webber, Melvin W.: "The Post-City Age," *Daedalus*, vol. 97, 1968.

Wright, Frank Lloyd: *The Living City*, Mentor-Horizon, New York, 1958.

INDEXES

NAME INDEX

Abbott, Walter, 118n.
Abrams, Charles, 273n., 365
Abu-Lughod, Janet, 396n., 399n.
Acker, Joan, 242
Adams, Robert, 25n., 26n., 27n.
Aiken, Michael, 246n., 247
Aird, John, 411n.
Alba, Richard, 190
Alihan, Milla, 104, 114
Alinsky, Saul, 266
Allman, T. D., 258n.
Alston, Jon, 234n.
Anderson, Martin, 271n.
Ando, Hikotaro, 415n.
Andre, Carolyn, 174n.
Aragon, Manny, 210n.
Aristotle, 31, 32, 291
Arsodol, Maurice, 121n.
Atchley, Robert C., 99n.
Austin, Sarah, 176n.

Babchuk, Nicholas, 250
Bacchus, J., 136n.
Baker, Newman, 318n.
Baldassare, Mark, 137n.
Banfield, Edward, 261, 262, 323n.
Baron, H. M., 249n.
Barraclough, Solon, 361n.
Beale, Calvin, 90n.
Beier, George, 337n.
Bell, Wendell, 121, 122, 139, 170n.
Bendix, Richard, 236n., 241n.
Bensman, Joseph, 11
Berger, Bennett, 171
Bergh, Andrew, 73n.
Berry, Brian J. L., 10n., 19n., 85n., 91n.,
    163n., 335, 347n.
Biderman, A. D., 136n.
Bienen, Henry, 385n.
Biggar, Jeanne, 95n., 96n.
Black, Donald, 268n.
Blake, Nelson M., 61n.
Blau, Peter, 240
Bogue, Donald, 71n., 230

Bollens, John C., 99n.
Bose, Nirmal, 406n.
Boserup, Ester, 390n.
Bott, Elizabeth, 149n.
Bradford, William, 54
Bradley, Donald, 289n.
Braidwood, Robert, 21n.
Breese, Gerald, 341n.
Bridenbaugh, Carl, 55, 66n.
Broom, Leonard, 243n.
Brown, A. Theodore, 57n., 68n., 71n., 75n.,
    312n.
Brown, Dee, 214n.
Bryce, James, 69n.
Bryson, Reid, 123n.
Buck, David, 412n.
Buckout, Robert, 136n.
Buder, Stanley, 314n.
Burby, Raymond, 326
Burgess, Ernest, 102, 103, 105–111, 114–117, 224
Burnham, Daniel, 316
Burnight, Robert, 234n.
Burton, Ian, 123n.

Calhoun, John, 137n.
Caplow, Theodore, 118, 154n., 249
Carcoping, Jerome, 35n.
Carns, Donald, 141
Casis, Anna, 346n.
Cayton, Horace, 198n.
Chadwick, Bruce, 218n.
Chase, Ivan, 243
Chon, Peter, 422n.
Chen, Pi-chao, 412n., 413n.
Chilcote, Ronald, 349n.
Childe, V. Gordon, 24, 27n.
Choldin, Harvey, 137n.
Chudacoff, Howard, 70n.
Clapp, J., 308n.
Clark, S. D., 169n.
Clark, Terry, 247n., 260
Cloward, Richard, 150n.
Coale, Ansley, 89n., 339n.
Cohen, Albert, 172

Colcord, Frank, 145n.
Coleman, James, 177n.
Coleman, Richard, 233, 234n.
Conway, William, 286n.
Costello, V. V., 397n.
Costells, Manuel, 257n.
Creel, H. G., 26, 27n.
Cressey, Paul, 68n.
Cresswell, Peter, 307n.
Cubell, Harold, 405n.
Curwin, E. Cecil, 11n.

Dahl, Robert, 245, 246
Dantzig, George, 433
Darley, J. M., 136n.
Dash, Leon, 384n.
Davie, Maurice, 115, 117
Davies, Ronald, 374n.
Davis, Kingsley, 3n., 8n., 27n., 28, 346n., 427
Deauz, George, 42n.
de Souza, Alfred, 404n.
Dickinson, Peter, 239n.
DiMaio, Alfred, 301n.
Donaldson, S., 169n.
Douglass, Frederick, 193
Downs, Anthony, 86n., 127, 128n.
Doxiadia, Constantinos, 433, 439, 440n.
Drake, St. Clair, 198n.
DuBois, W. E. B., 194
Ducoff, Louis, 361n.
Duncan, Beverly, 84n., 120
Duncan, Otis Dudley, 18, 19, 94, 98n., 104, 120, 122n., 240
Durand, John, 361n.
Durant, Seymour, 255n., 263n.
Durkeheim, Emile, 14, 129

Eggers, Frederick, 265n.
Elder, Glen, 243n.
Eldridge, Hopetisdale, 9n.
Ellis, David, 184n.
Engels, Friedrich, 14
Ennis, P. H., 267n.
Erbe, Brigitte, 201n.
Eschman, Donald, 122n.

Faltermayor, Edmund, 313n.
Farley, Reynolds, 166, 200
Featherman, David, 240n.
Firebaugh, Glenn, 341
Firey, Walter, 104
Fischer, Claude, 13, 137n., 154, 169n.
Flaming, Karl, 249n.
Flanagan, William, 389n., 390n.
Fogelson, R. M., 255n.
Forstall, R. C., 77n., 98n.
Fowler, Edmund P., 145n.
Fox, Gerald, 48n.
Frame, Richard, 56n.
Frank, Andrew, 369n.

Frey, William, 177
Fried, Joseph, 267n.
Fryer, D. W., 421n.
Fuguitt, Glen, 90n.
Fuller, Buckminster, 433
Fustel de Coulanges, Numa Dens, 29n.

Gakenheimer, Ralph, 355n.
Gale, Denis, 289n.
Galland, George, 266n.
Galston, Arthur, 415n.
Gans, Herbert, 135, 137, 139, 142n., 147, 163n., 171, 172, 275n., 276n., 323
George, Dorothy, 45n.
Gernet, J., 393n.
Gerth, H., 14n.
Gettys, Warner, 104n.
Gibbon, Edward, 33
Gibbs, Jack, 340
Ginsburg, Norton, 421n.
Gist, Noel, 118n., 403n.
Glabb, Charles C., 57n., 60n., 66n., 68n., 71n., 73n., 75n., 157n., 312n.
Glazer, Nathan, 190, 263n.
Glazier, William, 66n.
Glenn, Norval, 234n.
Glotz, Gustave, 29n.
Golden, Hilda, 346n.
Gomberg, Shostak, 172n.
Gomberg, W., 172n.
Gordon, Gregory, 282n.
Gordon, Milton, 190
Gordon, Wayne, 251n.
Gorham, William, 263n.
Gottmann, Jean, 79n., 89, 111n.
Grant, Madison, 189n.
Gras, N. B., 78n.
Greeley, Andrew, 190, 238n.
Green, C. M., 54n., 56n., 57n., 58n.
Green, Edward, 268n.
Greer, Colin, 241n.
Greer, Scott, 122, 145, 170, 190, 191, 277, 432
Gregory, Frances, 236
Guest, Avery, 166, 200n.
Gugler, Josef, 389n., 390n.
Guilhemin, Jeanne, 217n.
Guterbock, Thomas M., 177
Gutkind, Peter, 382n.
Gutman, Herbert, 236

Haggerty, Lee J., 116
Hall, Peter, 418–420
Hamdan, G., 374n.
Hammond, Mason, 36n.
Hance, William, 353, 375n., 382n., 383n., 390, 391
Hanna, Judith, 388n.
Hanna, William, 388n.
Hardoy, Jorge, 353n., 358n.
Harris, Chauncy, 98, 99, 115

Harris, Louis, 165
Hart, Gudmund, 21n.
Hartley, Shirley, 137n.
Hartman, Chester, 276n.
Hassan, S. S., 397n.
Hauser, Francis L., 118n.
Hauser, Philip, 3n., 255, 362n., 367
Hauser, Robert, 239, 240n.
Hawley, Amos, 7n., 28, 77, 78n., 84n., 104,
    161n., 178n.
Heberle, Rudolf, 357n.
Herman, Leon, 299n.
Hernandez, Jose, 211n.
Higham, John, 185n.
Hillery, G. A., 153n.
Hiorns, Frederick, 38
Hodge, Robert, 226n.
Hodges, Harold, 172
Hodgkin, T., 382n.
Hofstadter, Richard, 75
Hollingshead, A. B., 226, 234n.
Hollingsworth, Leslie, 199n.
Holzner, Lutz, 374n.
Homblin, Dora, 20n.
Hoselitz, Bert, 40n., 348n., 367
Howard, Ebenezer, 304-307
Hoyt, Homer, 114
Hudson, James, 288n.
Humphrey, Craig, 91n.
Hunter, Albert, 154
Hunter, Alfred, 122n.
Hunter, Floyd, 244, 245
Hurd, Richard, 68n.

Inkeles, Alex, 349n.
Isennberg, Irwin, 340n.
Issawi, Charles, 393n.

Jackson, Robert, 169n.
Jacobs, Jane, 319-321, 434
Janowitz, Morris, 145
Jefferson, Mark, 347n.
Jefferson, Thomas, 60, 72, 73
Johnson, Jerry, 217n.
Jones, K. O., 116n.
Jones, Lancaster, 243n.
July, Robert W., 22n., 24n.
Juppenlaty, Morris, 365n.
Jusenius, C. L., 97n.

Kafes, Robert, 123n.
Kahl, Joseph, 239
Kasarda, John D., 19n., 85n., 91n., 157n., 163n.
Keller, Suzanne, 154
Kelly, Sara D., 177n.
Kent, Calvin, 217n.
Kilbridge, Maurice, 343n.
Kitano, Harry, 219n.
Koffel, John, 239n.

Kramer, John, 180n.
Kuper, Leo, 374n.

Lake, Robert, 174n.
Lampara, Eric, 46n.
Langer, William, 41n., 42n.
Lapidus, Ira, 392n., 395n.
Latane, B., 136n.
Le Corbusier, 432
Ledebur, L. C., 97n.
Lee, Rose Hum, 39n.
Leeds, Anthony, 369
Leeds, Elizabeth, 369
LeMasters, E. E., 148n.
Lenski, Gerhardt, 22n., 235
Leslie, J. A., 387n.
Levasseur, Alain, 390n.
Lewis, Oscar, 367, 368
Lieberson, Stanley, 190n., 198
Liebow, Elliot, 151n.
Lineberry, Robert, 165, 167n., 168n.
Ling, Tai, 422n.
Linsky, Arnold, 347n.
Lipscomb, Andrew, 73n.
Lipset, Seymour, 236n., 241n., 243n.
Liversmore, Charles, 266n.
Lloyd, P. C., 389n.
Long, Larry, 171n.
Louria, M., 136n.
Lowe, Jeanne, 276n.
Lowry, Michael, 387n.
Luppo, Alan, 145n.
Lynd, Helen M., 154, 247, 248
Lynd, Robert S., 154, 247, 248n.

McCarthy, Kevin, 91n., 92n.
Machiavelli, Niccolo, 434
McKay, Henry, 268, 269n.
McKelveg, Blake, 61n., 66n.
MacLehose, Murray, 416n.
MacLeod, Celeste, 231n.
Macura, Milos, 6n.
Mangin, William, 365
Manners, Gerald, 86n.
Marcus, Melvin, 122n.
Marden, Parker, 234n.
Marston, Wilfred, 116, 201n.
Martin, Walter, 340
Marx, Karl, 14, 129
Matre, Marc, 116
Matza, David, 151n.
Mead, Margaret, 168
Meadows, Paul, 9n.
Mendelker, Daniel, 294n.
Merlin, Pierre, 309n.
Merton, Robert, 71, 217n.
Meyerson, Martin, 323n.
Michelson, William, 105, 163n.
Milgram, Stanley, 132
Miller, William, 236

Mizruchi, Ephraim, 9n.
Molotch, Harvey, 200
Moore, Joan, 206n., 208n.
Moore, John A., 177n., 367
Moore, Winston, 266n.
Morris, James, 365n.
Morrison, Peter, 29n., 91n.
Morsey, Ruth, 251n.
Mott, Paul, 246n., 247n.
Moynihan, Patrick, 190
Muller, Peter O., 160n.
Mumford, Lewis, 19, 20, 31, 45, 54n., 255
Mundy, John H., 40n.
Munro, William, 127
Murphey, Rhoads, 401n., 412n.
Myrdal, Gunnar, 192, 342n.

Neils, Elaine, 216n.
Neu, Irene, 236
Newman, Oscar, 281n., 329
Novak, Michael, 190

Ofshe, Richard, 137n.
Ogburn, William F., 134
O'Harrow, Dennis, 318n.
Olmstead, Frederick, 185n., 315
Oloo, Dick, 385n.
Osborn, Frederick, 305, 306n.

Palen, J. John, 116, 201n., 225, 249n.,
    379n., 431n.
Pankhurst, Richard, 379n.
Park, Robert E., 6n., 102, 103
Payne, Goeffrey, 377n.
Pelaez, Cesar, 361n.
Perry, David, 95n.
Petersen, William, 32n., 64n., 218, 219n.
Pettigrew, Thomas, 177n., 197n.
Pettler, Lynne, 260n.
Philips, Ulrich, 193n.
Piggot, Stuart, 28n.
Pinkerton, James, 117
Pirenne, Henri, 36, 37n., 38n.
Piven, Frances F., 150n.
Plato, 31
Plunkitt, George W., 70
Polsby, Nelson, 245n.
Pons, V. G., 377n.
Popenoe, David, 310n.
Poplin, Dennis, 146n.
Porter, Paul, 261
Portes, Alejandro, 349n.

Rainwater, Lee, 152n., 233, 234n., 280n.
Ramachandran, P., 404n.
Reckless, Walter, 109n.

Redfearn, George, 157n.
Redfield, Robert, 14, 15, 130, 131
Redlich, Fredrich, 234n.
Reed, Henry H., 62n.
Reid, Clifford, 265n.
Reilly, William, 296n.
Reinhold, Robert, 178n.
Reisenberg, Peter, 40n.
Reishauer, Edwin, 417n.
Rice, Lee R., 18n.
Riesman, David, 170
Riis, Jacob, 72, 317
Robertson, H. M., 375n.
Robinson, C. M., 314n.
Rock, Vincent, 77n.
Rodwin, Lloyd, 306n.
Rogoff, Natalie, 238
Ronchek, Dennis, 137n.
Roof, Wade, 199n.
Rörig, Fritz, 37n.
Rose, Harold, 201n.
Rosenfeld, Rachel, 243n.
Ross, E. A., 189n.
Ross, John, 123n.
Rossi, Alice, 242
Rossi, Peter, 226n.
Rubin, Irene, 260n.
Rush, Benjamin, 73
Russell, J. C., 39n.
Ryder, Norman, 427

Saalman, Howard, 45n., 294n.
Saatz, Thomas, 433
Safdie, Moshe, 434
St. Clair, David, 364n.
Sale, Kirkpatrick, 95
Sands, Sonia, 291n.
Scammon, Richard, 202n.
Schaffer, Frank, 306n.
Schlesinger, Arthur, 63n., 68, 70n.
Schmandt, Henry J., 99n., 437n.
Schnore, Leo, 3n., 9n., 79n., 104, 116n., 117,
    119,164, 201n., 224, 225n., 335, 336n.
Schwirian, Kent P., 116, 121n.
Scobie, James, 359n.
Seeley, John, 441
Sell, Ralph, 91n.
Sethuraman, S. U., 342n.
Sewell, William, 241, 242n.
Sexton, Brendan, 235n.
Sexton, Patricia, 235n.
Sharkansky, Ira, 168n.
Sharp, Harry, 174n.
Shaw, Cliford, 15n., 268, 269n.
Shevky, Eshref, 121
Sidenbladh, Goran, 308n.
Siegel, Paul M., 226n.
Siegfried, Andre, 41n.
Simkus, Albert, 120

Simmel, George, 129, 131, 132
Simonson, John, 265n.
Singer, Milton, 131
Sjoberg, Gideon, 43, 105, 117n., 119, 356, 388
Smelser, Neil, 133, 134n.
Smith, Joel, 225n.
Smith, John 54
Smith, T. Lynn, 79n., 353
Soja, Edward, 374n.
Soleri, Paolo, 433
Sorenson, Annemette, 199n.
Sorkin, Alan, 217n.
Sovani, N. V., 346n.
Sowell, Thomas, 193n., 194n.
Spectorsky, A. C., 173n.
Spinard, William, 172n.
Srole, Leo, 13n., 139n.
Starr, Joyce, 141
Starr, Roger, 256n.
Steffens, Lincoln, 70n., 72
Stegman, Michael, 279n.
Stein, Maurice, 12n.
Stern, S. M., 392n.
Sternlieb, George, 153n., 174n., 255
Stoddard, Ellwyn, 209n.
Strauss, Joseph, 218n.
Strong, Josiah, 64n., 74, 188
Suttles, Gerald, 143n., 144, 145n., 147
Sutton, Horace, 258n.
Swan, James, 136n.
Swanson, Albert, 282n.
Synookler, Helen, 326
Szelenyi, Ivan, 301, 303n.

Taeuber, Alma, 199
Taeuber, Conrad, 156n.
Taeuber, Karl, 174, 199, 201, 430n.
Taubman, William, 301n., 302
Tertius, Chandler, 48n.
Theodorson, George, 356n.
Thernstrom, Stephen, 154, 237, 238
Thomas, Ray, 307n.
Thomas, William, 15n.
Thomas, Wyndham, 307n.
Thomlinson, Ralph, 103n., 115, 294n., 347n.
Tien, Hung-Mao, 414n., 415n.
Tilly, Charles, 428
Tocqueville, Alexis de, 73
Toffler, Alvin, 132
Tönnies, Ferdinand, 14
Travis, Harry P., 239n.
Treas, Judith, 243
Trigger, Bruce, 20n.
Tull, Jethro, 47
Tunnard, Christopher, 62n., 314n.
Turkel, Studs, 144n.
Turner, Frederick J., 63, 74
Turner, John, 365
Tyree, Andrea, 243

Udry, Richard, 234n.
Ullman, Edward L., 99, 111n., 115
Ullman, M. B., 411n.

Valentine, Charles, 369
Van Valey, Thomas, 199n.
Vernon, Raymond, 86n.
Vidich, Arthur, 11
Vogel, Ezra, 412n.
von Eckardt, Wolf, 432, 433n.

Wade, Richard C., 63, 193n., 194n.
Walton, John, 246, 247
Ward, Sally, 247
Warner, Sam Bass, 59n., 62n., 68n., 188n.
Warner, W. Lloyd., 154, 227, 229
Warren, Roland, 154
Wattenberg, Ben, 202n.
Watts, Hilstan, 374n.
Webber, Melvin, 143, 440, 441
Weber, Adna F., 3n., 156
Weber, Max, 14, 31, 36n., 40, 129, 153, 393
Weiss, Shirley, 326
Weissbroud, Bernard, 273n.
Wekerle, Gerda, 141
Weller, Robert, 90
Wellisz, Slaneslaw, 346n.
Wheatley, Paul, 130n.
White, Andrew, 69
White, Gilbert, 123n.
White, Lucia, 73n.
White, Morton, 73n.
Whyte, William F., 134, 143n., 147, 169, 188
Wienk, Ronald, 265n.
Wilcox, Jerome, 199n.
Willmott, Peter, 149n.
Wilson, James O., 136n.
Wilson, William, 202
Wirth, Louis, 11, 15n., 43, 102, 113, 127, 131-133,
    183, 366, 386, 387
Woodward, C. Van, 194
Wright, Frank Lloyd, 432
Wurdock, Bud, 200n.

Young, Michael, 149n.

Zeisel, John, 329n.
Zelan, Joseph, 170n.
Zetterberg, Hans, 243n.
Zimmer, Basil, 82n., 161n., 178n.
Zimmerman, Erwin, 260n.
Zink, Harold, 70n., 71n.
Zopf, O. Paul, 79n.
Zorbaugh, Harvey, 15n., 113
Zuiches, James, 200n.

SUBJECT INDEX

Africa, 373–392
Age and crime rates, 267–268
Agricultural revolution, 20–21
Agriculture:
  in Africa, 384
  and the emergence of cities, 20–22
  and urban growth, 47–48
Ancient cities, 19–22
Arson, 266–267
Automobile:
  and dispersion, 67–68
  era of, 158–160

Babylon, 19, 27
"Back to city" movement, 288–291
Blacks, 191–203
  and crime, 268
  in poverty areas, 152–153
  powerlessness of, 249
  suburbanization and, 174–176, 430
Bombay 8, 404–405
Boston, 55, 59, 89, 147, 148
Brasilia, 295
Brownsville Housing Project, New York, 329
BUILD, 213

Cairo, 8, 10
Calcutta, 405–408
Central business district (CBD), 82
  changes in, 259–260
  communications in, 86
  decentralization and, 84–85
  in zonal hypothesis, 107–108
Central city:
  land value in, 105
  outmovement from, 82–84
Chicago, 63, 65, 67, 68, 111
Chicago school, 12, 113, 131–132
  Burgess's growth hypothesis, 105–109
  and human ecology, 103–105
China, 411–415
Cities, 257–258
  African, 374–388
  Asian, 401–423
  crime in, 267–269
  defining, 6–8
  emergence of, 19–49
    agricultural revolution and, 20–21
    population explosion and, 22–24
    social class and 26–27
    social organization of, 23–24, 25–27
  federal funding for, 431
  fiscal crisis of, 260–262
  functional specialization of, 98–99
  general characteristics of, 24–25
  growth of, 4–5
  growth hypothesis of, 105–107

Cities (Cont.):
  Hellenic, 29–32
  immigrants in, 187–188
  and immigration, 64, 71–72
  industrial, 48–50, 62–66
  Latin American, 353–369
  life-styles in, 139–144
  medieval, 37–42
  Mexican Americans in, 208–209
  middle eastern, 392–399
  native Americans in, 215–217
  passing of, 441
  preindustrial and industrial comparisons, 43–44
  primate, 347–350, 378, 382
  segregation in, 198–201
  slavery in, 193–194
  Sun Belt growth, 95–98
  in third world, 341–351
  urban concentrations in, 78–79
  U.S. (see United States, cities of)
"City beautiful" movement, 315–317
Columbia, Maryland, 325–326
Combat zone, 109–110
Communities:
  categories of, 145–147
  characteristics of, 16
  decision making in, 243–247
  definitions of, 153–154
Community of limited liability, 145
Condominiums, 284–285
Contrived community, 145
Cosmopolites, 140
Crime:
  in cities, 267–269
  in India, 407–408
Culture of poverty, 367–371
Current population survey, 119, 120

Decentralization in metropolitan areas, 82–87
Defended community, 145
"Demographic transition," 47
Density, 136–139
  and economic development, 344–345
  Indian, 404
Dependency theory, 349–350
Developing countries, 335–351
Discrimination in housing, 265–266
Drugs on skid row, 232

Ecological complex, 18–19
Ecology:
  factorial, 120–122
  human, 102–105
Elitists, 244–245
Employment:
  in Sun Belt cities, 97–98
  in the third world, 341–342

Enclosure Acts, 47
Energy, 430–431
Environment and urbanization, 122–123
Ethnic neighborhoods:
    family norms in, 148–149
    housing in, 149
    peer group orientation in, 147
    vulnerability of, 149–150
Ethnic villagers, 142–144
Expanded community, 145
Experimental Housing Allowance Program
    (EHAP), 283, 284
Exurbanites, 173–174

Factorial ecology, 120–122
Family in working class neighborhoods, 148–149
Federal Housing Authority (FHA), 161, 272–273
Federal programs for cities, 431
Feudal system, 36–37

Gangs, 212–213
Garden City, 305
Greece, urban planning in, 293
Greek city-states, 29–32

Homesteading, urban, 285–287
Hong Kong 416–417
Housing:
    condominiums, 284–285
    discrimination in, 265–266
    in Europe, 297–300
    Mexican American, 206–207
    public (see Public housing)
    in Singapore, 422
    in Soviet Union, 301
    in suburbs, 161–163
    trend in U.S., 428
    urban homesteading, 285–287
    U.S. government and, 271–291
    in working class neighborhoods, 149
Houston, 87
Human ecology, 102–105

Immigrants:
    new, 185–187
    old, 184
    and urban ills, 71–72
    in zone of transition, 111
Immigration, 184–189
    to cities, 64
    Japanese, 219
India, 403–410
Industrial Revolution, 48
Integration, 178–180
Internal migration, 428
Invasion, 112–113
Issei, 219–220

Japan, 417–420
Japanese Americans, 218–222
Jarmo, 21
Jim Crow laws, 194

Lagos, Nigeria, 383
Levittown, 172–173
Life-styles in cities, 139–144
Limited liability, community of, 145
London, 5, 48, 49
Los Angeles, 19

Medieval cities, 37–42
Megalopolis:
    definition of, 79
    descriptions of, 87–90
    in the future, 439–440
Mental health in urban places, 13–14
Metropolitan areas, 80–99
    decentralization in, 82–87
Metropolitan political systems, 436–437
Mexican Americans, 205–210
Middle East, 392–399
Middletown, 247–249
Migration:
    black, 195–198
    internal, 428
    Mexican American, 208–209
    native American, 215–217
Mobility, 236–243
    Japanese, 222
Multiple-nuclei theory, 115
Muslims, 393–395

Native Americans, 214–218
New towns:
    British, 304–308
    European, 308–310
    in U.S., 323–327
New York, 3, 55, 56, 59, 61, 65, 75, 89
Newburyport, Massachusetts, 237
Newport, Rhode Island, 55
Nisei, 219
Nonterritoriality, 440–441

Oak Park, Illinois, 179–180
Occupation:
    and mobility, 239–240
    and social class, 226–229
Overurbanization, 345–346

Park Forest South, Chicago, 178–179
Parks, 315
Peer group orientation, 147
Peking, 415
Philadelphia, 5, 56, 59

Plague, 40–42
Planning (see Urban planning)
Pluralists, 245
POET (population, organization, environment, and technology), 18–19
   to analyze Latin American cities, 357–358
Political bosses, 68–71
Pollution:
   in Hellenic cities, 31–32
   in nineteenth century, 66–67
Population:
   in defining urbanized areas, 7
   of India, 410
   of medieval cities, 38–39
   of metropolitan areas, 4
   in Roman Empire, 32–33
   to Sun Belt cities, 96
   in urban area, 3–4, 5–6
   and urban growth, 336–339, 427–428
   in U.S. cities, 59–60
Population explosion:
   in early settlements, 22–24
   in third world, 338–339
Poverty:
   black, 203
   culture of, 367–371
   and displacement, 290–291
   in India, 405
   in Latin America, 364–365
   Mexican American, 207
   in suburbs, 180–181
Power, 244–251
   in Africa, 389
   of blacks, 249–250
   women and, 250–251
Primate cities, 347–350, 378, 382
Pruitt-Igoe Project, St. Louis, 279–281
Public housing, 278–281
   in Hong Kong, 416
   use of space in, 328–331
Puerto Ricans, 210–214

Red light districts, 109, 110
Redlining, 263
Religion and social mobility, 238
Reservations, 216–217
Reston, Virginia, 324–325
Rome, ancient, 32–34
   urban planning in, 293–294
Rural life-styles, 92
"Rural renaissance," 91

St. Louis, 65, 170, 180
Sector theory, 114
Segregation, 198–201
Shanghai, 8, 413–415
Singapore, 421–423
Singles, 140–141

Skid row, 230–232
Slavery, 192–194
Slums, 150–153
Social-area analysis, 120–122
Social change, 389
Social class, 225–243
   blacks and, 201
   in prehistoric cities, 26–27
   in socialist countries, 303
Social disorganization:
   in Africa, 387
   in Hellenic cities, 29–30
   in prehistoric cities, 25–27
Social planning, 437–439
Social theory, urbanism and, 14–16
Soviet Union, 301
Squatter settlements, 342–344
   in Africa, 382–383
   in Latin America, 362–366
Standard Metropolitan Statistical Area (S.M.S.A.):
   definition of, 80–81
   economic functions of, 98–99
   growth of, 90–91
   rates of suburbanization in, 177
   suburban growth in, 156–157
Stevenage, 307
Stratification, 224–243
Street people, 231–232
Streetcar era, 158
Suburbanites, characteristics of, 166–167, 169–171
Suburbanization:
   of blacks, 430–431
   in Japan, 420
Suburbs:
   blacks in, 174–176, 430–431
   categories of, 164–167
   cause of, 161–163
   contemporary patterns of, 163–164
   and crime, 269
   growth of, 156–160
   integration in, 178–180
   in Japan, 420
   myth of, 167–169
   poverty in, 180–181
   zoning, 272–273
Succession, 113
Sun Belt cities, 95–98
Superterritoriality, 439

Technology:
   and city development, 45–47, 64–66
   and settlement patterns, 64
Tenement laws, 316
Third world, 335–351
Title 235 program, 281–283
Tokyo-Yokohama, 3, 5, 79, 418–420
Transition, zone of, 111
Transportation:
   and cities, 100

Transportation (*Cont.*):
  and decentralization, 84-85
  impact of, 64-66
  in Roman cities, 34-35
  (*See also* Automobile; Streetcar era)

United States:
  cities of: early images, 72
    growth of, 58-62
    planning, 313-314
    structure of, 102-104
    (*See also specific cities, for example:* Boston;
      New York)
  housing programs of, 271-291
  industrial growth in, 62-66
  internal migration in, 428
  population growth in twentieth century, 77-78
  power in, 244-247
    black, 249-250
    women, 250-251
  rural images in, 11
  stratification in, 224-243
  urban concentrations in, 78-79
  urban definitions in, 8
  urbanism in, 11-12
  urbanization of (*see* Urbanization, in U.S.)
United States Housing Authority, 271
Ur, 19, 27
Urban areas, definition of, 6-8
"Urban crisis," 255-256
Urban explosion, 5-6
Urban homesteading, 285-287
Urban life-styles, 129-130
Urban planning:
  historically, 293-294
  in Japan, 420
  in socialist countries, 300-303, 312-331
  in U.S., 313-314
  in western Europe, 297-300
Urban renewal, 273-278
"Urban revolution," 24-25
Urbanism:
  Chicago school and, 12

Urbanism (*Cont.*):
  definition of, 9
  vs. rural image, 12-14
  and social disorganization, 134-139
  in social theory, 14-16
  in the U.S., 11-12
Urbanization:
  in Africa, 373-374
  Chicago school and, 12
  in China, 412-413
  definition of, 8-9
  ecological complex and, 18-19
  and environment, 122-123
  in industrial Europe, 48-50
  in Japan, 417
  in preindustrial Europe, 35-48
  process of, 3-5
  in the third world, 335
  in U.S., 9-10
    colonial, 53-57
    industrial, 57-62
Urbanized area, definition of, 78

Van Dyke Housing Project, New York, 329, 330
Veterans Administration (VA), 161, 272-273

Washington, D.C., 89, 312
White ethnics, 184-191
Women:
  in Africa, 389-390
  mobility of, 242-243
  and power, 250-251
Working-class neighborhoods, 148-149

Zero population growth, 338
Zonal hypothesis, 105-109
  alternate theories, 114-115
  outside U.S., 117-120
Zone of transition, 111
Zoning, 318
  in suburbs, 272-273